ANNUAL REVIEW OF
POLITICAL SCIENCE

ANNUAL REVIEW OF POLITICAL SCIENCE

VOLUME 2, 1999

NELSON W. POLSBY, *Editor*
University of California, Berkeley

http://www.AnnualReviews.org   science@annurev.org   650-493-4400

ANNUAL REVIEWS   4139 EL CAMINO WAY   P.O. BOX 10139   PALO ALTO, CALIFORNIA 94303-0139

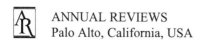 ANNUAL REVIEWS
Palo Alto, California, USA

International Standard Serial Number: 1094-2939
International Standard Book Number: 0-8243-3302-0

Annual Review and publication titles are registered trademarks of Annual Reviews.

The paper used in this publication meets the minimum requirements of American
National Standard for Information Sciences—Permanence of Paper for Printed
Library Materials, ANSI Z39.48-1992

Annual Reviews and the Editors of its publications assume no responsibility for the
statements expressed by the contributors to this *Annual Review.*

Typesetting by Ruth McCue Saavedra and the Annual Reviews Editorial Staff

PRINTED AND BOUND IN THE UNITED STATES OF AMERICA

PREFACE

As befits a loosely organized discipline, the topics taken up by articles in this second *Annual Review* vary quite a lot. Some seek to supply the best current answers to substantive propositions purporting to describe or account for a piece of the political world. Others summarize the state of play in a subfield, hence are about literature and ideas rather than directly about politics. Some explore the behavioral foundations of political phenomena in psychology or sociology. Some describe the institutional settings in which important political science work—teaching and research—is being done. We continue our interest in the contributions of exemplary and influential scholars and we hope, in due course, to consider or reconsider landmark works that have cast a shadow, or a searchlight, over the field.

In general, we try to urge our authors toward statements that can assist readers in orienting themselves to a body of literature, to the state of play, to alternative—if there are alternative—perspectives. Sometimes this does not work as intended, and what is required is another run some other year at the same topic by a different scholar whose work can be read in conjunction with the first. Thus, successive *Annual Reviews* can be read as an ongoing conversation, or group of conversations (a gargle?)—sometimes harmonious, sometimes antiphonal, sometimes cacophonous, sometimes, we suppose, downright hostile.

We think there is something quite attractive about the picture of a discipline that emerges from piecemeal contributions in all of these various modes, traditions, and voices. Political science sustains inquiry on some of the most significant issues facing human beings who must, of necessity, live together on a planet being shrunk by modern technology. Think of how fast a virus can spread around the globe in the age of jet-powered travel. Or an idea in the age of the internet. This is frightening, of course, but it is also intensely interesting, and leads to all sorts of questions and all sorts of answers. Political scientists all over the world constitute a community of scholars devoted to inventing some of these questions and discovering some of the answers. The purpose of organized scholarly communication, such as an *Annual Review*, is to invite many minds to focus on problems and to put proposed solutions to the test of peer review and evaluation.

NELSON W. POLSBY

EDITOR

Annual Review of Political Science
Volume 2 (1999)

CONTENTS

Annu. Rev. Polit. Sci. 1999. 2:1–23

STUDYING THE PRESIDENCY

Nigel Bowles

St. Anne's College, University of Oxford, Oxford OX2 6HS, England;
e-mail: Nigel.Bowles@st-annes.ox.ac.uk

KEY WORDS: methodology, presidency, archival methods

ABSTRACT

This essay identifies five schools of presidential study and argues that the presidency is better understood for the plurality of scholarly approaches embodied in them. The obstacles to the presidency's study notwithstanding, much more is now known about the presidency as an institution than was the case as recently as the mid-1970s. The essay argues that further research ought ideally to meet three conditions: It must be constitutionally informed and politically nuanced; it must be empirically rich, drawing on primary data in some form; and the investigation of particular cases should proceed with the cases' wider significance in mind, if not necessarily with the explicit intention of generating theory.

INTRODUCTION

Politics is too often marginalized in political science. Sensitivity to contingency and to the need to inflect a study's theoretical implications with awareness of contingent events' repercussions are prerequisites for robust political analysis. As Butler has recently observed, "the substance of great works can be lost in writing about writing about writing, where the essence of politics is lost in generalisations too broad and international and abstract to throw much light on what is actually happening" (Butler 1997:26).

Butler writes that the intellectual absorption of politics springs from its being in a "state of flux," that the scholar's subject matter is "constantly changing," and that as a result, "[v]ery few interesting generalisations are valid for more than a small space of territory and slice of time" (1997:26). In study of

1

1094-2939/98/0616-0001$08.00

executives in general and of the US presidency in particular, the subject's compelling interest and importance lies in nuance, complexity, contingency, and
discounting for the future. This claim does not comprise a plea for the exclusion of theoretical concerns; Ellis & Wildavsky (1991) are right to warn
against the indirection that may result from the assumption that there are as
many cases as there are presidents. The attempt to generalize as far as the
evidence permits is central to social science (and, indeed, to history). In
American politics, scholars frequently and properly generalize not only
about the federal government's fixed structural characteristics but about those
characteristics' implications for political processes. The structures of government have implications of their own, which are remarkably durable. Not
everything that is important flows from the three facts of the separation of
powers, of federalism, and of judicial review. Nor are their contents unchang-
ing. But much of importance does flow from them; as Krasner (1978) and
others have shown, it is difficult for a national government to be durably
strong amid such structural separation and fragmentation. When the cultural
variables of individualism and distrust of politicians are added to the three
structural conditions outlined, it is clear that the United States is a polity of a
special and distinctive sort among advanced democracies. Beyond the confines of structure in one system, however, the second-order implications for
process, stability, and durability become rarer; predictability accordingly becomes harder. There are usually too many variables to permit robust, comparative theories of political behavior and policy outcomes with cross-national and intertemporal explanatory applicability. As even the huge literatures
on comparative electoral behavior and party systems—the most theoretically sophisticated literatures within political science—demonstrate, the
limits to theory building (to say nothing of predictability) are severe. Neither
in voting behavior nor in party system change are there satisfactory systematic
accounts of related comparative generalizations with explanatory and predictive power.

Even within the familiar, strikingly stable structural setting of federal
government, Butler's warning about the flux of the political scientist's subject
matter and the paucity of broad, stable, valid observations is compelling. The
contingencies of events and circumstances need not be regarded as theoretically or logically prior to other considerations in attempts to explain executive
decision making; however, being both ever-present and of unpredictable
weight, they undermine nomothetic projects, whether of Marxism or of rational choice. Even middle-range theories of the presidency risk draining
political science of politics. Not all scholars have been so skeptical, however.
In *Studying the Presidency*, Edwards & Wayne (1983) examine the question of
why the US presidency has attracted so little theory building. Wayne argues
that for study of the institution to improve, scholars must approach their

analyses with refined conceptual awareness. Although identification of the independent and dependent variables and measurement of their effects remain "extremely difficult" tasks, he maintains that they are necessary ones if causal explanations are to be offered (Wayne 1983:20). It remains unclear whether such a task is achievable.

There is, however, a prior problem. The presidency is studied less than its governing importance merits. Heclo's (1977) measured plea, through a report commissioned by the Ford Foundation, for much more extensive work has met with a muted response. Heclo criticized the "lack of basic empirical research" on the presidency and thought that there had been "remarkably little in-depth research" on "the everyday work flow and operations of Presidential institutions and staff" (Heclo 1977:24). There has been progress; for example, the editors of and contributors to *Presidential Studies Quarterly* have achieved much in showing what political scientists using historical methods can do to advance knowledge and understanding. Nevertheless, presidency research rarely breaks through into certain of the most distinguished professional journals of political science; such research founded on historical methods does so even less often. The *American Political Science Review*, for example, publishes very few articles about the presidency, in part perhaps because the study of this political institution's operation is not straightforwardly susceptible to quantification.

The problem is not confined to the US presidency. It is also apparent in comparative studies of democratic executives, a subject whose status has diminished and whose literature has shrunk in important respects in the last quarter of the twentieth century. King's penetrating essay in Polsby & Greenstein's *Handbook of Political Science*, published in 1975, contained a measured argument for greater and more focused comparative research on executives (King 1975). Yet Goodin & Klingemann's *A New Handbook of Political Science*, published in 1996, contains no systematic discussion of executives. The book's index contains 100 references to rational choice, 14 to postmodernism, and 11 to Goodin himself, but none to executives (Goodin & Klingemann 1996). The inclusion of an essay about one of the arms of government rightly needed no justification in 1975; its exclusion in 1996 surely should. Yet Goodin & Klingemann's introduction makes no reference to the omission. Fuller consideration of the silence, in part the outcome of the disruptive currents of postmodernism and rational choice, lies beyond the scope of this article. But both currents eliminate much of what is most interesting about politics, the eternal problems of flux, change, and contingency, to which Butler rightly draws attention.

The obstacles to the study of chief executives are significant (Hart 1998). Four are especially problematic and are independent of passing academic fashion.

Sample Size

For Germany, Fifth Republic France, Britain, Spain, Australia, India, South Africa, and the United States, the explanation lies partly in the small samples of democratic chief executives. Only in Fourth Republic France, and in post-war Italy and Japan, have Prime Ministers been sufficiently numerous to permit internal and cross-national longitudinal comparison.

Definition of the Dependent Variable and the Problem of Quantification

It is difficult to know what the unit of analysis should be in comparative analysis of chief executives governing. Comparisons with study of elections and legislatures illustrate the point. In both, the dependent variables are clear (typically, a specified aggregation of votes) and readily expressed in quantified form. Study of political parties is less straightforward but specification of the unit of analysis rarely presents serious difficulty. Great advances in understanding of citizens' behavior in voting booths and of politicians' behavior in committee and on the floors of legislatures have flowed from investment of large intellectual and financial resources in quantification and statistical analysis. Quantification also has its application in studies of judiciaries, interest groups, and bureaucracies; even where schematic, as in Mayhew's (1986) indexation of party strength, it not only can be done but can systematically and usefully illustrate a scholarly argument. The point can be extended to almost all other subjects within comparative politics but not to chief executives (except with regard to their election and to proxy measures of executive success such as legislative votes). King's argument in 1975 retains its weight:

> In the case of legislatures..., the roll-call vote is readily available as a behavioral datum to which other kinds of data—attitudinal, situational, and so on—can be linked. But what is the comparable datum in the case of executives? The decision? The interaction? The initiative? The policy? All of these present formidable problems of conceptualization and operationalization. (King 1975:174)

Linguistic Weakness

In those branches of comparative politics where quantitative techniques drawing on survey data, votes, or campaign contributions are applicable, linguistic difficulties might be slight. In the comparative analysis of chief executives in government, however, difficulties in the specification of the unit of analysis and consequent impediments to quantification imply a reliance on the use of primary sources, which, in turn, requires not merely linguistic competence but linguistic fluency. Comparison of the sources of cohesion and incohesion in the central executives of Fourth Republic France, Italy, and Japan is a plausibly attractive research project. However, few indeed are the scholars with linguistic abilities sufficient even to contemplate undertaking primary archival research across those three states.

Secrecy

Executives conduct business mostly in secret. Whereas almost everything about legislatures and judiciaries is public, little is known about the procedures of executives (and almost nothing is known for certain). Except in extraordinary circumstances, legislatures in democratic societies cannot be relied on to serve democratic procedural principles when sitting *in camera*. Preservation of their legitimacy requires that they be at least formally open institutions to whose business citizens have full or nearly full access. Judiciaries in democratic countries, even where (as is usually the case) they are unelected, similarly cannot be relied on to serve purposes consistent with democratic principles of fairness and equality of treatment when sitting *in camera* (though, for compelling reasons, pretrial grand juries remain an exception). The legitimacy of both branches—the one elected, the other not—requires procedural transparency, both in order to facilitate access of properly interested parties (and of public-spirited citizens above all) and to demonstrate propriety, making those who hold a public trust accountable to those who grant it.

Executives typically neither follow such a pattern nor have such underlying purposes. Democratic executives are, to varying degrees, procedurally secret. The principle, normal in British and French executive branches, that files of government departments be released only after at least 30 years would, if applied to the House of Commons, the US Congress, or the courts of any democracy, not only shatter their operative principles and culture but nullify democracy itself. (However, while imposing freedom of access on the executive, neither the US House of Representatives nor the US Senate concedes this freedom with respect to its own committees' unpublished papers. The House retains committee papers for 30 years and the Senate for 20.) Study of executives, accordingly, proceeds under difficult circumstances. Information becomes available from executives in three circumstances: (*a*) when government officials release information selectively, either through leaks while in government or through memoirs and interviews after having left it, in order to promote their or their agency's interests; (*b*) when information is drawn from them as a result of legislative oversight procedures and press inquiries, as happens routinely in normal political times, or when it is forced from them in exceptional circumstances such as Watergate, Iran-Contra, and the Westland Affair; or (*c*) when scholars wait for the due time of papers' release.

There is considerable scope for further comparative work on executives through the use of legislative scrutiny or oversight and through the study of administrative law; too many reports of committee hearings in Europe and in

North America lie unexamined by scholars. Using such methods, the potential for comparative analysis of policy evaluation, and hence for fuller understanding of the bureaucracy, is substantial but largely unrealized. Although such work is often, paradoxically, effective only after administrative failure, the asymmetries of expertise that typically exist between executives and legislatures (even in the case of legislatures such as the US Congress with exceptional cognitive and technological resources) are reduced under such circumstances by the temporary political weakness of governments. (It is notable that operations of the executive branch should so often be revealed through the examination of the records of legislative committees and of court transcripts and judgments.)

Those scholars who rely on the third method, that of waiting for the review and declassification of papers, cannot depend on the completeness of their sources, regardless of their extent. Even less may they depend on papers' veracity. As all political historians know, the record of executive decision making that papers provide is partial in both senses of the word: It is neither complete nor dispassionate. Papers for meetings are drafted and their minutes compiled from many motives, but attachment to a principle of the disinterested recording of events is rarely prior to other, political, purposes. Papers are not themselves revealed truth, nor even competing truths. They may, however, expose falsehoods or demonstrate truths given researchers' appropriately acute interpretative skills. Interpretation of political context, purpose, calculation, and nuance is (or ought to be) the stuff of archival research—just as it is (or ought to be) of research based on interviews.

Even if, exceptionally, disinterestedness were to guide an official's or a staff member's record, minute, note, or briefing paper, it is not clear that the principle could knowingly be applied by policy makers (because honesty and disinterestedness are not synonymous qualities), nor that a disinterested paper would be recognized as such by scholars (because it would not necessarily carry distinguishing marks). Such epistemological questions pose genuine problems of method, but archival records are not alone in presenting problems of truth-value; the same questions arise, for example, about the meaning of a vote (not to mention that of aggregated votes). The problems of using archival records must be surmounted precisely because, for the reasons discussed above, scholars who study the executive have fewer alternative sources than do their colleagues whose subjects are elections, legislatures, or judiciaries.

In fact, the difficulty is more severe than even this account implies. The adequacy of paper records has been curtailed by the connected developments of communications and computing technologies. It is reduced further in governing cultures and institutions that either lack a tradition of committing minutes of conversations or meetings to paper or lack the routinized civil service procedures by which such minutes are taken. Both obstacles obtain in the US presidency, and hence in its study; White House structures and procedures are typically established anew not only between incumbents but within an incumbency. Those scholars who have studied the presidency as part of a wider set of problems in constitutional law have largely escaped this difficulty because they are able to draw their data from court cases. For scholars in the other four schools of presidency studies, the problem remains.

THE FIVE SCHOOLS

Study of the presidency can usefully be thought of as falling into five schools. The first is the constitutional history school, exemplified by the work of Corwin (1957), Fisher (1991), and Pious (1979) on positive and normative questions of presidential authority.

The second is the political history school, dominated by the many distinguished biographers of individual presidents, such as Morris (1979) on Theodore Roosevelt, Burns (1956, 1970) on Franklin Roosevelt, and Dallek (1991, 1998) on Lyndon Johnson. Its policy history variant focuses especially on budgetary, welfare, and foreign policy; *Nixon's Economy* (Matusow 1998) and *From Opportunity to Entitlement* (Davies 1996) are distinguished examples securely founded on primary historical sources. The third is the school of institutional history, to which major contributors have been Wilson, Neustadt, Skowronek, and Tulis (Wilson 1908, Tulis 1987, Skowronek 1993). This school has a comparative variant, with which Kallenbach (1966) and King (1975) are closely associated. The fourth is the school of political analysis, in which the major figure is Neustadt (1954, 1955, 1990). It contains a number of subschools, including that on presidential-congressional relations, whose contributors include Polsby (1971), and Peterson (1990).

The fifth is the psychological school of presidential analysis, of which the work of Alexander and Juliet George (1956), Barber (1972), and Simonton (1987) are prominent examples.

The School of Constitutional History

Were its adherents, such as Fisher and Pious, less modest scholars than they are, they could plausibly claim their framework to be intellectually prior to all others. Although not sufficient for understanding the system, it is foundational. Without knowledge of the history of the presidency's place within constitution and statute, of the contested understandings and changing interpretations to which that changing place gives rise, the presidency certainly cannot be understood. In *The President, Office and Powers, 1787–1957,* Corwin observed that "American constitutional law, far from being a closed system, often bristles with alternatives; and especially is this true of the segment of it with which these pages are concerned" (1957:vii). What presidents do, what they may do, what they may not do, what Congress and the courts may and may not do in relation to the presidency, are questions to which constitutional scholars have made major contributions. Members of the school are not guilty of the charge that their subject is individual presidents; on the contrary, their focus is on the institution of the presidency. Moreover, it is intrinsically comparative not only between and within administrations, but between the presidency and the other component parts of a separated system—Congress, courts, states, citizens.

The presidency has become what it is in part because of charged debates about its actual and proper scope under normal and abnormal circumstances. Most of Article II's constitutional provisions are unchanged from their drafting at Philadelphia in 1787. Yet the presidency's places in constitutional understanding, in congressional statutes, and in public expectation have undergone radical change. As with the departmental component of the executive branch, so with the presidential: It has become what it is primarily because Congress has willed it. Most of the powers that presidents exercise have accrued to the presidency through congressional conferment in statute. With such enumerated powers comes responsibility; indeed, most such powers also carry obligations. For example, the Employment Act of 1946 imposes a duty on the President to report annually to the Congress on the state of the economy; the Budget and Impoundment Control Act of 1974 both permitted and limited presidential discretion in the expenditure of appropriated funds by legitimizing two forms of impoundments, rescissions and deferrals, under specified conditions. The authority presidents exercise under statutory powers of this kind is contingent; Congress may alter or remove it. Congress does sometimes withhold such authority, as its unwillingness to extend fast-track authority to President Clinton in 1997 showed.

It is these questions and their implications with which Corwin was concerned and about which Fisher and Pious have continued to write. At its best, and it often is at its best, it is a school of deep scholarship and analytical refinement. Although the quality and depth of presidential scholarship are commonly thought disappointing, such a charge certainly cannot be made against constitutional studies of the presidency. Corwin's interpretation of the establishment and development of the powers of the presidency has been challenged but retains remarkable analytical purchase. His focus was on presidential authority, the growth of such authority, and the implications of that growth for the presidency's relations with Congress and the courts and with citizens. Corwin and his colleagues in the school were vitally concerned with the normative questions attending their study of the enlargement of presidential authority. Although much troubled by the presidency's expansion, Corwin expressed his anxieties with flashes of wit. No arid constitutionalist, he signified his misgivings about the presidency's aggrandizement by referring to Franklin Roosevelt as "Roosevelt II."

The general point about the centrality of normative considerations may be illustrated by the example of executive orders. Corwin considered what their limits actually are and whether such limits are justifiable (1957:213). His consideration of the role of "Administrative Chief" focused on the scope of the President's powers to appoint persons to office and to remove them from it (1957:69). His account of the President's role as Chief Executive was concerned with the general problem of agency. His particular focus was on the difficulty created for constitutional government by the President's "duty to the law" in the context of an extensive body of administrative regulation that requires federal officials to exercise discretion in the course of making rules that have binding effect. Corwin rightly insisted that the key implied question is the normative one. Barely concealing his distaste for the expanded presidency, he enquired "whether there are statable limits to this kind of thing, or available safeguards against the indefinite accumulation of power by this method in the hands of the President" (Corwin 1957:119).

Pious and Fisher have contributed to this literature from different perspectives. Unlike Corwin, Fisher is concerned not with what he terms the "general drift of authority and responsibility to the President over the past two centuries... [but with] executive activity cut loose from legislative moorings and constitutional restrictions—presidential action no longer tethered by law" (Fisher 1991:281). In the examples of Watergate, the CIA's abuse of its power in the 1970s, and the Iran-Contra scandal, even the judicious and sober Fisher finds that "those who fear executive power" have good cause for alarm. Worse, he thinks that "little has been learned except the capacity to repeat past mistakes" (1991:281).

The propositions I derive from this survey of the constitutional school are, therefore, that its members are concerned with the following:

1. the presidency's constitutional authority, its expansion, and the implications of such expansion for the President's relationship with the departments and agencies of the executive branch, with Congress, with the courts, and with the electorate;

2. Congress's responses to that expansionary process;

3. the growth of administrative law by volume and political significance;

4. the implications (both positive and normative) of these interlaced developments for constitutional law and a liberal republic.

These questions are certainly fundamental, but not exclusive; the authors' emphasis on authority and formal powers comes at the expense of considerations of power and influence. Moreover, leadership, a dependent variable in many accounts of executives within the United States and in other systems, is not so categorized by constitutional scholars. Neither Corwin nor Fisher nor Pious set out to consider how presidential leadership might be made effective. They have been criticized for that omission, but it is a criticism without conviction, for it is quite beside the point. If they are guilty of the charge, so were Madison and Jefferson. Some might think it a criticism of constitutional scholars to argue that the constitutional approach fails "readily [to] lend itself to hypothesis testing or theory building" (Wayne 1983:25). It might more convincingly be argued that such a "failure" raises more serious questions about the appropriateness of social scientists' criteria than it does about constitutional law.

The School of Political History

The profundity of political historians' contributions to scholarly understanding of presidents and their administrations is insufficiently acknowledged by political scientists. Historians' purposive contributions to understanding of the presidency as a political institution have been less distinctive, but few historians have had such a purpose. Although merely one of historians' vehicles, biography certainly carries the greatest public appeal and is likeliest to win the attention of literate lay-people. A historical study of a major component part of the Executive Office of the Presidency in order to cast light on the presidency in general may or may not have intellectual merit and coherence. It is, however, unlikely to gain as much attention from scholars of the presidency as a large biography of President Nixon is likely to do. That which is true of scholars is truer of the wider reading public. We know Eisenhower remarkably well through Ambrose (1984), and through the same author, Nixon (Ambrose 1987, 1989). We know a little of Lyndon Johnson through Caro's massive prosecution of him (1982, 1990) but much more through Dallek's measured assessment (1991, 1998). Scholarly knowledge of Truman similarly owes much to Donovan (1977, 1984) and McCullough (1982), as that of Reagan does to Cannon (1991).

By the same token, much that is known about individual presidents derives from studies of policies, events, and processes. We know a good deal about Andrew Johnson through Foner's (1990) much broader canvas on the Reconstruction; about Franklin Roosevelt through countless works on New Deal agencies and the Second World War; about Harry Truman through vast literatures on the Marshall Plan, on American policy toward the Soviet Union between 1945 and 1953, and on the Korean War; and about Woodrow Wilson through studies of Versailles and through King's (1995) work on segregation in federal employment. But the contributors to these rich histories have not had the presidency or some aspect of it as their dependent variable, not least because they do not usually think explicitly in such methodological categories.

That which separates most historians from most social scientists separates them in the study of presidents and the presidency. Most historians of US politics have not usually aimed to arrive at generalizable statements. For example, most historians' accounts of presidential command of the Korean War do not have as their wider purpose the creation of a theory of presidential war powers (though they may well test hypotheses derived from the scholarly literature about how President Truman conducted the Korean War). Hence, the charge Burns (1963:xi) leveled against scholarly understanding of the presidency—that much is known about presidents and almost nothing about the presidency—is one that many historians are likely to regard as beside the mark. How else, they may protest, is knowledge of the institution to advance other than through study of those entrusted with it? Among political scientists, by contrast, Burns's charge has typically been acknowledged as having force.

Two major recent works by political scientists employ historical methods to achieve ends which, because they are general claims about the presidency, can be considered social-scientific. The first, *The Rhetorical Presidency* (Tulis 1987), is a comparative longitudinal analysis of a particular presidential function, namely twentieth-century presidents' assumption of a duty to defend themselves and to promote policy initiatives (in this respect, Andrew Johnson was a precursor to twentieth-century practice). Tulis's elegant argument is that the "old logic" of the presidency has since Wilson's administration become detached from a new politics. Whereas (even in Jackson's case) presidents formerly engaged in limited but purposeful discourse directed to a deliberative form of governance, they have since 1913 engaged in a public rhetoric that reduces the prospects for deliberative decision making. In short, whereas in the nineteenth century campaigning was subordinated to governance, in the twentieth century governance has come to be subordinated to campaigning (Tulis 1987:183). In the first of two well-argued cases, the Senate's refusal to ratify the Versailles Treaty, Tulis shows how the old logic defeated the new politics. He argues that Wilson faced two rhetorical contexts: persuading the Senate to support the treaty and persuading citizens to pressure the Senate to support the treaty. The one contradicted the other (1987:158). In the second case, Lyndon Johnson's advocacy of the Economic Opportunity Act of 1964, Tulis shows how the new politics defeated the old logic through Johnson's rhetorical choices of symbolism and argument, which helped undermine the Act's implementation. Despite having only two case studies, neither of them deriving heavily from primary research, Tulis's is an attractive argument that poses interesting questions and develops stimulating answers.

The second work, *The Politics Presidents Make* (Skowronek 1993), is conceived on a grander scale. Skowronek's exploration of presidents' "differential impact" through an analytical framework of the presidency's development cast asynchronously in political time and chronological time is imaginative and thought-provoking. The author's intellectual ambition for his framework is so broad as to preclude more than a derivative historical knowledge of many of the 14 presidencies that comprise his study; his treatments of the presidencies of Hoover, Franklin Roosevelt, Lyndon Johnson, Carter, and Bush contain no references to unpublished papers. As Skowronek readily concedes, his framework is insufficient to accommodate certain important presidencies, notably Nixon's. Awkwardly, the intellectual problem Skowronek poses is neither altogether explicit nor precise. It appears to be that of how "leadership efforts...shape the political landscape and drive its transformation" (1993:3). The argument about that nebulous question is, partly in consequence, less securely founded than Tulis's; "Presidential action in history is politicized by the order-shattering, order-affirming, and order-creating impulses inherent in the institution itself" (Skowronek 1993:20). Conceptually, the work is weakened by his failure satisfactorily to define or systematically to explore "authority," and hence to counterpose it to "power." Nevertheless, Skowronek's book offers a thoughtful, novel, and penetrating reinterpretation of the dilemmas of presidential leadership, which reveals much about what he defines as the problem of political legitimacy and the rather different problems of public and political support.

Three propositions seem to derive from this discussion:

1. The scholarly quality of the best historical work on presidents and the presidency is exemplary. Although archival research is not free of methodological weakness, in skilled hands its robustness is unmatched by other methods.

2. The charge that historians have contributed more to knowledge and understanding of particular presidents or of particular episodes in history than they have to knowledge and understanding of the presidency, and the more general charge that historical methods do not meet the methodological requirements of many political scientists, have force. Those charges do not, however, undermine the historical method, its practitioners, or its findings.

3. To be convincing, historical analysis of the presidency requires the sifting of large quantities of primary evidence for its foundations. An approach that relies on a purely derivative literature cannot suffice.

The School of Institutional History

The institutional history school is distinguished and has proved intellectually durable. Woodrow Wilson is its patron. Wilson supplemented the study of constitutional and statute law with politics, changing his view of the presidency and Congress greatly as he did so and concerning himself increasingly with the politics of presidential leadership.

As indicated above, Neustadt's early academic writing was concerned not with the President but with a part of the institutionalized presidency, the Bureau of the Budget—and, in particular, with the Bureau's legislative clearance function (Neustadt 1954, 1955). Neustadt's argument about legislative clearance was entirely consistent with the broader argument he made later about presidential leadership: The legislative clearance function is more valuable to the presidency if individual presidents have the wisdom to sustain its distance from them in order to encourage the senior civil servants in charge of it to perform their aggregative fiscal tasks dispassionately. The distinctions between career and noncareer bureaucrats, institutional and personal staff, and political and nonpolitical appointees, which Louis Brownlow and Franklin Roosevelt had thought essential to the Bureau's position as a nondepartmental component of the Executive Office of the President (EOP), fell victim to Johnson's and Nixon's apparent inability to discern the Bureau's value to the office of which they were temporary custodians. Berman (1979) provides the best account of the development of both the Bureau of the Budget and its flawed successor, the Office of Management and Budget (OMB). Berman's short monograph is sensitive to political context, illustrates the centrality of the Bureau's functions to the processes of fiscal policy formation (and hence to the presidency), and is carefully argued. Although it lacks deep foundations in archival evidence, its value as a historical study lies in its marshaling of evidence in support of the essentially Neustadtian argument that "[t]he OMB is still the closest thing a President has to an interest-free perspective on Executive Branch policies, but only if the President distinguishes institutional from personal staff services" (Berman 1979:130).

Scholars both of governing structures and of policy process have been more drawn to foreign and security agencies and processes than to domestic ones. Consistent with this broad pattern, the National Security Council (NSC) has attracted more attention from institutional analysts than has the Budget Bureau. It must be said, however, that whatever the comparative attention given them, the NSC and its secretariat have been remarkably little studied. There is a large literature (contributed to by scholars, policy analysts, and former participants) about foreign policy decision making in general, and about the place of the National Security Adviser in foreign policy decision making (and the contending departmental and EOP influences on policy) in particular. Among the small scholarly literature on the Council as an institution is Shoemaker's *The NSC Staff* (1991). Shoemaker examines the question of how the "rise in power" of the NSC since 1947 is to be explained. He ascribes the primary position of the Council to the centrality in the decision-making process of the Council's staff.

Not until 1959, when Fenno published *The President's Cabinet*, was the Cabinet subjected to systematic scholarly examination. Like all of Fenno's work, *The President's Cabinet* still repays careful reading. Nevertheless, although the formation of Cabinets has its literature, it is disappointing that the structure and processes of the Cabinet have attracted so little academic attention in the succeeding 40 years (Polsby 1978). Whereas some Cabinets have at best been of marginal importance to policy formation, others have been more significant and are illuminated by archival data of high quality. Yet few scholars appear to have thought it worthwhile to exploit those data to explain how and why presidents' Cabinets operate as they do. Here, I think, is a gap in understanding of the executive. Before the Cabinet and its offshoots are dismissed as having no institutional significance, the evidence should be examined.

Jefferson claimed in his inaugural address that the President was the only national officer "who commands a view of the whole ground." Implausible as that characterization has become in the twentieth century, a similar claim might be made for the component parts of the EOP since 1939. The commanding views afforded by a presidential perspective, or that of EOP agencies, have attractions for scholars, too. The institutional approach to study of the presidency has the powerful attraction that, since Roosevelt signed Executive Order No. 8248 in 1939, which brought the Executive Office into being, its component parts have offered ready-made lenses on different aspects of policy-making processes. The examples of the NSC, Budget Bureau/OMB, Council of Economic Advisers (CEA), and Office of the United States Trade Representative (USTR) suggest that the institutionalist perspective may help to convert presidential scholarship from the study of individual presidents to patterned regularities of institutional behavior. Although presidents make of these agencies what they will, all four have since their creation been excellent vehicles for the analysis of presidential leadership of four large policy areas (each stipulated in law by Congress). Here is where policy is coordinated with departments and agencies, where presidential leadership is expressed most directly, and where the prospects for overcoming sectional rivalries are greatest. The EOP agencies are not all of a piece. They have been created, their remits modified, and their design altered by different Congresses under the control of different parties in different circumstances. By its passage of the National Security Act, for example, Congress granted presidents substantial discretion in determining how and whether the NSC is used, how NSC staff are employed to filter information and intelligence, and how the NSA's relations to the President are constructed.

The office of the USTR not only coordinates trade negotiations but is explicitly given the responsibility, by Kennedy's 1963 Executive Order, for leading the United States in those negotiations. No other unit in the EOP (to which the 1974 Trade Act transplanted the USTR) has one of its four most senior members permanently based abroad (in Geneva, home of the World Trade Organization). Further strengthened by Carter's 1980 Executive Order under the authority of the 1979 Reorganization Plan, the USTR is responsible for setting and administering overall trade policy. The USTR is now chief US representative for the World Trade Organization and for all other bilateral and multilateral negotiations concerning trade policy, direct investment incentives and disincentives to trade, and incentives and barriers to cross-border investment. Here is where future scholars of the presidency might fruitfully begin their analyses of the North American Free Trade Agreement (NAFTA) and of the American negotiating position in the Uruguay Round.

By the Employment Act of 1946, Congress did not grant the President comparable discretion regarding his use of the CEA (Bailey 1950). On the contrary, Congress forced President Truman to dilute his full employment legislation with respect to the definition of full employment, the extent of government control of the economy required to produce such an employment level, the relative weight accorded to manipulation of the federal budget in economic planning, and the desirability of according to the Keynesian Bureau of the Budget the decisively important role in the formulation of fiscal policy. Each marked a retreat toward conservative fiscal and political ground. That body was not at all what Truman had sought, with the result that he made little use of it (like the NSC) until, to his undisguised relief, its first chairman retired. The CEA offers a distinctive, and vital, perspective on economic policy making. The quality of its members' papers in the Presidential Libraries is often excellent. Yet, like the USTR, the CEA has drawn less scholarly interest than its key involvement in the processes of economic policy making merits. Flash's work is one of the few to examine the CEA's significance in the institutionalized presidency (1965).

One key proposition emerges from this account: As Neustadt demonstrated in his early work on the Bureau of the Budget, institutional analysis offers a powerful means of both describing the presidency and explaining the relationship between its formal structures and the policy processes in which its several parts engage. Yet many of the component parts of the EOP have drawn less scholarly attention than their importance merits.

The School of Political Analysis

For Neustadt, power is not a simple function of authority. In *Presidential Power and the Modern Presidents*, the 1990 edition of *Presidential Power*, he argued that President Nixon, in his conflict with Congress over impoundment, confused "the first bite of invoked authority with longer-run effects on power prospects" (Neustadt 1990:xi). Neustadt did not elide the concepts as he thought Nixon had the practices. Neustadt defined "power" as "personal influence of an effective sort on governmental action" and distinguished it from the "formal 'powers' vested in the Presidency by constitutional or statute law and custom," with which scholars of the constitutional school primarily concern themselves (Neustadt 1990:ix). Here, then, are Neustadt's first two steps toward a theory of presidential leadership. It is a theory built on an assumption that the presidency is a weak institution. Neustadt regarded this assumption as the "underlying theme of *Presidential Power*" upon publication of the first edition in 1960 and continued so to regard it 30 years later; "*weak,*" he wrote, was "the word with which to start" (1990:xix, italics in original). The central structure of Neustadt's theory remains in place. There are three sources of presidential influence: formal powers, professional reputation within Washington, and prestige or public standing.

The presidency was weak, he argued, first because its foundation in authority was insecure, and second because "effective personal influence" was "a risky thing—hard to consolidate, easy to dissipate, rarely assured" (Neustadt 1990:ix). Between 1960 and 1990, he concluded, four factors had increased presidents' difficulty in making their personal influence effective: (*a*) a rise in public expectations of the presidency; (*b*) an increase in the burden on presidents through the growth of their "clerkly tasks," many of them imposed on the executive by Congress; (*c*) a loosening of foreign alliances with the end of bipolarity; and (*d*) the further weakening of political parties (Neustadt 1990:ix).

Neustadt's work still reads as a work of penetrating insight. If a measure of a book's greatness is its capacity to reveal further analytical subtleties with each new reading, *Presidential Power* is great indeed. It is not a little ironic that at behavioralism's high tide in the United States, one of political science's classic non-behavioralist scholarly arguments should have been written in one of the United States's greatest departments of political science. Neustadt suffers the fate (especially among undergraduate students) of being more often quoted than either read or understood. But we can scarcely blame him for that. He is, in any case, in distinguished company, since the same is true of de Tocqueville, Weber, and Keynes (among others). But like those scholars, Neustadt's claims have achieved the status of truths. His subtle account of power and influence; his emphasis on the two elective branches as being not only independent but intertwined; his placing of the presidency in a maelstrom of shared governance comprising not only the White House and Congress but also courts, pressure groups, the states, and foreign interests; and his emphasis on the President's reputation and prestige as "the sources of his power, case by case" are now broadly accepted as points of analytical departure. Like de Tocqueville, Weber, and Keynes, he has been accused of harboring an unexamined assumption about free agency. That criticism appears, however, to rest on a misreading of Neustadt's argument.

For Neustadt, the art of leadership from the Oval Office was an honorable cause—hence the depth of his disappointment in the conduct of presidential

STUDYING THE PRESIDENCY 17

office by some of Kennedy's successors. Neustadt's decisive intellectual achievements were that he empathized with those who attempt to use office for the public good, while he also understood not only the subtleties of political motivation but why political calculation is essential if presidential leadership under democratic constraints is to be made effective. Indeed, he criticized Franklin Roosevelt, Kennedy, Nixon, and Reagan primarily for considering options for action without giving sufficient thought to the consequences of those actions for their later freedom to act. These presidents' points of failure were attributable to their failure to reflect on "the most important law at a President's disposal" (Neustadt 1990:50), namely Friedrich's "law of antici-pated reactions" (Friedrich 1940). They failed, in Neustadt's own words (1990:xviii), to look

> down the line and around corners. They did not think enough about prospec-tive power, not anyway in its symbolic and constitutional dimensions. For that they suffered something—Nixon everything—and so also did we, the rest of us, whether or not actively engaged in public life.

Such a perspective gives Neustadt's account intimacy, plausibility, and vi-tality. The account is intimate with respect to the author's proximity to power; it is plausible with respect to his capacity to convey in his writing proximity to power's exercise and to power's frustration; and it is vital in conveying a vivid sense of the importance for presidents and scholars of understanding presiden-tial power, its constraints, and its possibilities. These three factors, in combina-tion with Neustadt's integrity, also result in *Presidential Power* yielding new layers of meaning and understanding upon further rereadings. Far from being dewy-eyed about power, Neustadt was fully seized of the magnitude of presi-dential responsibilities and of the implications of failure. There is throughout his work a tone of anxiety about the risks to America in particular and the free world in general of temporary incumbents making consequential errors. Given the fragility of the structure of nuclear deterrence in the 1960s, he prudently emphasized and reemphasized both the responsibilities and the risks. But he did so while insisting that the constitutional context imposes an obligation on presidents and congresses to recognize each other's legitimacy in the shared processes of public policy making.

Neustadt wrote *Presidential Power* before rational choice achieved its recent fashion. In contrast to exponents of rational choice, he not only recog-nized the existence of the public interest but thought that those who serve in government carry a public trust and are to be trusted. In similarly sharp con-trast, he prized civil servants' primary resource of expertise. Indeed, he cele-brated that resource not only among the civil service but also among presidents (Neustadt 1954). The combination of his insistence on reciprocal obligations to recognize legitimacy and his prizing of expertise suggests why he took so poor a view of Nixon's fitness for the office of President. In Neustadt's view, President Nixon's incursion into Cambodia, his politicization of the Budget Bureau, and his impoundment of lawfully appropriated funds were attributable to his failure to distinguish "the crucial from the irritating. He also seems inexpert in distinguishing the implications over time from effects of the moment" (Neustadt 1990:214). Lyndon Johnson's commitment of ground troops to Vietnam in July 1965, and his repeated accessions thereafter to requests from his commanders for increases in their number, were further illustrations of the same cardinal error. In emphasizing that error's magnitude, Neustadt illuminated the wisdom of his underlying argument. The two presidents concerned, the institution of which they were temporary incumbents, and the American people themselves lost a good deal from the failure of both Kennedy's defeated opponent in 1960 and his successor in 1963 to read *Presidential Power* (as Kennedy had the humility to do) and to absorb its implications. As for scholars of the presidency, everyone who has written about it since 1960 has either worked broadly within Neustadt's paradigmatic framework or attempted (thus far, unsuccessfully) to displace it.

In attempting both to explain the presidency to students of American politics and to advise presidents and those around them of the nature of their task, Neustadt engaged in analysis and prescription. Remarkable as his work is, and respectable though his bridging of the divide between those who govern and those who study them, the fit between the two is not entirely comfortable. Wayne holds that Neustadt resolved the difficulty by offering a normative conception of presidential leadership based on "a stewardship model of duties and a Rooseveltian model of behavior. The president should be a calculating activist who gets his way through persuasion—gentle or otherwise" (Wayne 1983:33). If we accept Wayne's claim, we are faced with the implied consequential question of how presidential success is to be measured. Neither authority nor power nor influence can be quantified; therefore, as Wayne notes and as Neustadt implicitly acknowledged, and as in their different ways Edwards (1989) and Peterson (1990) have shown, we are obliged to use presidential success as a proxy measure, and we use secondary proxy measures such as congressional support scores and opinion poll measures because they are quantities. Consistent with a Neustadtian understanding of the presidency, Peterson stresses the importance of contextual factors shaping the legislative process, which bind presidency and Congress together in political relationships containing elements of conflict, competition, and cooperation. This perspective applies not only to direct relations between the presidency and Congress but also to the complex political networks linking the two elective institutions and their progeny, the federal bureaucracy.

The propositions I derive from this account are that the political analysis school's strengths lie in its

1. exhibiting a finely tuned sensitivity to political context and circumstance;

2. placing the presidency in an explicitly relational and competitive set-ting—to the other two branches, to the bureaucracy, to citizens, and to the external world.

School of Psychological Analysis

The work of authors within the school of psychological analysis is too mar-ginal to the purposes of this article to justify studying it at length. The quality of scholarship in the field varies considerably. At its best, as in Alexander and Juliet George's work, it is scrupulous in the use of evidence, theoretically sophisticated, and rigorous in the development of argument (A George & J George 1956). The Georges' work throws Wilson's presidency into clear relief while hinting at the broader explanatory possibilities of psychological tools in presidential analysis. The quality of later work has not, however, fulfilled that early promise; for example, the work of Barber is decidedly problematic. His major book, *The Presidential Character* (1972), has had a powerful impact on studies of the presidency, but the theoretical foundations of Barber's scheme are precarious (A George 1974).

Simonton (1987) has examined presidential success from the standpoint of a political psychologist. He evaluates measures of presidential performance by four quantified criteria (elections, public opinion polls, congressional rela-tions, and historians' evaluation of presidents) and coordinates the resulting findings about the patterns of presidential performance with independent vari-ables of personality, family background, occupation and political experience, and contextual factors. His commitment to theory building through rigorous quantitative research results in multiple correlations but in few convincing causal relationships. For example, Simonton (1987:231) claims that

> [m]ore intelligent presidents tend to enter office with a diminutive share of the popular vote and may not even receive a popular majority, as Woodrow Wilson discovered twice. Bright chief executives thus lack a strong mandate from the people. At the same time, the more intellectually brilliant the presi-dent the greater the odds of his going down in history as one of the all-time greats. Much of the esteem in which Jefferson is held can be ascribed to the likelihood that he was the only undoubted genius ever to live in the White House.

Notwithstanding his purported nomothetic commitment and reliance on "systematically collected data," too much of Simonton's work depends on sur-mise, loose conceptualization, and unargued claims (Simonton 1987:7). Here is what he has to say about what he terms person-context interaction: "[T]he president's birth order, by affecting his social development, may interact with the political zeitgeist, especially the key issues and crises of the day, to determine whether his time has come in history" (1987:234).

I derive the following propositions from this account:

1. At its best, the disciplinary rigor of psychology brings an analytical zest to explanation of why particular presidents behave as they do;

2. In less secure hands, disciplinary rigor is at risk of displacement by loose conceptualization and reliance on tenuous evidence.

CONCLUSION

The presidency remains the better understood for the plurality of scholarly approaches embodied in the five schools. Significant though the obstacles to the presidency's study are, scholars working within each school have achieved enough for both parts of Burns's claim that "[w]e know everything about the Presidents and nothing about the Presidency" to ring less true than they did when he made them (Burns 1963:xi). As more papers and audiotapes in archival collections are reviewed, declassified, and opened, it becomes clearer that much less is known about presidents and that much more is coming to be known about the presidency than was previously thought.

Regardless of the school in question, fuller understanding of presidents and the presidency will be assisted by the meeting of three conditions for research.

The first is that all research should at least be constitutionally informed and always politically nuanced. Sensitivity to the constitutional constraints on presidents, to their dynamic political purposes and those of their political competitors, and to contingency is necessary if politics is not to be marginalized in political science. Shorn of constitutional context and sensitivity to political flux, the presidency and its place in policy making and political change simply cannot be understood. Such context is necessarily relational; as Jones (1994, 1995) has demonstrated, in a separated system one must explore the complex relations of competition, conflict, and cooperation that presidents maintain with the federal bureaucracy, Congress, courts, public opinion, and interest groups.

The second condition for research is that the work be empirically rich, drawing on primary data in some form. The archives of the Presidential Libraries are the most important source of such data, but much material is also now available in published form (Haldeman 1994, Beschloss 1997, Kutler 1997). Hart (1998) has argued that the geographical dispersal of Presidential Libraries impedes inter-temporal research on the presidency. Awkward though such dispersal is, it cannot help explain why (for example) the superb collection of White House papers at the Nixon Presidential Project, housed at the National Archives II just outside Washington, DC, does not attract more political scientists. This may have more to do with the reluctance of many political scientists to exploit archival sources, itself a symptom of the methodological estrangement between the disciplines of political science and political history. Recent advances of historical institutionalism notwithstanding, the divide between the two disciplines has harmed both, and obstructed fuller understanding of the presidency. Heclo's (1977) complaint that too little is known about the presidency is being remedied—but more often by political historians than by political scientists. Davies (1996) and Matusow (1998) demonstrate anew that politically nuanced accounts of the presidency and its place in policy making can be developed on the foundations of deep and extensive archival research. Each author meets the challenge of providing ample information about certain key policy processes with which Presidents Johnson and Nixon (respectively) were concerned, while developing analyses of their origins, development, and significance.

The third condition is that scholars investigating particular cases should always be alive to the cases' wider significance, but they need not be constrained by a prior obligation to generate theory. Employing case studies has value only if it is clear what larger problem the particular study illuminates; nevertheless, if Wayne's stipulation that scholarship on the presidency should "readily lend itself to hypothesis testing or theory building" were to be complied with, constitutional scholarship might not meet the standard (Wayne 1983:25). While taking full account of political contexts, ambitions, and pressures, scholars need to be cognizant of Evans's injunction that "a compelling interpretation of a particular case is only interesting if it points to ways of understanding other cases as well" (Evans 1995:4). Searching for broader patterns and for wider significance of particular findings is a scholarly imperative in political history as much as in political science, but to require scholarly activity to meet methodological criteria of investigation derived from certain experimental sciences risks constraining legitimate avenues of inquiry and, indeed, entire schools of study. Constitutional scholars such as Corwin and Fisher, political scientists such as Neustadt, and political historians such as Davies and Matusow have not sought to build theory; they have, however, had as a prime object understanding the presidency through study of presidents. In other words, scholars from different schools, using different methods, and studying different kinds of problems have, through their particular studies, arrived at larger truths about the presidency and presidential policy making in the United States. In a field sometimes characterized as infertile, that is a considerable achievement on which there is every reason to continue to build.

Visit the *Annual Reviews home page* at
http://www.AnnualReviews.org.

Literature Cited

Ambrose SE. 1984. *Eisenhower: The President*. New York: Simon & Schuster

Ambrose SE. 1987. *Nixon: The Education of a Politician, 1913–1962*. New York: Simon & Schuster

Ambrose SE. 1989. *Nixon: The Triumph of a Politician, 1962–1972*. New York: Simon & Schuster

Bailey S. 1950. *Congress Makes a Law*. New York: Columbia Univ. Press

Barber JD. 1972. *The Presidential Character*. Englewood Cliffs, NJ: Prentice-Hall

Berman L. 1979. *The Office of Management and Budget and the Presidency, 1921–1979*. Princeton, NJ: Princeton Univ. Press

Beschloss MR. 1997. *Taking Charge*. New York: Simon & Schuster

Burns JM. 1956. *The Lion and the Fox*. New York: Harcourt, Brace & Co

Burns JM. 1963. *The Deadlock of Democracy*. Englewood Cliffs, NJ: Prentice-Hall

Burns JM. 1970. *The Soldier of Freedom*. New York: Harcourt, Brace & Co

Butler DE. 1997. How the party mood can shift. In *Times Higher Educ. Suppl.*, Oct. 3, p. 26

Cannon L. 1991. *President Reagan*. New York: Simon & Schuster

Caro RA. 1982. *The Years of Lyndon Johnson*. London: Collins

Caro RA. 1990. *Means of Ascent*. London: Bodley Head

Corwin ES. 1957. *The President, Office and Powers, 1787–1957*. New York: NY Univ. Press

Dallek R. 1991. *Lone Star Rising*. New York: Oxford Univ. Press

Dallek R. 1998. *Flawed Giant*. New York: Oxford Univ. Press

Davies G. 1996. *From Opportunity to Entitlement*. Lawrence: Univ. Kansas Press

Donovan RJ. 1977. *Conflict and Crisis*. New York: Norton

Donovan RJ. 1984. *Tumultuous Years*. New York: Norton

Edwards GC. 1989. *At the Margins*. New Haven, CT: Yale Univ. Press

Edwards GC, Wayne S. 1983. *Studying the Presidency*. Knoxville: Univ. Tenn. Press

Ellis RJ, Wildavsky A. 1991. *Dilemmas of Presidential Leadership*. New Brunswick, NJ: Transaction

Evans R. 1995. The role of theory in comparative politics. *World Polit.* 48:2–10

Fenno R. 1959. *The President's Cabinet*. Cambridge, MA: Harvard Univ. Press

Fisher L. 1991. *Constitutional Conflicts Between Congress and the President*. Lawrence: Univ. Kansas Press. 3rd ed.

Flash ES. 1965. *Economic Advice and Presidential Leadership*. New York: Columbia Univ. Press

Foner E. 1990. *Reconstruction*. New York: Harper & Row

Friedrich CJ. 1940. Public policy and the nature of administrative responsibility. *Public Policy* 1:1

George A. 1974. Assessing presidential character. *World Polit.* 26:234–282

George A, George J. 1956. *Woodrow Wilson and Colonel House*. New York: Day

Goodin RE, Klingemann H-D. 1996. *A New Handbook of Political Science*. New York: Oxford Univ. Press

Haldeman HR. 1994. *The Haldeman Diaries*. New York: Putnam

Hart J. 1998. Neglected aspects of the study of the presidency. *Annu. Rev. Polit. Sci.* 1: 379–99

Heclo H. 1977. *Studying the Presidency*. New York: Ford Found.

Jones CO. 1994. *The Presidency in a Separated System*. Washington, DC: Brookings Inst.

Jones CO. 1995. *Separate But Equal Branches*. Chatham, NJ: Chatham House

Kallenbach JE. 1966. *The American Chief Executive: the Presidency and the Governorship*. New York: Harper & Row

King A. 1975. Executives. In *Handbook of Political Science*, ed. NW Polsby, FI Greenstein, 5:173–256. Reading, MA: Addison-Wesley

King DS. 1995. *Separate and Unequal*. Oxford, UK: Oxford Univ. Press

Krasner S. 1978. *Defending the National Interest*. Princeton, NJ: Princeton Univ. Press

Kutler SI. 1997. *Abuse of Power*. New York: Simon & Schuster

Matusow A. 1998. *Nixon's Economy*. Lawrence: Univ. Kansas Press

Mayhew D. 1986. *Placing Parties in American Politics*. Princeton, NJ: Princeton Univ. Press

McCullough D. 1982. *Truman*. New York: Simon & Schuster

Morris E. 1979. *The Rise of Theodore Roosevelt*. London: Collins

Neustadt RE. 1954. Presidency and legislation: the growth of central clearance. *Am. Polit. Sci. Rev.* 48:641–671

Neustadt RE. 1955. Presidency and legislation: planning the President's program. *Am. Polit. Sci. Rev.* 49:980–1021

Neustadt RE. 1990. *Presidential Power and the Modern Presidents*. New York: Free

Peterson MA. 1990. *Legislating Together*. Cambridge, MA: Harvard Univ. Press

Pious R. 1979. *The American Presidency*. New York: Basic Books

Polsby NW. 1971. *Congress and the Presidency*. Englewood Cliffs, NJ: Prentice-Hall

Polsby NW. 1978. Presidential cabinet making. *Polit. Sci. Q.* 93:15–25

Shoemaker C. 1991. *The NSC Staff*. Boulder, CO: Westview

Simonton K. 1987. *Why Presidents Succeed*. New Haven, CT: Yale Univ. Press

Skowronek S. 1993. *The Politics Presidents Make*. Cambridge, MA: Belknap

Tulis J. 1987. *The Rhetorical Presidency*. Princeton, NJ: Princeton Univ. Press

Wayne SJ. 1983. Approaches. See Edwards & Wayne, pp. 17–49

Wilson W. 1908. *Constitutional Government in the United States*. New York: Columbia Univ. Press

Annu. Rev. Polit. Sci. 1999. 2:25–48

DETERRENCE AND INTERNATIONAL CONFLICT: Empirical Findings and Theoretical Debates

Paul K. Huth

Political Science Department and Institute for Social Research, University of
Michigan, Ann Arbor, Michigan 48106; e-mail: phuth@umich.edu

KEY WORDS: deterrence, credible threats, rational choice, prevention of war and crises

ABSTRACT

The utility of military threats as a means to deter international crises and war
has been a central topic of international relations research. Rational choice
models have provided the foundation for theorizing about the conditions under which conventional deterrence is likely to succeed or fail. Rational deterrence theorists have focused on four sets of variables: the balance of military
forces, costly signaling and bargaining behavior, reputations, and interests at
stake. Over the past two decades, scholars have tested propositions from rational deterrence theory utilizing both statistical and comparative case study
methods. Although the empirical results from these tests have supported a
number of hypotheses derived from the theoretical literature, they have also
challenged some theoretical arguments and have sparked vigorous debates
about both theory and research designs for conducting empirical research.

INTRODUCTION

The causes of international crises and the outbreak of war have been a central
topic in the field of international relations (IR). Whether wars and crises can be
prevented by policies of deterrence has also been a question of continuing interest to scholars, who have developed a substantial body of theoretical and
empirical work seeking to understand the conditions under which deterrent
threats are likely to succeed or fail. With the development of nuclear weapons

1094-2939/99/0616-0025$08.00

and the emergence of the Cold War, academic analyses of deterrence initially centered on questions of nuclear strategy and the credibility of US nuclear threats to protect allies in Europe and Asia (e.g. Kaufman 1956; Kissinger 1957; Brodie 1959; Ellsberg 1961; Wohlstetter 1959; Schelling 1960, 1966; Snyder 1961; Kahn 1965). In subsequent scholarship, the focus began to broaden to include the theory and practice of conventional deterrence. Analysts sought to develop more general models of deterrence and to draw upon the historical record of deterrence as practiced by states to test hypotheses about deterrence (e.g. Russett 1963, 1967; Quester 1966; George & Smoke 1974; Whiting 1975; for a review, see Jervis 1979). Over the past two decades, analysts have continued to study both nuclear and conventional deterrence and, as a result, the literature on deterrence is now characterized by a diversity of theoretical approaches and hypotheses as well as methods of empirical analysis and findings.

This chapter evaluates the scholarly literature of the past two decades that has focused on the study of conventional deterrence from a rational choice perspective. The findings from empirical tests and research are considered in order to evaluate various hypotheses and theoretical propositions about rational deterrence theory. Critiques of rational deterrence theory have in general drawn upon organizational theory and cognitive psychology to question the capacity of individual decision makers and military organizations to act rationally. A careful review of this literature is not possible in this chapter but good examples of each tradition are Sagan (1993) and Lebow & Stein (1989).

I first discuss the concept of deterrence, and in the second section I summarize rational deterrence theory and present hypotheses about the success and failure of deterrent threats. In the third section I review empirical studies of deterrence and in the concluding section I consider an agenda for future theoretical and empirical work on deterrence.

CONCEPT OF DETERRENCE

The concept of deterrence can be defined as the use of threats by one party to convince another party to refrain from initiating some course of action. A threat serves as a deterrent to the extent that it convinces its target not to carry out the intended action because of the costs and losses the target would incur. In IR scholarship, a policy of deterrence generally refers to threats of military retaliation directed by the leaders of one country to the leaders of another in an attempt to prevent the other country from resorting to the threat or use of military force in pursuit of its foreign policy goals. It should be clear, however, that policies of deterrence in international politics can include both military and non-military threats that are intended to prevent both military and non-military courses of action by other states. My analysis of the scholarly literature is restricted in its scope to those works that focus on the use of military threats by states to prevent other countries from resorting to the threat or use of military force.

Cases of Deterrence

A policy of deterrence can be directed at preventing an armed attack against a country's own territory (direct deterrence) or that of another country (extended deterrence). In addition, deterrent threats may be issued in response to a pressing short-term threat of attack (immediate deterrence), or a deterrent policy may seek to prevent such short-term crises and militarized conflict from arising (general deterrence). Combining these two dimensions of deterrence policies, we have four situations in which deterrence can be pursued by states: (*a*) direct-immediate deterrence, (*b*) direct-general deterrence, (*c*) extended-immediate deterrence, and (*d*) extended-general deterrence (Morgan 1977).

Major powers have been the primary states to practice extended deterrence. In a study of extended-immediate deterrence from 1885 to 1984, 48 out of 58 cases of attempted deterrence (83%) involved major powers as defenders (Huth 1988). Examples of extended-immediate deterrence include the crises leading to the outbreak of World Wars I and II, in which Great Britain failed to deter Germany. Following the end of the Korean War, the United States established an alliance and military presence in South Korea in support of a policy of extended-general deterrence against the threat of another invasion by North Korea.

Situations of direct deterrence often center on territorial conflicts between neighboring states in which the major powers do not directly intervene. In the Arab-Israeli conflict, Israel has relied on its own military forces to attempt deterrence against hostile Arab neighbors. For example, since the end of the Six-Day War of 1967, in which Israel occupied the Golan Heights, Israel has generally been successful in its efforts to deter Syria from attempting to retake the Golan by force of arms. In October of 1973, however, Israeli policies of general and then immediate deterrence failed as Syria launched a large-scale attack against Israeli forces in the Golan Heights.

Although the theoretical literature has considered both extended and direct deterrence situations extensively, hypotheses typically focus on deterrent threats in the context of immediate deterrence. A similar focus can be found in the empirical literature. As a result, the theoretical and empirical study of general deterrence is less extensive and less well developed than is the body of work on immediate deterrence.

Deterrence Outcomes

A successful policy of deterrence must be understood in both political and military terms. Militarily, general deterrence success refers to preventing state leaders from issuing military threats and actions that escalate peacetime diplomatic and military competition into a crisis or militarized confrontation which threatens armed conflict and possibly war. Immediate deterrence success is defined as preventing state leaders who have already threatened force in a crisis or militarized confrontation from resorting to the large-scale use of military force. The prevention of crises or wars, however, is not the only goal of deterrence. In addition, defenders must be able to resist the political and military demands of a potential attacker. If armed conflict is avoided at the price of diplomatic concessions to the maximum demands of the potential attacker under the threat of war, then we cannot claim that deterrence has succeeded. Deterrence failures, then, include the initiation of crises or militarized disputes (general deterrence failure); their escalation to war (immediate deterrence failure); or the avoidance of crises and war by defender states who make far-reaching concessions to the potential attacker (both general and immediate deterrence failures).

A further refinement would be to conceive of deterrence outcomes as ranging along a continuum of success/failure. Thus, general deterrence outcomes would be anchored at one end of the scale by complete success, defined as the absence of any military threats or political demands for a change in the status quo. The opposite end of the scale would be characterized by explicit demands for maximum changes in the status quo, which are supported by extensive military preparations for the large-scale use of force. Intermediate levels of challenges to general deterrence would include small-scale military probes and threats of force that are accompanied by demands for more restricted changes in the status quo. The same logic would apply to immediate deterrence outcomes. Complete success would entail potential attackers backing away from threats of escalation without resorting to any use of force and without securing any demanded changes in the status quo. Complete failure would involve escalation by the attacker, including a large-scale attack, or capitulation by the defender to the attacker's maximum demands as the price for avoiding war. Partial success/failure would be represented by the attacker initiating only limited uses of force and defending states offering concessions only on issues of secondary interest to the attacker.

RATIONAL DETERRENCE THEORY

The predominant approach to theorizing about deterrence has entailed the use of rational choice and game-theoretic models of decision making. Examples include the early efforts of Schelling (1960, 1966), Snyder (1961), and Ellsberg (1961), as well as more recent work by Zagare (1987), Brams (1985, Brams & Kilgour 1988), Nalebuff (1991), Powell (1990), Wagner (1982, 1991), and Fearon (1994b). In this rational choice tradition, state leaders considering the use of military force compare the expected utility of using force with that of refraining from a military challenge to the status quo, and they select the option with greater expected utility. A potential attacker considers the possible gains to be secured by the use of military force to change the status quo and evaluates the likelihood that force can be used successfully. This estimate of the expected utility for military conflict is then compared with the anticipated gains (or losses) associated with not using force and an estimate of how probable those gains/losses would be.

Rational deterrence theory focuses on how military threats can reduce the attacker's expected utility for using force by persuading the attacker that the outcome of a military confrontation will be both costly and unsuccessful. In addition, some deterrence theorists have studied the effects of defenders' policies on attackers' expected utility of not using force. Scholars have analyzed whether deterrent threats can lead to preemptive strikes by an attacker who fears that a defender's deterrent threats are actually a prelude to offensive attack. This literature examines the conditions under which the security dilemma might operate and produce fears of a first-strike advantage (e.g. Schelling 1960, Jervis 1978, Powell 1990, Wagner 1991, Kydd 1997, Glaser 1997). Some scholars have given attention to the role of positive inducements in combination with deterrent threats as a way to make the diplomatic and political status quo, with no military confrontation, more attractive to potential attackers (e.g. Huth 1988, Leng 1993). In theoretical terms, the most effective deterrent policies are those that decrease the expected utility of using force while not reducing the expected utility of the status quo; optimally, deterrent policies would even increase the expected utility of not using force. The most interesting theoretical questions are "When is it most important for defending states to strike a balance between credibly threatening war while also making continued peace acceptable to the attacker?" and "What policies are most likely to achieve such a balance?" The theoretical challenge for analysts is to develop models in which defenders offer enough positive inducements to make the expected utility of not using force acceptable to potential attackers, while not sacrificing vital security interests or undermining the credibility of the threat to use force.

Deterrence theorists have consistently argued that deterrence success is more likely if a defender's deterrent threat is credible to an attacker. A threat is considered credible if the defender possesses the military capabilities to inflict substantial costs on an attacker in an armed conflict and if the attacker believes that the defender is resolved to use its available military forces. However, deterrence theorists do not agree on what military capabilities, interests at stake, and past and current actions by a defender create a credible threat. There is no single set of accepted theoretical answers to the question of what factors produce credible deterrent threats. Nevertheless, a number of hypotheses and convergent lines of argument can be identified among rational choice analysts. Below, I focus on these areas of convergence and summarize some of the main propositions in four areas: military capabilities, signaling and bargaining behavior, reputations, and interests at stake.

The Military Balance

Deterrent policies have often been attempted in the context of territorial disputes between countries. This reflects the fact that territorial disputes have been a primary cause of crises and wars between states. (For a review of much of the literature on war and territorial disputes, see Vasquez 1993:123–52.) Deterrence is often directed against state leaders who have specific territorial goals that they seek to attain either by seizing disputed territory in a limited military attack or by occupying disputed territory after the decisive defeat of an adversary's armed forces.[1] In either case, the strategic orientation of potential attackers is generally short-term and driven by concerns about military costs and mission effectiveness. Thus, attacking states prefer to utilize military force quickly to achieve military-territorial goals without suffering heavy attrition of manpower and weapons. The arguments of Mearsheimer (1983), Huth (1988), and Glaser & Kaufmann (1998) lead to the hypothesis that a defending state needs the military capacity to respond quickly and in strength to a range of military contingencies, and thus to be able to deny the attacker its military objectives at the outset or very early stages of an armed offensive. When defending forces lack the strength and mobility to blunt an attack at or near its point of origin, the attacking state's prospects of a rapid advance into enemy territory and the overrunning of opposing forces greatly increase the confidence of political and military leaders that military costs will not be extensive and that military successes can be translated into concrete territorial gains. In sum, advantages for attacking states in the determinants of the "immediate" and "short-term" balance of forces can convince leaders that an offensive military strategy can be successful at low cost.

Signaling and Bargaining Behavior

The central problem for a state that seeks to communicate a credible deterrent threat through diplomatic and military actions is that all defending states have an incentive to act as if they are determined to resist an attack, in the hope that a challenger will back away from military conflict with a seemingly resolved adversary. If all defenders have such incentives, then potential attackers may discount statements and the movement of military forces as mere bluffs. Resolved

---

[1]One study finds that between 1950 and 1990 there were 129 territorial disputes between states (Huth 1996).

defenders want to distinguish themselves from states that are bluffing in order to establish the credibility of their threats. Attackers want to identify truly resolved defenders so that a decision to escalate is not based on the mistaken belief that the defender will capitulate under the threat of war.

Rational deterrence theorists have argued that "costly" signals are required to communicate credibly a defender's resolve. Schelling's classic work (1966) on the manipulation of risk and commitment strategies provides the foundation for this line of argument, but other scholars have refined and extended his initial insights (e.g. Jervis 1970; Nalebuff 1991; Powell 1990; Fearon 1994a,b, 1997). Costly signals are those actions and statements that clearly increase the risk of a military conflict and also increase the costs of backing down from a deterrent threat, thereby revealing information about the actual commitment of a state to defend against an attack. States that are bluffing will be unwilling to cross a certain threshold of threat and military actions in a crisis for fear of committing themselves to armed conflict. Fearon (1994a) offers an interesting extension of the costly signaling approach with applications to deterrence. He hypothesizes that leaders of democratic states are more capable of communicating credible threats in a crisis because democratic leaders face higher domestic political costs for backing down in a crisis (political opposition would be able to hold them accountable for such a foreign policy setback). The implication for deterrence is that crisis bargaining by democratic defenders should be a more effective deterrent than comparable bargaining moves by nondemocratic leaders, for whom bluffing is less politically dangerous.

Although the concept of costly signals and the manipulation of risk represent critical contributions to rational deterrence theory, scholars have also argued that political constraints may limit the willingness of state leaders to send costly signals and that there may even be strategic drawbacks associated with such policies. For example, the security dilemma may induce defenders to be cautious about what types of military actions are to be taken in a crisis for fear of provoking the attacker into a preemptive strike. Fearon (1997) summarizes several reasons why state leaders may send less than fully committing signals: (*a*) uncertainty about the degree of domestic political support for such a policy, (*b*) concerns that the ability to moderate the policies of allies will be weakened if unqualified support is given to them, or (*c*) the risk that rigid diplomatic and military policies may generate high political costs for the adversary in backing down. One possible theoretical answer is for defending states to send signals that are likely to balance the competing demands of crisis credibility and stability. Huth (1988) and Leng (1984, 1993), for example, have argued that diplomatic and military policies relying on reciprocity and conditional cooperation are likely to achieve these varied goals of signaling resolve without generating very high political or military costs for attackers if they back down in a crisis.

Reputations for Resolve

Three different arguments have been developed with respect to the role of reputations in influencing deterrence outcomes (see Huth 1997 for a more detailed summary).[2] The first argument, which I label the strong-inter-dependence-of-commitments position, is drawn from Schelling (1966). His hypothesis is that a defender's past behavior in international disputes and crises creates strong beliefs in a potential attacker about the defender's expected behavior in future conflicts. The credibilities of a defender's deterrence policies are linked over time, and reputations for resolve have a powerful causal impact on an attacker's decision whether to challenge either general or immediate deterrence.

The logical foundations for Schelling's interdependence-of-commitments argument are not well developed. Although Schelling is clear about what behaviors to expect, he does not develop a compelling logical foundation to explain why we should expect such behaviors. The weakest element in the argument is the claim that reputations are a powerful causal variable relative to what I term case-specific determinants of credibility, such as the balance of forces, interests at stake, or crisis bargaining behavior. Because deterrence analysts argue that the credibility of threats varies across situations, we would expect potential attackers to pay close attention to contextual determinants of defender behavior. What are the logical grounds, then, for weighing reputational inferences so heavily relative to other sources of information about the resolve of the defender? Scholars working in this tradition have not presented tight theoretical arguments to sustain strong claims about the interdependence of commitments.

The second approach to reputations in deterrence theory is the "case-specific credibility position." In contrast to Schelling, proponents of this position argue that reputations have a limited impact on deterrence outcomes because the credibility of deterrence is so heavily determined by the specific configuration of military capabilities, interests at stake, and political constraints faced by a defender in a given situation of attempted deterrence. The argument of this school is that potential attackers are not likely to draw strong inferences about a defender's resolve from prior conflicts because potential attackers do not believe that a defender's past behavior is a reliable predictor of future behavior. Instead, potential attackers reason that a defender's behavior

---

[2]I focus on defenders' reputations for resolve to use force, although other types of reputations have also been addressed in the literature (much less extensively)—for example, reputations relating to the quality of military leadership and combat effectiveness of troops or reputations for honesty when communicating through diplomatic exchanges. On the latter, see Sartori (1998). I do not review Mercer's (1996) theory of reputations because it is based on insights from cognitive psychology and therefore is not part of the rational choice literature.

is largely a function of case-specific variables, and therefore their decisions about whether to challenge general or immediate deterrence should be only weakly influenced by a defender's reputation.

The case-specific credibility approach has a strong logical foundation, since it is premised on the argument that the credibility of threats can vary substantially across deterrence situations and that potential attackers are aware of this. As a result, the general theoretical implication that we should not expect reputations to have a consistent and strong causal effect is convincing. The weakness of this second school is that scholars neglect the possibility that the impact of reputational variables might be important but only under more limited conditions.

This shortcoming is addressed in the third tradition of theorizing about reputations, which I refer to as the qualified-interdependence-of-commitments position. This approach argues that potential attackers are likely to draw reputational inferences about resolve from the past behavior of defenders only under certain conditions. The reasoning is that reputations are likely to form only when the behavior of a defender runs counter to the expectations of the potential attacker. If, for example, the potential attacker expects the defender to use force but the defender fails to do so, the potential attacker may infer that the defender lacks resolve for reasons that are not case-specific but instead reflect some general enduring trait. (The formal modeling literature on costly signals and bargaining described above uses similar logic in arguing that only certain actions are informative because they help decision makers to distinguish between different types of states.) The insight is that we should expect decision makers to use only certain types of information when drawing inferences about reputations. From this perspective, much information about the behavior of a defender is irrelevant to the formation of reputational inferences by a potential attacker. Therefore, in attempting to predict when such inferences will be drawn, the analyst must first identify the potential attacker's initial expectations or prior beliefs about the defender's likely response. The hypothesis is that a potential attacker updates and revises his beliefs when the unanticipated behavior of the defender cannot be explained by case-specific variables. The updating and revising of beliefs in such a situation can be understood as the potential attacker's process of drawing reputational inferences.

This third school of thought stakes out a position on reputations that is intermediate between the first two. Reputations can form and be important but only under certain conditions. Logically, reputations could form on the basis of defender actions in a broad range of past conflicts, as long as the defender's actions ran counter to the potential attacker's expectations. It also seems logical to argue that if reputational inferences are drawn, they are quite strong in terms of causal impact on subsequent decisions to challenge the defender, since the inference itself is based on the idea that some characteristic of the defender was powerful enough to override situational variables in a past case.

Interests at Stake

Although the costly signaling argument is well established in rational deterrence theory, scholars (e.g. George & Smoke 1974, Maxwell 1968) have questioned the explanatory power of such arguments by proposing that attackers may look beyond the short-term bargaining tactics of a defender and ask, "What are the interests at stake for the defender that would justify the risks of a military conflict?" These critics reason that when state leaders have vital interests at stake in a dispute they will be more resolved to use force and more willing to endure military losses in order to secure those interests. The claim, therefore, is that the "balance of interests" plays a very important role in determining deterrence outcomes. The next step, however, of specifying what interests are most salient to national leaders is not well established in the literature. Scholars have drawn distinctions between international reputational interests, domestic political interests, and various intrinsic security and non-security interests (e.g. Jervis 1970; Desch 1993; Fearon 1994a, 1997), but it has been difficult to develop convincing logical arguments about how to rank order or compare the relative saliency of such interests. In addition, critics of balance-of-interests logic are concerned that such arguments risk reliance on interpersonal comparisons of utilities or questionable claims about the attacker's recognition of the legitimacy of the status quo, and may employ tautological reasoning to make inferences about interests given known deterrence outcomes (see Wagner 1982, Betts 1987:132–44). As a result, claims that the balance of interests is critical to explaining deterrence outcomes (e.g. Lieberman 1994, Bar-Joseph 1998, George & Smoke 1974, Jervis 1979:314–19) seem questionable on theoretical grounds.

This is not to deny that the interests at stake for states in a dispute are theoretically important variables to include in an analysis of deterrence. There is no doubt that potential attackers have beliefs about what issues are at stake for themselves as well as for defending states, but translating those separate beliefs into an integrated comparative assessment of what scholars call the balance of interests is quite problematic. Until stronger logical arguments are developed about the rank ordering of interests and other problems raised by critics are addressed, claims about the balance of interests should be avoided. Instead, propositions should be developed positing that the presence/absence of certain interests for attacker and defender have a systematic impact on their expected-utility calculations without implying that state leaders have made a direct comparison and evaluation of relative interests.

EMPIRICAL FINDINGS ON DETERRENCE

The body of empirical research on conventional deterrence has increased substantially over the past two decades. Scholars have employed both statistical and comparative case study methods to produce new findings. Most studies have examined cases of immediate deterrence (both direct and extended) with cross-sectional research designs, but the use of time-series approaches is increasing. Findings on immediate deterrence require special attention to the potential problems posed by selection effects for causal inference in empirical research, problems that have become more widely understood by political scientists in the past decade (Achen & Snidal 1989, Fearon 1994b). In addition, scholars have debated the strengths and weaknesses of various approaches to constructing data sets for testing hypotheses about deterrence (Lebow & Stein 1990, Huth & Russett 1990, Harvey 1997:19–46). The result is that we now have a range of empirical studies to draw on in evaluating hypotheses derived from rational deterrence theory.

The Military Balance

Several empirical studies have found that the balance of military power is an important but not overriding determinant of deterrence success and failure. The findings indicate that when defenders have the military capabilities to repulse a large-scale attack from the very outset, the prospects of immediate deterrence success increase significantly, as potential attackers recognize that it will be difficult and costly to achieve specific military missions and territorial goals (e.g. Mearsheimer 1983; Shimshoni 1988; Lieberman 1994, 1995; Huth 1988, 1996; Bueno de Mesquita et al 1997). Attackers generally seek to utilize military force in relatively quick and decisive military operations; if the defender has the military capacity to counter an attack from the outset, an attacker risks a quick defeat or a prolonged war of attrition.

However, studies of Israeli policies of deterrence against Syria and Egypt (Lieberman 1994, 1995; Shimshoni 1988; Bar-Joseph 1998) suggest that attackers will adjust to their relative military weakness by moderating their territorial goals and by developing less ambitious operational plans for future attacks. As a result, while Israel was able to deter a general Arab offensive with the goal of penetrating deep into Israeli territory, the challenge of immediate deterrence for Israel shifted to preventing attacks in contested demilitarized zones and occupied territories. Thus, over time, although an Israeli advantage in the balance of forces did not ensure immediate deterrence success, it did serve to lower significantly the military aspirations of Arab leaders and the levels of subsequent attack when deterrence did fail.

The strategic perspective of attackers poses a difficult challenge for defenders attempting extended-immediate deterrence. Although major powers have historically been the states to practice immediate deterrence most frequently, their ability to project military forces beyond their own national borders quickly and in large numbers is a demanding military task. In most cases, such states can mobilize and transport substantial forces over a longer period of time, but extended-immediate deterrence success places a premium on the rapid movement of forces into position to repulse an attack. Thus, major powers may fail in their attempts at extended-immediate deterrence, even though they are able to apply decisive force after a more protracted military buildup. (For example, contrast the absence of US ground forces in Kuwait in July 1990, prior to the Iraqi invasion, with the massive US buildup in Saudi Arabia by January 1991.) Furthermore, the timely projection of military power with forward deployments of ground forces can be undercut by domestic and regional political constraints that preclude extensive military preparations early in a crisis, when they are most critical. The broader implication is that while scholars have identified many of the military conditions conducive to immediate deterrence success, they have also found that defenders are often hampered by political constraints, which prevent leaders from implementing more effective policies of immediate deterrence.

In general deterrence situations, the balance of military strength has weaker deterrent effects. It is difficult for defenders to deter low-level military probes and threats of force because attackers avoid committing large forces and can pull back if the defender responds quickly with a powerful military buildup. George & Smoke (1974), in their classic study, found that attackers often devised ways to test and probe the strength of US extended deterrent forces by the calculated use of limited force. Similarly, studies of Israel's attempts to deter its Arab neighbors concluded that small-scale border raids and skirmishes were frequent and not easily deterred by Israeli reprisal strikes (Lieberman 1994, 1995; Shimshoni 1988; Bar-Joseph 1998; Morris 1993). Finally, in two studies of enduring rivalries involving either great powers or regional adversaries (Huth et al 1992, Huth & Russett 1993), the conventional balance of military forces had a weak effect at best in preventing challenges to general deterrence.

The final set of findings focuses on critical misperceptions or miscalculations about the military balance that have contributed to immediate deterrence failures. Two types of misperceptions can be identified in the literature (e.g. Lebow 1981, Stein 1985, Paul 1994): (a) Attackers are overconfident of their ability to translate short-term military advantages into quick and favorable diplomatic and political settlements; (b) attackers are overconfident that short-term military advantages will result in a very quick and decisive military victory. The problem seems to be that attackers either underestimate the likelihood of military intervention by defenders when their allies have suffered heavy initial military losses, or they underestimate the military and political capacity of larger states to withstand initial military setbacks and continue fighting. Although scholars generally agree on the consequences of such miscalculations for deterrence, they disagree on the sources of the miscalculations (see Orme 1987 vs Lebow 1987). Are they caused by uncertainty about the military capabilities of states, or do they reflect more fundamental errors in decision making due to various cognitive biases?

Crisis Bargaining and Interests at Stake

Deterrence theorists have argued that potential attackers trying to estimate the interests at stake for defenders will consider two sources of information about the defenders' likely resolve. The first source consists of direct indicators of intrinsic interests, such as whether defenders risk losing territory with known economic or strategic value or losing beneficial economic or military ties with an ally. The second, more indirect information source is a defender's bargaining behavior, which conveys a signal as to the defender's interests at stake and resolve. That is, a defender with important interests at stake is presumably more likely to send costly signals, and crisis bargaining moves can create domestic and international audience costs that in turn affect the defender's political interests at stake.

Let me begin by reviewing findings on bargaining behavior. Studies of crisis bargaining indicate that the military and diplomatic actions of defenders can have strong effects on whether deterrence succeeds or fails (Huth 1988; Leng 1984, 1993; Gelpi 1997). This finding provides general support for the role of bargaining behavior as an effective means for states to signal their intentions and to communicate resolve in short-term confrontations. The finding is also consistent with the rational choice claim that bargaining moves as informative signals can allow attackers to update their beliefs about a defender's resolve. Existing empirical studies, however, do not provide clear evidence whether attackers utilize the defender's bargaining behavior to update beliefs about the defender's intrinsic interests at stake or to conclude that increased audience costs have stiffened the resolve of the defender.

Although the findings of Huth, Leng, and Gelpi lend support to rationalist arguments about crisis signaling, they do not clearly substantiate Schelling-type arguments about the manipulation of risk and inflexible commitment tactics. The reason is that these scholars conclude that diplomatic policies of firm but flexible bargaining that combines reciprocity with conditional compromise or military policies of tit-for-tat escalation are more effective as deterrents than are more intransigent and bold policies of diplomatic and military response.

More tempered policies of reciprocating the military actions of attackers seem more effective in deterring the escalation of crises to wars. In contrast, policies of caution or aggressiveness in the level of military response are more likely to lead to crisis escalation and deterrence failure. It is important to rec-

ognize that such tit-for-tat policies of military response have not often produced spirals of escalation culminating in preemptive strikes. In the past two
centuries, the outbreak of war has very rarely been triggered by preemptive
attacks by states (Reiter 1995).

As noted, another important finding related to crisis bargaining is that diplomatic policies that include elements of accommodation and positive inducements can significantly increase the likelihood of deterrence success. In particular, diplomatic policies that include flexibility and a willingness to compromise and negotiate on secondary issues, combined with a refusal to concede on vital security issues, increase the likelihood of deterrence success.
These firm but flexible diplomatic strategies can help leaders of attacker states
to retreat from their threats by reducing the domestic or international political
costs of backing away from a military confrontation. Leaders can claim that
defender concessions on certain issues were a major gain, or that a defender's
willingness to negotiate was a promising diplomatic development. In either
case, foreign policy leaders can use even limited accommodative diplomatic
actions of the defender to fend off domestic or foreign political adversaries
who claim that the government of the would-be attacker state has retreated
under pressure.

Leng (1984, 1993) has also presented evidence that the combination of
threats and limited positive inducements is more effective in preventing crisis
escalation than are deterrent threats alone. The deterrent value of this carrot-
and-stick approach reflects the fact that such a policy seeks to alter both aspects of an attacker's expected-utility calculation. The use of the stick can persuade the attacker that a military conflict will be costly and risky, while the
carrot provides some favorable, even if limited, political changes that can
convince leaders that in the absence of a military conflict there exists an acceptable status quo.

In sum, early arguments about the strategic advantages of the manipulation
of risk and commitment strategies have not been fully supported by empirical
research. Instead, more moderate bargaining moves seem to serve as effective
signals because attackers often distrust defenders' claims of defensive intentions and they must also face the audience costs associated with backing
down.

When we turn to empirical research that tests hypotheses about how the intrinsic interests of either defenders or attackers influence deterrence outcomes,
it is critical to consider selection effects (Fearon 1994b). For example, if
analysts focus on observable measures such as alliance or economic ties as indicators of interests at stake for defenders in situations of extended deterrence
(Huth & Russett 1984, Huth 1988), then such variables should have their most
powerful deterrent effects at the stage of general deterrence and have attenuated effects at the stage of immediate deterrence. Unfortunately, no empirical

studies of immediate deterrence have systematically analyzed the conditions that initially shaped the attacker's decision to issue a threat. As a result, we cannot compare the substantive impact of variables measuring intrinsic interests across different stages of deterrence or control for such selection effects in statistical analyses of immediate deterrence.

Available results about intrinsic interests at stake, then, are drawn from situations of immediate deterrence and must be interpreted with potential selection effects in mind. Studies have reported that military alliances and cooperative military ties do not have a strong deterrent effect in situations of extended-immediate deterrence (Huth 1988). Selection effects may account for these weak findings. For example, it may be that attackers believe that defenders will honor their alliance commitments if their allies are attacked (Fearon 1994b). Thus, if we observe a crisis in which an attacker threatens a state that has alliance ties, the attacker must be highly resolved to use force, since it knows that the defender will most likely be supported by its ally if attacked. Highly resolved attackers would be more likely to challenge immediate deterrence, so the presence of an alliance should be correlated with the failure of extended-immediate deterrence.[3] A different explanation (Smith 1996) is that attackers believe that the credibility of alliance commitments varies substantially, and therefore attackers only threaten states having alliance ties when they believe that the defender is not a reliable alliance partner. As a result, the attacker is more likely to risk a war by threatening the allied state, based on the expectation that the defender is unlikely to come to the military aid of its ally.

The fact that alliance ties fail to promote extended-immediate deterrence, however, does not necessarily imply that they are also ineffective as an extended-general deterrent. Indeed, the very logic of the two arguments just presented suggests that military alliances and other types of military ties act as powerful deterrents and prevent attackers from challenging general deterrence. For example, alliances that include the peacetime deployment of defender forces on the territory of an ally should act as the most powerful deterrents. In a study of challenger states seeking to overturn the territorial status quo by threats of force, alliance ties had only a modest deterrent impact (Huth 1996). However, this study made no attempt to code whether alliances were supported by foreign deployments. There are, then, no existing studies that directly and carefully test for the extended-general deterrent value of alliances. Given the limited empirical evidence available on alliances, it is not possible to reach clear conclusions about their utility as extended deterrents. What evi-

---

[3]In a statistical analysis, whether the coefficient for the alliance variable shifts from its expected positive sign to negative depends on (a) the strength of the correlation between the alliance measure and the unobserved variable of the attacker's resolve, and (b) the substantive impact of the unobserved variable on deterrence outcomes.

dence does exist suggests that their deterrent value in situations of immediate deterrence is limited.

Several studies present evidence that control of disputed territory, particularly homeland territory, is considered particularly salient by national leaders. These studies report a strong relationship between territorial disputes and international conflict. Territorial disputes are associated with the initiation of international crises, the emergence of enduring rivalries, and the escalation of crises and militarized disputes to the outbreak of war (Hensel 1996a,b; Leng 1993; Brecher 1993:72; Brecher & Wilkenfeld 1997:821; Kocs 1995; Senese 1996; Vasquez 1995). Furthermore, disputed territory that has military value or is populated by ethnic conationals is most likely to escalate to the level of military confrontations (Huth 1996). In sum, policies of extended and direct deterrence are more likely to fail when challenger states seek to gain territory they view as part of their national homeland.

The final finding to consider is that a declining status quo position is an important reason why states initiate challenges to the deterrent policies of defenders. The rational choice literature has not given careful attention to this topic. As noted, most of the literature is directed at the question of how defenders can increase the credibility of deterrent threats and therefore convince potential attackers that the expected value of using force is low. Recent work on audience costs is a promising avenue for developing hypotheses about the costs of inaction for states, but the idea that a deteriorating status quo position acts as a powerful cause of challenges to deterrence is different from the logic of audience costs.

The theoretical inattention to evaluations of the status quo as a cause of general deterrence failure may reflect in part the Cold War context in which scholarship on deterrence developed. In the United States, initial efforts at theorizing and building deterrence models typically treated the Soviet Union as the strategically aggressive potential attacker. Another limitation, on the empirical side, may have been the difficulty of constructing data sets to test hypotheses about general deterrence and crisis initiation. As a result, both theory and empirical work often started with a situation of immediate deterrence and did not include a careful analysis of the conditions that prompted the attacker to challenge deterrence.

A useful contribution from empirical studies of deterrence in regional conflicts is the finding that a declining domestic political position or a deteriorating international security position has caused leaders to challenge deterrence (e.g. Lebow 1981; Stein 1985, 1996; Paul 1994; Huth & Russett 1993). Similarly, a study of territorial disputes found that defending states' political, military, and economic efforts to consolidate their control over disputed territory are one significant cause of challengers' decisions to use military force (Huth 1996:130–32).

Both supporters and critics of deterrence agree that an unfavorable assessment of the domestic or international status quo by leaders can undermine or severely test deterrence. However, there are different theoretical explanations for these empirical findings. A theoretical debate exists concerning the causal process by which leaders' concerns about the status quo lead to challenges to deterrence. In a rational choice approach, if the expected utility of not using force is reduced by a declining status quo position, then deterrence failure is more likely, since the alternative option of using force becomes relatively more attractive. Rational choice analysts could argue that the risks of a crisis or war may be acceptable to decision makers when the alternative is the loss of political power or the anticipated weakening of their country's international security position. Conversely, psychological theories of motivated misperceptions or risk taking in prospect theory[4] could question this expected-utility explanation and provide an interpretation of leader decisions in which an attacker's expected-utility calculations are biased in favor of using force.

The theoretical debate about the role of misperceptions and risk taking in failures of deterrence will not be easily resolved through empirical testing of contending propositions. Researchers will have to design empirical tests that answer such difficult questions as how much information was available to leaders when decisions were made, what were reasonable inferences to draw from the information, how did decision makers define the status quo position of their country domestically and internationally, and how risky was it for decision makers to have initiated a crisis or large-scale attack.

The debate over evidence and the interpretation of historical cases should not obscure the larger area of agreement between rational deterrence analysts and their critics, which is that deterrence is more likely to fail if leaders of potential attacker states believe they will incur substantial political and/or military costs if they fail to pursue a more aggressive foreign policy.

Reputations

The number of studies that have produced findings on reputations is limited, and therefore the conclusions drawn from these studies should be regarded as tentative and requiring further confirmation. There is little support for the strong-interdependence-of-commitment argument that potential attackers infer the defender's reputation for resolve from its prior behavior in disputes with other states across a broad range of geographic locations.[5] Huth & Rus-

---

[4]For a review of prospect theory and its applications to international relations see Levy (1997).

[5]Sartori (1998) finds that states do seem to acquire general reputations for honesty in communicating their intentions through diplomacy. This finding does not directly support the Schelling argument, however, because Sartori focuses on reputations for bluffing and not reputations for resolve.

sett's (1984) study of 54 cases of extended deterrence from 1900 to 1980 indicated that the past behavior of the defender in disputes with other states had no significant impact on deterrence outcomes. Mercer's (1996) analysis of international crises in the decade prior to World War I found no consistent pattern of European leaders inferring reputations from previous crisis outcomes. Finally, Hopf (1994) concluded that Soviet assessments of the credibility of US extended-deterrent commitments in Europe and Asia were essentially unaffected by US behavior in the Third World.

Orme (1992) makes the strongest claims in support of the strong-interdependence-of-commitments argument. He argues that periods of more active and confrontational Soviet behavior during the Cold War were influenced by Soviet perceptions of US resolve based on prior US involvement in international conflicts. A close examination of the data indicates, however, that the general pattern was one of Soviet leaders inferring from US actions in the Third World that their country could intervene in other Third World conflicts, or that US actions in a particular region indicated a reputation for resolve only in that region. Orme does not argue that US failures to act more forcefully in the Third World, or in areas where US deterrence commitments were not well established, resulted in Soviet leaders' challenging US primary deterrent commitments in Western Europe or the Far East. What Orme's evidence shows is that the US reputation for irresolution in the Third World, or in regions where a US sphere of influence was not well established, did encourage the Soviets to act more forcefully in those areas.

Thus, although support for the strong-interdependence-of-commitments position is weak, there is stronger evidence for a more limited claim about the interdependence of commitments. Within dyads interacting in a given region, reputations may form on the basis of past behavior. For example, past retreats by defenders in disputes with a particular potential attacker have been consistently correlated with subsequent militarized dispute initiation or crisis escalation by that same potential attacker (Huth 1988, Huth et al 1992, Huth et al 1993). In studies of the Arab-Israeli conflict (Shimshoni 1988; Lieberman 1994, 1995; Evron 1987), scholars have argued that the Israeli reputation for resolve was formed on the basis of the direct experience of Arab states in past wars and border skirmishes with Israel. The regional dimension to the interdependence of commitments is evident in Orme's study (above), in the work on Israel's reputation with its Arab neighbors, and in the various studies by Huth, in which many of the cases linking the defender's past behavior to the potential attacker's current conflict behavior were situated in the same region. In sum, to the extent that these findings support the notion that reputations do form, they indicate that reputations tend to arise from the past record of interactions between the same defender and the same potential attacker within the same geographic region.

The strongest claim of the case-specific credibility school, namely that the effects of reputational variables are insignificant, is not supported by the available findings. On the one hand, there is substantial evidence that situational determinants of deterrence outcomes are very important. On the other hand, there is ample evidence that, under certain conditions, reputational influences can be important as well. Thus, several scholars conclude that reputations are important to take into account in explaining the success or failure of deterrence (e.g. Huth 1988; Huth et al 1993; Lieberman 1994, 1995; Orme 1992; Shimshoni 1988). Several statistical studies have reported that the substantive impact of reputational variables is quite comparable to the impact of situational variables such as relative military strength, interests at stake, and crisis bargaining strategies (Huth 1988; Huth et al 1992, 1993). One possible way to summarize these results is that although situational variables are more consistently important determinants of deterrence outcomes than reputational influences, when reputational inferences are drawn by potential attackers, they have causal effects similar to those of situational variables.

The duration of these reputational effects, however, may not be extensive, as studies of Israeli deterrence policies suggest. Lieberman (1994, 1995) and Shimshoni (1988) argue that although Arab leaders did learn lessons about Israeli resolve from past military confrontations, these reputational inferences were not long-lived. These authors also note that changing military technologies and new military planning could render past lessons less relevant. Stein (1996) is even more doubtful about the longevity and impact of reputations on deterrence outcomes, based on her analysis of challenges to deterrence by Arab countries. Another possible conclusion is that when reputations do form they may have important effects on attacker calculations but only for a relatively short period of time. The importance of reputations may well fade as the international strategic environment changes over time and as new leaders assume power within defender states.

An important gap in the empirical literature is the failure to test the qualified-interdependence-of-commitments argument. This is unfortunate because, as argued above, the qualified-interdependence-of-commitments position is built on a stronger logical foundation than the more widely tested strong-interdependence-of-commitments argument. A priority for future empirical work, then, should be to think about what type of research designs and data would be appropriate to test the qualified-interdependence position. Given the centrality of initial potential-attacker expectations about the actions of defenders in this approach, the first requirement will be to construct a data base cast at the level of the individual policy maker. One of the most promising areas for future research, therefore, will be tests that assess the relative explanatory power of the strong- and qualified-interdependence-of-commitments arguments.

CONCLUSION

Problems of conventional deterrence remain pressing security issues for a number of states in the post–Cold War international system. Territorial disputes that could escalate to higher levels of international conflict persist in such regions as the Balkans, the Middle East, South Asia, and the Far East. The collapse of domestic political order within states threatens military intervention by neighboring states and greater involvement by NATO and UN peacekeeping forces. Wars and international crises will continue to occur and state leaders will attempt to maintain national security against external military threats by means of a range of diplomatic and military policies. Multilateral peacekeeping operations will also be confronted with more demanding military missions in which deterrence will be a more central policy objective.

The continuing relevance of deterrence underscores the need for further research on the causes of conventional deterrence success and failure. Although research on deterrence has advanced considerably over the past two decades, there are still important limits to our knowledge. An agenda for research would include the following:

1. Much further theoretical work on identifying when reputations form and what impact they have on deterrence. In addition, careful empirical work is required to test arguments about reputation formation and its causal impact. Policy makers often justify policies of immediate deterrence as necessary to avoid damage to their country's international reputation, but in fact our understanding of the importance of reputations to deterrence, though improving, remains quite rudimentary. Recent work on reputations for honesty in diplomacy provides interesting new arguments and findings (Sartori 1998), and their implications for existing research on reputations for resolve is one promising area for future research.

2. The domestic political sources of defender and attacker policy choices in situations of deterrence is a very promising area for research. Recent work has found strong evidence that domestic conditions can (*a*) be causes of initial challenges to general deterrence, (*b*) constrain and shape the defender's deterrent response to the attacker's threats, and (*c*) influence the attacker's decision to escalate an immediate-deterrence confrontation to war. In each of these areas, scholarly debates exist about how and to what degree domestic factors shape state behavior. One example is the interesting theoretical question of comparing the relative causal impact of high domestic costs of inaction for potential attackers vs high military costs of using force. A promising area for empirical research is in devising empirical tests to discriminate between explanations drawn from rational choice models of audience costs, prospect theory, and the motivated misperception literature as to

how an unfavorable domestic political position would lead to deterrence failures.

3. More research should be directed toward analyzing the conditions under which threats and rewards can be combined into a coherent and effective deterrent policy. Recent research suggests that reciprocating as well as carrot-and-stick bargaining strategies enhance the prospects of deterrence success, but much greater refinements can be made in identifying effective strategies and the conditions under which they are most effective (Peterson 1996). For example, how robust are firm-but-flexible and carrot-and-stick bargaining strategies under varying degrees of severity of the security dilemma? How robust are they when attackers view themselves as operating in the domain of losses according to prospect theory? Another topic that has not systematically been addressed, either theoretically or empirically, is the relationship between deterrence outcomes and conflict resolution. It is important to recognize that deterrence success cannot be equated with successful conflict resolution. The avoidance of crises and wars between states by means of deterrence may not be accompanied by a settlement of the underlying issues in dispute between adversaries. Whether, in the absence of armed conflict, two disputing parties can settle their differences is largely a question of diplomatic bargaining and the ability of state leaders to devise agreements that they can accept and that they believe will be upheld by their adversary. Deterrent policies may contribute to conflict resolution indirectly by persuading states that there is no viable military solution to a dispute. However, notions of a "hurting stalemate" in recent studies of international mediation (Bercovitch 1997) and findings about military defeats and the settlement of territorial disputes (Huth 1996:164–71) suggest that deterrence failures and the resulting high costs of war and armed conflict push parties toward settlements. This suggests that successful deterrence might actually impede conflict resolution.

4. Situations of general deterrence require much more extensive empirical analysis. States devote considerable diplomatic and financial resources as well as manpower to support general deterrence, but there are too few empirical studies of the subject. For example, there is a need for more extensive theoretical and empirical work on the relationship between arms races and challenges to general deterrence. Recent works on the security dilemma (Glaser 1992, 1994/1995, 1997; Kydd 1997) provide a stronger theoretical foundation for empirical work (e.g. Sample 1997, 1998) by clarifying the causal pathways that connect the consequences of arms races to deterrence outcomes. There are potentially multiple causal pathways from arms races to crises and war (Downs 1991), and empirical tests need to be designed to trace those different pathways. A rich historical record is available to schol-

ars, and the results of such research should significantly advance our understanding of how conflicts first emerge and what compels leaders to risk military confrontations by challenging deterrence.

Literature Cited

Achen C, Snidal D. 1989. Rational deterrence theory and comparative case studies. *World Polit.* 41:143–69

Bar-Joseph U. 1998. The conceptualization of deterrence in Israeli strategic thinking. *Secur. Stud.* 7:145–81

Bercovitch J. 1997. Mediation in international conflict. In *Peacemaking in International Conflict*, ed. IW Zartman, JL Rasmussen, pp. 125–54. Washington, DC: US Inst. Peace. 412 pp.

Betts R. 1987. *Nuclear Blackmail and Nuclear Balance.* Washington, DC: Brookings Inst. 240 pp.

Brams S. 1985. *Superpower Games.* New Haven, CT: Yale Univ. Press. 176 pp.

Brams S, Kilgour DM. 1988. *Game Theory and National Security.* New York: Blackwell. 199 pp.

Brecher M. 1993. *Crises in World Politics.* New York: Pergamon. 676 pp.

Brecher M, Wilkenfeld J. 1997. *A Study of Crisis.* Ann Arbor: Univ. Mich. Press. 1064 pp.

Brodie B. 1959. *Strategy in the Missile Age.* Princeton, NJ: Princeton Univ. Press. 423 pp.

Bueno de Mesquita B, Morrow J, Zorick E. 1997. Capabilities, perception, and escalation. *Am. Polit. Sci. Rev.* 91:15–27

Desch M. 1993. *When the Third World Matters.* Baltimore, MD: Johns Hopkins Univ. Press. 218 pp.

Downs G. 1991. Arms race and war. In *Behavior, Society, and Nuclear War*, ed. P Tetlock, JL Husbands, R Jervis, P Stern, C. Tilly, 11:73–109. New York: Oxford Univ. Press

Ellsberg D. 1961. The crude analysis of strategic choice. *Am. Econ. Rev.* 51:472–78

Evron Y. 1987. *War and Intervention in Lebanon.* Baltimore, MD: John Hopkins Univ. Press. 246 pp.

Fearon J. 1994a. Domestic political audiences and the escalation of international disputes. *Am. Polit. Sci. Rev.* 88:577–92

Fearon J. 1994b. Signaling versus the balance of power and interests. *J. Confl. Resolut.* 38:236–69

Fearon J. 1997. Signaling foreign policy interests. *J. Confl. Resolut.* 41:68–90

Gelpi C. 1997. Crime and punishment. *Am. Polit. Sci. Rev.* 91:339–60

George A, Smoke R. 1974. *Deterrence in American Foreign Policy.* New York: Columbia Univ. Press. 666 pp.

Glaser C. 1992. The political consequences of military strategy. *World Polit.* 44:497–538

Glaser C. 1994/1995. Realists as optimists. *Int. Secur.* 19:50–90

Glaser C. 1997. The security dilemma revisited. *World Polit.* 50:171–201

Glaser C, Kaufmann C. 1998. What is the offense-defense balance and how can we measure it? *Int. Secur.* 22:44–82

Harvey F. 1997. *The Future's Back.* Montreal: McGill-Queens Univ. Press. 192 pp.

Hensel P. 1996a. *The evolution of interstate rivalry.* PhD thesis. Univ. Ill., Urbana-Champaign. 207 pp.

Hensel P. 1996b. Charting a course to conflict. *Confl. Manage. Peace Sci.* 15:43–74

Hopf T. 1994. *Peripheral Visions.* Ann Arbor: Univ. Mich. Press. 306 pp.

Huth P. 1988. *Extended Deterrence and the Prevention of War.* New Haven, CT: Yale Univ. Press. 227 pp.

Huth P. 1996. *Standing Your Ground.* Ann Arbor: Univ. Mich. Press. 275 pp.

Huth P. 1997. Reputations and deterrence. *Secur. Stud.* 7:72–99

Huth P, Bennett DS, Gelpi C. 1992. System uncertainty, risk propensity, and international conflict. *J. Confl. Resolut.* 36:478–517

Huth P, Gelpi C, Bennett DS. 1993. The escalation of great power militarized disputes. *Am. Polit. Sci. Rev.* 87:609–23

Huth P, Russett B. 1984. What makes deterrence work? Cases from 1900 to 1980. *World Polit.* 36:496–526

Huth P, Russett B. 1990. Testing deterrence theory. *World Polit.* 42:466–501

Huth P, Russett B. 1993. General deterrence between enduring rivals. *Am. Polit. Sci. Rev.* 87:61–73

Jervis R. 1970. *The Logic of Images.* Princeton, NJ: Princeton Univ. Press. 281 pp.

Jervis R. 1978. Cooperation under the security dilemma. *World Polit.* 30:167–214

Jervis R. 1979. Deterrence theory revisited. *World Polit.* 31:289–324

Kahn H. 1965. *On Escalation.* New York: Praeger. 308 pp.

Kaufman W, ed. 1956. *Military Policy and National Security.* Princeton, NJ: Princeton Univ. Press. 274 pp.

Kissinger H. 1957. *Nuclear Weapons and Foreign Policy.* New York: Counc. Foreign Relat. 455 pp.

Kocs S. 1995. Territorial disputes and international war. *J. Polit.* 57:159–75

Kydd A. 1997. Game theory and the spiral model. *World Polit.* 49:371–400

Lebow RN. 1981. *Between Peace and War.* Baltimore, MD: Johns Hopkins Univ. Press. 350 pp.

Lebow RN. 1987. Deterrence failure revisited. *Int. Secur. Stud.* 12:197–213

Lebow RN, Stein JG. 1989. Rational deterrence theory. *World Polit.* 41:208–24

Lebow RN, Stein JG. 1990. Deterrence, the elusive dependent variable. *World Polit.* 42:336–69

Leng R. 1984. Reagan and the Russians. *Am. Polit. Sci. Rev.* 78:338–55

Leng R. 1993. *Interstate Crisis Bargaining Behavior, 1816–1980.* Cambridge, UK: Cambridge Univ. Press. 259 pp.

Levy J. 1997. Prospect theory, rational choice, and international relations. *Int. Stud. Q.* 41:87–112

Lieberman E. 1994. The rational deterrence theory debate. *Secur. Stud.* 3:384–427

Lieberman E. 1995. What makes deterrence work? *Secur. Stud.* 4:833–92

Maxwell S. 1968. Rationality in deterrence. *Adelphi Papers.* London: Instit. Strateg. Stud. 19 pp.

Mearsheimer J. 1983. *Conventional Deterrence.* Ithaca, NY: Cornell Univ. Press. 296 pp.

Mercer J. 1996. *Reputation and International Politics.* Ithaca, NY: Cornell Univ. Press. 236 pp.

Morgan P. 1977. *Deterrence.* Beverly Hills, CA: Sage. 216 pp.

Morris B. 1993. *Israel's Border Wars.* Oxford, UK: Clarendon. 469 pp.

Nalebuff B. 1991. Deterrence in an imperfect world. *World Polit.* 43:313–35

Orme J. 1987. Deterrence failures. *Int. Secur.* 11:96–124

Orme J. 1992. *Deterrence, Reputation and Cold-War Cycles.* New York: Macmillan. 168 pp.

Paul TV. 1994. *Asymmetric Conflicts.* Cambridge, UK: Cambridge Univ. Press. 248 pp.

Peterson S. 1996. *Crisis Bargaining and the State.* Ann Arbor: Univ. Mich. Press. 208 pp.

Powell R. 1990. *Nuclear Deterrence Theory.* Cambridge, UK: Cambridge Univ. Press. 230 pp.

Quester G. 1966. *Deterrence Before Hiroshima.* New York: Wiley. 196 pp.

Reiter D. 1995. Exploding the powder keg myth. *Int. Secur.* 20:5–34

Russett B. 1963. The calculus of deterrence. *J Confl. Resolut.* 7:97–109

Russett B. 1967. Pearl Harbor. *J. Peace Res.* 4:89–105

Sagan S. 1993. *The Limits of Safety.* Princeton, NJ: Princeton Univ. Press. 286 pp.

Sample S. 1997. Arms races and dispute escalation. *J. Peace Res.* 34:7–22

Sample S. 1998. Military buildups, war, and realpolitik. *J. Confl. Resolut.* 42:156–75

Sartori A. 1998. *Deterrence by diplomacy.* PhD thesis. Univ. Mich. 185 pp.

Schelling T. 1960. *Strategy of Conflict.* Cambridge, MA: Harvard Univ. Press. 309 pp.

Schelling T. 1966. *Arms and Influence.* New Haven, CT: Yale Univ. Press. 293 pp.

Senese P. 1996. Geographical proximity and issue salience. *Confl. Manage. Peace Sci.* 15:133–61

Shimshoni J. 1988. *Israel and Conventional Deterrence.* Ithaca, NY: Cornell Univ. Press. 247 pp.

Smith A. 1996. To intervene or not to intervene. *J. Confl. Resolut.* 40:16–40

Snyder G. 1961. *Deterrence and Defense.* Princeton, NJ: Princeton Univ. Press. 294 pp.

Stein J.G. 1985. Calculation, miscalculation, and conventional deterrence I. In *Psychology & Deterrence*, ed. R Jervis, RN Lebow, JG Stein, pp. 34–59. Baltimore, MD: Johns Hopkins Univ. Press.

Stein JG. 1996. Deterrence and learning in an enduring rivalry. *Secur. Stud.* 6:104–52

Vasquez J. 1993. *The War Puzzle.* Cambridge, UK: Cambridge Univ. Press. 378 pp.

Vasquez J. 1995. Why do neighbors fight? *J. Peace Res.* 32:277–93

Wagner H. 1982. Deterrence and bargaining. *J. Confl. Resolut.* 26:329–58

Wagner H. 1991. Nuclear deterrence, counterforce strategies, and the incentive to strike first. *Am. Polit. Sci. Rev.* 85:727–49

Whiting A. 1975. *The Chinese Calculus of Deterrence*. Ann Arbor: Univ. Mich. Press. 299 pp.

Wohlstetter A. 1959. The delicate balance of terror. *Foreign Aff.* 37:211–34

Zagare F. 1987. *The Dynamics of Deterrence*. Chicago: Univ. Chicago Press. 194 pp.

Annu. Rev. Polit. Sci. 1999. 2:49–73

ENDING REVOLUTIONS AND BUILDING NEW GOVERNMENTS

Arthur L. Stinchcombe

American Bar Foundation, Chicago, Illinois 60611; e-mail: a-stinch@nwu.edu

KEY WORDS: leviathan, stability, thermidor, totatalitarianism, democracy

---

ABSTRACT

Revolutions may be defined as periods in which the rate of change of power positions of factions, social groups, or armed bodies changes rapidly and unpredictably. Revolutions then come to an end to the degree that political uncertainty is reduced by building enough bargains into a political structure that can maintain those bargains. The paper summarizes what we know about the structures that can produce such decreases in uncertainty: conservative authoritarianism, independence, occupation government, totalitarianism, democracy, and *caudillismo*. The essay describes these governmental types by how they increase certainty of power distributions in the short and medium run and so bring revolutions to an end.

ON ENDING REVOLUTION

Writing on the Restoration of Charles II coming in 1660, after the death of Oliver Cromwell, Hallam, a historian sensitive to the "defensible claims" of parties to the English Revolution, described the problem of constructing a government as follows (Hallam 1854 2:286–87, footnotes omitted):

> [E]veryone spoke of the King's restoration as imminent, yet none could distinctly perceive by what means it would be effected, and much less how the difficulties of such a settlement could be overcome. As the moment approached, men turned their attention more to the obstacles and dangers that lay in their way. The restoration of a banished family, concerning whom they knew little, and what they knew not entirely to their satisfaction; with ruined, perhaps revengeful, followers; the returning ascendance of a distressed party, who had sustained losses that could not be repaired without fresh changes of property, injuries that could not be atoned without fresh severi-

49

ties; the conflicting pretensions of two churches—one loth to release its claim [Church of England], the other to yield its possession [Presbyterians]; the unsettled dissensions between crown and parliament; all seemed pregnant with such difficulties, that prudent men could hardly look forward to the impending revolution [i.e. the Restoration] without some hesitation and anxiety.[1]

The passage gives a synopsis of the difficulties of finding a set of bargains among the interests contending in a revolution and a reliable apparatus to enforce them, of adapting those bargains thereafter to changing circumstances, and so of stably regenerating the authority of the government being created. Each party to the Restoration (or other government-creating bargain) had to balance the uncertainties of trying to continue the revolution and trying to get in on a stable regime being bargained out.

In general, the more autonomous coercive power a party has in the revolution (as military bodies often have), the more precarious the balance between the bargains proposed by the new regime and what they can expect by continued revolution. A major assumption of my argument below is that many of these bargains are not stable treaties bargained among the warring parties (Licklides 1995). The best portrait I know of the process of bargaining on the creation of governments in revolutionary situations is Elster's study (1994, especially pp. 210–53) of the discourse of the late eighteenth-century constitutional conventions in the United States and France; I comment on the stability of both bargains below.

We conceive the core of revolution to be uncertainty about who, and what policies, will rule in the near and medium-run future—a Hobbesian state of the war of each against all. As Hallam argues, creating a Leviathan to get out of such a situation is not a matter of political philosophy so much as of each party comparing the proposed constitutional bargain and its coercive imposition with what one can expect in a continued state of anarchy. The better one is situated in the revolutionary "state of nature," the more suspicious one is of the creation of a Leviathan.

In fact, the Leviathan of Charles II did not last long, although no doubt 28 years seemed longer to his contemporaries than it does to us three centuries later. Some of the other postrevolutionary regimes analyzed below had medium-run instabilities. God be praised, not all thousand-year reichs last a millennium.

The recent literature on building new governments has mostly used the language of "regime transition" rather than the language of revolution. This suggests that, although there may be a "time of transition," it is the natural order of

---

[1] Actually, there had been three recent kinds of parliaments: a revolutionary parliament with many political tendencies excluded, a parliament with an equalized franchise, and the parliament then sitting with the prerevolutionary franchise.

things that people and territories have governments. In the extreme, one might bargain with an existing government about what sort of constitution a new government might have (Przeworski 1986, Linz & Stepan 1996, O'Donnell et al 1986, Linz 1978b). In much of world history, empires seldom bargained with colonies about bringing their own sovereignty to an end; conquerors in world wars did not rebuild democratic regimes using occupation governments; military juntas did not peacefully organize elections and bargain about the constitution under which such elections would take place; and totalitarian governments did not explicitly introduce *perestroika*. In much of the world they still do not. O'Donnell & Schmitter (1986) recognize that in modern transitions, it is very uncertain when and how a government will be created. But they implicitly do not consider the state of uncertainty, and the special problem of creating certainty when a revolution is going on, to be the central phenomenon.

This essay generally bypasses the literature on transitions because I believe that revolutions in the past seldom ended in a way naturally described as a transition, as if one knew where one was headed. I will also confine myself mostly to revolutions of Europe and the Americas. I do not know how far my conceptions of the alternative types of governments that can decrease the uncertainty of revolution are shaped by the fact that my learning is almost confined to Europe and the Americas. I do not know enough about recent Eastern European or Asian and African revolutions to generalize about them.

A DEFINITION OF REVOLUTION

By a political revolution I mean a time of rapid, often erratic, change in the relative power of social classes, ethnicities, regions, political parties, legislatures, military groups, royal or noble lineages, and so on. I believe this definition includes most of what we ordinarily call revolutions.[2] For such instability of relative power to continue, different groups and people have to have different estimates of how it will all come out; otherwise they would make deals in light of who was going to win and so produce stability. In a stable government, most groups do not believe they can unexpectedly win big, and so there is approximate certainty about power distribution over the next few decades. Great uncertainty about power distribution, then, preserves the condition of rapid changes of relative power—preserves revolution.[3]

[2]"In [a routine power struggle] the fight, by common agreement, takes place within the borders of the possible; in [a revolution] the fight concerns how those borders should be drawn" (Elster 1978:50). This captures well the equal standing of solid middle-of-the-road bargains and utopian visions during revolutions.
[3]However, most contemporary revolutions end in the first year or two; those that continue, on average, increase their level of violence, getting further from stable government (Poe & Tate 1994:865).

This definition will seem odd because the general messiness and random violence of revolution does not come through in political science and sociological analysis. It has never been captured better than by Sorokin (1967 [1925]). But Sorokin so obviously hated revolutionaries that his stance was taken as political bigotry; he was a positivist but too strongly driven by his hostile ideas. A cooler positivist tone, addressing minor urban civil disorders rather than revolutions, shows the same spread of random disorder (Gurr et al 1977:651–76). Similarly, Kelley & Klein (1981) show that social mobility is more random during revolution than before or after, and Shultz (1995) argues that revolution itself creates greater and more intractable ethnic conflict.

Sorokin gave us an image of increased speed of all sorts of unpredictable uses of power, like the increased speed of molecules in boiling water. Much the same image, but with enthusiasm for boiling, comes through in Trotsky's great *History of the Russian Revolution* (1933). Trotsky did not have Sorokin's reaction because he was protected by the Marxist teleology of revolution, seeing future order where Sorokin saw chaos, and was encouraged in that teleology by his knowledge of how in fact there came to be a Soviet government in the end.

Revolution continues because it is hard for any group to build a government. All aspects of government tend to be unsettled and difficult to manage: which ethnicity will dominate a nation, where state and subnationality boundaries will be drawn, which classes will be mobilized into politics or collective bargaining under the regime, who will pay taxes to which political budgets, which property will be secure, how economic going concerns will be created and governed, who will recruit and sustain armies to fight whom, who will arrest juvenile delinquents or organize them into gangs, who will back the promises of commercial contracts with force, and who will select legislative bodies or authorities to make policy on all these matters. Building a government means increasing the certainty of the answers to all such questions. Building a terror apparatus on an irregular basis to create a "revolutionary" government generally does not build a government that can last into the future (O'Kane 1991, Chirot 1994), although a totalitarian ending to a revolution (described below) achieves this to some extent.

Solving one such stabilizing problem need not solve the others. The Irish revolution may have "ended," for most of the British, with drawing the national boundary of independent Ireland and confirming it in a treaty—but the relative power of urban versus rural Catholicism, the certainty of the boundary with Ulster, who got to organize military and terrorist bodies to coerce others in Ulster or in the internal contest for power in Eire, all remained uncertain for years or decades afterward. More people have been killed in the continuing parts of that revolution than in the winning of independence (Keogh 1994: 1–63, O'Brien 1972, Bell 1972). But with independence came a major reduction in uncertainty through the elimination of the major contender for power, and there is obvious good sense in calling this an end of the revolution, if perhaps also the beginning of a new civil war. The degree to which a government can be created that controls all the power uncertainties at a given turning point in a revolution is obviously a continuous variable, and even a drastic reduction in uncertainty with independence may leave much undecided.

Further, the causes or political projects that first brought on the crisis within which the uncertainty of power grew, may have little to do with the causes or political projects within which a government that ends a revolution can grow. Napoleon largely organized the project that settled many aspects of relative power in France for several decades; some parts of that solution are still more or less in place. But it is hard to imagine Napoleon storming the Bastille or organizing neighborhood sections in Paris. Eckstein (1976) has shown much the same precarious connection between the similar causal origins and the different consequences of two Latin American revolutions.

Coups d'etat and "transitions" are distinct from revolutions in that they establish quickly who is to govern, so that the uncertainty about how relative power can be changed only obtains for a short period. However, coups happening during revolutions, although they by definition do not destroy the powers of the government they take over, do not resolve the uncertainties of relative power elsewhere. The several coups d'etat in Paris during the French Revolution did not disturb the continued uncertainty in the countryside about which feudal dues were converted into legitimate bourgeois rents, and which of those legitimate rents were factually collectable, and what the next legislation from Paris would say about it (Markoff 1996). Therefore, neither did the coups in Paris resolve the uncertainty about when the next coup would take place.

Similarly, the Bolsheviks in 1917 could gain a majority in the urban soviets and dominate the soviet military committee without resolving the wider uncertainty of whether and when they would overturn the Provisional Government. When they carried out a coup d'etat and took control of that government, they did not much disturb the relative powers (what few were left by that time) of that government, though they still did not determine the powers of the white armies, or of provincial soviets, or of the already-elected Constituent Assembly. They did not even determine whether the soviet government so created would have the boundaries that the Russian Empire had had (Trotsky 1933 3:302–43).[4] The uncertainty of relative powers declined continuously in the course of the postrevolutionary civil war, growing out from a core of relative certainty in St. Petersburg and Moscow.

---

[4]In fact, the soviet government never ruled Finland, which had been part of the Russian Empire.

The general plan of this review is to define revolution as the rapid and erratic rate of change of relative power and the uncertainty of powers that maintains that rapid rate. The central argument of the review is that revolution ends to the degree that governments are built that can slow down rates of change of relative power and decrease uncertainty about who, and what policies, will rule in the near and medium-range future. I summarize what we know about various devices for slowing the rate of change of relative power in revolutions and decreasing its uncertainty. I refer to this stabilization of power uncertainties as the process of building a government or occasionally as building a Leviathan; Hallam showed that Hobbes oversimplified that problem. I first present a typology of the resulting governments, which will sound familiar, but I characterize them according to the alternative devices by which they slow the rate of change and increase the certainty of relative power distributions on which government authority rests.

STABILIZATION OF RELATIVE POWERS AND TYPES OF GOVERNMENTS

When revolutions end depends on the mechanisms of creating governments that can stabilize power distributions and increase certainty. Stabilizing power distributions is arranging the nesting of powers in such a fashion that if one power starts to fail, sufficient power resources from elsewhere will be supplied to shore it up. Such nested powers make a challenger face overwhelming power because reserves are called up that were not busy elsewhere (AL Stinchcombe 1968:158–63; for a critique, Przeworski 1986:50–53). In a revolution, reserve powers are too busy elsewhere. If a government's power will fade next year, paying its taxes or joining its army is not the best way to preserve one's own powers. My typology classifies stabilizing devices in terms that suggest the kinds of governments they give rise to as follows: (*a*) Thermidor, or conservative authoritarianism; (*b*) independence; (*c*) military defeat and occupation government; (*d*) totalitarianism; (*e*) democracy; and (*f*) *caudillismo*.

Thermidor and Conservative Authoritarianism

Thermidor was the revolutionaries' name for the month in which a middle-of-the-road coup was carried out against the Jacobins, leading to Napoleon's regime. The next section, "Conservative Authoritarianism as a Support for Bargained Coalitions," uses Brinton's (1965 [1953]:205–36) analysis of Thermidorian reaction as a stage in the natural history of revolution. Prerevolutionary status and power relations are integrated into a postrevolutionary government.

Conservative authoritarianism incorporates much of the elite of the prerevolutionary regime (propertied classes, nobility, ecclesiastical bodies, guilds, officer corps, colonists, etc). Return to normalcy, high living, style, and restarting manufacturing, trade, and agriculture are characteristic. The reimposition of slavery and planter government in Guadeloupe after the French Revolution (Bangou 1989) is the ugly side. A modern example is the Franco government in Spain (Linz 1973, 1978a). Old regime status, property, and authority relations serve as templates of local, corporate, or property-holding powers.

Independence

A big step in anticolonial revolutions is the empire granting independence, often accompanied by an agreement to introduce the new government into the international system. The Treaty of Paris (1783) between the British and the United States, which detached the United States from its alliance with France (WC Stinchcombe 1969:183–213) and formed a basis for England's nonintervention in the States until 1812, is an early example. Many of the nationalist revolutions in the European and US empires after World War II ended with international covenants on international relations after independence.

Defeat and Occupation Governments

Military defeat, with postwar occupation governments imposed by the victors, redistributed and stabilized power after the revolution of the slave states in the United States in the 1860s. Much of the stabilization is known as Reconstruction, and much of the rest was carried out in a further "treaty" in 1876 (Woodward 1974 [1957]; on the courts, see Brandwein 1994). Similarly, the occupation governments in Germany and Japan after World War II set the major terms of relative powers in those countries. In some cases, "colonies" originated as occupation governments after intervention in internal revolutions (e.g. after the 1898 US intervention in Cuba's independence movement, the United States arranged powers in "independent" Cuba).

Totalitarianism

Sometimes revolutionary mobilization of new groups continues after a revolutionary government takes power. An evangelistic corporatism spreads the revolution into the crannies of the society, and often abroad through "liberating" revolutions. When Bonapartism was not Thermidorian, it was a relatively mild form of authoritarian and imperialistic political evangelism. The full form is what is usually called the totalitarianism of the Nazi, the Soviet, and the Maoist revolutions. Continuous mobilization and continuous terror made these regimes a continuation of the revolution. A high degree of corporatist organization of mobilization is often maintained, in spite of recurrent purges, campaigns, and cultural revolutions. Some of the most solid postrevolutionary governments have come out of totalitarian stabilization, particularly in the Soviet Bloc before the recent transitions.

Democracy

Democracy can be defined as a system in which a set of citizens is consensually established who can defeat a sitting government and substitute another by legal means alone. In this review I call the consensual definition of citizenship "nationalism." I call the effectiveness of legal means alone in changing governments "legal democracy" and distinguish it from "revolutionary democracy." I argue that legal democracy is an unlikely outcome of revolutionary processes alone, without the help of conquest. The main exceptions are rare cases in which a revolutionary movement already has an internal legal-democratic culture and structure.

Caudillismo

A very different sort of semipermanent revolution is continued fragility of governments and a continued, somewhat anarchical, building up of cosmopolitan power by local chiefs who are in turn torn down. Sudden independence after a revolution of colonial societies whose government had not been politically deeply embedded in local society is one of the origins of such permanent semi-anarchy of personal coteries (Safford 1985; AL Stinchcombe 1995a:286–318).

Sometimes new revolutionary governments are so fragile that coups d'etat do not actually greatly decrease the interval to the next coup, as in Bolivia, Haiti, the Dominican Republic, or the Congo. But sometimes these rates of power shifts fall drastically with *caudillo* governments of intermediate stability. More stable similar structures have been common in the former Spanish colonies of South and Central America, in central Africa, and in the Sicilian Mafia and related gangster quasi-governments in southern Italy (Gambetta 1993). I classify such "stable anarchies" as ways out of revolution only because the typical uncertainty about how far and how long a *caudillo* can extend his power is not of the same scale as in a revolution.

CONSERVATIVE AUTHORITARIANISM AS A SUPPORT FOR BARGAINED COALITIONS

Because power cannot easily be concentrated behind political or economic projects in revolution, coalitions based on a flow of medium-run rewards cannot provide that flow. Short-run military projects to gain power or ideological projects to terrorize enemy classes or parties dominate revolutionary attempts to construct governments. People who wanted more food, more fun, more education for jobs, or more products from the factories, tend to drop out of revolutionary politics because contenders for governing coalitions produce fighting and speechmaking rather than food, fun, jobs, or clothing. The connections between political projects and people's projects for their own lives tend to be severed.

A political general, often back from pacification of a colony or foreign conquest, can make coalitions possible. If revolutionary parliamentary bargaining were oriented to paying projects rather than zero-sum contention for power, a Napoleon or Franco or Chiang Kai Chek would not be necessary. Generals, like foreign kings, can appear more nonpartisan and so can be trusted by potential coalition members to deliver the benefits of coalitions. Kann (1968), who describes many such instances, takes partial incorporation of revolutionary achievements to be essential to such restorations (also Goldstone 1991: 416–58, Sperber 1994:195–259).

The efflorescence of consumption, fun, production, property markets, and speculation characteristic of Thermidor and the Restoration (Brinton 1965 [1953]:205–36, Robiquet 1962 [1942], Bergeron 1981:119–58) is a sign that people believe they can keep the benefits and property they get hold of. For Napoleon, "[O]ne of the essential and conclusive results of the Revolution, achieved in the legislation of [his] Consulate, was to render all transfers of property originating in the Revolutionary confiscations henceforth untouchable" (Bergeron 1981:125–26).

One of the most explicit of such coalitions was the Concordat of Napoleon with the papacy. It required Napoleon rather than a revolutionary legislature. "Napoleon had certainly restored religion, but rather after the fashion in which a road full of pot-holes is repaired by driving a roller over it" (Robiquet 1962 [1942]:50). Napoleon paid salaries to both non-juring priests who had resisted the Revolution and those who took the oath to it. All could say mass publicly, and parishioners could celebrate mass, be married, and be buried. Napoleon got a coalition with the Church on his own terms and stopped the Church support for religious rebellion. But the pope thought he would get what he was promised, a stop to revolutionary anticlericalism, which he could not get before. A comparable deal was negotiated by Franco in Spain.

Very roughly speaking, Napoleon reinforced the balance of powers and property as defended by the Directorate, an attempt at centrist authoritarianism administered as a republic (instituted in the month of Thermidor). But by making those balances into a deal that he (as the government) backed, people could enjoy and plan with their income and property; priests with diverse convictions could collect their state salaries; and the bourgeois families could strut and display their wealth. It was not, then, "normalcy" in the sense of *status quo ante* but rather in the sense that, wherever people had ended up through revolutionary processes, they could start there and go on with their lives—a normalcy of "picking up the pieces."

Compared with the flurries of contradictory ideology of the revolution, the tone of the higher government of Thermidor was enforcing sober bargains and technocratic problem solving (see Woloch 1994, especially his brilliant study of administering conscription, pp. 380–426). Napoleon's founding of higher technical schools to educate the higher military and civil servant classes, and his own technical artillery origin, are an early model of the technocratic thrust of Pinochet's bringing in the Chicago boys. A discourse of accounts and technical drawings, leading to the production and distribution of material benefits, tends to dominate the bureaucratic levels just below the military summit government.

Repression of the intransigent wings and rewriting of history so that revolutionaries or counterrevolutionaries are not the heroes of their respective sides reduce uncertainty of such deals, as outlined below. Sometimes this repression is part of the deal of coalition formation. It was certainly implicit in both Napoleon's and Franco's concordats that the Church hierarchy would not support the most intransigent priests against the dictator. When many of the political groups in a system have recently had factions that proposed to raise violent rebellion, the creation of an incentive system favoring compromise often involves repression of those who opppose compromise. The conservative authoritarianism of Thermidorian reaction does not ordinarily involve giving authority to the most extreme right-wing forces (the Russian Tsar after 1905, the Austrian Hapsburg regime after 1848, and Hitler after 1933 are exceptions).

Repression, Order, and Imposed Bargains

Political bargains during revolutions are unstable because extreme and unbargained methods of conflict are roughly as powerful after the bargains as before. In stable political systems, "legitimacy" means that the outcomes of votes, contacts, court decisions, and administrative procedures have a substantial political advantage over "illegitimate" outcomes.

In conservative authoritarianism after revolutions, repression takes two forms simultaneously: (*a*) repressing extremist unbargained outcomes and dual power methods of political conflict that challenge who the government will be, and (*b*) favoring those political and property interests incorporated into the regime. The first form justifies the label "authoritarian," the second "conservative." In particular, interests are protected that cannot be represented effectively unless spontaneous forces exercising autonomous power are disadvantaged and "disorder" is repressed.

One of the principal devices for choosing reliable bargaining representatives within the resulting regimes is corporatist organization. Corporatist bargaining units are organized either by the government itself or through a political party attached to the regime (e.g. the Institutional Revolutionary Party, the PRI, after the Mexican Revolution). The key feature is a continuous bargain between the regime and the interests within a corporatist structure about what means are legitimate to gain bargaining power. The repression of Emiliano Zapata's movement and the creation of the peasant section of the PRI more under the Mexican President's thumb is one example. A church incorporating both revolutionary and counterrevolutionary priests, whose leadership was acceptable to Napoleon, is another.

Corporatism gives a much stronger reward for acceptance of a semi-imposed bargain and a stronger punishment for intransigence than are available during a revolution. This depends on the imposition of a constitution in which long-run power positions are not changeable by extremism. Short-run imposed bargains, and the repression of power plays outside the bounds, are usually determined authoritatively by the chief and his coterie. An extraordinary chief or coterie may produce long-run changes by, for example, stabilizing uncertain landed properties by a cadastral survey (Napoleon) or organizing a stable autonomous federal judicial system (John Marshall in the United States). A detailed look at such constructions usually shows an implicit rather than explicit strategy, a piecewise adjustment of means and ends, so as not to raise constitutional issues.

The usual fate of attempted conservative authoritarianism is probably simple failure to impose bargains, and thus failure to create incentives for moderation (e.g. von Papen in Weimar Germany). But a key long-run vulnerability is arbitrary authority overreaching its means. On the average, only half or less of participants in international wars earn more in legitimacy and resources than the war cost. Multiple wars therefore increase the chance of net losses. Even Napoleon, who had enormous advantages in most of his wars, lost once to a large but minor power on Europe's periphery (Russia) and once, on land, to a much smaller naval power (England). He had a great run of luck, but no one could stop him from overreaching his resources. Franco was in this respect wiser, though weaker, than his big fascist allies. Chiang Kai Chek at least finally stopped at defeating the Formosan natives and so did not lose as much as he might have. When people realize what wars have cost and how little has been won, tyrants often have even more trouble than Churchill after World War II or Roosevelt in 1944.

INDEPENDENCE

Let us step back from the picture of revolutionary anarchy to analyze why deals made between an empire and a new independent government can produce major stabilization. Coercion (other than massacres) ultimately involves moving troops and establishing intelligence networks (e.g. courts, secret police, tax assessors). This means that revolutions tend to be territorial on a small scale, because central control of complex long-distance networks and dispersed troops is precarious during revolution. Whenever revolutions segment coercion by establishing separate smaller states, then regional segmentation of governments increases coercive reliability for each segment. If networks (and troop loyalties) are sharply bounded by language, religion, previous experience with federal government, and distance, then revolutionary uncertainty segments power regionally or communally. The extreme of segmentation of government is ordinarily called independence. Revolution itself increases the degree of independence of regions, religions, and language groups.

In practice, then, the treaty that ends revolution by independence is often the recognition of de facto regional independence developed during the revolution. The region is making a treaty with a power that recently thought it might manage to rule by winning and that therefore bargains from strength. For example, England, having granted the United States independence in 1782 (confirmed in 1783), easily conducted a devastating punitive expedition against it in 1812 as only a minor episode in the Napoleonic wars. Similarly, Irish independence was conditional on noninterference with Ulster. Neocolonialism is independence with conditions on the property rights and trading privileges of imperial citizens.

In particular, such treaties are always made with a potential government of the newly independent segment, or there would be no one to put conditions on. This obviously gives an advantage to the revolutionary faction recognized as the government; many of the most active revolutionaries in Cuba, for example, were not so recognized when the United States signed the treaty with Spain granting Cuban independence.

A treaty of independence does not resolve all conflicts. But this commonplace does not undermine the central fact that Britain, France, the United States, and Russia are not fighting revolutions in India, Pakistan, Australia, Jamaica, Algeria, the Ivory Coast, the Philippines, or Finland. If European powers did not care much about imposing conditions, as in Uganda, the Congo, or the Central African Empire, they withdrew even without establishing much of a government to deal with.

The revolution may effectually end in only one of two segments whose separateness was exaggerated by revolution. The Irish rural fundamentalist-Catholic romantic revolution (against the partition in the treaty, the Irish parliament, and courts) continued after independence. The federalist settlement within the United States followed several years of internal segmentation in the Articles of Confederation, and even the settlement of the present Constitution broke apart in the 1860s, while England went on merrily winning at Waterloo and running an empire.

After independence, the chances of establishing a new government often do go up. Effective revolutions often involve regions with relatively strong ethnic, religious, or provincial government boundaries. For the same reasons, effective ends to revolution are often established in those regions after independence, for networks of information and integrated armies prove easier to establish in the revolutionary parts than they had been in the empire.

OCCUPATION GOVERNMENTS

Defeat in war automatically creates a psychological and sociological revolutionary situation, a suspended state of uncertainty about the future government. It is suspended only because the occupying army is in control. If the occupiers leave without encouraging the construction of a government, a revolution in the ordinary sense is a frequent outcome. The prewar regime is humiliated by defeat. The cascade of appeals to the occupiers' overwhelming coercion, which could stabilize solid governments, has foreigners at the top rather than one of the contending revolutionary parties, and perhaps rather than anyone who wants to govern. When the occupiers go home, no legitimate monopoly of violence may remain.

Remarkably many "democratic" regimes have been established by occupation governments [see Stepan (1986:66–67) for several, starting perhaps with the Dutch invasion of England under William of Orange in 1688]. The treaty that established his kingship was largely created by the Whigs (insofar as that distinction held at the time) in Parliament, and it put severe constraints on the conqueror. William's was not exactly an occupation government. Nevertheless it was more nearly democratic than James II's. The same democratic outcome obtained in the Adenauer Christian Democratic government in Germany and the Liberal Democratic government in Japan after World War II (an excellent analysis of the imposition of a bargain among social classes by the MacArthur occupation government of Japan is Dore 1984 [1959]). A flurry of somewhat democratic governments were established by the Bonapartist Empire in Europe.

An ambiguous case is the American Reconstruction after the Civil War, roughly from 1865 to 1876. It is ambiguous because, first, if one is willing to ignore the exclusion of women, slaves, and aborigines (as we do for ancient Athens), the slave states maintained democratic governments before and through the Civil War. Second, the gradual disenfranchisement and the decrease of free labor relations in the black belt through share tenancy (roughly from 1876 to 1900) point to the instability of the democratic institutions (in the modern sense) established by the Reconstruction. The Reconstruction did create substantial democratic government in the South and brought about a permanent end of the southern rebellion. Its short-run democratic effects should be counted as evidence of the importance of occupation governments for creating democratic regimes out of revolution, although a democracy with powerful plantation owners is nearly a political impossibility.

Such occupation governments control the ultimate backup of authority by armed force. This makes bargaining among the conquered more advantageous to various interests than trying to construct autonomous paramilitary bodies. For democratic endings of revolutions, more than for other kinds, it is important that bargains have a political advantage over the parties' autonomous military action. This is also fairly central to conservative authoritarianism. Occupation governments creating conservative authoritarian outcomes were fairly frequent in the dynastic revolutions in Europe before 1800.

Thus, an occupation government is somewhat similar in effect to the early modern city-states and aristocratic kingdoms calling in a foreign prince, not attached to local interests, so that revolutionary bargaining would not lead to civil war or despotism. Douglas MacArthur as a foreign prince in Japan after World War II, a William of Orange perhaps, has a certain ring to it.

The democratic outcome is perhaps more likely when institutions for bargaining among the local elite are well developed. The Parliament of England worked out the terms of the treaty that recognized William of Orange as the conqueror, for example, attaching a bill of rights. The Reconstruction governments of the South left many of the pre–Civil War democratic arrangements in place. The post–World War II government of West Germany drew on many arrangements of the Weimar Republic, including even some of its main political parties. If bargaining institutions are already in the repertoire of the society, especially in elected legislatures, they stand ready to function when appeals to revolutionary coercion are excluded by the occupier.

However, conquests can also set up gangster governments, leave anarchy behind by destroying all possible governments (as has often occurred in the Middle East in the twentieth century), establish endogamous ruling castes of foreign extraction (e.g. colonial Peru), grant the kingship to a relative of the conqueror (e.g. Bonapartist Mexico), establish branch totalitarian governments (e.g. Eastern Europe after World War II and Outer Mongolia earlier), or simply add the conquest to an empire [Maoz (1984) shows that thorough conquering by an empire gives more stable outcomes than negotiated agreements do]. Being conquered is no sure route to peaceful democratic government and prosperity. But conquest often stops revolution. The extreme of good luck is to have one's conqueror impose democracy but forbid an army, so the military budget can be devoted to investment while one's conquerors engage in an arms race, as in modern Germany and Japan.

TOTALITARIAN "STABILIZATION"

Totalitarian endings of revolutions are analogous to conservative authoritarian ones except for special social structures preserving ideological mobilization under regime control. Our model cases are Nazi Germany, the USSR, and Maoist China. Totalitarian endings impose bargains by authoritarian methods but preserve and incorporate revolutionary structures of dual power into a quasigovernmental party structure devoted to further ideological transformation (one of the best descriptions is still Neumann 1965 [1942]).

Although the Weimar Republic and the First Republic of Austria are not conventionally called revolutionary, they satisfy our definition (rapidly and erratically changing positions of power). They also satisfy the more conventional definitions of revolution, having dual armed (though sometimes only with clubs) powers outside the state that have the purpose of constructing governments (e.g. the German *Freikorps*, the SA of the Nazi Party, the Austrian Heimwehr, various "defensive" socialist military formations, and the recent and well-remembered postwar left socialist revolutions). Another symptom of revolution was that important constitutional issues were continually raised without being solved, such as parliamentary control over the military, the enforcement of the treaties of World War I, and, for Austria, sovereignty versus being part of Germany (Bracher 1957, Simon 1978). In the elegant language of Bessel (1991), by 1933 both the revolution and the counterrevolution had failed without being defeated.

The incorporation of one part of the extremist dual power structures from the revolution into the regime is best summarized by a phrase of Reinhard Bendix: a structure for "mobilizing assent from below." Both Nazis and communists built extensive "cells," responsive to higher bodies in the party, that were supposed to mobilize ideological assent and enthusiastic discipline in the corporatist structures [see Bendix (1956:341–433) for postwar East Germany; Granick (1954) for the Soviet Union; and Hayes (1987) for Nazi Germany, including Austria]. Comparable parallel structures for mobilization and control of the army are documented for the USSR (Fedotoff-White 1944) and Nazi Germany (Shils & Janowitz 1948). Similarly, city and province or republic governments were penetrated by neighborhood cells and local party organizations.

The clearest case for the possibility of renewed anti-state revolution is the Great Proletarian Cultural Revolution in Maoist China. The transformation of the German Gestapo by an infusion of Nazi Party activists, especially from the SA, and the consequent creation of the genocidal bureaucracy (Arendt 1967 [1951], 1963) are of similar significance, as is the Soviet collectivization of agriculture in the 1930s.

Yet Brinton (1965 [1953]) was not wrong to see in the first years of the Soviet regime a "Thermidorean" reaction that lasted on into Stalin's dictatorship. It involved repression of white armies on a massive scale, as well as repression of anarchists and Trotskyists. Much of the passion of the fascist movements in Italy and Spain was hatred and fear of leftist revolution, leading to repression similar to the Thermidorian repression of Jacobins.

The distinction is that, in the totalitarian outcome, the new authoritarians keep in reserve a revolutionary corporatist apparatus, so that a one-sided revolution can be started up again at any time. Authoritarian heads of such structures cannot seem to resist tweaking the dual structure, to make sure it still works, in periodic purges. However, Linz & Stepan (1996:42–51) are correct to see a later, watered-down version of totalitarianism in former communist states in Eastern Europe, better classified as authoritarian (and actually quite Thermidorian) rather than totalitarian.

Totalitarianism with controlled mobilization structures should be distinguished from simple brutal tyranny or gangster government continuing a revolutionary condition. The key is whether the tyrant or gangster constructs a systematic policy, incorporating various interests outside the apparatus of terror into structures with government backing. If the only governmental apparatus is entirely devoted to terror, as was more or less true of Idi Amin's regime in Uganda [Chirot 1994:373–93; Bienen (1993) argues that gangster violence without imposed bargains among social forces is common among African leaders], then the revolution is not stopped; anarchy is merely centralized.

Perhaps the most sensitive low-level indicator of whether there is a government at all within a tyranny is whether the roads that might move troops to distant parts of the realm are built and maintained. Any real government maintains the means of systematic repression so that its policies can be enforced; roads to move troops are an elementary requirement of systematic repression. A comparison of Mobutu's Zaire with nearby Zimbabwe, of Idi Amin's Uganda with Tanzania or Kenya, of Papa Doc Duvalier's Haiti with Rafael Trujillo's Dominican Republic, would show the first in each pair with declining kilometers of effective roads, the second with increasing kilometers. Roads are rarely built and maintained during revolutions or gangster governments.

Further, when revolution is renewed in totalitarian regimes by activating mobilization by the dual structure, state administration of essential services, road building, and systematic private production are disturbed as during revolutions. The Great Proletarian Cultural Revolution in Maoist China was a direct cause of famine, as was the collectivization of peasant farms and of nomadic herding in the USSR. But a totalitarian regime afterward goes back to producing public goods, building roads, and producing food, often with the unchanged dual totalitarian mobilization apparatus attached to the government. Gangster governments, like revolutions and totalitarian-managed revolutionary periods, keep people hungry.

NATIONALISM AND DEMOCRACY

During a revolution, agreement to a democratic constitution is necessarily an agreement to regard the votes of fellow citizens as binding on issues affecting one's welfare. Entrusting one's welfare to the votes of others, mostly strangers, requires an "imagined community" with those others [Anderson 1991 (1983) applied the phrase to nationalism; see also Dahl 1970:59–67, Greenfield 1992]. Entrusting one's welfare to the votes of others is the central continuation of the uncertainty of the revolution into a democratic end of revolution (Przeworski 1986).

For example, in the postrevolutionary United States in the late eighteenth century, southern, largely Anglican, plantation owners were quite unwilling to entrust their welfare to the votes of sectarian (even Quaker) northern merchants and small farmers. For holders of bonds of the revolutionary government, entrusting the repayment of the debt to provincial legislatures was problematic, but a central regime with indirect election and (eventually) a central bank looked better. The Constitution had to be delicately balanced to be decentralized enough for the plantation owners but centralized enough for bondholders. In the 1860s, the worries of southerners temporarily broke up the federal government. In the 1830s, the safety of creditors of the central government was precarious in the hands of those who had voted for Andrew Jackson. That is, the Madisonian worriers of the Articles of Confederation (valid 1781–1789)[5] and of the 1787 Constitution turned out to be right.

If we think of political nationalism as entrusting one's welfare to the votes of strangers, and democracy as a system of government requiring that trust, then the relation of nationalism to democratic outcomes of revolution is obvious. When nationalists themselves do not entrust their welfare to the votes of many of their fellow citizens (as Nazis and conservative nationalists in Weimar Germany and Austria did not), and when socialists do not trust the nationalists, then a democratic way out of "revolutionary" instability is difficult.

For democracy, then, nationalism has two faces. One is that nationalism's political project is a boundary excluding those to whose vote citizens do not entrust their welfare; the other is that it is a boundary within which a vote may be binding. Clearly, not permitting the American South to draw such a boundary excluding the North led to the Civil War. Permitting Ireland to draw such a boundary with British supervision made at least British democracy more stable and eventually Irish democracy as well (not yet Ulster democracy). In both cases, I am in favor of the outcome—independence of Ireland and continued dependence of the American South. But seeing the cost of challenging the South, one may understand, if not approve of, the compromises of the Articles of Confederation and of the Constitution, without which the Civil War might have taken place in the 1780s.

The extension of the right to govern one's own welfare to the votes of a national polity has historically depended on qualified majorities (e.g. both houses of Congress) and limited jurisdictions (separation of powers). By excluding some issues from national democracy (e.g. by federalism), by excluding some voters (e.g. the poor or slaves), and by requiring greater majorities for

---

[5]The Articles of Confederation were actually written early in the revolution, but even this relatively unified revolution could not adopt its constitution without a struggle.

constitutional innovations, groups have protected themselves against democracy in order to adopt it. Some of these excluded issues were liberties (as for example the Bill of Rights), and some were rights to oppress others (as when Southern states governed "labor relations"). Some such limited democracies have been extremely effective defenses of oppression of workers and minority ethnicities, as in the American South, South Africa after World War II, Israel, and many settler colonies in their relations to the aboriginals (e.g. Australia, the United States, the democratic Cossack communities of the Russian Empire).

When the powers in play during a revolution do not see regional independence as a solution to problems of regional, ethnic, religious, or linguistic pluralism, persuading people to trust conationals is extremely difficult.[6] Lijphart (1977; cf Dahl 1973:18–25) suggests four conditions for stable democratic government in segmented polities [extended by Linz & Stepan (1996:24–37) to democratic "transitional" situations]: (a) a government in which all contending segments are represented; (b) an effective veto in general government policies for each important minority; (c) proportionality of allocations (e.g. of money, government posts, local offices) and of participation in interpretation and implementation of policies; and (d) "federalist" policy making, with each group effectively running its own local or communal affairs, protected by requirements of large majorities for central penetration of localities or communities.

Let us compare ending the American Revolution and the Irish Revolution as nationalist problems for a democratic outcome (with the American South from the 1780s to 1860 and "Ireland in Great Britain" from the 1880s to the 1910s as the nonmajority crucial segments). First, the American central government had southerners in crucial positions in legislative, federal court, and executive (particularly military) branches until 1860; Ireland had only a small minority parliamentary representation, with no real role in Tory governments, a bit in Liberal ones. Second, the South had an effective veto in Congress as long as new free states were paired with new slave states, i.e. until about the 1850s; Ireland had a veto only when a Liberal government depended on them for a majority. Third, the American Senate represented states equally, and somewhat proportional patronage was customary by respecting state delegations in appointments ("senatorial courtesy"); in Ireland, suffrage for Catholics for parliamentary seats, and so approximate proportionality of representation, was introduced during the period but there was no tradition of equal allocation of posts or resources. Finally, internal affairs of the South, especially about slavery, were formally left to the separate states until the 1863 Emancipation Proc-

---

[6]Fearon & Laitin (1996) show, in contrast, that communities quite commonly get along outside politics; these authors have a political explanation below the level of states.

lamation; Home Rule for Ireland was carried by a Liberal government in the Commons but stopped in the Lords—the decision of the Irish parliamentary delegation to sit as a parliament for Ireland was a central revolutionary act.

The solution for Ireland was independence of much of the island, and the continuation of the revolution within Ireland was importantly about accepting the partition in the treaty and accepting the final fixing of the boundary in 1925–1926. For the American South, of course, independence was not recognized, and an extremely bloody civil war and reconstruction followed. But if one considers the South in the period from the 1780s to 1860 as a democracy (except of course for slaves, women, and aboriginals), it was more stable and more democratic than any democracy that included Ireland in the relevant period. Both Ireland and Britain have been fairly democratic, and England was stable after Irish independence. In short, Lijphart's (1977) theory illuminates the different democratic ends (with and without independence) of these two revolutions in deeply segmented societies, where nationalistic trust in fellow citizens was problematic.

Most of our evidence on the failure of democracy in deeply plural societies comes from states put together, from segments with separate histories and languages, by colonial powers. The relations between segments were largely managed by the empire rather than by grand coalitions among the ethnicities and regions; no subject group had veto power over the empire policy; allocation of posts and benefits was predominantly to the metropole rather than being proportional; and "indirect rule" is not really federalism. Nationalist revolutions did not have much experience of managing segmented democratic polities. Most of the postcolonial democracies have failed, sometimes by genocide. One can be right not to trust a majority segment with one's welfare.

Trust failed in many of those states. Nigerian Ibos did not entrust their welfare to the votes of Fulani, nor vice versa; western-educated professionals did not trust judgments of their competence by tribal magicians; nor did unionized workers entrust their fates to policies backed by the International Monetary Fund, however democratically the coercive dictates were adopted.

Law and Democracy

The ballot and vote are instruments of coercion (coercing especially the defeated party) created entirely by law and having their effects by law. Ballots and votes are especially central to the two main ways of introducing innovation and adjustment into democratic politics, namely replacement of governments (or the continuation of regimes by succession) and legislation. Voting only makes political sense if it has legal effects and if the effects can change when the votes are different. The ballot is, however, only the most extreme form of democracy's substitution of legal devices for arms in the organization of coercion. In modern democracies, contracts, bureaucratic regulation, and administrative and judicial discretion all have their primary effects by way of law rather than arms. Many of these legal devices are also central to most modern authoritarian governments. But it is characteristic of revolutionary situations that law is an especially precarious device: People in revolutions want to turn their legal paper money into gold, have their contracts backed by a mafia, and set up machine gun nests on boundaries within which they claim jurisdiction. A law seems a paltry thing.

Law tends to have its effects more reliably when it has existed for some time, so that the bugs are worked out and responses to its main difficulties are built into it; so that people have come to know they cannot avoid it; and so that its operation is routine. The notion that something as ephemeral, as "spiritual," as a ballot could determine great questions is almost inconceivable in the midst of a revolution, when if there are laws at all they are the decisions of the last few months.

As a way out of revolution, democracy depends more on law than do conquest, totalitarianism, or independence. Conservative authoritarianism is also often quite legalistic. Conquests by democracies may create legalized occupation governments; for example, after the union of East and West Germany (not exactly a conquest), many more lawyers were required in the East (Blankenberg 1995:237–42).

The key requirement of a government of laws is that few disputes lead to contests of coercive power. The anarchy of revolution can be redescribed for our purposes here as a condition in which nearly all serious disputes lead to tests of coercive power; that is, revolution is a situation in which law is ineffective. The creation of the certainty of the law, after a situation in which the law was very uncertain, is central to the possibility of a democratic way out of a revolution.

Revolutionary "Democracy"

The preeminently legal character of the establishment of a democratic government after a revolution distinguishes it from so-called democracy during a revolution. Revolutions mobilize new groups into legislatures. This may sometimes lead to the establishment of legal citizenship, ballots, elections, and legally constituted legislatures, but it may not. In a revolution, the various "parties" often aim to become, and often proclaim themselves as, governments. They present what are much like party conventions as sovereign. The distinction between parties as proposed programs of governments and parties as governments is elided. In revolutions, laws do not gainsay a party program becoming a constitution by force of arms.

Revolutionary "democratic" movements often show their partisan character by creating laws declaring opponents to be traitors, by conducting trials in the legislature, by setting up apparatuses of terror (O'Kane 1991, AL

Stinchcombe 1995b), by entering into secret negotiations with foreign governments, by purging mobilized partisans who disagree with the current majority, or by setting up oaths of allegiance to which their opponents will not agree as a qualification for office. It would be amusing, if it were not so tragic, to see purges, exclusions, and treason trials of comembers create a national legislature that is a radical or reactionary rump of the original. But such a process shows that, for example, the revolutionary soviets in the Russian Revolution were a different sort of democracy from the Tsarist Duma dissolved by the Provisional Government and the Constituent Assembly that the soviet government dissolved; they needed very few lawyers in order to govern.

The overall conclusion of this section is that legal democracy is an inherently unlikely end of revolution, absent conquest. This conclusion is, however, undermined by the "transitions" of Eastern Europe in recent times.

CAUDILLISMO

Caudillismo and its analogues slow down the rate of change of power positions by building governments out of coteries and personal dependents. The key feature is that the forces that are called in when necessary to support authority and repress dissent are assembled by a leader of the state from patron-client relations. The King Arthur of English mythology is a good model of a *caudillo*. Armed men recruited sporadically through networks of military comradeship, kinship, and exchange of favors for loyalty, in a sort of ramshackle pyramid, are the main administrative apparatus of the state. At the core might be semipermanent coteries of the form of Knights of the Round Table. Such networks of armed men in shifting contracts of loyalty, with central governments of varying degrees of effectiveness, were characteristic of European feudalism before it was reconceived as a stable legal defense of the aristocracy's autonomy from the King. Perhaps the precariously centralized Sicilian Mafia is a better image (Gambetta 1993).

Such precarious pyramids of personal political contracts tend to exist after revolutions if the rebuilding of the previous state structure is completely impossible (AL Stinchcombe 1995a:288–311). After the Haitian Revolution, consisting of slave revolt, had defeated all the major slave powers in wars on the island, it could not build a new state on the basis of French plantation owners and royal representatives reintroducing slavery. Napoleon did that in Guadeloupe by conquest but was defeated in Haiti. Personal ties with local power centers tied to coteries of revolutionary generals substituted for historical traditions. Nineteenth-century Haitian governments looked much like *caudillismo*.

Similarly, the Spanish structure of rule through *peninsulares* from Spain, excluding almost all creoles from political power, could not be rebuilt in Spanish America after the independence revolutions. Some reduction of random violence and competition for power could be achieved through personal mobilization of somewhat erratic coteries and pyramids of clients (Safford 1985: 348–49, 375–83; Hoetink 1982 [1972]). As in feudalism, the clients were often regional leaders with their own militarized coteries (for the problems of building an army with such materials, see AL Stinchcombe 1995a:295–99).

In *caudillo* governments, the ties between central and local powers are not built of social and moral materials about what the center should be and do. Instead, the relations between patron and client, hero and follower, are the cultural materials of government. Center and periphery are tied together by interpersonal loyalty and exchanges rather than by public services to be performed, responsibilities to localities to be discharged, or elections by localities on the basis of national programs to be recognized. The position of the center is "nonlegitimate domination." When former principles of legitimacy are impossible to build with, coteries and patron-client relations may be the best one can do to get out of a revolution.

In Spanish America, such models of rule were in continuing competition with democratic forms, often borrowed from the United States or France: legislatures, elections, political parties, presidents, and the like. Alexander Hamilton consulted on the constitution of Haiti at one time. He advised that one might want a president-for-life to establish stability. Many short-lived *caudillos* became presidents-for-life, and others followed Napoleon's model and became emperors.

Caudillismo looks too much like a continuation of the uncertainty of revolution to seem like an ending. I think we see less stability than is really there because it is much less than in the societies where there are professorships of political science. The mean time to failure of Bolivian governments in the nineteenth and early twentieth century was only a bit longer than that in the middle of the French Revolution. And the most stable *caudillo* dictators sometimes look more like totalitarians than *caudillos* (e.g. Trujillo in the Dominican Republic). Democratic stability of a kind came out of a system of personalized rural power centers by forming a loose antiurban *Blanco* political party in rural Uruguay by the late nineteenth century.

That is, some unstable personalized pyramidal networks may be thought of as a transition phase out of revolution toward one of the alternative types of postrevolutionary governments (democratic, totalitarian, conservative authoritarian) outlined in this review. Thus, the above theory of ends of revolutions may also apply to transitions from *caudillismo*. The way many *caudillos* have had to truck and barter with followers to get the resources to run a government does not look very authoritarian on the ground—unpleasant and unreliable, yes; authoritarian, no.

CONCLUSION

In most cases, the explanation of there being a revolution this month is that there was a revolution last month and it has not stopped. Consequently, a central causal component in explaining revolutions is the set of devices by which they are stopped. The slogan of this review is that they are stopped by building a government. The mechanisms of building a government are those of rendering the distribution of powers more certain than they are during a revolution but not so rigid or illegitimate that the government cannot maintain itself.

The devices that end revolutions increase the degree to which major political policies are bargained out; the degree to which, once negotiated, they have a political advantage over extremism or recalcitrance; the degree to which the connections between cosmopolitan or national powers and segmental powers are shaped by the purposes and functions of the central government; the degree to which bargains are enforced by powers that can call up reserves that are large and compared to the powers of the parties; and the degree to which subsystems that can govern themselves achieve independence. Such mechanisms contribute to the certainty and continuity of the outcomes of political bargains. They are devices that create governments in troubled times.

The Leviathan must consist of such devices if it is to make war among factions less attractive. But all these devices, and the types of nascent governments to which they give rise, rely on a peculiar source of legitimacy: that very many people get sick of revolution and the disruption of the creation of public goods that civil wars entail. Being sick of revolution was, after all, how Hobbes originally was recruited to Leviathan's cause. I doubt he would have been enthusiastic about some of the Leviathans to end revolution outlined above; I myself have preferences among them, not quite the same as Hobbes's. But the fact is that many people in many parts of the world have ended revolutions one way or another. To establish the solutions described here, many people must have reckoned they were better than revolution. That fact lends considerable historical force to Hobbes' problem, if perhaps not to his solution.

ACKNOWLEDGEMENTS

This essay was written at Australian National University. Bob Goodin, Susanne Karstedt, John Markoff, and Charles Tilly have convinced me that most of this essay should be reservations, cautions, and contrary cases. In particular, I have left out the government apparatus, the supply of political personnel, money, amount and kind of armaments of paramilitary groups, and control of territory near boundaries, all critical to the processes I study. I could not take all their suggestions, though I thank them for the few I could. So I publish to be damned.

Literature Cited

Anderson BRO. 1991 (1983). *Imagined Communities: Reflections on the Origin and Spread of Nationalism.* London: Verso. 239 pp.

Arendt H. (1951) 1967. *The Origins of Totalitarianism.* London: Allen & Unwin. 493 pp. 3rd ed.

Arendt H. 1963. *Eichman in Jerusalem: A Report on the Banality of Evil.* London: Faber & Faber. 275 pp.

Bangou H. 1989. *La Revolution et l'Esclavage a la Guadeloupe 1789–1802: Epopee Noir et Genocide.* Paris: Messidor/Ed. Sociales

Bell JB. 1972. Societal patterns and lessons: the Irish case. In *Civil Wars in the 20th Century,* ed. RDS Higham pp. 217–27. Lexington: Univ. Ky. Press. 260 pp.

Bendix R. 1956. *Work and Authority in Industry: Ideologies of Management in the Course of Industrialization.* New York: Wiley. 486 pp.

Bergeron L. 1981. *France Under Napoleon.* Transl. R Palmer, 1972. Princeton, NJ: Princeton Univ. Press (From French)

Bessel R. 1991. 1933: a failed counter-revolution. In *Revolution and Counter-revolution,* ed. EE Rice, pp. 109–28. Oxford, UK: Blackwell. 223 pp.

Bienen H. 1993. Leaders, violence and the absence of change in Africa. *Polit. Sci. Q.* 108(2):271–82

Blankenberg E. 1995. The purge of lawyers after the breakdown of the East German communist regime. *Law Soc. Inq.* 20(1): 223–43

Bracher KD. 1957. *Die Auflösung der Weimarer Republik: Eine Studie zum Problem des Machtverfalls in der Demokratie.* Stuttgart: Ring

Brandwein P. 1994. *Reconstructing reconstruction: the Supreme Court and the production of historical knowledge.* PhD thesis. Northwestern Univ., Evanston, IL

Brinton CC. 1965 (1953). *The Anatomy of Revolution.* New York: Vintage Books

Chirot D. 1994. *Modern Tyrants: The Power and Prevalence of Evil in Our Age.* New York: Free. 510 pp.

Dahl RA. 1970. *After the Revolution? Authority in a Good Society.* New Haven, CT: Yale Univ. Press. 178 pp.

Dahl RA, ed. 1973. *Regimes and Oppositions.* New Haven, CT: Yale Univ. Press. 415 pp.

Dore RP. (1959) 1984. *Land Reform in Japan.* London: Athlone. 527 pp.

Eckstein S. 1976. *The Impact of Revolution: A Comparative Analysis of Mexico and Bolivia.* London: Sage. 55 pp.

Elster J. 1978. *Logic and Society: Contradictions and Possible Worlds.* New York: Wiley. 248 pp.

Elster J. 1994. Argumenter et negocier dans deux assemblées constituantes. *Rev. Fr. Sci. Polit.* 44(2):187–256

Fearon JP, Laitin DD. 1996. Explaining interethnic cooperation. *Am. Polit. Sci. Rev.* 90(4):715–35

Fedotoff-White D. 1944. *The Growth of the Red Army.* Princeton, NJ: Princeton Univ. Press

Gambetta D. 1993. *The Sicilian Mafia: the Business of Private Protection.* Cambridge, MA: Harvard Univ. Press. 441 pp.

Goldstone J. 1991. *Revolution and Rebellion in the Early Modern World.* Berkeley: Univ. Calif. Press. 637 pp.

Granick D. 1954. *Management of the Industrial Firm in the U.S.S.R.* New York: Columbia Univ. Press

Greenfield L. 1992. *Nationalism: Five Roads to Modernity.* Cambridge, MA: Harvard Univ. Press. 581 pp.

Gurr TR, Grabosky PN, Hula RC. 1977. *The Politics of Crime and Conflict: A Comparative History of Four Cities.* Beverly Hills, CA: Sage

Hallam H. 1854. *The Constitutional History of England: From the Accession of Henry VII to the Death of George II.* Vol 2. London: Murray. 473 pp. 3rd ed

Hayes P. 1987. *Industry and Ideology: I. G. Farben in the Nazi Era.* Cambridge, UK: Cambridge Univ. Press. 439 pp.

Hoetink H. 1982 (1972). *The Dominican [Republic] People 1850–1900.* Transl. S Ault, 1982. Baltimore, MD: Johns Hopkins Univ. Press (From Spanish)

Kann RA. 1968. *The Problem of Restoration: A Study in Comparative Political History.* Berkeley: Univ. Calif. Press.

Kelley J, Klein HS. 1981. *Revolution and the Rebirth of Inequality: A Theory Applied to* the *National Revolution in Bolivia.* Berkeley: Univ. Calif. Press. 285 pp.

Keogh D. 1994. *Twentieth-Century Ireland: Nation and State.* New York: St. Martin. 527 pp.

Licklides R. 1995. The consequences of negotiated settlements in civil wars, 1945–1993. *Am. Polit. Sci. Rev.* 89(3): 681–87

Lijphart A. 1977. *Democracry in Plural Societies.* New Haven, CT: Yale Univ. Press

Linz JJ. 1973. Opposition in and under an authoritarian regime: the case of Spain. See Dahl 1973, pp. 171–259

Linz JJ. 1978a. From great hopes to civil war: the breakdown of democracy in Spain. See Linz & Stepan 1978, pp. 142–215

Linz JJ. 1978b. *The Breakdown of Democratic Regimes: Crisis, Breakdown, and Reequilibration.* Baltimore, MD: Johns Hopkins Univ. Press.

Linz JJ, Stepan A, eds. 1978. *The Breakdown of Democratic Regimes: Europe.* Baltimore, MD: Johns Hopkins Univ. Press. 237 pp.

Linz JJ, Stepan A. 1996. Theoretical overview. In *Problems of Democratic Transition and Consolidation: Southern Europe, South America, and Post-Communist Europe,* ed. JJ Linz, A Stepan, pp. 1–83. Baltimore, MD: Johns Hopkins Univ. Press. 499 pp.

Markoff J. 1996. *The Abolition of Feudalism: Peasants, Lords and Legislators in the French Revolution.* University Park, PA: Penn. State Univ. Press.

Maoz Z. 1984. Peace by empire: conflict outcomes and international stability, 1816–1976. *J. Peace Res.* 21(3):227–41

Neumann S. 1965 (1942). *Permanent Revolution: Totalitarianism in the Age of International Civil War.* London: Pall Mall

O'Brien CC. 1972. *States of Ireland.* London: Hutchinson

O'Donnell GA, Schmitter PC. 1986. Introducing uncertainty. See O'Donnell et al 1986, pp. 1–78

O'Donnell GA, Schmitter PC, Whitehead L. 1986. *Transitions from Authoritarian Rule: Prospects for Democracy.* Baltimore, MD: Johns Hopkins Univ. Press. 746 pp.

O'Kane RHT. 1991. *The Revolutionary Reign of Terror: The Role of Violence in Political Change.* Aldershot, UK: Edward Elgar. 312 pp.

Poe SC, Tate N. 1994. Repression of human rights to personal integrity in the 1980s: a

global analysis. *Am. Polit. Sci. Rev.* 88(4): 853–72

Przeworski A. 1986. Some problems in the study of the transition to democracy. See O'Donnell et al 1986, pp. 47–63

Robiquet J. 1942. *Daily Life in France Under Napoleon.* Transl. VM MacDonald, 1962. London: Allen & Unwin. 230 pp. (From French)

Safford F. 1985. Politics, ideology and society in post-independence Spanish America. In *The Cambridge History of Latin America,* Vol. 3, ed. L Bethell, pp. 347–421. Cambridge, UK: Cambridge Univ Press. 960 pp.

Shils EA, Janowitz MP. 1948. Cohesion and disintegration in the Wehrmacht in World War II. *Pub. Opin. Q.* pp. 280–315

Shultz RH. 1995. State disintegration and ethnic conflict: a framework for analysis. *Ann. Am. Acad. Polit. Soc. Sci.* 541:75–88

Simon WB. 1978. Democracy in the shadow of imposed sovereignty: the First Republic of Austria. See Linz & Stepan 1978, pp. 80–121

Sorokin PA 1967 (1925). *Sociology of Revolution.* New York: H Fertig. 436 pp.

Sperber J. 1994. *The European Revolutions, 1848–1851.* Cambridge, UK: Cambridge Univ. Press

Stepan A. 1986. Paths toward redemocratization: theoretical and comparative considerations. See O'Donnell et al 1986, pp. 64–84

Stinchcombe AL. 1968. *Constructing Social Theories.* Chicago: Univ. Chicago Press. 318 pp.

Stinchcombe AL. 1995a. *Sugar Island Slavery in the Age of Enlightenment: The Political Economy of the Caribbean World.* Princeton, NJ: Princeton Univ. Press. 379 pp.

Stinchcombe AL. 1995b. Lustration as a problem of the social basis of constitutionalism. *Law Soc. Inq.* 20(1):245–73

Stinchcombe WC. 1969. *The American Revolution and the French Alliance.* Syracuse, NY: Syracuse Univ. Press

Trotsky LB. 1933. *The History of the Russian Revolution.* Transl. M Eastman, 1933. Ann Arbor: Univ. Mich. Press/London: Victor Gollancz. 1406 pp. (From Russian)

Woloch I. 1994. *The New Regime: Transformations of the French Civic Order.* New York: Norton. 536 pp.

Woodward CV. 1974 (1957). *The Strange Career of Jim Crow.* New York: Oxford Univ. Press. 250 pp.

Annu. Rev. Polit. Sci. 1999. 2:75–89

HAROLD D. LASSWELL'S LEGACY TO MAINSTREAM POLITICAL SCIENCE: A Neglected Agenda

Heinz Eulau

Stanford University, Stanford, California 94305; e-mail: heulau@leland.stanford.edu

Susan Zlomke

Emory and Henry College, Emory, Virginia 24327; e-mail: sz@ehc.edu

KEY WORDS: political behavior, empirical theory, values, methodology

ABSTRACT

Harold D. Lasswell's extensive and wide-ranging books and essays are extraordinarily rich sources of ideas, methods, and topics for the study of political behavior. Whether and how the legacy of his writings is used by contemporary political scientists and theorists is reported here by way of an investigation of references to his work appearing in mainstream political science journals (available through JSTOR) for the 17 years following the end of his academic career. We find that most references to Lasswell are superficial (perfunctory, suggestive, deferential), although a few are more substantial (critical, extending). We conclude that Lasswell's legacy is today undervalued and underused, to the discipline's detriment.

INTRODUCTION

"If you want a book to become a 'classic,'" Harold Lasswell once told Heinz Eulau, "there are two strategies.[1] One strategy is to have it published in very small quantity by an obscure university press that has no budget for advertising. That will soon make your book an addition to a 'rare book room' in some university library and guarantee something out of it being repeatedly quoted

---

[1] Lasswell was strong on "strategy" long before game theory invaded the social sciences. It was a word he had undoubtedly picked up as a close student of another great scholar, Lenin, who had applied it to the politics of the class struggle and revolution. But that is another story.

1094-2939/99/0616-0075$08.00

without having been read, like Havelock Ellis on sexuality."[2] Lasswell grinned, sniffed his after-dinner Courvoisier, and had a sip before going on. "The other strategy is to mass-market your opus. A notorious Athenian, Socrates by name, was rather good at that. Originally his messages were spread by word of mouth, until some entrepreneur by the name of Plato—one of his students—came along, and then there was no end to the fame of *The Republic*. The great virtue of this strategy is that this kind of stuff [another favorite Lasswell expression] does not require any attribution."

That Harold Dwight Lasswell was, during his lifetime, an omnipresence as the most original and eminent of political scientists is beyond doubt. The eulogies upon his death in 1978 were ecstatic, as befits a "living legend." Lasswell's memorials are also noteworthy for their predictions of his continuing importance. [For a compilation of eulogies, see *Harold Dwight Lasswell, 1902–1978: In Commemoration and Continuing Commitment* (Yale Law School 1979).] Lasswell's extensive and wide-ranging books, essays, and other publications remain extraordinarily rich sources of ideas, methods, and topics for the study of political behavior. Those ideas, methods, and topics—i.e. the substance of his "classic" writings—are his legacy. Whether and how that legacy has been substantively used by subsequent political scientists is the question that kindles our curiosity here.[3]

How does one go about determining the fruition of a prolific scholar's legacy, regardless of which "strategy" lifted his works to the status of "classic"? A count of the lines or inches devoted to Lasswell's name in the *Social Science Citation Index*, for example, yields far fewer references than we would expect—not that he aspired to become a *SSCI* superstar. Besides, we do not believe that the reputation of a person, especially if departed, is a function of so simple a measure as number of citations. On the contrary, intellectual influence is sometimes so pervasive and encompassing that attribution is unnecessary. As Alfred North Whitehead advised,[4]

[2]In the United States, until 1935, Ellis's works were legally available only to the medical profession. According to the Encyclopedia Britannica's *Micropaedia* (III:860), "a legal dispute over [a volume of Ellis's *Studies in the Psychology of Sex*] led the judge...to call claims for the book's scientific value 'a pretense, adopted for the purpose of selling a filthy publication....' Ellis's work helped to foster open discussion of sexual problems, and he became known as a champion of women's rights and of sex education." Although Lasswell was not a learned practitioner of medicine, he evidently had access to Ellis's books and relied on them.

[3]We are not about to launch another rehearsal of Lasswell's personal and intellectual biography or a tedious explication of his political science. There exist two excellent essays written before his death in 1978 (Smith 1969, Marvick 1977) and another of more recent vintage (Muth 1990). The Muth volume is primarily an annotated bibliography of Lasswell's writings but also includes a long list of "analytical," biographical, and "further" references to his work.

[4]Lasswell once acknowledged that his own terminology "owes something to the Cambridge Logical School, and especially to A.N. Whitehead. The debt is evident in the use of such expressions as 'event' and 'event manifold'" (Lasswell [1939] 1948b:195).

When you are criticizing the philosophy of an epoch, do not chiefly direct your attention to those intellectual positions which its exponents feel it necessary explicitly to defend. There will be some fundamental assumptions which adherents of all the various systems within the epoch unconsciously presuppose. Such assumptions appear so obvious that people do not know what they are assuming because no other way of putting things has ever occurred to them. With these assumptions a certain limited number of types of philosophic systems are possible, and this group of systems constitutes the philosophy of an epoch. (Whitehead 1948:49–50)

When a Lasswellian *piece de resistance* is cited, what usually gets quoted (we might add, ad nauseam) is either "who gets what, when, and how" or the clinical formula known as the displacement hypothesis, which, he told us, "expresses the developmental facts about the fully developed political man":

$$p \} d \} r = P,$$

where p = private motives, d = displacement onto a public object, r = rationalization in terms of the public interest, P = the political man, and $\}$ signifies "is transformed into" (1930:75).

Not often cited are other Lasswellian adages, like this brash proverb from the book that made Lasswell notorious in the established circles of his time (*Psychopathology and Politics*):

Political science without biography is a form of taxidermy. (1930:1)

Or the first sentence in his most original book, *World Politics and Personal Insecurity:*

Political analysis is the study of changes in the shape and composition of the value patterns of society. (1935:3)

Or the "premature" formula of the "social process" that should make every rationally inclined neo-institutionalist's mouth water:

Man
pursues *Values*
through *Institutions*
on *Resources*. (1948a:17)

Or, finally, the triumphant welcome to the dawning age of computer-guided policy making:

....even in an automatizing world some top-level choices must be made. In that sense at least discretion is here to stay. (1955:399)

Although absolute and relative numbers of attributions are suggestive and thus of interest (we report some below), our peek at Lasswell's legacy to political science—whether and how it has been substantively used—rests on an examination of the context of those attributions.

READING LASSWELL BACKWARD

An intellectual legacy, unlike a pot of gold, is not constant in nature. We read our intellectual heroes backward—from the perspective of our own interests and curiosities rather than from the perspective of the legator. We pick and choose from the "objective" legacy only what seems relevant as our own interests change. At times, we may even read into an earlier work what we need to find for our own work. And the more diverse and comprehensive the earlier source is, the more likely it is to be interpreted and reinterpreted, used and misused, picked at and sifted. Such has been the fate of Lasswell's legacy, a particularly wide-ranging and equally suggestive body of work by an especially ecumenical social scientist (see Muth 1990 for Lasswell's extensive bibliography).

Our survey thus turns on a simple question: If one knows about Lasswell only by reading the citations or references to him in the political science literature, what does his legacy seem to be? (We suggest that the more technically inclined reader repair to the Appendix, where we spell out our investigative procedures.)

A BOTTOMLESS BOTTOM LINE

Before detailing what we retrieved as tapped, praised, cherished, critiqued, misplaced, or abused, a look at the "bottom line" is appropriate. Lasswell's legacy is undervalued and underemployed. Frankly, we were disappointed not to find more and better utilization of the rich intellectual heritage Lasswell left behind.

We think it not accidental that of Lasswell's books the most frequently referenced (with only 15 mentions) is *Power and Society* (1950), which in many respects is not a book at all but an inventory of definitions and propositions that are easily lifted for literary exploitation without requiring the reading of anything else in the volume (for instance, its illuminating introduction, which deals with "political science, philosophy, and policy" and "political inquiry"). The next most often cited book, *Politics: Who Gets What, When, How* (1936), with 14 mentions, is the most accessible of Lasswell's books (heavily edited and possibly rewritten by one of Lasswell's most devoted students). Its title provides a conveniently concise and flashy definition of politics. The absence of citations to particular pages strongly suggests that the book has far fewer actual readers than admirers of its title. What has survived from *Psychopathology and Politics* (1930), referenced 11 times, is largely some restatement—sometimes correct, sometimes incorrect—of the displacement hypothesis, an obviously suggestive target for latter-day riposte. But these numbers are of interest mainly when contrasted with the mere five references to

Lasswell's most seminal and extended work, *World Politics and Personal Insecurity* (1935). Although this book is intellectually complex and difficult to read, it not only reflects what Lasswell conceived in the first decade of his professional life but also anticipates almost all of his later formulations and deliberations on power, revolution, institutions, context, configurative analysis, developmental constructs, elites and symbols, values, decision making, and more.

Of Lasswell's other major works, *Power and Personality* (1948a) was referenced six times and the coauthored *Power, Corruption, and Rectitude* (Rogow & Lasswell 1963) four times. The essay "Democratic Character" (1951) was alluded to twice, and another nine sundry items were each mentioned once. Two works presumably of particular interest to political scientists, *The Future of Political Science* (1963) and *A Pre-View of Policy Sciences* (1971), did not appear among references or citations in the 75 JSTOR articles.

Suffice it to say that of the references to Lasswell's name and works that we record in the following five categories, few are substantial. In some cases there is no citation at all from the book referenced, or the citation does not specify the page where the quotation is presumably located, or the citation is not to the original edition of the book.

Perfunctory Treatment

Most references to Lasswell are perfunctory or, to be less generous, superficial, ornamental, even irrelevant. The addition of Lasswell's name to a text, a footnote, or a bibliography does not substantively contribute to an author's argument. The worst and most common offenders have simply quoted what is taken to be Lasswell's definition of politics—"who gets what, when, and how"—and then blithely moved on to their particular concern. For example: "Any attempt to remove politics from the reorganization process, however, is bound to fail. Politics, as Harold Lasswell opined, is the process that determines who gets what, when, and how. The reorganization act neither eliminates nor diminishes politics; it merely alters the rules..." (Fisher & Moe 1981:310). Another example deals with an approach to the study of municipal services. "It focuses on the levels of municipal services provided to different groups in the metropolis. Rooted in the academic tradition of Harold Lasswell's definition of politics, the attention to 'who gets what' in public service is termed the study of service distribution" (Jones et al 1978:333). A third case uses Lasswell's name in a manner that is largely gratuitous. "Years ago, Harold Lasswell defined politics as 'the study of influence and the influential.' But we have arbitrarily narrowed the discipline of political science to the study of government. Perhaps we should reconsider Professor Lasswell's advice and rededicate ourselves to the study of the origins of public policy..." (Dye 1978:330–31).

Suggestive Influence

A cousin of the perfunctory reference to Lasswell's legacy is the "suggestive influence" of his ideas. These references or citations are more contextual (i.e. connected to the whole of Lasswell's text) and directly related to an author's research or theoretical argument. They are "suggestions" from Lasswell used for an author's own purposes, rather than literal attributions drawn from some single module in the Lasswellian legacy.

Our first example is of the suggestive influence of Lasswell's *Power and Personality* (1948a). One researcher, concerned with the influence of self-esteem on judicial decision making, pointed out that "the process is somewhat more complex than envisaged by Lasswell," clearly stimulated by the Lasswellian postulate that office seeking may be a compensatory device for overcoming low self-esteem (Gibson 1981:105–6).

"Unconventional political behavior" has rarely been a major item on the agenda of mainstream political science. Of the "early" political behavioralists, only Lasswell concerned himself with such problems as violence, coercion, corruption, protest, and legitimacy as topics for systematic study. That his work in this area is suggestive, especially his examination of the difficult-to-research topic of corruption, is to be expected. The following example illustrates what we consider suggestive influence.

> Definitions of political corruption based on notions of the public or common interest significantly broaden the range of behavior one might investigate. Consider the definition proposed by Arnold Rogow and Harold Lasswell: "A corrupt act violates responsibility toward at least one system of public or civic order and is in fact incompatible with (destructive of) any such system" [Rogow & Lasswell 1963:132–33]. While this definition focuses our attention on any act or set of acts which threaten to destroy a political system, the researcher has the responsibility of determining what the public or common interest is before assessing whether a particular act is corrupt. (Peters & Welch 1978:975)

A final example of suggestive influence stems from Lasswell's writings on epistemology and methodology. In this case, an author reported the familiar allegation that the historical study of political theory was inimical to "the development of modern scientific political theory" (Sabia 1984:985). A footnote then illustrated his argument by referring to a string of scholars—Merriam, Catlin, Munro, Lasswell, Dahl, and perhaps Easton—who presumably held this view.[5] He then quoted Lasswell from as obscure a source as one could find: "Lasswell's comments are typical: In the recent past, said he, historians

---

[5]The author qualifies his statement in the case of Easton, suggesting that he might be interpreted differently. He seems not to know that Merriam (1903, 1920) and Catlin (1939) wrote ponderous works on the history of political theory.

of political theory 'were so weighed down with the burden of genteel erudition that they had little intellectual energy left with which to evolve original theory.... Hence empirical work in political science received a minimum of constructive aid from scholars formally responsible for political theory' [Lasswell 1954:201]" (Sabia 1984:985–86). But the quotation is neither "typical" of the other scholars named nor representative of the argument it was presumably designed to illustrate. Instead, it seems to have served the author as a negative catalyst.

Thus, as these quotations demonstrate, something in one or another of Lasswell's writings can suggest an idea or concern to a later author, even if neither Lasswell nor the author originally had that idea or concern in mind.[6]

Critical Appraisal

Some authors have engaged in a more or less careful and judicious evaluation—whether positive or negative—of some aspect of Lasswell's work. Unlike a perfunctory or suggestive reference, critical analysis entails a serious look at the substance of Lasswell's ideas. This critical appraisal may result in the adoption, adaptation, or rejection of his legacy.

The silliest critique of Lasswell characterized him as "that notorious radical skeptic" among an earlier generation of political scientists, including Woodrow Wilson and Charles Beard. These gentlemen, compared with the later devotees of "relevance" in political science, were "much more interested in shaping and guiding the public agenda through the authority of the new discipline and its research products" (Seidelman 1990:598). Lasswell may have been notorious and certainly was radical, but, by the evidence of the quoted statement itself, a skeptic he was not.

Worse than silly due to its bald inaccuracy is this sweeping, polemical characterization of the "behavioral generation," including such scholars as Almond and Key, as atheoretical: "Even Lasswell, the most theoretically inclined of that generation—probably the most erudite—did not sit down and write a theoretical work. His publications were empirical (e.g. *Psychopathology and Politics* [1960]), encyclopedic (*Power and Society* [1950]), or methodological..." (Lowi 1988:886). This author's conception of "theory" and empiricism are so idiosyncratic as to draw the reader away from a significant portion of Lasswell's opus.

A less objectionable evaluation concerns the overquoted, even overheated, *Politics: Who Gets What, When, How.* Werlin (1990) was not altogether off base in trying to link what is sometimes called "interest group pluralism" to

---

[6]A few references to Lasswell are neither perfunctory nor suggestive; they are only bibliographical. Frequently appearing in a footnote, these mentions of Lasswell's writings are simply part of a string of literature citations.

Lasswell's book. "To see politics in this way is as misleading as to see the Olympics as nothing more than competing individuals and teams, neglecting the organizational arrangements and consensus on rules..." (Werlin 1990: 251). One might say "amen," were it not for the fact that Lasswell's conception of politics—perhaps we should say "conceptions"—went far beyond the "who gets what, when, how" formula, a fact that most of those appropriating the phrase rarely acknowledge.

But other critical appraisals of Lasswell's legacy are more thoughtful. For example, Lane observed that the American public values wealth more than power and that this "is the threat to Lasswell's plural-valued man that is most significant.... [W]here the market is dominant over other value-giving institutions, eroding their value positions, employing its superior resources against them, these other institutions cannot give sustenance to the plural values of the citizen, starving, in effect, Lasswellian man" (1978:24). Similarly, Sears & Lau (1983) noted that social scientists "from Lasswell (1930) on" have found that voters disguise their self-interested behavior by claiming to act in the public interest. They continued: "However, our interpretation would turn Lasswell on his head: people seem instead to claim to be self-interested...." (Sears & Lau 1983:247). These are both significant critiques of Lasswell's early psychological formulations.

Extension or Test

The most significant and exciting use of Lasswell's legacy is the attempt to extend his theories or methods to new areas of political research. When scholars apply a Lasswellian concept, method, or theory to their own research concerns, they are doing two things. First, they are implicitly, if not explicitly, affirming the validity of Lasswell's work as it stands. Second, they are testing whether that validity is maintained in a different context. An intellectual legacy could not hope for a better use, and Lasswell's has warranted several examples.

Baas (1979) examined Lasswell's displacement hypothesis in an intensive, one-subject study of the constitution as a secondary-world symbol. He found that "[t]he entire pattern of [the research subject] Smith's object world can be explained by some variant of Lasswell's theory" (Baas 1979:110). Other authors used Lasswell's distinction between inducements and constraints in an effort to "disaggregate" corporatism (Collier & Collier 1979), correlated Lasswell's psychological understanding of "political man" with human biochemical markers (Madsen 1985), incorporated Lasswell and Kaplan's distinction between "welfare" and "deference" values into a collective-goods analysis of neighborhood organizations (Rich 1980), and applied Lasswell's psychological profile of a democracy's ruling elite to Harry Truman, born to the middle class (Hamby 1991).

Of course, sometimes tests succeed by disproving a theory, and Lasswell's legacy has experienced this use too. In their research into the psychological motives of state and local politicians, Clarke & Donovan (1980:542,545) found that

> [h]igh-esteem politicans are attracted to power because it allows them to control events and move people—not, it appears, because it serves as compensation against estimates of the self as 'unloved, shameful, guilty, and weak,' as Lasswell claimed (1948, p. 45)....There was, again, no evidence that this group exercises power as compensation, as Lasswell (1930, 1948) suggested in his earlier work. To the contrary, this group finds little emotional solace in the exercise of power, and public life makes them uncomfortable.

Deferential Posture

Some references to Lasswell simply pay tribute to his brilliance and entrepreneurship. He is honored for his theoretical achievements, his historical importance at a critical turning point in the social sciences, his disciplinary vision, his methodological contributions, his inspirational activities. Here is an example of the respect accorded him by those who knew him best, from a discussion of rationality in human behavior by the discipline's only Nobel prize winner: "But [the reader] may feel that I have not gone far enough in my skepticism about reason in political behavior. Surely even the concept of bounded rationality does not capture the whole role of passion and unreason in human affairs. Don't we need to listen to Lasswell and Freud as well as to Wallas and James? Assuredly we do" (Simon 1985:301). Some accolades are perverse, in that Lasswell is being lauded for work with which the author does not agree. We consider this a tribute nevertheless. In a defense of the rationality of voter turnout, Jackman (1993:279) argued that "[d]espite the plausibility of this [rational choice] perspective, casting political behavior as rational continues to generate considerable resistance.... Since at least Lasswell (1930), many have preferred to see political behavior as motivated by subconscious nonrational drives without purpose. The impact on the field of Lasswell's emphasis on the psychopathology of politics has been monumental in this regard." A third author compared Lasswell's conceptual precision unfavorably to more recent theorists of legitimacy: "...[these] problems have been exacerbated by the lack of explicit distinction in the usage of the terms *interest* and *value*, particularly since Lasswell 1959 [sic]"[7] (Razi 1990:72; emphasis in original).

Linked with such homages to Lasswell's accomplishments are appeals to Lasswell as a learned authority. As the innovative and prolific developer of a comprehensive theory of political behavior, Lasswell is used to give authors'

---

[7]Actually Lasswell 1936.

arguments the weight of his mastery. This use is more than a eulogistic acknowledgement of his work; it incorporates the validity of his legacy into another writer's work. In the 1970s, for example, when community studies pursuing Dahl's question, "Who Governs?," had proved inconclusive and "a new generation of community studies...focused on outcomes" rather than decision making, one such study asserted, "Although this [new] literature is little more than a decade old, its roots are firmly based in Harold Lasswell's definition of politics: Who gets what, when, and how" (Boyle & Jacobs 1982:372). Since Lasswell's conception of politics was taken to be superior to others, this claim implied that these latter-day community studies were credible and promising. Similarly, Baldwin (1978:1231) blamed the incompleteness of exchange theorists' concept of power on their inattention to Lasswell (and Dahl): "Obviously, the exchange theorists use a narrower concept of power than Dahl does. It is interesting to note that neither Blau (1964) nor Homans (1964) cites Dahl (1957, 1968) or Lasswell and Kaplan (1950)." Because they don't use Lasswell, it was hinted, their theories are suspect.

COMING FULL CIRCLE

Some 60 years ago, in its June 1935 issue, the staid *American Political Science Review* carried what has probably remained the most devastating critique of a book (namely *World Politics and Personal Insecurity*) ever to appear in its pages. A few sentences convey the review's aroma:

> ....In this excellently printed, tempestuous, and obstreperous volume, Dr. Lasswell leaps about the cosmos of sociological-psychobiological-obstetrical-psychiatric political science with the abandon of a flock of sparrows at a horse-show. The title may seem to include everything from here to there, but the book actually does so, and with a rattling fusilade of partially related footnotes.....What this book contributes is the author's modernist-cubist anfractuosities of dialectical metaphysic. It is hard to see how our universities can help our laboring, lumbering democracy by telling people what they know in language they will not understand, and burdened by a cluttering universality of casual allusion. There is an adequate index. (Whittlesey 1935:500–1)

There is one truth in this polemic: Lasswell was his own worst messenger and representative. He is difficult to read and understand, which is ironic because he saw himself as a herald of a better world. Understanding him requires a willingness to learn his language, patience in letting his formulations sink in, sympathy with his intentions and goals, and a readiness not to take every one of his words at face value. Much commentary along these lines was published in his lifetime (e.g. Smith 1969, Marvick 1977, Muth 1990); to repeat it here would be redundant.

Our look at the uses made of Lasswell's work in the mainstream journals since his death shows that, just as he was an enigma to the "traditional" political scientists during his early decades, so he has remained an enigma to contemporary political scientists, with one difference: Whereas in the 1930s and 1940s he could be easily ignored as a cocky upstart whose verbal effusions would fade away, his latter-day status as a kind of patron of avant-garde disciplinary discourse makes his works count even as they seem to elude serious understanding. After considering how his legacy has been received in mainstream political science, we suspect that many of those who quote his most popular adages or maxims do not really know the works in which they appear.

APPENDIX

Our detailed inspection of the uses to which Lasswell's contributions have been put in the research and writings of his legatees took place in several steps. We used JSTOR to access the following mainstream journals: *American Political Science Review*, the *American (Midwest) Journal of Political Science*, the *Journal of Politics, Political Science Quarterly*, and *World Politics*. We first examined all references to Lasswell's name in articles published in the 17 years after his death (actually after his stroke in December 1977, which ended his scholarly career and permitted us to include the 1978 calendar year). The 17-year span was dictated by the fact that the current JSTOR inventory ceases after 1994.

To get a handle on the number of references, we made two comparisons. First, we looked at the articles in which his name appeared in the 17 years prior to his year of death, taking us back to 1961. Then we compared these two 17-year ranges with the equivalent ones for EE Schattschneider (who died in 1971). We chose Schattschneider because he was Lasswell's close academic contemporary, following him, for instance, in the presidency of the American Political Science Association (Lasswell, 1955–1956; Schattschneider, 1956–1957). In our primitive calculations, Schattschneider unexpectedly outdistanced Lasswell. In the 17 years after their respective deaths, Schattschneider's name appears in 127 articles, Lasswell's in only 70. (In this comparison we omitted *World Politics* because Schattschneider is referenced in it only four times over the entire period of 34 years.) Looking at the 17 years prior to their deaths, it appears that Lasswell's "stock" went down (from 206 to 70 references) while Schattschneider's went up (from 73 to 127). Although we could speculate about intellectual and contextual factors that might account for this "interesting" result, we do not make much of these nonvital statistics.

Our second step was to classify the potpourri of topics in the JSTOR-provided articles, paying some attention to the relative incidence of the different interests of Lasswell's legatees. Here are our roughly defined topics and multiply-coded counts:

1. Conventional politics and political behavior or institutions: Theory and/or research on political participation, voting behavior, legislatures and legislative behavior, representation, administrative structures and decision making, and so on ($N = 8$).

2. Unconventional politics and political behavior: Theory and/or research on issues of legitimacy, corruption, coercion, violence, revolution, etc ($N = 6$).

3. Social and/or political change: Theory and/or research on time and developmental constructs such as world revolutionary change, garrison state, elite circulation, skill revolution, symbol transformation, etc ($N = 12$).

4. Political processes: Theory and/or research on power situations, exchange, bargaining, rational choice, decision making, conflict, communication, professionalization, group identification, etc ($N = 8$).

5. Public policy: Theory and/or research on substantive policy arenas (e.g. foreign affairs, welfare), "policy science," politics and economics, the "good regime," etc ($N = 7$).

6. Political psychology: Theory and/or research on "human nature," political personality, "perspective" (identifications, demands, expectations), socialization, interpersonal relations, attitudes, political culture, values and value orientations, etc ($N = 22$).

7. International and comparative politics: Theory and/or research on "the state" (as interaction and/or "subjective event"), diplomacy, international law, etc ($N = 3$).

8. Analytic theory, methodology and epistemology: Theory and/or research on political science as discipline, education, causation, contextual analysis, configurative analysis, "individual and society," value-institutional approach, etc ($N = 16$).

Finally and most importantly, we categorized the ways in which Lasswell's ideas, concepts, formulas, approaches and so on seem to have been used. After a good deal of "mental experimentation" with categories and subcategories, we arrived at the five used above. Here we again provide our rough counts (including multiple codings) without vouching for their eternal reliability: (*a*) Perfunctory ($N = 27$); (*b*) Suggestive ($N = 20$); (*c*) Critical ($N = 11$); (*d*) Extending ($N = 8$); and (*e*) Deferential ($N = 9$). Before our "field research" through the grasslands of the JSTOR system, we had naively hoped to be able to crosstabulate the eight topical groupings with these five analytical catego-

Table 1   References to Lasswell in books published since 1978 in the field of American politics

Subject Matter	Number of Books	Number Mentioning Lasswell
Political behavior and public opinion	8	4
Political parties and national politics	7	1
Elite and class	5	1
Presidency and Cabinet	4	1
Voting and electoral behavior	4	2
Congress and legislative behavior	4	0
Democracy and political values	10	0
Interest groups and organizations	4	2
Race relations	2	0
Rational and public choice	10	0
Information processing	3	0
Total	61	11

ries. We were quickly cured of our naivete as we encountered one of the social scientist's worst nightmares—the "many variables, few cases" problem. As we ended up with 40 cells but only 75 usable references, our noble intentions had to be jettisoned.

Just to assure ourselves that Lasswell's low profile in the journals is not a fluke, we looked at 61 books published since 1978 in the broad field of American politics, casually pulled down from our personal library shelves. What we found was even more stultifying than the results of the journals survey. Overall, of the 61 books, an appalling 50 had no references to Lasswell in either their indices or bibliographies. Table 1 shows the breakdown by topics.

Perusal of the 11 "ordained" books reveals that only three authors made creative use of some fundamental part of the Lasswellian legacy. The rest of the references are as inane as those found in the journals, being perfunctory or explicative, unnecessary to the author's point.

Visit the *Annual Reviews home page* at
http://www.AnnualReviews.org.

Literature Cited

Baas LR. 1979. The constitution as symbol: the interpersonal sources of meaning of a secondary symbol. *Am. J. Polit. Sci.* 23: 101–20

Baldwin DA. 1978. Power and social exchange. *Am. Polit. Sci. Rev.* 72:1229–42

Blau, PM. 1964. *Exchange and Power in Social Life.* New York: Wiley. 352 pp.

Boyle J, Jacobs D. 1982. The intracity distribution of services: a multivariate analysis. *Am. Polit. Sci. Rev.* 76:371–79

Catlin G. 1939. *The Story of the Political Philosophers.* New York: McGraw-Hill. 802 pp.

Clarke JW, Donovan MM. 1980. Personal needs and political incentives: some observations on self-esteem. *Am. J. Polit. Sci.* 24:536–52

Collier RB, Collier D. 1979. Inducements versus constraints: disaggregating 'corporatism.' *Am. Polit. Sci. Rev.* 73:967–86

Dahl RA. 1957. The concept of power. *Behav. Sci.* 2:201–15

Dahl RA. 1968. Power. In *International Encyclopedia of the Social Sciences.* 12: 405–15. New York: Free

Dye TR. 1978. Oligarchic tendencies in national policy-making: the role of the private policy-planning organizations. *J. Polit.* 40:309–31

Fisher L, Moe RC. 1981. Presidential reorganization authority: Is it worth the cost? *Polit. Sci. Q.* 96:301–18

Gibson JL. 1981. Personality and elite political behavior: the influence of self esteem on judicial decision making. *J. Polit.* 43: 104–25

Hamby AL. 1991. An American democrat: a reevaluation of the personality of Harry S. Truman. *Polit. Sci. Q.* 106:33–55

Homans GC. 1964. *Social Behavior: Its Elementary Forms* New York: Harcourt, Brace, Jovanovich. 386 pp. Rev. ed.

Jackman RW. 1993. Response to Aldrich's "rational choice and turnout": rationality and political participation. *Am. J. Polit. Sci.* 37:279–90

Jones BD, Greenberg SR, Kaufman C, Drew J. 1978. Service delivery rules and the distribution of local government services: three Detroit bureaucracies. *J. Polit.* 40:332–68

Lane RE. 1978. Autonomy, felicity, futility: the effects of the market economy on political personality. *J. Polit.* 40:2–24

Lasswell HD. 1930. *Psychopathology and Politics.* Chicago: Univ. Chicago Press. 282 pp.

Lasswell HD. 1935. *World Politics and Personal Insecurity.* New York: McGraw-Hill. 307 pp.

Lasswell HD. 1936. *Politics: Who Gets What, When, How.* New York: McGraw-Hill. 264 pp.

Lasswell HD. 1948a. *Power and Personality.* New York: Norton. 262 pp.

Lasswell HD. 1948b (1939). General framework: person, personality, group, culture. [*Psychiatry* 2:533–61]. In *The Analysis of Political Behavior,* ed. HD Lasswell, pp. 195–234. New York: Oxford Univ. Press

Lasswell HD. 1951. Democratic character. In *The Political Writings of Harold D. Lasswell,* pp. 463–525. Glencoe, IL: Free

Lasswell HD. 1954. Selective effects of personality on political participation. In *Studies in the Scope and Method of "The Authoritarian Personality,"* ed. R Christie, M Jahoda. pp. 197–225. Glencoe, IL: Free

Lasswell HD. 1955. Current studies in the decision process: automation versus creativity. *West. Polit. Q.* 8:381–99

Lasswell HD. 1963. *The Future of Political Science.* New York: Atherton. 256 pp.

Lasswell HD. 1971. *A Pre-View of the Policy Sciences.* New York: American Elsevier. 173 pp.

Lasswell HD, Kaplan A. 1950. *Power and Society: A Framework for Political Inquiry.* New Haven, CT: Yale Univ. Press. 295 pp.

Lowi TJ. 1988. The return to the state. *Am. Polit. Sci. Rev.* 82:885–91

Madsen D. 1985. A biochemical property relating to power seeking in humans. *Am. Polit. Sci. Rev.* 79:448–57

Marvick D. 1977. Introduction: contexts, problems, and methods. In *Harold D. Lasswell on Political Sociology,* ed. D Marvick, pp. 1–72. Chicago: Univ. Chicago Press

Merriam CE. 1903. *A History of American Political Theories.* New York: Macmillan. 364 pp.

Merriam CE. 1920. *American Political Ideas: Studies in the Development of American Political Thought, 1865–1917.* New York: Macmillan. 481 pp.

Muth R. 1990. Harold Dwight Lasswell: a biographical profile. In *Harold D. Lasswell: An Annotated Bibliography,* ed. R Muth, MF Finley, MF Muth, pp. 1–48. New Haven, CT: New Haven Press; Dordrecht, the Netherlands: Kluwer

Peters JG, Welch S. 1978. Political corruption in America: a search for definitions and a theory. *Am. Polit. Sci. Rev.* 72:974–84

Razi GH. 1990. Legitimacy, religion, and nationalism in the Middle East. *Am. Polit. Sci. Rev.* 84:69–91

Rich RC. 1980. A political-economy approach to the study of neighborhood organizations. *Am. J. Polit. Sci.* 24:559–92

Rogow AA, Lasswell HD. 1963. *Power, Corruption, and Rectitude.* Englewood Cliffs, NJ: Prentice-Hall. 138 pp.

Sabia DR Jr. 1984. Political education and the history of political thought. *Am. Polit. Sci. Rev.* 78:985–99

Sears DO, Lau RR. 1983. Inducing apparently self-interested political preferences. *Am. J. Polit. Sci.* 27:223–52

Seidelman R. 1990. Can political science history be neutral? *Am. Polit. Sci. Rev.* 84: 596–600

Simon HA. 1985. Human nature in politics: the dialogue of psychology with political science. *Am. Polit. Sci. Rev.* 79:293–304

Smith BL. 1969. The mystifying intellectual history of Harold D. Lasswell. In *Politics, Personality, and Social Science in the Twentieth Century,* ed. AA Rogow. pp. 41–105. Chicago: Univ. Chicago Press

Werlin HH. 1990. Political culture and political change. *Am. Polit. Sci. Rev.* 84:249–53

Whitehead AN. 1948 (1925). *Science and the Modern World.* New York: Pelican Mentor. 212 pp.

Whittlesey WL. 1935. Review of HD Lasswell, "World Politics and Personal Insecurity." *Am. Polit. Sci. Rev.* 29: 500–1

Yale Law School, Policy Sciences Center. 1979. *Harold Dwight Lasswell, 1902–1978: In Commemoration and Continuing Commitment.* New Haven, CT: Yale Law School, Policy Sci. Cent., Ogden Found.

Annu. Rev. Polit. Sci. 1999. 2:91–114

THE POLITICAL ECONOMY OF INTERNATIONAL TRADE

Helen V. Milner

Department of Political Science, Columbia University, New York, New York 10027;
e-mail: Hvm1@columbia.edu

KEY WORDS: trade policy, protectionism, preferences, institutions, international politics

---

ABSTRACT

One of the most salient changes in the world economy since 1980 has been
the move toward freer trade among countries across the globe. How do existing theories about trade policy explain this puzzle? Three sets of explanations are prominent. First, many focus on changes in trade policy preferences
among domestic actors, either societal groups or political leaders. Second,
scholars examine changes in political institutions to account for such policy
change. Third, they seek explanations in changes in the international political system. Large-scale changes in political institutions, especially in the
direction of democracy, may be necessary for the kind of massive trade liberalization that has occurred. But changes in preferences cannot be overlooked
in explaining the rush to free trade. Moreover, the influence of international
institutions has been important. Finally, the reciprocal impact of trade on domestic politics and the international political system is important. If the rush
to free trade is sustained, will its impact be benign or malign?

INTRODUCTION

One of the most salient changes in the world economy since 1980 has been the
move toward freer trade among countries across the globe. Countries as diverse as Mexico, India, Poland, Turkey, Ghana, Morocco, and Spain—not to
mention Chile, which moved earlier in the 1970s—have all chosen to liberalize unilaterally their trade policies.[1] In addition, the successful conclusion of
the multilateral trade negotiations under the General Agreement on Tariffs and

---

[1]Many of these trade liberalizations occurred within the context of larger economic reform
packages. Here I discuss only the trade liberalization component.

1094-2939/99/0616-0091$08.00

Trade (GATT), the Uruguay Round, in 1994 further liberalized trade among many developed countries and between them and developing ones. This global "rush to free trade," as Rodrik (1994) has called it, is an anomaly politically. As he describes it (1994:62), "Since the early 1980s, developing countries have flocked to free trade as if it were the Holy Grail of economic development.… Together with the historic transformation and opening of the Eastern European economies, these developments represent a genuine revolution in policymaking. The puzzle is why is it occurring now and why in so many countries all at once?" The purpose of this essay is to ask whether and how the existing theories we have about trade policy can explain this puzzle.

The scholarly literature on international trade is vast. Both economists and political scientists have contributed much to it, as recent surveys by economists such as Reizman & Wilson (1995) and Rodrik (1995) and political scientists such as Cohen (1990) and Lake (1993) demonstrate. But their approaches have tended to differ. Economists have focused on explaining trade flows. Why certain countries import and export particular goods or services to certain other countries has been a central question for them. Much theory in international trade addresses this question; for instance, one of the central theorems in trade theory, the Heckscher-Ohlin theorem, explains trade flows. Economists have also devoted attention to the issue of trade barriers. The central theoretical conclusion of the field, of course, has been that free trade is the best policy for most countries most of the time. Thus, economists have puzzled over why, given this finding, countries invariably employ at least some protectionist policies. They have tended to ask why countries protect certain of their industries when free trade would be better economically. By and large, their answer has focused on the preferences of domestic actors for protection. Using the Stopler-Samuelson theorem and other economic theories, they have explored why certain domestic groups would prefer protection and why they would expend resources to lobby for it. This has resulted in a large empirical literature examining levels of protection across industries and, recently, in the development of models of such protection. Ultimately, then, economists have been pushed into studying the politics of trade. How well have they done in modeling such politics? Moreover, have they been able to explain the rush to free trade that has occurred?

In contrast, political scientists have rarely focused on explaining the pattern of trade flows. Only some recent work has explored the political roots of import and export flows among countries. Moreover, political scientists have tended to see protection as the norm and have puzzled over why a country would ever liberalize its trade policy or adopt free trade. Politically, protectionism seems eminently reasonable. Explaining both protectionist and free trade policies and their changes over time has occupied political scientists. Indeed, the prevailing theories of the 1970s and early 1980s would have predicted the opposite of the rush to free trade. As I argue below, many systemic theories, such as hegemonic stability and dependency theory, seemed to forecast growing protectionism in the world economy. For many political scientists, then, the rush to free trade has been unexpected.

Here I explore four sets of issues that are central to understanding trade politics. First, what do we know about the preferences of domestic groups for protection or free trade? Why do some groups favor protection, and some favor free trade? Do these preferences change over time? And if so, why? Can changes in preferences explain the rush to free trade?

Second, how do political institutions affect the ways in which the preferences of actors are translated into policy? How important are institutions in aggregating preferences and supplying policy? How much do changes in institutions affect trade policy, and can they explain the rush to free trade?

Third, what factors at the international level shape trade policy choices? How do relations among countries and the structure of the international system affect domestic choices about trade? Have changes such as the end of the bipolar Cold War system been responsible for the recent trend toward trade liberalization?

Finally, how does international trade itself affect states and the international political system? Do rising trade flows produce important changes in domestic preferences, institutions, and policies?

I examine each of these issues to see if they can provide us with some answers to the most significant aspect of trade policy today: the widespread liberalization of trade policies that has taken place since the early 1980s.

WHAT DO WE KNOW ABOUT TRADE AND TRADE POLICY?[2]

Since World War II, the main instrument of trade policy, tariffs, among advanced industrial countries have been reduced to insignificant levels. After the latest round of international trade negotiations, the Uruguay Round, completed in 1994, the average tariff for the developed countries was reduced from 6.3% to 3.8% [World Trade Organization (WTO) 1996:31]. On the other hand, non-tariff barriers—which include quantitative restrictions, price controls, subsidies, voluntary export restraints, etc—have proliferated, in part making

---

[2]"Trade policies" refers to all policies that have a direct impact on the domestic prices of tradables, that is, goods and services traded across national boundaries as imports and/or exports. Such policies include not only import tariffs, which are taxes on imports, but also export taxes, which under certain conditions have the same effects as import taxes. Likewise, import and export subsidies count. Exchange rate policy also affects trade flows, but I leave this subject for others to discuss.

up for the decline in tariffs. But again the Uruguay Round slowed or reversed this, helping to reduce quotas, subsidies, and voluntary export restraints across a wide range of industries and to convert these barriers into more transparent tariffs (WTO 1996:32).

For most of the postwar period, less developed countries (LDCs) have used trade barriers extensively, many for the explicit purpose of import-substituting industrialization (ISI). But beginning in the 1980s especially, many developing countries began to liberalize trade and to adopt export-oriented policies [International Monetary Fund (IMF) 1992]. The conclusion of the Uruguay Round promoted this by reducing trade barriers in many areas of key interest to the LDCs, such as textiles and agriculture; it also brought many new developing countries into the international trade organization, the WTO, inducing them to follow its rules. In addition, the transition from communist economies to market-based ones by many countries in the early 1990s further accelerated the trend toward global trade liberalization. All of these changes have resulted in one striking fact about the period since 1980: There has been a far-reaching liberalization of trade barriers across the globe (WTO 1996, Rodrik 1994). Why has this occurred? And will it last?

Concomitantly and in part consequentially, the growth of world trade has surged. For most of the postwar period, the growth of trade has outpaced growth in world output. Also important are changes in the nature of global trade. There has been tremendous growth in intra-industry trade and in intrafirm trade. Intra-industry trade, which involves the exchange of goods from within the same industry, say Toyotas for BMWs, now accounts for between 55% and 75% of trade in advanced industrial countries (Greenaway & Milner 1986:Table 5-3); for the United States, this figure was 83% in 1990 (Bergsten & Noland 1993:66). Intrafirm trade, which involves transfers of goods within one company across national boundaries, has also grown; it now accounts for over 40% of total US imports and 30% of US exports (Encarnation 1992:28). These two types of trade are important because they tend to have different effects than standard, interindustry trade. Generally, they are associated with fewer displacement effects and less conflict. As Lipson (1982:453) argues, "intra-industry trade provides a powerful new source of multilateral interest in the liberal trade regime: diminished adjustment costs in some sectors, and higher net gains from trade as a result." Finally, there has been a significant regionalization of trade. Intraregional trade flows within the European Union, East Asia, North America, and Latin America especially have become more important as a share of total trade. This is partially a result of the regional integration agreements signed by these countries in the past two decades—e.g. the single market in Europe, the North American Free Trade Agreement (NAFTA), the Association of South East Asian Nations (ASEAN), the Asia Pacific Economic Cooperation (APEC), and Mercosur (WTO 1996:17–22).

TRADE POLICY PREFERENCES

Some of the earliest models explaining trade policy have focused on "pressure group politics." That is, they explain the recourse to protection by governments as a function of the demands made by domestic groups. Domestic groups seek protection or liberalization because such policies increase their incomes. The distributional consequences of trade policy thus become the explanation for its causes. Adam Smith (1937 [1776]) may have been one of the first to recognize this when he noted that the subversion of the national interest in free trade is the frequent outcome of collusion among businessmen. Schattschneider (1935) was another early proponent of the view that special economic interests were mainly responsible for the choice of protectionism; he showed how these pressure groups hijacked the US Congress in 1929–1930 and produced one of the highest tariffs in US history, the Smoot-Hawley tariff.

Since then, development of the pressure group model has attempted to delineate more specifically the groups who should favor and oppose protection and the conditions under which they may be most influential. One motive for this has been the observation that the extent of protection and the demands for it vary both across industries and across countries. If all domestic groups favored protection, then such variance should not exist. Explaining this variance has been a key feature of the literature. The main divide has been between so-called factoral versus sectoral or firm-based theories of preferences. In both cases, preferences are deduced as a result of the changes in income that accrue to different actors when policy changes from free trade to protection or vice versa. Factoral theories rely on the Stopler-Samuelson theorem (1941), which shows that when factors of production, such as labor and capital, can move freely among sectors, a change from free trade to protection will raise the income of factors that are relatively scarce in a country and lower the income of relatively abundant factors. Thus, scarce factors will support protection, whereas abundant ones will oppose it. Rogowski (1989) has developed one of the most interesting political extensions of this, claiming that increasing (decreasing) exposure to trade sets off either increasing class conflict or urban-rural conflict according to the factor endowments of different countries.

In contrast, sectoral and firm-based theories of trade preferences follow from the Ricardo-Viner model of trade—also called the specific-factors model—in which, because at least one factor is immobile, all factors attached to import-competing sectors lose from trade liberalization while those in export-oriented sectors gain. Conflict over trade policy thus pits labor, capital, and landowners in sectors besieged by imports against those who export their production. How closely factors are tied to their sectors—i.e. the degree of factor specificity—is the key difference between these two models (Alt et al

1996). A number of studies have tested these two models, sometimes singly and sometimes simultaneously. Irwin (1994, 1996), Magee et al (1989), and Frieden (1990) have found evidence in support of the specific-factors model; in contrast, E Beaulieu (unpublished manuscript), Balestreri (1997), Rogowski (1989), Midford (1993), and Scheve & Slaughter (1998) find support for the Stolper-Samuelson–type factoral models.

In addition to these models of trade preferences, others have looked at how particular characteristics of industries affect patterns of protection. Caves (1976), Pincus (1975), Baldwin (1986), Anderson (1980), Marvel & Ray (1983), Ray (1981), and Trefler (1993) have shown how specific characteristics make an industry more likely not only to desire protection but also to be able to induce policy makers to provide it. These regression analyses tend to straddle the debate between sectoral and factoral models of trade politics. Their comparison across industries suggests a sectoral type of model, but many of their findings do not disagree with those of a more factoral view of the world. For example, they tend to demonstrate that low-skill, labor-intensive industries with high and rising import penetration are frequently associated with high protection. In addition, many show that export-oriented industries and multinationals tend to favor freer trade and to be associated with less protection (Milner 1988). The attention to antiprotectionist groups is particularly interesting given the global move toward trade liberalization; one question is whether this movement has been due to the growth in importance of these types of groups domestically.

Can these models of societal preferences explain the rush to free trade? As Rodrik (1994:78) points out, "Focusing on the distributional consequences of trade policy provides one potential key to the puzzle. Perhaps the powerful interests that benefited from protection and had successfully blocked reform were weakened by the debt crises of the 1980s, which would explain the general move toward liberal policies." He concludes that such evidence would be difficult to find. But others have argued that the distributional politics of trade can explain this change in policy.

Frieden & Rogowski (1996:40), for example, argue that exogenous changes have brought about a reduction in the costs of trade and have thus made trade more important relative to any domestic economy, increasing the costs of protection. They then point out that this

> exogenous easing of international trade [i.e. internationalization] increases potential benefits to capitalists and skilled workers in the advanced countries, to skilled and unskilled workers in the NICs [newly industrializing countries], and to unskilled workers in LDCs—all of whom are predicted to mobilize on behalf of liberalization. At the same time, easier trade threatens unskilled workers in advanced economies, local capitalists in NICs, and owners of both physical and human capital in LDCs—all of whom will

heighten their demands for protection or compensation. Wood (1994) has argued that we observe exactly this in the economic history of the last twenty years. (Frieden & Rogowski 1996:40)

Reductions in the costs of trade have thus heightened the opportunity costs of protection, creating new pressures for freer trade. Exactly why and how the proponents of trade liberalization have gained political advantage over those demanding protection is less clear. Indeed, as Rodrik (1994:66–67) notes, "the prospect of too much redistribution may be the central political difficulty in trade reform.... Taking income away from one group is rarely easy for a politician to accomplish." Why did policy makers around the globe choose to do this, and how were they able to overcome opposition to the sizable income redistribution wrought by embracing freer trade?

One argument made to explain this is that various exogenous conditions created new actors who preferred freer trade, thus shifting the balance of power in their favor. Many LDCs began their experiment with trade liberalization as part of a package of reforms designed to pull their economies out of severe economic crises. The crises themselves helped decimate sectors of the economy and created government budget crises, which in turn meant an end to subsidies for some domestic industries. Both of these changes eliminated many import-competing firms and put a premium on creating exporting firms that could generate foreign exchange (Haggard 1995:16–19). Thus, in many LDCs, the crises may have not only created new groups with preferences for freer trade but also eliminated supporters of protection. For the advanced industrial countries, such changes in the nature of the actors and in their influence may have come from a different source. Frieden & Rogowski (1996) claim that exogenous change, often in the form of technological change, may have altered the interest group politics of trade. Here one could cite the growing component of intra-industry trade among the developed countries and the new support for trade liberalization it might generate. In any case, interest group explanations of the rush to free trade remain incomplete unless they can somehow specify how an exogenous force shifted political influence away from protectionists and in favor of those preferring free trade.

The preferences of other domestic actors have also received some attention. Many authors assume that individual voters take their preferences from their role as consumers. Because consumers gain from free trade, they should favor it (e.g. Grossman & Helpman 1994). Other models of individual preferences contradict this. Mayer (1984), for example, introduces an electoral component into the determination of trade policy. Trade policy is determined by the median voter's preferences, which depend on his factor endowments. The better endowed he is in the factor used intensively for production of import-competing goods, the more protectionist he will be. Scheve & Slaughter (1998) add a new component by asking how asset ownership is affected by trade policy.

They show that the preferences of individual voters depend on how trade affects their assets. Individuals living in regions with a high concentration of import-competing industries tend to favor protection because, as imports rise, economic activity in the region will fall, causing their housing assets to fall in value. Some surveys have also shown that voters respond positively toward protection out of sympathy for workers who lose their jobs because of import competition. Thus, whether individual voters favor protection or free trade is an area demanding further research, especially in democracies where elections are often linked to trade policy decisions. Moreover, understanding changes in these preferences may help us account for the recent rush to free trade.

A number of scholars have argued that the preferences of interest groups and voters are less important in determining trade policy than are those of the policy makers themselves. Bauer et al (1972) were among the first to make this point. From their surveys, they concluded that constituents rarely had strong preferences about trade policy and even more rarely communicated these to their political representatives. Trade policy depended much more on the personal preferences and ideas of politicians. Baldwin (1986) and Goldstein (1988) have also argued that it is the ideas of policy makers about trade policy that matter most. Rather than material factors determining preferences, ideational factors are paramount. Interestingly, Krueger (1997) argues that "ideas with regard to trade policy and economic development are among those [factors] that have changed most radically" from 1950 to the 1990s and that help explain the rush to free trade. A key example of this change is Fernando Henrique Cardoso. As coauthor of one of the most important books on dependency theory in the 1970s, he argued for the continuation of ISI policies to shelter LDCs from the capitalist world economy (Cardoso & Faletto 1979). In the 1990s, however, Cardoso was elected president of Brazil and initiated a major economic reform program, including extensive trade liberalization. How could his ideas about the proper policies for LDCs have changed so much? What factors explain this dramatic change in ideas among political leaders in the developing world?

Given that belief in the superiority of free trade has existed for centuries among economists, it is also important to question why this change occurred when it did. Krueger appears to retreat to more material factors to explain its timing; the failures of ISI and the success of the relatively open NIC economies convinced policy makers that new trade policies were necessary. Others focus on the economic crises of the early 1980s and the growing influence of international institutions and the United States.

Although Krueger and others, such as Rodrik (1995), Haggard & Kaufman (1995), and Bates & Krueger (1993), attribute trade policy reform to crises and economic downturns, another strand of literature on the macroeconomics of trade policy concludes in the opposite direction. Many scholars consider bad economic times a prelude to rising demands for protection and increasing levels of protection. Takacs (1981), Gallarotti (1985), Cassing et al (1986), Magee & Young (1987), and Wallerstein (1987) all found that declines in economic growth or capacity utilization and/or increases in unemployment and imports tend to increase the demand and supply of protection. This earlier literature saw policy makers responding increasingly to the rising demands for protection from domestic groups in bad economic times.

The more recent literature, however, implies that bad economic times allow policy makers more freedom to maneuver so that they can overturn existing protectionist policies by blaming them for the bad times. For example, Rodrik (1992:88–89) finds it "paradoxical that the 1980s should have become the decade of trade liberalization in the developing countries. Thanks to the debt crisis, the 1980s have also been a decade of intense macroeconomic instability. Common sense would suggest that the conventional benefits of liberalization become muted, if not completely offset, under conditions of macro instability." But he claims that "a time of crisis occasionally enables radical reforms that would have been unthinkable in calmer times" (1992:89). Rodrik argues that the prolonged macroeconomic crises of the 1980s were so bad that "the overall gain from restoring the economy's health [in part via trade liberalization] became so large that it swamped distributional considerations [raised by such reforms]" (1994:79).

On the other hand, others, especially Haggard (1995), have argued that crises reduce the maneuvering room of political leaders. They suggest that in the 1980s these leaders were almost forced to liberalize trade (and make other reforms) because of the lack of options and international pressures. Noting the difference between the 1930s and 1980s crises, Haggard (1995:16–19) points out that

> why external shocks and corresponding macroeconomic policy adjustments might also be associated with trade and investment liberalization…is puzzling. In the 1930s, balance of payments and debt crises spurred the substitution of imports…and gave rise to a more autarchic and interventionist policy stance. In the 1980s, by contrast, an inward-looking policy seemed foreclosed…. The opportunities for continued import substitution were limited, and ties to the world economy had become more varied, complex and difficult to sever.

The effect of economic crises on countries' decisions to liberalize trade, then, seems contingent on other factors, such as the prevailing ideas about trade, the extent of openness existing at the time, and the influence of international factors.

A similar debate seems to exist concerning the exchange rate. Appreciation of the exchange rate may increase protectionist pressures because it increases imports and decreases exports, thus affecting the balance of trade preferences domestically (Mansfield & Busch 1995). Others suggest that the effects of an exchange rate change may have little impact. For instance, Rodrik (1994:73) shows that a devaluation, which is the opposite of an appreciation, increases the domestic price of all tradables—imports and exports—thereby allowing both import-competing and export-oriented sectors to benefit. But under certain conditions, e.g. when foreign exchange is rationed, devaluations can work just like trade liberalization, prompting demands for new protection from import-competing sectors. Some studies reveal such an association between periods of currency devaluations and rising tariffs; Simmons (1994) points out that many, though not all, of the same conditions that drove states to devalue also pushed them to increase tariffs in the interwar period. Both policies were intended to increase demand for domestic output, thus counteracting the effects of the depression. Much debate continues over the macroeconomic conditions that produce increasing pressures for protection and/or that induce policy makers to relent to or resist such pressures.

Can these preference-based theories explain the rush to free trade we have witnessed recently? As noted above, large changes in relative factor endowments or increasing exposure to international markets could perhaps explain changes in preferences in liberalizing countries. But relative factor endowments do not seem to have changed much; and greater exposure to international markets, which Frieden & Rogowski (1996) cite as paramount, has had more effect on the developed countries, since over the prior 30 years many LDCs have actually reduced their exposure to trade through their ISI policies. Frieden & Rogowski would counter that the opportunity costs of such closure have been increasing nevertheless and should have propelled greater demands for liberalization. Moreover, various exogenous changes may have created new actors who favor free trade, shifting the domestic balance of power in favor of liberalization. Numerous studies, however, suggest that many interest groups in LDCs opposed trade liberalization and few supported it (e.g. Bates & Krueger 1993, Haggard & Webb 1994). Nonetheless, many scholars recognize that the support of societal groups favoring free trade is an essential element of the reform process, if not for its initiation at least for its implementation. "Governments seeking to liberalize trade clearly gain by building ties to private sector organizations with export interests and by weakening institutions that provide access for firms in the import-substituting sector" (Haggard & Webb 1994:19).

The changing preferences of policy makers may have played a greater role. But our models of such preferences seem the most underspecified and post hoc. There are few theories about the conditions under which policy makers will abandon ideas that produce "bad" results and what ideas they will adopt in their stead. Furthermore, such theories suggest that the recent liberalization process may not be long-lived; changes in leaders or their preferences, or the onset of bad economic conditions, may lead to the revival of protectionism. In sum, theories of trade preferences seem to provide only poor explanations for the major change in trade policy that has occurred globally in the past decade.

POLITICAL INSTITUTIONS

Can theories that focus on the supply side of trade policy do any better? What role do political institutions play in trade policy making? And are changes in them responsible for the rush to free trade?

A number of scholars have argued that political institutions, rather than preferences, are crucial in explaining trade policy. Although preferences play a role in these arguments, the main claim is that institutions aggregate such preferences and different institutions do so differently, thus leading to distinct policies. Understanding institutions is necessary to explain the actual supply of protection, rather than simply its demand (Nelson 1988). On the domestic side, different institutions empower different actors. Some institutions, for example, tend to give special interest groups greater access to policy makers, rendering their demands harder to resist. For example, many scholars believe that the fact that the US Congress controlled trade policy exclusively before 1934 made it very susceptible to protectionist pressures from interest groups (Destler 1986, Haggard 1988, Baldwin 1986, Goldstein 1993). Other institutions insulate policy makers from these demands, allowing them more leeway in setting policy. Thus, some authors argue that giving the executive branch greater control over trade after the Reciprocal Trade Act of 1934 made trade policy less susceptible to these influences and more free-trade oriented. In general, concentrating trade-policy–making capabilities in the executive branch seems to be associated with the adoption of trade liberalization in a wide variety of countries (e.g. Haggard & Kaufman 1995:199). As Haggard & Webb (1994:13) have noted about trade liberalization in numerous LDCs, "In every successful reform effort, politicians delegated decisionmaking authority to units within the government that were insulated from routine bureaucratic processes, from legislative and interest group pressures, and even from executive pressure."

Other aspects of political regimes may make them more or less insulated from societal pressures. Rogowski (1987), for example, has argued that policy makers should be most insulated from domestic pressures for protection in countries having large electoral districts and proportional representation (PR) systems. Mansfield & Busch (1995), however, find that such institutional insulation does indeed matter but often in exactly the opposite direction—greater insulation (i.e. larger districts and a PR system) leads to more protection. Similarly, D Rodrik (unpublished paper) shows that "political regimes with lower executive autonomy and more participatory institutions handle exogenous shocks better," and this may include their response to shocks via trade policy. Thus, it is not clear that greater insulation of policy makers always produces policies that promote trade liberalization; the preferences of those policy makers also matter.

The administrative capacity of the state is also seen as an important factor shaping trade policy. It is well established that developed countries tend to have fewer trade barriers than do lesser developed countries (Magee et al 1989:230–41; IMF 1992; Conybeare 1982, 1983; Rodrik 1995:1483). Part of the reason is that taxes on trade are fairly easy to collect and thus, in LDCs where the apparatus of the state is poorly developed, such taxes may account for a substantial portion of total state revenues (between a quarter and a half, according to Rodrik 1994:77). As countries develop, their institutional capacity may also grow, reducing their need to depend on import taxes for revenue.[3] For example, the introduction of the personal income tax in 1913 in the United States made trade taxes much less important for the government, which permitted their later reduction. Thus, changes in political institutions may help explain changes in trade policy.

Large institutional differences in countries' political regime types also may be associated with different trade policy profiles. Some scholars have argued that democratic countries are less likely to be able to pursue protectionist policies. Wintrobe (1998) claims that autocratic countries are more rent-seeking and that protection is simply one form of rent-seeking. Mansfield et al (1997, 1998) also show that democratic pairs of countries tend to be more likely to cooperate to lower trade barriers and to sign trade liberalizing agreements than are autocratic ones. On the other hand, Verdier (1998) argues that, because of the political conflict engendered by trade, democracies may be less likely to pursue free trade and more likely to adopt protection against each other, except when intra-industry trade dominates their trade flows. "The postwar democratic convergence among OECD countries did not hurt trade because similarity in endowments, combined with the presence of scale economies, allowed these countries to engage in intra-industry trade—a form of trade with few, if any, wealth effects…. The current wave of democratization endangers trade. Only in the presence of scale economies [and thus intra-industry trade] can democratic convergence sustain trade" (Verdier 1998:18–19). Haggard & Kaufmann (1995) are more circumspect, arguing that the presence of crises and the form of autocracy may influence the ability to adopt economic reforms (such as trade liberalization) more than does regime type alone. Debates over the impact of regime type on trade policy have just begun.

---

[3]Political leaders may also favor trade liberalization simply because it increases government revenues. Liberalization may generate more revenues because of the increased economic activity and higher volumes of trade it produces, even at lower tariff rates.

The structure of the government and the nature of the party system have also been seen as important institutional factors shaping trade policy. Parties very often take specific stands on trade policy, and their movement in and out of government may explain trade policy changes, as many authors have contended about the United States (e.g. Epstein & O'Halloran 1996). If so, then countries with highly polarized party systems, in which the main parties are separated by large ideological differences, may experience huge swings in policy and generally produce unsustainable trade reforms. On the other hand, countries with large numbers of parties may frequently experience coalition governments, which may be unable to change the status quo. Haggard & Kaufman (1995:170) predict that countries with fragmented and/or polarized party systems will be unable to initiate economic policy reforms, including trade liberalization, let alone to sustain them. In general, these perspectives suggest that fragmented political systems are similar to ones with many veto players, and like them are resistant to change (Tsebelis 1995).

Party systems also interact with the structure of the government. For example, Lohmann & O'Halloran (1994) and O'Halloran (1994) have argued that when government in presidential systems, such as the United States, is divided—i.e. when one party controls the legislature and the other controls the executive branch—protectionism is likely to be higher. Milner & Rosendorff (1996) also argue that divided government in any country is likely to make the lowering of trade barriers, either domestically or internationally, harder in most cases. In sum, "political systems with weak executives and fragmented party systems, divided government, and decentralized political structures responded poorly to crises" and were unable to mobilize the support necessary for the initiation of economic reforms such as trade liberalization (Haggard & Kaufman 1995:378). In all of these cases, however, the trade policy preferences of the parties matter for the outcome. Political institutions tend more to affect which preferences, if any, will become dominant in policy making.

Many of these institutional arguments thus depend on prior claims about actors' preferences. For instance, many of the arguments about insulation assume that the policy makers (usually executives) who are insulated from societal demands are free traders. But, as Mansfield & Busch (1995) show, they may actually be protectionists, in which case insulation allows greater protection. The arguments about divided government, party systems, and democracies also rest to some extent on assumptions about each actor's preferences. Divided government matters most when preferences of the parties differ, and differences in the preferences of autocratic leaders and democratic ones may be important for the implications of different regime types. Thus, theories that incorporate both preferences and institutions seem most valuable, since we know that both matter. Very few studies, however, try to bring together theories of preference formation and institutional influence; Gilligan (1997) and

Milner (1997) are examples. Moreover, the matter of which comes first, preferences or institutions, is far from settled. Scholars who focus on preferences tend to argue that institutions are often shaped by the preferences of those in power; those who emphasize institutions argue that institutions may actually shape actors' preferences. The growing consensus is that both matter and are jointly determined, but parsimoniously modeling and testing this is an area for future research.

Do these arguments about the role of institutions help explain the recent rush to free trade across the globe? They suggest that large institutional changes should have preceded this change in policy. Have trade-policy–making institutions become more or less insulated across a variety of countries in the past two decades? Compared with the monetary area, where independent central banks and currency boards have sprung up widely, there is limited evidence for such a change in trade. Although Haggard & Webb (1994:13) point to such evidence for some LDCs, little evidence exists that developed countries have changed their trade policy structures much in the past 20 years. Moreover, it is unclear whether more or less insulation of policy makers induces trade liberalization.

There is one area where change has occurred that may be linked to this rush to free trade. Many of the countries that have embraced trade liberalization have also democratized. Mexico is a prime case. The growth of political competition and the decline of the hegemonic status of the governing party, the PRI, seem to have gone hand in hand with the liberalization of trade policy beginning in the 1980s. However, trade reform in many LDCs occurred before the transition to democracy and was often more successful when it did occur this way (Haggard & Webb 1994). Chile, Turkey, Taiwan, and South Korea all began their trade liberalization processes before their democratic transitions. Rodrik argues more generally that any change in political regime is likely to induce trade reforms. "Historically sharp changes in trade policy have almost always been preceded (or accompanied) by changes in the political regime.... Not all political transformations result in trade reform, but sharp changes in trade policy are typically the result of such transformations" (Rodrik 1994:69). Although strong evidence has not yet been presented, at this point changes in political regimes, and specifically the spread of democracy, may be the institutional change that best helps explain the rush to free trade.

INTERNATIONAL POLITICS

Trade policy is not only affected by domestic forces. A number of factors in the international system have been connected to countries' trade policy choices. A favored argument among Realists has been that the distribution of capabilities in the international system has a fundamental effect on trade. The so-called theory of hegemonic stability (HST) posited that when the international system or economy was dominated by one country, a hegemon, then free trade would be most likely (Krasner 1976, Gilpin 1987, Lake 1988, Gowa 1994). Many critics have challenged this claim both theoretically and empirically (Lake 1993, Keohane 1997). Conybeare (1984) has shown that large countries should favor optimal tariffs, not free trade, even if others retaliate; Snidal (1985) and others have claimed that small numbers of powerful countries could maintain an open system just as well as a single hegemon could. The theory has also faced empirical challenges implying that a hegemon is neither necessary nor sufficient for an open trading system (e.g. Krasner 1976, Mansfield 1994). In light of these results, HST has been modified as scholars examine more closely the dynamics of interaction among countries in the trading system.

Perhaps the most interesting point about this theory is that it tries to explain change over time in the overall level of openness in the trading system; that is, it looks at the sum of countries' trade policy choices. In terms of our puzzle of explaining the rush to free trade, HST seems to hold much potential. Changes in the distribution of capabilities over time should provide clues to this puzzle. In the 1980s, however, many political scientists argued that the decline of American hegemony from its zenith after World War II would lead to a rise in protectionism and perhaps the fragmentation of the international economy into rival blocs (e.g. Gilpin 1987). This prediction does not seem to explain the rush to free trade witnessed since the mid-1980s.

One possible retort, however, is that US hegemony has risen, not declined, since 1980, as Russett (1985) and Strange (1987) have argued. Thus, the renewal of American preeminence in the international system explains the turn away from protectionism. This argument fits well with a broader claim concerning the dominance of American ideas about free markets and trade, and the impact of those ideas on other countries' trade policy choices. After all, the package of market-oriented reforms, including trade liberalization, that has been proposed for the LDCs and ex-communist countries is called the Washington consensus. Finally, Haggard (1995) argues that changes in US trade policy in the 1980s help explain the move toward free trade. The United States began exerting strong bilateral pressure on LDCs to liberalize their economies or face closure of the American market to their exports. American hegemony and the renewed will to exert influence may help account for the rush to free trade.

Other scholars have felt that aspects of the international security environment best explain the pattern of trade. Gowa (1994) has argued that countries that are military allies trade more with each other, and that this is especially true of countries within the same alliance in bipolar system. That is, when countries are allies in a system featuring one other major opposing alliance group, as was the case during the Cold War, they tend to trade the most freely among themselves. The security externalities of trade drive their behavior, inducing them to help their allies while punishing their enemies. Gowa & Mansfield (1994) and Mansfield & Bronson (1997) provide strong evidence for this effect. How would this argument deal with the rush to free trade? Unlike other arguments, it directly links trade policy to the end of the Cold War and the dissolution of the Eastern bloc. Unfortunately, however, the argument suggests that protectionism should rise, not decline, with the demise of bipolarity. Predictions from this model seem to be inaccurate or at least incomplete. A description of the current structure of the international system might be one of either multipolarity, in which case the model is inaccurate, or unipolarity, in which case Gowa has no prediction.

Another aspect of the international system that scholars have noted for its effect on trade policy is the presence and influence of international institutions. Although a long debate has occurred over whether international institutions matter, many scholars conclude that the willingness of states to set up and participate in such institutions implies that they do matter (e.g. Ruggie 1983, Keohane 1984). In the trade area, a number of institutions provide support for an open, multilateral trading system; these include the GATT and its successor, the WTO, as well as the IMF and World Bank. Although regional trade institutions may have a more ambiguous effect on the multilateral system (E Mansfield, H Milner, unpublished manuscript), some of them, including the European Union (EU), NAFTA, and ASEAN, seem to have positive effects on lowering trade barriers and reinforcing unilateral moves toward freer trade.

These institutions are postulated to have a number of different effects on countries' trade policy choices. Some authors suggest that their main role is to provide information about other countries' behavior and compliance with the rules of the game (e.g. Keohane 1984). Others see these institutions as providing a forum for dispute resolution so that partners in trade can feel more secure and thus more likely to trade (e.g. Yarbrough & Yarbrough 1992). Still others view such international institutions as encapsulating the norms by which countries agree to play the trading game, which again provides a common framework for sustaining trade flows (e.g. Ruggie 1983). All of these arguments hypothesize that the presence of these institutions should be associated with a freer trade environment; moreover, they imply that the depth and breadth of these institutions should be positively related to trade liberalization and the expansion of trade. Can these arguments help explain the rush to free trade since the 1980s?

Certainly the presence of institutions like the GATT and IMF have added leverage to arguments for trade liberalization; the IMF and World Bank, for instance, have often made loans conditional on trade policy reform. But these institutions have existed since the 1940s, and thus their mere presence cannot explain the current move toward liberalization. The fact that many countries have been in severe economic crisis and needed external financing may help explain the added influence that these institutions have exerted since the 1980s. As Rodrik (1992:89) points out, "The 1980s were a decade of great leverage for these institutions [i.e. the IMF and World Bank] vis-à-vis debtor governments, especially where poorer African governments are concerned. The trade policy recommendations of the World Bank were adopted by cash-starved governments frequently with little conviction of their ultimate benefits." But he also notes that, once the crisis is over, governments may return to their old protectionist ways. Others tend to argue that international institutions help lock in such domestic reforms. For example, Mexican unilateral trade liberalization seems much more secure now that Mexico is part of NAFTA and the WTO.

Finally, the creation of the WTO out of the GATT Uruguay Round represents a step toward the deeper institutionalization of an open trading system. This change could be associated with growing pressure for domestic trade liberalization. But the WTO's birth occurred in the wake of changed preferences for freer trade, not as a precursor to them. By the early 1990s, many countries were already convinced that trade liberalization was the right policy. In sum, the growing influence of these international institutions seems to have depended either on the desperation of debtors or on changing domestic preferences and ideas about trade. Although there is little doubt that these institutions helped support trade liberalization globally, it is less certain that they provided the crucial impetus for this liberalization process (Haggard & Kaufman 1995:199). But, as with domestic political support, these institutions may be necessary for the reforms to be long lasting.

One might presume that international-level explanations would better account for a global movement like the rush to free trade. But the main political-economy arguments reviewed here have an awkward time explaining this trend. The distribution of capabilities certainly has changed since the early 1980s, but the direction of this change does not account for the trend in trade policies. If we have witnessed a move away from American hegemony or from bipolarity to multipolarity, then we should see a decrease in the openness and extent of trade. Only if we argue that American hegemony has returned to its postwar levels can we explain the rush to free trade more confidently. The constant presence of international institutions to guide trade, such as the GATT and IMF, is also a poor explanation for the global change in policy that has occurred since the 1980s. The increased influence that these institutions had in the 1980s because of the economic crises that many LDCs underwent may account for some of the change, but again, this combination had been present before the 1980s and had not led to such a U-turn in trade policy. These international institutions, however, may help to ensure that this liberalization process is not easily reversible.

EFFECT OF TRADE ON COUNTRIES AND THE INTERNATIONAL SYSTEM

A final area of interest in the political economy of trade policy is the reciprocal effect of international trade on domestic and international politics. Once countries have liberalized or protected their economies, what might be the effects of such choices? Scholars have examined this question with attention to at least three aspects of the domestic political economy. First, some have argued that trade liberalization can change domestic preferences about trade. As countries liberalize, the tradables sector of the economy should grow along with exposure to international economic pressures. Rogowski (1989) has argued that this should lead to greater or new political cleavages and conflicts between scarce and abundant factors domestically. These new cleavages in turn will alter domestic politics, as for example new parties arise to represent these groups or new coalitions form. Milner (1988) also argues that increasing openness to trade changes preferences domestically. Openness raises the potential number of supporters of free trade as exporters and multinational firms multiply; it may also reduce import-competing firms as they succumb to foreign competition. Hathaway (1998:606) presents a dynamic model showing that trade liberalization "has a positive feedback effect on policy preferences and political strategies of domestic producer groups. As industries adjust to more competitive market conditions, their characteristics change in ways that reduce the likelihood that they will demand protection in the future." James & Lake (1989) suggest an ingenious argument that repeal of the protectionist Corn Laws in the United Kingdom created the necessary conditions for the creation of a successful coalition for free trade in the United States. Each of these arguments in distinct ways suggests that increasing exposure to trade leads to increasing pressure against protection, thus creating a virtuous cycle of rising demand for freer trade. As an explanation for trade policy in the advanced industrial countries over the past few decades, this type of argument seems very plausible. The abrupt rejection of ISI and protectionism by developing countries seems less explicable in these terms.

A second aspect of domestic politics that increased trade may affect involves the character of national political institutions. Among the advanced industrial countries, Cameron (1978) long ago noted the relationship between those that were very open to international trade and those with large governments. He and Katzenstein (1985) attributed this correlation to the need for governments with open economies to provide extensive domestic compensation to the losers from trade and to employ flexible adjustment strategies for their industries. Rodrik (1997) has found strong evidence of this relationship around the globe. He claims that greater exposure to external risk, which trade promotes, increases the volatility of the domestic economy and thus that "societies that expose themselves to greater amounts of external risk demand (and receive) a larger government role as shelter from the vicissitudes of global markets" (1997:53). Increasing exposure to international trade may thus create demands for more government intervention and a larger welfare state, which in turn are necessary to sustain public support for an open economy.

Rogowski (1987:212) has argued that as countries become more open to trade, they will find it increasingly advantageous to devise institutions that maximize "the state's insulation, autonomy and stability." For him, this implies parliamentary systems with strong parties, proportional representation (PR), and large districts. He finds a strong relationship especially between openness and PR systems. Haldenius (1992) also finds that trade may have effects on domestic institutions. He argues that exposure to international trade brings higher rates of economic growth, which, through the development process, may translate into better conditions for the emergence of democracy. Thus, trade liberalization may over time foster conditions conducive to political liberalization. This again suggests a virtuous cycle—trade liberalization fosters democratization and democracy in turn may promote more trade liberalization, and so on.

Besides its effects on preferences and institutions, trade may constrain the policy choices available to decision makers. The recent literature on internationalization, or globalization, suggests this constraining influence. Rodrik (1997) provides some of the most direct evidence that greater openness may force governments to relinquish the use of various policy instruments. In particular, he notes that openness often makes governments cut spending on social programs and reduce taxes on capital. In order to maintain competitiveness, governments are prevented from using many of the fiscal policy measures they once could.[4] Whether such constraints are good or bad depends on the value one places on government intervention in the economy. For some, like Rodrik (1997), this constraint is worrisome because it reduces the government's ability to shelter its citizens from external volatility and thus may erode the public's support for openness. Here the impact of trade liberalization may not be benign. It may produce a backlash, creating pressures for protection and closure.

In terms of international politics, trade liberalization may also have important effects. As countries become more open to the international economy, it may affect their political relations with other countries. In particular, scholars have asked whether increased trade promotes peace between countries or increases their chances of conflict. Several scholars, such as Polachek (1980),

---

[4]Many scholars have noted that in the presence of high capital mobility—another condition of globalization—governments also lose control of their monetary policy, especially if they desire to fix their exchange rates (e.g. Garrett 1998).

Gasioworski (1986), and Russett et al (1998), have found that increases in trade flows among countries (or between pairs of them) decrease the chances that those countries will be involved in political or military conflicts with each other. Others, such as Waltz (1979) and Barbieri (1996), argue that increased trade and the interdependence it creates either increase conflict or have little effect on it. One way the rush to free trade might affect the international political system, then, is by increasing or decreasing the level of political-military conflicts. The different arguments, however, imply different feedback mechanisms. If trade promotes pacific relations among trading nations, then such a pacific environment is likely to stimulate further trade liberalization and flows; on the other hand, if trade produces more conflict, then we might expect more protectionism and less openness in the future.

These more dynamic models of how international trade and domestic politics interact are an important area of research. They may tell us a good deal about what the rush to free trade, if sustained, may mean for the future. Will the global liberalization process bring increasing pressures for more openness and for democracy? Or will it undermine itself and breed demands for closure and a backlash against governments and the international institutions that support openness? Will openness produce a peaceful international system or one prone to increasing political conflict? The answers to these questions will in turn tell us much about the future direction of trade policy globally.

CONCLUSION

The question that I set out to address was why nations around the globe have liberalized their trade policies since 1980. I examined the preeminent theories of trade policy to see if they could help explain this monumental shift in policy. In this section I assess how well they have done and where future research might be useful.

Why have trade barriers been declining globally since 1980? Existing theories suggest at least three plausible answers. The first involves changing preferences about trade policy among domestic actors. Clearly, in the 1980s, many political leaders and some societal groups in countries around the globe changed their views on what their best trade policy choice was. Political leaders in the LDCs launched ambitious, unilateral economic reforms that included massive trade liberalization, while leaders in the advanced industrial countries undertook large-scale, multilateral efforts to reduce trade barriers. For the latter group, it is hard to pinpoint changes in political institutions or democratization as playing a major role. Instead, the virtuous cycle—growing trade creating more groups in favor of trade liberalization, which in turn created more impetus for greater liberalization and more trade—seems to be a key factor. For the LDCs, on the other hand, changes in leaders' preferences and in political institutions appear more important. The failure of ISI, economic crises, the success of the relatively open Asian NICs, and the demise of a socialist alternative all combined to make leaders favor economic reforms that included trade liberalization. Democratization in some countries also fostered this process. Large-scale changes in political institutions, especially in the direction of democracy, may be necessary for the kind of massive trade liberalization that occurred in some LDCs. But changes in preferences cannot be overlooked in explaining the rush to free trade.

One might think that international factors would play a major role in this global change in policy. But it is harder to argue this. Certainly, the collapse of socialist and communist economies, which was part and parcel of the end of the Cold War and the demise of the Eastern bloc, had an effect. Leaders could no longer plausibly appeal to such models to justify their protectionist policies. But it is important to remember that many of the unilateral reforms toward liberalization began in the early or mid 1980s, before the collapse of the Eastern bloc. They also began at a time when many observers thought American hegemony was long past, especially economically. Perhaps most important was the role of international institutions. For the advanced industrial countries, the GATT allowed countries to design wide-ranging packages of reciprocal trade concessions that fostered broad liberalization; in addition, the EU helped promote liberalization within an ever-growing Europe. For the LDCs, the role of the IMF and World Bank may have played a larger role. Economic distress forced countries to turn to these institutions for help, and part of the price was a prescription of trade liberalization. Although for some leaders this prescription fit with new trade preferences, for others it was a bitter pill to swallow and one they would not have taken without external pressure.

Thus, changing preferences among political leaders and societal groups, institutional changes (especially democratization), and the increased influence of international institutions that supported trade liberalization may best explain the global rush to free trade witnessed since 1980. Research on this puzzle is certainly not complete, however. None of our existing theories by itself seems to do very well in explaining this movement, the most important change in trade policy globally since the end of World War II, and none appears to have predicted it. A better understanding of how political leaders form their trade preferences and how these preferences are connected to societal ones is essential. Moreover, theories about the relationship between democracy and trade are in their infancy. Knowledge of the conditions under which international institutions are able to exert greater (or less) influence over countries is necessary.

Finally, we need to know whether the rush to free trade will be sustained or reversed. Will trade barriers remain as low as they are and keep declining, or will protectionism return? Again, I suspect that the factors that are responsible for the initial change may have some bearing on this. If leaders' or social groups' preferences for free trade are maintained or grow, then we might expect liberalization to remain in place. Factors, such as economic crises, that cause actors to question these preferences will limit their sustainability. We might also expect that the return of authoritarian governments would be associated with the return to protection, but democracy itself is not a sufficient condition for liberalization. Finally, the role of international institutions seems to be heightened by the severity of domestic economic crises. This suggests that, as good times return, political leaders who do not favor free trade may reject the policies forced on them by their lenders and turn protectionist. These and other factors will be important for understanding the sustainability of trade liberalization. Our existing theories are perhaps even less helpful in explaining sustainability than they are in explaining why countries liberalized in the first place.

ACKNOWLEDGMENTS

I wish to thank David Baldwin, Jeffry Frieden, Stephan Haggard, Robert Jervis, and Dani Rodrik for their very helpful comments on an earlier draft of this paper.

Visit the *Annual Reviews home page* at
http://www.AnnualReviews.org.

Literature Cited

Alt J, Freiden J, Gilligan M, Rodrik D, Rogowski R. 1996. The political economy of international trade. *Comp. Polit. Stud.* 29: 689–717

Anderson K. 1980. The political market for government assistance to Australian manufacturing industries. *Econ. Rec.* 56:132–44

Baldwin R. 1986. *The Political Economy of US Import Policy.* Cambridge, MA: MIT Press

Balestreri E. 1997. The performance of the Heckscher-Ohlin-Vanek model in predicting endogenous policy forces at the individual level. *Can. J. Econ.* 30:1–17

Barbieri K. 1996. Economic interdependence. *J. Peace Res.* 33:29–49

Bates R, Krueger A, eds. 1993. *Political and Economic Interactions in Economic Policy Reform.* Cambridge, MA: Blackwell

Bauer R, Pool I, Dexter L. 1972. *American Business and Public Policy.* Chicago: Aldine Atherton

Bergsten CF, Noland M. 1993. *Reconcilable Differences?* Washington, DC: Inst. Int. Econ.

Cameron D. 1978. The expansion of the public economy. *Am. Polit. Sci. Rev.* 72:1243–61

Cardoso FH, E Faletto. 1979. *Dependency and Development in Latin America.* Berkeley: Univ. Calif. Press

Cassing J, McKeown T, Ochs J. 1986. The political economy of the tariff cycle. *Am. Polit. Sci. Rev.* 80:843–62

Caves R. 1976. Economic models of political choice. *Can. J. Econ.* 9:278–300

Cohen BJ. 1990. The political economy of international trade. *Int. Organ.* 44:261–81

Conybeare J. 1982. The rent-seeking state and revenue diversification. *World Polit.* 35: 25–42

Conybeare J. 1983. Tariff protection in developed and developing countries. *Int. Organ.* 37:441–63

Conybeare J. 1984. Public goods, prisoners dilemma and the international political economy. *Int. Stud. Q.* 28:5–22

Destler IM. 1986. *American Trade Politics*. Washington, DC: Inst. Int. Econ.

Encarnation D.1992. *Rivals Beyond Trade*. Ithaca, NY: Cornell Univ. Press

Epstein D, O'Halloran S. 1996. The partisan paradox and the US tariff, 1877–1934. *Int. Organ.* 50:301–24

Frieden J. 1990. *Debt, Development and Democracy*. Princeton, NJ: Princeton Univ. Press

Frieden J, Rogowski R. 1996. The impact of the international economy on national policies. In *Internationalization and Domestic Politics*, ed. R Keohane, H Milner, pp. 25–47. New York: Cambridge Univ. Press

Gallarotti G. 1985. Toward a business cycle model of tariffs. *Int. Organ.* 39:155–87

Garrett G. 1998. *Partisan Politics in the Global Economy*. New York: Cambridge Univ. Press

Gasioworski M. 1986. Economic interdependence and international conflict. *Int. Stud. Q.* 30:23–38

Gilligan M. 1997. *Empowering Exporters*. Ann Arbor: Univ. Mich. Press

Gilpin R. 1987. *The Political Economy of International Relations*. Princeton, NJ: Princeton Univ. Press

Goldstein J. 1988. Ideas, institutions and American trade policy. *Int. Organ.* 42:179–218

Goldstein J. 1993. *Ideas, Interests and American Trade Policy*. Ithaca, NY: Cornell Univ. Press

Gowa J. 1994. *Allies, Adversaries, and International Trade*. Princeton, NJ: Princeton Univ. Press

Gowa J, Mansfield E. 1993. Power politics and international trade. *Am. Polit. Sci. Rev.* 87: 408–20

Greenaway D, Milner C. 1986. *The Economics of Intraindustry Trade*. Oxford, UK: Blackwell

Grossman GM, Helpman E. 1994. Protection for sale. *Am. Econ. Rev.* 84:833–50

Haggard S. 1988. The institutional foundations of hegemony: explaining the Reciprocal Trade Agreements Act of 1934. *Int. Organ.* 42:91–120

Haggard S. 1995. *Developing Nations and the Politics of Global Integration*. Washington, DC: Brookings Inst.

Haggard S, Kaufman R. 1995. *The Political Economy of Democratic Transitions*. Princeton, NJ: Princeton Univ. Press

Haggard S, Webb S, eds. 1994. *Voting for Reform: Democracy, Political Liberalization, and Economic Adjustment*. New York: Oxford Univ. Press

Haldenius A.1992. *Democracy and Development*. New York: Cambridge Univ. Press

Hathaway O. 1998. Positive feedback. *Int. Organ.* 52:575–612

IMF. 1992. *Issues and Developments in International Trade Policy*. Washington, DC: IMF

Irwin D. 1994. The political economy of free trade. *J. Law Econ.* 37:75–108

Irwin D. 1996. Industry or class cleavages over trade policy? In *The Political Economy of Trade Policy*, ed. Feenstra et al, pp. 53–75. Cambridge, MA: MIT Press

James S, Lake D. 1989. The second face of hegemony. *Int. Organ.* 43:1–30

Katzenstein P. 1985. *Small States in World Markets*. Ithaca, NY: Cornell Univ. Press

Keohane R. 1984. *After Hegemony*. Princeton, NJ: Princeton Univ. Press

Keohane R. 1997. Problem lucidity: Stephen Krasner's "State Power and the Structure of International Trade." *World Polit.* 50: 150–70

Krasner S. 1976. State power and the structure of international trade. *World Polit.* 28: 317–47

Krueger A. 1997. Trade policy and economic development: how we learn. *Am. Econ. Rev.* 87: 1–22

Lake D. 1988. *Power, Protection and Free Trade*. Ithaca, NY: Cornell Univ. Press

Lake D. 1993. Leadership, hegemony and the international economy. *Int. Stud. Q.* 37: 459–89

Lipson C. 1982. The transformation of trade. *Int. Organ.* 36:417–56

Lohmann S, O'Halloran S. 1994. Divided government and US trade policy: theory and evidence. *Int. Organ.* 48:595–632

Magee S. 1978. Three simple tests of the Stopler-Samuelson Theorem. In *Issues in International Economics*, ed. P Oppenheimer, pp. 138–53. London: Oriel

Magee S, Brock W, Young L. 1989. *Black Hole Tariffs and Endogenous Policy Theory*. New York: Cambridge Univ. Press

Magee S, Young L. 1987. Endogenous protection in the US. In *US Trade Policies in a Changing World Economy*, ed. R Stern, pp. 145–95. Cambridge, MA: MIT Press

Mansfield E. 1994. *Power, Trade and War*. Princeton, NJ: Princeton Univ. Press

Mansfield E, Bronson R. 1997. Alliances, preferential trading arrangements, and international trade. *Am. Polit. Sci. Rev.* 91: 94–107

Mansfield E, Busch M. 1995. The political economy of nontariff barriers: a cross-national analysis. *Int. Organ.* 49:723–49

Mansfield E, Milner H, Rosendorff BP. 1997. *Free to trade: democracies and international trade negotiations*. Presented at

Annu. Meet. Am. Polit. Sci. Assoc., Washington, DC, Sept. 1997

Mansfield E, Milner H, Rosendorff BP. 1998. *Why do democracies cooperate more: electoral control and international trade negotiations.* Presented at Annu. Meet. Am. Polit. Sci. Assoc., San Francisco, Sept. 1998

Marvel H, Ray E. 1983. The Kennedy round. *Am. Econ. Rev.* 73:190–97

Mayer W. 1984. Endogenous tariff formation. *Am. Econ. Rev.* 74:970–85

Midford P. 1993. International trade and domestic politics. *Int. Organ.* 47:535–64

Milner H. 1988. *Resisting Protectionism.* Princeton, NJ: Princeton Univ. Press

Milner H. 1997. *Interests, Institutions, and Information.* Princeton, NJ: Princeton Univ. Press

Milner H, Rosendorff BP. 1996. Trade negotiations, information and domestic politics. *Econ. Polit.* 8:145–89

Nelson D. 1988. Endogenous tariff theory: a critical survey. *Am. J. Polit. Sci.* 32:796–837

O'Halloran S. 1994. *Politics, Process and American Trade Policy.* Ann Arbor: Univ. Mich. Press

Pincus J. 1975. Pressure groups and the pattern of tariffs. *J. Polit. Econ.* 83:757–78

Polachek SW. 1980. Conflict and trade. *J. Conflict Resol.* 24:55–78

Ray E. 1981. Determinants of tariff and nontariff restrictions in the US. *J. Polit. Econ.* 89:105–21

Reizman D, Wilson J. 1995. Politics and trade policy. In *Modern Political Economy*, ed. J Banks, E Hanuschek, pp. 108–44. New York: Cambridge Univ. Press

Rodrik D. 1992. The limits to trade policy reform in LDCs. *J. Econ. Perspect.* 6:87–105

Rodrik D. 1994. The rush to free trade in the developing world. Why so late? Why now? Will it last? In *Voting for Reform: Democracy, Political Liberalization, and Economic Adjustment*, ed. S Haggard, S Webb, pp. 61–88. New York: Oxford Univ. Press

Rodrik D. 1995. Political economy of trade policy. In *Handbook of International Economics*, Vol. 3, ed. G Grossman, K Rogoff, pp. 1457–94. Netherlands: Elsevier

Rodrik D. 1997. *Has Globalization Gone Too Far?* Washington, DC: Inst. Int. Econ.

Rogowski R. 1987. Trade and the variety of democratic institutions. *Int. Organ.* 41:203–24

Rogowski R. 1989. *Commerce and Coalitions.* Princeton, NJ: Princeton Univ. Press

Ruggie J. 1983. International regimes, transactions and change. In *International Regimes*, ed. S Krasner, pp. 196–232. Ithaca, NY: Cornell Univ. Press

Russett B. 1985. The mysterious case of vanishing hegemony; or is Mark Twain really dead? *Int. Organ.* 39:207–32

Russett B, Oneal J, Davis D. 1998. The third leg of the Kantian tripod for peace. *Int. Organ.* 52:441–68

Schattschneider EE. 1935. *Politics, Pressures and the Tariff.* Englewood Cliffs, NJ: Prentice-Hall

Scheve K, Slaughter M. 1998. *What determines individual trade policy preferences?* Natl. Bur. Econ. Res. Work. Pap. No. 6531

Simmons B. 1994. *Who Adjusts?* Princeton, NJ: Princeton Univ. Press

Smith A. 1937 (1776). *The Wealth of Nations.* New York: Modern Library

Snidal D. 1985. The limits of hegemonic stability theory. *Int. Organ.* 39:579–614

Stolper W, Samuelson P. 1941. Protection and real wages. *Rev. Econ. Stud.* 9:58–73

Strange S. 1987. The persistent myth of lost hegemony. *Int. Organ.* 41:551–74

Takacs W. 1981. Pressures for protection. *Econ. Inq.* 19:687–93

Trefler D. 1993. Trade liberalization and the theory of endogenous protection. *J. Polit. Econ.* 101:138–60

Tsebelis G. 1995. Decision-making in political systems: veto players in presidentialism, parliamentarism, multicameralism and multipartism. *Br. J. Polit. Sci.* 25:289–325

Verdier D. 1998. Democratic convergence and free trade? *Int. Stud. Q.* 42:1–24

Wallerstein M. 1987. Unemployment, collective bargaining and the demand for protection. *Am. J. Polit. Sci.* 31:729–52

Waltz K. 1979. *Theory of International Politics.* Reading, MA: Addison-Wesley

Wintrobe R. 1998. *The Political Economy of Dictatorship.* New York: Cambridge Univ. Press

Wood A. 1994. *North-South Trade, Unemployment and Inequality.* Oxford, UK: Clarendon

WTO. 1996. *Annual Report 1996: Trade and Foreign Direct Investment.* Vol. 1. Geneva: World Trade Organ.

Yarbrough BV, Yarbrough RM. 1992. *Cooperation and Governance in International Trade: The Strategic Organizational Approach.* Princeton, NJ: Princeton Univ. Press

Annu. Rev. Polit. Sci. 1999. 2:115–44

WHAT DO WE KNOW ABOUT DEMOCRATIZATION AFTER TWENTY YEARS?

Barbara Geddes

Department of Political Science, University of California at Los Angeles, Los Angeles, California 90095-1472; e-mail: geddes@ucla.edu

KEY WORDS: democratization, transition, regime, authoritarian, military

ABSTRACT

This essay synthesizes the results of the large number of studies of late–20th-century democratization published during the last 20 years. Strong evidence supports the claims that democracy is more likely in more developed countries and that regime transitions of all kinds are more likely during economic downturns. Very few of the other arguments advanced in the transitions literature, however, appear to be generally true. This study proposes a theoretical model, rooted in characteristics of different types of authoritarian regimes, to explain many of the differences in democratization experience across cases in different regions. Evidence drawn from a data set that includes 163 authoritarian regimes offers preliminary support for the model proposed.

INTRODUCTION

As the twentieth century ends, elected officials govern more countries than at any previous time in human history. Transitions to democracy have occurred with surprising frequency during the past 20 years, and a great deal has been written on the subject by enthusiastic and intrigued observers. This essay summarizes what we have learned about such transitions and proposes a theory that makes sense of a number of apparently disparate findings.

Since 1974, identified by Huntington (1991) as the beginning of the "third wave" of democratization, 85 authoritarian regimes have ended. These transitions have resulted in 30 surviving and mostly quite stable democracies (not including democracies in some of the new states created as a consequence of

115

regime change); 9 democracies that lasted only a very short time before being overthrown; 8 cases in which there have been elections and leadership changes but in which either democracy appears very unstable or important groups are excluded from competition; 4 descents into warlordism; and 34 new authoritarian regimes.[1]

Four regime changes led directly to the break-up of states, and 3 to the reunion of previously divided nations. Of the 21 new states created in the wake of regime changes, 5 seem at this point to be full democracies and 8 have held competitive elections but remain in important respects undemocratic. In 8, either elections have not been held or competition has been severely constrained. Six have been ravaged by civil war or impoverished by war with neighbors.

Thirty-two countries that either had authoritarian regimes in 1974 or have succumbed to them since then remain authoritarian, though most of them have taken some steps in the direction of political liberalization. In an additional 7 countries, long-ruling parties or rulers who had previously reinforced their dominance by fraud, limitations on competition, and selective repression have held competitive elections considered free and fair by observers, but have not been turned out of office. These regimes are hard to classify because well-entrenched incumbents have so many advantages with regard to control of state resources and the media that the lifting of restrictions on competition may not create a level playing field. Though several appear to have started irreversably down the road to democracy, it is impossible to know whether such long-ruling parties and leaders will really step down if voted out of office until we see them do so.

Nearly a quarter of a century has passed since the beginning of the third wave, so perhaps the owl of Minerva is waking up and readying its wings for flight. With all the years for study and all these cases to explore, what have we learned about late–twentieth-century regime transition and democratization?

---

[1]Figures here and elsewhere are drawn from a data set collected by the author, which includes all authoritarian regimes (except monarchies) lasting three years or more that either existed in 1946 or came to power after 1946, in countries that achieved independence before 1990 and have a million or more inhabitants. Regimes are defined as sets of formal and informal rules and procedures for selecting national leaders and policies. Using this definition, periods of instability and temporary "moderating" military interventions (Stepan 1971) are considered interregna, not regimes. The three-year threshold is simply a way of excluding such periods from the data set. This cut-off point was chosen, after considerable empirical investigation of very short-lived authoritarian interludes, as the one that introduced the least misclassification into the data. I counted an authoritarian regime as defunct if either the dictator and his supporters had been ousted from office or if a negotiated transition resulted in reasonably fair, competitive elections and a change in the party or individual occupying executive office. Cases in which elections deemed free and fair by outside observers have been held but have not led to a turnover in personnel are treated here as uncertain outcomes because, until they actually step down, we do not know if long-ruling parties such as the Partido Revolucionario Institucional (PRI) in Mexico or the Revolutionary Party of Tanzania (CCM) in Tanzania really will relinquish power.

Scholars have greeted the increasing number of democratizations with delight, intense attention, and theoretical puzzlement. It seems as though there should be a parsimonious and compelling explanation of the transitions, but the explanations proposed thus far have been confusingly complicated, careless about basic methodological details, often more useful as description than explanation, and surprisingly inconsistent with each other. The basic problem faced by analysts is that the process of democratization varies enormously from case to case and region to region. Generalizations proposed have failed either to accommodate all the real-world variation or to explain it.

This essay first reviews several of the most prominent arguments about the causes of democratization and briefly considers the evidence supporting and challenging them. It then suggests that different kinds of authoritarianism break down in characteristically different ways and sketches the theoretical underpinnings for this difference. Many of the contradictory conclusions reached by analysts who focus primarily on one region or another make sense once we take into account the predominance of different forms of authoritarianism in different parts of the world and the systematic differences in the ways these different forms disintegrate. A study of 163 authoritarian regimes in 94 countries provides evidence that the differences in breakdown patterns hypothesized actually do exist.

PAST RESEARCH

One of the few stylized facts to emerge from studies of regime transition is that democracy is more likely in more developed countries. The positive relationship between democratic government and economic development was empirically established beyond reasonable doubt by Jackman (1973) and Bollen (1979) and has been confirmed more recently by Burkhart & Lewis-Beck (1994). Several recent studies have increased our understanding of the process that results in this relationship. Using sophisticated statistical models to capture the complicated interaction between regime type and economic growth, Londregan & Poole (1990, 1996) have shown that the most important predictor of transitions to authoritarianism, whether from democracy or from other forms of authoritarianism, is poverty. Working in the same vein, Przeworski & Limongi (1997) show that once democratization has occurred, for whatever reason, it survives in countries above a certain level of economic development. Among countries below that threshold, the probability of a reversion to authoritarianism rises as the level of economic development falls.

Przeworski & Limongi interpret their findings as a challenge to modernization theory, though it seems to me a revisionist confirmation—in fact, the strongest empirical confirmation ever. Noting that transitions to democracy can occur for many reasons, they argue that the observed relationship between democracy and development is caused not so much by the greater likelihood that more developed countries will democratize as by the improbability of authoritarian interventions in developed countries. This argument challenges all previous work on democratization; from Lipset (1959) and others associ- ated with the early articulation of modernization theory to Moore (1966) and his descendants to those who have advocated a focus on contingent choices, *fortuna*, and *virtu* in the study of transitions (most notably O'Donnell et al 1986), all analysts have focused their attention on transitions *to* democracy. Przeworski & Limongi's findings do not, however, disconfirm the basic argu- ments made by any of these schools of thought unless it turns out that moderni- zation, the class composition of society, or contingent choices have no effect on the probability of transitions to authoritarianism, which seems unlikely.

From a large number of studies based on large numbers of cases covering several different time periods, the best of which use very sophisticated statisti- cal models, we can conclude that a positive relationship exists between eco- nomic development and the likelihood of democratic government. A useful way to think about this relationship is shown in Figure 1.

This graphic image of modernization theory helps to interpret both standard observations and those that might otherwise be puzzling. First, we note that

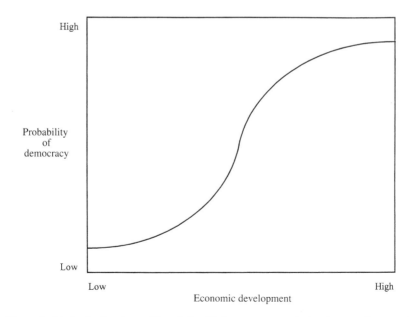

Figure 1   Modernization theory. The relationship between economic development (*horizontal axis*) and the probability of democracy (*vertical axis*) is nonlinear, taking on the standard "S" shape we expect when the dependent variable is a probability ranging between zero and one.

among countries above a certain level of development, the probability of democracy is close to 100%, consistent with both casual observation and the findings of Przeworski & Limongi (1997). The probability of authoritarianism is similarly close to 100% below some threshold. Few countries currently remain below that threshold, but we can interpret it as consistent with the overwhelming historical prevalence of authoritarianism since the invention of states. The middle area of the graph is in many ways more interesting. Here, the probability of democracy is close to 50%, and we should not be surprised that countries at middle levels of development tend to alternate between different regime types. This is the group of countries in which transitions to both democracy and authoritarianism should be most common. It is also the group of countries in which human choices and serendipitous events—*virtu* and *fortuna*—could most easily affect outcomes, since underlying structural causes are fairly evenly balanced.

Of course, not all countries have the form of government this graph would lead us to expect. At the moment (summer 1998), Mongolia, Benin, and Madagascar have what appear to be viable democratic governments, and Singapore remains authoritarian. But we do not expect any social science theory to explain everything or predict perfectly, and certainly "modernization theory," whatever underlying process it actually reflects, does not.

In short, after 20 years of observation and analysis during the third wave of academic interest in democratization, we can be reasonably certain that a positive relationship between development and democracy exists, though we do not know why.

A second stylized fact is also reasonably well established. Virtually all transition specialists believe that poor economic performance increases the likelihood of authoritarian breakdown, as it increases democratic breakdown and defeat of incumbents in stable democracies (e.g. Diamond & Linz 1989, Bermeo 1990). Most quantitative studies support their view. Przeworski & Limongi (1997) find the expected relationship between low economic growth and transition. Haggard & Kaufman (1995) emphasize the effects of economic crisis on regime change.

I turn now to a consideration of some of the more controversial arguments proposed by scholars. The body of literature on transitions now includes hundreds, if not thousands, of case studies of particular transitions; dozens of comparisons among small numbers of cases; and at least half a dozen important efforts at theoretically informed general synthesis. Many of the finest minds in comparative politics have worked on the subject. Virtually every suggested generalization to arise from this literature, however, has been challenged. Should social scientists throw in the towel, or is there some way to integrate the findings of different specialists working on different parts of the world and different time periods?

Until recently, one of the most widely accepted generalizations was that "there is no transition whose beginning is not the consequence—direct or indirect—of important divisions within the authoritarian regime itself" (O'Donnell & Schmitter 1986:19). Carefully documented case studies of a number of Latin American transitions supported the idea that the first steps toward what eventually became democratization could be traced to splits within military governments. The transition from military rule in Greece also fit. Analogous studies of the roots of transition in Spain and Portugal showed the existence of similar splits within the old regimes and were thus not seen as challenging the argument, though they brought some anomalies to analysts' attention.

The democratizations that occurred in the wake of the Soviet collapse, however, could not in most cases be traced to splits within the old regime. Nor can most regime transitions in Africa. Bratton & van de Walle conclude from a study of 42 African countries that "transitions in Africa seem to be occurring more commonly from below.... [R]ulers are driven by calculations of personal political survival: They resist political openings for as long as possible" (1997:83).

In keeping with the argument about elite-initiated democratization, most observers of Latin American transitions assign little importance to popular mobilization as a cause of democratization. Popular mobilizations took place in many countries, but they usually occurred relatively late in the process, when democratization was well underway and the risks of opposition had diminished. Popular protest may have pushed democratization farther and faster than regime elites initially intended (Collier & Mahoney 1997; Bermeo 1997; R Collier, unpublished manuscript), but in most Latin American cases it did not cause the initiation of liberalization. In contrast, popular protest was the main reason old-regime elites agreed to begin negotiation in a number of East European and African cases (Bratton & van de Walle 1992, 1997).

Another often repeated claim is that pacts between elites facilitate successful transition to democracy (Burton et al 1992, Karl 1990). Pacts, as the term is used in the transitions literature, are agreements among contending elites that establish formulas for sharing or alternating in office, distributing the spoils of office, and constraining policy choice in areas of high salience to the groups involved, while excluding other groups from office, spoils, and influence over policy. Arguments about the usefulness of pacts have arisen from studies of Latin American and European cases of democratization, but, again, Bratton & van de Walle (1997) find no evidence of pacts in their African cases.

Yet another common argument is that "stronger" outgoing regimes are able to negotiate transition outcomes more favorable to themselves than those forced out by crisis. Agüero (1992, 1995), for example, argues that military governments that have ruled more effectively, such as those in Chile and Brazil, are able to secure a continuing role for officers in the policy process and safeguard themselves from prosecution for crimes committed in office, whereas those that lose wars or otherwise leave in disgrace, such as the Argentine and Greek militaries, have little leverage. Haggard & Kaufman (1995, 1997) concur with Agüero about military bargaining power, though they disagree about which regimes were stronger. Further, they maintain that regimes exiting during economic crisis have less ability to obtain opposition agreement to institutions that are conducive to the moderate future politics and policies they prefer. It has to be true that actors with more bargaining power can get more in negotiations, so this argument is highly plausible if not earthshaking. It has been challenged, however, not by evidence from a larger number of cases, but by the passage of time. Stronger outgoing leaders can certainly get more during negotiations, but what they get may only matter for a short time after the transition.

THEORETICAL SYTHESIS

One of the reasons regime transitions have proved so theoretically intractable is that different kinds of authoritarianism differ from each other as much as they differ from democracy. They draw on different groups to staff government offices and different segments of society for support. They have different procedures for making decisions, different ways of handling the choice of leaders and succession, and different ways of responding to society and opponents. Because comparativists have not studied these differences systematically, what theorizing exists about authoritarian regimes is posed at a highly abstract level, and few authors have considered how characteristics of dictatorships affect transitions. These differences, however, cause authoritarian regimes to break down in systematically different ways, and they affect transition outcomes. Here I propose theoretical foundations for explaining these differences among types of authoritarianism.

As virtually all close observers of authoritarian governments have noted, politics in such regimes, as in all others, involves factionalism, competition, and struggle. The competition among rival factions, however, takes different forms in different kinds of authoritarian regimes and has different consequences.

To facilitate the analysis of these differences, I classify authoritarian regimes as personalist, military, single-party, or amalgams of the pure types. In military regimes, a group of officers decides who will rule and exercises some influence on policy. In single-party regimes, access to political office and control over policy are dominated by one party, though other parties may legally exist and compete in elections. Personalist regimes differ from both military and single-party in that access to office and the fruits of office depends much more on the discretion of an individual leader. The leader may be an officer and may have created a party to support himself, but neither the military nor the party exercises independent decision-making power insulated from the whims of the ruler (see Bratton & van de Walle 1997:61–96, Linz & Chehabi 1998:4–45, Snyder 1998).[2]

Military regimes, as shown below, carry within them the seeds of their own disintegration; transitions from military rule usually begin with splits within the ruling military elite, as noted by much of the literature on Latin American transitions. In contrast, rival factions within single-party and personalist regimes have stronger incentives to cooperate with each other. Single-party regimes are quite resilient and tend to be brought down by exogenous events rather than internal splits (cf Haggard & Kaufman 1995, Huntington 1991). Personalist regimes are also relatively immune to internal splits except when calamitous economic conditions disrupt the material underpinnings of regime loyalty. They are especially vulnerable, however, to the death of the leader and to violent overthrow (Huntington 1991). The lower probability that internal splits will lead to regime breakdown in non-military forms of authoritarianism explains why observers of transitions in Africa and Eastern Europe usually find the beginnings of change outside the regime rather than inside. Below I elaborate these arguments.

To explain why military regimes are more susceptible to internal disintegration, I focus here on rivalries and relationships within the ruling entity of an authoritarian government: the officer corps, single party, clique surrounding the ruler, or some amalgam of two or more of these three. Action within the ruling entity, of course, tells only a part of the story of regime change. Opposition from outside the ruling group and exogenous shocks [e.g. Soviet collapse, international economic crisis, International Monetary Fund (IMF)-induced economic reform] affect, sometimes decisively, regime survival. However, by focusing on political dynamics within different kinds of authoritarian regimes, I aim to show precisely how exogenous shocks and popular mobilization affect different kinds of regimes and thus the likelihood of transition. Building a theoretical foundation for understanding different kinds of authoritarian regimes makes it possible to move beyond lists of causes that sometimes matter (found in many studies of transitions) and toward systematic statements about when particular causes are likely to matter.

Most authoritarian regimes are established through either military intervention or the elimination of competition by a party that has gained office via election. What I call personalist regimes generally develop after the actual seizure

---

[2]Many authoritarian regimes go through changes over time that affect their classification. It is common for officers who seize power in military coups, for example, to attempt to concentrate power in their own individual hands, to hold plebiscitary elections to legitimate their personal rule, and to create parties to organize their supporters. In these ways, they sometimes succeed in changing basic features of the regime. Where such changes occurred over time, I used the later, in most cases stabler, period as the basis for classification.

of office, as a consequence of the struggle for power among rival leaders. In most military and some single-party regimes, struggles among factions, one backing the leader and others led by potential rivals, become visible to observers within the first few months after the seizure of power. When one individual wins such a struggle, successfully continuing to draw support from the organization that brought him to power but limiting his supporters' influence on policy and personnel decisions, I label the regime personalist. Winning the initial struggle is no guarantee of long-term security, but individual leaders sometimes achieve a position from which, with continuous monitoring and rapid, shrewd, and unscrupulous responses to incipient opposition, they can for a time prevent serious challenges from arising.

Coup plotters, especially those with past experience in power, can often foresee the possibility of regime personalization, and they attempt in various ways to prevent it. Institutional arrangements designed to insure power sharing and consultation among high-ranking officers can be very elaborate. It took months for the various factions within the Argentine armed forces to hammer out power-sharing arrangements before the 1976 coup, and the resultant complicated and cumbersome governing institutions all but immobilized decision making at various times (Fontana 1987). As another way to reduce the probability that one officer will succeed in consolidating personal power at the expense of his colleagues, plotters often choose an officer known for correctness, adherence to rules, fairness, lack of personal ambition, and low charisma to lead the junta or military command council. General Augusto Pinochet, for example, was chosen to lead what was supposed to be a collegial junta in Chile because he had the most seniority within the junta, and his colleagues thought him a safe choice precisely because of his professionalism, respect for rules, and wooden, uncharismatic demeanor. Their assessment of his character was mistaken, as many others have been before and since. But power does not always corrupt; General Humberto Castello Branco, chosen to lead the first military government in Brazil for much the same reasons, lived up to expectations and resisted the temptation to consolidate personal power. Groups that seize power extraconstitutionally often try to prevent the personalization of the regime, but pre-coup contracts are often unenforceable.

Classification Issues

Although most authoritarian regimes are easy to classify, some are not. The criteria for classification used here emphasize control over access to power and influence rather than formal institutional characteristics. A military regime, in contrast to a personalist dictatorship led by a military officer, is one in which a group of officers determines who will lead the country and has some influence on policy. In an institutionalized military regime (many are not), senior officers have agreed on some formula for sharing or rotating power, and consultation is somewhat routinized. Military hierarchy is respected, perhaps after an initial purge of supporters of the previous government. Examples of military regimes include the Brazilian (1964–1985), in which senior officers, in consultation with a small number of civilians, picked each successive president in keeping with rules specified by the institutions of the authoritarian regime; the Argentine (1976–1983), in which senior officers never completely lost the power to choose the president, despite intense factional struggle and the efforts of the first military president to renege on pre-coup agreements among the conspirators to rotate the office; and the Salvadoran (1948–1984), in which military manipulation of elections insured that the officer selected by the military as its candidate always won the presidency.

In contrast to these cases, many regimes headed by military officers are not in reality controlled by a group of senior officers. It is common for military interventions to lead to short periods of military rule followed by the consolidation of power by a single officer and the political marginalization of much of the rest of the officer corps. These are personal dictatorships, even though the leader wears a uniform. Regimes such as Rafael Trujillo's in the Dominican Republic (1930–1961), Idi Amin's in Uganda (1971–1979), and Jean-Bédel Bokassa's in the Central African Republic (1966–1979) are somewhat extreme instances of the transformation of military intervention into personal tyranny. Others, such as Pinochet's in Chile and Suharto's in Indonesia, are harder to classify because the military institution retained some autonomy and influence. Here I classify them in intermediate categories (on Chile, see Remmer 1989 and Arriagada 1988; on Indonesia, see Jenkins 1984, Liddle 1989).

Because many dictators form parties to support themselves, distinguishing between "real" and nominal single-party regimes involves the same careful judgments as distinguishing between military regimes and personalist ones led by officers. In the ideal-type single-party regime, a party organization exercises some power over the leader at least part of the time, controls the career paths of officials, organizes the distribution of benefits to supporters, and mobilizes citizens to vote and show support for party leaders in other ways. Holding regular elections in which there is some competition, either from opposition parties or within the dominant party, is a strong indication that a party has achieved a level of organization and influence sufficient to be taken seriously as a political actor. Examples of single-party regimes include that of the Partido Revolucionario Institucional (PRI) in Mexico, the Revolutionary Party of Tanzania (CCM), and the Leninist parties in various East European countries. Regimes such as Juan Perón's in Argentina, in which the leader himself maintains a near monopoly over policy and personnel decisions despite having founded a support party, are personalist.

Area experts' criteria for distinguishing dominant-party authoritarian regimes from democracies vary by region. Latin Americanists generally consider Mexico authoritarian at least until 1996, but most African specialists consider Botswana, Senegal, and even Zimbabwe democratic. To compare across regions, the same set of criteria must be applied everywhere. In this study, regimes are considered authoritarian and labeled single-party if other parties have been banned or subjected to serious harassment or institutional disadvantage, or if the dominant party has never lost control of the executive since coming to power and usually wins more than two thirds of the seats in the legislature. Once a regime is labeled single-party, I do not consider it fully democratized until one turnover of executive power has occurred. Where it appears that conclusions might be affected by the considerable stringency of these criteria, I also show results using a less demanding rule.[3]

Theoretical Foundations

Standard theories of politics in democratic regimes begin with two simplifying assumptions: (*a*) Politicians want to get into office and remain there; (*b*) the best strategy for doing so is to give constituents what they want. Both of these assumptions need modification in the context of authoritarianism. Although even very coercive regimes cannot survive without some support, in the absence of routine ways for citizens to remove authoritarian leaders from office, questions of who exactly their constituents are, how satisfied they have to be, and what factors besides satisfaction with regime performance affect their level of acquiescence require empirical investigation and cannot be answered in the abstract. Moreover, before questions about the identity of constituents and how to keep them acquiescent can be relevant, we need to ask whether it is plausible to assume that potential authoritarian leaders always want to achieve office and, once having achieved it, always try to hold onto power. If they do not, we need a new theory to account for their behavior. One of the central arguments of this essay is that military officers, in contrast to leaders in single-party and personalist regimes, often do not.

The Interests of Military Officers

Research on the attitudes and preferences of military officers in many different societies shows that officers in different countries come from different socioeconomic, ethnic, and educational backgrounds. They have different ideologies and feel sympathetic toward different societal interests. No generalizations can be made about the interests or policies they are likely to support.

---

[3]These regime type classifications are similar to Huntington's (1991), and my "coding" judgments are very close to his. My decision rule for determining whether a political system had crossed the threshold to democracy is essentially the same as that of Przeworski & Limongi (1997). The biggest difference between my classification scheme and that of Linz & Stepan (1996) is that I collapse what they call sultanistic and civilianized regimes into one category, personalist. Which classification scheme is most useful depends on the purpose to which it is being put.

There is, however, a consensus in the literature that most professional soldiers place a higher value on the survival and efficacy of the military itself than on anything else (Janowitz 1960, 1977; Finer 1975; Bienen 1978; DeCalo 1976; Kennedy 1974; Van Doorn 1968, 1969).

This corporate interest implies a concern with the maintenance of hierarchy, discipline, and cohesiveness within the military; autonomy from civilian intervention; and budgets sufficient to attract high-quality recruits and buy state-of-the-art weapons. Officers also value highly the territorial integrity of the nation and internal order, but they feel unable to pursue these goals effectively unless the military itself remains unified and adequately supplied (Stepan 1971, Nordlinger 1977, de Oliveira 1978, Barros 1978). In countries in which joining the military has become a standard path to personal enrichment (for example, Bolivia for a time, Panama, Nicaragua under Somoza, Guatemala, Ghana before 1981, Nigeria, Thailand, Congo), acquisitive motives can be assumed to rank high in most officers' preferences—highest for some, and second or third for most, if only because the continued existence of lucrative opportunities for officers may depend on the survival of the military as an effective organization.

Such preferences imply that officers agree to join coup conspiracies only if they believe that the civilian government prevents the achievement of their main goals, and that many, in fact, will only join if they believe that the military institution itself is threatened. These preferences are thus consistent with Stepan's (1971) and Nordlinger's (1977) observations about the importance of threats to the military as an institution in the decisions of officers to join coup conspiracies.

> Only a small proportion originally entered the military in the hope of attaining governmental offices. Many praetorians took up the reins of government with little enthusiasm. Most of them would probably have much preferred to remain in the barracks if their objectives, particularly the defense or enhancement of the military's corporate interests, could have been realized from that vantage point. (Nordlinger 1977:142).

The worst possible outcome for the military as an institution is civil war in which one part of the armed forces fights another. Consequently, the most important concern for many officers deciding whether to join a coup conspiracy is their assessment of how many others will join.

What Nordlinger, Stepan, and others are describing is similar to a classic Battle of the Sexes game. The insight behind Battle of the Sexes games comes from the following scenario: One member of a couple would prefer to go to a movie and the other would prefer the opera, but each would prefer doing something together to doing something alone. Going to either event together is a potential equilibrium, but no dominant strategy exists, since the best outcome for either player always depends on what the other does.

The logic of decisions about seizing power or returning to the barracks is the same. Some officers are tempted to intervene, others have legalist values that preclude intervention except in the most extreme circumstances, and most are located somewhere in between—but almost all care most about the survival and efficacy of the military and thus want the military to move either in or out of power as a cohesive whole. Figure 2 depicts this set of preferences as a game.

In the game shown in Figure 2, the majority prefers to remain in the barracks. A minority would prefer to intervene, but would be far worse off if they tried to intervene without support from the majority than if they remained unhappily in the barracks. Participants in an unsuccessful coup attempt face possible demotion, discharge, court martial, and execution for treason, so their payoff is shown as a negative number. The majority faction that opposed the coup is also likely to be worse off after the attempt, since the armed forces will have been weakened, and the government is likely to respond with greater oversight, reorganization, and interference with promotions and postings to try to insure greater loyalty, all of which reduce military autonomy. The final possible outcome is a successful coup carried out despite minority opposition. In this event the minority that remains loyal to the civilian government is likely to face the same costs as unsuccessful conspirators: demotion, discharge, prison, death. The winners achieve power, but a weakened military institution reduces their chances of keeping it. Future conspiracies supported by those demoted or discharged after the coup become more likely. Once factions of the military take up arms against each other, it takes years or decades to restore unity and trust.

This is a coordination game; once the military is either in power (*upper left cell*) or out of power (*lower right cell*), neither faction can improve its position unilaterally. Each faction must have the other's cooperation in order to secure its preferred option. When the military is out of power, even if the majority

Minority Faction

		intervene	barracks
	intervene	4, 5	0, -10
Majority Faction			
	barracks	3, -20	5, 4

Figure 2   Game between military factions. The two numbers in each cell represent the respective pay-offs to the two factions. *Upper left cell*: pay-offs of a successful intervention by the unified military. *Lower right cell*: pay-offs of remaining in or returning to the barracks. *Lower left cell*: pay-offs of an unsuccessful coup attempt by a minority faction. *Upper right cell*: pay-offs of a successful coup carried out despite minority opposition.

comes to believe it should intervene, it cannot shift equilibria without cooperation from the minority.

Where interventionists have wide support and an open political system
makes plotting relatively safe and easy, coups are often preceded by extensive
consultation among officers, delays until almost total consensus within the
officer corps is achieved, and elaborate negotiations over power sharing and
rotation in office. These consultations and negotiations aim to insure the cooperation of all major factions in the intervention. Such elaborate efforts to
achieve coordination have been described, e.g. in Brazil leading to the 1964
coup (Stepan 1971), in Argentina prior to the1976 coup (Fontana 1987), and in
Chile in 1973 (Valenzuela 1978).

Where interventionists have only minority support and plotting is more difficult, another, though riskier, strategy is available. Conspirators can keep the
plot secret from all but a few key officers and hope that the rest will go along
once key central institutions have been seized. (Often the presidential palace,
garrisons in and around the capital city, radio and TV stations, central tele-
phone and telegraph exchanges, and the airport will suffice.) This is the strategy Nordlinger (1977) identifies as most common. It often succeeds precisely
because most of the officer corps cares more about military unity than about
whether officers control government or not. It is a characteristic of games like
Battle of the Sexes that the actor who succeeds in moving first can always get
what he or she wants. In the real world, however, the first-mover strategy
sometimes fails, usually because the first mover fails to persuade the rest that
most other officers will support the coup.

The attempted Spanish coup in 1981 is an example of a failed first-mover
strategy. Passive support for intervention was widespread within the Spanish
military, mostly because of the threat to national integrity posed by the Suárez
government's willingness to negotiate with Basque and Catalán nationalists.
The small group of active conspirators believed that once they had seized control of the Cortes and key installations in Madrid, King Juan Carlos and the rest
of the officer corps would go along with the fait accompli. The evidence available suggests that most of the officer corps would have gone along if the king
had not immediately begun telephoning the captains-general and other high-
ranking officers to inform them that he would resist the coup (Colomer 1995).
For some officers, loyalty to the king was stronger than other values and led
them to oppose the intervention. For others, the king's unequivocal opposition
indicated which position the rest of the officer corps was likely to take, and this
information led them to resist intervention in order to end up on the same side.
The coup might well have succeeded if the king's access to telephones and
television had been blocked. Colomer (1995:121) quotes one of the erstwhile
conspirators as saying, "The next time, cut the King's phone line!"

For some military leaders, the game changes after a successful seizure of power, but most officers always see their situation as resembling a Battle of the Sexes game, even in the most politicized and factionalized militaries. Repeated coups by different factions, as in Syria prior to 1970 or Benin (Dahomey) before 1972, would not be possible if most of the army did not go along with the first mover, either in seizing power or in handing it back.

The Interests of Party Cadres in Single-Party Regimes

The preferences of party cadres are much simpler than those of officers. Like democratic politicians, they simply want to hold office. Some value office because they want to control policy, some for the pure enjoyment of influence and power, and some for the illicit material gains that come with office in some countries. The game between party leaders and cadres, sometimes called Staghunt, is shown in Figure 3. (The insight behind the Staghunt game is that in a primitive stag hunt, everyone's cooperation is needed in order to encircle and kill the prey. If anyone wanders off, leaving a hole in the circle, all including the wanderer are worse off.)

The minority's pay-off in opposition is lower than when the party holds power because the opposition has fewer opportunities to exercise influence or line pockets. If the minority faction is excluded from office but the party continues in power, the minority continues to receive some benefits, since its policy preferences are pursued and party connections are likely to bring various opportunities.

Factions form in single-party regimes around policy differences and competition for leadership positions, but everyone is better off if all factions remain united and in office. This is why cooptation rather than exclusion is the rule in established single-party regimes. Neither faction would be better off ruling alone, and neither would voluntarily withdraw from office unless ex-

		Majority **(Leader's Faction)**	
		in office	out of office
Rival **Faction**	in office	8, 10	5, 1
	out of office	3, 9	0, 0

Figure 3   Staghunt game between factions in single-party regimes. The best outcome for everyone is for both factions to hold office (*upper left cell*). The worst outcome occurs when both are out of power (*lower right cell*). *Upper right cell*: the pay-off to the minority of holding office in the opposition (i.e. after the dominant party no longer rules), and to the majority out of office. *Lower left cell*: The minority faction is excluded from office, but the party continues in power.

ogenous events changed the costs and benefits of cooperating with each other (and hence the game itself)—a possibility to which I return below.

The Interests of Members of Cliques

Membership in personalist cliques tends to be more fluid and harder to identify than membership in parties or the officer corps. During and after a seizure of power, personalist cliques are often formed from the network of friends, relatives, and allies that surrounds every political leader. In personalist regimes, one individual dominates both the military and state apparatus. As in single-party regimes, factions form around potential rivals to the leader, but during normal times they have strong reasons to continue supporting the regime and leader.

> [I]nsiders in a patrimonial ruling coalition are unlikely to promote reform.... Recruited and sustained with material inducements, lacking an independent political base, and thoroughly compromised in the regime's corruption, they are dependent on the survival of the incumbent. Insiders typically have risen through the ranks of political service and, apart from top leaders who may have invested in private capital holdings, derive livelihood principally from state or party offices. Because they face the prospect of losing all visible means of support in a political transition, they have little option but to cling to the regime, to sink or swim with it. (Bratton & van de Walle 1997:86)

In game-theoretic terms, this description means that the pay-offs to members of personalist cliques differ from the pay-offs in the game between factions in single-party regimes in two ways. First, the pay-off to members of a minority faction excluded from office is likely to be much lower, in part because this faction is unlikely to receive benefits from the leader's policy choices. Factions excluded from the inner circle by a personalist leader often face poverty, exile, prison, or the risk of assassination. Second, the majority faction may actually increase benefits to itself by excluding the minority from participation. Where the main benefits of participation in the government come from access to rents and illicit profit opportunities, benefits to individual members of the ruling group may be higher if they need not be shared too widely. It may also be easier to keep damage to the economy below the meltdown threshold, and thus increase the likelihood of regime survival, if the predatory group is relatively small. Despite these differences, however, the basic logic of the game is similar to that in single-party regimes. Neither faction would voluntarily leave office.

THE EFFECT OF CADRE INTERESTS ON REGIME BREAKDOWN

The interests described above determine whether the splits and rivalries that exist within all kinds of governments lead to regime breakdown. Because most military officers view their interests as following a logic similar to that of a Battle of the Sexes game, they acquiesce in continued intervention regardless of whether military rule becomes institutionalized, the leader concentrates power in his own hands, or a rival ousts the original leader. The officer corps will not, however, go along with disintegration of the military into openly competing factions. If elite splits threaten military unity and efficacy, most of the officer corps will opt for a return to the barracks.

Military regimes thus contain the seeds of their own destruction. When elite rivalries or policy differences become intense and factional splits become threatening, a return to the barracks becomes an attractive option for most officers. For officers, there is life after democracy, as all but the highest regime officials can usually return to the barracks with their status and careers untarnished and their salaries and budgets often increased by nervous transitional governments (Nordlinger 1977, Huntington 1991).

Leaders of single-party regimes also face competition from rivals, but most of the time, as in personalist regimes, the benefits of cooperation are sufficiently large to insure continued support from all factions. Leadership struggles and succession crises occur, but except in some extraordinary situations, ordinary cadres always want to remain in power. During leadership struggles, most ordinary cadres just keep their heads down and wait to see who wins. Thus, in contrast to military regimes, leadership struggles within single-party regimes do not usually result in transitions.

This difference explains why the early transitions literature, drawing insights primarily from the transitions from military rule in Latin America, emphasized splits within the regime as causes of the initiation of democratization. In other parts of the world, where rule by the military as an institution is less common, factions and splits could be identified within authoritarian regimes but did not seem to result in transition. Instead, observers emphasize the importance of economic crisis (Haggard & Kaufman 1995), external pressure (Huntington 1991), and popular protest (Bratton & van de Walle 1992, 1997; Casper & Taylor 1996) in bringing down long-standing dictatorships.

Because military regimes have more endogenous sources of instability than do personalist or single-party regimes, they are more fragile. Military regimes in existence at any time between 1946 and the present have lasted on average about 9 years.[4] Personalist regimes survived about 15 years on average, and single-party regimes (excluding those maintained by direct foreign occupation or military threat) endured on average almost 23 years. Even more dramatic

---

[4]The data set excludes regimes formed since 1995 (in keeping with the three-year rule) and all regimes in states formed since 1990. The vast majority of temporary authoritarian interludes excluded by the three-year rule are military. If they were included, the average duration of military regimes would be much lower. Nordlinger, who did not exclude them from his calculations, found that military regimes last five years on average (1977:139).

are the differences in the ages of currently surviving regimes of different types. The average age of military regimes still in existence in 1998 is 7 years; personalist regimes, almost 19 years; and single-party regimes, 35 years.[5] Table 1 shows the average duration and survival rates of all regime types, including hybrids.

Survival rates for different types of regime also differ markedly. Only about 11% of the military regimes that have existed since 1946 still exist in 1998. The proportion of surviving personalist regimes is not much higher (15%). In contrast, 50% of single-party regimes continue to exist. The proportion of each type of regime that ended during each five-year period after 1945 is shown in Table 2. This chronological presentation reveals the effects of exogenous shocks, such as the economic crisis of the 1980s, that affect all regimes. On average, the proportion of military regimes that fell during any particular five years between 1945 and 1994 was about 50% higher than the proportion of personalist regimes and about four times the proportion of single-party regimes .

Personalist regimes are less vulnerable to internal splits than are military regimes, but three characteristics make them less robust than single-party regimes. First, personalist regimes rarely survive long after the death of the leader, perhaps because, in their effort to defend themselves from potential rivals, leaders so assiduously eliminate followers who demonstrate high levels of ability and ambition. Of the 51 personalist regimes included in my data set, only four survived more than a short time after the dictator's death or ouster: Salazar's in Portugal, Somoza's in Nicaragua, Tubman's in Liberia, and Duvalier's in Haiti. These exceptions underscore the importance of the elimination of able potential rivals as an explanation for why personalist regimes so seldom last longer than their founders. Salazar was incapacitated two years before his death and personally chose Marcello Caetano as his successor, thus lending him the old man's personal protection during the initial stage of his administration. Caetano, who lasted six years, has been described as "a follower, not a leader. His caution, legalism, and indecision proved fatal to the regime he headed. He had stood too long in the shadow of a mentor who rewarded diligence but distrusted initiative" (Maxwell 1986:112). Somoza and Duvalier passed the scepter to their sons and Tubman to his son-in-law, perhaps the only potential successors likely to be tolerated for long by most personalist dictators.

Personalist regimes arise when the military and party are not sufficiently developed or autonomous to prevent the leader from taking personal control of decisions and the selection of regime personnel. The fear of potential rivals leads such rulers to undermine these and other institutions that might serve as power bases for challenges (Linz & Chehabi 1998, Snyder 1998). Personalist

---

[5]Figures were calculated using stringent criteria for democratization. Table 1 also shows regime lengths when less stringent criteria are used.

Table 1   Durability of different types of authoritarian regime[a]

Regime Type	Average Length of Rule (years)[b]	Average Age of Surviving Regimes[c]	Percent of Regimes Surviving in 1998
Military	8.8 (31)[d]	7.3 (4)	11.4%
Military/Personal	10.3 (3)	12.3 (3)	19.8
Personal[e]	15.1 (43)	18.8 (8)	15.7
Single-Party/Personal	15.0 (8)	39.0 (3)	27.0
Single-Party (stringent transition criteria)[f]	22.7 (17)	35.1 (17)	50.0
Single-Party (less stringent criteria)	25.7 (22)	33.5 (11)	33.3
Single-Party/Military	23.8 (4)	— (0)	0.0
Single-Party/ Military/ Personal	31.0 (2)	37.3 (3)	60.0

[a]Regimes imposed and maintained by foreign occupation or military threat are excluded.

[b]Includes all regimes that had ended by 1998.

[c]Includes regimes in existence in 1946, or that have come into existence since then, that still survived in 1998.

[d]The number of regimes on which averages are based is shown in parentheses.

[e]One case classified as a surviving regime here is ambiguous: the Rawlings government in Ghana. Ghana held elections deemed free and fair by international observers in 1996 (and elections boycotted by the opposition in 1992), and voters reelected Rawlings. It might seem reasonable to classify Ghana as having made a transition to democracy at that time. The only reason not to do so is that some observers have expressed doubts both about whether Rawlings would have stepped down if he had been defeated and the levelness of the playing field. If Ghana were classified as having made a transition, it would increase the average age of surviving regimes by a tenth of a year.

[f]Six countries in this category have held elections deemed free and fair by international observers, but nevertheless returned the ruling party to power. The results if these countries are classified as having democratized are shown immediately below.

rulers rely instead on informal and often quite unstable personal networks, sometimes based on kinship, ethnicity, or region, within which particularistic favors are exchanged for loyalty. Typically, regime personnel are rotated frequently to prevent them from developing autonomous bases of support, and erstwhile supporters who become rivals or dissidents are quickly and unceremoniously excluded from office, influence, and sometimes life (Bratton & van de Walle 1994, 1997). Currently, Saddam Hussein provides a vivid example of a personalist dictator in action. "[S]enior officers have been switched, fired, executed or so tarred with Mr. Hussein's brush that they have no future outside his orbit" (*Economist* 1995:46).

The second characteristic that affects the longevity of personalist regimes is the relative narrowness of their support bases. They distribute benefits and office to a smaller proportion of citizens than do single-party regimes, and the group of beneficiaries is more likely to be dominated by a single familial, clan, ethnic, or regional group. With both rewards for loyalty and penalties for

Table 2   Failure rate of authoritarian regimes

Date	Single-Party	Personalist	Military
1945–1949	0.14^a (7)^b	0.11 (9)	0.25 (4)
1950–1954	0.0 (8)	0.0 (12)	0.33 (3)
1955–1959	0.0 (11)	0.27 (15)	0.40 (5)
1960–1964	0.05 (21)	0.19 (16)	0.13 (8)
1965–1969	0.04 (24)	0.21 (24)	0.31 (13)
1970–1974	0.13 (24)	0.13 (24)	0.20 (15)
1975–1979	0.04 (27)	0.35 (26)	0.40 (15)
1980–1984	0.12 (26)	0.14 (22)	0.55 (11)
1985–1989	0.04 (23)	0.18 (22)	0.50 (8)
1990–1994	0.26 (23)	0.42 (19)	0.43 (7)
Average mortality rate per 5-year period	0.08	0.20	0.35

^{a}Proportion of the total number of each kind of regime in existence, or that came into existence during the time period, that ended during each five-year time span.
^{b}Number of regimes in each category during each five-year period.

unsuccessful defection very high, internal splits become unlikely. But groups excluded from participation and benefits may be tempted to challenge the regime, even though the penalty for unsuccessful attempts is grave for them too.

Because personalist regimes sustain the loyalty of their supporters by providing access to material rewards, they are vulnerable to economic catastrophe—a salient fact in the current international economy. Poor economic performance does not destabilize them, since performance need not be good in order to reward those who benefit from inefficient policies. Disasters of such magnitude that public employees and soldiers cannot be paid, however, are another matter. Economic reforms that reduce state intervention and hence rent-seeking opportunities can also undermine regime support, though people are pretty inventive about finding ways to benefit from reforms.

Single-party regimes also have few endogenous sources of instability and, in addition, can usually weather the death of founders and leaders. Through their control over the allocation of educational opportunities, jobs, and positions in government, single parties can typically claim the loyalty (or at least acquiescence) of many of the most able, ambitious, and upwardly mobile individuals in society, especially those from peasant and urban marginal backgrounds whose social mobility might otherwise have been quite limited. Single parties are more likely to be open to all loyal citizens than are personalist regimes and are less likely to limit their clientele to particular clan, regional, or ethnic groups. In the absence of exogenous shocks, they are unlikely to be destabilized by either internal rivalries or external opposition, as shown by their remarkably low average five-year morbidity rate prior to 1990 (see Table

2.) Of the single-party regimes that either existed in 1946 or were formed after that date, 50% still exist in 1998.

Single-party regimes survive in part because their institutional structures make it relatively easy for them to allow greater participation and popular influence on policy without giving up their dominant role in the political system. Most single-party governments have legalized opposition parties and increased the space for political contestation. Six (in Botswana, Mexico, Taiwan, Tanzania, Angola, and Mozambique) have been certified by outside observers as having held free and fair elections, but in only two does the party seem to be in danger of losing its hegemonic position.

When faced with unexpected problems, military regimes tend to split, personalist regimes to circle the wagons, and single parties to try to coopt their critics. Consequently, violent overthrow is much more likely to end personalist than military or single-party regimes. The modal ending for personalist regimes is a coup, and insurgency, assassination, popular uprising, or invasion are important causes of breakdown in more than half (see Skocpol & Goodwin 1994). Such endings are relatively uncommon for military and single-party regimes. Coups are fairly common in military governments, but they usually do not end the regime. They are primarily a way of changing leadership while maintaining the regime itself.

Economic crises threaten the survival of all forms of government, democratic and authoritarian. Military governments are more vulnerable to economic downturns than are other authoritarianisms because poor economic performance is likely to precipitate or worsen splits in the officer corps. On average, military governments can survive only moderate amounts of economic bad news, whereas single-party governments are remarkably resilient in the face of disastrous economic performance. Among military regimes that fell between 1946 and 1993, per capita income grew on average 0.4% during the year prior to the fall.[6] Such low per capita growth is never good news, but neither is it an economic crisis. Per capita income declined by an average of 0.5% during the year before transitions from personalist rule, suggesting that personalist regimes are somewhat more resilient to economic decline than are military. In single-party regimes that broke down before 1993, in

---

[6]The most recent transitions had to be excluded from these calculations because of data limitations. The year before a transition seems to be the best indicator of relevant economic performance. Growth rates in transition years sometimes decline steeply as a consequence of chaos and violence associated with the transition itself and sometimes rise sharply in response to public euphoria and renewed optimism; both possibilities make them poor indicators of the old regime's economic performance. Przeworski & Limongi (1997) tested various longer-term and lagged indicators of economic performance on the probability of transition and found that only the preceding year had an effect. Tests of the effect of economic performance on US voting behavior have also shown that citizens have short memories.

striking contrast, per capita income fell by about 4% on average during the year prior to the transition.[7]

Because military governments are more likely to decide to step down before conditions in the country have reached crisis, military governments are also more likely to negotiate orderly transitions. The modal pattern of transition from military rule is negotiation, sometimes preceded by a bloodless coup against the military faction in power by officers determined to return to the barracks (Huntington 1991). Democracies are created by negotiation. It is very rare for them to emerge directly from popular insurgency, rebellion, or civil war.

Thirty-one percent of transitions from military rule since 1945 have resulted in stable, long-lived democracies, and another 43% in short-lived, unstable, or exclusionary democracies. In contrast, only 16% of the breakdowns of personalist regimes have led to stable democracies. Forty-nine percent of transitions from personalist regimes have resulted in new authoritarianisms. The higher average level of economic development in countries with military regimes accounts for some of this difference, but the effect of type of authoritarianism on regime outcome, though reduced, remains statistically significant when level of economic development is controlled for.

Because negotiation is more likely to play an important role in transitions from military rule than in the typically more rapid and chaotic transitions from personalist rule, it might seem that pacts would be more likely during transitions from military rule. It turns out, however, that explicit pacts of the kind emphasized in studies of the Venezuelan, Colombian, and Spanish transitions (Karl 1986, 1990) are extremely uncommon in comparative perspective, and many successful democratizations have occurred without them. Efforts to form pacts usually fail, and the ones that succeed may be a reflection of underlying political and social conditions conducive to stable democracy rather than an independent cause of later stability.[8] Successful pact making seems to require the prior existence of well-organized parties able to make and keep commitments, whose membership encompasses most potential political elites. The ability to keep commitments implies a reasonable degree of party control over the rival factions within each party. Such prior party development is uncommon in countries with little democratic experience.

[7]As elsewhere in this essay, regimes maintained in power by direct foreign military threat are excluded from calculations.

[8]The study of the effects of pacts has been affected by selection bias. Most observers are only aware of the pacts that have lasted a reasonably long time. Those that failed, such as the Honduran pact, patterned explicitly after the Colombian National Front and expected to guarantee the success of the transition to democracy in 1971, are almost never studied. The Honduran democratic experiment of 1971 was overthrown in 1972.

Although explicit pacts to share power, exclude others from office, and limit the policy space have been uncommon during transitions from all kinds of authoritarian regimes, negotiations and bargaining have played a role in most transitions from military rule. Some outgoing governments have been able to negotiate amnesties for themselves, limitations on future political competition, and changes in democratic political institutions designed to disadvantage leftist or extremist parties. These guarantees seemed very important at the time and may well have hastened the transitions. From the perspective of 1998, however, they seem less important. No democratic government has prosecuted more than a few people for crimes committed during authoritarian regimes, whether an amnesty was agreed to or not, and the majority have prosecuted no one. Korea, one of the countries in which the military was considered the most successful, has carried out more severe punishments of former military rulers than have most countries whose departing rulers were considered weak.

Similarly, efforts to manipulate the future political spectrum have proved both less effective (except in Chile) and less important than expected. Voters in the vast majority of new democracies have opted for centrist political leaders, and center-right parties have done better than expected (Bermeo 1990). Where democracies have survived, initial exclusionary arrangements have been allowed to lapse. During the third wave, threats to private property have arisen not from the left, but from ineffective economic policy, the breakdown of public order, and civil war.

Later transitions have faced different challenges than earlier ones. While military regimes, most but not all conservative, predominated among the early breakdowns, later breakdowns were much more likely to involve left-leaning regimes. In addition, the collapse of the Soviet Union simply changed perceptions; as the appeal of socialist options declined, so did the leftist threat and the apparent need for institutional arrangements to limit leftist influence.

The basic problem facing exiting dictatorships is that the agreements they make during transitions are usually unenforceable once the transition is complete. Much of their bargaining power disappears the minute they leave office. Militaries can enforce compliance with amnesties and other deals, but only if they can make credible threats to respond with violence if the new government reneges. The ability to make such credible threats does not depend on whether an amnesty was signed at the time of the transition; it depends on the condition of the military at the time the threat is needed (Hunter 1997). Former dominant parties and ruling cliques have even less ability to enforce agreements once out of power. Their only real resource is popular support.

The success of exiting dictators' efforts to lock in preferred policies or limit future political participation also depends on what happens after the transition (Pion-Berlin 1992, Zagorski 1994, Millett 1995, Hunter 1995, Ruhle 1996, Pion-Berlin & Arceneaux 1998). A number of dictators have imposed changes in traditional political institutions aimed at creating long-term disadvantages for their opponents. Most of these efforts have been short-sighted and unsophisticated, leading either to the kind of strategic voting so elegantly described in O'Donnell's (1973) analysis of Argentine politics during the 1960s or to other unforeseen consequences. Furthermore, institutions can be changed, and once authoritarians have stepped down, democratic politicians have strong incentives to change any that truly disadvantage large groups of citizens. Authoritarian regimes have successfully locked in policies only where a substantial number of citizens benefits from them. Even in Chile, Pinochet's multiple reinforcing institutional innovations depend for their survival on about a third of the voters continuing to favor conservative parties.

THE EFFECTS OF EXOGENOUS SHOCKS

Authoritarian governments need some support and a good deal of acquiescence to remain in power. A very cohesive dictatorship willing to use force can survive despite widespread opposition for a limited period but not indefinitely and not if deserted by its own cadres. Authoritarian governments, like others, need to be able to distribute benefits to active supporters and coalition partners, to achieve passable economic performance in order to sustain mass acquiescence, and to maintain adequate coercive capacity to get through the inevitable times when they fail to deliver. The exogenous shocks that undermine authoritarian regimes are those that prevent passable economic performance, impede the distribution of benefits to supporters and allies, and destroy coercive capacity.

As shown in Table 2, the rate of breakdown for authoritarian regimes rises in the context of external shocks. These shocks were both geopolitical and economic. Beginning with the second oil crisis in the late 1970s and worsened by the debt crisis, changes in the international economy made it increasingly difficult for governments to supply passable economic performance. This worldwide economic crisis hit the countries of Africa and Latin America hardest but also reduced consumption in communist Europe and elsewhere. Of the 14 military regimes in power just prior to the second oil crisis, all had fallen by 1988, about a decade later. I do not suggest that the economic crisis caused these breakdowns, but it worsened preexisting splits within the military, greatly increased popular protest against military regimes, and cast doubt on the competence of military governments, even in the eyes of officers. In the face of popular opposition and increasing internal factionalism, a return to the barracks became increasingly attractive to officers in many countries.

All kinds of authoritarian regimes were eventually affected by the economic crisis, as populations plunging into poverty blamed their governments and gradually took the risk of demanding change. As the crisis deepened,

IMF-induced economic reforms forced governments to reduce benefits to traditional supporters. By the late 1980s, regime stalwarts were losing their government jobs and facing wage cuts in many developing countries, trade liberalization was undermining the support of both labor and capital in the import-substitution sector in many economies (much of it previously nurtured by government subsidy), and various economic reforms were cutting profit opportunities out from under rent seekers all over the world. Economic reform reduced benefits to regime supporters at the same time that the crisis itself reduced acquiescence among ordinary citizens.

Personalist regimes began to fall at an increased rate in the early 1990s. As long as economies functioned well enough for personalist leaders to provide supporters with access to opportunities and resources, the supporters remained committed to the regime. During the 1990s, however, "the economic crisis undercut the material foundations of patrimonial rule: With ever fewer resources to distribute, political elites faced a growing problem of how to maintain control of clientelist networks" (Bratton & van de Walle 1997:100). Pressure from donors and lenders forced rulers to reduce precisely the kinds of state spending that had been most politically useful and to change state interventionist policies that had traditionally supplied politically necessary rents. Without these material inducements, allies and supporters deserted their leaders.

The timing of the big increase in the morbidity rate of African personalist regimes in the early 1990s suggests that these breakdowns were caused not by poor economic performance per se (which had begun in most countries at least 10 years earlier) but rather by the combination of external pressures and reforms that have cut benefits to regime cadres.[9] Although few African countries have made full transitions to democracy, many authoritarian regimes have fallen. At this point, one can feel confident that few African personalist regimes of the early 1980s will see the new century, but what is likely to follow them is not clear.

On average, single-party regimes have been remarkably resilient even in the face of long, severe economic crises. A few (in Malaysia, Singapore, and Taiwan) continued to prosper until very recently, but they are the exceptions. The collapse of the Soviet empire destroyed coercive capacity in Eastern Europe and caused a rapid rise in economic distress throughout the Soviet trading bloc. It is estimated that incomes in Cuba fell by 50% as a result of the withdrawal of Soviet subsidies (Pastor 1994). In response to the end of the threat of Soviet intervention, East European regimes fell like rotten fruit in late summer. However, many single-party regimes outside Soviet invasion dis-

---

[9]Bratton & van de Walle's (1997) statistical results might seem to challenge this conclusion, but they seek to explain democratization (defined as the occurrence of a founding election), not authoritarian breakdown.

tance, both communist and non-communist, have shown greater robustness in the face of economic crises far worse than those in Eastern Europe—an indication that the regime type has great stamina when not dependent on an external power for enforcement. Eighty-five percent of the autonomous single-party regimes in power at the beginning of the second oil crisis still existed a decade later, and 59% still survive today. The games analyzed above help explain why single-party regimes are more resilient than military ones, and thus why even serious exogenous shocks may not bring them down.

CONCLUSION

This essay began by sketching several fairly widely accepted arguments about regime transition. It then considered the evidence supporting and challenging each argument. A few could be confirmed, a few could not.

Strong evidence supports the argument that economic development increases the likelihood of democratic politics. Available evidence also supports the claim that authoritarian regimes are more likely to break down during economic crisis, though some forms of authoritarianism are more susceptible to economic downturns than others.

I found little evidence in a set of 163 regime transitions, however, for the claim that pacts increase the likelihood of democracy. They may have had that effect in a few cases, but we cannot rule out the possibility that the likelihood of both pacts and stable democracy is increased by the existence of well established, coherent parties capable of making credible commitments to abide by pacts.

Although not enough time has passed to be certain, I also found little evidence to support the idea that amnesties and other implicit contracts between outgoing authoritarian rulers and opposition leaders have substantial long-term effects. All outgoing authoritarians face serious future contract-enforcement problems.

The primary original contribution of this study is to propose a theoretical innovation that subsumes a number of apparently contradictory arguments. I began this section with a simple game-theoretic portrayal of the incentives facing officers in military regimes as contrasted with the incentives of cadres in single-party and personalist regimes. If the incentives shown in the games are, on average, accurate, then we can understand why the process of transition from military regimes differs from that of single-party and personalist regimes. Because most officers value the unity and capacity of the military institution more than they value holding office, military regimes cling less tightly to power than do other kinds of authoritarianism and, in fact, often initiate transitions.

This basic insight leads to explanations for many of the differences between early transitions, mostly from military rule, and later transitions, mostly from personalist rule. Most military transitions begin, as O'Donnell & Schmitter (1986) note, with internal disagreements and splits. Most personalist regimes, however, maintain their grip on power as long as possible. As a result, they are more likely to be overthrown by popular uprising or rebellion. Popular protest seems about equally likely to occur at some point during transition from any kind of regime, but it is often the first indicator of impending transition from personalist rule, whereas transitions from military rule are usually well underway before protests swell.

Most military regimes end in negotiation, which accounts for the emphasis on bargaining and the advantages of moderation in the early literature on transitions. Most personalist regimes, however, end in coups, many of them accompanied by widespread violence. If opposition to many personalist regimes had remained moderate, they might have survived until the dictator, or even his grandsons, died of old age. Leaders of personalist regimes also negotiate when under pressure from lenders or faced with widespread public protest, but the proportion who renege on the deals they make has been very high.

Transitions from single-party rule, though the subject of numerous case studies, have not played a major role in the comparative transitions literature because few have occurred besides those that resulted directly from the Soviet collapse. Single-party regimes under pressure from donors and popular opposition are more inclined to negotiation than are personalist regimes. Like officers, single-party cadres can expect life as they know it to continue after liberalization or even regime change. If they cannot avoid regime change, they are better off in a democracy than in some other form of authoritarianism. Previously hegemonic parties have remained important in political life wherever countries have fully democratized, but they have been outlawed and repressed in several that did not. Consequently, they have good reason to negotiate an extrication rather than risking a more violent ouster. Outside the area affected by the Soviet collapse, single-party regimes have tried to negotiate institutional changes that allow the opposition some participation and satisfy international donors and lenders, while not actually giving up control of the government and the resources attached to it. It is too soon to know whether most of these liberalizations will progress to full transitions or stabilize as mostly "free and fair" single-party dominant systems, as regime leaders hope.

Since the great surge from 1989 to 1992, the pace of transitions has slackened. Observers can catch their breaths and take stock of what they have learned. Democratization has compelled scholarly attention for at least the past 20 years but has resisted yielding up its theoretical secrets. Despite the high quality of much of the work cited here, our theoretical understanding remains thin. We have, however, amassed an astonishing amount of "data," mostly in the form of case studies. The time may have come to begin finding the patterns that were less obvious earlier. I have focused here on one hitherto obscure pattern that seems to make sense of several apparently contradictory observations from different regions. Other patterns await discovery.

ACKNOWLEDGMENTS

My work on this project has benefitted from conversations with many colleagues over the years. I am especially grateful to David Laitin, Alan Ware, David Collier, and John Zaller for their insight and attention to detail. My thanks also to Dean Scott Waugh of UCLA, who provided the research funds that made the data collection for this project possible, and to my research assistants: Allyson Benton, Johanna Birnir, Kimberly Niles, Cathy Sweet, and John Quinn.

> Visit the *Annual Reviews home page* at
> http://www.AnnualReviews.org.

Literature Cited

Agüero F. 1992. The military and the limits to democratization in South America. In *Issues in Democratic Consolidation: The New South American Democracies in Comparative Perspective*, ed. S Mainwaring, G O'Donnell, JS Valenzuela, pp. 153–98. Notre Dame, IN: Univ. Notre Dame Press

Agüero F. 1995. *Soldiers, Civilians, and Democracy: Post-Franco Spain in Comparative Perspective.* Baltimore, MD: Johns Hopkins Univ. Press. 316 pp.

Arriagada G. 1988. *Pinochet: The Politics of Power.* Transl. N Morris. Boston: Unwin Hyman. 196 pp. (From Spanish)

Barros ASC. 1978. *The Brazilian military: professional socialization, political performance and state building.* PhD thesis. Univ. Chicago. 439 pp.

Bermeo N. 1990. Rethinking regime change. *Comp. Polit.* 22:359–77

Bermeo N. 1997. Myths of moderation: confrontation and conflict during democratic transitions. *Comp. Polit.* 29:305–22

Bienen H. 1978. *Armies and Parties in Africa.* New York: Africana. 278 pp.

Bollen K. 1979. Political democracy and the timing of development. *Am. Sociol. Rev.* 44:572–87

Bratton M, van de Walle N. 1992. Popular protest and political reform in Africa. *Comp. Polit.* 24:419–42

Bratton M, van de Walle N. 1994. Patrimonial regimes and political transitions in Africa. *World Polit.* 46:453–89

Bratton M, van de Walle N. 1997. *Democratic Experiments in Africa: Regime Transitions in Comparative Perspective.* Cambridge, UK: Cambridge Univ. Press. 307 pp.

Burkhart R, Lewis-Beck M. 1994. Comparative democracy: the economic development thesis. *Am. Polit. Sci. Rev.* 88:903–10

Burton M, Gunther R, Higley J. 1992. Introduction: elite transformation and democratic regimes. In *Elites and Democratic Consolidation in Latin America and Southern Europe*, ed. J Higley, R Gunther, pp. 1–37. Cambridge, UK: Cambridge Univ. Press. 354 pp.

Casper G, Taylor M. 1996. *Negotiating Democracy.* Pittsburgh, PA: Pittsburgh Univ. Press. 287 pp.

Collier R, Mahoney J. 1997. Adding collective actors to collective outcomes: labor and recent democratization in South America and Southern Europe. *Comp. Polit.* 29: 285–303

Colomer J. 1995. *Game Theory and the Transition to Democracy: The Spanish Model.* Aldershot, UK: Edward Elgar. 134 pp.

Decalo S. 1976. *Coups and Army Rule in Africa: Studies in Military Style.* New Haven, CT: Yale Univ. Press. 284 pp.

de Oliveira ER. 1978. *As Forças Armadas: Política e Ideologia no Brasil (1964–1969).* Petrópolis, Brazil: Vozes. 133 pp.

Diamond L, Linz JJ. 1989. Introduction: politics, society, and democracy in Latin America. In *Democracy in Developing Countries: Latin America,* ed. L Diamond, JJ Linz, SM Lipset. Boulder, CO: Lynne Rienner. 515 pp.

Economist. 1995. Saddam sacks a henchman. July 22, p. 46

Finer S. 1975. *The Man on Horseback: The Role of the Military in Politics.* Harmondsworth, UK: Penguin. 305 pp. 2nd ed.

Fontana A. 1987. *Political decision-making by a military corporation: Argentina, 1976–83.* PhD thesis. Univ. Texas. 218 pp.

Haggard S, Kaufman RR. 1995. *The Political Economy of Democratic Transitions.* Princeton, NJ: Princeton Univ. Press. 391 pp.

Haggard S, Kaufman RR. 1997. The political economy of democratic transitions. *Comp. Polit.* 29:263–83

Hunter W. 1995. Politicians against soldiers: contesting the military in postauthoritarian Brazil. *Comp. Polit.* 27:425–45

Hunter W. 1997. *Eroding Military Influence in Brazil: Politicians Against Soldiers.* Chapel Hill, NC: Univ. North Carolina Press. 243 pp.

Huntington SP. 1991. *The Third Wave: Democratization in the Late Twentieth Century.* Norman: Univ. Okla. Press. 366 pp.

Jackman RW. 1973. On the relations of economic development to democratic performance. *Am. J. Polit. Sci.* 17:611–21

Janowitz M. 1960. *The Professional Soldier: A Social and Political Portrait.* Glencoe, IL: Free. 464 pp.

Janowitz M. 1977. *Military Institutions and Coercion in the Developing Nations.* Chicago: Univ. Chicago Press. 211 pp.

Jenkins D. 1984. *Suharto and His Generals: Indonesian Military Politics, 1975–83.* Ithaca, NY: Cornell Univ. Press. 280 pp.

Karl TL. 1986. Petroleum and political pacts: the transition to democracy in Venezuela. See O'Donnell et al 1986, 3:196–219

Karl TL. 1990. Dilemmas of democratization in Latin America. *Comp. Polit.* 23:1–21

Kennedy G. 1974. *The Military in the Third World.* New York: Charles Scribner's Sons. 368 pp.

Liddle WR. 1989. *The relative autonomy of the third world politician: Soeharto and Indonesian economic development in comparative perspective.* Presented at Annu. Meet. Am. Polit. Sci. Assoc., Atlanta

Linz JJ, Chehabi HE, eds. 1998. *Sultanistic Regimes.* Baltimore, MD: Johns Hopkins Univ. Press. 284 pp.

Linz JJ, Stepan A. 1996. *Problems of Democratic Transition and Consolidation: Southern Europe, South America, and Post-Communist Europe.* Baltimore, MD: Johns Hopkins Univ. Press. 479 pp.

Lipset SM. 1959. Some social requisites of democracy: economic development and political legitimacy. *Am. Polit. Sci. Rev.* 53: 69–105

Londregan JB, Poole K. 1990. Poverty, the coup trap, and the seizure of executive power. *World Polit.* 42:151–83

Londregan JB, Poole K. 1996. Does high income promote democracy? *World Polit.* 49:1–30

Maxwell K. 1986. Regime overthrow and the prospects for democratic transition in Portugal. See O'Donnell et al 1986, 2:109–37

Millett RL. 1995. An end to militarism? Democracy and the armed forces in Central America. *Curr. Hist.* 94:71–75

Moore B. 1966. *Social Origins of Dictatorship and Democracy: Lord and Peasant in the Making of the Modern World.* Boston: Beacon. 559 pp.

Nordlinger E. 1977. *Soldiers in Politics: Military Coups and Governments.* Englewood Cliffs, NJ: Prentice-Hall. 224 pp.

O'Donnell G. 1973. *Modernization and Bureaucratic-Authoritarianism.* Berkeley: Univ. California Inst. Intl. Stud.

O'Donnell G, Schmitter P. 1986. *Transitions from Authoritarian Rule: Tentative Conclusions about Uncertain Democracies.* Baltimore, MD: Johns Hopkins Univ. Press. 81pp.

O'Donnell G, Schmitter P, Whitehead L, eds. 1986. *Transitions from Authoritarian Rule.* 4 vols. Baltimore, MD: Johns Hopkins Univ. Press

Pastor M. 1994. Waiting for change: adjustment and reform in Cuba. *World Dev.* 23: 705–21

Pion-Berlin D. 1992. Military autonomy and emerging democracies in South America. *Comp. Polit.* 25:83–102

Pion-Berlin D, Arceneaux C. 1998. Tipping the civil-military balance: institutions and human rights policy in democratic Argentina and Chile. *Comp. Polit. Stud.* 31: 633–61

Przeworski A, Limongi F. 1997. Modernization: theories and facts. *World Polit.* 49:
155–83
Remmer K. 1989. *Military Rule in Latin
America.* New York: Unwin Hymen. 213
pp.
Ruhle JM. 1996. Redefining civil-military relations in Honduras. *J. Interam. Stud.
World Aff.* 38:33–66
Skocpol T, Goodwin J. 1994. Explaining revolutions in the contemporary Third World.
In *Social Revolutions in the Modern
World,* T Skocpol, pp. 259–78. Cambridge, UK: Cambridge Univ. Press. 354
pp.
Snyder R. 1998. Paths out of sultanistic regimes: combining structural and volun-
tarist perspectives. See Linz & Chehabi
1998, pp. 49–81

Stepan A. 1971. *The Military in Politics:
Changing Patterns in Brazil.* Princeton,
NJ: Princeton Univ. Press. 312 pp.
Valenzuela A. 1978. *The Breakdown of Demo-
cratic Regimes: Chile.* Baltimore, MD:
Johns Hopkins Univ. Press. 140 pp.
Van Doorn J, ed. 1968. *Armed Forces and So-
ciety: Sociological Essays.* The Hague:
Mouton. 386 pp.
Van Doorn J, ed. 1969. *Military Profession
and Military Regimes: Commitments and
Conflicts.* The Hague: Mouton. 304 pp.
Zagorski P. 1994. Civil-military relations and
Argentine democracy: the armed forces
under the Menem government. *Armed
Forces Soc.* 20:423–37

Annu. Rev. Polit. Sci. 1999. 2:145–61

ELECTORAL RULES AND ELECTORAL COORDINATION

G. Cox

Department of Political Science, University of California at San Diego, La Jolla, California 92093-0521; e-mail: gcox@weber.ucsd.edu

KEY WORDS: electoral systems, political parties, party systems

ABSTRACT

Electoral coordination occurs at two main levels: (*a*) within individual electoral districts, where competitors coordinate entry and citizens coordinate votes; and (*b*) across districts, as competitors from different districts ally to form regional or national parties. We know a fair amount about district-level electoral coordination for single-tier electoral systems. In particular, when political actors are primarily concerned with the current election and have good information about the relative chances of potential competitors, two different $M+1$ rules apply in an M-seat district. First, the number of competitors entering a given race tends to be no more than $M+1$; second, when more than $M+1$ competitors do enter a race, votes tend to concentrate on at most $M+1$ of them. We know much less about cross-district coordination, in which potentially separate local party systems merge to form a national party system. This essay focuses on the latter, relatively neglected topic.

INTRODUCTION

The laws and practices regulating electoral competition can affect the behavior of voters, contributors, candidates, factions, parties, and alliances in various and sometimes profound ways. In this essay, I consider how differing electoral rules affect electoral competitors' incentives to coordinate their efforts and resources.

Every electoral system stipulates, among other things, how votes are converted into elective offices. But any method of translating votes into seats will pose coordination problems, of varying difficulty, for electoral competitors. These coordination problems arise because there are fewer seats to be filled

145

1094-2939/99/0616-0145$08.00

than there are potential candidates wishing to fill them. Those who win the seats will be those who succeed in amassing a sufficient level of support in the electorate. One way of amassing support is by persuading voters that a particular candidate or party is better in some respect than the alternatives. But what if there are 15 possibly competent and more-or-less social democratic parties willing to enter the electoral fray? In this case, amassing sufficient votes in the left-of-center segment of the electorate will require either limiting the number of actual competitors (e.g. via joint lists or fusion candidacies), limiting the number of competitors for whom voters actually vote (strategic voting), or both. The process of limiting either entry or vote dispersion entails coordinating the actions of more than one person.

Once elections have been held, there may be further rounds of coordination, as seats in the assembly are translated into portfolios in government. ("Portfolio" here refers to any position that carries a substantially greater influence over governmental policies than a mere seat in the assembly. Committee chairs in the US Congress are portfolios, as are ministerial positions in parliamentary and some presidential systems.) The rules structuring how seats are converted into portfolios may be partly electoral (e.g. the new Israeli system directly elects the Prime Minister and puts significant restrictions on how governments are formed) and partly nonelectoral (e.g. some constitutions require a legislative vote of investiture).

Figure 1 provides a schematic picture of the coordination problems this essay considers. Within each district (*bottom row of boxes*), votes are converted into seats in accordance with the particular rules obtaining in the system under consideration. These rules set up what I call the local coordination problem. India's use of plurality rule in single-member districts, for example, provides strong incentives to coordinate entry and voting, whereas the Brazilian system (which uses proportional representation in large multi-member districts) provides weak incentives.

Figure 1 also depicts how the votes and seats from the various districts may be sorted (*lower arrows*) into a smaller number of categories corresponding to parties (*middle boxes*), before flowing into the national assembly (*upper arrows to top box*). The extent of the sorting depends both on how fragmented the votes are in each district and on whether the parties in one district are the same as those in another, or what I have elsewhere called linkage (Cox 1997). Linking some of the potentially separate local parties to form a national party poses a second coordination problem.

Once linked groups of legislators elected from various districts enter the assembly, a third process of coordination occurs, as the various parties jostle for positions in government. In this essay I ignore this problem of government formation and deal only with the first two coordination problems (local coordination and linkage).

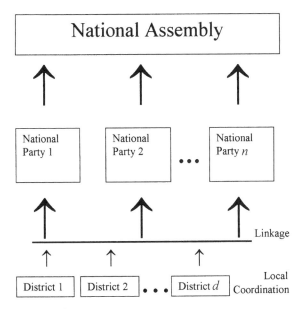

Figure 1   The structure of party systems.

The rest of the essay proceeds as follows. First, I define its main explanandum: the size of national and local party systems. Efforts at coordination can have various consequences; when they succeed, one prominent effect is that the number of electoral competitors shrinks. It is on this reductive effect that I concentrate here. Second, I review recent work concerning the local coordination problem, focusing in particular on the issue of strategic entry. Third, I sketch out elements of a research program on the understudied issue of linkage.

THE SIZE OF NATIONAL AND LOCAL PARTY SYSTEMS

Party systems are complex and can be categorized in many different ways (Mair 1996). Here, I focus on the criterion most widely used to classify party systems: the number of viable parties competing. After considering how to define and count parties, I discuss the processes that generate a given number of parties at different levels (local and national).

Defining and Counting

Although classifying party systems by the number of parties competing within them seems straightforward, it remains in some ways ambiguous. One point of ambiguity concerns how to define parties and what to do with factions and alliances. The factions of Japan's Liberal Democratic Party (LDP) act for many purposes like parties. Should the LDP be counted as a single party or as five parties in alliance? The *Concertación* alliance in Chile acts for many purposes like a single party. Should it be considered a party or should its component members be counted separately? Having decided how to define parties, one still has to decide how to count them. Should small parties count as much as large parties, for example? Although these important issues deserve continued attention (see Morgenstern 1996 for a more extended consideration), here I adopt standard solutions to both.

The standard solution to the first problem is to define a party as any group competing for election under a common label (Epstein 1980). This definition still leaves some cases ambiguous, such as Uruguay, but is a manageable start in the right direction.

The standard solution to the second problem is to count big parties more than small ones. Just as an industry with 100 firms, one of which makes 95% of all sales, is essentially a monopoly despite its 100 firms, so one might say that an election with 100 candidates, one of whom garners 95% of the vote, has not much more than one "real" candidate. The notion of an "effective number of parties" (Laakso & Taagepera 1979), is one attempt to count "real" candidates and parties. If v_j is the vote share of the jth party, then the effective number of parties (ENP) is $1/\left(\sum v_j^2\right)$, the reciprocal of the Hirschman-Herfindahl index used in economics to measure industrial concentration. The Laakso-Taagepera index has the property that, if there are n equally sized parties, then ENP = n. As inequalities in vote share among the n parties grow, ENP shrinks. Ultimately, if one of the n parties secures all the votes, ENP = 1.

The Determinants of Local and National Party System Size

Having clarified what I mean by the size of a party system—simply the effective number of parties in that system—the next step is to consider the determinants of party system size. The almost universal approach in comparative electoral studies is to calculate the effective number of parties using national aggregate vote figures. The resulting number—call it ENP$_{nat}$—is then related to various electoral system features, such as the average district magnitude (i.e. the average number of seats per electoral district) or the electoral formula (used to translate votes into seats).

What is odd about this analytic procedure is that most features of an electoral system affect politics within, rather than across, districts. Different voting options, district magnitudes, and electoral formulas directly affect the translation of electoral support into seats within districts; they do not, at least not in the simplest systems, affect linkage. Thus, theoretically, electoral system features should be related to the average effective number of parties in the various districts (ENP$_{avg}$), but they may be rather less closely related to ENP$_{nat}$. ENP$_{avg}$ reflects the average size of the local party systems in a given country, an attribute that is directly conditioned by electoral rules. ENP$_{nat}$ reflects both how large the local party systems are, on average, and how much they overlap. There is currently little or no explicit theory about how electoral system features affect the similarity of a country's local party systems. Thus, if we seek to measure the effects of differing electoral institutions, the relevant measure of party system size is ENP$_{avg}$, not ENP$_{nat}$.

Of course, some scholars may not be interested primarily in measuring the effects of differing electoral rules. Instead, they may be interested in explaining variations in the number of national parties competing in different systems (i.e. explaining ENP$_{nat}$). Even if explaining the number of national parties is the ultimate end, however, conceptually the best approach may be to divide ENP$_{nat}$ into two components. The first component is the average size of the local party systems; the larger these are, the larger the national party system will be. The second component reflects the inflation of the national party system, above the baseline level expected from ENP$_{avg}$, due to poor linkage across districts. We might measure this inflation by the difference $D = $ ENP$_{nat}$ $-$ ENP$_{avg}$ (Chhibber & Kollman 1998, Samuels 1998).

Thought of in this way, explaining variations in the size of national party systems breaks down into two separate analytical tasks: first, explaining variations in the average size of the local party systems in a country; second, explaining variations in the extent of linkage in a system. The first task pertains to coordination within districts, the second to coordination across districts.

LOCAL COORDINATION

The two main subheadings under the rubric of local coordination are strategic entry and strategic voting. In both terms, "strategic" refers to actions that are primarily instrumental as opposed to consummatory—that is, actions taken because of their perceived impact on the final outcome of the election, rather than because of any intrinsic value they may have.

Strategic Entry

If candidates and parties decide whether or not to enter a race partly on the basis of their chance of winning a seat (or seats), then expectations about who will win under various entry scenarios are crucial in determining who will actually enter. For example, if party A believes that it will surely lose if it enters when party B does too, then A will enter only if it expects that B will not.

SINGLE-MEMBER DISTRICTS   The simplest example of a strategic entry game can be constructed by imagining a single-member district with two parties. Suppose there is a single candidate for the Right party's nomination but two candidates for the Left party's nomination (whether these nominations are awarded via primary elections or some internal party procedure is left unspecified). Suppose further that, if both Left candidates enter the race (i.e. whichever loses the battle for the Left nomination enters the race anyway as an independent), then the probability that the Right candidate will win the seat is p, whereas if only a single Left candidate enters then the probability that the Right will win is q.

Suppose $p = 1$ and $q = 0$, so that the Left wins the seat if and only if it manages to coordinate on a single candidate. This is the situation tacitly assumed by Duverger (1954) and most of the succeeding literature to characterize competitive single-member districts. The incentive for the Left to get its act together is clear. The literature has generally argued that one should expect parties in this sort of situation to react to this incentive and, one way or another, ensure that only a single candidate emerges from their side.

It is instructive to underscore some of the key assumptions that underlie this analysis. First, everyone must agree that there are really only two parties with realistic chances of winning. In some countries using single-member districts, such as Papua New Guinea, this assumption clearly does not hold. Expectations there appear chaotic, with no clear advantage for two or even a small number of parties or candidates, with the result that in 1987 (a typical year) the average number of candidates per district was almost 14 (Dorney 1990:59).

Second, it is important that the Left's two potential candidates have the expectations stipulated above, $p = 1$ and $q = 0$. If one of them thinks $p = 0$—the Right will lose even if both Left candidates enter—he or she may enter regardless of who wins the Left's nomination. If both of them think $p = 0$, then we have the situation commonly envisioned in studies of one-party regions, e.g. the Solid South in the United States. The practical result in this case seems not to be double entries in the general election but increased competition for the dominant party's nomination, hence increased factional activity (Key 1964).

Third, even with two parties and common expectations that $p = 1$ and $q = 0$, it is important that both Left candidates care mostly about the outcome of the current election. If these two candidates represent competing factions within the Left party, both vying for long-term dominance of the party, then each may view the coordination game not as a one-shot affair but as a repeated interaction. Optimal strategies in repeated coordination games, however, typically entail being "tough" in the early rounds. By sending forth a candidate to do battle, even though this will lead to a bad result in the current election (a Right victory), each faction demonstrates its patience and commitment. If the other faction backs down eventually, the victor will be left in possession of the spoils for an extended period (assuming that incumbents are easily renominated). This sort of early posturing might be especially likely in highly uncertain conditions, such as those in many new democracies.

Nomination control is of course only one aspect of electoral coordination. One can put different players into the game sketched above and generate coordination problems with a family resemblance. Instead of two contenders for the Left nomination, for example, suppose there are two leftist parties. Now the issue is whether they will agree on a joint nominee. Differing electoral rules can make agreement easier or harder. Fusion candidacies (whereby different parties nominate the same candidate, with the names of all nominating parties appearing on the ballot) make it easier. So do two-round systems (see Tsebelis 1990).

Now suppose there are not two parties but an established Left party and a group that might or might not form a new party on the left. Here again the issues are similar. The more permeable the nomination procedure of the established party, and the higher the electoral threshold, the more likely it is that the group will choose to enter the established party as a faction, rather than enter the party system as a new party (Epstein 1986, Cox 1997:ch. 8).

MULTI-MEMBER DISTRICTS   Somewhat more elaborate coordination problems arise in connection with the control of nominations in multi-member districts. There is a small literature on the strategy of nomination under cumulative voting, to which Goldburg (1994) is a convenient access. There has also been some consideration of nomination under the limited vote system (Lijphart et al 1986). A somewhat larger literature exists on the regulation of nominations in Japan.

From 1947 to 1993, Japan used mostly three-, four-, and five-seat districts, with each voter casting a single vote for a candidate and the top three, four, or five candidates winning seats. This system posed coordination problems similar to those arising in single-member plurality districts. If a party had enough supporters in a district to elect just one member, then the situation essentially reduced to the single-member case. More than one faction within the party would presumably have liked to secure the seat but if more than one candidate actually entered the general election, the party risked splitting its support too thin and winning no seats at all.

The situation was not much more complicated if a party had votes enough for two seats. If at least three politicians were seeking the party nomination, and all entered, the party might win fewer than two seats; but it would rarely be agreed which of the potential candidates should withdraw.

More generally, a party might have votes enough for c out of the M seats at stake in a particular district, but $d > c$ competitors for the nomination. When $M = 1$, $c = 1$, and $d = 2$, we have the Duvergerian single-member scenario discussed above. For larger values of M, c, and d, more complicated coordination problems arise.

The fundamental issue in studies of coordination in Japan has been the parties' success. Were they able to limit their nominations? Were they able to prevent disappointed nomination seekers from entering the general election as independents? Most studies have focused on the long-ruling Liberal Democratic Party (LDP). The basic finding is that the LDP overnominated frequently in the first election (1958) held after its formation as an alliance of two preexisting parties (in 1955) but improved steadily thereafter (Reed 1991, Cox & Niou 1994). The party was less successful in preventing independent candidacies, which continued to be a common feature of LDP politics throughout the postwar era. But even here they did have some success, as overnominations in the "conservative camp" (LDP plus independents) also declined (Cox & Rosenbluth 1994, Christensen & Johnson 1995).

The LDP's increasingly successful coordination was an important factor pushing the Japanese system as a whole toward an equilibrium in which only $M + 1$ serious candidates entered the fray in an M-seat district (Reed 1991). The logic of this $M + 1$ result is a direct generalization of Duverger's argument regarding entry in single-member districts. If expectations about the candidates' order of finish in the poll are clear enough, then the top $M - 1$ seats may be "sewn up." The only uncertainty, hence competition, will concern the last-allocated, or Mth, seat. For this last-allocated seat, there are typically at most two viable competitors—the expected last winner and the expected first loser—just as there are typically at most two viable competitors for the last-allocated (and only) seat in a single-member district. Thus, one typically expects a total of $(M - 1) + 2 = M + 1$ viable candidates to enter. This result depends, of course, on assumptions similar to those underlying Duverger's original analysis: There must be precise expectations about prospective candidates' vote shares at the time entry decisions are made; and potential entrants must care mostly about the outcome of the current election (as opposed to the outcomes of future elections or non–outcome-related matters).

Beyond the basic issue of whether entry in Japanese districts has tended to equilibrate over time at $M + 1$ serious candidates, several other issues concerning the nature of electoral coordination in Japan have arisen. One question concerns whether the downward trend in LDP overnominations, and the concomitant downward trend in the average number of entrants per district, is evidence of learning or not. Reed (1991) has argued that Japanese candidates do not appear to have understood the implications of their electoral system as quickly as a standard rational choice account would have it. As an alternative, he proposes that candidates and parties were muddling through, slowly learning from painful experience, and adapting.

Certainly there are cases in which assuming that actors can correctly deduce the full consequences of a given set of rules is not warranted, and incremental adaptation rings true. However, I am not sure that Japan's experience with nomination under its former electoral system is one of those cases. The electoral system had been in use since 1925 (with a gap during and after the war).

The Japanese had borrowed a preexisting nonpolitical word, *tomodaore* ("falling down together"), specifically to denote the bad consequence of overnomination; this word expresses the problem quite pithily and came into political usage some time ago. Finally, a number of rounds of overnomination is what one would expect under a completely standard repeated coordination game, in which candidates fully understood the likely outcome of overnomination but in which expectations about candidates' viability had not crystallized. Given the uncertain conditions that prevailed in early postwar Japan, it is not surprising that coordination would take a long time. I thus prefer to view Japan's early postwar experience as a case similar to that of Eastern Europe now: There is no lack of deductive capacity, simply a lack of the clarity in expectations required to support equilibrium.

A second issue, related to the LDP's increasing success at controlling overnomination, has to do with scholarly assessments of the LDP's popularity. Standard accounts of postwar political history have routinely noted the LDP's declining share of the national vote during the 1960s and interpreted it as a loss of popularity. Kohno (1998, unpublished manuscript) has noted that this interpretation raises two questions. First, incumbent governments are generally thought to benefit from good economic times (e.g. Lewis-Beck 1988), and Japan was undergoing an economic miracle during the 1960s—so is Japan an exception to the general rule? Second, mass surveys from the 1960s show no decline in the LDP's popularity, so how does one reconcile stable polls with declining votes? Kohno proposes that the decline in the LDP's vote share was a simple consequence of the party running fewer candidates as the coordination battles in the districts sorted themselves out. His evidence is straightforward: Between 1960 and 1963, for example, the LDP vote declined little in districts in which the party continued to run the same number of candidates, but it declined substantially where the party ran fewer candidates. In most of the places where the party ran fewer candidates, it did so in response to overnomination experiences (or near misses) in the previous election. Thus, the decline in the party's vote resulted largely from strategic coordination rather than any decline in popularity.

MULTI-MEMBER DISTRICTS WITH LISTS   Thus far I have considered only multi-member districts in which seats are awarded only to candidates. Similar issues arise in multi-member districts in which intermediate seat allocations are made to lists. A good example is Chile, which currently uses two-member districts and awards seats to lists by the d'Hondt method of proportional representation. Given that there are only two seats per district, the d'Hondt method amounts to the following rules: The first seat in any district goes to the list with the highest vote total. If this list has more than double the vote total of the second-place list, then it also wins the second seat; otherwise the second-place list does.

These rules set up a clear coordination problem on the left and on the right. (Some other features of the Chilean system are secondary for present purposes—e.g. that voters vote for candidates, with each candidate's votes automatically counting for his or her list; and that any seats allocated to a list are then reallocated to the candidates on that list by plurality rule.) Suppose, for example, that the Right has about 40% of the vote in a particular district and faces a unified Left. If the Right fields one list, it will win a seat, but if it fields two lists that split the vote more or less evenly, then the Left will win both seats. The current Chilean solution to this coordination problem takes the form of two alliances of parties, the *Concertación* on the left and a variously named coalition on the right. These alliances ensure that there is only one serious list from the left and one from the right in most districts.

It is worth emphasizing that the impact of the electoral system in Chile, as in all electoral systems, falls on electoral competitors—i.e. candidates and lists—not on parties. When Chile's former dictator, Augusto Pinochet, introduced a new electoral system, the number of lists in Chile reacted quickly to the new electoral incentives when democratic elections were resumed, producing two-list competition in most districts. Because Chile's lists are joint (containing candidates from more than one party), however, the reductive impact of the electoral rules has not fallen directly on the party system.

Strategic Voting

If the prospective candidates in a district are all primarily interested in winning a seat in the election at hand, and they will not enter if their chances are not good enough, then electoral coordination may end at the elite level. For example, voters in a single-member district may be presented with only two choices on the ballot, obviating any need for strategic voting. If, on the other hand, some minor-party or independent candidates enter regardless of their chances at winning—or if the Right (or Left) fails to coordinate on an appropriate number of candidates or lists—then voters may be faced with incentives to vote strategically.

The voters who will in fact face such an incentive are those who care mostly about who wins seats in the current election. Voters who care about expressing their true preferences, or about affecting the outcome of future elections, may vote for a candidate even if they recognize that he or she has little chance of winning in the current contest.

We now know a fair amount about the equilibrium consequences of strategic voting in a world where all voters do care mostly about who wins seats in the current election, at least in simple electoral systems where all seat allocations are made at the district level. The general finding is embodied in the $M+1$ rule, which says, loosely, that in an M-seat district there can be at most $M+1$

viable candidates (in systems where citizens cast a single vote directly for a candidate) or lists (in systems where citizens cast a single vote for a list).

Because the logic behind and evidence for this generalization have recently been extensively reviewed (Cox 1997), here I make only two remarks. First, the $M + 1$ rule coincides, in the case $M = 1$, with Duverger's observation that multi-candidate elections in single-member districts tend to reduce to two-candidate affairs. Second, this $M + 1$ rule is logically distinct from, although related to, the tendency for there to be $M + 1$ candidates (noted in the previous subsection). When in fact only $M + 1$ candidates enter a race, then strategic voting is unnecessary. When entry coordination rule fails, however, and more than $M + 1$ candidates enter, then there is an opportunity for strategic voting. The $M + 1$ rule says that, under specified conditions, strategic voting will reduce contests with more than $M + 1$ candidates to contests in which at most $M + 1$ candidates are seriously in the running for seats. Thus, the $M + 1$ rule as it applies to strategic voting concerns the equilibrium degree of vote concentration in multi-candidate contests, not the number of candidates who enter. Of course, anticipation of strategic voting may be crucial in convincing some potential candidates to forego entering the race to begin with, so that the issues of vote concentration and entry are closely related.

LINKAGE

The coordinative activities discussed above all occur within individual electoral districts. The end result is a series of local party systems, each with a given effective number of parties.

The next step in the process of creating a national party system is linking the members of the various local party systems into national parties. At one extreme, each party in a country might field candidates in just one district, so that every local party system was sui generis. In this case, the national party system would be considerably larger than the average of the local party systems. At the opposite extreme, every party might run candidates in every district, so that every local party system was a microcosm of the national party system. In this case, the effective number of parties in the national system would more nearly equal the average number in the local systems.

Thus, as mentioned, the difference between the effective number of parties in the national party system and the average effective number of parties in the local party systems, $D = \text{ENP}_{nat} - \text{ENP}_{avg}$, can be used as an inverse measure of linkage. As D gets larger, linkage is poorer, and the consequent inflation of the national party system over the local baseline is larger. By dividing the gap between the national and mean local figures by ENP_{nat}, and multiplying by 100, we get $I = 100(\text{ENP}_{nat} - \text{ENP}_{avg})/\text{ENP}_{nat}$, a measure of party system inflation on a percentage basis. If I is 10, for example, about 10% of the overall size of the national party system can be attributed to different parties obtaining votes in different parts of the country (poor linkage), with the other 90% due to the average size of the local party systems.[1]

Table 1 provides some examples of inverse linkage (or inflation) scores from a sample of seven countries. One feature of the data worth noting at the outset is that the correlation between the median district magnitude and the average effective number of parties in the districts (ENP_{avg}) is +0.86, whereas the correlation between median district magnitude and the effective number of parties calculated at the national level (ENP_{nat}) is only +0.66. The number of observations is insufficient to make this difference statistically significant, but it is in the direction expected from the discussion above: Electoral system features such as district magnitude are expected to affect the average size of the local party systems in a country (i.e. ENP_{avg}), but there is no clear theoretical reason to expect them to affect linkage, hence less reason to expect them to affect the size of the national party system (i.e. ENP_{nat}).

Now consider linkage. As Table 1 shows, there is considerable variation in the inflation scores of the national party systems displayed. At one end of the scale, Austria has just as large a national party system as one would expect were each local party system a microcosm of the whole (0% inflation). At the other end of the scale, Brazil and India have substantially larger national party systems than one would expect were their local party systems largely the same throughout the nation (38–48% inflation). Between these extremes is a middle group consisting of Finland, Japan, Spain, and the United Kingdom, with inflation rates in the 7–15% range.

Explaining Variation in Linkage: Institutional Factors

What explains variations in linkage? Some likely explanations pertain to economies of scale and have the following abstract form: Some group seeks to accomplish a task that requires the help of a large number of legislators or legislative candidates; this group therefore seeks to induce would-be legislators from many different districts to participate in a larger organization (Cox 1997). Different versions of the story emerge as the task is changed. Here I consider

---

[1]One wrinkle to note here is that ENP_{avg} should be calculated as a weighted rather than a simple average, where each district is weighted by the share of assembly seats elected from within that district. If one defines perfect linkage as a situation in which each party obtains the same vote share in every district, then ENP_j will be the same for all districts j, and it will not matter whether a simple or weighted average is used. When linkage is perfect by this standard, ENP_{avg} will equal ENP_{nat} for either sort of average. If one thinks that the effective number of parties in a district will be a function of district magnitude, then a different standard for perfect linkage is suggested: If party A wins votes in a district of magnitude M, then it wins votes in all districts of higher magnitude. By this standard, there is no guarantee that ENP_{avg} will equal ENP_{nat} when linkage is perfect. But one comes closer to this condition with weighted averages.

Table 1   Some inverse linkage scores from seven countries

Country (years)	Median district magnitude	Avg. ENP_{nat}	Avg. ENP_{avg}	Avg. D	Avg. I
Austria (1994)	13	3.74	3.74	0.0	0%
Brazil (1945–1962, 1990–1994)	11	6.3	3.3	3.0	48%
Finland (1995)	13	5.78	4.94	0.84	15%
India (1957–1977)	1	4.2	2.6	1.6	38%
Japan (1958–1993)	4	2.9	2.7	0.2	7%
Spain (1986)	5	3.59	3.20	0.39	11%
United Kingdom (1955–1992)	1	2.70	2.39	0.31	11%

just two tasks: (*a*) securing more legislative seats or a better chance at winning the presidency, and (*b*) securing control of the central government.

One reason to form cross-district alliances of politicians has to do with the existence of upper tiers in legislative elections or vote distribution requirements in presidential elections. Upper tiers are secondary electoral districts, such as states, regions, or the whole nation, within which unused votes (and sometimes unallocated seats) from primary electoral districts are aggregated and distributed. From the perspective of electoral competitors, upper tiers offer an opportunity to pool votes that are wasted or excess in a given district, in a way that will fetch seats. Typically, laws implementing upper tiers require an explicit legal linkage of the lists or candidates wishing to pool their votes at the stipulated higher level. Thus, they provide an obvious incentive to politicians to ally across district boundaries. Vote distribution requirements in presidential elections, such as Algeria's requirement that the winning candidate must get specified support levels in the different regions of the country, provide similar incentives.

Another closely related reason to form cross-district alliances is to improve one's chances of controlling the central government. How much effort one is willing to exert to attain this goal depends on, among other things, how centralized power is in the polity and to what degree this power is at stake all at once electorally. Thus, one expects better linkage in states that are more unitary and worse linkage in states that are more federal, especially if state and federal elections are held at separate times. Similarly, one expects better linkage in states that are unicameral and worse linkage in states that are bicameral, especially if the two houses of the legislature are elected at separate times. The nature of the executive (presidential or parliamentary) has a more ambiguous affect. On the one hand, presidential elections may present a large and important prize that is awarded in an essentially winner-take-all fashion. On the other hand, presidentialism divides and hence decentralizes power within the central government.

These two broad factors —whether there are upper tiers or vote distribution requirements, and the centralization of power/unification of elections—seem to make sense of Table 1. Austria is the only system in the table with upper tiers, and it has a zero inflation score; each of Austria's nine districts is more or less a microcosm of the national party system. Brazil and India are the most highly federalized states in the table, and they have very high inflation scores. Finland, Japan, Spain, and the United Kingdom are less federalized, and these four have lower scores.

These observations are suggestive but hardly sufficient to establish that upper tiers or federalism are generally important in explaining linkage. Some further evidence bearing on the importance of federalism can, however, be culled from two recent studies (the only such studies currently available) that explicitly address the issue of linkage.

INDIA AND THE UNITED STATES   Chhibber & Kollman (1998) present figures on ENP_{nat} and ENP_{avg} for India and the United States over a number of years. In India, the average effective number of parties in the districts (ENP_{avg}) has fluctuated from year to year between 2 and 3. In contrast, ENP_{nat} is always above 3 and sometimes above 5. There is thus typically a substantial gap in India between the size of the national party system and the average size of the local party system—i.e. between ENP_{nat} and ENP_{avg}.

In the United States, ENP_{avg} has always (since 1790) hovered around 2, but ENP_{nat} occasionally ranged above 5 in the nineteenth century and was above 3 as late as 1912. The gap between ENP_{nat} and ENP_{avg}, which Chhibber & Kollman use to measure linkage, does not fall permanently to low levels until the 1920s.

For both India and the United States, Chhibber & Kollman also present figures on nondefense spending by the federal government as a percentage of total nondefense spending by all levels of government. In the case of the United States, there was a substantial increase in the central government's share of total spending with the onset of the New Deal, which, Chhibber & Kollman argue, explains why regional parties disappeared permanently thereafter. Looking over the full range of US history, they show that the effective number of national parties (ENP_{nat}) is statistically related to fiscal centralization. The evidence for India is less clear but the argument is the same: Chhibber & Kollman view the ups and downs in ENP_{nat} as related to levels of centralization (especially high under Indira Gandhi, lower before and after). They conclude that "the degree of political and economic centralization can influence the number of national parties in single-member simple-plurality systems" (1998:329).

BRAZIL   Another study that looks explicitly at linkage is Samuels' (1998) study of Brazil. Brazil has an even larger problem of national integration of its local party systems than does India, at least judging by the figure given in Table 1 (which is from Samuels). This is important to note, given that the previous literature has generally accounted for the large number of Brazilian parties in terms of its electoral system (large-magnitude proportional representation). But the average effective number of parties in Brazil's states (which act as districts) is only 3.3, not much more than the corresponding figure for India (2.6). Nearly half the 6.3 effective parties that appear on the national stage in Brazil arise because parties have state- or region-specific strongholds.

Although Samuels' main purpose is not to explain the gap between ENP_{nat} and ENP_{avg} in Brazil, the main theme of his work is the power of state governments (especially governors) in Brazil, the related state-centeredness of political careers, and the relative weakness of the national government and party system. He points out in particular that, during its democratic periods, Brazil has been one of the most fiscally decentralized countries in the world. His work thus fits well with the Chhibber-Kollman thesis and extends it beyond the single-member plurality case.

Explaining Variations in Linkage: Social Cleavages

If we should think of national party systems as being created in a two-step process, then we should also consider how social cleavages work through this two-step process. Ordeshook & Shvetsova (1994) and Amorim Neto & Cox (1997) have shown that ENP_{nat} is best modeled as an interactive function of social heterogeneity and the permissiveness of the electoral system. Neither study, however, empirically explores the stage at which the cleavage structure matters. Do more complex cleavage structures increase the size of the local party systems in a country, depress the level of linkage, or both?

Theoretically, there are reasons to expect both effects. At the local level, the story is simply that, as the number of distinct religious, ethnic, or linguistic groups in a district increases, the chances of malcoordination (hence of an increase in the number of entrants) also increase. Jones (1997) provides some support for this view in a study of Louisianan elections.

At the national level, the story is a bit more complex. Social diversity matters for linkage when Basques are concentrated in one region of Spain, Swedes are concentrated in one region of Finland, and Scots are concentrated in one region of Britain. But the relevant level of concentration depends on where district lines are drawn and on the relevant electoral thresholds.

To see this point, imagine a number of organized groups, each with its own political interests. Where a particular group is above the electoral threshold, it is more likely to enter as a separate party. Where it is below the electoral threshold, it is more likely to join an alliance. The groups' adjustment to local electoral realities may thus accentuate the differences between the parties contesting in different districts. Instead of parties 1 and 2 contesting in both districts *a* and *b*, party 1 contests only in *a* and party 2 only in *b*, pursuant to some mutual withdrawal pact. This pact increases the diversity of local party systems as measured by received votes, hence increases ENP_{nat}. With more permissive electoral rules and a more homogeneous distribution of all groups, there is less need for this sort of adjustment to local electoral realities, and local party systems are more like microcosms of the national system.

CONCLUSION

Electoral systems affect the coordination of political forces at two main levels: (*a*) within individual electoral districts when candidates and lists enter the electoral fray and voters distribute their votes among them; and (*b*) across these districts (within the nation as a whole) as potentially autonomous candidates and lists from different districts ally with one another to form regional or national parties. A third and final stage of coordination is less directly affected by electoral rules, namely the forming and sustaining of governments.

We know a fair amount about district-level electoral coordination problems for the simplest electoral systems (in which all seats are awarded at the district level, without regional or national compensatory seats or other adjustments). In particular, when political actors are primarily concerned with the outcome of the current election, and good information about the relative chances of actual and potential competitors is publicly available, two different $M + 1$ rules apply. First, the number of candidates or lists entering a given race tends to be no more than $M + 1$; second, when more than $M + 1$ candidates or lists do enter a race, votes tend to concentrate on at most $M + 1$ of them. In cases where political actors take a longer-term view, or where information about relative chances is poor, the number of entrants and the dispersion of votes across them can both increase. More specific and detailed analyses—focusing on either entry or vote concentration in the context of a particular electoral system—support these general observations.

We also know a fair amount about the political coordination of forces in parliament necessary to form or sustain a government. This essay has not addressed such matters but a good introduction can be found in Laver & Schofield (1990).

We know much less about the intermediate stage of coordination, in which potentially separate local parties and party systems merge to some degree, forming a national party system. This essay has noted some issues involved in exploring this neglected topic further.

Visit the *Annual Reviews home page* at
http://www.AnnualReviews.org.

Literature Cited

Amorim Neto O, Cox GW. 1997. Electoral institutions, cleavage structures and the number of parties. *Am. J. Polit. Sci.* 41: 149–74

Chhibber P, Kollman K. 1998. Party aggregation and the number of parties in India and the United States. *Am. Polit. Sci. Rev.* 92: 329–42

Christensen RV, Johnson PE. 1995. Toward a context-rich analysis of electoral systems: the Japanese example. *Am. J. Polit. Sci.* 39:575–98

Cox GW. 1997. *Making Votes Count: Strategic Coordination in the World's Electoral Systems.* Cambridge, UK: Cambridge Univ. Press

Cox GW, Niou EMS. 1994. Seat bonuses under the single non-transferable vote system: evidence from Japan and Taiwan. *Comp. Polit.* 26:221–36

Cox GW, Rosenbluth F. 1994. Reducing nomination errors: factional competition and party strategy in Japan. *Elect. Stud.* 13:4–16

Cox GW, Rosenbluth F. 1996. Factional competition for the party endorsement: the case of Japan's Liberal Democratic Party. *Br. J. Polit. Sci.* 26:259–97

Dorney S. 1990. *Papua New Guinea: People, Politics, and History Since 1975.* Sydney: Random House. 345 pp.

Duverger M. 1954. *Political Parties.* New York: Wiley. 439 pp.

Epstein LD. 1980. *Political Parties in Western Democracies.* New Brunswick, NJ: Transaction Publishers. 374 pp.

Epstein LD. 1986. *Political Parties in the American Mold.* Madison: Univ. Wisc. Press. 440 pp.

Goldburg CB. 1994. The accuracy of game theory predictions for political behavior: cumulative voting in Illinois revisited. *J. Polit.* 56:885–900

Jones MP. 1997. Racial heterogeneity and the effective number of candidates in majority runoff elections: evidence from Louisiana. *Elect. Stud.* 16:349–58

Key VO. 1964. *Southern Politics in State and Nation.* New York: Knopf. 675 pp.

Laakso M, Taagepera R. 1979. *Proportional Representation and Effective Number of Parties in Finland. Social Sciences Research Reports, 42b.* School of Soc. Sci., Univ. Calif., Irvine

Laver M, Schofield N. 1990. *Multiparty Government: The Politics of Coalition in Europe.* Oxford/New York: Oxford Univ. Press. 308 pp.

Lewis-Beck MS. 1988. *Economics and Elections: The Major Western Democracies.* Ann Arbor: Univ. Mich. Press. 183 pp.

Lijphart A, Lopez Pintor R, Sone Y. 1986. The limited vote and the single nontransferable vote: lessons from the Japanese and Spanish examples. In *Electoral Laws and Their Political Consequences,* ed. B Grofman, A Lijphart, pp. 154–69. New York: Agathon. 273 pp.

Mair P. 1996. Party systems and structures of competition. In *Comparing Democracies,* ed. L LeDuc, RG Niemi, P Norris, pp. 83–106. London: Sage. 428 pp.

Morgenstern S. 1996. *The electoral connection and the legislative process in Latin America: factions, parties, and alliances in theory and practice.* PhD thesis. Univ. Calif., San Diego. 265 pp.

Ordeshook PC, Shvetsova OV. 1994. Ethnic heterogeneity, district magnitude, and the number of parties. *Am. J. Polit. Sci.* 38: 100–23

Reed SR. 1991. Structure and behavior: extending Duverger's Law to the Japanese case. *Br. J. Polit. Sci.* 29:335–56

Samuels DJ. 1998. *Careerism and its consequences: federalism, elections, and policymaking in Brazil.* PhD thesis. Univ. Calif., San Diego. 358 pp.

Tsebelis G. 1990. *Nested Games: Rational Choice in Comparative Politics.* Berkeley: Univ. Calif. Press. 274 pp.

Annu. Rev. Polit. Sci. 1999. 2:163–88

TERM LIMITS

Bruce E. Cain and Marc A. Levin

Institute of Governmental Studies, University of California at Berkeley, Berkeley,
California 94720; e-mail: bruce@cain.berkeley.edu; mlevin@library.berkeley.edu

KEY WORDS: legislators, progressivism, populism, republicanism, libertarianism

ABSTRACT

The literature on term limits has burgeoned in recent years. This paper looks
at both the empirical and normative studies, exploring how the term-limit debate is confounded by both fact and value disagreements. We identify four
schools of thought with respect to the desirability of term limits and conclude
that, because people start from different normative perspectives, findings
about term-limit effects can be interpreted in very different ways. Reviewing
the literature on electoral impacts, we discovered that term limits have increased turnover most noticeably in the more professionalized legislatures.
The length of term limitations and the types of legislatures that adopt them
are critical explanatory variables. The implications for the internal workings
of legislatures and the balance of power are less well documented by scholars, but there is a great deal of testimony from legislators and lobbyists that
term limits have changed their operations in important ways.

INTRODUCTION

When the legislative term-limit debate began in the early 1990s, political scientists were asked to predict what would happen if the term-limit measures under consideration in the various states passed and to offer opinions on whether
term limits were a good or bad idea. At that time, there was very little serious
research on legislative term limits from which to draw. Those who entered the
fray had to rely largely on their own judgment and intuition, informed by a
small literature on executive term limits and related work on incumbency, seniority, voting behavior, and the like.

Almost a decade later, the work specifically on legislative term limits has
burgeoned. We now know more about the effects of term limits than we did

163

1094-2939/99/0616-0163$08.00

before. But having a more solid factual basis has not changed a lot of minds about the pros and cons of term limits. For the most part, in both academia and politics, positions have hardened in the intervening years. The only exception seems to be certain Republican members of Congress who, to the dismay of their followers, have abandoned their pledge to apply term limits to Congress (and, by implication, themselves). It is unlikely, however, that political scientists or their research had much to do with those conversions. On the whole, experience and self-interest are more persuasive teachers for elected officials than are the best-crafted academic studies.

Our influence on politicians aside, the idea of term limits, whether good or bad, has presented a wonderful research opportunity. Term limits are to political science what war injuries were for medical science in an earlier period. When bombs ripped open the bodies of combatants or caused unusual neurological damage, physicians were able to learn things that would otherwise have required unimaginably unethical experiments. Similarly, the drastic changes that term limits have inflicted on the body politic—especially on incumbency and the seniority system—provide a valuable opportunity to understand more about how legislatures operate and adjust to radical change. Although many political scientists do not share Petracca and Kristol's enthusiasm for the term-limitation movement (e.g. Petracca 1992, 1996; Kristol 1993), they have nonetheless profited professionally and intellectually from the fascinating experiment that it has created in numerous state and local governments.

Although our overall knowledge is better today than it was 10 years ago, as we shall see shortly, progress in this area has not been even. Because most term-limit legislation was written so that the tenure clocks for returning and new members were set identically at the time of enactment, the effects of term limits have been delayed by the time it has taken to rotate old members out and bring new ones in. As a consequence, we tend to know more about the characteristics of pre- and post–term-limitation candidates than we do about the impact of term limits on legislative competence or the balance of power between the governmental branches. Even in the latter category, however, evidence is beginning to emerge as some of the first states with the shortest limits (e.g. California) have finally "termed out" their original members.

The purpose of this essay is not only to summarize the state of knowledge about term limits to date but also to make some points about the big picture. Many predictions were offered in the early days of the term-limit debate. As was pointed out some years back, every term-limit prediction in one direction was matched by a prediction with equal confidence in the counter direction (Cain 1996b).

Some of the things that happened subsequently were as predicted (e.g. turnover rates increased). Some things occurred that, in retrospect, should have been predicted but were not (e.g. the increasing number of special elections as members left their offices early to run for other offices or take private-sector opportunities). Some effects, however, were unforeseen simply because they were harder to anticipate, such as the redistribution of power between lower and upper houses and the equilibrium adjustments that legislatures have made to compensate for the changes inflicted by term limits. This serves to remind us about an essential characteristic of our fortuitous political science experiment: It is not completely controlled in the way that pure science demands. Neither, of course, were the injury experiments that advanced medical science, which gives us hope that we will learn much despite the limitations of our design.

THE PASSAGE OF TERM LIMITS

As institutional innovations go, term-limit laws have spread quite rapidly, especially considering that they were put in place by the separate actions of state and local jurisdictions and were not centrally imposed by the federal government. As of May 1998, 21 states have adopted state legislative term limits, which remain in effect in 18 of those states and have been thrown out by the courts of the other 3. Congressional limits have also passed in many states but have so far been deemed unconstitutional by the US Supreme Court (US Term Limits vs Thornton, 115 S. Ct. 1842, 1995). A study in the early 1990s estimated that 32% of all cities with populations above 250,000 also adopted term limits, as did many county boards (Petracca & Jump 1992). In this essay, we focus mainly on state legislative and proposed congressional term limits because that is where the bulk of political science research has concentrated.

Although we refer to term limitation as a general category, it in fact encompasses a wide diversity of measures. Term limits vary in features that may have causal significance. Most important, there are variations in the length of the limits imposed, ranging from 6 to 12 years. Shorter terms, it would seem, should have more pronounced effects than longer ones, but so far there has not been enough direct attention to this (Cain 1996b). Twelve states limit by consecutive years of service, whereas the others do not. Some states, like California, include a lifetime ban, but others merely require that the office holder rotate out for a period of time. In most states, limits apply to service in a given chamber of the legislature, but in Oklahoma, limits apply to legislative service in either or both chambers. To date, there is no research that tells us which of these differences matter and why.

As the Council of State Governments points out (Chi & Leatherby 1998), the regional distribution of term limits is skewed heavily to the West. Only one western state, Washington, failed to pass legislative term limits by 1998. By contrast, Maine is the only state in the East with term limits in place after the

Massachusetts Supreme Court's invalidation of the Massachusetts term limits in 1997 (Chi & Leatherby 1998). What should we make of this? Above all, this is probably an artifact of the initiative process. In all cases but one, term limits were passed through the initiative process, the only exception being Utah in 1994. Given term limits' unpopularity with sitting members and the high level of general public dissatisfaction with politics, it is not surprising that this reform has a better chance in states where voters get to decide directly than in states where the decisions rest with the office holders themselves.

Although the debate over congressional term limits still rages, most of the ferment in the states occurred between 1992 and 1994. After winning in Oklahoma, Colorado, and California in 1990, term limits quickly spread to other states, with 17 measures passing in a span of 3 years. Even though, as we shall discuss shortly, a majority of political scientists are skeptical about the wisdom of term limits, the public's enthusiasm is indisputable. Quite possibly, if all the states had had the initiative option, term limits would have passed everywhere. Aside from perhaps campaign finance reform, no other reform has produced as wide a discrepancy between public and professional political science opinion as has term limits.

What do we know about the bases of public support for term limits? Most of the political science work in this area has focused on micro-level explanations, using survey data. The results vary somewhat by state, but there is a general consensus that partisanship, cynicism, and underrepresentation have had the strongest effects. Party affiliation seems to have mattered most (i.e. there were higher levels of support among Republicans than among Democrats) in California's Proposition 140 vote (Donovan & Snipp 1994), but it was also measurably significant in a National Election Studies (NES) survey asking about support for congressional term limits (Karp 1995, Southwell 1995) and in an aggregate analysis of 13 states that considered term-limitation proposals in 1992 (Boeckelman & Corell 1996). However, partisanship seems not to have been a factor in Wyoming (King 1993) or Florida (Karp 1995).

The evidence that cynicism and alienation influence the term-limit vote is somewhat more consistent. Donovan & Snipp find greater support among young and female voters in California, suggesting that underrepresentation may be the common factor. Southwell (1995) and Karp (1995) find that those who score highly on a political cynicism scale (measuring people's dissatisfaction with the process and outcomes of government) are more likely to vote for term-limit measures. Surprisingly, Karp finds that term-limit support is not related to dissatisfaction with the performance of the legislature specifically or of particular incumbents. Rather, he argues, it is generic distrust of the political system that matters.

Finally, although term limits per se passed in a variety of states with different levels of professionalism and various types of partisanship, there is some evidence that the harshness of the limits varied with the turnover rate in the state legislature (Chadha & Bernstein 1996). States that had experienced lower rates of turnover in the years preceding the passage of term limits tended to pass measures that were more restrictive by an index that included both the length of the term and the permanence of the ban. Even so, this accounts for only a small portion of the variance: mostly these laws seem to be motivated by a generic concern and dissatisfaction with the political system.

The finding that term limits are most popular with those who were most disillusioned with and cynical about the political system agrees with journalistic accounts of these measures and ties in with the normative perspective that proponents have taken (see below). Supporters promoted term limitation as the quick and easy solution to a multitude of contemporary political problems, from incumbency advantage to the stifling effects of the seniority system. Term limits became the catch basin for the flow of public discontent unleashed in the post-Watergate period and fed by frustration in the 1980s over divided government.

THE COMPLEX INTERPLAY OF NORMATIVE AND EMPIRICAL ISSUES

The debate over the desirability of term limits has both an empirical and a normative dimension. Empirically, there are questions about how term limits affect the incentives of legislators, the pool of likely candidates, turnover, re-election rates, and the like. Agreeing about likely effects is hard enough, but people often do not agree on the many values and goals implicit in the debate—e.g. what representatives should do in office, how expert they need to be about policies, and the role of new faces in the legislature. Hence, even when proponents and opponents agree on what the facts are, they do not always agree on what the facts mean, or even on whether they are good or bad. To someone who thinks that less government is better governance, diminished legislative expertise (if that is the effect of term limits) may be a good fact. For those who favor executive-led government over a strict division of power, a well-staffed, knowledgeable legislature is a bad fact—and so on. Discussion about term limits becomes complex because proving a fact cannot convince an opponent whose values fundamentally differ, and asserting a value does not always succeed if people perceive the likely effects to be different.

Four Normative Perspectives

This normative-empirical confusion and its importance to the debate have not escaped the notice of political scientists. Somewhat ambitiously, Kurfirst

(1996) has tried to categorize the different normative perspectives of term-limit proponents into four types.

TERM-LIMIT PROGRESSIVISM   Kurfirst's first type of normative perspective on term limits, term-limit progressivism, upholds the progressive movement's ideal of an expert professional legislature but maintains that it has been corrupted by representatives who put their own reelection and the interests of their campaign donors above the public good. Term limitation is a means to an end, namely restoring good government through systematic rotation within the framework of a still professionalized legislature. Kurfirst classifies Petracca as a term-limit progressive.

Kurfirst thought of his scheme as applying to proponents, but we can use it to talk about the critics as well. As Petracca himself has acknowledged, most political scientists are at least skeptical of, if not outright opposed to, term limits. Petracca speculates that this is because political scientists have long been advocates of professionalism and see term limits as a threat to "their self-proclaimed status as professionals; i.e. that the rejection of their advice is taken as a rejection of their professional expertise" (Petracca 1992). He also speculates that party politics and an unwarranted skepticism about the competence of voters play a role. Using the Kurfirst typology, we can locate the term-limit critics—Polsby (1991), Mann (1992), Ornstein (1990), etc—in this first category of legislative progressives. They believe that a strong, competent legislature is an important check on executive power and that, deprived of indefinite terms of office, the legislature will lack the expertise to be an effective player.

Disagreements about term limits among those who share this normative framework are primarily factual. What is disputed is whether term limits detract from legislative professionalism, not whether the detraction from professionalism is desirable. Of course, political actors and scholars do not always remain neatly within the confines of conceptual categories such as these. At times, for instance, Petracca seems to be arguing that the factual fears of political scientists (e.g. that term limits will weaken the committee system and internal leadership) are baseless, and that legislatures will not be greatly weakened. On other occasions, he seems to favor a more amateur legislature (which would put him in a different normative category). Slippage between normative paradigms complicates the debate further.

Term-limitation proponents who share the progressive perspective view term limits as a means of getting back to the professional ideal. Things have gotten out of balance, and term limits are simply a necessary means of restoring what was lost.

TERM-LIMIT POPULISM   Term-limit populism, Kurfirst argues (1996), rejects the professional legislative ideal in favor of amateurism. The ultimate goal is to end political elitism and encourage more citizen participation. At times Petracca belongs in the term-limit populist category, as do Strubble & Jahre (1991). Kurfirst suggests that those who hold this position tend also to believe that representatives should be delegates and not trustees. They may even think that the legislature should not be coequal with the executive branch.

The empirical theory behind the populist position is that term limits open up office-holding opportunities that would otherwise be closed by the incumbency advantage. This in turn brings in new faces and fresh perspectives, which serve to make the legislature more representative of the people. The greater participation by the citizenry in office holding is a good in itself, which more than offsets whatever loss of expertise and institutional memory might occur. One of the reasons, Petracca claims, that political scientists tend to oppose term limits is that they prefer stability and efficiency to participation, and he links this preference to the low regard that political scientists have for the average citizen's abilities and knowledge.

Holding the populist as opposed to the progressive perspective can matter a great deal when judging whether an empirical claim is good or bad, independent of whether it is true or false. For the populists, rotation is important per se, because it indicates that more citizens are being drawn into the process. The higher the turnover, the healthier the system and the more likely it is to respond accurately to the needs of the populace (Petracca & Smith 1990). From the professionalist perspective, an overemphasis on rotation misses an important point about elections, namely that they screen out the more competent candidates from the less competent (Mondak 1995a,b). If the screening mechanism is working properly, more qualified candidates and more competent incumbents will be reelected at higher rates than others in any given election. If so, the cumulative effect of sequential elections is to weed out the less able, i.e. a survival-of-the-politically-fittest effect. Mondak argues that empirical evidence supports this claim. Under term limitation, therefore, an unrestricted repetitive-screening system that on average rewards the ablest with reelection is replaced by a restricted repetitive-screening system that cannot filter out the weak and incompetent as adequately because it has fewer screens. Hence, Mondak predicts that term limits will produce a decline in the quality of congressional representatives.

There are two major components to this argument. The first is the greater weight that populists give to rotation in itself versus the greater importance that Mondak implicitly assigns to competence. The other is Mondak's empirical assertion that reelection is positively correlated with legislative competence. Obviously, if that is not true, then his argument loses validity. Factual disagreements can be verified and resolved, but value differences are harder to resolve. The preference for higher participation over competence or stability is the kind of value judgment that underlies stable, ongoing political disagreements. Facts will not change people's value judgments. Hence, even if the populists could be persuaded that elections act as competence filters, it might not be enough to offset the participatory value of rotation in their minds.

TERM-LIMIT REPUBLICANISM   The third perspective is term-limit republicanism (Kurfirst 1996), best exemplified by George Will (1992). In contrast to the populists, Will deplores political professionalism for destroying the distance between representatives and their followers that is necessary for truly deliberative decisions. Whereas the populists want their representatives to be accurate reflections of public sentiment, term-limit republicans want representatives to be more like trustees, acting on behalf of their constituents' best interests rather than slavishly following public whims. Decisions should be based on merits, not on career considerations and electoral pressures. The purpose of term-limit reform is to promote reason and deliberation by freeing representatives of career considerations and the oppressive need to win reelection—in effect, to insulate representatives to a greater degree from electoral pressures.

Two observations spring immediately to mind. First, one has to marvel that the same reform can arise from two such disparate justifications as populism and republicanism. The populists believe that term limits bring the legislature closer to the people and make it more reflective of the electorate. The term-limit republicans believe that limited tenure frees the representative from constituency pressures. Clearly, what unites these two positions in support of term limits is a fundamental disagreement over the facts—were they to agree on the empirical implications of term limits, they would not be in the same camp. Only their empirical disagreement binds them. This may not be unique in politics, but it is certainly unusual in analytic discourse.

The second observation is that, even granting the republican premise that limited tenure frees the representative from electoral pressures, that does not guarantee that representatives will make better, wiser, more deliberative decisions. Game theorists, for instance, remind us that, in cooperative situations, the incentives of the end game (e.g. the lame-duck term) can be disruptive. Consider the argument of Cohen & Spitzer (1996). If we conceive the relation between voters and their representative to be like a Prisoner's Dilemma, in which constituents cooperate by giving their votes in exchange for legislative assistance in the form of serving the constituent interests, then a legislator in the final period has a strong incentive to defect—i.e. to shirk—since it does not matter what will happen in the next election. Even more ominously, if term limitation flattens the reward structure (i.e. by allowing new members to rise to leadership positions much sooner), it will remove a critical institutional incentive for cooperation within the legislature, namely, the reward of leadership posts in exchange for years of loyalty. With the weakened internal reward structure will come a weakening of cooperative norms and behavior.

Whether the claim is empirically true or not, it serves to make a valuable point: Will's argument hinges crucially on an empirical prediction that might not be right. Polsby (1993a,b) points out that Will mostly "delves only anecdotally into individual actions, some horrible, some trivial, invariably assigning base motives" and ignores the fact that "Congress as an organizational entity does its work by deliberating" (1993a:1518–19). Limited tenure might not promote deliberation and concern for the public good, and, if it does not, term limits will fail to achieve Will's republican goals.

TERM-LIMIT LIBERTARIANISM   The last of the four perspectives is that of the term-limit libertarians (Kurfirst 1996). Their position is similar to the populists' in its opposition to a professionalized, strong legislature. However, there is an important difference between their reasons for opposing professionalism; whereas the populists value participation and closeness to the people, the libertarians want the legislature to be less effective in order to preserve a minimalist government. A number of the conservative polemical studies illustrate this point (Bandow 1996, Crane 1991, Fund 1990), using the following argument. There is broad electoral support for a conservative agenda that would reduce the size of government. The translation of that broad support into political victories (particularly before 1994) has been slowed by the incumbency advantage. Moreover, the careerism of contemporary legislative politics attracts those who are predisposed to solve problems through government and distorts the perspectives of those who get elected to office. Careerists are less likely to have life experiences and thus are less competent to run a fiscally solvent state. If representatives are doing their job properly, they do not need a great deal of technical policy or parliamentary expertise. They need mainly to be able to grasp the big picture. By limiting terms, one eliminates career incentives and changes the mix of people who run for office. The end result will be people in office who run government more efficiently.

Libertarians oppose the professional legislative model because they assume that there is an empirical connection between tenure and a preference for larger government (Payne 1991). Amateurism is valued not so much for its own sake as for the types of policies it is likely to produce. As noted earlier, professionalists and populists disagree about the comparative value of participation versus competence, but both, unlike the libertarians, are neutral regarding the types of policies they want to see a legislature pass. By contrast, libertarians explicitly base their institutional preferences on their policy preferences and on their assumptions about the connection between the two. Like Will's term-limit republican position, the libertarian position rests on disputable facts. Is it true that tenure in office biases lawmakers towards proactive government?

Some recent work in political science suggests maybe not (Stein & Bickers 1994, Alvarez & Saving 1997, Moore & Hibbing 1996). All three studies find that there is no relation between a district representative's tenure in office and the district's level of federal spending. On the other hand, mean tenure of the state's federal delegation may affect a state's share of federal money. Noting that there was press speculation that Washington State voters rejected congressional term limits for fear that their state would be punished by having a less experienced delegation, Moore & Hibbing (1996) find evidence in the House of Representatives that the mean tenure of the state's House delegation (but not its Senators) is related to the state's per capita federal outlays. So the factual hypothesis on which the libertarian position rests is not clearly proven or unproven at the moment.

There is, then, a complicated overlay of empirical fact and value underlying the position for and against term limits. It is helpful to separate these out in order to ascertain the fundamental sources of conflict. The intricacy of fact and value relations also implies that, even if political scientists were to learn all that they could about term limits and their effects on the political system, they would not necessarily close the gap between the different sides of the term-limit question. Indeed, some factual findings could actually exacerbate differences because the same finding could be read in different ways; proof that term limits weaken legislative competence would strengthen opposition among the professionalists (and possibly even the deliberationists), but the same evidence would strengthen support for term limits among populists and libertarians. In short, knowing more in this case might sharpen and not lessen disagreements.

THE ELECTORAL EFFECTS ASSESSED

A number of the predictions made about term limits had to do with their potential for affecting the electoral system. Term-limit professionalists (i.e. those who wanted to save the modern, professional legislature from the corrupting effects of electoral insulation) predicted that term limits would increase turnover and competitiveness, thereby weakening the incumbency effect and offsetting the influence of special interests and money.

Term-limit populists went one step further, arguing that term limits would change the incentives of those who might consider running for office, creating new opportunities for non-careerists, previously underrepresented in legislatures. Leaving aside the normative issues about whether these would be good or bad effects, the empirical question is whether these predictions are correct.

Seemingly, the most straightforward prediction would be that limiting terms should increase the rate of legislative turnover. In the simplest sense of eliminating incumbents who stay on past a certain number of years, this is true by definition. But in the sense of altering the mean tenure of representatives, the matter is not so straightforward. Whether the limit imposed by law changes average tenure rates will depend on such factors as the length of the term, the rate of turnover in the legislative body before term limits, and the opportunities for advancement perceived by incumbents. Depending on these characteristics, term limits can have either a dramatic or null impact on average turnover.

Trying to get an early handle on the impact that term limits would have on state legislatures and Congress, a few political scientists looked at the experience local governments had with term limits (Cain 1996a, Fay & Christman 1994). Because many of the local jurisdictions adopted 12-year limits and the rate of turnover in these bodies was high to begin with, it should come as no surprise that term limits did not affect mean turnover at the local level very much. The Cain study found that the mean time in office in a sample of California cities and counties that adopted term limits was already less than the legal limit the law imposed. The main target of these measures seemed to be the career politicians who remain in office for decades and seemingly could be removed only by means of term limits.

Fay & Christman (1994) also conclude that local government limits, "unlike limits on congress and state legislators, will have little effect; the turnover rates already are high" (Fay & Christman 1994). They found that only 2.3% of 2177 elected city officials in California and 2% of the 296 California county supervisors that they studied remained in office 20 years after they were first elected. Only 14.6% of the city officials and 27% of the county officials were still in office after 10 years. Revealingly, supervisors elected in the most populous counties had a measurable tendency to stay in office longer.

As we move from local governments to state legislatures, it is important to note differences in the types of state legislatures and how these affect turnover rates. Professional legislatures (full-time with a large staff) tend to have lower pre–term-limit turnover than do citizen legislatures (part-time, small staff). One study found that in professional legislatures, the percentage of members remaining in lower chambers after 6 years was 63% and after 12 years was 40%, but the numbers for citizen legislatures were 48% and 19%, respectively (Moncrief et al 1992). In upper chambers, the figures were 69.5% and 40% for professional legislatures and 54% and 26% for citizen bodies. The authors predicted, quite reasonably, that term limits would affect professionalized legislatures more.

Not surprisingly, therefore, Proposition 140 (the California initiative that imposed six- and eight-year limits on the State's Assembly and Senate Representatives) has had a dramatic impact on legislative turnover in California. Petracca (1996) reports that, between 1972 and 1992, the average turnover (i.e. the percentage of new members entering the legislature) was 20% in the Assembly and 12% in the State Senate. Since the passage of Proposition 140, the corresponding figures for the Assembly and State Senate are 36% and 17%, respectively (Petracca 1996). Another study of the California legislature also reports a 20% increase in the number of incumbents seeking voluntary retirement and an increase in the number of special elections from an average of 1 per year between 1980 and 1989 to 10 per year between 1990 and 1993, including 16 in 1993 alone (Caress 1996).

Projecting the turnover effects of term limits onto Congress is a trickier enterprise for all the obvious reasons. Any such counterfactual prediction would depend heavily on its assumptions. Nonetheless, the exercise is revealing, even if the final numbers should be taken lightly. Reed & Schansberg (1995) looked at historical turnover rates for congressional cohorts at points subsequent to their initial election. Applying 6- and 12-year limits, they project that the average length of stay among representatives would decrease from 13 to 3.8 years for the 6-year limit and to 6.1 years for the 12-year limit. Even more important, they warn of the problem of freshman superclasses, created by the lumpiness of cohorts turning over at the end of their terms. This means that there would be periods when the House would be particularly inexperienced. This problem has led one scholar to propose a staggering of terms in order to spread out the superclasses and facilitate intercohort learning (Cohen 1995, Cohen & Spitzer 1996). Reed & Schansberg (1994) also claim that if a three-term limit were imposed on Congress, Republicans would receive a slight boost—between 5 and 14 seats. Gilmour & Rothstein (1994) also project modest gains for the Republicans, especially under a three-term limit.

As various critics of these analyses have pointed out, it could well be that these mathematical models underestimate the true turnover rate, given their somewhat restrictive assumptions. In particular, there could be secondary effects that increase the turnover rate, such as the higher value of other opportunities or the diminished value of holding office in the House without career expectations. Francis & Kenny (1997) make this point in their study of state legislatures; they find that the direct effects of eight-year term limits lead to an expected turnover rate of 36%, but when the indirect effects are added, the number increases to over 50%. In addition, term limits at the lower levels (local governments and state legislatures) will likely increase the pool of potential congressional challengers, which could affect congressional turnover rates further (Fett & Ponder 1993).

Apart from turnover, many term-limit proponents also predicted that there would be more competitive races in a term-limited world than in one without term limits for at least two reasons: first, there would be more open seats; second, incumbency advantages could be cumulative (e.g. if name recognition grows with years of service). The growth of the incumbency advantage in Congress is well documented [see the seminal studies of Erikson (1971) and Mayhew (1974)]. Cox & Morgenstern (1993) argue that the same trend appears in the state legislatures, a phenomenon they linked statistically to the size of a legislature's operating budget—which is likely to be another measure of legislative professionalism.

There is some evidence now that term limits have increased the competitiveness of races. Once again, the best work on this point has been done in California. Daniel & Lott (1997) use a multivariate model to test whether term limits (controlling for other effects, such as redistricting, running in a presidential election year, the tenure of the incumbent, etc) affected various measures of competitiveness, including whether the incumbent was defeated, the number of candidates running, the absolute margin between the two top candidates, and the number of unopposed races. In all cases, the term-limit effect was statistically significant, indicating that there was a change in these indicators toward more competitiveness after the passage of Proposition 140. They conclude, "By any measure, term limits have coincided with large changes in the level of political competition, and these changes occurred even before term limits have even forcibly removed one politician from office" (Daniel & Lott 1997:182).

As mentioned above, term-limit populists and libertarians predicted that, in addition to increased turnover and more new faces in the legislature, there would be new types of people elected to office. Groups that had been historically underrepresented, for instance, would be able to take advantage of the new openings, resulting in a more representative legislature. Moncrief & Thompson (1992), however, concluded that the effects on women and minorities are likely to be more mixed. Despite more opportunities for women and minorities to be elected in greater numbers, there is an offsetting negative effect, namely that some women and minorities have had to give up newly acquired positions of power sooner than they would have otherwise. For instance, they found that women who stayed in office longer than 12 years had a 54% chance of being in the leadership of lower houses of state legislatures and a 71% chance of attaining leadership in the upper houses. Petracca (1996), predictably, focuses more on the first effect than the second. He finds that the percentage of women elected to the California Assembly rose from 18% to 25% as a result of term limits. On the other hand, he finds little change in the number of women elected to the State Senate after the passage of Proposition 140.

Petracca (1996) also examines the legislators' occupational backgrounds before and after term limitation and notes that there have been some changes. His data show a dramatic decrease in the number of legislators who call themselves full-time legislators, from 36% in 1986 to 3.4% in 1995. On the other hand, he finds an increase in the number of local government officials holding legislative office. So although fewer are willing to call themselves full-time legislators, there are still many who are following a traditional political career path up the ladder. There also seems to be a significant increase in the number of legislators who call themselves business owners, but it is hard to tell whether that is a fashionable listing in an antipolitics era or a trend that reveals something about the opportunities and incentives of serving in a term-limited world.

The increased number of local elected officials in the California legislature brings to mind a very important point. A number of the predictive term-limit analyses assumed a static model of ambition—that people built up human capital that allowed them to get reelected to the same office continuously over time. If the possibility of continuous reelection is removed, these analyses reasoned, static ambition would be thwarted, and the door would be opened for nonprofessionals. But if the ambition is not static but progressive, then careerists will still see running for a term-limited office as desirable, both because it gives them a step up the ladder and because skills acquired in one office are transferable to other offices (Garrett 1996).

A political career can still be pursued in a term-limited world if one is willing to seize opportunities to move to different offices when they become open. The problems with the amateurization hypothesis are that it assumes a wrong theory of ambition and underestimates other forces in the political system that favor those with political experience and connections. The local government official will have an advantage over the mere citizen in terms of name recognition, fund-raising connections, familiarity with the law-making process, and knowledge of how to run a campaign (Weintraub 1997). It is clear that term limits will produce more rotation in professionalized legislatures. However, term limits will not deprofessionalize politics in those states nor open up an era of amateurization.

The experience of California is illustrative. The lower house has more people who are learning on the job, but the leadership positions are going to those with prior governmental experience. Moreover, many are leaving the lower house to run for State Senate seats, Congress, and constitutional offices when the opportunity arises—hence the big rise in the number of special elections. There may be more inexperienced legislators in the Assembly, but are they inexperienced would-be professionals who are looking to move up, or are they a new breed of amateurs who are ready to get off the political track as soon as their terms are up? Recent experience suggests the former. Clearly, the next round of research needs to address this issue in more detail.

Effects on the Operation of the Legislature

A great deal of the term-limit controversy hinges on whether term limitation weakens or enhances legislative competence. Except for the libertarians, who view effective government as the enemy, most proponents believe that term limits will at least preserve and even possibly improve legislative effectiveness. The critical concept at the core of this debate is expertise. Term-limit critics argue that expertise is central to the effectiveness of a strong legislature;

without experienced members who have expertise in policy areas, the legislature cannot hope to compete effectively with the executive branch. Also, experience fosters familiarity between the members, encouraging norms of collegiality and reciprocity. Some term-limit proponents do not acknowledge a connection between experience, expertise, and effectiveness, believing that the legislature's internal norms only interfere with the legitimate ties between members and their constituents. Others, as we have said, concede the causal relationship but want it severed in order to limit the total amount of governmental activity.

Another way to think of legislative competence is in terms of a learning curve about legislative procedures, political skills, and policy knowledge. We could, of course, separate these three dimensions, expecting to find some variance across them and among new members. A former county supervisor who gets elected to the state legislature is likely to have fairly well-developed political skills and a head start in terms of familiarity with certain issue areas (local taxes, schools, etc) compared with a local businessman who has never held office before. Even regarding legislative procedures, the local official will see more parallels between the processes used in the county board and the new processes to be learned in the legislature than will the businessman or housewife with no prior elected-office experience. So, in one sense, the increasing numbers of local government officials who have chosen to run for legislative seats are an equilibrating adjustment that recaptures some of the lost experience caused by senior members terming out.

Given the knowledge with which individual representatives start, the second consideration is how quickly new members get up to speed in these three areas: legislative procedures, political skills, and policy knowledge. Those who acquire the relevant skills and knowledge rapidly are said to have steep learning curves, and those who acquire these things more slowly have flatter ones. Another way of framing the debate between term-limit proponents and opponents who believe in effective legislatures is as a dispute over the likely shapes of representatives' learning curves. If the learning curves are steep, or can be made steeper by throwing members into positions of greater responsibility sooner, then term limits might not weaken legislative competence—indeed, they might even strengthen it, as George Will predicts, by giving members the incentive to learn faster. If there are real constraints on how quickly people can get up to speed in a legislative environment, then term limits could be enormously detrimental to legislative effectiveness. As with the electoral effects, much will depend on the exact features of the limits adopted and of the political culture on which the limits are imposed; shorter terms require steeper learning curves, and professional legislatures in larger states require longer learning curves than do small state legislatures, comprised of citizen legislators, or local city councils.

One reason many political scientists were skeptical about the claim that term limits would give us greater electoral responsiveness with little loss of legislative competence is the strong evidence that learning the ropes in a professionalized legislature takes time and effort. The best example of this is Hibbing's (1991) study of congressional careers. Hibbing found that legislative involvement (measured by a variety of indices) seemed to be correlated with tenure in office and "that there is now even more variation in legislative involvement from early-career stages to late than there was thirty years ago." This was particularly true of the measures of legislative specialization and efficiency, even though the norm of apprenticeship had waned considerably in Congress and opportunities to hold leadership positions were given to members earlier in their careers. Hibbing concluded that, if term limits were imposed on Congress, it would result in "a devastating loss of legislative acumen, expertise and activity." Moreover, he believed his evidence showed that "simply doling out formal positions to the junior members who remain after the senior members have been exiled will in no way take up the slack created by these legislative departures" (Hibbing 1991:180).

As before, congressional scholars are constrained to speculate about the effects that term limits would have, because they have not yet been and may never be imposed on Congress. Hence, we must look where the light already shines to discover more about the impact of term limits on legislative competence. We must look at those state legislatures that now have had several years of experience with term limits. To date, little formal political science research has been done on this subject. With the exception of a recent dissertation (Noah 1998), no one has yet systematically studied the effects of term limits on legislative learning curves. There is, however, a growing body of testimony from the legislators and their professional organizations that political scientists can use as a point of departure. We review some of this work to point out some possible hypotheses that are worth exploring. The point of this exercise is not to argue that the testimony of state legislators and staff is unbiased but rather that it constitutes a body of information for political scientists, who can then try to develop more impartial tests of the theses offered.

It is fair to say that most veteran state legislators and leaders give a gloomy analysis of the effect of term limits on their work environments. Leaving aside for the moment the strong possibility that this assessment is at least partly the resentment of those who feel cast aside, it is incumbent upon our profession to check out the validity of these claims. Hansen (1997a:50) summarizes their views as follows:

> Legislative leaders in states with term limits give a sobering view of what term limits may mean to legislatures: no institutional memory in elected officials; discord among legislators who try to maneuver for leadership positions; disrupted balance of power in which the executive branch becomes, by

default, stronger; state agencies where career officials need merely out-wait lawmakers with whom they disagree; special interest lobbies more capable of wielding influence over inexperienced lawmakers; a loss of rural and minority influence.

But legislators also reveal another side to this story; namely, that adjustments have been made to cope with the changes term limits have brought upon them. For the moment, however, we examine each of these claims more closely.

TERM LIMITS HAVE DESTROYED INSTITUTIONAL MEMORY AND EXPERTISE
A number of legislators complain that the terming out of experienced, senior members has severely diminished institutional memory and policy expertise. Only senior staff, to the extent that they remain, can draw from the experiences of previous legislative sessions. Massachusetts Representative John McDonough said, "I think institutional memory is very important, to have people who remember as far back as possible to avoid mistakes and to have people who were witnesses to what has happened before" (Hansen 1997b). Schrag (1996), in his assessment of term limits in California, suggests that there has been a decline not only in legislators' knowledge about policy but in the quality of the information available to them. "Previously, committee bill analyses were, for the most part, objective statements that laid out the arguments on a bill.... Now they tend increasingly to be taken verbatim from the lobbyists pushing or opposing the measure, or simply from fantasy" (Schrag 1996:28).

To the populists and libertarians, these developments, if true, are not normatively problematic. Populists would say that being responsive to what the people want is more important than recalling what was done in the past, and libertarians would say that the less legislators know about the past, the better. This trend—less institutional memory and expertise—is a problem only for deliberationists and professionalists, who want the legislature to be transformative, to borrow Polsby's term (Polsby 1975). It is conceivable that institutional memory could be measured by member surveys. Ideally, the design would be dynamic, so that we could track the acquisition of institutional memory, since it is possible that new members now start with less but acquire it more rapidly. The latter is plausible because two of the adjustments that state legislatures have made to term limitation are to expand training and new-member orientation for freshman legislators and to give them committee assignments that groom them for leadership earlier than in the past. Arkansas, Michigan, and Colorado have expanded their training, bringing in former representatives and policy experts from the state to offer orientation talks (Hansen 1997b).

The National Conference of State Legislatures has developed recommendations that exemplify how legislatures can adjust by speeding up the learning process. They suggest (*a*) reorganizations that encourage earlier specialization and modernization of facilities that provide information; (*b*) more up-front training of members and more demands on staff to develop the institutional memory and policy expertise that is lacking; (*c*) stable, routinized paths to leadership that give new members apprenticeship roles; and (*d*) upgrading staff capabilities. Any future studies by political scientists need to examine not only the disruptions caused by term limits but also the efficacy of the adjustments that legislatures make to maintain effectiveness.

TERM LIMITS HAVE CAUSED A DECLINE IN COLLEGIALITY AND COOPERATION
A second concern expressed by legislators and journalists is the apparent decline in collegiality and norms of cooperation. Normatively, this is less controversial than the previous point. Except perhaps for the most radical libertarians, few if any would wish bickering and bitter partisan struggles on a legislative body. The questions, then, are whether collegiality and cooperation have been undermined by term limits, and if so, why?

Logically, the connection could go either way, i.e. toward greater or less collegiality. The argument for the former is that new legislators who come to office are blank slates, without the grudges and legacies of past disputes. The argument for less collegiality is that people who interact with one another over time are more likely to develop understandings about reciprocity, civility, and cooperation. Game theorists remind us that the incentives for cooperation in repeat game situations are stronger than in single-play games or terminal periods (Cohen & Spitzer 1992, 1996). The testimony of state legislators and journalists is strongly on the side of declining collegiality.

The California Assembly is a paradigmatic case. Schrag (1996:26) describes the post–term-limit 1995 session in the Assembly as "the most mean-spirited and unproductive in memory, a unique combination of instability, bad behavior, political frenzy and legislative paralysis." In one year, California had three Assembly speakers, two Republican Assembly leaders, two Republican Senate leaders, and three recalls. Schrag reports a higher level of partisanship, exacerbated by the attitude of new members that people in government have "screwed it all up; I'm going to fix it" (1996:27). Another veteran reporter blames the growing divisiveness on the poisonous mixture of term limits and district nesting; term limits create the incentive to find new offices to run for, and nesting (the alignment of two Assembly districts with each Senate district) directly pits colleagues against one another for those positions (Block 1993).

However, California is by no means the only state that reports a decline in collegiality. Former Michigan House Speaker Paul Hillegonds has said, "There is much more jockeying for leadership and much less collegiality.... This has an impact on the leader's ability to hold his caucus together and work on consensus building" (Hansen 1997a:50). Arizona's minority leader Art

Hamilton reports that, in his state, "there is a clear loss of collegiality and much more contentiousness between the House and Senate" (Hansen 1997a:50). Similar observations have been made about the Michigan and Maine legislatures (Bell 1998, Brunelle 1997).

This, then, is another area that cries out for systematic research. The increasing-partisanship hypothesis can be tested by examining party-line votes before and after term limitations. Collegiality, for instance, might be measured in terms of rates of cosponsorship of bills. But regardless of whether these are the best indicators and tests, our point is simply that it is, in principle, possible to measure term-limit–induced changes in collegiality and cooperation.

TERM LIMITS HAVE CAUSED CHANGES IN CAREER INCENTIVES AND POLICY HORIZONS   Deliberationists and libertarians had high hopes that term limits would change legislative incentives for the better. Freed from the need to pursue a political career and the attendant obsession with reelection, proponents (e.g. Will) hoped that legislators would spend less time on casework, pork barreling, and credit claiming and more time deliberating in the public interest or thinking of ways to keep government small. The key consideration is the incentives of a limited versus a potentially unlimited stay in office. Critics argue that term limitation proliferates the number of lame ducks, who then make lame policies. Proponents argue that limited tenure liberates the legislator from the necessity of pleasing voters when it is not in the public interest.

Once again, the verdict from state legislators is negative. Most believe that career and policy incentives have taken a turn for the worse. Gurwitt (1996) reports that legislators in the six-year tenure go through a predictable career cycle, "learning their way around in the first term; concentrating on legislating in their second; and shifting their attention to whatever job they hope to hold next in their third." Being a lame duck not only diverts the representative's attention, some claim, but it also makes it harder to get the attention of other representatives; in the words of Arkansas Speaker Bobby Hogue, "You take a freshman coming into this arena, and the first year, he's got to find out what's going on, the second, he might have a little influence over the bureaucracy, the third year he's a lame duck so why should the bureaucrats listen to him anyway" (Hansen 1997a:53). Knowing this tends to compress the legislator's time horizons. Says one Nebraska Senator, "if you've only got so many years, then you can't take on some projects that will be long term" (Hansen 1997a:53).

Measuring oversight capability and the time horizons of policy making are not simple tasks, and perhaps this is why there are no recorded attempts by political scientists to do so. In theory, the casework literature in the 1980s provides some guidance about oversight. It turns out that a good deal of oversight is informational, and its success in influencing the bureaucratic decisions as opposed to winning political credit is questionable (Cain et al 1987). Nonetheless, the ability to ask questions about a bureaucracy is important. The problem with the time-horizon hypothesis is that it rests on the static ambition theory—i.e. that people are not acting to maximize their political chances for other offices. Those doing future work in this area may want to consider whether the prospects of a career in another office counteract lame-duck incentives to some degree.

TERM LIMITS CAUSE POWER SHIFTS   Two types of power shifts are reported by legislators. The first is from one house to the other or from one branch to another. As we noted earlier, certain populists tend to prefer executive-led government to a division of power. At first glance, it would seem that libertarians should prefer coequal branches as the best means of preserving checks and balances and guaranteeing minimal government. In reality, they tend to see the legislature as the culprit in big government, relying heavily on the postwar experience with divided government (i.e. Democratic legislatures and Republican executives). In theory, however, weakening the division of power and placing more power in the hands of the executive branch could be an even more potent recipe for expanded government than the current system.

The shifting of power from lower to upper houses is one of the surprising effects of term limits. In the words of one California legislator, "it's hard to quantify it, but lobbyists are clearly going to the Senate for their serious conversations. You have to conclude that the psychological center of the legislature has shifted" (Gurwitt 1996:16). In the golden era of the California legislature, the Assembly was the incubator of policy innovation and the springboard for ambitious lawmakers (Muir 1983). The State Senate was the sleepy backwater for the less ambitious. Term limits have changed all that. The standard career path now flows from the Assembly to the Senate: the lower house is where lawmakers learn their craft, and the upper house is where they practice it.

In a sense, this is another example of legislative resiliency. Term limits have given new meaning to bicameralism. In an era of unlimited terms, bicameralism seemed an outmoded institutional vestige. Given the Court's "one person, one vote" decisions in the 1960s, one could no longer justify having two houses by the need to represent different constituencies, since both now have to be based on the equal-population principle. After the enaction of term limits, a state with two houses—one with a 6-year and the other an 8-year limit—offers a combined 14-year track. The combined tenure of a two-house career track more than accommodates the span of the average legislative learning curve.

The other important shift that might have been caused by term limits is from legislators to interest groups (Polsby 1991). We have already cited several legislators and journalists who believe that lobbyists and interest groups have been empowered by term limits, either in the sense that their expertise is more heavily relied on or because new legislators lack the institutional knowledge and expertise to counteract them. However, lobbyists themselves find the new environment somewhat unsettling because they do not always know who their friends and enemies are with so many new faces (Capell 1996).

There needs to be a more refined discrimination between types of interest groups. Groups that rely heavily on stable relationships, trust, and the exchange of information are weakened by term limits, whereas those that rely on campaign contributions are in no worse a position, and possibly even a better one, to influence legislative decision making. Common Cause concluded recently, "Proposition 140 promised a new breed of citizen legislators, independent of special interests and accountable to constituents. The reality is far different. Freshman are raising record amounts of money because they will be in positions of power the longest" (Hansen 1997a:55). Future work needs to differentiate between types of special interest more closely.

TERM LIMITS HAVE UNDERCUT LEGISLATIVE LEADERSHIP   In one sense, this is a corollary of the earlier principle about expertise and institutional knowledge and thus does not deserve extensive separate treatment. However, finding and training leaders is particularly critical in a system that relies on the decentralization of power into committees and subcommittees. It demands a deep bench, so to speak, in order to have enough individuals to take on the many leadership assignments in an elaborated committee structure and strong incentives at the disposal of those at the top to pull together diverse coalitions in order to get action. As noted above, the loss of experienced leadership is primarily the concern of the professionalists, who want the legislature to be transformative. Legislatures tend to draw their leaders from the most experienced and senior members; in 1993, the average length of service was 12 years for lower houses and 11 years for state senates, and only two states, Arizona and Maine, had leaders with less than 6 years. Clearly, 8- and 6-year term limits would drastically change the experience profile of legislative leaders.

One of the important tasks for political scientists is to examine more closely the strategies that legislatures adopt to compensate for the loss of the pool of experienced legislators. In some cases, particularly citizen legislatures in small states, the system may operate adequately without experienced and strong leadership. This is unlikely to be the case in larger states that have a history of strong, centralized leadership. There the challenge is to find a system that grooms leaders more rapidly. A couple of states, Wyoming and Florida, have for some years used an apprenticeship system that culminates in a one-term speakership. Such an apprenticeship would include giving members significant posts in their early terms so that they are ready when their time comes (Hodson et al 1995).

It may also include a designated-heir system. In the Wyoming Senate, for instance, future leaders move from vice president to majority floor leader to president. In the Florida system, candidates declare themselves candidates for the speakership for the succeeding biennium two weeks after the November election and are chosen a year and a half before they actually are sworn in. Will such systems prove to be effective ways of countering term limits? Will they work in the seven lower houses that have six-year terms? These are questions that political scientists should address in the future.

CONCLUSION

Political scientists have good reason to be suspicious about term limits. In both the normative and empirical assumptions that proponents make, there is much to quarrel with. However, the public verdict is in, and wherever the initiative process allowed these measures to be placed on the ballot, they have passed. Term limits are a fact of life at the state and local levels. The battle over Congress may go on for some time (although it is settled for now by US Term Limits vs Thornton, 115 S. Ct. 1842, 1995), but one cannot rule out the possibility of a constitutional amendment succeeding in the future. In the meantime, it is important for our profession to switch gears and learn what we can from this fortuitous natural experiment. Legislatures will probably prove resilient in the face of problems presented by term limits. Their coping strategies should be. The concept of a strong, transformative legislature is not necessarily dead if the proper coping strategies are implemented and if the features of term limits are reasonably crafted.

> **Visit the *Annual Reviews home page* at**
> **http://www.AnnualReviews.org.**

Literature Cited

Alvarez RM, Saving JL. 1997. Deficits, Democrats, and distributive benefits: congressional elections and the pork barrel in the 1980s. *Polit. Res. Q.* 50:809–32

Bandow D. 1996. *The Political Revolution That Wasn't: Why Term Limits Are Needed Now More Than Ever.* Policy Anal. 259. Washington, DC: Cato Inst. 21 pp.

Bell D. 1998. Time's up: let the experiment begin as the Michigan legislature says farewell to experience. *State Legis.* 24:24–29

Block A. 1993. "Nesting" in the Assembly

does not refer to a comfort zone. *Calif. J.* 24:25–29

Boeckelman K, Corell G. 1996. An analysis of term limitation elections. See Grofman 1996, pp. 187–97

Brunelle J. 1997. The reign in Maine. *State Legis.* 23:28–29

Cain BE. 1996a. Term limits and local governments in California. See Grofman 1996, pp. 309–19

Cain BE. 1996b. The varying impact of legislative term limits. See Grofman 1996, pp. 21–36

Cain BE, Ferejohn J, Fiorina M. 1987. *The Personal Vote: Constituency Service and Electoral Independence.* Cambridge, MA: Harvard Univ. Press. 268 pp.

Capell EA. 1996. The impact of term limits on the California Legislature: an interest group perspective. See Grofman 1996, pp. 67–85

Caress S. 1996. The impact of term limits on legislative behavior: an examination of transitional legislature. *PS: Polit. Sci. Polit.* 29:671–77

Chadha A, Bernstein R. 1996. Why incumbents are treated so harshly: term limits for state legislators. *Am. Polit. Q.* 24:363–77

Chi K, Leatherby D. 1998. State legislative term limits. *Solutions*, Vol. 6. Lexington, KY: Counc. State Gov. 38 pp.

Cohen LR. 1995. Terms of office, legislative structure, and collective incentives. In *Constitutional Reform in California: Making State Government More Effective and Responsive,* BE Cain, RG Noll, pp. 239–61. Berkeley, CA: Inst. Gov. Stud.

Cohen LR, Spitzer ML. 1992. Term limits. *Georgetown Law J.* 80:477–522

Cohen LR, Spitzer ML. 1996. Term limits and representation. See Grofman 1996, pp. 47–65

Cox G, Morgenstern S. 1993. The increasing advantage of incumbency in the US states. *Legis. Stud. Q.* 18:495–514

Crane EH. 1991. Six and twelve: the case for serious term limits. *Natl. Civic Rev.* 80: 248–55

Daniel K, Lott JR. 1997. Term limits and electoral competitiveness: evidence from California's state legislative races. *Public Choice* 90:165–84

Donovan T, Snipp J. 1994. Support for legislative term limitations in California: group representation, partisanship, and campaign information. *J. Polit.* 56:492–501

Erikson RS. 1971. The advantage of incumbency in congressional elections. *Polity* 3: 395–405

Fay J, Christman R. 1994. Hell no, we won't go! California's local pols confront term limits. *Natl. Civic Rev.* 83:54–61

Fett PJ, Ponder DE. 1993. Congressional term limits, state legislative term limits and congressional turnover: a theory of change. *PS: Polit. Sci. Polit.* 26:211–16

Francis W, Kenny L. 1997. Equilibrium projections of the consequences of term limits upon expected tenure, institutional turnover, and membership experience. *J. Polit.* 59:240–52

Fund JH. 1990. *Term Limitation: an Idea Whose Time Has Come.* Policy Anal. 141. Washington, DC: Cato Inst. 29 pp.

Garrett E. 1996. Term limitations and the myth of the citizen-legislator. *Cornell Law Rev.* 81:623–97

Gilmour J, Rothstein P. 1994. Term limitation in a dynamic model of partisan balance. *Am. J. Polit. Sci.* 38:770–96

Grofman B, ed. 1996. *Legislative Term Limits: Public Choice Perspectives.* Boston: Kluwer. 385 pp.

Gurwitt R. 1996. Greenhorn government. *Governing* 9:15–19

Hansen K. 1997a. Term limits for better or worse. *State Legis.* 23:50–57

Hansen K. 1997b. The third revolution. *State Legis.* 23:20–26

Hibbing JR. 1991. *Congressional Careers: Contours of Life in the U.S. House of Representatives.* Chapel Hill, NC: Univ. NC Press. 213 pp.

Hodson T, Jones R, Kurtz K, Moncrief G. 1995. Leaders and limits: changing patterns of state legislative leadership under term limits. *Spectrum* 68:6–15

Karp J. 1995. Explaining public support for legislative term limits. *Public Opin. Q.* 59: 373–91

King J. 1993. Term limits in Wyoming. *Comp. State Polit.* 14:1–18

Kristol W. 1993. Term limitations: breaking up the iron triangle. *Harvard J. Law Public Policy* 16:95–100

Kurfirst R. 1996. Term-limit logic: paradigms and paradoxes. *Polity* 29:119–41

Mann T. 1992. The wrong medicine: term limits won't cure what ails congressional elections. *Brookings Rev.* 10:23–25

Mayhew D. 1974. *Congress: The Electoral Connection.* New Haven, CT: Yale Univ. Press. 194 pp.

Moncrief GF, Thompson JA, eds. 1992. *Changing Patterns in State Legislative Careers.* Ann Arbor: Univ. Michigan. 237 pp.

Moncrief G, Thompson J, Haddon M, Hoyer R. 1992. For whom the bell tolls: term limits and state legislatures. *Legis. Stud. Q.* 17:37–47

Mondak J. 1995a. Focusing the term limits debate. *Polit. Res. Q.* 48:741–50

Mondak J. 1995b. Elections as filters: term limits and the composition of the US House. *Polit. Res. Q.* 48:701–27

Moore M, Hibbing J. 1996. Length of congressional tenure and federal spending: Were the voters of Washington State correct? *Am. Polit. Q.* 24:131–49

Muir WK. 1983. *Legislature: California's School for Politics.* Chicago: Univ. Chicago Press. 219 pp.

Noah RL. 1998. *The limited legislature: the effects of term limits on state legislative or-*

ganization. PhD thesis. Univ. Calif., Berkeley. 245 pp.

Ornstein NJ. 1990. The permanent Democratic Congress. *Public Interest* 100:24–45

Payne J. 1991. Limiting government by limiting congressional terms. *Public Interest* 103:106–17

Petracca M. 1992. *Why Political Scientists Oppose Term Limits.* Briefing Pap. 14. Washington, DC: Cato Inst. 10 pp.

Petracca M. 1996. *A Legislature in Transition: The California Experience with Term Limits.* Working Pap. 96-1. Berkeley, CA: Inst. Gov. Stud. 47 pp.

Petracca M, Jump D. 1992. From coast to coast: the term limitation express. *Natl. Civic Rev.* 81:352–65

Petracca M, Smith P. 1990. How frequent is frequent enough? An appraisal of the four-year term for House members. *Congr. Pres.* 17:46–66

Polsby NW. 1975. Legislatures. In *Handbook of Political Science: Governmental Institutions and Processes,* 5:257–319. Reading, MA: Addison-Wesley

Polsby NW. 1991. Constitutional mischief:

what's wrong with term limitations. *Am. Prosp.* 6:40–43

Polsby NW. 1993a. Restoration comedy: book review. *Yale Law J.* 102:1515–26

Polsby NW. 1993b. Some arguments against congressional term limitations. *Harvard J. Law Public Policy* 16:101–7

Reed WR, Schansberg DE. 1994. An analysis of the impact of congressional term limits. *Econ. Inq.* 32:79–91

Reed WR, Schansberg DE. 1995. The House under term limits: focusing on the big picture. *Soc. Sci. Q.* 76:734—40

Schrag P. 1996. The populist road to hell. *Am. Prosp.* 24:24–30

Southwell P. 1995. "Throwing the rascals out" versus "throwing in the towel": alienation, support for term limits, and congressional voting behavior. *Soc. Sci. Q.* 76:741–48

Stein RM, Bickers KN. 1994. Congressional elections and the pork barrel. *J. Polit.* 56: 377–400

Strubble R, Jahre ZW. 1991. Rotation in office: rapid but restricted to the House. *Polit. Sci. Polit.* 24:34–37

Literature Consulted But Not Cited

Ainsworth B. 1993. Battle of the branches: the Supreme Court vs. the legislature. *Calif. J.* 24:21–23

Barcellona MM, Grose AP. 1994. *Term Limits: a Political Dilemma.* San Francisco: Westrends. 18 pp.

Benjamin G, Malbin MJ. 1992. *Limiting Legislative Terms.* Washington, DC: Congr. Q. Books. 324 pp.

Block A. 1989. The puzzling lack of leadership. *Calif. J.* 20:233–37

Boeckelman KA. 1993. Term limitation, responsiveness, and the public interest. *Polity* 26:189–205

Bond J. 1995. *Temporizing Term Limits: the Speaker Likes 12 Years, Not 6.* Briefing Pap. 22. Washington, DC: Cato Inst. 10 pp.

Borland J. 1996. Third house rising. *Calif. J.* 27:28–31

Borland J. 1997. Stopping the clock. *Calif. J.* 28:36–41

Brown W. 1991. Legislative term limits: altering the balance of power. *J. Law Polit.* 7:747–55

Calamita FP. 1992. Solving voters' dilemma:

the case for legislative term-limitation. *J. Law Polit.* 8:559–607

Carey JM. 1996. *Term Limits and Legislative Representation.* New York/London: Cambridge Univ. Press 216 pp.

Carey JM, Niemi RG, Powell LW. 1998. The effects of term limits on state legislatures. *Legis. Stud. Q.* 23:271–300

Copland GW, Rausch JD. 1993. Sendin' 'em home early: Oklahoma and legislative term limitations. *Okla. Polit.* 2:33–50

Corwin E. 1991. Limits on legislative terms: legal and policy implications. *Harvard J. Legis.* 28:569–608

Cox G, Morgenstern S. 1995. The incumbency advantage in multimember districts: evidence from US states. *Legisl. Stud. Q.* 20: 329–49

Coyne JK, Fund JH. 1992. *Cleaning House: America's Campaign for Term Limits.* Washington, DC: Regnery Gateway. 235 pp.

Crane EH, Pilon R. 1994. *The Politics and Law of Term Limits.* Washington, DC: Cato Inst. 162 pp.

Dillon R, DuBay A, Yee BT. 1990. *Proposition 140: The Schabarum Initiative, Analysis of Provisions and Implications. Sacramento: Calif. Senate Off. Res. 72 pp.

Dire A. 1998. The clock strikes 12 in Colorado: the term-limits law has just about wiped out the top legislative leadership in the Centennial State. State Legis. 24: 32–38

Elving R. 1990. Congress braces for fallout from state measures. Congr. Q.Wkly. Rep. 48:3144–47

Elving R. 1991. Foley helps put the brakes on drive for term limits. Congr. Wkly. Rep. 49:3261–64

Elving R. 1991. National drive to limit terms casts shadow over congress. Congr. Q. Wkly. Rep. 49:3101–6

Ericson S. 1993. A bulwark against faction: James Madison's case for term limits. Policy Rev. 63:76–78

Foster D. 1994. The lame-duck state. State Legis. 20:32–39

Fowler L. 1995. Why history hates term limits. State Gov. News 38:14–16

Frenzel B. 1992. Term limits and the immortal Congress: how to make congressional elections competitive again. Brookings Rev. 10:18–22

Fund JH. 1991. Term Limits for New York State: Expanding Democracy Through a Citizen Legislature. Albany, NY: Empire Found. Policy Res. 19 pp.

Gilmour J, Rothstein P. 1996. A dynamic model of loss, retirement, and tenure in the US House of Representatives. J. Polit. 58: 54–68

Glaeser EL. 1997. Self-imposed term limits. Public Choice 93:389–94

Gorush N, Guzman M. 1992. Will the Gentleman Please Yield?: A Defense of the Constitutionality of State-Imposed Term Limitations. Policy Anal. 178. Washington, DC: Cato Inst. 32 pp.

Hansen K. 1997. Living with the limits. State Legis. 23:13–19

Hickok EW. 1992. The Reform of the State Legislatures and the Changing Character of Representation. Lanham, MD: Univ. Press Am. 159 pp.

Hummel M. 1998. The empire strikes back: a history of political and judicial attacks on term limits. Term Limits Outlook Ser. 6. Washington, DC: US Term Limits. 54 pp.

Katches M, Weintraub D. 1997. The tremors of term limits. State Legis. 23:21–25

Katz J. 1991. The uncharted realm of term limitation. Governing 4:35–39

Kesler C. 1990. Bad house keeping: the case against congressional term limits. Polit. Rev. 53:20–25

Klein M. 1989. The Twenty-Second Amendment: Term Limitation in the Executive Branch. Washington, DC: Am. Limit Congr. Terms. 7 pp.

Klein M. 1989. Limiting Congressional Terms: an Historical Perspective. Washington, DC: Am. Limit Congr. Terms 8 pp.

Kobach, K. 1994. Rethinking Article V: term limits and the Seventeenth and Nineteenth Amendments. Yale Law J. 103:1971–2007

Kurtz K. 1992. Limiting terms: what's in store? State Legis. 18:32–34

Lee L. 1994. The end of an era in Ohio. State Legis. 20:24–29

Lewis C. 1991. The Proposition 140 aftermath: was the golden handshake a boon or a bust? Calif. J. 22:249–54

Mitchell CD. 1991. Limiting congressional terms: a return to fundamental democracy. J. Law Polit. 7:733–46

Montgomery P. 1990. Should congressional terms be limited? Common Cause Mag. 16:31–33

Moore D. 1995. Failure of term limits bill unlikely to cause repercussions. Gallup Poll Mon. 355:15–16

Peery G. 1996. Transcending term limits. State Legis. 22:20–25

Petracca M. 1993. A new defense of state-imposed congressional term limits. Polit. Sci.Polit. 26:700–5

Petracca M. 1995. A comment on "elections as filters". Polit. Res. Q. 48:729–40

Petracca M, O'Brien KM. 1994. Municipal term limits in Orange County, California. Natl. Civic Rev. 83:183–95

Price C. 1993. Advocacy in the age of term limits: lobbying after Proposition 140. Calif. J. 24:31–34

Price C, Bacciocco E. 1994. Is this a far, far better thing than we have ever done before? Calif. J. 21:497–99

Reed WR, Schansberg DE. 1996. Term limits, responsiveness and the failures of increased competition. In Legislative Term Limits: Public Choice Perspectives, ed. B Grofman, pp. 101–16. Boston: Kluwer

Reed WR, Schansberg DE, Wilbanks J, Zhu Z. 1998. The relationship between congressional spending and tenure with an application to term limits. Public Choice 94:85–104

Scott S. 1996. Sacramento's Youth Movement. Calif. J. 27:16–21

Southwell P, Waquespack D. 1997. Support for term limits and voting behavior in congressional elections. Soc. Sci. J. 34: 81–89

Squire P. 1992. Legislative professionalization and membership diversity in state legislatures. Legis. Stud. Q. 17:69–79

Sullivan K. 1995. Dueling sovereignties: US Term Limits, Inc. *v* Thornton. *Harvard Law Rev.* 109:78–109

Thomas JC. 1995. The term limitations movement in US cities. *Natl. Civic Rev.* 81:155–74 *U.S. Term Limits v. Thornton*, 115 *S. Ct.* 1842 (1995). St. Paul, MN: West

Weintraub D. 1991. Limits stand in California. *State Legis.* 17:12–13

Weintraub D. 1994. California leaders look at limits. *State Legis.* 20:40–44

Annu. Rev. Polit. Sci. 1999. 2:189–210

MISPERCEPTIONS ABOUT PERCEPTUAL BIAS

Alan Gerber and Donald Green

Department of Political Science, Yale University, New Haven, Connecticut 06520;
e-mail: alan.gerber@yale.edu; donald.green@yale.edu

KEY WORDS: learning, public opinion, cognition, bias, Bayes' rule

ABSTRACT

Do people assimilate new information in an efficient and unbiased manner—that is, do they update prior beliefs in accordance with Bayes' rule? Or are they selective in the way that they gather and absorb new information? Although many classic studies in political science and psychology contend that people resist discordant information, more recent research has tended to call the selective perception hypothesis into question. We synthesize the literatures on biased assimilation and belief polarization using a formal model that encompasses both Bayesian and biased learning. The analysis reveals (*a*) the conditions under which these phenomena may be consistent with Bayesian learning, (*b*) the methodological inadequacy of certain research designs that fail to control for preferences or prior information, and (*c*) the limited support that exists for the more extreme variants of the selective perception hypothesis.

INTRODUCTION

Central to the study of democratic politics is the subject of how voters learn. Politics is an unending stream of events, and each day the public is presented with news about the economy, current policy concerns, scandal, and a welter of other information. Granted, much of what appears in the first section of the newspaper fails to attract the attention of the typical citizen (Neuman 1986; Patterson & McClure 1976). Granted, too, relatively few people possess detailed knowledge of political terminology or proper nouns, and many are grossly misinformed about the amounts that government spends on foreign aid or welfare (Delli Carpini & Keeter 1996). Nonetheless, the public does seem to update its perceptions in the wake of events. When unemployment rises, the public's assessment of economic conditions sours, and when economic opti-

189

1094-2939/99/0616-0189$08.00

mism fades, the public's evaluation of presidential performance deteriorates (Tufte 1976). As expenditures on national defense change or as crime policies become more draconian, the public alters its desire to press government action further in these areas (Page & Shapiro 1992). Hunger for tax cuts seems to subside after tax rates fall (Sears & Citrin 1985). Learning seems to occur. The question is, what kind of learning?

Do people assimilate new information in an efficient and unbiased manner—that is, do they update their prior beliefs in accordance with Bayes' rule? Or are they selective in the way that they gather and absorb new information? A Bayesian public may be ignorant or inattentive, but it is not incapable of being persuaded by new information. If the economy's vital signs are widely reported to be deteriorating during a Democratic administration, Democratic and Republican voters with equivalent amounts of prior information will both tend to revise downward their assessment of the Democrats' economic stewardship. Democrats might greet the bad economic news with disappointment, but they nonetheless acknowledge its implications when evaluating political leaders.

For decades, leading scholars of electoral politics have argued that voter learning departs from this Bayesian characterization. One set of claims, which falls under the heading of selective perception, holds that citizens' interpretations of events are slanted toward their previously held convictions. Evidence for this phenomenon is drawn from a variety of sources. In Lord et al's classic experiment (1979), opponents of the death penalty were more likely to find fault with a study suggesting that it deters serious crime; death penalty supporters were similarly resistant to a study that drew the opposite conclusion. In fact, exposure to discordant evidence only made people more set in their ways. In a similar vein, several studies have found that viewers of presidential debates tend to think that their predebate favorite carried the day (Katz & Feldman 1962, Sigelman & Sigelman 1984). The economy is given more favorable marks by supporters of the incumbent president (Kinder & Mebane 1983), and people of different ideological stripe harbor different impressions about who is or is not a credible source of factual information (Sears 1969).

The most influential statement of the hypothesis that citizens with different political orientations form different impressions of the same set of facts concerns the distorting influences of partisan attachments. "Identification with a party," Campbell et al contend (1960:133), "raises a perceptual screen through which the individual tends to see what is favorable to his partisan orientation." Important recent work by Zaller (1992) extends this argument, proposing that, among the more politically aware segments of the public, "partisan resistance" causes voters to filter out information when it does not conform to their existing political predispositions. If this politically aware subset of the public is sufficiently large, a flurry of new information will generate a polarization of public opinion, since "people tend to accept what is congenial to their partisan values and to reject what is not" (Zaller 1992:241; see also 1992:144).[1]

In part, this characterization of partisan biases reflects the extensive research literatures in psychology concerning persuasion and the persistence of attitudes. Early work on selective perception emphasized the cognitive costs of holding inconsistent views (Festinger 1957). By this account, an individual is motivated by a desire to maintain harmony among his or her beliefs. Merrill & Lowenstein (1971:226–27) wrote,

> The sensible individual...will build up his own complex 'safety mechanism' for screening information; he will see less and less that does not agree with his dominant dispositions (selective exposure)...he uses propaganda to simply reinforce—not challenge—his basic attitudes and predispositions. If he did not do this, he would quickly fly into a million emotional pieces in the face of unverifiable and disharmonic information and opinion that surround him every day.

Later, psychologists such as Nisbett & Ross (1980) downplayed the role of consistency-seeking motivation and emphasized instead cognitive biases in the ways that self-styled "objective" observers interpret evidence. Currently, psychologists who argue on behalf of selective perception tend to cite both motivational and cognitive mechanisms (e.g. Pomerantz et al 1995).

Theories of biased learning in political science also draw upon a much deeper tradition of skepticism about human capacities for objectivity. Francis Bacon's view that "human understanding when it has once adopted an opinion (either as being received opinion or as being agreeable to itself) draws all things else to support and agree with it" (quoted in Lundgren & Prislin 1998:715) is echoed in Madison's [1937 (1787):56] observation, "No man is allowed to be a judge in his own cause because his interest would certainly bias his judgment." Stubbornness and self-interest cause people to hew to facts that confirm what they wish to believe. As a consequence, beliefs are not easily altered through reasoned, dispassionate discussion of evidence.

---

[1]A related form of biased learning is selective exposure, the tendency to expose oneself to evidence and viewpoints with which one is predisposed to agree. Supporters of Christian fundamentalism are more likely to tune in to church-sponsored cable news networks and less likely to read *Mother Jones*. Selectivity may be deliberate or incidental. Some liberals may make a conscious effort to avoid the blandishments of conservative radio commentators; others may find themselves in areas or social milieux where conservative views are simply absent from the airwaves or casual conversation. Like selective perception, selective exposure acts to reinforce existing beliefs. If conservative media are more likely to attract Republican viewers and more likely to present and emphasize information that is damaging to a Democratic administration, the net effect, according to this theory, will be to amplify the audience's negative assessments of the president. And if the converse process occurs among liberal media and Democratic audiences, the electorate as a whole becomes more polarized by the flow of information. Empirical studies summarized by Sears (1969), Sears & Whitney (1973), Chaffee & Miyo (1983), and Frey (1986) tend to offer little support to the notion that citizens avoid or seek political information depending on its anticipated content.

Whatever its cognitive or motivational origins, selective perception implies that when the political fortunes wane for one party, its supporters nonetheless maintain their prior beliefs and evaluations; supporters of the other party, on the other hand, absorb the favorable news. This asymmetry widens the gap between the perceptions of Democrats and Republicans. As Berelson et al (1954:223) explain in their classic book *Voting,*

> The more intensely one holds a vote position, the more likely he is to see the political environment as favorable to himself, as conforming to his own beliefs. He is less likely to perceive uncongenial and contradictory events or points of view and hence presumably less likely to revise his own original position. In this manner, perception can play a major role in the spiraling effect of political reinforcement.

This "spiraling effect of political reinforcement" is the opposite of what a Bayesian model would predict about the trajectory of partisans' opinions over time. The Bayesian hypothesis holds that new information moves people with different partisan affinities (but similar levels of prior information) in the same direction and to approximately the same extent.

The purpose of this review essay is to situate the existing research on political learning within an analytic framework that encompasses both the Bayesian and biased learning perspectives.[2] In the first section, we explicate the Bayesian model. Next, we relax some of its assumptions in order to accommodate the hypothesis that people resist or ignore information that is at variance with their prior views or their partisan predispositions. Using these models to interpret the range of findings in political science and social psychology, we find that most of the studies purporting to demonstrate biased learning are either theoretically indeterminate or consistent with a Bayesian model. Moreover, although biased learning doubtless occurs, important aggregate time series, such as approval of the incumbent president, reveal little evidence of it. The phenomenon of biased learning in the form of selective perception has less empirical support than is often supposed. We conclude by discussing some of the conditions under which selective perception may shape political opinions and behavior.

MODELING VOTER LEARNING

With rare exceptions, scholars have advanced hypotheses about biased perception in informal terms. In this section, we attempt to translate the central propositions concerning biased learning into a mathematical form that permits

---

[2]For an earlier attempt to use Bayesian learning as an interpretive framework, see Ajzen & Fishbein (1975). The analytics of this essay, however, were found wanting (Fischhoff & Lichtenstein 1978). For discussion of non-Bayesian processes of perception, see Jervis (1976).

clearer exposition while elucidating their empirical implications. One of the most important by-products of this exercise is to distinguish between very different empirical claims that are sometimes conflated in discussions of biased learning. Bayesian models do not preclude the possibility that Democrats and Republicans bring different prior beliefs to the evaluation of new evidence. Nor are they inconsistent with the observation that supporters of different parties sometimes apply different evaluative criteria when assessing the performance of public officials, policies, or institutions. (If Democrats care about equity and Republicans efficiency, they may form very different assessments of a privatization or deregulation initiative.) Nor does the Bayesian framework rule out the possibility that Democrats find evidence of a Democratic scandal less credible than do Republicans. The prediction that distinguishes Bayesian models from biased learning models has to do with whether Democrats and Republicans who possess equivalent levels of prior uncertainty and assign a given information source equal credibility ex ante are equally affected by the new information.

Model of Bayesian Learning

When we speak of learning, we have in mind the process by which people assimilate information so as to form new beliefs or reinforce old ones. Beliefs are defined as an individual's assessment of the likelihood that given factual statements are true. For example, individuals have beliefs about the likelihood that cigarettes cause cancer, that it will be sunny on Sunday, or that their legislator trades votes for campaign contributions. This section presents a simple mathematical model of learning to explain precisely what we mean by our contrast between the Bayesian learning ("unbiased learning") and selective perception ("biased learning") hypotheses, which posit different ways in which beliefs adjust to new information. It is important to distinguish beliefs, which measure a voter's assessments of objective characteristics of the political world, and preferences, which describe what the voter likes and dislikes. Quite often, the opinions that political scientists track over time are a mixture of beliefs and preferences. The question "Which political party is best able to manage economic affairs?" taps not only one's beliefs about the objective capabilities of the political parties but also the criteria one uses to judge which party is "best." Some voters may prefer economic stewardship that maintains low rates of unemployment; others may care only about low interest rates. For the moment, the model we present focuses on the dynamics of beliefs, but the distinction between beliefs and evaluations will become crucial later on as we consider empirical applications.

As an example of how beliefs change in response to new information, consider voter assessments of whether a politician is honest or corrupt. Before receiving new information, individuals start with some preconceptions. Suppose an individual's prior beliefs can be represented by a normal distribution, with a mean value set to the individual's estimate of the politician's honesty and a variance capturing the uncertainty of this estimate. Let the variable θ stand for the politician's (unobserved) level of honesty. The voter's prior belief about the relative likelihood that the politician has various ethical standards is denoted by the probability distribution $\pi(\theta)$, which is distributed $N(\mu,\sigma_0^2)$.

Over time, a range of new information about the politician's ethics reaches the voter. The contents of this information are a function of both the truth and random sources of distortion. We model this new information by a second normally distributed random variable, with a mean equal to the truth about the politician and a variance that depends on the degree of uncertainty associated with the information. The new information is denoted x and is a draw from the probability distribution $N(\theta, \sigma^2_1)$. The variance, σ^2_1, captures how definitive the new information is. For example, if the new information is the result of a thorough and credible investigation, then the variance of this signal is very small, and the truth about the politician may be almost entirely revealed by the new evidence. Alternatively, if the new information is the number of rumors over a given period, this signal is only slightly informative, since it may be only weakly correlated with the truth about the politician.

Learning is how prior beliefs change in light of the new evidence. Using standard results from statistics, Bayes' rule implies that $\pi(\theta \mid x)$, the posterior distribution, is distributed $N(\mu(x), \rho)$, where

$$\mu(x)=\mu+(x-\mu)\frac{\sigma^2_0}{\sigma^2_0+\sigma^2_1}, \qquad\qquad 1.$$

$$\rho=\frac{\sigma^2_0\,\sigma^2_1}{\sigma^2_0+\sigma^2_1}. \qquad\qquad 2.$$

After observing x, the voter's best guess as to the legislator's level of honesty is $\mu(x)$. The degree to which the voter adjusts her beliefs in response to new information is a function of how much the new information deviates from her prior best guess, the precision of the new information, and the voter's confidence in her original guess. When additional new information arrives, the subject incorporates the information according to the same algorithm described in Equations 1 and 2, with the posterior mean and variance replacing the prior mean and variance in the formulas.

Model of Selective Perception

Over time, the voter observes a variety of pieces of new information, $\{x_1, x_2,...\}$, each with an associated variance, $\{\sigma^2_1, \sigma^2_2,...\}$. Let H_t denote the collection of new information available to the Bayesian learner at t, where t is an index of the number of pieces of new information observed. To formalize selective perception, we posit that partisans will minimize evidence that contradicts their partisan predispositions. To continue with the example of the honest or corrupt politician, suppose the politician in question is a Republican. Let higher values of x indicate higher levels of corruption, and let a value of $x = 0$ be a neutral reading. Then one interpretation of selective perception is that Republican partisans will look at $x > 0$ and see αx, where α is some number less than 1 ($x > 0$ is evidence of some corruption and so is one way to characterize "bad news" for a Republican partisan).

How does this bias in learning affect the updating of the prior beliefs? Using Equations 1 and 2, we can see that in the case of Bayesian learning, the mean value of the posterior beliefs given the history H_t is

$$\mu(H_t) = \rho(H_t)\left[\frac{x_0}{\sigma^2_0} + \sum_{i=1}^{t}\left(\frac{x_i}{\sigma^2_i}\right)\right], \qquad\qquad 3.$$

where $\rho(H_t)$ is the variance of the posterior distribution. To take into account the possibility of partisan perceptual bias, we rewrite this expression as

$$\mu(H_t) = \rho(H_t)\left[\frac{x_0}{\sigma^2_0} + \alpha\sum_{i=1}^{n}\left(\frac{x_i}{\sigma^2_i}\right) + \sum_{i=n+1}^{t}\left(\frac{x_i}{\sigma^2_i}\right)\right],$$

where the voter's information is grouped into the n cases where $x < 0$ and the $t-n$ cases where $x > 0$. In the interpretation of selective perception depicted in Equation 3a, partisans minimize the bad news in any report by viewing the evidence as less odious than it really is. One interpretation of this type of bias is "selective attention," in which the voter systematically fails to attend to the negative portions of the information. Another interpretation is "selective exposure," in which voters avoid television, radio, or newspaper accounts of untoward news (Sears & Whitney 1973) and so observe a version of reality in which much of the bad news is already filtered out. Indeed, the beauty of this formal treatment is that both forms of selectivity—selective exposure and perception—can be modeled within a common analytic framework.

EMPIRICAL ASSESSMENTS

Biased Assimilation

Lord et al (1979) used the term biased assimilation to describe the process by which an individual's prior beliefs determine whether he or she finds new information convincing. The claim that an individual's attachments and interests give rise to a tendentious interpretation of evidence has been borne out in decades of social-psychological research (Festinger 1957). Hastorf & Cantril (1954) found that when reviewing films of a rough football game between Dartmouth and Princeton, students from the two schools had disparate assessments of the number and severity of infractions committed by each team. Lord et al (1979) found that subjects who favored capital punishment were more likely to endorse a particular methodology if the study that used it found evidence for the deterrent effect of the death penalty; the same methodology was regarded as inferior when it generated the opposite conclusion. This finding was replicated by Houston & Fazio (1989), who found it particularly pronounced among subjects whose attitudes toward the death penalty were cognitively "accessible." In yet another death penalty study, Schuette & Fazio (1995) found a high correlation between preexisting attitudes and evaluations of the presented research results, except among those subjects who were told that the accuracy of their scientific evaluations would be judged against that of a "blue ribbon panel" of experts.

Moving outside the purview of death penalty research, Miller et al (1993, Experiment 3) found that proponents of affirmative action rated essays favoring the policy as more persuasive than opposing essays; the converse was true for opponents of the policy. Kunda (1987) examined the perceived harmfulness of coffee consumption. Selecting coffee drinkers and nondrinkers with roughly equivalent prior opinions about the adverse effects of coffee, Kunda studied the consequences of reading scientific evidence purporting to show that coffee consumption does or does not produce adverse health effects in women. Women coffee drinkers were less convinced by evidence showing adverse consequences. Chen et al (1992) found that students who were threatened by the immediate institution of proficiency exams were less persuaded by advocates of those exams than were students who expected to be grandfathered in under the current system. Koehler (1993) found that both parapsychologists and critics of parapsychology gave lower ratings to studies that disagreed with their positions on extrasensory perception. This pattern was also confirmed by a controlled experiment in which preconceptions about fictitious scientific issues were induced before subjects rated the soundness of research that supported or contradicted these preconceptions (Koehler 1993).

Findings of this sort abound in public opinion research as well, particularly in studies examining perceptions of prejudice and discrimination. Such studies invariably find that members of dominant groups believe job and housing discrimination to be less commonplace than do members of minority groups (Kluegel & Smith 1986) and that racial groups perceive new events (such as incidents of police brutality, race riots, and trials of prominent minorities) in markedly different ways.[3] Similarly, hostility and stereotyping of homosexuals is strongly related to students' receptivity toward scientific evidence confirming or disconfirming these beliefs (Munro & Ditto 1997).

---

[3]One of the more famous studies of biased assimilation (Vidmar & Rokeach 1974) found that more prejudiced viewers of *All in the Family*, a television series designed to denigrate bigotry, were more likely to admire the bigoted main character, whereas less prejudiced viewers admired his liberal antagonist.

Examples also abound in the world of partisan politics, as Democrats and Republicans often differ markedly in their perceptions of political and economic affairs. Early survey researchers noted in 1936 that 83% of Republicans felt that President Roosevelt's policies were leading the country down the road to dictatorship, a view shared by only 9% of Democrats (Key 1963:246). This theme figures prominently in the classic works *The American Voter* and *Elections and the Political Order* (Campbell et al 1960, 1966), which stress the role of partisanship as a filter of political information. Stokes (1966:127), for example, argues that "for most people the tie between party identification and voting behavior involves subtle processes of perceptual adjustment by which the individual assembles an image of current politics consistent with his partisan allegiance."

Although widespread consensus exists about the capacity of preexisting beliefs to structure the assimilation of new information, the implications for "biased" judgment remain unclear. In one sense, judgment may be said to be biased when observers with different preconceptions interpret the same piece of evidence in ways that conform to their initial views. This process of putting a favorable spin on a piece of news comports with Key's observation that Democrats and Republicans "discover virtues and strengths far beyond those actually possessed" by their party's leader (1961:244). On the other hand, one could argue that the process of evaluating new information in light of what is previously believed is consistent with rational information processing.

A Bayesian Interpretation of Biased Assimilation

The fact that individuals (*a*) tend to reject evidence that conflicts with their initial opinions and (*b*) tend to doubt the accuracy of studies that present unexpected findings is often interpreted as evidence of biased information processing. This reasoning is particularly common among those who study "motivated reasoning" and conclude, for example, that "[d]efensiveness, or a motivation to protect self-relevant attitudes, results in deeper and more favorable elaboration of arguments supporting those attitudes than arguments opposing them" (Lundgren & Prislin 1998:715). Although a slanted interpretation of evidence could indicate a departure from Bayesian learning, it is not inherently incompatible with Bayesian learning. This issue is treated formally below, but a simple example explains the basic point. Suppose that you are supervising an employee, and you have questions about the employee's competence. After reviewing the employee's work over the past year and speaking to a dozen of his co-workers, you conclude that the employee is not doing a good job. Just as you are about to call him into your office, you hear back from a final co-worker who says that, in his opinion, the employee is very capable. Although there is no reason a priori to consider this new report any less reliable than the dozen reports already given, it is hardly convincing evidence that the employee is in fact a good worker. It is far more likely that the new report is wrong and that the final co-worker either has poor evaluation skills (this co-worker's "study" has a methodological flaw) or has observed an uncharacteristic performance (the co-worker's "study" presents misleading findings due to "random error").

Before proceeding with a more formal analysis, we need to define what would lead an experimental subject to say that evidence was "weak" or "unconvincing." There are two conditions that might generate this response. First, the evidence could be methodologically suspect, even if what the evidence suggests is likely to be true. For example, a poorly designed study showing that smoking was linked to lung cancer might be deemed unconvincing. Second, evidence might be termed unconvincing if it supports a seemingly false conclusion. A witness who says that he saw someone commit a crime, when contradicted by 10 other witnesses who place the accused far from the crime scene, might be said to provide unconvincing testimony. Because many of the experiments that deal with learning provide subjects with evidence of equal methodological quality on both sides of the issue, we restrict our definition of "unconvincing" or "weak" evidence to mean evidence that supports a conclusion that is perceived to be false.

Returning to the example of an individual assessing the honesty of a politician, suppose a subject receives the information x^*. According to Equation 1, after considering x^*, the subject updates his beliefs in the direction of x^* and ends with a posterior distribution $N(\mu(x^*), \rho)$. One way to gauge the extent to which the subject deems x^* an accurate reflection of the truth about the politician is to ask how likely it is that, given the posterior distribution, an exhaustive further investigation would reveal that x^* is far from the truth. Consider the case where $x^* > \mu(x^*)$. Given the posterior distribution described by Equations 1 and 2, the probability that the politician's true level of corruption is equal to or greater than x^* is $1 - \Phi(z)$, where

$$z = \frac{x^* - \mu(x^*)}{\sqrt{(\sigma^2_0 + \sigma^2_1)}}\left(\sigma_1/\sigma_0\right) = \frac{x^* - \mu(x^*)}{\sqrt{\left(1 + \frac{\sigma_0^2}{\sigma_1^2}\right)}}. \qquad 4.$$

We say that x^* is too extreme to be convincing evidence if this probability is sufficiently low. Notice that the form of the z value is similar, though not identical, to the z value that would be used to test for a "difference of means" between two samples, where the prior and the new information are estimates of the means, with variances equal to σ^2_0 and σ^2_1, respectively.

Whenever z is large, new evidence can be regarded as unconvincing. Using Equation 4, we find that this occurs when the new evidence x^* is too different from our posterior beliefs. For any given degree of deviation from our posterior beliefs, x^* is more convincing when our prior beliefs are weak (i.e. σ^2_0 is large) or when the new evidence is very accurate (i.e. σ^2_1 is small). It is important to note that all of this is perfectly consistent with, and in fact derived from, a model of Bayesian learning.

This demonstration shows that in the Bayesian model, even unconvincing evidence is used in forming beliefs. Observers update their beliefs in the direction of the unconvincing evidence. Therefore, although it is not inconsistent with Bayesian learning for observers to comment that contrary information is unconvincing, in the simple version of Bayesian learning, we do not expect critics of new information to be altogether unmoved by it. Nor do we expect them to pick out only those features of the new information that are congenial to their view and to become more convinced of their original viewpoint, a process that Lord et al (1979) describe as polarization. Except in unusual circumstances (described below), polarization is inconsistent with the Bayesian model.

Polarization

More arresting than the hypothesis of biased assimilation is the notion that, when people with different prior attitudes encounter new information, the gap between their beliefs grows larger. When, for example, proponents and opponents of the death penalty were shown an identical set of mixed evidence, the apparent result was to "increase further the gap between their views" (Lord et al 1979:2105). Subjects in this experiment seemed to attend to findings congenial to their original point of view. Instead of bringing the two groups closer together (or at any rate, moving them in the same direction), the new evidence caused the groups to polarize further.

Before getting into the details of this and other studies, let us step back and reflect on the conditions under which such a pattern would be consistent with Bayesian processing. Using Equation 3, we see that beliefs change in a positive direction if $\mu(H_t) > x_0$, regardless of the exact value of one's prior beliefs. Equation 3 says that the posterior mean equals a weighted average of the prior and the observed values of x. Observations with a small variance are given greater weight. It is somewhat difficult to get a sense of the magnitude of $\mu(H_t)$ for the general case. However, when we assume that the variances associated with each piece of information are the same, Equation 3 simplifies to

$$\mu(H_t) = \frac{\rho(H_t)}{\sigma^2}\left[x_0 + \sum_{i=1}^{t}(x_i)\right],$$

where $\rho(H_t)$ is the variance of the posterior distribution after H_t. Since $\rho(H_t) = \sigma^2/t$, this can be written as

$$\mu(H_t) = \frac{\sum_{i=0}^{t}(x_i)}{t}.$$

Last, the change in beliefs in response to H_t is

$$\frac{t-1}{t}\left[\sum_{i=1}^{t}\frac{x_i}{t-1}-x_0\right].$$

5.

Equation 5 shows that, regardless of the value of the prior belief, the voter updates it in the direction of the new information If the average of the new information (i.e. $\frac{1}{t}\sum x_i$) is greater than the prior, the voter adjusts beliefs upward; if the average of the new information is less than the prior, the adjustment is in the opposite direction. That being the case, under what conditions might one expect to see a polarization of opinion in response to new information? There are two possibilities. First, voters may apply different evaluative criteria to the same set of evidence. Suppose that voters see two studies on capital punishment. One shows that capital punishment has a strong deterrent effect against murder, and the second shows that sometimes innocent people are executed. This new information may cause voters to draw different conclusions even if they started out with the same prior beliefs and updated these beliefs in accordance with Bayes' rule. A voter who is horrified by the possibility of errors may move away from supporting capital punishment, whereas a voter for whom reducing the murder rate is a priority will show increased support.

Second, voters might differ in their assessments of new information. As the model has shown, the amount of weight placed on any new information is inversely proportional to the variance associated with it. If voters attribute different variances to the same information, they will assign different weights to the same piece of news. This implies that if there is at least one component of the information pulling voters in each direction, voters' beliefs might move in opposite directions, depending on which component of the new information is considered more precise. This theoretical possibility might be relevant to the world of international relations, where perceptions of states' intentions are subject to markedly different interpretations (Jervis 1996, Kydd 1997). This concern, however, does not seem to apply to polarization in laboratory experiments. Even if voters ascribe different variances to each piece of new information, in the absence of selective perception there is no tendency to overweight positive or underweight negative information. Therefore, results should average out across voters (particularly since these experiments randomize the methodology associated with each fictitious study), leaving only a small subset of voters moving in the "wrong" direction.

How persuasive is the polarization hypothesis? Taken at face value, the Lord et al (1979) study indicates that, after reading conflicting research reports, supporters of the death penalty were more likely than opponents to characterize their views as more strongly pro–death-penalty than before reading the reports. The catch is that self-described opinion change is not quite the same thing as opinion change. Ordinarily, when we think of opinion change, we have in mind a before-and-after study in which beliefs are assessed at each point in time. As Miller et al (1993) point out, the Lord et al study does not measure opinions before and after presentation of evidence; instead, the authors rely entirely on the subjects' assessments of whether their views have become more pro– or anti–death-penalty. Tellingly, Miller et al find that when pretreatment and posttreatment opinions are measured directly, the polarization hypothesis receives no support [in contrast to the capital punishment study reported by Pomerantz et al (1995)]. Moreover, Miller et al (1993) asked subjects to write posttreatment essays about their views and compared the content of these essays to their prior attitudes and reported attitude change. Based on essays about capital punishment and affirmative action, Miller et al (1993:571) found "very minimal behavioral consequences to subjects' reports of attitude polarization."

Much the same pattern of findings emerges in Munro & Ditto's (1997) experiments on anti-homosexual stereotyping and exposure to scientific evidence confirming or disconfirming these stereotypes. Self-reported belief change across a pair of experiments comports with the polarization hypothesis; directly measured pre- and posttreatment beliefs reveal no evidence of polarization.

What about other studies in which opinion change is measured directly both before and after the introduction of new information? Such studies are not as abundant as one might suppose, given the number of decades that biased learning theories have been in currency. As Chaiken et al observe (1989:232),

> Surprisingly, the biasing effects of prior attitudes have received little attention by contemporary cognitively-oriented researchers, even though earlier persuasion researchers often accorded prior attitudes an important theoretical role.... Most contemporary studies do not even assess prior attitudes. In these "after-only" experiments, subjects' pre-experimental attitudes typically are assumed to be opposed to the message's advocacy. Moreover, when prior attitudes are assessed, they are rarely represented in the analytic design.

Indeed, evidence confirming the polarization hypothesis boils down to just two studies in addition to the Pomerantz et al (1995) capital punishment study mentioned above.

Using the "fibrocystic disease threat" experiment crafted by Kunda (1987), Liberman & Chaiken (1992) examined the reactions of female coffee drinkers and nondrinkers to scientific evidence purporting to show that coffee consumption does or does not produce adverse health effects in women. Drinkers and nondrinkers were selected for the study on the basis of their roughly equivalent prior beliefs about fibrocystic disease. After seeing a study that supported the fibrocystic disease theory, both coffee drinkers and nondrinkers adjusted their beliefs in the same direction. But although both groups became more convinced by the soundness of the claim that fibrocystic disease is a real health threat to women, the nondrinkers moved farther in the direction of accepting the claims of the theory. Strangely, however, nondrinkers exposed instead to scientific evidence disputing the fibrocystic disease hypothesis also became more convinced of the disease's adverse health effects. In the second study (Batson 1975), 11 Christian believers and 8 nonbelievers accepted as factual a fictitious story of archeological evidence disproving the Bible's account of the Resurrection; the believers became somewhat more firm in their religious conviction, whereas the nonbelievers became more skeptical after reading this report. Batson reported this asymmetric pattern of belief change to be statistically significant, despite the small sample sizes involved.

Taken together, these findings do not go very far in establishing the case for polarization, particularly when combined with the countervailing evidence presented by Miller et al (1993) and Munro & Ditto (1997). Applicability to the realm of politics is dubious as well. The experiments that do purport to show polarization make no attempt to establish the external validity of laboratory findings. Subjects in these experiments were quizzed about their beliefs immediately after exposure to the new information. It is unclear whether the polarization effects would have persisted over a longer period of time, amid further reflection or discussion with others. The issue of external validity is troubling because, to our knowledge, no field studies of the sort described by Wilson et al (1992) have turned up evidence of polarization.[4] In light of this concern, we now briefly examine the most widely studied time series in the study of American politics, namely approval of the incumbent president, to see whether Democrats and Republicans respond differently to political and economic developments.

A BRIEF LOOK AT AGGREGATE PUBLIC OPINION

Presidential Approval

Theories of party identification have often emphasized the extent to which party attachments operate as perceptual filters, causing partisans to assign disproportionate weight to evidence favoring their party. Stokes (1966:127), for example, contends that the "capacity of party identification to color perceptions holds the key to understanding why the unfolding of new events, the emergence of new issues, the appearance of new political figures fails to produce wider swings of party fortune. To a remarkable extent these swings are damped by processes of selective perception." Public opinion moves

---

[4]Wilson et al (1992) randomly assigned more than 1000 adults to an experimental condition in which they watched a movie designed to sensitize viewers to the plight of rape victims. Although the authors expected to find males in the treatment group to be less receptive to this message than females, evidence of polarization proved not to be significant.

sluggishly because supporters of the party disfavored by current events take no heed of unfavorable news or construe it as favorable.

Testing the claim that Democrats and Republicans weigh the same evidence differently requires a longitudinal research design. At any given point in time, those who identify with the Republican Party are much more likely than their Democratic counterparts to approve of a Republican president or disapprove of a Democratic one. These divergent evaluations do not in themselves make the case for biased perception because they may well reflect the different policy orientations of the two groups of partisans. A more telling assessment of perceptual bias tracks presidential approval over time. Are events interpreted differently by Democrats, Republicans, and Independents, such that approval rises among one partisan group while falling or remaining unchanged among others?

Edwards' (1990) compendium of presidential Gallup approval ratings classified by respondents' party provides a readily accessible means for answering this question. Edwards presents annual figures on the percentage of Democrats, Republicans, and Independents who approve of the way the president is handling his job for the period 1952–1988 (Figure 1). The trajectories of presidential approval track quite closely across the three partisan groups. Indeed, when we look at annual changes in approval (discarding, necessarily, the first year of each presidency), we find very high correlations between the ways in which the partisan groups update their assessments. Annual percentage-point changes in presidential approval among Democrats and Republicans correlate 0.77 (n = 29); this figure rises to 0.79 when changes are recalculated in terms of shifts in log-odds.

The correspondence across partisan groups can be assessed more rigorously by examining the extent to which change in partisans' opinions tracks change in the opinions of Independents. Independents provide a useful benchmark because they lack the motivation to slant news in a particular direction. To examine whether partisans adjust their evaluations in the same manner as Independents, we estimated a system of equations in which change in the log-odds of approval among Democrats or Republicans is regressed on change in the log-odds of approval among Independents, plus an interaction term (scored 1 or −1) that indicates whether Independents are moving in a direction that signals unfavorable news. (A pro-Republican shift, from the standpoint of Democratic partisans, occurs when Independents' approval of a Democratic president falls or their approval of a Republican president rises). Adding in random disturbance terms, we may write these equations as follows:

Δ log-odds of approval among Republicans = $a + b$ (Δ log-odds of approval among Independents) + c (indicator variable scored 1 if Independents' approval is changing in a pro-Republican direction and −1 otherwise) * (Δ log-odds of approval among Independents) + μ,

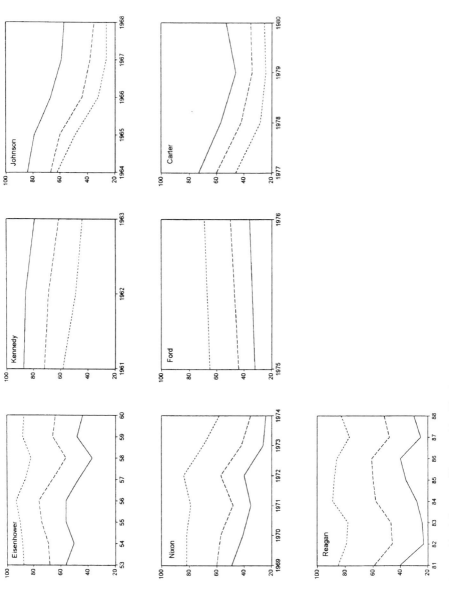

Figure 1 Presidential approval by party identification, 1953–1988 (Edwards 1990). Solid line, Democrats' approval; short-dashed line, Republicans' approval; long-dashed line, Independents' approval.

Table 1 Regression analysis of selective perception in presidential approval among partisans[1]

	Dependent Variable	
	Δlog-odds of approval: Democrats	Δlog-odds of approval: Republicans
Intercept	−0.016 (0.030)	0.014 (0.035)
Δ log-odds of approval: Independents	1.094 (0.133)	1.114 (0.111)
Δ log-odds of approval: Independents dummy scored 1 if change among Independents signals unfavorable news and 0 otherwise	−0.125 (0.163)	−0.006 (0.187)
Adjusted R^2	0.853	0.840

[1]N = 29 annually aggregated observations of presidential approval, deleting observations in which a president has just assumed office. Standard errors in parentheses.

and

Δ log-odds of approval among Democrats = $\alpha + \beta$ (Δ log-odds of approval among Independents) + γ (indicator variable scored 1 if Independents' approval is changing in a pro-Democratic direction and −1 otherwise) * (Δ log-odds of approval among Independents) + ε.

Selective perception implies that the parameters c and γ will be negative—untoward information reduces the impact of the opinion change among Independents. Indeed, in its strongest formulation, selective perception implies that $b + c = 0$ and $\beta + \gamma = 0$; unfavorable information is ignored altogether. A Bayesian model, on the other hand, expects b and β to be 1 and c and γ to be zero.

Table 1 reports the results of these regressions. Both c and γ are found to be small, and neither is statistically distinguishable from zero. A Wald test of the coefficient restrictions associated with the Bayesian null hypothesis that $b = \beta = 1$ and $c = \gamma = 0$ produces a chi-square of 2.12, which is nonsignificant ($p = 0.71$). In sum, only the faintest traces of selective perception are evident from partisan trends in presidential approval. All three partisan groups move together—sometimes markedly—as party fortunes change. These data are inconsistent with the claim that partisanship "dampens" the effects of new information, as well as the broader thesis (Slovic & Lichtenstein 1971) that people update their beliefs in an overly conservative manner. Beliefs and evaluations do change, and they change to approximately the same degree among those with different political allegiances.

CONCLUSION

One of the most difficult aspects of studying biased learning is drawing appropriate links between theory and evidence. That previous scholarship has sometimes lent support to the biased learning model suggests the inadequacy of tests that fail to track beliefs and evaluations over time. The mere fact that Democrats and Republicans each tend to declare their party's presidential nominee the more effective debater (Katz & Feldman 1962, Sigelman & Sigelman 1984) is not convincing evidence of selective perception because each group of partisans doubtless applies different ideological criteria when evaluating the candidates' ideas. Holding tastes constant is a critical component of an effective research design. If, in a college dormitory, half the students like Mexican cuisine and the other half do not, we would not cite mixed reviews of the lunch menu when tacos are served as evidence of perceptual bias. The issue of perceptual bias hinges on how evaluations change when the same dish is prepared by a gourmet chef.

By the same token, the fact that people with different preconceptions form different opinions about the same piece of evidence—so-called "biased assimilation"—is not inconsistent with Bayesian information processing. As Lord et al (1979:2107) acknowledge, it may be entirely rational for those with strong prior beliefs to downplay the value of new information. Making sense of the literature on biased learning requires a sharp distinction between studies that examine the credence subjects place in an argument and studies that examine how new evidence changes existing beliefs. Only the latter type offers a compelling test of whether learning departs from a Bayesian characterization.

Bayesian learning models are called into question by evidence of belief polarization because the Bayesian model predicts polarization only in very unusual circumstances. Although the Lord et al (1979) study has been cited with approval on hundreds of occasions, its central empirical claim is not well supported. Granted, subjects who evaluate mixed scientific evidence may report that their beliefs have grown more extreme, but direct assessments of change often fail to show evidence of polarization. Moving beyond the confines of laboratory experiments on undergraduates to public opinion surveys, we see surprisingly little indication that Democrats, Republicans, and Independents respond to current events differently. Presidential approval seems to rise and fall among all partisan groups to a similar extent. This finding accords with Gerber & Green's (1997) analysis of panel survey data, in which Democrats, Republicans, and Independents moved together in their evaluations of which party was best able to handle the nation's economy.[5] It accords also with Page

<hr />

[5]Based on their survey analysis of economic perceptions, Peffley et al (1987:103) conclude that "people appear to be extremely conservative information processors, revising their beliefs to a much more limited degree than Bayes' theorem prescribes." Whether voters change their beliefs to a sufficient degree is difficult to establish empirically, since it requires precise measurements of prior beliefs and exposure to new information. Suffice it to say, "beliefs about party economic competence may change fairly appreciably over the course of two year's time" (Peffley et al 1987:105), a finding consistent with results presented by Gerber & Green (1997).

& Shapiro's (1992) extensive evidence that the opinions of opposing ideological, social, and economic groups seldom polarize over time.

Such findings are more suggestive than definitive, and there may be important circumstances in which biased learning surfaces. Selective perception may be more apparent in people's immediate reactions to new information. The polarizing effects of information that have occasionally been observed in the laboratory may simply be too short-lived to manifest themselves in aggregate time series spanning months or years. Analyses that track evaluations over shorter time spans, when beliefs and the criteria by which to gauge the quality of incoming information are uncertain and unformed, may turn up more evidence of asymmetrical opinion change. Haight & Brod's (1977) analysis of opinion during political crises is suggestive of such short-run effects. It may also be that, in the cases we have studied, selective perception is restricted to a small portion of the electorate; although present, its effects escape detection. If motives arising from deep-seated ideological commitment engender selective perception, perhaps the United States, with its famously narrow band of ideological variation, is a limiting case.

As the study of voter learning moves forward, at least three lines of research and methodological innovation present themselves. The first is the study of more emotionally charged issues or ideologically committed individuals. As one tracks the beliefs of rival groups in a political or ethnic conflict, do perceptions converge as new evidence comes to light, or do these groups react in an asymmetric fashion to new information? Relatedly, in what ways do social processes—discussion, opinion leadership, and other processes that are generally overlooked in laboratory studies of belief change—contribute to or mitigate polarization (see Liu & Latane 1998)?

Second, a thorough empirical analysis of Bayesian learning (and departures therefrom) requires greater attention to the measurement of prior beliefs. Not only is it important to have reliable information about the location of these beliefs, it is also important to gauge the uncertainty with which they are held. The term selective perception, coined in political science by Berelson et al (1954), originally described the fact that voters' perceptions of candidate stances were colored by their own policy preferences: "In almost every instance, respondents perceive their candidate's stand on the issues as similar to their own and the opponent's stand as dissimilar—whatever their own position" (1954:220). Although Democrats and Republicans have broadly similar impressions of where the candidates stand, "Overlaying the base of objective observation is the distortion effect—distortion in harmony with political predispositions" (1954:220). Without disputing the existence of this phenomenon, which has been observed by other scholars (Markus 1982), we would argue that this sort of "projection" is much as the Bayesian model would expect among those who lack information. As the focus shifts from prior beliefs to learning, it is telling that Berelson et al themselves demonstrate a powerful relationship between respondents' exposure to campaign information and the accuracy with which they describe the candidates' platforms (1954:228; see also Sears 1969 on the inverse relationship between the clarity of a stimulus and the degree of perceptual distortion).[6] Very few studies take seriously interpersonal variation in uncertainty.

Finally, and perhaps most importantly, students of voter learning must devote greater attention to the measurement and conceptualization of beliefs. To date, researchers have been content to take verbal expressions of beliefs at face value. People are assumed to believe the survey response option that they select. The question arises, however, whether such responses actually constitute the premises on which people would be prepared to act. Consider, for example, respondents' retrospective appraisals of economic conditions in the 1980 and 1992 National Election Studies. In 1980, Democrats were more likely than Republicans to claim that the economy had improved over the preceding 12 months; in 1992, Republicans were more likely to do so than Democrats. Leaving aside the issue of whether Democrats and Republicans might have been applying different economic criteria when evaluating the nation's well-being, there remains the possibility that these statements reflect something other than genuine convictions about the state of the economy. If the Democrats really felt more sanguine about the economy in 1980, did these beliefs manifest themselves in terms of consumption or investment? Did Republicans' consumption decline and Democrats' surge between 1992 and 1993, when the Democrats regained control of the presidency? In the study of beliefs as elsewhere, seeing is believing.

> Visit the Annual Reviews home page at
> http://www.AnnualReviews.org.

---

[6]Berelson et al summarize (1954:229), "It seems that communication exposure clarifies perception probably more than any other factor...[T]he more reading and listening people do on campaign matters, the more likely they are to come to recognize the positions the candidates take on major issues. It is as though the weight of the media is sufficient to 'impose' a certain amount of correct perception, regardless of the barrier presented by the voter's party preference."

Literature Cited

Ajzen I, Fishbein M. 1975. A Bayesian analysis of attribution processes. *Psychol. Bull.* 82:261–77

Batson CD. 1975. Rational processing or rationalization? The effect of disconfirming information on stated religious belief. *J. Pers. Soc. Psychol.* 32:176–84

Berelson R, Lazarsfeld PF, McPhee WN. 1954. *Voting: A Study of Opinion Formation in a Presidential Campaign.* Chicago: Univ. Chicago Press

Campbell A, Converse PE, Miller WE, Stokes DE. 1960. *The American Voter.* New York: Wiley

Campbell A, Converse PE, Miller WE, Stokes DE. 1966. *Elections and the Political Order.* New York: Wiley

Chaffee SH, Miyo Y. 1983. Selective exposure and the reinforcement hypothesis: an intergenerational panel study of the 1980 presidential campaign. *Commun. Res.* 10: 3–36

Chaiken S, Liberman A, Eagly AH. 1989. Heuristic and systematic processing within and beyond the persuasion context. In *Unintended Thought*, ed. JS Uleman, JA Bargh, pp. 212–52. New York: Guilford

Chen HC, Reardon R, Rea C, Moore DJ. 1992. Forewarning of content and involvement: consequences for persuasion and resistance to persuasion. *J. Exp. Soc. Psychol.* 28:523–41

Delli Carpini MX, Keeter S. 1996. *What Americans Know about Politics and Why It Matters.* New Haven, CT: Yale Univ. Press

Edwards GC III. 1990. *Presidential Approval: A Sourcebook.* Baltimore, MD: Johns Hopkins Univ. Press

Festinger L. 1957. *A Theory of Cognitive Dissonance.* Stanford, CA: Stanford Univ. Press

Fischhoff B, Lichtenstein S. 1978. Don't attribute this to Reverend Bayes. *Psychol. Bull.* 85:239–43

Frey D. 1986. Recent research on selective exposure to information. In *Advances in Experimental Social Psychology*, 19:40–80, ed. L Berkowitz. New York: Academic

Gerber A, Green DP. 1997. Rational learning and partisan attitudes. *Am. J. Polit. Sci.* 42:794–818

Haight TR, Brody RA. 1977. The mass media and presidential popularity. *Commun. Res.* 4:41–60

Hastorf AH, Cantril H. 1954. They saw a game: a case study. *J. Abnorm. Soc. Psychol.* 49:129–34

Houston DA, Fazio RH. 1989. Biased processing as a function of attitude accessibility: making objective judgements subjectively. *Soc. Cogn.* 7:51–66

Jervis R. 1976. *Perception and Misperception in International Politics.* Princeton, NJ: Princeton Univ. Press

Katz E, Feldman JJ. 1962. The debates in light of research: a survey of surveys. In *The Great Debates*, ed. S Kraus, pp. 173–223. Bloomington: Indiana Univ. Press

Key VO Jr. 1961. *Public Opinion and American Democracy.* New York: Knopf

Kinder DR, Mebane W. 1983. Politics and economics in everyday life. In *The Political Process and Economic Change*, ed. KR Monroe, pp. 141–180. New York: Agathon

Kluegel JR, Smith ER. 1986. *Beliefs about Inequality: Americans' Views of What Is and What Ought to Be.* New York: De Gruyter

Koehler JJ. 1993. The influence of prior beliefs on scientific judgement of evidence quality. *Organ. Behav. Hum. Decision Process.* 56:28–55

Kunda Z. 1987. Motivated inference: self-serving generation and evaluation of causal theories. *J. Pers. Soc. Psychol.* 53: 636–47

Kydd A. 1997. Game theory and the spiral model. *World Polit.* 49:371–400

Liberman A, Chaiken S. 1992. Defensive processing of personally relevant health messages. *Pers. Soc. Psychol. Bull.* 18: 669–79

Liu JH, Latane B. 1998. Extremitization of attitudes: Does thought- and discussion-induced polarization cumulate? *Basic Appl. Soc. Psychol.* 20:103–10

Lord CG, Ross L, Lepper M. 1979. Biased assimilation and attitude polarization: the effects of prior theories on subsequently considered evidence. *J. Pers. Soc. Psychol.* 37:2098–109

Lundgren SR, Prislin R. 1998. Motivated cognition and attitude change. *Pers. Soc. Psychol. Bull.* 24:715–26

Madison J. 1937 (1787). The Federalist No. 10. In *The Federalist*, A Hamilton, J Jay, J Madison. New York: Random House

Markus GB. 1982. Political attitudes during an election year: a report on the 1980 NES panel study. *Am. Polit. Sci. Rev.* 76: 538–60

Merrill JC, Lowenstein RL. 1971. *Media, Messages, and Men.* New York: McKay

Miller AG, McHoskey JW, Bane CM, Dowd

TG. 1993. The attitude polarization phenomenon: the role of response measure, attitude extremity, and behavioral consequences of reported attitude change. *J. Pers. Soc. Psychol.* 64:561–74

Munro GD, Ditto PH. 1997. Biased assimilation, attitude polarization, and affect in reactions to stereotype-relevant scientific information. *Pers. Soc. Psychol. Bull.* 23: 636–53

Neuman R. 1986. *The Paradox of Mass Politics: Knowledge and Opinion in the American Electorate.* Cambridge, MA: Harvard Univ. Press

Nisbett R, Ross L. 1980. *Human Inference: Strategies and Shortcomings of Human Judgment.* Engelwood Cliffs, NJ: Prentice Hall

Page BI, Shapiro RY. 1992. *The Rational Public: Fifty Years of Trends in Americans' Policy Preferences.* Chicago: Univ. Chicago Press

Patterson T, McClure RD. 1976. *The Unseeing Eye: The Myth of Television Power in National Elections.* New York: Putnam

Peffley M, Feldman S, Sigelman L. 1987. Economic conditions and party competence: processes of belief revision. *J. Polit.* 49: 100–21

Pomerantz EM, Chaiken S, Tordesillas RS. 1995. Attitude strength and resistance processes. *J. Pers. Soc. Psychol.* 69:408–19

Schuette RA, Fazio RH. 1995. Attitude accessibility and motivation as determinants of biased processing: a test of the MODE model. *Pers. Soc. Psychol. Bull.* 21: 704–10

Sears DO. 1969. Political behavior. In *Handbook of Social Psychology*, ed. G Lindzey, E Aronson, 5:315–458. Reading, MA: Addison-Wesley. 2nd ed.

Sears DO, Whitney RE. 1973. *Political Persuasion.* Morristown, NJ: General Learning

Sears DO, Citrin J. 1985. *Tax Revolt: Something for Nothing in California.* Cambridge, MA: Harvard Univ. Press

Sigelman L, Sigelman CK. 1984. Judgments of the Carter-Reagan debate: the eyes of the beholders. *Public Opin. Q.* 48:624–28

Slovic P, Lichtenstein S. 1971. Comparison of Bayesian and regression approaches to the study of human information processing in judgment. *Organ. Behav. Hum. Perform.* 6:649–744

Stokes DE. 1966. Party loyalty and the likelihood of deviating elections. In *Elections and the Political Order*, ed. A Campbell, PE Converse, WE Miller, DE Stokes, pp. 125–35. New York: Wiley

Tufte ER. 1976. *Political Control of the Economy.* Princeton, NJ: Princeton Univ. Press

Vidmar N, Rokeach M. 1974. Archie Bunker's bigotry: a study in selective perception and exposure. *J. Commun.* 24:36–47

Wilson BJ, Linz D, Donnerstein E, Stipp H. 1992. The impact of social issue television programming on attitudes toward rape. *Hum. Commun. Res.* 19:179–208

Zaller JR. 1992. *The Nature and Origins of Mass Opinion.* Cambridge, UK: Cambridge Univ. Press

Annu. Rev. Polit. Sci. 1999. 2:211–41

CIVIL-MILITARY RELATIONS[1]

Peter D. Feaver

Department of Political Science, Duke University, Durham, North Carolina 27708-
0204; e-mail: pfeaver@duke.edu

KEY WORDS: civilian control, coups, military politics, defense policy, armed forces,
            principal-agent relations

ABSTRACT

Who will guard the guardians? Political scientists since Plato have sought to
answer this, the central question of the civil-military relations subfield. Although civil-military relations is a very broad subject, encompassing the entire range of relationships between the military and civilian society at every
level, the field largely focuses on the control or direction of the military by
the highest civilian authorities in nation-states. This essay surveys political
science's contribution to our understanding of civil-military relations, providing a rough taxonomy for cataloguing the field and discussing the recent
renaissance in the literature as well as fruitful avenues for future research.
The essay focuses on theoretical developments, slighting (for reasons of
space) the many case studies and empirical treatments that have also made
important contributions to our knowledge.

INTRODUCTION

Civil-military relations is one of the truly interdisciplinary fields of study in
social science. Historians, sociologists, political scientists, and policy analysts
all have made major contributions to the field and, perhaps more surprising,
regularly read and respond to each other's work in this area. The interdisciplinary nature is neatly captured in the subfield's indispensable lead journal,
Armed Forces & Society, and may help explain why nominally mainstream but
increasingly insular political science journals such as *American Political Science Review* have made less of a contribution to the subfield in the past few
decades.

---

[1]This essay adapts materials published variously in Feaver 1995, 1997a, and 1997b with the per-
mission of the Center for Strategic and International Studies, Transaction Publishers, and Funda-
ción Arias para la Paz y el Progreso Humano, respectively.

1094-2939/99/0616-0211$08.00

This essay focuses on the political science component of the subfield, making mention of associated disciplines as necessary. Political scientists, as distinct from historians, tend to look for patterned generalizations of cause and effect. Political scientists seek not so much to describe what happened in a particular instance as to explain what happens in general and, if possible, predict what is likely to happen in the next case, given the ceteris paribus constraint. As distinct from sociologists, political scientists focus primarily on institutions of political control. Factors of direct concern to sociologists—for instance, the integration of the military with society—are of interest only insofar as they may relate causally to the primary political question of who decides what, when, how, and with what effect. Sociologists and historians would no doubt balk at the prominence given to political science theory in this essay. The nomothetic versus ideographic debate plays out in this area as in others, and it is not clear that political science is the lead discipline in the study of civil-military relations anyway. But sociologists and historians are likely to pay greater attention to political theoretical developments in this field than they would in other political science subfields. This is, then, an unabashedly parochial review of the political science civil-military literature, but one with at least an eye directed at associated disciplines.

Although relations between civilian and martial spheres, broadly construed, have preoccupied political philosophers for thousands of years, the modern intellectual history largely dates to the pre–World War II literature on antimilitarism, especially Vagts (1937) and Lasswell (1941). The second large wave of literature came in the early Cold War period, as American social scientists struggled to reconcile the need for a permanent and large standing army with America's traditional suspicions of the threats to liberty posed by standing armies (Kerwin 1948, Smith 1951, Lasswell 1950, Ekirch 1956, Mills 1956, Millis et al 1958). Huntington's landmark study, *The Soldier and the State* (1957), was the capstone to this early work, and most of what has been written since has been an explicit or implicit response to his argument.

After Huntington, the field split along two distinct tracks. The first and arguably more fruitful was a sociologically oriented examination of the military, first in the United States and then extending to other countries. The landmark study, Janowitz's *The Professional Soldier* (1960), spawned literally hundreds of follow-on studies exploring the relationship between society and the armed forces (Moskos 1970, 1971; Larson 1974; Segal et al 1974; Sarkesian 1975; Segal 1975; Bachman et al 1977; Janowitz 1977; Moskos 1977; Segal 1986; Moskos & Wood 1988; Edmonds 1988; Burk 1993; Sarkesian et al 1995). The second track was an institutionally oriented examination of postcolonial civil-military relations in developing countries, a project dominated by political scientists (Finer 1962; Huntington 1968; Stepan 1971, 1988; Perlmutter 1977; Welch 1976; Nordlinger 1977) and largely focused on the problem of coups; this track has spawned numerous specialty literatures considering civil-military relations in specific contexts—in communist regimes (Kolkowicz 1966, Herspring & Volgyes 1978, Colton 1979, Rice 1984, Colton & Gustafson 1990, Zisk 1993, Herspring 1996), in ethnically divided polities (Horowitz 1980, 1985), in authoritarian and postauthoritarian regimes (Rouquie 1982, Frazer 1994, Aguero 1995), and so on.[2] Although this essay addresses the literature across the board, special attention will be given to civil-military relations within democracies and, within that set, civil-military relations in the United States because the American case has figured so prominently in the theoretical development of the field.

Although the sociological school dominated the study of American civil-military relations, the Vietnam War trauma produced a flurry of empirically rich studies by political scientists that remain important even 20 or 30 years later (Kolodziej 1966, Yarmolinsky 1971, 1974; Russett & Stepan 1973; Russett & Hanson 1975; Betts 1977). The literature continued to prove fruitful, especially its analyses of the implications of the end of the draft, gender issues, and the role of public opinion (Stiehm 1981, 1989, 1996; Cohen 1985; Petraeus 1987; Russett 1990). This literature greatly contributed to our understanding of civil-military issues but did not present a direct theoretical challenge to the dominant Huntingtonian or Janowitzean paradigms. As discussed in the penultimate section of this essay, however, the end of the Cold War has sparked a renaissance of attention to civil-military relations in the United States, much of it as theoretically ambitious as the early work of Huntington and Janowitz. If the past is any guide, this new work, which began as a response to questions raised in the American context, will generate a larger literature treating comparative questions in a new way.

The essay proceeds in seven parts. I begin with a discussion of the central problem underlying all analyses of civil-military relations, which I call the civil-military problematique. I then identify the three forms of analysis—normative, descriptive, and theoretical—that comprise political science's contribution to our understanding of civil-military relations. The next two sections briefly review the political science literature on civil-military relations, parsing scholars according to the different dependent and independent variables stressed in their work. The antepenultimate section addresses in more detail the range of civilian control mechanisms identified by the literature. The penultimate section highlights the recent renaissance in the study of American civil-military relations. I conclude with a brief discussion of promising questions for future research.

---

[2]A third track, though further removed from the development of civil-military theory, is the large literature on the interrelationship between war, the military, and state development (Tilly 1975, Downing 1991, Goldstone 1991, Holsti 1996).

THE PROBLEMATIQUE

The civil-military problematique is a simple paradox: The very institution created to protect the polity is given sufficient power to become a threat to the polity.[3] This derives from the agency inherent in civilization. We form communities precisely because we cannot provide for all our needs and therefore must depend on other people or institutions to do our bidding. Civilization involves delegation, assigning decision making from the individual to the collective (in the form of a leader or leaders) and consigning the societal protection function from the leader to specialists or institutions responsible for violence.

The civil-military problematique is so vexing because it involves balancing two vital and potentially conflicting societal desiderata. On the one hand, the military must be strong enough to prevail in war. One purpose behind establishing the military in the first place is the need, or perceived need, for military force, either to attack other groups or to ward off attacks by others. Like an automobile's airbag, the military primarily exists as a guard against disaster. It should be always ready even if it is never used. Moreover, military strength should be sized appropriately to meet the threats confronting the polity. It serves no purpose to establish a protection force and then to vitiate it to the point where it can no longer protect. Indeed, an inadequate military institution may be worse than none at all. It could be a paper tiger inviting outside aggression—strong enough in appearance to threaten powerful enemies but not strong enough in fact to defend against their predations. Alternatively, it could lull leaders into a false confidence, leading them to rash behavior and then failing in the ultimate military contest.

On the other hand, just as the military must protect the polity from enemies, so must it conduct its own affairs so as not to destroy or prey on the society it is intended to protect. Because the military must face enemies, it must have coercive power, the ability to force its will on others. But coercive power often gives it the capability to enforce its will on the community that created it. A direct seizure of political power by the military is the traditional worry of civil-military relations theory and a consistent pattern in human history. Less obvious, but just as sinister, is the possibility that a parasitic military will destroy society by draining it of resources in a quest for ever greater strength as a hedge against the enemies of the state. Yet another concern is that a rogue military could involve the polity in wars and conflicts contrary to society's interests or expressed will. And, finally, there is a concern over the simple matter of obedi-

---

[3]Of course, the military may not be established solely to protect the polity against external threats. Other motivations, e.g. preserving the regime's power over the masses or creating the trappings of the modern state for symbolic purposes, may also come into play. Nevertheless, regardless of the motivation for creating the institution, once created, the military raises the same control problematique described in the text.

ence: Even if the military does not destroy society, will it obey its civilian masters, or will it use its considerable coercive power to resist civilian direction and pursue its own interests?

This is a variant of the basic problem of governance that lies at the core of political science: making the government strong enough to protect the citizens but not so strong as to become tyrannical. The tension between the two desiderata is inherent in any civilization, but it is especially acute in democracies, where the protectees' prerogatives are thought to trump the protectors' at every turn—where the metaphorical delegation of political authority to agents is enacted at regular intervals through the ballot box.[4] Democratic theory is summed in the epigram that the governed should govern. People may choose political agents to act on their behalf, but that should in no way mean that the people have forfeited their political privileges. Most of democratic theory is concerned with devising ways to insure that the people remain in control even as professionals conduct the business of government. Civil-military relations are just a special, extreme case for democratic theory, involving designated political agents controlling designated military agents.

It follows that, in a democracy, the hierarchy of de jure authority favors civilians over the military, even in cases where the underlying distribution of de facto power favors the military. Regardless of how strong the military is, civilians are supposed to remain the political masters. While decision making may in fact be politics as usual—the exercise of power in pursuit of ends—it is politics within the context of a particular normative conception of whose will should prevail. Civilian competence in the general sense extends even beyond their competence in a particular sense; that is, civilians are morally and politically competent to make the decisions even if they do not possess the relevant technical competence in the form of expertise (Dahl 1985). This is the core of the democratic alternative to Plato's philosopher king. Although the expert may understand the issue better, the expert is not in a position to determine the value that the people attach to different issue outcomes. In the civil-military context, this means that the military may be best able to identify the threat and the appropriate responses to that threat for a given level of risk, but only the civilian can set the level of acceptable risk for society. The military can propose the level of armaments necessary to have a certain probability of successful de-

---

[4]This tension is also present in authoritarian regimes and even military dictatorships. The very existence of political power creates the delegation-agency problem. In military regimes, even though political leaders and fighting groups alike wear uniforms, responsibility is divided between those who do the fighting and those who remain behind to wield political power. Wearing the same uniform does not prevent those who stay behind from worrying about whether the fighters are adequate to defend them or whether the fighters are liable to turn around and unseat them, as the many coups and countercoups in military dictatorships attest. This is what Stepan (1971) has called the distinction between the "military as an institution" and the "military as government."

fense against our enemies, but only the civilian can say what probability of success society is willing to underwrite. The military can describe in some detail the nature of the threat posed by a particular enemy, but only the civilian can decide whether to feel threatened, and if so, how or even whether to respond. The military assesses the risk, the civilian judges it.

The democratic imperative insists that this precedence applies even if civilians are woefully underequipped to understand the technical issues at stake. Regardless of how superior the military view of a situation may be, the civilian view trumps it. Civilians should get what they ask for, even if it is not what they really want. In other words, civilians have a right to be wrong.

The two central desiderata—protection by the military and protection from the military—are in tension because efforts to assure the one complicate efforts to assure the other. If a society relentlessly pursues protection from external enemies, it can bankrupt itself. If society minimizes the strength of the military so as to guard against a military seizure of political power, it can leave itself vulnerable to predations from external enemies. It may be possible to procure a goodly amount of both kinds of protection—certainly the United States seems to have had success in securing a large measure of protection both by and from the military—but tradeoffs at the margins are inevitable.

Even if a society achieves adequate levels of assurance against utter collapse at either extreme, battlefield defeat and coup, there is a range of problematic activities in which the military can engage. It remains difficult to ensure that the military is both capable of doing and willing to do what civilians ask. Thus, "solving" the problem of coups does not neutralize the general problem of control on an ongoing basis.

THREE FORMS OF ANALYSIS

In general, political science consists of three forms of analysis: normative, empirical/descriptive, and theoretical. Each component makes important contributions to the study of civil-military relations. Normative analysis asks what ought to be done, how much civilian control is enough, and what can be done to improve civil-military relations. Because civilian control of the military is of such great policy importance, the normative approach often plays a central role in the study of civil-military relations. Political science's answers to the normative questions are various criteria concerning how much control (and of what type) is enough to satisfy the definition of civilian control or civilian supremacy (Huntington 1957, Colton 1979, Edmonds 1988, Aguero 1995, Kemp & Hudlin 1992, Ben Meir 1995, Kohn 1997, Boene 1997).

The normative lens draws explicitly on the empirical/descriptive lens, which seeks to describe cases in accurate detail. Applied to the problem of civil-military relations, the empirical/descriptive lens involves developing typologies of various forms of civilian control or lack thereof—for instance, Welch's (1976) distinction between military influence and military control or Ben Meir's (1995) fivefold typology of military roles (advisory, representative, executive, advocacy, and substantive). The key task for this kind of analysis is distinguishing between reality and rhetoric, between what appears to be the case and what in fact is the case. Measured by sheer volume, the bulk of the civil-military relations literature consists of empirical/descriptive treatments of the civil-military scene in different countries or regions. Area studies specialists have long noted the centrality of civil-military issues to political life in various regions—indeed, civil-military relations is a central preoccupation in most area studies subliteratures, except those dealing with the United States and Western Europe. As a consequence, there is a rich literature describing the ebb and flow of relations between the armed forces and the polity (Boene 1990, Zagorski 1992, Danopoulos & Watson 1996, Diamond & Plattner 1996, Lovell & Albright 1997, Zamora 1997).

Also implicit in the normative lens are conclusions drawn from the third form of analysis, the theoretical lens. The theoretical approach may also begin with typology development, but then it moves on to advance propositional statements of cause and effect. It is impossible to recommend a certain course of action without making an implicit predictive claim of cause and effect: A state should do X because then Y will happen, and otherwise Z will happen (where Y is "better" than Z). The theoretical approach distinguishes between the things to be explained/predicted, called dependent variables (DVs)—for example, coups or robustness of civilian control—and the things doing the explaining/predicting, called independent or explanatory variables (IVs), such as the degree of military professionalism or the type of civilian governmental structure. The theoretical approach specifies ways in which changes in the IVs are reflected in changes in the DVs. As the following two sections document, political science's contribution to the subfield of civil-military relations can be evaluated in terms of successive theoretical debates over what the most important DVs and IVs are.

WHAT IS THE DEPENDENT VARIABLE?

Traditionally, civil-military relations theory has focused on the direct seizure of political power by the military, i.e. the coup. With the remarkable spread of democratic governance over the past several decades, the question of coups remains interesting, but it is by no means the only interesting civil-military phenomenon to be explained. Accordingly, it makes sense to distinguish between a variety of DVs, any one of which might be the most important or interesting in a particular region at a particular time. The next five subsections describe a list of DVs adapted from Desch (1999). The evaluation of the list is my own.

Coups

Coups are the traditional focus of civil-military relations because they so dramatically symbolize the central problem of the military exploiting their coercive strength to displace civilian rulers. Under the general heading of coups, political scientists have looked at two related but distinct questions: on the one hand, the instance or frequency of coups (or coups attempted), and on the other hand, the probability that a coup will be successful. Classical civil-military relations theory has primarily addressed the former. Both Huntington (1957) and his earliest critic, Finer (1962), address the propensity of military institutions to coup, as do subsequent studies by Bienen (1968), Nordlinger (1977), Horowitz (1980), Thompson (1975, 1976), Jackman (1978), Perlmutter (1977), O'Kane (1981), Zimmermann (1983), Johnson et al (1984), Bienen & Van de Walle (1990), Londregan & Poole (1990), and Frazer (1994). Luttwak (1979), in an iconoclastic analysis, addressed the second question of how to conduct a coup successfully, and coup success is also covered in Zimmermann (1983), Bienen & Van de Walle (1990), and Frazer (1994).

Coups are a problematic focus for future studies of civil-military relations, however, because looking only at coups can underestimate military influence. A coup may indicate military strength, at least compared to the other political actors the military suppresses. But it can also indicate military weakness, reflecting the military's inability to get what it wants through the normal political process. In this way, the dog that does not bark may be the more powerful and, for ascertaining whether or not the democracy is robust, the more important dog. Moreover, while coups have not entirely disappeared, they are certainly less frequent in many regions, and the coup success rate has also fallen (Zagorski 1996, Hunter 1998). Thus, theories explaining the propensity to coup would yield fairly consistent null predictions in many cases, missing interesting and important changes in the nature of civil-military relations over time. Most recent work on civil-military relations, therefore, has focused on other issues.

Military Influence

Because the coup/no-coup dichotomy misses much of the interesting give and take in civil-military relations, some theorists have preferred to study military influence instead. Whereas the coup variable is dichotomous, the influence variable is continuous, or at least offers more than two gradations. The focus on military influence captures the idea that the military institution may be politically powerful even (or perhaps especially) when it does not seize direct power through a forceful takeover.

Even the classic texts on civil-military relations recognized that the problem of civil-military relations was larger than a question of coups. Huntington

(1957:20) observed, for instance, that "the problem of the modern state is not armed revolt but the relation of the expert to the politician." Finer (1962) and Janowitz (1960) likewise acknowledged the utility of a non-dichotomous variable. Finer added a third possibility, covert intervention, and Janowitz, although not explicit on the point, treated civil-military relations as a continuum. Subsequent theorists, including Stepan (1971, 1988), Welch (1976), Nordlinger (1977), Colton (1979), Rice (1984), Pion-Berlin (1992), and Brooks (1999), all add additional gradations to the military influence variable.

Military influence is much harder to measure than coups, however, and the measurement problem limits its theoretical usefulness. Nordlinger (1977) addressed this problem by inventing a tripartite typology of praetorianism, consisting of moderators, guardians, and rulers. His typology, however, only captures varieties of overt military control and misses the far more nuanced and more interesting situation where the military is able to shape government actions without directly controlling them. Stepan's (1988) second measure of civilian control, the extent of military institutional prerogatives, is a superior gauge of influence because it explicitly includes military behavior short of insubordination by force. Stepan traces prerogatives through 11 issue areas ranging from defense policy to the legal system. As Stepan defines civilian control, however, it is not a very sensitive metric; he allows for essentially only two codings—low and high (he also has a "moderate" category in three instances: active military participation in the cabinet, the role of the police, and the military role in state enterprises). Colton (1979) offers a still more sensitive operationalization of the influence DV by distinguishing between four types of policy issues over which the military exercises influence (internal, institutional, intermediate, and societal) and by distinguishing between the four means used (official prerogative, expert advice, political bargaining, and force). Colton's approach offers considerable analytical leverage over questions of military influence short of a coup, but it is not clear that he successfully overcomes the problem of hidden influence and civilian abdication.

A related problem of the influence DV is that a particular normative claim of what ought to be the proper sphere of military influence is often implicit in the concept. While the normative line may be easy to draw in the coup setting, it is debatable in other settings. Should the military decide tactical questions only? What about tactical questions of special importance, such as nuclear tactics? In some countries, most notably the United States, the challenge of designing the proper division of labor between "military matters" and "civilian matters" has driven much of the civil-military conflict (Feaver 1992, 1996). Indeed, the oldest debate in civil-military relations concerns fusionism, the argument that the line between the military and the political has become so blurred that the distinction has lost its meaning (Boene 1990).

Fusionism arose out of the public management school as a logical response to the World War II experience of total war, and appeared even more reasonable in the face of such Cold War exigencies as a permanent and large military establishment and the threat of nuclear annihilation (Sapin & Snyder 1954). Huntington (1957) positioned his treatise as a self-conscious rejection of fusionism. Every half decade or so since, someone revives fusionism as the inevitable consequence of whatever military mission seems ascendant at that time: nuclear strategy and limited war (Lyons 1961, Janowitz 1960), counterinsurgency (Barrett 1965, Russett & Stepan 1973, Slater 1977), crisis management (Betts 1977), or peacekeeping operations (Tarr & Roman 1995, Roman & Tarr 1995, Hahn 1997). What is puzzling in fusionism's cyclical rebirth is that it is not clear who is killing it; in other words, why must the fusionist insight be revived every five years? My own answer is that fusionism is self-negating. It overreaches by confusing overlap between the functions of the civilian and military spheres with a merging of the spheres themselves. The spheres are necessarily analytically distinct—a distinction that derives from democratic theory and the agency inherent in political community—and so every fusionist scholar finds him- or herself beginning anew from the same point of departure. The spheres are also necessarily distinct in practice—it matters whether the policy maker wears a uniform or not—and so fusionist scholars find that their subjects repeatedly revive the idea of difference even as they provide evidence of overlaps with the activities of actors from different spheres. In short, what makes the overlap of functions interesting is the fact that it is overlaid on an even more fundamental separation (Williams 1997). This is not to say that fusionism provides no insights. On the contrary, it is a logical point of departure for descriptive empirical work, and some of the best empirical work on the subject is fusionist (Ben Meir 1995, Tarr & Roman 1995). It has, however, proven less fruitful for theory development.

Civil-Military Friction

A focus on civil-military conflict compensates for the difficulties that attend the coup and influence DVs. Even in a coup-free society, there are still likely to be episodes of friction and conflict, so this DV is generalizable. Indeed, the recent renaissance of the study of American civil-military relations discussed in the penultimate section of this essay has been triggered by the heightened acrimony that has characterized the civil-military relationship over the past five or six years. Stepan (1988) makes friction an integral part of his analysis of Brazilian civil-military relations, calling it "military contestation," and it is central to Ben Meir's (1995) analysis of the Israeli case as well. Friction can be measured as the degree to which the military is willing to display public opposition to an announced civilian policy. Moreover, friction is not a trivial concern. Too much friction could be indications and warnings of a coup in the offing. In contrast with "military influence," it has the virtue of being relatively easy to measure, since evidence of friction and conflict is likely to find its way into the public record.

Yet it seems a second-order consideration, at least in terms of the central civil-military problematique of agency and control. Friction is more a consequence of different patterns of civilian control than it is a civilian control issue itself. It is worthwhile relating different forms of control to the presence of friction, but the presence or absence of friction does not directly capture the problem of civilian control.

Military Compliance

Because of the problems attending these DVs, more recent work focuses on yet a fourth formulation: whether military or civilian preferences prevail when there is a policy dispute (Kemp & Hudlin 1992, Weigley 1993, Kohn 1994, Desch 1999, Feaver 1998a). This DV has the obvious advantage of reflecting the essence of the normative democratic principle that the will of civilians should prevail in all cases. It also has the empirical advantage of varying across different democracies and different periods of time; even in "mature" democracies like the United States, there are instances of the military prevailing against civilian leaders on certain policy questions, as the 1993 debate over gays in the military showed. Moreover, there are many times when civilian governments defer to a military demand rather than test military subordination.

Military compliance is not without analytical limitations as a DV, however. For starters, it suffers from something like the "dog that does not bark" problem afflicting the coups DV. Once a dispute has gone public, it is possible, though not necessarily easy, to determine whose preferences prevail at the decision-making stage. It is much more difficult, however, to determine whose preferences are prevailing on the countless issues that are resolved before a dispute gains public attention. A particularly adept military could enjoy enough political influence to shape policy without the issue gaining salience as a major policy dispute. Likewise, focusing on the policy-decision stage risks missing compliance issues that arise at the later policy implementation stage.

Delegation and Monitoring

Some recent work also considers yet another aspect of civil-military relations, the degree of delegation and the types of monitoring mechanisms used by civilian society (P Feaver, unpublished manuscript). This DV is tailored for the American case, where many of the traditional DVs (e.g. coups) simply are not very interesting. Therefore, a theoretical focus on delegation and monitoring may be a particularly fruitful line of analysis for newly stable democracies, offering explanatory leverage over civil-military relations even (or especially) in cases where the basic problem of ensuring civilian rule seems to be solved. At the same time, conceptualizing the DV as delegation and monitoring may sidestep questions of direct policy interest, such as whether the military is going to coup and/or whether the military is going to comply with civilian direction. The delegation and monitoring focus is not irrelevant to those questions—indeed, different patterns of delegation and monitoring influence the degree to which the military has incentives to comply with civilian direction—but its relationship is indirect. To the extent that the study is motivated by a desire to answer those questions, one of the other conceptualizations of the DV may be more profitable.

WHAT ARE THE INDEPENDENT VARIABLES?

Explanatory factors can be differentiated according to whether they are external or internal to the country. External factors that require a large army (such as the presence of a security threat), or pressure in the form of targeted aid and "advice" from particularly influential great powers, can influence the shape of a country's civil-military relations. Internal factors include such determinants as the nature of dominant cleavages in society, whether the society faces an internal threat or civil war, the nature of the domestic political system, and the distribution of wealth. A few scholars, notably Huntington (1957), Lasswell (1941, 1950), and Bueno de Mesquita & Siverson (1995), emphasize the importance of external systemic factors in shaping civil-military relations. Similarly, Aguero (1995) concluded that the presence of an external threat against which transitional civilian leaders could focus defense policy was an important factor explaining the success of transitions from authoritarian to democratic regimes. In general, however, political scientists (including Aguero) have found greater explanatory leverage from internal factors (Colton 1979, Colton & Gustafson 1990, Finer 1962, Horowitz 1980, Horowitz 1985, Janowitz 1960, Nordlinger 1977, Perlmutter 1977, Rouquie 1982, Stepan 1971, Stepan 1988, Vagts 1937, Welch 1976), and some of the most interesting recent work attempts to integrate both internal and external factors (Desch 1999).

Explanatory variables internal to the state can be further differentiated according to the civilian/military distinction itself: Does the causal factor relate to features of civilian society or to features of the military? For instance, Huntington's (1957, 1968) two classic works touching on civil-military relations constitute something of a debate between explanatory variables; his early work emphasizes a military factor, namely the degree of professionalism in the officer corps, and his later work emphasizes a civilian factor, namely the degree of institutionalization within civilian society. Nordlinger (1977) locates the primary causal factors for coups in the political sociology of the officer corps. In contrast, Welch (1976) emphasizes the legitimacy and efficiency of civilian government as an important deterrent to coups.

Within the civilian sphere, it is possible to distinguish still further between ethnocultural, economic, ideological, and political factors. Enloe (1980) emphasizes ethnic identity and ethnic cleavages as the dominant shaping force in civil-military relations. Campbell (1990), on the other hand, emphasizes the economic pressure of fiscal stringency and its impact on Soviet civil-military relations. Huntington (1957) emphasizes the different ways in which three competing ideologies, liberalism, conservatism, and Marxism, conceive military affairs and how these conceptions lead to different patterns of civil-military relations in liberal, conservative, and communist societies. Aguero (1995) combines a variety of economic and organizational factors into an index of relative civilian and military political power.

A final set of IVs deserves mention: factors arising from the transition from authoritarianism to democracy (Danopoulos 1988a,b, 1992).[5] The conventional wisdom holds that the age and robustness of the democracy are important in determining the country's pattern of civil-military relations. At least where civilian control of the military is concerned, success breeds success and failure breeds failure. But the nature (as distinct from the newness) of the transition to democracy may also be a causal factor shaping civil-military relations. Frazer (1994) offers the counterintuitive finding that, at least in Africa, a peaceful transition from the colonial period to independence augurs less well for enduring civilian control than does a violent transition. She argues that civilians who inherit power peacefully have not developed the necessary institutional counterweights to forestall future coups by the military. In contrast, a state resulting from an armed struggle with the colonial power will have sufficient experience in maintaining political control over the military or, more importantly, may have inadvertently created strong armed counterweights to the traditional military and so will be able to keep the military in check. A similar logic may also hold in transitions from authoritarian regimes; institutional solutions developed during the transition in response to civil-military conflict, in the form of contested policy goals, can ultimately strengthen the hand of civilian authorities over the long run (Trinkunas 1999).

Busza (1996) has compared the experience of Poland and Russia and traced how leaders make key policy choices during the transition to democracy about the rules that will govern civil-military affairs. The institutional rules then shape civilian and military preferences, creating incentives either for subordination or for insubordination. Aguero (1995) likewise emphasizes the policy

[5]The transition literature is vast, and reviewing it is beyond the scope of this essay. I discuss only the literature of greatest relevance to the civilian control question, narrowly defined. For a broader treatment of the transition literature, see O'Donnell et al (1986).

trajectory established during the transition, tracing the endurance of civilian supremacy to the following five factors: whether the authoritarian regime had been militarized or civilianized; whether the transition was gradual or precipitous; the relative degree of internal unity of the civilian and military actors; the degree of mass public support for emerging civilian structures; and the extent to which civilians were able to develop expertise on defense matters. The record of the various former–Warsaw Pact countries suggests that another important issue may be whether establishing civilian control structures becomes a de facto prerequisite for the transitioning state to join a desirable organization such as NATO (Danopoulos & Zirker 1996, Michta 1997).

One of the weaknesses in the civil-military relations literature is that there are relatively few efforts to systematically compare explanatory factors or to identify the conditions under which one set of factors has more explanatory leverage than another. Even where different sets of factors are pitted against each other, it is rare for the analyst to do more than give rough comparable weights to one or the other. Zimmermann's (1983) excellent review of the literature on coups catalogues 18 determinants of coups, ranging from economic factors to social mobilization to external military aid. Although he stops short of providing clear weighting for each factor, he does show that the study of coups has progressed the farthest in comparing explanatory variables, perhaps because for that issue area the DV is relatively easy to operationalize. Desch (1999) is another compelling example of an effort to specify rigorously the conditions under which one set of factors has better explanatory leverage over civil-military relations than another.

It is worth noting that civil-military relationships can themselves serve as explanatory factors, IVs explaining other political phenomena of interest. Of course, inherent in the civil-military problematique is the notion that different patterns of relations differentially contributed to military effectiveness and the provision of adequate national security (Huntington 1957); more recently, this idea has been operationalized in a study comparing the abilities of states to exploit advantages in military technology (Biddle & Zirkle 1996). Studies show that different patterns of civil-military relations lead to different forms of nuclear command and control and therefore to differentially dangerous forms of nuclear proliferation (Feaver 1992, 1992/1993; Sagan 1994). Other studies argue that pathologies in civil-military relationships may make a state prone to war, or at least likely to adopt offensive strategies (Snyder 1984, Van Evera 1984). Still others have explored whether different patterns of civil-military relations lead to differential propensities to innovate in doctrine (Avant 1994; Kier 1997; Posen 1984; Rosen 1991, 1996; Zisk 1993). And, of course, patterns of civil-military relations can be used to explain defense spending and weapons procurement decisions (Rosen 1973, Jackman 1976, Zuk & Thompson 1982, Londregan & Poole 1990).

WHAT ARE THE CONTROL MECHANISMS?

As the preceding sections document, the literature has progressed from the original DV of coups and the original IV of military professionalism. Yet, while empirical and theoretical treatments of civil-military relations have progressed, the normative focus underlying the field has remained remarkably constant: How can civilians exercise better control over the military? This normative impulse begs the prior question of how civilians do exercise control over the military. Although political science has not produced the definitive answer, it has assisted the effort by cataloguing and evaluating different control mechanisms.

Civilian control techniques can be grouped into two broad categories: (*a*) those that affect the ability of the military to subvert control and (*b*) those that affect the disposition of the military to be insubordinate (Finer 1962, Welch 1976).

The options under the first category are inherently limited. Most countries employ some sort of constitutional and administrative restraints that legally bind the military in a subservient position (Damrosch 1995). These measures, however, only restrain the military insofar as the military abides by the measures. They are legal frameworks for civilian control, but they are not really mechanisms that affect the ability of the military to subvert. In an effort to force potentially reluctant militaries to respect the legal framework, the civilian government can choose to deploy the military far from the centers of political power, as in the ancient Roman practice of garrisoning troops on the periphery of the empire. Alternatively, or in tandem, the civilian government can keep the army divided and weak relative to the civilian government. Societies that do not face grave external threats may choose to keep the regular army small in size or rely on a mobilized citizenry for defense; this was the preferred option of the United States until the twentieth century. This approach is risky, however, for (depending on geography and/or technology) it may make the country vulnerable to outside threats.

Countries that face an external threat, or regimes that feel the need for large forces to preserve power, may deploy sizable armed forces but keep them divided, perhaps by setting various branches against each other or using secret police and other parallel chains of command to keep the military in check (Frazer 1994, Belkin 1998). In fact, the use of countervailing institutions such as border guards, secret police, paramilitary forces, militias, presidential guards, and so on is one of the most common forms of control, used both by autocracies (the Ottoman Empire) and democracies (Switzerland and the United States). Of course, even this effort may erode the ability of the military to execute its primary function of defending the society against external threats (Biddle & Zirkle 1996).

Welch (1976) suggests that, by developing a high degree of specialization in the army, a country may reduce the military's capacity to intervene without affecting its capacity to defend the republic. A large and highly specialized military might find it difficult to pull off a coup simply due to coordination problems. Thus, modern armed forces might be optimized for battlefield performance—each specialist performing his or her role in synchrony with the others—and yet be unable to execute a domestic power grab because all the parts would not know how to coordinate in this novel operation. Welch is correct only if the specialized military does not decide to devote training time to such power grabs. As Welch himself notes, increased functional specialization only increases the complexity of a coup plot. There is nothing inherently limiting about size or role specification that would frustrate a determined military.

Since most efforts to reduce the *ability* of the military to subvert civilian government simultaneously weaken it vis-à-vis external threats, theorists have emphasized instead efforts to reduce the military's *disposition* to intervene. Any military strong enough to defend civilian society is also strong enough to destroy it. It is therefore essential that the military choose not to exploit its advantage, voluntarily submitting to civilian control. Finer (1962), noting that civilian control of the military is not "natural," argues that, given the political strengths of the military, the real puzzle is how civilians are able at all to exercise control—and the key to the puzzle, Finer says, is military disposition.

Under this category, the most prominent mechanism is the principle itself, which is variously called the "cult of obedience," the "norm of civilian control," or simply "professionalism" (Welch 1976, Smith 1951, Huntington 1957). Hendrickson (1988) concludes that no amount of institutional tinkering can ensure civilian control; the real basis of civilian control is the ethic that governs the relationship between civilians and the military. This is what organizational theorists call nonhierarchical control (Bouchard 1991).

The necessity of focusing on the military's disposition to intervene turns the civil-military problem into what can be understood as a form of the classic principal-agent relationship, with civilian principals seeking ways to ensure that the military agents are choosing to act appropriately even though they have the ability to shirk (Feaver 1998a). To develop this norm of obedience, civilians can employ two basic techniques, which follow the traditional principal-agent pattern: efforts to minimize either the adverse selection problem or the moral hazard problem. In civil-military terms, this translates to (*a*) adjusting the ascriptive characteristics of the military so that it will be populated by people inclined to obey, and (*b*) adjusting the incentives of the military so that, regardless of their nature, the members will prefer to obey.

Virtually all societies have used accession policy to influence ascriptive features of the military. For instance, European countries restricted military service, and especially officer commissions, to privileged castes such as the aristocracy or particular religious groups (e.g. Catholics in France). Americans adopted the mirror opposite approach, expanding military service through the militia in order to have the military reflect as much as possible the republican virtues of citizen-soldiers.[6] Different mixes of selected service, short-term universal service, and merit-based commissions are likewise effective in reducing the military's disposition to subvert civilian control by changing the character of the people that make up the military. The sociological school of civil-military relations embraces this tool and operationalizes it in terms of integrating the military with society (Larson 1974, Moskos & Wood 1988, Moskos & Butler 1996). A variant of this approach is prominent in communist and fascist countries, which have used party membership and political commissars to shape the attitudinal structure of the senior officer corps, if not the lower ranks (Kolkowicz 1966, Herspring & Volgyes 1978, Colton 1979, Herspring 1996).

There are limits to the accession tool, however. As Huntington (1957) argues, tinkering with ascriptive characteristics, an element of what he calls "subjective control," can politicize the military such that it becomes an arena for the political struggle of the various civilian groups represented or not represented in the accession policy. Without using the term, Vagts (1937) goes into more detail on these "subjective" measures of civilian control and shows how they can politicize the military in unhealthy ways.

One way to gain some of the benefits of restrictive accession policy without the negative side effects of subjective control is through training. Thus, every recruit, regardless of social origin, is molded by careful training to adopt the characteristics desired by society—in this case, every recruit is indoctrinated with the ideal of civilian control. This approach is implicit in Huntington's (1957) emphasis on professionalism. Training is also the long pole in the civilian control tent of Janowitz (1960) and the sociological school.

Yet, there is considerable difficulty in operationalizing civilian control of the military by changing the ethic of the military. Arguably, training officers in liberal arts colleges as a complement to the official military academies constitutes an important, albeit subtle, form of civilian control. Officers so trained are likely to bring to their jobs a wider world view, certainly more "civilian" in perspective than their purely military peers. However, as opposition to ROTC programs in the United States shows, it is possible to view these programs not as instruments of civilian control but as evidence of creeping militarism in civilian society: enshrining military influence and opportunities for propaganda within the walls of the liberal (civilian) bastion (Ekirch 1956, Sherry 1995). A strong ROTC program can either be an indication of subtle civilian control

---

[6]As noted above, the militia also serves to reduce the ability of the military to subvert by creating a competing power source.

over the composition of the military or weak capitulation of civilian society to an all-pervasive military value structure.

If the civilians cannot completely change the nature of the military, they can seek to adjust the military's incentives to encourage proper subordination. Some versions of this are particularly base. For instance, the Romans essentially bribed the capitol garrison to keep it out of politics. Political loyalty is similarly bought among many developing world armed forces, where substantial corruption opportunities give them a stake in the survival of the civilian regime. Guarantees of wages and benefits function much like these bribes— guarantees that, if broken, are a likely trigger for coup attempts. Bribes are very problematic as a tool of civilian control (Brooks 1998). At some level they are inherently corrupting of the military institution, and the loyalty they buy may be allegiance to the bribe, not to the civilian institution doing the bribing.

A more noble version of incentive adjustments forms the heart of traditional civil-military relations theory: a social contract between civilians and the military enshrined in a "proper" division of labor. By this division of labor, the civilians structure a set of incentives for the military that rewards subordination with autonomy. Some division of labor is inevitable; indeed, the very term civil-military relations assumes that there is something called civilian and that it is different from the thing called military. However, as used here, the division of labor is more a normative than a descriptive concept. It derives from Clausewitz's (1976) principle that war is the continuation of politics by other means. This is what Clausewitz meant by the aphorism, "[War's] grammar, indeed, may be its own but not its logic." The logic of war must come from the political masters of the military.

Clausewitzean logic assigns a role for civilians and implies, in turn, a role for the military. The military are, in Clausewitzean phraseology, the grammarians of war. This makes operations the exclusive province of the military. The argument asserts that some issues are not political; that is, some issues are purely technical, best decided by the experts, in this case, the military.

This division of labor is implied in Huntington's (1957) preferred method of civilian control, "objective control." Objective control means maximizing the professionalism of the military; because obedience to civilians is at the heart of professionalism (Huntington claims), this will insure civilian control. Maximizing professionalism is best achieved by getting the military out of politics and, similarly, getting the politicians out of the military, that is, getting the politicians out of directing tactical and operational matters. Welch (1976) is even more explicit about the quid pro quo aspect of the division of labor. He advocates a hands-off approach as the most effective and achievable path to civilian control. Civilians grant autonomy to the military in matters of lesser import in exchange for military acceptance of the ethic of subordination. Such a deal was crucial, for instance, in preserving civilian control during the early French Republic; the army was granted autonomy over accession policy (which the army exploited to limit commissions to the aristocracy and to Catholics) in exchange for a cult of obedience.

The disposition of the military to intervene can be reduced in yet another way—by strengthening the legitimacy of the civilian government (Holsti 1996). A vigorous and effective civilian government eliminates a powerful coup motive, namely the military conviction that they can rule better than incompetent or corrupt civilians. Such a government also makes insubordination and coups more costly because it raises the expectation that the mass civilian society will support the civilian leaders against the military.[7]

Finally, civilians can adopt numerous monitoring mechanisms, which, while not making insubordination impossible, nevertheless raise the costs and so may affect the military's disposition to intervene (P Feaver, unpublished manuscript). Monitoring mechanisms include such activities as audits, investigations, rules of engagement; civilian staffs with expertise and oversight responsibilities; and such extragovernmental institutions as the media and defense think tanks. Essentially, monitoring mechanisms enhance civilian control by bringing military conduct to the attention of responsible civilians. Monitoring mechanisms like this presume a certain level of civilian control—they are not going to secure civilian control in the face of a coup-prone military. They are essentially the practical implementation of the constitutional/legal provisions discussed above, suffering from the same limitations. Indeed, they may even be self-limiting; monitoring mechanisms can take the form of "getting in the military's knickers," provoking more harm in military resentment than benefit they gain in civilian oversight. Properly implemented, however, monitoring mechanisms can raise the costs of military insubordination or noncompliant behavior simply by making it more difficult for such action to go unnoticed.

The greater the willingness of civilian leaders to punish noncompliant behavior, the more effective the monitoring mechanisms are in securing civilian control. Yet, even with weak and uneven punishment, the monitoring mechanisms can support civilian control. Especially in the face of a global norm supporting democratic traditions, it always costs the military more to disobey in public than to do so in private. Although monitoring mechanisms may not ensure compliance in cases where military interests dictate large benefits from noncompliance, they can affect cost-benefit calculations at the margins.

---

[7]Although this affects the perceived ability of the military to be insubordinate, its primary causal relationship is with the military disposition to intervene. The military may decide not to coup because they calculate they cannot govern, even though they have the wherewithal to seize power temporarily.

More to the point, they are the critical arena for civil-military relations in mature democracies. As the norm and the fact of civilian control become more deeply entrenched, the day-to-day practice of civil-military relations (and hence the focus of the study of civil-military relations) will increasingly center on monitoring and oversight of the delegation relationship. As the field shifts in this direction, however, care should be taken to make precise and sufficiently limited claims. Conclusively establishing which monitoring mechanisms are more effective than others—or identifying the conditions under which one kind of monitoring mechanism is superior to another—is notoriously difficult. Just as it is difficult to know whether deterrence is working, the absence of civil-military problems may be evidence for the effectiveness of the control mechanism or it may reflect the underlying stability of the political structure, or luck, or indeed all three factors.

AN AMERICAN RENAISSANCE

The casual observer might be surprised to learn that the civil-military problematique is the focus of renewed attention among scholars and observers of the American case. An outsider might assume that if any country has solved this problem, surely it must be the United States, which boasts unchallenged superpower status and a 200-plus–year record without a coup or attempted coup. In fact, however, the question of the robustness and efficacy of civilian control in the United States is very much a live issue in policy-making circles, and this has precipitated a renewed interest in the academic subfield.

Shortly after the end of the Cold War, and well before President Clinton's much-discussed problems with the military became manifest, a number of scholars and analysts began to express concern about the health and direction of civil-military relations. The alarms were somewhat ironic because the peaceful end of the Cold War and the operational success of the coalition forces in the 1990–1991 Gulf War seemed to augur nothing but good things for the future of the national security establishment. Nevertheless, experts found things to worry about: an overly vigorous Joint Staff with a politically savvy Chairman who seems to dominate defense policy debates (Campbell 1991, Weigley 1993, Kohn 1994); a civilian society that overutilizes the military for missions that politicize the military and divert them from their primary warfighting focus (Dunlap 1992/1993, 1994); a growing gap between the experiences, outlook, and ideology of the military and those of civilian society, especially civilian policy makers (Ricks 1997; Holsti 1997; Kohn & Bacevich 1997; Gibson & Snider 1998). Of course, the Clinton problem exacerbated these concerns in the form of an apparently weak and vacillating civilian leadership, personified by a president who had avoided military service and knew little about military affairs (Bacevich 1993, 1994/1995, Luttwak 1994, Owen 1994/1995, Lane 1995, Johnson & Metz 1995, Johnson 1996, Korb 1996).

The basic political questions of "who decides?" and "what should they decide?" played out in a variety of well-publicized policy fights and scandals: debates over whether or how to use force in Bosnia, Haiti, Somalia, Iraq, and Rwanda; the debate over whether to allow homosexuals to serve openly in the military; the debate over whether to open combat duties to women; and the various sexual harassment and sexual peccadilloes scandals (charges of sexual harassment at the 1991 Tailhook Convention, allegations of sexual harassment at the Aberdeen training facility, the issue of Kelly Flinn's adultery and fraternization, the withdrawal of General Ralston's nomination for Chairman of the Joint Chiefs of Staff after his own adulterous affair came to light, etc) (Snider & Carlton-Carew 1995).

The newsworthiness of American civil-military relations has naturally attracted the attention of a new generation of scholars, who, expressing frustration with the old Huntington and Janowitz theoretical frameworks, have offered a range of broad-gauged alternatives.

Avant (1994, 1996/1997, 1998) offers a principal-agent interpretation, contrasting divided-principal settings like the United States, where military agents have the opportunity to play civilian principals off of each other, with unified principal settings like Britain, where such opportunities are more limited. Militaries in the former setting are less likely to embrace civilian-led doctrinal innovations than are militaries under a unified principal. My own work (P Feaver, unpublished manuscript; 1998a) also draws on the principal-agent literature. I develop a deductively grounded model of civil-military relations as a game of strategic interaction between civilian principals, who must decide how intrusively to monitor the military, and military agents, who decide whether to work or shirk in light of the monitoring regime and exogenously determined expectations of punishment. Weiner (1995), Zegart (1996), and Brooks (1999) also use the principal-agent approach to explore variations in how political-military institutions are formed and reformed. The framework has particular appeal because it is deductively grounded (and therefore able to generate parsimonious hypotheses) and because it nests the civil-military relationship within other political institutions and political relationships (and therefore offers opportunities to link the issue of political control of the military to concerns about the political control of other institutions).

Desch (1998a, 1999) offers a structural theory that treats military compliance with civilian directives as a function of the configuration of external and internal threats confronting a state; in the US case, Desch argues, moving from the Cold War setting of a high-external/low-internal threat environment to a post–Cold War low/low environment eroded the external orientation of the American military and encouraged them to engage in internal political squabbles. Dauber (1998), coming from the field of communications studies, offers an interpretation of civil-military relations as a contest in which standards of argumentation—public, private, or expert—will dominate policy making. Schiff (1995) offers "concordance theory," which explains changes in military subordination as a function of different patterns of relations among the governmental elite, the mass public, and the military. In a rare example of competitive theory testing, a number of the different frameworks have been applied to a common case in the hope of clarifying the uses and limitations of each framework (Bacevich 1998, Burk 1998, Desch 1998b, Feaver 1998b).[8]

The recent work is distinctive for its explicit emphasis on theory building, theory testing, and building bridges to other debates within political science. The traditional emphasis in the civil-military relations subfield has been on rich description and inductive case studies. It has been ideographic rather than nomothetic in orientation. This has had the advantage of producing a body of common knowledge accessible to a variety of disciplines, including history, sociology, and area studies. It has had the disadvantage, however, of limiting the theoretical development of the subfield. In contrast, the new work has generated clear, falsifiable, and generalizable hypotheses grounded in a consistent deductive logic: Patterns of military compliance vary according to different configurations of internal and external threat; the costs of monitoring and prospects for punishment influence the way the military responds to civilian direction; divisions among principals make the military less responsive to innovation; and so on. It is too soon to know whether future research will reinforce or undermine these hypotheses and the broader theories from which they derive, but the focus on theory, rather than description, opens the door to the kind of cumulation expected in normal science. Moreover, the recent work offers the chance to integrate the subfield more profitably with the rest of political science. Much of the new work in civil-military relations makes use of concepts and methods common in other political science literatures (structural theory, the principal-agent framework, game theory, etc) and thereby enhances the possibility for fruitful interactions between those who study civil-military relations and those who study other political phenomena.

The newsworthiness has also generated at least three major collaborative research projects, involving scores of researchers from academia, the military, and the civilian policy arena. Harvard's Olin Institute sponsored a multiyear Project on US Post–Cold War Civil-Military Relations that resulted in some 30 books, articles, book chapters, and working papers. The Triangle Institute for Security Studies has a follow-on project, Bridging the Gap: Assuring Military Effectiveness When Military Culture Diverges from Civilian Society, that will

---

[8]The revival within political science has been matched by several equally ambitious efforts within the sociological school to reorient the study of civil-military relations. Miller (1994, 1997a,b, 1998) has explored changing attitudes on class, gender, and sexual orientation, and the impact of those attitudes on military operations (see also Miller & Moskos 1995, Harrell & Miller 1997).

produce several original surveys of civilian and military opinion as well as over 15 article-length analyses of the nature, origin, and significance of any differences or similarities between civilian and military cultures. The Center for Strategic and International Studies is conducting a companion study, American Military Culture in the Twenty-First Century, that will explore how the traditions, values, customs, and leadership behaviors of the military influence military effectiveness. As the project titles suggest, one of the key points of emphasis for current research is the role of culture (both military and civilian), the extent to which those cultural forms are immutable, and the ways in which they interact with the challenge of ensuring the need for protection from and by the military (Burk 1999).

CONCLUSIONS AND DIRECTIONS FOR FUTURE RESEARCH

These separate but reinforcing investigations ensure that the American case will receive due attention. In the broader civil-military subfield, future research might profitably focus on at least three additional faultlines in the existing literature. One concerns whether measures targeting the ability of would-be military insubordinates are more effective than those targeting the disposition. The conventional answer is that measures aimed at reducing military leaders' ability to be insubordinate are inherently limited because they also leave a state more vulnerable to external threats. Thus, traditional theorists such as Huntington (1957), Janowitz (1960), and Welch (1976) all emphasize various (and sometimes contradictory) measures aimed at the disposition of the military: professionalizing it and/or keeping it integrated with society, establishing social contracts that delineate spheres of influence, and so on. Recently, however, some political scientists have given greater weight to measures designed to check the ability of military organizations to intervene. As noted above, Frazer (1994) explicitly advocates that civilians establish competing institutions with coercive capabilities (such as separate paramilitary groups), which can serve as counterweights deterring military insubordination and/or compelling military compliance with civilian authorities. Likewise, Belkin (1998) concludes that all alternative strategies are inadequate and so a coup-prone state will perforce rely on these institutional counterweights, what he calls counterbalancing. This debate provides an interesting contrast with the trend elsewhere in political science. The fad in other subfields is the constructivist project, exploring ideational and norm-based explanations for political phenomena. The civil-military field has been dominated by ideational and norm-based explanations for 40 years, and some of the best new work is instead exploring the rationalist and interest-based aspects of civil-military relations. This debate also has obvious policy relevance, especially in transitioning democracies, where civilian control measures are still in their infancy. Thus far, these analyses have focused on coups, and so one priority is to apply the interest-based approach to the other dependent variables discussed in this essay.

A second faultline, also of great relevance to the vast democratization project, concerns whether to focus reforms on the civilian or on the military side of the relationship. Perlmutter (1977:281) concludes that a "stable, sustaining, and institutionalized political regime can hardly succumb to military pressure and rule," whereas no degree of professionalism can be counted on to guarantee military compliance in the face of the utter collapse of the civilian regime. By implication, any effort to improve civilian control must focus on improving the civilian side of the house. Stepan (1988), although not necessarily sympathetic to Perlmutter's approach, nevertheless pursues the civilian-side agenda even further. He argues for the strengthening of civilian military expertise by creating independent think tanks and stronger permanent committees in the parliament with routinized oversight responsibilities and sufficient staff to carry them out.

Welch (1976), in contrast, emphasizes efforts aimed at the military institution itself. Although he concedes that civilian legitimacy is important, he argues that efforts to improve civilian legitimacy (what he calls Strategy 1) are doomed by forces well beyond the control of most states: the vitality of the economy, the dominant social cleavages, and the general weakness of civilian institutions. Hence, Welch favors Strategy 2, tailoring the boundaries, mission, values, organization, recruitment, and socialization of the military so as to foster "a mutual sense of political restraint on the part of officers and politicians alike" (1976:317). The debate so far has taken the form of dueling anecdotes and competing laundry lists, however, and the field would greatly benefit from carefully specified theory testing. Special emphasis should be placed on identifying the conditions under which civilian-based or military-based reforms are more fruitful, and, if both are pursued simultaneously, the circumstances under which one set of reforms can undermine efforts in the other area.

A third faultline concerns the other side of the problematique, the linkage between patterns of civil-military relations and military effectiveness (Biddle & Zirkle 1996). Most American military officers accept as an article of faith the general Huntingtonian assertion that respect for military autonomy is necessary for military effectiveness, but it has never been established through rigorous empirical testing. It relies on anecdotes, like the botched Iranian hostage rescue mission, and myths, like the belief that President Johnson's micromanagement of the bombing campaigns prevented air power from deciding the Vietnam War (this myth has been rather convincingly rebutted in Pape 1996). A priority for future research would be to subject this and related claims to serious empirical study. Does civilian meddling uniformly result in disaster, or is such assertive control conducive to better strategy and operations under certain conditions?

Likewise, scholars should explore more fully the linkages between patterns of civil-military relations and the propensity to use force. The linkage has been investigated in the case of World War I (Van Evera 1984, Snyder 1984), especially the possibility that inadequate civilian control let military strategists push Germany and France into adopting inappropriately offense-oriented doctrines. The existing political science literature, however, is not very sophisticated in its understanding of civil-military relations. It tends to treat civil-military relations as a dichotomous variable—civilians in control/not in control—and does not explore the different causal effects of other forms of societal-military relations. For instance, is a country more prone to use force if it has an all-volunteer army, which can be deployed almost as mercenary force, or does the existence of mass-based conscription constrain leaders to follow swings in public opinion rather than the more prudent dictates of raison d'état? What if civilian decision makers increasingly come to positions of power without any personal experience with the military? Will they be ignorant of the limits of military power and prone to use the military in inappropriate ways or under unnecessarily dangerous circumstances? Or will they be overly sensitive to casualties, fearful that they lack the moral authority to order other men into danger, and thereby underutilize force when its application is called for? And if strategists are correct about a coming revolutionary change in war and military practice occasioned by the integration of advanced information technology into the armed forces, what does this portend for the way civilian decision makers control military institutions and for the way the armed forces relate to society?

Finally, I argue that one longstanding line of inquiry is not fruitful and should be abandoned: the linkage between professionalism and military subordination to civilian control. Huntington (1957) inaugurated this line of study with his argument that professionalism was the key to civilian control. But he included in his definition of professionalism acceptance of the ethic of subordination, so his argument (at least on this point) was in some sense tautological and defined away the problem. For this he has been roundly criticized (Finer 1962, Abrahamsson 1972). Janowitz (1960), however, did much the same thing, hinging political control on "professional ethics," and has received much less criticism for it (Abrahamsson 1972, Larson 1974). In my view, the analytical utility of the umbrella concept has been exhausted, and it now serves to obscure interesting debates—for instance, whether rational-interest factors are more influential than values-based factors in determining military behavior—rather than to illuminate them. Future research should focus on teasing out the explanatory force of the different component factors of what has been called professionalism and leave the synthetic concept at the rhetorical level, where it belongs. Sociologists have already embraced this approach, tracing changes in the nature of professionalism with the switch from draft-based service, which produced a traditional or "institutional" model of service, to an all-volunteer form of ascription, which produced an "occupational" model of service (Moskos 1977, Segal 1986, Moskos & Wood 1988).

The foregoing underscores the relatively weak cumulation in the political science theory of civil-military relations. The field has simply not produced a large body of consensus findings that enjoy widespread support and that would apply with equal force to a wide range of countries. Part of the problem may be an epistemological one that bedevils all of political science, the problem of self-negating predictions. Unlike electrons and atoms, the subjects of political science are themselves volitional actors. It makes sense for physicists to assume that particles are simply reacting to forces affecting them. The subjects of political science theory, however, are acting, reacting, and counteracting. And just as physics has its Heisenberg principle, which acknowledges the confounding influence of human measurement, so too does political science, but at an even more fundamental level.

Civil-military theorists must recognize that our subjects are thinking about the same problems, perhaps drawing similar conclusions about cause-effect relationships, and adjusting their behavior accordingly. Even a sensible policy prescription based on a reliable prediction that is itself based on a robust theory of cause and effect can be wrong if the political players understand the process and adjust their behavior successfully. Thus, seemingly weak civilian governments can compensate for their weakness to preserve civilian control, just as seemingly weak military actors can compensate to threaten even an apparently stable civilian regime. In short, even the best political science will offer only tentative predictions and qualified assessments.

Yet, the literature could be stronger than it is. The literature offers a rich resource of civil-military case studies but relatively few rigorous attempts to test hypotheses against these data. The sophistication and methodological self-awareness of the more recent studies augurs well in this regard, however. And the confluence of two trends in the real world—the spread of democracies and the remarkable disharmony within America's political and military elite—has made the study of civil-military relations more interesting and more salient than at any time since the end of the Vietnam War.

Visit the *Annual Reviews home page* at
http://www.AnnualReviews.org.

Literature Cited

Abrahamsson B. 1972. *Military Professionalization and Political Power*. Beverly Hills, CA: Sage

Aguero F. 1995. *Soldiers, Civilians, and Democracy: Post-Franco Spain in Comparative Perspective*. Baltimore, MD: Johns Hopkins Univ. Press

Avant DD. 1994. *Political Institutions and Military Change: Lessons from Peripheral Wars*. Ithaca, NY: Cornell Univ. Press

Avant DD. 1996/1997. US military reluctance to respond to post–Cold War low-level threats. *Secur. Stud.* 6(2):51–90

Avant DD. 1998. Conflicting indicators of "crisis" in American civil-military relations. *Armed Forces Soc.* 24(3):375–88

Bacevich AJ. 1993. Clinton's military problem—and ours. *Natl. Rev.* 45(24):36–40

Bacevich AJ. 1994/1995. Civilian control: a useful fiction? *Joint Forces Q.* 6(Autumn/Winter):76–83

Bacevich AJ. 1998. Absent history: a comment on Dauber, Desch and Feaver. *Armed Forces Soc.* 24(3):447–54

Bachman JG, Blair JD, Segal DR. 1977. *The All-Volunteer Force*. Ann Arbor: Univ. Mich. Press

Barrett RJ. 1965. Partners in policymaking. *Mil. Rev.* 45(10):84–88

Belkin A. 1998. *Performing the national security state: civil-military relations as a cause of international conflict*. PhD thesis. Univ. Calif., Berkeley. 273 pp.

Ben Meir Y. 1995. *Civil Military Relations in Israel*. New York: Columbia Univ. Press

Betts RK. 1977. *Soldiers, Statesmen, and Cold War Crises*. Cambridge, MA: Harvard Univ. Press

Biddle S, Zirkle R. 1996. Technology, civil-military relations and warfare in the developing world. *J. Strat. Stud.* 19:171–212

Bienen H. 1968. *The Military Intervenes: Case Studies in Political Development*. New York: Russell Sage Found.

Bienen H, Van de Walle N. 1990. Poverty, the coup trap, and the seizure of executive power. *World Polit.* 42:151–83

Boene B. 1990. How "unique" should the military be? A review of representative literature and outline of a synthetic formulation. *Eur. J. Soc.* 31(1):3–59

Boene B. 1997. *Western-type civil-military relations revisited*. Presented at Hebrew Univ. Jerus., Dec. 2–3

Bouchard J. 1991. *Command in Crisis: Four Case Studies*. New York: Columbia Univ. Press

Brooks RA .1998. *Political-military relations and the stability of Arab regimes*. Adelphi Pap., Int. Inst. Strat. Stud.

Brooks RA. 1999. *The domestic origins and international effects of political-military institutions*. PhD thesis. Univ. Calif., San Diego

Bueno de Mesquita B, Siverson R. 1995. War and the survival of political leaders: a comparative study of regime types and political accountability. *Am. Polit. Sci. Rev.* 89:841–56

Burk J. 1993. Morris Janowitz and the origins of sociological research on armed forces and society. *Armed Forces Soc.* 19(2):167–86

Burk J. 1998. The logic of crisis and civil-military relations theory: a comment on Desch, Feaver, and Dauber. *Armed Forces Soc.* 24(3):455–62

Burk J. 1999. Military culture. In *Encyclopedia of Violence, Peace and Conflict*, ed. L Kurtz. San Diego, CA: Academic

Busza E. 1996. Transition and civil-military relations in Poland and Russia. *Communist Post-Communist Stud.* 29(2):167–84

Campbell K. 1991. All rise for chairman Powell. *Natl. Interest* 23(Spring): 51–60

Campbell R. 1990. Resource stringency and civil-military resource allocation. In *Soldiers and the Soviet State*, ed. TJ Colton, T Gustafson, pp. 126–63. Princeton, NJ: Princeton Univ. Press

Clausewitz KV. 1976. *On War*. Ed./Transl. M Howard, P Paret. Princeton, NJ: Princeton Univ. Press

Cohen EA. 1985. *Citizens and Soldiers: The Dilemmas of Military Service*. Ithaca, NY: Cornell Univ. Press

Colton TJ. 1979. *Commissars, Commanders and Civilian Authority: The Structure of Soviet Military Politics*. Cambridge, MA: Harvard Univ. Press

Colton TJ, Gustafson T, eds. 1990. *Soldiers and the Soviet State: Civil-Military Relations from Brezhnev to Gorbachev*. Princeton, NJ: Princeton Univ. Press

Dahl R. 1985. *Controlling Nuclear Weapons*. Syracuse, NY: Syracuse Univ. Press

Damrosch L. 1995. Constitutional control over war powers: a common core of accountability in democratic societies? *Univ. Miami Law Rev.* 50(Oct.):181–99

Danopoulos CP. 1988a. *The Decline of Military Regimes: The Civilian Influence*. Boulder, CO: Westview

Danopoulos CP. 1988b. *Military Disengagement from Politics*. New York: Routledge

Danopoulos CP. 1992. *From Military to Civilian Rule.* New York: Routledge

Danopoulos CP, Watson C. 1996. *The Political Role of the Military: An International Handbook.* Westport, CT: Greenwood

Danopoulos CP, Zirker D. 1996. *Civil-Military Relations in the Soviet and Yugoslav Successor States.* Boulder, CO: Westview

Dauber C. 1998. The practice of argument: reading the condition of civil-military relations. *Armed Forces Soc.* 24(3):435–46

Desch MC. 1998a. Soldiers, states, and structures: the end of the Cold War and weakening US civilian control. *Armed Forces Soc.* 24(3):389–406

Desch MC. 1998b. A historian's fallacies: a reply to Bacevich. *Armed Forces Soc.* 24(4):587–92

Desch MC. 1999. *Soldiers, States, and Structure: Civilian Control of the Military in a Changing Security Environment.* Baltimore, MD: Johns Hopkins Univ. Press

Diamond L, Plattner MF, eds. 1996. *Civil-Military Relations and Democracy.* Baltimore, MD: Johns Hopkins Univ. Press

Downing B. 1991. *The Military Revolution and Political Change: Origins of Democracy and Autocracy in Early Modern Europe.* Princeton, NJ: Princeton Univ. Press

Dunlap C. 1992/1993. The origins of the American military coup of 2012. *Parameters* 22(Winter):2–20

Dunlap C. 1994. Welcome to the junta: the erosion of civilian control of the US military. *Wake Forest Law Rev.* 29(2):341–92

Edmonds M. 1988. *Armed Services and Society.* Boulder, CO: Westview

Ekirch AA Jr. 1956. *The Civilian and the Military.* New York: Oxford Univ. Press

Enloe CH. 1980. *Ethnic Soldiers: State Security in Divided Societies.* Athens: Univ. Georgia Press

Feaver PD. 1992. *Guarding the Guardians: Civilian Control of Nuclear Weapons in the United States.* Ithaca, NY: Cornell Univ. Press

Feaver PD. 1992/1993. Command and control in emerging nuclear nations. *Int. Secur.* 17(3):160–87

Feaver PD. 1995. Civil-military conflict and the use of force. In *U.S. Civil-Military Relations: In Crisis or Transition?*, ed. D Snider, MA Carlton-Carew, pp. 113–44. Washington, DC: Cent. Strat. Int. Stud.

Feaver PD. 1996. An American crisis in civilian control and civil-military relations? Historical and conceptual roots. *Tocqueville Rev.* 17(1):159–84

Feaver PD. 1997a. The civil-military problematique: Huntington, Janowitz, and the question of civilian control. *Armed Forces Soc.* 23(2):149–78

Feaver PD. 1997b. El control civil en pequeñas democracias: la contribución de las ciencias politicas. See Zamora 1997, pp. 67–106

Feaver PD. 1998a. Crisis as shirking: an agency theory explanation of the souring of American civil-military relations. *Armed Forces Soc.* 24(3):407–34

Feaver PD. 1998b. Modeling civil-military relations: a reply to Burk and Bacevich. *Armed Forces Soc.* 24(4):593–600

Finer SE. 1962. *The Man on Horseback: The Role of the Military in Politics.* London: Pall Mall

Frazer JE. 1994. *Sustaining civilian control in Africa: the use of armed counterweights in regime stability.* PhD thesis. Stanford Univ., Palo Alto, CA

Snider DM, Gibson CP. 1997. Explaining post-Cold War civil-military relations: a new institutionalist approach. *John M Olin Inst. Strat. Stud., Proj. US Post Cold-War Civil-Mil. Relat., Work. Pap. No. 8*

Snider DM, Gibson CP. 1998. Civil-military relations and the ability to influence: a look at the national security decisionmaking process. *Armed Forces Soc.* 25

Goldstone J. 1991. *Revolution and Rebellion in the Early Modern World.* Berkeley: Univ. Calif. Press

Hahn RF. 1997. Politics for warriors: the political education of professional military officers. *John M Olin Inst. Strat. Stud., Proj. US Post Cold-War Civil-Mil. Relat., Work. Pap. No. 12*

Harrell MC, Miller LL. 1997. *New Opportunities for Military Women: Effects on Readiness, Cohesion and Morale.* Santa Monica, CA: RAND

Hendrickson D. 1988. *Reforming Defense: The State of American Civil-military Relations.* Baltimore, MD: Johns Hopkins Univ. Press

Herspring DR. 1996. *Russian Civil-Military Relations.* Bloomington: Indiana Univ. Press

Herspring DR, Volgyes I. 1978. *Civil-Military Relations in Communist Systems.* Boulder, CO: Westview

Holsti KJ. 1996. *The State, War, and the State of War.* Cambridge, UK: Cambridge Univ. Press

Holsti O. 1997. A widening gap between the military and society? Some evidence, 1976–1996. *John M Olin Inst. Strat. Stud., Proj. US Post Cold-War Civil-Mil. Relat., Work. Pap. No. 13*

Horowitz D. 1980. *Coup Theories and Officers' Motives: Sri Lanka in Comparative Perspective*. Princeton, NJ: Princeton Univ. Press

Horowitz D. 1985. *Ethnic Groups in Conflict*. Berkeley: Univ. Calif. Press

Hunter W. 1998. Negotiating civil-military relations in post-authoritarian Argentina and Chile. *Int. Stud. Q.* 42:295–318

Huntington SP. 1957. *The Soldier and the State: The Theory and Politics of Civil-Military Relations*. Cambridge, MA: Harvard Univ. Press

Huntington SP. 1968. *Political Order in Changing Societies*. New Haven, CT: Yale Univ. Press

Jackman RW. 1976. Politicians in uniform: military governments and social change in the Third World. *Am. Polit. Sci. Rev.* 70:1078–97

Jackman RW. 1978. The predictability of coups d'état: a model with African data. *Am. Polit. Sci. Rev.* 72:1262–75

Janowitz M. 1960. *The Professional Soldier: A Social and Political Portrait*. Glencoe, IL: Free

Janowitz M. 1977. *Military Institutions and Coercion in the Developing Nations*. Chicago: Univ. Chicago Press

Johnson DE. 1996. Wielding the terrible swift sword: the American military paradigm and civil-military relations. *John M Olin Inst. Strat. Stud., Proj. US Post Cold-War Civil-Mil. Relat., Work. Pap. No. 7*

Johnson DV II, Metz S. 1995. American civil-military relations: new issues, enduring problems. *Strat. Stud. Inst.* 24 (April)

Johnson TH, Slater RO, McGowan P. 1984. Explaining African military coups d'état. *Am. Polit. Sci. Rev.* 78:622–40

Kemp KW, Hudlin C. 1992. Civil supremacy over the military: its nature and limits. *Armed Forces Soc.* 19(1):7–26

Kerwin JG. 1948. *Civil-Military Relationships in American Life*. Chicago: Univ. Chicago Press

Kier E. 1997. *Imagining War: French and British Military Doctrine Between the Wars*. Princeton, NJ: Princeton Univ. Press

Kohn RH. 1994. Out of control: the crisis in civil-military relations. *Nat. Interest* 35:3–18

Kohn RH. 1997. How democracies control the military. *J. Democr.* 8:140–53

Kohn RH, Bacevich AJ. 1997. Grand army of the Republicans. *New Republic* 4,325:22–25

Kolkowicz R. 1966. *The Soviet Military and the Communist Party*. Princeton, NJ: Princeton Univ. Press

Kolodziej E. 1966. *The Uncommon Defense and Congress, 1945–1963*. Columbus: Ohio State Univ. Press

Korb L. 1996. The military and social change. *John M Olin Inst. Strat. Stud., Proj. US Post Cold-War Civil-Mil. Relat., Work. Pap. No. 5*

Lane C. 1995. The legend of Colin Powell. *New Republic* 17(April):20–32

Larson AD. 1974. Military professionalism and civil control: a comparative analysis of two interpretations. *J. Polit. Mil. Sociol.* 2:57–72

Lasswell HD. 1941. The garrison state and specialists on violence. *Am. J. Sociol.* 46:455–68

Lasswell HD. 1950. *National Security and Individual Freedom*. New York: McGraw-Hill

Londregan JB, Poole KT. 1990. Poverty, the coup trap and the seizure of executive power. *World Polit.* 42:151–83

Lovell JP, Albright DE. 1997. *To Sheathe the Sword: Civil-Military Relations in the Quest for Democracy*. Westport, CT: Greenwood

Luttwak E. 1979. *Coup d'Etat: A Practical Handbook*. Cambridge, MA: Harvard Univ. Press

Luttwak E. 1994. Washington's biggest scandal. *Commentary* 100(5):29–33

Lyons GM. 1961. The new civil-military relations. *Am. Polit. Sci. Rev.* 55:153–63

Michta AA. 1997. *The Soldier-Citizen: The Politics of the Polish Army After Communism*. New York: St. Martin's

Miller LL. 1994. Fighting for a just cause: soldiers' attitudes on gays in the military. In *Gays and Lesbians in the Military: Issues, Concerns, and Contrasts*, ed. WJ Scott, SC Stanley, pp. 69–85. New York: Aldine de Gruyter

Miller LL. 1997a. Not just weapons of the weak: gender harassment as a form of protest for army men. *Soc. Psychol. Q.* 60:32–51

Miller LL. 1997b. Do soldiers hate peacekeeping? The case of preventive diplomacy operations in Macedonia. *Armed Forces Soc.* 23:415–50

Miller LL. 1998. Feminism and the exclusion of army women from combat. *Gender Issues* 16:33–64

Miller LL, Moskos CC. 1995. Humanitarians or warriors? Race, gender and combat status in Operation Restore Hope. *Armed Forces Soc.* 21:615–37

Millis CW. 1956. *The Power Elite*. New York: Oxford Univ. Press

Millis W, Mansfield H, Stein H. 1958. *Arms and the State: Civil-Military Elements in*

National Policy. New York: 20th Cent. Fund.

Mills CW. 1956. *The Power Elite.* New York: Oxford Univ. Press

Moskos CC. 1970. *The American Enlisted Man: The Rank and File in Today's Military.* New York: Russell Sage Found.

Moskos CC, ed. 1971. *Public Opinion and the Military Establishment.* Beverly Hills, CA: Sage

Moskos CC. 1977. From institution to occupation: trends in the military organization. *Armed Forces Soc.* 4(1):41–50

Moskos CC, Butler JS. 1996. *All That We Can Be: Black Leadership and Racial Integration the Army Way.* New York: Basic Books

Moskos CC, Wood FR, eds. 1988. *The Military: More Than Just a Job?* Washington, DC: Pergamon-Brassey's

Nordlinger E. 1977. *Soldiers in Politics: Military Coups and Governments.* New York: Prentice-Hall

O'Donnell G, Schmitter PC, Whitehead L, eds. 1986. *Transitions from Authoritarian Rule: Comparative Perspectives.* Baltimore, MD: Johns Hopkins Univ. Press

O'Kane R. 1981. A probabilistic approach to the causes of coups d'état. *Br. J. Polit. Sci.* 11:287–308

Owen MT. 1994/1995. Civilian control: a national crisis? *Joint Forces Q.* Winter: 80–83

Pape RA. 1996. *Bombing to Win: Air Power and Coercion in War.* Ithaca, NY: Cornell Univ. Press

Perlmutter A. 1977. *The Military and Politics in Modern Times: On Professionals, Praetorians, and Revolutionary Soldiers.* New Haven, CT: Yale Univ. Press

Petraeus DH. 1987. *The American military and the lessons of Vietnam.* PhD dissertation. Princeton Univ., Princeton, NJ

Pion-Berlin D. 1992. Military autonomy and emerging democracies in South America. *Comp. Polit.* 25:83–103

Posen BR. 1984. *The Sources of Military Doctrine: France, Britain, and Germany Between the World Wars.* Ithaca, NY: Cornell Univ. Press

Rice C. 1984. *The Soviet Union and the Czechoslovak Army, 1948–1983: Uncertain Allegiance.* Princeton, NJ: Princeton Univ. Press

Ricks T. 1997. *Making the Corps.* New York: Scribner

Roman PJ, Tarr DW. 1995. *Soldiers, presidents, and the use of force in the post Cold War.* Presented at Am. Polit. Sci. Assoc. Annu. Meet., Chicago, Aug. 31–Sept. 3

Rosen S. 1973. *Testing the Theory of the Military-Industrial Complex.* Lexington, MA: Lexington Books

Rosen SP. 1991. *Winning the Next War.* Ithaca, NY: Cornell Univ. Press

Rosen SP. 1996. *Societies and Military Power: India and Its Armies.* Ithaca, NY: Cornell Univ. Press

Rouquie A. 1982. *The Military and the State in Latin America.* Transl. PE Sigmund. Berkeley: Univ. Calif. Press

Russett BM. 1990. *Controlling the Sword: The Democratic Governance of National Security.* Cambridge, MA: Harvard Univ. Press

Russett BM, Hanson EC. 1975. *Interest and Ideology: The Foreign Policy Beliefs of American Businessmen.* San Francisco: Freeman

Russett BM, Stepan A. 1973. *Military Force and American Society.* New York: Harper & Row

Sagan SD. 1994. The perils of proliferation: organization theory, deterrence theory, and the spread of nuclear weapons. *Int. Secur.* 18(4):66–107

Sapin BM, Snyder RC. 1954. *The Role of the Military in American Foreign Policy.* Garden City, NY: Doubleday

Sarkesian SC. 1975. *The Professional Army Officer in a Changing Society.* Chicago: Nelson-Hall

Sarkesian SC, Williams JA, Bryant FB. 1995. *Soldiers, Society and National Security.* Boulder, CO: Lynne Rienner

Schiff R. 1995. Civil-military relations reconsidered: a theory of concordance. *Armed Forces Soc.* 22(1):7–24

Segal DR. 1975. Civil-military relations in the mass public. *Armed Forces Soc.* 1:215–29

Segal DR. 1986. Measuring the institutional/occupational change thesis. *Armed Forces Soc.* 12(3): 351–76

Segal DR, Blair J, Newport F, Stephens S. 1974. Convergence, isomorphism, and interdependence at the civil-military interface. *J. Polit. Mil. Soc.* 2:157–72

Sherry MS. 1995. *In the Shadow of War: The United States Since the 1930s.* Princeton, NJ: Princeton Univ. Press

Slater J. 1977. Apolitical warrior or soldier-statesman: the military and the foreign policy process in the post-Vietnam era. *Armed Forces Soc.* 4(1):101–18

Smith L. 1951. *American Democracy and Military Power.* Chicago: Univ. Chicago Press

Snider D, Carlton-Carew MA. 1995. *US Civil-Military Relations: In Crisis or Transition?* Washington, DC: Cent. Strat. Int. Stud.

Snyder J. 1984. *The Ideology of the Offensive: Military Decisionmaking and the Disas-*

ters of 1914. Ithaca, NY: Cornell Univ. Press

Stepan A. 1971. *The Military in Politics: Changing Patterns in Brazil.* Princeton, NJ: Princeton Univ. Press

Stepan A. 1988. *Rethinking Military Politics: Brazil and the Southern Cone.* Princeton, NJ: Princeton Univ. Press

Stiehm JH. 1981. *Bring Me Men and Women: Mandated Change at the US Air Force Academy.* Berkeley: Univ. Calif. Press

Stiehm JH. 1989. *Arms and the Enlisted Woman.* Philadelphia: Temple Univ. Press

Stiehm JH. 1996. *It's Our Military, Too!: Women and the US Military.* Philadelphia: Temple Univ. Press

Tarr DW, Roman PJ. 1995. *Serving the commander-in-chief: advice and dissent.* Presented at Am. Polit. Sci. Assoc. Annu. Meet., Chicago, Aug. 31– Sept. 3

Thompson WR. 1975. Regime vulnerability and the military coup. *Comp. Polit.* 7: 459–87

Thompson WR. 1976. Organizational cohesion and military coup outcomes. *Comp. Polit.* 9:255–76

Tilly C, ed. 1975. *The Formation of National States in Western Europe.* Princeton, NJ: Princeton Univ. Press

Trinkunas HA. 1999. *Constructing civilian control of the armed forces in new democracies: the cases of Argentina and Venezuela.* PhD thesis. Stanford Univ., Palo Alto, CA

Vagts A. 1937. *A History of Militarism: A Romance and Realities of a Profession.* New York: Norton

Van Evera S. 1984. The cult of the offensive and the origins of the First World War. *Int. Secur.* 9(1):58–107

Weigley RF. 1993. The American military and the principle of civilian control from McClellan to Powell. *J. Mil. Hist.* 57: 27–58

Weiner SK. 1995. The changing of the guard: the role of Congress in defense organization and reorganization in the Cold War. *John M Olin Inst. Strat. Stud., Proj. US Post Cold-War Civil-Mil. Relat., Work. Pap. No. 10*

Welch C, ed. 1976. *Civilian Control of the Military.* New York: State Univ. New York Press

Williams JA. 1997. The new military professionals. *Proc. Nav. Inst. Press* 122:42–48

Yarmolinsky A. 1971. *The Military Establishment: Its Impacts on American Society.* New York: Harper & Row

Yarmolinsky A. 1974. Civilian control: new perspectives for new problems. *Indiana Law J.* 49:654–71

Zagorski PW. 1992. *Democracy vs. National Security: Civil-Military Relations in Latin America.* Boulder, CO: Lynne Rienner

Zagorski PW. 1996. *The Latin American military and politics: retrospect and prospects.* Presented at Annu. Meet. Midwest Polit. Sci. Assoc. Apr. 18–20, Chicago, IL

Zamora KC. 1997. *Relaciones Cívico-Militares Comparadas: Entendiendo los Mecanismos de Control Civil en Pequeñas Democracias.* San Jose, CR: Fund. Arias Paz Progreso Humano

Zegart AB. 1996. *In whose interest? The making of American national security agencies.* PhD thesis. Stanford Univ., Palo Alto, CA

Zimmermann E. 1983. *Political Violence, Crises, and Revolutions: Theories and Research.* Cambridge, MA: Schenkman

Zisk KM. 1993. *Engaging the Enemy: Organization Theory and Soviet Military Innovation, 1955–1991.* Princeton, NJ: Princeton Univ. Press

Zuk G, Thompson WR. 1982. The post-coup military spending question: a pooled cross-sectional time series analysis. *Am. Polit. Sci. Rev.* 76:60–74

Annu. Rev. Polit. Sci. 1999. 2:243–67

POLITICAL PARTIES AND DEMOCRACY

S. C. Stokes

Department of Political Science, University of Chicago, Chicago, Illinois 60637;
e-mail: s-stokes@uchicago.edu

KEY WORDS: political parties, democracy, responsiveness, representation, elections

---

ABSTRACT

A central claim of democratic theory is that democracy induces governments
to be responsive to the preferences of the people. Political parties organize
politics in every modern democracy, and some observers claim that parties
are what induce democracies to be responsive. Yet, according to others, parties give voice to extremists and reduce the responsiveness of governments
to the citizenry. The debate about parties and democracy takes on renewed
importance as new democracies around the globe struggle with issues of representation and governability. I show that our view of the impact of parties
on democratic responsiveness hinges on what parties are—their objectives
and organization. I review competing theories of parties, sketch their testable
implications, and note the empirical findings that may help adjudicate among
these theories. I also review debates about the origins of parties, about the
determinants of party-system size and characteristics, and about party competition.

Political parties created democracy...modern democracy is unthinkable save
in terms of the parties.

E. E. Schattschneider (1942)

INTRODUCTION

Schattschneider believed that political parties "created" American democracy
out of a "small experiment in republicanism" (1942:3) by drawing the masses
into political life. Despite this achievement, Schattschneider complained, po-

1094-2939/99/0616-0243$08.00

litical theorists were at the founding, and remained a century and a half later, silent on parties.[1] The founders of the American republic tried to create institutions in which parties and "factions" would wither; yet parties appeared when American democracy was still in its infancy, just as they have reappeared in every democracy on earth. Later normative theorists, many of them no less skeptical than Madison or Jefferson of parties as promoters of the public good, seem to regard political parties as an unpleasant reality, a hardy weed that sprouts up in what would otherwise be the well-tended garden of democratic institutions.

Among positive theorists and empirical students of democracy, regard for political parties is higher. Early postwar political scientists in the United States yearned for a strengthening of parties that would allow "party government"; their aspirations are echoed today by observers of new democracies in Eastern Europe and Latin America who blame the shortfalls of these democracies on the absence or weakness of political parties. Perhaps because their normative world is ordered not around notions of the public good but around the effective representation of inevitably conflicting interests, positive democratic theorists are more likely to view parties not as a weed but as a necessary microbe lodged deep in the digestive tract—not pretty, but vital to keeping the body politic in good health. In one view, parties promote interests that are partial (note the common etymology) or extremist; in the other, parties are the link between citizen interests and government actions. In addition to inducing governments to be responsive to citizens, parties are reputed to give order to legislative processes, reduce problems of multidimensionality of the issue space, and permit voters an object to hold to account. The debate over political parties—are they an inevitable evil? Are they what makes democracy democratic?—remains unsettled. It will not be settled until some agreement is reached about the nature of parties—what their objectives are and how they are structured. In this review, I outline the competing positions in this debate and suggest directions for empirical research that may help settle it, or at least move it to a fully normative plane. I turn to that task in the second section. In the first section I review prominent currents of research about political parties in postwar political science.

I restrict my discussion to political parties in democracies [i.e. political systems in which important governmental posts are decided by fair, competitive elections held on a regular schedule, freedoms of association and speech are protected, and the franchise is extended to nearly all adult citizens (see Dahl 1971)]. For discussions of parties in nondemocratic systems, see Duverger 1963, LaPalombara & Weiner 1966, and Janda 1993. Space limitations force

---

[1]The silence persists. The encyclopedic *Democracy and its Critics* (Dahl 1989), a 400-page volume, devotes seven pages to political parties.

me to ignore some streams of research, in particular the burgeoning literature on the behavior of legislative parties. For a sampling of recent contributions, see Rohde 1991; Cox & McCubbins 1992; Schickler & Rich 1997; Krehbiel 1993; and JM Snyder & T Groseclose, unpublished manuscript.

RESEARCH ON POLITICAL PARTIES: WHAT ARE THE ISSUES?

The Origins of Political Parties

Political parties are endemic to democracy. However, they are not part of the formal definition of democracy; nor do the constitutions of most democracies dictate a role for parties. Indeed, in most countries, parties operate in a realm little regulated by statutory law. In the United States, the founders were dead set against parties. Madison, in Federalist 10, drew no distinction between parties and factions—"a minority or majority" united by "some common impulse of passion, or of interest, adverse to the rights of other citizens, or to the permanent and aggregate interests of the community" (1982 [1787]:43)—but he realized that the price paid in liberty of eliminating the cause of parties would be too great. Parties, then, were an inevitable by-product of the liberties associated with a republican community combined with the human propensity toward division and conflict; "where no substantial occasion presents itself, the most frivolous and fanciful distinctions have been sufficient to kindle their unfriendly passions" (1982 [1787]:44). Despite the efforts of founders, including the authors of the Federalist papers, to design institutions to control parties and factions, within a decade of the birth of the American state they had begun to organize the new nation's political life (see Hofstadter 1969).

Many contemporary students of democracy give a more upbeat answer to the question, "Why parties?" A leading answer is that legislative politics is unstable without parties; hence, legislators who want to get something done and who want their preferred policies to prevail will form parties. Far from an unfortunate consequence of human nature plus liberal freedoms, parties introduce effectiveness into democratic institutions.

A recent book entitled *Why Parties?* (Aldrich 1995) explores the origins of the US party system. Members of Congress faced important decisions about debt repayment and the future structure of government. It became clear even to anti-party thinkers such as Hamilton and Jefferson that there were advantages to be gained from coordinating votes over a number of issues among congressmen with similar (though not identical) preferences. The formation of parties in the legislature was a natural reaction to the problem of a multidimensional issue space and the resulting instability and issue cycling. The minority legislative party then had an interest in mobilizing votes to enhance its position in the legislature, leading to the transformation of legislative parties into mass parties. Aldrich (1995) echoes Schattschneider's (1942) explanation of the natural advantages of party organization in legislatures, and he draws on theories of instability of decisions under majority rule (Condorcet in Black 1958; Arrow 1963; McKelvey 1976; Riker 1982; Schwartz 1986; MO Jackson, B Moselle, unpublished manuscript).

The universality of the scenario whereby parties originate in legislatures and then extend themselves to the electorate has not been established. In countries where military dictatorships suppressed parties for long periods, when a transition to democracy begins, parties often spring up before legislative politics is underway (see e.g. Linz & Stepan 1996). In these instances, the advantage of party organization seems to arise out of the dynamics of a negotiated transition from authoritarian rule, a process that may or may not have much in common with normal legislative processes. To settle the debate, which may mean establishing not the origins of parties but the conditions under which either elite politics or popular mobilization will engender political parties, we need better, more social-scientifically informed historical research into the origins of parties (see Vincent 1966, Cox 1987).

The extension-of-legislative-politics answer to the "why parties?" question competes in contemporary scholarship with several up-from-the-bottom explanations (see next section). By one account, parties are the projection into the political realm of historically inherited social cleavages. By another, parties arise out of district-level competition for office; there are heuristic and coordination advantages to organizing this competition along partisan lines, particularly in the leap from local to national parties. Note that the effect of parties in normative terms is still, contra Madison, good: although they do not stabilize legislative politics, they give more effective expression to the people's interests and solidarities.

Party Systems, Social Cleavages, and Electoral Rules

Parties are endemic to democracy. Yet their number, degree of institutionalization, and structure vary enormously from continent to continent and from country to country. The size of a party system (how many parties regularly compete in elections) and its scope (which cleavages and identities are politicized, which are not)— have profound normative implications. If parties convey the preferences, opinions, and interests of constituencies to government, then the expression of societal interests or their suppression via the party system will critically influence the quality of democracy.

In the debate over the determinants of the nature and size of party systems, one side champions a "comparative sociology of politics" (Lipset & Rokkan 1967:1), the other side an institutional analysis. The political sociology contingent explains variations in party systems in terms of the nature of underlying social cleavages (Campbell 1958, Grumm 1958, Lipson 1964, Lipset & Rokkan 1967, Rokkan 1970, Nohlen 1981, Beyme 1985, Solari 1986). In Lipset & Rokkan's (1967) formulation, the party system that emerged in European countries was the consequence of alliances struck in the wake of critical historical events—the Reformation, the construction of nation-states, and the industrial revolution. Although the sociological approach is sometimes caricatured as ignoring the impact of electoral rules on party systems, it often, in fact, acknowledges the force of institutions on party systems. Lipset & Rokkan, for example, recognize the centrality of the "rules of the electoral game" (1967:30) and make some gestures toward explaining how these rules arise out of preexisting societal cleavages. Recent scholarship has carried this project further. Boix (1997), with a strategic-action orientation, explains the choice of majoritarian versus proportional systems in European countries at the moment when workers were enfranchised and socialist parties appeared. Liberal voters and parties faced the dilemma of how to retain control of legislative seats. If one of the preexisting liberal parties dominated the other electorally, this party could serve as a focal point for liberal voters, and majority rule remained attractive. If two preexisting liberal parties tended to divide the vote equally, the liberal leadership would prefer to shift to a proportional system to assure continued liberal representation.

Boix's (1997) analysis is a welcome innovation on a comparative sociology of politics that was weak on agency. Comparative sociologists never accounted satisfactorily for the emergence and persistence of one set of cleavages over another. The claim that some social cleavages were simply more central than others ignores extensive evidence of the non-mobilization of differences that, from a logical or historical standpoint, might well be politicized (see Laitin 1986). When comparative sociologists seek to explain why one or another cleavage is expressed in the party system, they link these cleavages to alliances and divisions in the distant past without taking sufficient account of party-system volatility and the decline of parties affecting many democracies (see Mair 1997). Kalyvas (1996) shows that divisions around religion, for example, are not fixed but can remake themselves from one period to the next, with drastic effects on party systems. He shows that liberal anticlericalism at the end of the nineteenth century led the Church to self-defensive strategies, with the eventual outcome—unintended by the Church—of the establishment of Christian Democratic parties. As long as agency persists, there is little reason to believe that party systems will remain immutable.

Institutionalism has developed as an alternative to the comparative sociology of political systems. Yet, as we shall see, instituionalists are better at answering the question "How many parties?" than "What kinds of parties?" Institutionalism originated in the writing of Duverger (1951, 1966). "Duverg-

er's law" holds that single-member districts in which a simple plurality is required to win the seat produces two-party systems at the level of the electoral
district. Duverger reasoned that voters would not waste votes on parties with
little chance of gaining representation and that parties that failed to mobilize
votes would become discouraged and disband. The same reasoning was extended by Leys (1959) and Sartori (1968) to multi-member districts in which
seats are allocated by proportional representation. Proportional representation
produces systems with three or more parties, depending on the number of seats
in districts and the minimum number of votes required to gain any legislative
representation.

A large literature extends and refines Duverger's insights (see e.g. Leys
1959; Wildavsky 1959; Sartori 1968, 1976; Gibbard 1973; Satterthwaite 1975;
Riker 1982; Lijphart 1994). The most important advance in this area since
Duverger is Cox's *Making Votes Count* (1997). In the context of a broader discussion of strategic voting, Cox shows that Duverger's law should be understood as placing an upper limit on the number of parties. Through an analysis
of the impact of distinct electoral rules (single-member simple majority,
single-member with run-offs, proportional representation of various kinds),
Cox concludes that electoral rules interact with "social diversity" to determine
the effective number of parties in a system. Social diversity comes into the
story in the linkage between district party systems and national systems. Consider single-member districts with a simple majority rule. Duverger's law obviously produces bipartism in individual districts, but why might the national
party system repeat this same two-party structure? Cox (1997:186) suggests
that "Some preexisting group, that is already of national scope or perspective,
seeks to accomplish a task that requires the help of a large number of legislators or legislative candidates; this group therefore seeks to induce would-be
legislators from many different districts to participate in a larger organization." The preexisting groups may be labor unions, religious sects, ethnic
groups, or regional interests. The prominence of one group or another is not
caused by electoral rules. The empirical findings, like those of Taagepera &
Grofman (1985), Powell (1982), and Ordeshook & Shvetsova (1994), support the conclusion that local-level district magnitude, itself determined by
electoral rules, places an upper bound on the number of effective parties; this
institutional effect then interacts with social heterogeneity to produce the
effective number of parties. In the end, institutionalism needs a comparative
sociology to give a full account of party systems. The work of Boix and Kalyvas suggests a more vital, strategically sensitive comparative sociology.

Parties and the Mobilization of Voters

How do parties mobilize voter support? Postwar political science offers competing answers with distinct implications for the impact of parties on democ-

racy. Do parties reveal and aggregate voters' preferences such that governments are responsive to citizens? Or do parties form oligopolies of competitors
with interests and preferences at odds with those of voters?

The leading early studies of voting behavior saw parties as organizations
that mobilized voters through ties of socialization and affect. Drawing heavily
on social psychology, scholars in the Michigan school in the 1960s developed
the notion of party identification as an emotional tie to a political party, which
is inculcated early and which, barring major partisan realignments, shapes voting behavior throughout a person's life (Campbell et al 1960, 1966; Converse
1969, 1976; Edelman 1964; Clarke & Stewart 1998). Later this perspective
was displaced by ones in which parties competed for the support of voters
whose posture was more rational and instrumental. Downs (1957) had posited
that voters choose whom to vote for based on the proximity of a party's issue
position to their policy ideal point (for a recent review see Ferejohn 1995).
Downs offered some remarks suggesting that party labels may play a heuristic
role in allowing voters to locate candidates on an issue space even when they
lack detailed information about the past policies of incumbents or the proposals of challengers. Key (1966) is the father of contemporary theories of retrospective voting, where citizens assess not issue positions but past performance
of governments in deciding how to vote. Here, too, the role of the party label is
heuristic. The "running tally" (Fiorina 1981) view of parties, according to
which party labels summarize the past performance of governments under a
particular party's leadership, is an extension of this perspective (see also
Zechman 1978, Alt 1984, Popkin 1991, Achen 1992).

A different kind of cognitive role for parties is proposed by Rabinowitz
and Macdonald (Rabinowitz & Macdonald 1989, Rabinowitzet al 1991). Beginning with the observation that Downs's prediction of convergence of parties at the preferred position of the median voter is not borne out in the real
world (see below), and following the lead of D Stokes (1966), who underscored the importance of "valence" as opposed to position issues,[2] they
posit that voters perceive politics in dichotomous terms. Parties can adopt either "my" side of an issue or the "other" side. In order to clearly signal which
side a party is on, parties send relatively "intense" messages—ones which, in
spatial terms, might be termed extreme. Rabinowitz et al provide some empiri-

---

[2]Spatial issues are ones in which positions can be defined across a Euclidean space. An example
is taxes; in theory, people's ideal points can fall at any point between 0% and 100% tax rates.
Valence issues are ones that "involve the linking of the parties with some condition that is
positively or negatively valued by the electorate" (D Stokes 1966:170–71). An example is
prosperity or corruption. Whereas strategy on spatial issues is conceived as a matter of locating the
party at a point proximate to some set of voters whose support the party wants to mobilize, party
strategy on valence issues is to try to establish a bond in the public's mind between the party and the
issue with positive valence, e.g. to be known as the prosperity or anti-corruption party.

cal evidence from the United States for their "directional theory" of party competition.

Iversen (1994a,b) notes the diverging predictions of directional theory and spatial models. If directional theory is correct, parties should adopt more extreme (or intense) positions than those of voters. In Downs's spatial model, party programs are predicted to converge to the same point, the one preferred by the median voter.[3] Iversen explores these predictions with evidence from European democracies. He finds that, contrary to the predictions of spatial models, leaders of left-wing and right-wing parties hold policy positions that are extreme relative to those of their constituents and even of party activists. Only centrist parties occupy positions that converge on the median of their constituents. The finding lends support to the directional model, as well as to a "mobilizational" perspective (see Przeworski & Sprague 1986), wherein parties pursue both short-term electoral gains and longer-term changes in the political identities and beliefs of their target constituents. Iversen's exploration of party positioning suggests that voters' preferences are shaped by electoral politics and party competition and that they respond not only to positional cues about what a government plans do to but also, potentially, to deeper appeals for social transformation.

POLITICAL PARTIES AND DEMOCRACY

What Are Political Parties?

Democracy induces governments to be responsive to the preferences of the people. This, at least, is a central claim of many democratic theorists. According to Dahl (1971:1), "continuing responsiveness of the government to the preferences of its citizens [is] a key characteristic of democracy," and equivalent claims abound. Yet, just as responsiveness of governments to the people's will is normatively controversial, the degree of responsiveness of elected governments is disputed (see S Stokes 1998a, Przeworski et al 1999). Postwar democratic theory often asserts that political parties transmit popular preferences into policy. Echoing Schattschneider, Key wrote that an "essential function" of parties is to obtain "popular consent to the course of public policy" (1958:12). Yet here again much rides on one's view of political parties. By some accounts, parties force elected governments to be responsive to constitu-

---

[3]The prediction assumes that voters' utility functions are single-peaked and decline asymmetrically as policy moves away from their ideal point, an assumption challenged in the directional model. For discussions of the extension of Downs's model to multidimensional issue spaces, multiparty systems, and a variety of electoral rules, see Hinich & Munger (1994) and Cox (1990, 1997).

Table 1   Two dimensions in the conceptualization of political parties

Internal structure	Objectives	
	Winning office	Pursuing policies
Unified	Spatial theory	Modified spatial theory Directional theory Mobilization
Divided	Incumbent hegemony	Overlapping genera- tions Curvilinear disparity

ents. Others claim parties make governments unresponsive. Much is at stake in the competing perspectives on political parties.

Scholars impute to parties different characteristics on two dimensions, namely their objectives and their internal structure. Parties' objectives may be exclusively to win office or may also include implementing their preferred policies; parties' internal structure may be unified or divided.[4] A two-by-two table illustrates these two dimensions and locates major theories of political parties simultaneously on both dimensions (Table 1).

Unified Parties

SPATIAL THEORY   Beginning in the northwest cell of Table 1, spatial theory in its early form assumed parties that were single-mindedly interested in attaining office and were internally unified around this goal. Downs invoked the metaphor of parties as teams (Downs 1957, Black 1958). Parties were assumed to move freely across the policy space in pursuit of votes. The prediction that parties would converge at a single point (the position of the median voter) raised troubling questions about the degree of choice voters faced. Yet, for the most part, ideological displacement in pursuit of votes was regarded as what made governments responsive. Electoral competition induced parties, and hence governments, to give voters what they wanted, just as economic competition induced firms to produce what consumers wanted. Barry (1978:99–100) noted the parallel between spatial theory and the invisible hand: "[J]ust as the baker provides us with bread not out of the goodness of his heart but in return for payment, so the politician supplies the policies we want not to make us happy but to get our votes."

MODIFICATIONS   Moving to the northeast cell, a later set of writers, still influenced by spatial theory, relaxes the assumption of preference- or ideology-free

---

[4]Strom (1990) suggests that distinct party objectives are not static features of parties but are endogenous to the institutional environment.

parties and explores the implications for party competition when parties care about policies as well as about winning (Wittman 1977, 1983; Calvert 1985; Chappell & Keech 1986). Calvert shows that if the distribution of voters across the policy space is known, even parties with ideological commitments will converge around the position of the median voter. The prediction is identical to that of Downs under the assumption of office-seeking parties [Ledyard (1984), Coughlin (1984), and Hinich (1977) show that the convergence result is more general than the median voter theorem]. Calvert reasons that unless a party wins the election, its opportunities to pursue its preferred policies are nonexistent; hence it will be willing to (almost) entirely give away its preferred position in order to win. Thus, the original spatial model's prediction of party responsiveness to voter preferences generalizes to the case of ideological parties.[5]

The nearest approach to a theory in which parties care about expressing policy positions but are indifferent to winning is Edelman's (1964). Such parties can be thought of as gaining consumer utility from the expression of a preference or ideology, but few examples of such behavior among political parties are to be found.

The story is different if the distribution of voter preferences is unknown. In this case, the behavior of office-seeking versus ideological parties should diverge. Office-seeking parties are expected to use available information to form a belief about the median voter's ideal point and adopt that position; assuming the available information is the same, both parties will form the same conjecture and arrive at the same position. [Ferejohn & Noll (1978) derive a result of nonconvergence when parties are purely office-seeking, are uncertain about the outcome of elections, and use different information to formulate predictions about electoral outcomes; see below.]

What about ideological parties? Uncertainty about the ideal point of the median voter means that the outcome of elections is uncertain. Parties must choose policy positions on the basis of their expected utility. Assuming that a party's campaign position is binding on its behavior in office (see below), the expected utility of adopting a given position is

$$E(U/x_a) = Pw(V_x) + (1-Pw)(V_y),$$ 1.

where x_a is the policy announced in the campaign, Pw is the probability of winning the election, V_x is value the party derives from implementation of its preferred policies, and V_y is the value the party derives from the implementation of the other parties' preferred policies.

---

[5]Additional assumptions are that voters' preferences are formed by processes other than party competition and, relatedly, that parties are focused on the current election—assumptions that are challenged by mobilization theory, as noted above.

Calvert shows that the degree of divergence in campaigns depends on pa-
rameter values. In particular, the greater the value derived from one's own
policies compared with those of one's opponent, the wider the gap between
platforms. Note then that ideological parties under uncertainty are less responsive to voters than they are in spatial models, in which parties just want to hold
office. Now their own ideological predispositions, as well as the preferences of
voters, determine their policy position.

The result gains relevance if we acknowledge that some of the uncertainty
about electoral outcomes is because voters' preferences are partly determined
by electoral politics. This was the point of mobilization theory, a point that has
been strengthened by recent work exploring the impact of party messages on
public opinion (Zaller 1994, Gerber & Jackson 1990). Politicians consider
voter preferences sensitive to campaigns; otherwise they would not waste their
time and money campaigning.[6] Under the assumption of partially endogenous
voter preferences, parties must make two projections: about the distribution of
voter preferences before the campaign and about the persuasiveness of messages (and hence the distribution of preferences on election day). Viewed this
way, the assumption of uncertainty regarding electoral results seems realistic.
Still, we have much to learn about the formation of voter preferences, and endogeneity of voter preferences raises difficult problems for normative democratic theory.

Divided Parties

The bottom half of Table 1 is occupied by theories that explore the implications
of party competition if parties are composed of actors with conflicting objectives. But below this level of abstraction, these models are miles apart. In overlapping generation models, parties induce governments to be responsive to
voters; in incumbent hegemony and curvilinear disparity models, parties make
governments less responsive to voters than they would be without parties.

OVERLAPPING GENERATIONS   Overlapping generation models conceptualize
political parties as composed of individuals who want to win office but once in
office desire to impose their own preferences, which are distinct from those of
the median voter. Fellow party members, however, induce them not to indulge
their ideological preferences and to remain responsive to voters.

Following Alesina & Spear (1988), assume a political party whose individual members all have policy ideal points that are eccentric in comparison with
the median voter. Party members know that their preferences deviate from the
median voter's, although they do not know the exact distribution of voter

---

[6]The other explanation for campaigns is to induce participation in settings in which voting is
not compulsory. But even where it is compulsory, such as in parts of Latin America, substantial
sums are spent on sending out policy-relevant messages.

preferences. Party members, for these purposes, are defined as individuals of sufficiently high rank that they realistically anticipate running for office in the future. Members have a finite number of years remaining in their careers, and when they retire, young, new recruits will take their place. For simplicity, consider a party with three members. Member 1 has one political term remaining in her career; she will run for office now and retire at the end of the term. Member 2 has two terms left; his turn to run for office will come upon the retirement of Member 1, one term from now. Member 3, the youngest, has three terms remaining and gets to run at the end of the term that would correspond to Member 2. If, counterfactually, Member 1 were not constrained by a party, she would use office as a tool for her ideological commitments and impose her ideal policy, x_p, which (by assumption) is different from the ideal point of the median voter.

Alesina (1988) shows that if office holders are not bound in some way, any announced policy position will be inconsistent over time and hence incredible to voters. Voters expect office holders to impose their own preferred policies and hence expect government policy to diverge from campaign positions (see also Ferejohn 1986). Voters only believe campaign statements that reflect the candidate's true ideal point; candidates announce their true positions, and their campaigns (and policies) diverge from each other and from the preferences of the median voter.

But Member 1 *is* a party member, and Members 2 and 3 may have some ways of controlling her behavior in office. They can force her to adopt policies in office (and in her now-credible campaign) that match those preferred by the median voter. They want to because their own future electoral prospects are diminished if voters associate their party with unpopular policies of the past. Alesina & Spear (1988) posit that parties compensate incumbents by offering them services in exchange for policy moderation, such as helping to get the leader's agenda through the legislature or defending her before the press and public. Zielinsky (unpublished manuscript) shows that internal party democracy has the same effect of compelling incumbents to be responsive to voters. If the party in government chooses policy by majority vote of party members, then the incumbent Member 1, whose instinct is to indulge her own ideological predisposition, is outvoted by Members 2 and 3, who want to hold office in the future; by a two-to-one vote, the party chooses the policy preferred by the median voter (x_v) over the one preferred by Member 1 (x_p). Whether the mechanism of control is internal democracy or exchange of services, the impact of the party is to make government responsive to voters and not to the whims of individual office holders or the ideological commitments of parties.

INCUMBENT HEGEMONY   Now consider a cleavage between incumbents and non-office-holding party leaders, similar to the one described above except that incumbents care mainly about retaining office and are unconstrained by nonincumbent members when they choose their platform. Parties will be responsive to the median voter in the districts they already represent. But many voters, potentially a majority, will be deprived of representatives with more proximate policy stances than those of their actual representatives.

What I call the incumbent hegemony model has been developed by Snyder (1994) and S Ansolabehere & JM Snyder (unpublished manuscript) (see also Austen-Smith 1984). Political parties are composed of incumbents and would-be incumbents in a multidistrict legislature, where each district is represented by a single member. There are two parties. In this model, unlike overlapping generation models, would-be incumbents have no power to influence party platforms. Incumbents care about retaining office, and their careers are modeled as infinite. They also care, but less, about the size of their party's majority in the legislature. Snyder (1994:205) describes the utility function of Party X's candidate in district i as

$$u(w_i, W) = w_i \left[\alpha + \beta(W) \right],\qquad\qquad 2.$$

where w_i is an indicator variable that is 1 if Party X's candidate wins and 0 if Party Y's candidate wins, and W is the total number of seats Party X wins. Note that the party member derives no utility if she loses the election. As an incumbent, she prefers a larger number of copartisans in the legislature over a smaller number, but she is unwilling to reduce her prospects of reelection in favor of adding members to her party's legislative contingent.

The party platform is chosen by party members who are incumbents immediately before the election. Platforms are assumed to be binding. Given Party Y's platform, Party X chooses a platform that cannot be defeated by any alternative in a pairwise vote; Party Y uses the same procedure. The process for determining the platform is entirely democratic, at least as far as office holders are concerned. Under these assumptions, party platforms diverge; incumbents want voters to be able to easily distinguish their party from the other. The intuition, as explained by Snyder (1994), is that representatives from inner-city Democratic districts want voters to identify them as liberals, just as Republicans from affluent suburban districts want voters to identify them as conservatives. Divergence allows incumbents to retain safe districts.

A critical finding is that, to the extent that incumbents are more concerned about protecting their seats than about increasing their party's numbers in the legislature, a majority may not agree to change the platform in order to take advantage of new seats the party might pick up at the cost of a reduced probability of retaining seats it already holds. Under conditions specified by S Ansolabehere & JM Snyder (unpublished manuscript), parties will forgo opportunities to increase their seats, even dramatically, and the legislature may be made up of representatives whose policy positions are less responsive to the full set of district medians than would be the case if parties were more sensitive to changes in public opinion.

CURVILINEAR DISPARITY   Returning to the southeast cell of Table 1, consider finally the curvilinear disparity view of parties. In this account of parties, as in the overlapping generation model, leaders' preferences diverge from those of members. Yet the effect is not to force leaders, despite their preferences, to be responsive to voters, but rather to force leaders, despite their preferences, to be *unresponsive* to voters.

In both models, party leaders are people who run for and sometimes hold office. Members, in the curvilinear disparity view, are defined as activists or militants, people who are unlikely ever to hold office themselves. Most important, they are people with intense policy preferences that are more extreme than those of most voters. In Hirschman's (1970) formulation, this is not an ad hoc assumption but flows from the tenets of spatial theory. If, as Downs showed, vote-maximizing parties converge on the position of the median voter, then people whose policy preferences are far from the median face a dilemma: How to force politicians to consider their preferences? "Exit" is not an attractive option (Hirschman 1970). If they abstain, they only increase the weight of the opinions of people whom they disagree with. If they protest by voting for a party whose position is even farther from their own, they are supporting politicians whose views are even more obnoxious than the more proximate party's.

Hirschman's (1970) solution is that extremists join parties. They can then exercise "voice"—harass, harangue, and keep their leaders awake at night until they shift policy positions. If ideological extremists disproportionately join political parties, then the median position of party activists will be extreme in comparison with the position of the median voter. And if activists use voice effectively to shift their party's leaders toward their position, party leaders (and governments) will be drawn away from the median voter and end up somewhere between voters and party activists—hence the term curvilinear disparity, coined by May (1973). This disparity is the observable implication of parties staffed by extremists under the assumptions of classic spatial theory of party competition. Hirschman (1970) thus supplies another plausible condition under which party platforms diverge, namely when party activists use voice to pressure leaders away from the median. The critical point is that, in curvilinear disparity models, parties reduce the responsiveness of candidates/governments to the median voter, whereas in overlapping generation models they impose that responsiveness.

An objection to the law of curvilinear disparity challenges its assumptions about the ideological differences between leaders and activists. Where do leaders come from, after all, if not from the ranks of parties? Is it realistic to maintain that leaders do not share the ideological agenda of activists? The answer suggests a modification of Hirschman's formulation (1970), one that allows leaders' primitive or pre-electoral preferences to be identical to those of activists; it is the allure of office, rather than fundamental (and theoretically ad hoc) differences in ideology, that creates a potential conflict between activists and leaders.

Consider the leader of Party 1. She wants to win office both because it allows her to implement her preferred policies and because she values the prestige and perks attached to it; in the phrase of Rogoff & Sibert (1988), she seeks "ego-rents." The value of holding office for its own sake is denoted by k. The precise distribution of voters' preferences is unknown. Following Alesina & Spear (1988), the goal of party leaders in choosing a campaign position is to maximize the sum of the expected utility of implementing their preferred policy and the expected utility of holding office for its own sake. Alesina & Spear (1988) show that the Nash equilibrium of a game with two parties is found by solving the following problems:

$$\max_{x} w^1 = \alpha\{P(x,y)u(x) + [1 - P(x,y)]u(y)\} + (1 - \alpha)P(x,y)k$$

3.

for Candidate 1, and

$$\max_{y} w^2 = \alpha\{P(x,y)v(y) + [1 - P(x,y)]v(x)\} + (1 - \alpha)P(x,y)k$$

4.

for Candidate 2. In the above equations, w^1 and w^2 are the utility of policy positions adopted by Parties 1 and 2, respectively. $P(x,y)$ is the probability of winning given campaign positions x and y. $u(x)$ and $u(y)$ are the value that the leader of Party 1 derives from the implementation of her program or her opponent's, respectively; $v(x)$ and $v(y)$ are the value that the leader of Party 2 derives. α is the value each leader derives from implementation of her preferred program relative to the value derived from holding office ($0 \leq \alpha \leq 1$). Alesina & Spear (1988) show that the more the party leaders care about policies as opposed to office (the larger α is relative to $1 - \alpha$), the greater the divergence between platforms. At the same time, if the value derived from office (k) is large enough, then policy positions will converge even when α is large. The more the party leaders approximate pure office seekers, the more responsive their platforms are to the preferences of the median voter; the closer they are to being pure ideologues who are indifferent to office for its own sake, the farther their platforms from the preferences of the median voter.

Party activists, in Hirschman's (1970) world, are people for whom the allure of office approaches zero. Few of them will rise in the ranks to hold office themselves; their entire motivation for getting involved in politics is to hold party leaders to an ideological vision. In the terms of the model above, for activists both k and α approach zero. The party's leaders were ideologically identical to the activists when they were low-level activists themselves, but as they rise organizationally, so does the value of their party's winning office apart from the good works that it will allow them to carry out. k becomes a non-zero value and α begins to rise. In this model, parties' policy positions reflect distinct ideological orientations of activists and leaders, and these orientations are endogenous to their structural positions in the party organization.

Evaluating Models of Political Parties

Spatial theory's prediction of programatic convergence is unsustainable, even for two-party systems, where the prediction is clearest. Because of this anomaly, the authors whose work I have reviewed went looking for alternatives. Recent research confirms that political parties in two- and multiparty systems occupy persistently different policy positions, as expressed both in their campaigns (see e.g. Klingemann et al 1994) and in the policies they adopt (see e.g. Iversen & Wren 1998, Boix 1998). Modifying spatial models so that parties care about winning but are uncertain about the distribution of voters yields divergence only when parties formulate different predictions about the location of the median voter (Ferejohn & Noll 1978). It is possible that parties would have private information, perhaps from their own polls, about the preferences of the electorate; but such private information is insufficient to account for the broadly divergent policies adopted decade after decade by liberal, social democratic, and confessional parties in Europe, or by Democrats and Republicans in the United States. Either parties care about policies as well as office or they have more complex sets of constituencies than the median voter to whom they appeal.

Overlapping generation, incumbent hegemony, and curvilinear disparity models may help us make sense of parties under democracy. These models diverge in assumptions and predictions; hence, with appropriate data, we should be able to adjudicate among them (see Table 2).

Several of the predictions in Table 2 have been subjected to extensive research, though usually not in an attempt to understand parties. We have extensive knowledge of the impact of manifestos and platforms on policy but little more than scattered evidence on what turns out to be a crucial issue: "Who controls the platform?" The lacuna is regrettable because our three models make sharply distinct predictions. Future candidates exercise majority control over the platform, according to overlapping generation models; incumbents have control according to the incumbent hegemony model; and leaders plus activists have control in the curvilinear disparity model. We would also benefit from more systematic study of the relationship between national party platforms and the ways that individual candidates from parties run. Incumbent he-

Table 2   Divergent assumptions/predictions of three models of parties

	Overlapping generations	Incumbent hegemony	Curvilinear disparity
Who controls the platform?	Leaders (future candidates)	Incumbents	Leaders and activists
Mechanism of control over incumbent	Services from party leaders	No control	"Voice"—pressure from activists
Preferences of distinct party actors	Induced preferences same	Divergence: incumbents vs non-incumbent leaders	Activists more extreme than leaders
Government responsive to whom?	Median voter	Median voter in districts, not over-all median	Median voter and median party member
Dynamic responsiveness?	Policy changes with public opinion	Policy stable despite changes in public opinion	Policy changes with public opinion but moderated by activist opinion
Last term effects?	No	Yes, toward overall median voter	Yes, toward office-holder's preferences
Stability of relative party strength in legislature	No prediction	Stable	Changes with voter/party preference change

gemony posits platforms that are national in the sense that all candidates from a single party run on the same platform and voters identify all party candidates with this set of positions. Alternatively, if a party's platform is aggregated from individual candidate platforms, the results posited by S Ansolabehere & JM Snyder (unpublished manuscript) do not follow (see Austen-Smith 1984).

The same lament applies to the question, "What are the mechanisms of control that parties exert over office holders?" Future research might profitably focus on these mechanisms. In incumbent hegemony, there is no control; in curvilinear disparity, voice is the mechanism of control. Overlapping generation models posit services—defense of the office holder in public opinion and the press, help getting his agenda through the legislature—or internal party democracy. Any of these mechanisms could be treated as an independent variable whose value could vary over time within a given system or across systems. One could then test for variation in dependent variables, such as last-term effects, policy congruence between incumbents and potential future office holders from the same party, and congruence between voters' preferences and government policy. Furthermore, in overlapping generation models, governments are induced to be responsive by party leaders who are worried about future elections. Office holders' responsiveness should be less in countries where democracy and party careers are periodically interrupted by coups. If overlapping generation models have the mechanisms right, comparative research ought to reveal an association between the age of parties and the age of democracy, on one hand, and government responsiveness, on the other. A common complaint about new democracies is that governments are unresponsive (see e.g. O'Donnell 1994). More theoretically informed research on parties in these as opposed to stable democratic systems may well turn up evidence in favor of overlapping generations.

Some systematic research has addressed the question, "Do distinct sorts of actors in parties have distinct policy preferences?" In overlapping generation models, party members may all have the same primitive policy preferences; retiring incumbents would want to indulge these preferences, but they are kept to the median voter position by younger party leaders. Hence the "induced" policy preferences of current and future office holders—preferences they will report publicly and attempt to pursue in office—will be the same. In incumbent hegemony models, no party actor need care much about policy and all care most about office; a conflict should be observable between a party's incumbent legislators and would-be legislators from districts controlled by the other party, the latter wishing to shift the party's platform in a direction that would enhance their chances of winning. Curvilinear disparity predicts activists who are extremist in relation to most voters and party leaders who fall in between.

Iversen (1994a,b) finds evidence from Europe contradictory to this prediction. Yet one must worry about his data on party leaders' policy preferences, reported in surveys taken at party congresses. These ultrastrategic actors may wish to appear bold in their ideological positions in the eyes of the activists who populate such congresses, and this strategic posture could influence their answers to survey questions. Bruce et al (1991) present evidence that leaders of "presidential parties" are ideologically more extreme than the parties' constituents, and they conclude that parties are interested in "advocacy" rather than office maximization or representation, a finding seemingly at odds with overlapping generation predictions and more in line with curvilinear disparity. The difficulty is that Bruce et al's "leaders"—county campaign directors— seem suspiciously like Hirschman's (1970) activists. The critical question is how likely they are to ever run for office.

Government responsiveness, defined as a shift in government policy in response to a prior shift of preference of some other actors, is a well-researched topic. The prediction of overlapping generation models is that incumbents will be induced by future candidates to be responsive to the median voter. The prediction of incumbent hegemony models is different; government as a whole, such as an entire legislature, may be distinctly unresponsive to the electorate as a whole. But a given party's program should reflect the preferences of the median of district median voters in districts under that party's control. Curvilinear disparity predicts a kind of muffled responsiveness; governments may, for example, change their position when the median voter's preferences change, but all policy responsiveness is mediated by activists, who by assumption are extreme. Researchers have used widely different strategies to scrutinize responsiveness. In the United States, an early, organizing essay by Miller & Stokes (1966) found members of Congress to be responsive to (or ideologically predisposed to agree with) voters in their districts. Later research shifted to an aggregated level, the overall responsiveness of branches of government to shifts in public opinion (Stimson et al 1995, Page & Shapiro 1992, Mishler & Sheehan 1993, Bartels 1991, Jackson & King 1989). Their basic finding is that American government is responsive to changes in public opinion. Stimson et al (1995), for example, show that between 1950 and 1990, a one-point shift of public opinion to the left or right on an ideological scale was followed by a 0.74-point shift in the same direction by the president and a 1.01-point shift in the same direction by the House of Representatives. So powerful were shifts in public opinion that they dwarfed the effect of changing partisan composition of the House; a 1% increase in Democrats (about 4 additional Democratic members) produced only a 0.48% increase in policy liberalism.

Note that the change in the research strategy, from disaggregation at the level of individual districts to aggregation at the level of general public opinion and government as a whole, changes the significance of these findings for theories of parties. To choose between overlapping generation and incumbent hegemony models, we need to know whether the responsiveness of individual legislators to their districts is more or less powerful than the responsiveness of the government as a whole to the electorate.

Another way that political scientists have investigated responsiveness is by examining the predictive power of pre-electoral policy positions and post-electoral government policy: "mandate-responsiveness" (S Stokes 1999). Their reasoning is that manifestos and campaigns express voters' preferences as interpreted and aggregated by parties, so that remaining true to campaign positions is equivalent to remaining responsive to voters. Most studies do find a substantial consistency between campaigns or pre-election manifestos, on the one hand, and government policy, on the other (Krukones 1984, Fishel 1985, Budge et al 1987, Keeler 1993, Klingemann et al 1994). The Comparative Manifestos Project finds that manifestos predict policy; the authors credit this responsiveness to political parties.

The theoretical significance of mandate responsiveness depends on one's view of parties. As shown above, according to curvilinear disparity, party leaders' (induced) policy preferences diverge in the direction of the median voter from the more extreme position of activists from their own party. Activists may use party manifestos as a contract between themselves and party leaders, a common understanding of the position they were able to get candidates to adopt in exchange for a quieting of voice. If parties are only partially responsive to voters, and if manifestos are a testament to the gap between party activists and voters, the policy predictiveness of manifestos may indicate the opposite of responsiveness to voters.

Consideration of theories of parties should raise awareness of the potential for differences between what politicians say in campaign speeches, debates, and nominating conventions, which are directed at voters, and the program they run on, which may have more to do with their relationship with their party. Manifestos are not generally widely disseminated to voters. Studies of the responsiveness of parties to their campaign positions have scrutinized actual policy in relation either to campaign "speech" (Krukones 1984, Fishel 1985, Keeler 1993) or to written manifestos (Budge et al 1987, Klingemann et al 1994), or both (S Stokes 1998b) without considering the potential for systematic slippage between speech and manifestos. A possible implication of the law of curvilinear disparity, and of the modification I suggested above, is a consistent difference between the two, with speech more responsive and manifestos less responsive to voters.

Another rival prediction supported by some data concerns last-term effects, a shift in an office holder's behavior when he does not face reelection at the end of the term. Last-term effects are predicted to be minimal in overlapping generation models: if services, defense before the media, and the like are effective, then younger members should be able to induce retiring incumbents not to depart from the policies the party advertised in its campaign. The other models predict significant last-term effects. If the law of curvilinear disparity has force, leaders in their last term may well return to their primitive or pre-electoral preference, which should (like those of activists) be more extreme than most voters'. Predictions of incumbent hegemony are less clear. By assumption, office holders do not retire. If they do retire and if their vote on the party platform still counts, they may favor a shift in the direction of the electorate median and away from the median of district medians in order to increase their party's number of seats in the legislature. For the United States, there are some empirical findings on last-term effects, namely that they are small; no major change in roll-call behavior is observed among members of Congress who are not seeking reelection (see Lott & Bronars 1993 and citations therein).[7] The absence of last-term effects favors overlapping generation models, but we need more data.

The preceding suggests future lines of research that may help adjudicate the parties-as-cause-of-responsiveness and parties-as-cause-of-unresponsiveness debate. Still, combination may be as fruitful as adjudication. What if both overlapping generation and curvilinear disparity models are accurate portrayals of different parts of political parties? Perhaps parties are composed of cur-

---

[7]They do, however, vote less. Last-term members of Congress are not "ideological shirkers" but plain shirkers!

rent candidates or incumbents, future candidates who have an interest in keeping current incumbents in line with voter preferences, and activists who have no prospect of holding office, care most about ideology and policy, and have ways of inducing candidates away from the median voter. If this is the right picture, then certain dynamic patterns ought to appear. When a party leader is actively seeking office or holds office and can seek reelection, she ought to ally with other leaders who will someday be candidates and distance herself from activists. When she is a last-termer, her natural allies should be the party activists, and her natural antagonists should be party leaders who will run in the future. A horizontal pattern of party cohesion should be in evidence when a leader is reeligible; a vertical pattern of cohesion, linking office holders with activists against the leadership, should appear when the leader is ineligible.

PARTIES AND DEMOCRACY: CONCLUDING REMARKS

Today, more of the world's population lives under democracy than ever before. Hence, it is more urgent than ever before to understand how democracy works and assess how well it performs the functions imputed to it, such as responsiveness, representation, accountability, and realization of the public good. Observers of the myriad new democracies around the globe (but not they alone) complain of the ineffectiveness of democracy in achieving these functions. They not infrequently cast the blame on weak political parties (see e.g. Mainwaring & Scully 1994). Conversely, when observers detect a strengthening of parties in new democracies, they expect representation and responsiveness to be similarly strengthened (see e.g. Dix 1992).

Certainly it is hard to shake off the intuition that the more political parties are in evidence, the more consolidated the democracy. Yet it may well be that parties are markers of democracy, inevitable expressions of its advance, without being causally connected to all that is presumed good about democracy. If the foregoing stroll through empirical democratic theory taught us anything, it is that the connection between political parties and the responsiveness of elected governments is not at all settled. Some contemporary models of political parties reinforce the fears of early theorists that political parties would intervene between elected governments and the achievement of the public good. In the original conception, parties were partial and bound to the passions and prejudices of local public opinion; in some recent conceptions, parties are partial to their own conception of the good and unconstrained by public opinion.

It is clear that parties are here to stay, an unavoidable part of democracy. Whether, as Schattschneider believed, political parties made modern democracy, or whether they are an inextricable weed in its garden, is a question that social science research does not yet answer.

ACKNOWLEDGMENTS

I am grateful to Rob Boatwright, David Laitin, and Margaret Levi for their comments.

> **Visit the *Annual Reviews home page* at http://www.AnnualReviews.org.**

Literature Cited

Achen CH. 1992. Social psychology, demographic variables, and linear regression: breaking the iron triangle in voting research. *Polit. Behav.* 14:195–212

Aldrich JH. 1995. *Why Parties? The Origin and Transformation of Political Parties in America.* Chicago: Univ. Chicago

Alesina A. 1988. Credibility and convergence in a two-party system with rational voters. *Am. Econ. Rev.* 78:796–805

Alesina A, Spear SE. 1988. An overlapping generation model of electoral competition. *J. Public Econ.* 37(3):359–79

Alt JE. 1984. Dealignment and the dynamics of partisanship in Britain. In *Electoral Change in Advanced Industrial Societies: Realignment or Dealignment?*, ed. RJ Dalton, SC Flanagan, PA Beck, pp. 298–329. Princeton, NJ: Princeton Univ. Press

Arrow KJ. 1963. *Social Choice and Individual Values.* New Haven, CT: Yale Univ. Press. 2nd ed.

Austen-Smith D. 1984. Two-party competition with many constituencies. *Math. Soc. Sci.* 7:177–98

Barry B. 1978. *Economists, Sociologists, and Democracy.* Chicago: Univ. Chicago Press

Bartels LM. 1991. Constituency opinion and congressional policy making: the Reagan defense build-up. *Am. Polit. Sci. Rev.* 85: 457–74

Black D. 1958. *The Theory of Committees and Elections.* Cambridge, UK: Cambridge Univ. Press

Beyme KV. 1985. *Political Parties in Western Democracies.* Transl. E Martin. New York: St. Martin's

Boix C. 1997. Choosing electoral rules: structural factors or political calculations. Presented at Annu. Meet. Am. Polit. Sci. Assoc., Washington, DC

Boix C. 1998. *Political Parties, Growth, and Equality: Conservative and Social Democratic Strategies in the World Economy.* New York: Cambridge Univ. Press

Bruce JM, Clark JA, Kessel JH. 1991. Advocacy politics in presidential parties. *Am. Polit. Sci. Rev.* 85(4):1089–1105

Budge I, Robertson D, Hearl D, eds. 1987. *Ideology, Strategy, and Party Change: Spatial Analysis of Post-War Programs in Nineteen Democracies.* London: Cambridge Univ. Press

Calvert R. 1985. Robustness of the multidimensional voting model: candidates' motivations, uncertainty, and convergence. *Am. J. Polit. Sci.* 29:69–95

Campbell A, Converse PE, Miller WE, Stokes DE. 1960. *The American Voter.* New York: Wiley

Campbell A, Converse PE, Miller WE, Stokes, DE. 1966. *Elections and the Political Order.* New York: Wiley

Campbell P. 1958. *The Electoral Systems and Elections 1789–1957.* London: Faber & Faber

Chapell HW Jr, Keech WR. 1986. Policy motivation and party differences in a dynamic spatial model of party competition. *Am. Polit. Sci. Rev.* 80:881–99

Clarke HD, Stewart MC. 1998. The decline of parties in the minds of citizens. *Annu. Rev. Polit. Sci.* 1:357–78

Converse PE. 1969. Of time and partisan stability. *Comp. Polit. Stud.* 2:139–71

Converse PE. 1976. *The Dynamics of Party Support: Cohort-Analyzing Party Identification.* Beverly Hills, CA: Sage

Coughlin P. 1984. Expectations about voter choices: a comment. *Public Choice* 44: 49–59

Cox G. 1987. Electoral equilibria under alternative voting institutions. *Am. J.Polit. Sci.* 31:82–108

Cox G. 1990. Centripetal and centrifugal incentives in electoral systems. *Am. J. Polit. Sci.* 34:903–35

Cox G. 1997. *Making Votes Count: Strategic Coordination in the World's Electoral Systems.* Cambridge, UK: Cambridge Univ. Press

Cox G, McCubbins MD. 1992. *Legislative Leviathan: Party Government in the House.* Berkeley: Univ. Calif. Press

Dahl R. 1971. *Polyarchy: Participation and Opposition.* New Haven, CT: Yale Univ. Press

Dahl R. 1989. *Democracy and its Critics.* New Haven, CT: Yale Univ. Press

Dix RH. 1992. Democratization and the institutionalization of Latin American political parties. *Comp. Polit. Stud.* 24:488–511

Downs A. 1957. *An Economic Theory of Democracy.* New York: Harper & Row

Duverger M. 1951. *Political Parties.* New York: Wiley

Duverger M. 1966. *Political Parties and Pressure Groups: A Comparative Introduction.* New York: Wiley

Edelman M. 1964. *The Symbolic Uses of Politics.* Urbana: Univ. Ill.

Ferejohn J. 1986. Incumbent performance and electoral control. *Public Choice* 50:5–25

Ferejohn J. 1995. The spatial model and elections. In *Information, Participation, and Choice: An Economic Theory of Democracy in Perspective,* ed. B Grofman, pp. 107–24. Ann Arbor: Univ. Mich. Press

Ferejohn J, Noll RG. 1978. Uncertainty and the formal theory of political campaigns. *Am. Polit. Sci. Rev.* 72:492–505

Fiorina MP. 1981. *Retrospective Voting in American National Elections.* New Haven, CT: Yale Univ. Press

Fishel J. 1985. *Platforms and Promises.* Washington, DC: Congr. Q. Press

Gerber ER, Jackson JE. 1990. *Endogenous preferences and the study of institutions.* Presented at Annu. Meet. Am. Polit. Sci. Assoc., San Francisco

Janda K. 1993. Comparative political parties: research and theory. In *The State of the Discipline II,* ed. AW Finifter, pp. 163–92. Washington, DC: Am. Polit. Sci. Assoc.

Gibbard A. 1973. Manipulation of voting schemes: a general result. *Econometrica* 41:587–601

Grumm JG. 1958. Theories of electoral systems. *Midwest J. Polit. Sci.* 38:357–76

Hinich M. 1977. Equilibrium in spatial voting: the medium voter result is an artifact. *J. Econ. Theory* 16:208–19

Hinich M, Munger M. 1994. *Ideology and the Theory of Political Choice.* Ann Arbor: Univ. Mich. Press

Hirschman AO. 1970. *Exit, Voice, and Loyalty.* Cambridge, MA: Harvard Univ. Press

Hofstadter R. 1969. *The Idea of a Party System: The Rise of Legitimate Opposition in the United States, 1780–1840.* Berkeley: Univ. Calif. Press

Iversen T. 1994a. The logics of electoral politics: spatial, directional, and mobilizational effects. *Comp. Polit. Stud.* 27(2): 155–89

Iversen T. 1994b. Political leadership and representation in West European democracies: a test of three models of voting. *Am. J. Polit. Sci.* 38:45–74

Iversen T, Wren A. 1998. Equality, employment, and budgetary restraint: the trilemma of the service economy. *World Polit.*

Jackson JE, King DC. 1989. Public goods, private interests, and representation. *Am. Polit. Sci. Rev.* 83:1143–64

Kalyvas S. 1996. *The Rise of Christian Democracy in Europe.* Ithaca, NY: Cornell Univ. Press

Keeler JTS. 1993. Opening the window for reform: mandates, crises, and extraordinary decision-making. *Comp. Polit. Stud.* 25(4):433–86

Key VO Jr. 1958. *Politics, Parties, and Pressure Groups.* New York: Crowell

Key VO Jr. 1966. *The Responsible Electorate.* New York: Vintage

Klingemann H-D, Hofferbert RI, Budge I. 1994. *Parties, Policies, and Democracy.* Boulder, CO: Westview

Krehbiel K. 1993. Where's the party? *Br. J. Polit. Sci.* 23:235–66

Krukones MG. 1984. *Promises and Performance: Presidential Campaigns as Policy Predictors.* Lanham, MD: Univ. Press Am.

Laitin D. 1986. *Hegemony and Culture: Politics and Religious Change among the Yoruba.* Chicago: Univ. Chicago Press

LaPalombara J, Weiner M, eds. 1966. *Political Parties and Political Development.* Princeton, NJ: Princeton Univ. Press

Ledyard J. 1984. The pure theory of large two-candidate elections. *Public Choice* 48: 7–41

Leys C. 1959. Models, theories and the theory of political parties. *Polit. Stud.* 7:127–46

Lijphart A. 1994. *Electoral Systems and Party Systems: A Study of Twenty-Seven Democracies, 1945–1990.* Oxford, UK: Oxford Univ. Press

Linz JJ. Stepan A. 1996. *Problems of Democratic Transition and Consolidation.* Baltimore, MD: Johns Hopkins Univ. Press

Lipset SM, Rokkan S. 1967. Cleavages structures, party systems, and voter alignments: an introduction. In *Party Systems and*

Voter Alignments: Cross-National Perspectives, ed. SM Lipset, S Rokkan, pp. 1–64. New York: Free

Lipson L. 1964. *The Democratic Civilization.* New York: Oxford Univ. Press

Lott J, Bronars S. 1993. A critical review and an extension of the political shirking literature. *Public Choice* 74:125–49

Madison J. 1982 (1787). *The Federalist Papers.* Ed. by G Wills. New York: Bantam

Mainwaring S, Scully TR. 1995. Introduction: party systems in Latin America. In *Building Democratic Institutions: Party Systems in Latin America*, ed. S Mainwaring, TR Scully, pp. 1–34. Stanford, CA: Stanford Univ. Press

Mair P. 1997. *Party System Change: Approaches and Interpretations.* New York: Oxford Univ. Press

May JD. 1973. Opinion structure of political parties: the special law of curvilinear disparity. *Polit. Stud.* 21(2):133–51

McKelvy RD. 1976. Intransitivities in multidimensional voting models and some implications for agenda control. *J. Econ. Theory* 12:472–82

Miller WE, Stokes DE. 1966. Constituency influence in Congress. See Campbell et al 1966, pp. 351–72

Mishler W, Sheehan RS. 1993. The supreme court as a countermajoritarian institution? The impact of public opinion on Supreme Court decisions. *Am. Polit. Sci. Rev.* 87: 87–101

Nohlen D. 1981. *Sistemas Electorales del Mundo.* Transl. R García Cotarelo. Madrid: Cent. Estud. Const.

O'Donnell G. 1994. Delegative democracy? *J. Democr.* 5(1):55–69

Ordeshook PC, Shvetsova O. 1994. Ethnic heterogeneity, district magnitude, and the number of parties. *Am. J. Polit. Sci.* 38: 100–23

Page BI, Shapiro RY. 1992. *The Rational Public: Fifty Years of Trends in American Policy Preferences.* Chicago: Univ. Chicago Press

Popkin S. 1991. *The Reasoning Voter: Communication and Persuasion.* Chicago: Univ. Chicago Press

Powell GB Jr. 1982. *Contemporary Democracies: Participation, Stability and Violence.* Cambridge, MA: Harvard Univ. Press

Przeworski A, Stokes S, Manin B. 1999. *Democracy, Accountability, and Representation.* Cambridge, UK: Cambridge Univ. Press

Przeworski A, Sprague J. 1986. *Paper Stones: A History of Electoral Socialism.* Chicago: Univ. Chicago Press

Rabinowitz G, Macdonald SE. 1989. A directional theory of issue voting. *Am. Polit. Sci. Rev.* 83:93–121

Rabinowitz G, Macdonald SE, Listhaug O. 1991. New players in an old game: party strategy in multiparty systems. *Comp. Polit. Stud.* 24:147–85

Riker WH. 1982. *Liberalism Against Populism: A Confrontation Between the Theory of Democracy and the Theory of Social Choice.* Prospect Heights, IL: Waveland

Rogoff K, Siebert A. 1988. Elections and macroeconomic policy cycles. *Rev. Econ. Stud.* 80:1–16

Rohde DW. 1991. *Parties and Leaders in the Postreform House.* Chicago: Univ. Chicago Press

Rokkan S. 1970. *Citizens, Elections, Parties.* New York: Mackay

Sartori G. 1968. Political development and political engineering. In *Public Policy*, ed. JD Montgomery, AO Hirschman, pp. 262–76. Cambridge, UK: Cambridge Univ. Press

Sartori G. 1976. *Parties and Party Systems: A Framework for Analysis*, Vol. 1. Cambridge, UK: Cambridge Univ. Press

Satterthwaite MA. 1975. Strategy-proofness and Arrow's conditions: existence and correspondence theorems for voting procedures and social welfare functions. *J. Econ. Theory* 10:1–7

Schattschneider EE. 1942. *Party Government.* New York: Rinehart

Schickler E, Rich A. 1997. Controlling the floor: parties as procedural coalitions in the House. *Am. J. Polit. Sci.* 41:1319–39

Schwartz T. 1986. *The Logic of Collective Choice.* New York: Columbia Univ. Press

Solari AE. 1986. El sistema de partidos y regimen electoral en el Uruguay. In *El Sistema Electoral Uruguayo: Peculiaridades y Perspectivas*, ed. R Franco. 2:117–50. Montevideo, Uruguay: Fund. Hanns-Seidel

Snyder JM Jr. 1994. The logic of platform difference. *Econ. Polit.* 6(3):201–11

Stimson JA, Mackuen MB, Erikson RS. 1995. Dynamic representation. *Am. Polit. Sci. Rev.* 89:543–65

Stokes DE. 1966. Spatial models of party competition. See Campbell et al 1966, pp. 161–79

Stokes SC. 1998a. *Mandates and Democracy.* Chicago Cent. Democr. Work. Pap. No. 20. Chicago: Univ. Chicago

Stokes SC. 1998b. Constituency influence and representation. *Elect. Stud.* 17(3):351–67

Stokes SC. 1999. What do policy switches tell us about democracy? In *Democracy, Accountability, and Representation*, ed. A Przeworski, SC Stokes, B Manin. Cambridge, UK: Cambridge Univ. Press. In press

Strom K. 1990. A behavioral theory of competitive political parties. *Am. J. Polit. Sci.* 34(2):565–98

Taagepera R, Grofman B. 1985. Rethinking Duverger's law: predicting the effective number of parties in plurality and PR systems—parties minus issues equals one. *Eur. J. Polit. Res.* 13:341–52

Vincent J. 1966. *The Formation of the British Liberal Party.* New York: Scribner

Wildavsky A. 1959. A methodological critique of Duverger's *Political Parties. J. Polit.* 21:303–18

Wittman D. 1977. Candidates with policy preferences: a dynamic model. *J. Econ. Theory* 14:180–89

Wittman D. 1983. Candidate motivation: a synthesis of alternative theories. *Am. Polit. Sci. Rev.* 77(1):142–57

Wittman DA. 1989. Why democracies produce efficient results. *J. Polit. Econ.* 97:1395–1424

Zaller JR. 1994. *The Nature and Origins of Mass Opinion.* Cambridge, UK: Cambridge Univ. Press

Zechman MJ. 1978. *Dynamic Models of Voting Behavior and Spatial Models of Party Competition.* Chapel Hill, NC: Inst. Res. Soc. Sci. Press

Annu. Rev. Polit. Sci. 1999. 2:269–95

THE ROCHESTER SCHOOL: The Origins of Positive Political Theory

S. M. Amadae

Office for the History of Science, University of California, Berkeley, California
94720; e-mail: amadae@socrates.berkeley.edu

Bruce Bueno de Mesquita

Hoover Institution, Stanford University, Stanford, California 94305;
e-mail: bdm@hoover.stanford.edu

KEY WORDS: decision making, rational choice, game theory, spatial models

ABSTRACT

The Rochester school of political science, led by William H Riker, pioneered
the new method of positive political theory. Positive political theory, or rational choice theory, represents the attempt to build formal models of collective decision-making processes, often relying on the assumption of self-
interested rational action. This method has been used to study such political
processes as elections, legislative behavior, public goods, and treaty formation and diplomatic strategy in international relations. In this article, we provide a retrospective account of the Rochester school, which discusses Riker's theoretical synthesis and his institution building in the 1950s, 1960s, and
1970s. We discuss some of the most important Rochester school contributions related to spatial models of voting, agenda setting, structure-induced
equilibria, heresthetics, game theory, and political theory. We also briefly
situate positive political theory within the larger context of political science
and economics.

INTRODUCTION

Over the past three decades, positive political theory has become a central and
widely accepted method for studying politics. At the beginning of the 1960s,
however, the Rochester school, which launched the positive political theory
revolution in political science, was no more than the idea of a lone intellec-

269

tual, William H Riker. He was the visionary and institution builder who founded and established the Rochester school of political science with the aid of his University of Rochester colleagues and students. Because Riker master-minded positive political theory himself, and because he trained so many of the political scientists who spread the Rochester approach to other universities and established it as mainstream within the field of political science, to a large extent the name William H Riker is synonymous with the Rochester school.

The Rochester approach to political science, which Riker called positive political theory, and which in contemporary parlance is a variant of rational choice theory, has two essential elements. First, it upholds a methodological commitment to placing political science on the same foundation as other scientific disciplines, such as the physical sciences or economics. Thus, it holds that political theory should be comprised of statements deduced from basic principles that accurately describe the world of political events. The goal of positive political theorists is to make positive statements about political phenomena, or descriptive generalizations that can be subjected to empirical verification. This commitment to scientifically explaining political processes involves the use of formal language, including set theory, mathematical models, statistical analysis, game theory, and decision theory, as well as historical narrative and experiments.

Second, positive political theory looks to individual decision making as the source of collective political outcomes and postulates that the individual functions according to the logic of rational self-interest. Individuals are thought to rank their preferences consistently over a set of possible outcomes, taking risk and uncertainty into consideration and acting to maximize their expected payoffs (Austen-Smith & Banks 1998). Through the assumptions of rational self-interest, positive political theory postulates a specific motivational foundation for behavior. Interests, as opposed to attitudes, which are the subject of study in much behavioral research, are thought to be the well-spring of action.

The goal of positive political theorists is to build models that predict how individuals' self-oriented actions combine to yield collective outcomes. This method is applied to political processes (such as elections and the platform formation of political parties), legislative behavior (such as coalition formation and bargaining), public goods (such as the "tragedy of the commons" and the "free rider"), and treaty formation and diplomatic strategy in international relations. Using game theory and formal models, positive political theorists strive to determine whether these complex, strategic political interactions have predictable, law-like outcomes that exhibit stability. Stable outcomes, referred to as equilibria, signify that agents' actions combine in such a way that, given the collective social outcome of agents' self-oriented actions, no individual could achieve a greater (expected) payoff if he had unilaterally selected an alternative course of action. Equilibria are significant to positive political theorists because they indicate that the political processes under investigation result in predictable, stable social outcomes that best serve individuals' constituent interests, given the constraints imposed by the situation. The sequence of strategic choices that form an equilibrium and that imply specific outcome events constitutes the core of a predictive science of politics. The motivation to maximize expected payoffs provides the explanation of political action and provides the basis for predictions about processes that lead to outcomes.

This essay covers several aspects of the Rochester school. In order to contrast the accomplishments of positive political theory with its early competitors in the 1950s, we discuss the state of political science during Riker's training and early academic career. This is followed by a discussion of Riker's theoretical synthesis, which occurred between 1955 and 1962. This section, which culminates with *The Theory of Political Coalitions*, shows the breadth and consistency of Riker's vision for political science, and identifies the preexisting tools he used in developing the method of positive political theory. A brief discussion of the Public Choice Society is included to show that although Riker was a solitary pioneer within political science, other disciplines (such as mathematics, economics, psychology, sociology, philosophy, and public policy) also had rational choice pioneers, who could bolster and critique each other's efforts by providing a common, supportive network, and supplying institutional support to an emerging cross-disciplinary shared method. Riker's vital period of institution building at the University of Rochester occurred between 1963 and 1973, by which time positive political theory existed as an identifiable, if not widely shared, scientific paradigm. The next section highlights the institutional milestones between 1975 and the 1990s, by which time positive political theory must be acknowledged as a dominant force within political science. We then discuss the content of the scholarship contributed by the Rochester theorists. It includes spatial models of collective choice over one or more issues; coalition building; agenda formation; structure induced equilibria and heresthetics; cooperative and noncooperative game theory; democratic theory; and epistemological advances. Each of these general areas of inquiry has resulted in theoretical and empirical insights about American politics, comparative politics, and international relations. Two concluding sections revisit the "economics imperialism" thesis and touch on the nature of recent controversies in which positive political theory (within political science) has become embroiled.

STATE OF POLITICAL SCIENCE 1945–1955

Following World War II, political science lacked a unifying method. Instead, American political scientists debated over the appropriate method and substance of their field, leading some to despair, "The political sciences are a very fair illustration of the following: as a whole they are sure neither of their methods nor even of their subject matter, but [are] hesitant and groping; and further, taking it all in all, can they really boast of a sufficiently abundant harvest of achievement to resolve doubts about their essential premises?" (Eisenmann 1950:91). In the postwar period there were two articulated, mutually opposed tendencies in the field. Some political scientists sought to "emulat[e]...the natural sciences.... Objective description and precise measurement have become their ideals." Others promoted political science as a normative enterprise in which the study of particular political institutions is guided by values and ethical postulates (Cook 1950:75). Variants of political science practice included the historical, case-study approach that resonated with then-popular public law and public administration studies (exemplified by the work of Leonard D White); public opinion and survey research (Walter Lippman); psychological approaches (Harold D Lasswell); political and democratic theory (John Dewey); and the growing behaviorist approach emphasizing surveys and statistics (Charles E Merriam and David Easton).

Although there was already a clear tendency to promote statistical methods and quantitative techniques, especially evident in the behavioral school, nothing on the intellectual map of political science remotely resembled what would come to be known as positive political theory or rational choice theory. (For detailed analysis of the forces behind increasing formalization of the American social sciences including political science during the twentieth century, see Klausner & Lidz 1986.) Its seemingly closest cousin, the then-flourishing behavioral approach, emphasized statistical correlation and empirical testing but lacked the concept of axiomatic treatment of human behavior and the reliance on minimalist assumptions that yield general laws. The behavioral approach instead generally focused on psychological attitudes to derive empirical generalizations.

RIKER'S THEORETICAL SYNTHESIS AND THE ORIGINS OF POSITIVE POLITICAL THEORY (1955–1962)

Riker graduated with his PhD in political science from Harvard University in 1948, studying under Carl Friedrich. His dissertation, on the Council of Industrial Organizations, reflected the then-popular case-study approach. Upon completion of his graduate studies, Riker accepted a faculty position at Lawrence College in Wisconsin in 1949. There he remained for the next decade, building up a small political science department and striving to articulate his thoughts on political science methodology. During this period he was awarded two fellowships: a Ford Foundation education grant, which he relied on while writing his first textbook, and a Rockefeller fellowship, which he used to assemble his thoughts on a new approach to the science of politics.

As significant as the contrast would be between Riker's work and other work characteristic of political science in the 1950s, Riker's textbook, *Democracy in the United States* (1953), shows that an equally dramatic shift occurred within his own thinking. Whereas all his writings after 1955 exhibited a remarkable consistency, this textbook is indicative of Riker's own roots in a discipline of political science governed by normative conclusions. In this text, Riker proclaims, "Democracy is self-respect for everybody. Within this simple phrase is all that is and ought to be the democratic ideal.... If self-respect is the democratic good, then all things that prevent its attainment are democratic evils" (1953:19). Riker's upcoming dramatic personal conversion to the vocabulary of self-interested rational action would signify the profound change in the language that would increasingly come to structure insights into politics.

Ever since his days as a graduate student, Riker had been intellectually dissatisfied with the dominant case-study approach, which political science shared with the overlapping fields of legal history and public administration. He was casting about for a new method to serve as the platform on which to build a sturdy science of politics. In 1954, two RAND scholars, LS Shapley and Martin Shubik, published a paper with a formal treatment of what they called a power index. This paper defined the power index as a mathematical formula expressing a legislator's power as a function of his ability to swing decisions (Shapley & Shubik 1954). It exemplified a new vein of literature that addressed political processes in the language of mathematics, including the work of John von Neumann and Oskar Morgenstern, Duncan Black, Kenneth Arrow, and Anthony Downs. Riker rapidly introduced this work into his curriculum at Lawrence College and used it as the basis for his new science of politics.

Von Neumann & Morgenstern's *The Theory of Games and Economic Behavior* (1944), Black's "On the Rationale of Group Decision Making" (1948), Arrow's *Social Choice and Individual Values* (1963 [1951]), and Downs's *An Economic Theory of Democracy* (1957), which have subsequently earned a reputation as the first texts of the rational choice canon, served as rich fertilizer for Riker's ambitious program of placing political science on a scientific footing. Each text contributed to the brew of ideas that Riker fermented to produce positive political theory.

Von Neumann & Morgenstern's classic text served as the definitive point of origin of a rational choice theory of human action because this text axiomatized the principles of rational agency. It took the hubris of von Neumann, a Hungarian-trained physicist and mathematician, to announce, "We wish to find the mathematically complete principles which define 'rational behavior' for the participants in a social economy.... The immediate concept of a solution is plausibly a set of rules for each participant which will tell him how to behave in every situation which might conceivably arise" (von Neumann & Morgenstern 1944:31). *The Theory of Games and Economic Behavior* was innovative in its set-theoretic presentation, which was unprecedented in the social sciences; it was path-breaking in modeling an economy as a deliberate, strategic competition; and it developed game theory as a new form of mathematics. However, although this text was certainly foundational, its target audience, economists, found it of little value, in part because it concentrated on a two-person, zero-sum game of dubious relevance to voluntary market exchange. The book received little attention outside of the RAND Corporation, where mathematicians were assigned the task of exploring its relevance for nuclear brinkmanship (see Leonard 1992).

Black's "On the Rationale of Group Decision Making" (1948) contributed a new way of considering the problem of collective outcomes reached by non-market means such as voting. Black revisited the eighteenth-century Condorcet paradox, which demonstrated that if three individuals democratically vote among three possible outcomes, there is no guarantee that the final result is independent from the means by which the votes are aggregated. Specifically, consider the case in which a collective choice is to be made among three options, A, B, and C. Suppose that one decision maker prefers A to B and B to C; a second prefers B to C and C to A; and the third prefers C to A and A to B. Given these individual preference orderings, following majority rule, the resulting collective preference ordering is intransitive; that is, A is preferred to B, B is preferred to C, *and* C is preferred to A. This intransitive collective preference, with no definitive winner, is said to cycle. The existence of such cycles, arising from preference aggregation, alerted Riker to the importance of agenda setting in politics and raised for him a persistent desire to understand how the cycling phenomenon predicted in theory related to actual political practice.

Black (1948) saw a way out of the Condorcet paradox, although his solution assumes a restriction on freedom of choice. He extended the discussion of the voting paradox to n voters, and he proved that the arbitrariness of the result could be avoided by stipulating that voters' preferences be single-peaked, so that if, for instance, A, B, and C are aligned in that order, then it is not possible to least prefer B. Black was original in addressing the voting problem as a spatial model using the formal language of individual preference orderings, and he recognized the power of mathematical analysis to provide insight into the problem of arriving at collective decisions through non-market means.

Arrow's classic *Social Choice and Individual Values* (1951), which grew out of the earlier paper "A Difficulty in the Concept of Social Welfare" (1950), was the product of three disparate approaches. Working in the late 1940s at RAND, where game theory was in vogue, Arrow was drawn to von Neumann & Morgenstern's set theoretic treatment of rationality. Arrow's boss at RAND, Olaf Helmer, assigned him the task of deriving a single mathematical function that would predict the collective political outcomes for the entire Soviet Union. In attempting to meet this challenge, Arrow drew on his familiarity with the Bergsonian social welfare function that attempted to translate private preferences into a single public choice. It is also likely that Arrow encountered a copy of Black's "On the Rationale of Group Decision Making" when he served as a reviewer for *Econometrica* (for more information on the priority dispute between Black and Arrow, see Coase 1998). Combining these three approaches—a set-theoretic treatment of decision making, the social welfare function, and a formal analysis of voting—led Arrow to derive his famous Impossibility Theorem. Arrow's Impossibility Theorem proved that Condorcet's paradox of three voters and three outcomes could be extended to *n* voters, showing that democratic voting procedures obeying the most limited strictures do not necessarily result in meaningful, nonarbitrary, collective outcomes. Arrow's text would spawn a vast literature and transform the foundations of welfare economics, but it was wholly unrecognized as relevant to political science. For instance, *The American Political Science Review* did not review the book.

Arrow's student, Anthony Downs, published his dissertation, *An Economic Theory of Democracy,* in 1957. Downs argued that in studying democratic institutions, the ends that government serves must be evaluated in terms of the individuals comprising it. In arguing that political agents must be thought of as seeking their own gains, he challenged the concepts of public interest and public service. Downs concluded that in seeking to win elections and maximize their votes, political parties move to the center in order to cater to the median voter.

In the mid-1950s, Riker had a stimulating collection of approaches to the study of political phenomena, including methodological individualism, an emphasis on micro-foundations, game theory, spatial models, axiomatic set-theoretic treatment of rational action, and generalized Condorcet results questioning the validity of processes for collective decision making. However, these approaches and results were marginal in their own fields, and they required disciplined and unifying development before they could be recognized as the canonical works of a new tradition. Between 1957 and 1962, Riker wrote three formal papers indicating tentative steps toward his eventual theoretical synthesis. Two of these papers drew on Shapley & Shubik's formulation of the power index (Riker & Schaps 1957), and the third set about determining whether Arrow's Impossibility Theorem, which predicted that *n*-person voting procedures for more than two outcomes should demonstrate an inherent instability, pertained to actual voting practices (Riker 1958, 1959a). Although these papers were mathematical and attempted to draw generalized conclusions by combining theoretical deduction with empirical tests, they did not yet put together the pieces that would later characterize positive political theory. Notably, even though Riker was engaging in experiments in coalition formation using a game-theoretic structure, neither game theory nor an explicit rational-action model was relevant to these early papers.

Riker also authored two papers published in philosophy journals before the close of the decade. These papers discuss the importance of carefully circumscribing the events defining a scientific study and the need to base science on "descriptive generalizations" (1957, 1959b). Although these articles were not earth-shattering to the philosophical community, they did reveal Riker's grasp of the philosophical and conceptual issues necessary to ground his developing positive approach to politics. In them, Riker challenged the standard view in political science that promoted the study of the idiosyncratic details of rare and influential events. This challenge to the case-study method and to so-called thick analysis remains at the core of methodological debates today.

The earliest indication that Riker's theoretical synthesis was complete is found in his application as a nominee to Stanford's Center for Advanced Study in the Behavioral Sciences, submitted in 1959 (CASBS file, William H Riker papers, University of Rochester[1]). In this application, Riker distanced himself from his earlier work on federalism and stated, "I describe the field in which I expect to be working at the Center as 'formal, positive, political theory.'" He elaborated, "By formal, I mean the expression of the theory in algebraic rather than verbal symbols. By positive, I mean the expression of descriptive rather than normative propositions." This document demonstrates Riker's own sense of intellectual development, as well as his reflective and unabashed program for political science.

> I visualize the growth in political science of a body of theory somewhat similar to...the neo-classical theory of value in economics. It seems to be that a number of propositions from the mathematical theory of games can perhaps be woven into a theory of politics. Hence, my main interest at present is attempting to use game theory for the construction of political theory.

Riker was a fellow at the Stanford Center in the 1960–1961 academic year. In this fertile year away from the responsibilities of teaching, Riker wrote *The Theory of Political Coalitions*, which served as the manifesto for his freshly articulated positive political theory.

The Theory of Political Coalitions (1963) is highly innovative and accompanies the aforementioned texts by von Neumann & Morgenstern, Black, Arrow, and Downs as part of the rational choice canon. This canon also includes Buchanan & Tullock's *The Calculus of Consent* (1962) and Olson's *The Logic of Collective Action* (1965). Riker's opening chapter, entitled "The Prospect of a Science of Politics," puts forth how a science should be built up of deductive structures derived from intuitively justified axioms that are subject to empirical tests. Riker proposed studying politics by analyzing its micro-foundations in the decision making of agents whose actions could be modeled like those of

---

[1]The William H Riker papers at the University of Rochester are hereafter cited as "WHR papers."

particles in motion. Just as a particle's trajectory could be traced by knowing its momentum and the force on it, so an agent's actions can be predicted by knowing her preferences and the environment structuring her choices. Then the political scientist could model the results of collective actions through analysis of the parameters of individual decision making.

Riker adopted Easton's definition of politics as the authoritative allocation of value and made the crucial point that distinguished his theory of politics from economic theory. Whereas collective outcomes that occur in the market-place are made in "a quasi-mechanical way," collective outcomes that are the stuff of politics are made by conscious processes (Riker 1963:11). This is a crucial distinction because the rational actor in political arenas intentionally calculates how to achieve aims in a strategic environment with other strategically acting agents. Riker drew heavily on von Neumann & Morgenstern's (1944) formulation of human rationality, as well as their zero-sum, n-person game theory.

Besides introducing positive political theory to political science, the main point of Riker's book was to construct a positive theory of political coalitions. To this end he proposed the size principle, which held that

> In n-person, zero-sum games, where side-payments are permitted, where players are rational, and where they have perfect information, only minimum winning coalitions occur. (Riker 1963:32)

The size principle, which embodied the idea that political science could give rise to general laws, was a response to Downs's argument (1957) that political parties strive to maximize votes. In Downs's model, parties or political coalitions seek to attain a maximum number of votes without limit. Riker first deductively argued that rational agents, such as party leaders, create minimum winning coalitions so that a minimum of compromise is necessary, and the spoils of victory is divided among fewer coalition members. Then he strove to use his principle to explain the outcomes of political processes. His empirical tests included discursive discussions of the evolution of the American two-party system, which on occasion had briefly had three parties, and empirical evidence of coalition formation gathered from his experiments on undergraduates at Lawrence College.

When *The Theory of Political Coalitions* was published in the early 1960s, few in political science were in a position to appreciate it. Still, the book created a significant stir precisely because Riker not only exhorted the discipline to become more scientific but also showed how to do it. As one reviewer noted, "Although Riker's particular approach is not the answer to all of the discipline's woes, he has certainly succeeded in challenging us by example. Those who would accept the challenge had better come prepared with a well sharpened kit of tools. For, either to emulate or attack, nothing less will suffice"

(Fagen 1963:446–47). One of the remarkable achievements of the Rochester school has been that Riker's nudges and pushes have produced several generations of scholars with just such well-honed tool kits. Riker was the first non-RAND theoretician to recognize the potential of game theory to explain political interactions. It was Riker who bestowed on game theory the promise of a new life after RAND defense strategists concluded it had little merit for studying warfare, and before economists grasped its promise for grounding a new mathematics of the market.

PUBLIC CHOICE SOCIETY, EARLY 1960s

Although it is remarkable that Riker, working first as a lone scholar and then as a leader of a single school of thought, would exert so much impact on an entire field, it is also remarkable that the rational choice cradle was shared by fringe scholars in other disciplines. These scholars, working on the peripheries of their own fields, recognized their shared research interests and formed a community that fostered the rise of rational choice theory as a cross-disciplinary phenomenon. In the early 1960s, a meeting of minds occurred, resulting in the founding of the Public Choice Society (originally called the Committee on Nonmarket Decision Making). Researchers active in its early meetings included subsequent Nobelists Herbert Simon (economics and public administration), John Harsanyi (mathematics), and James Buchanan (public finance), as well as Gordon Tullock (public finance), John Rawls (philosophy), James S Coleman (sociology) and, of course, William Riker. The Public Choice Society is noteworthy for helping to generate the critical mass required to establish the rational choice approach as an academy-wide method of inquiry. In founding the society, members ensured that their newly wrought discipline would benefit from an active network of similarly minded intellects. To further this end, annual meetings were held. The society also initiated an enduring journal, *Public Choice*, which was one of the first signs that the formal approach to non-market collective decisions was maturing into a recognizable program of research.

BUILDING A DEPARTMENT, 1963–1973

It took imagination and vision to synthesize the leads provided by von Neumann, Morgenstern, Black, Arrow, and Downs into a coherent theory of politics based on the idea of methodological individualism encapsulated in a theory of rational, strategic action modeled by n-person game theory. However, brilliant vision does not inevitably lead to achievement. Riker's ambitious platform for reorienting political science may have gone little further than his personal bibliography had he not tirelessly and deftly built up a graduate program specifically geared toward generating theorists ultimately capable of transforming the entire discipline of political science. A unique constellation of circumstances provided Riker with the resources and institutional infrastructure requisite to carry out his program for reform.

Shortly before setting forth to the Stanford Center in 1960, Riker caught the eye of administrators at the University of Rochester who sought to establish social science graduate programs with national standing. The University of Rochester, throughout most of the 1960s, was flush with capital provided by Joseph Wilson, head trustee of the Haloid-Xerox Corporation, who was committed to science as a means of bettering human lives. Thanks to this beneficence, the University of Rochester's endowment was the nation's third highest for much of the 1960s, surpassed only by Harvard's and Yale's. Support abounded on campus to build up the social science departments by emphasizing programs oriented toward rigorous quantitative analysis resembling the successful programs in the physical sciences. Riker, whose work admirably fit this bill, was hired to create a graduate program in political science. Also newly appointed were Lionel McKenzie, brought in to chair the Economics Department and build its graduate program, and W Allen Wallis, formerly Dean of the Chicago Business School, to head the University of Rochester as chancellor. Wallis and McKenzie, too, were committed to the development of analytic and formal social science and would become close colleagues and active supporters of Riker.

Riker rapidly outlined a strategy for building the Rochester political science department. His strategy emphasized both behavioral methods and positive theory. He sought to rival the then-nationally-significant programs at Yale, Chicago, Northwestern, MIT, and the Michigan Survey Research Center. The result was an entirely new curriculum of 14 courses and seminars: the scope of political science, theories of strategy, positive political theory, techniques of research in political science, theories of decision making, theories of organization, problems in measurement of political events, political parties, legislative behavior, political sociology, comparative politics, problems in constitutional interpretation, national security policy, and recent political philosophy. Riker, always highly self-conscious of his goals and methods, wrote to the graduate dean, "What is proposed here is the creation of another department to join the half-dozen just mentioned in seeking and creating a discipline." He stated that he was placing a "two-fold emphasis...on (1) objective methods of verifying hypothesis (i.e., 'political behavior') and (2) positivistic (i.e., non-normative) theories of politics" (Riker's proposal for the new graduate program in political science as submitted to SDS Spragg, WHR papers).The new PhD program's requirements stressed quantification and formal analysis. In an unprecedented move, Riker persuaded the graduate dean to accept the substitution of statistics for a modern language. Whereas other programs emphasized the literature, Riker's focused on developing tools for rigorous research into the theoretical properties and empirical laws of politics.

Faculty recruitment was Riker's next priority. When he arrived at the University of Rochester, the political science department had three active faculty: Richard Fenno, Ted Bluhm, and Peter Regenstrief. Over the years, Riker added Jerry Kramer, Arthur Goldberg, John Mueller, Richard Niemi, Alvin Rabushka, Gordon Black, and G Bingham Powell. Along with faculty, Riker worked to recruit students. Whereas in 1959 the Rochester political science department did not graduate a single undergraduate major, by the early 1970s it was flourishing with over 100 undergraduates and between 25 and 30 graduate students. As of June 1973, the department had graduated 26 doctoral students and 49 master's students; it moved up in the American Council of Education ratings from being unrated in 1965 to holding fourteenth place in 1970. In student placement during the 1960–1972 period, Rochester's political science program was second only to Yale's; Yale placed 62% of its total placements in American Council of Education–rated departments, and Rochester placed 58%. The students trained in the first decade of Riker's leadership of the department would take up appointments in the next decade at numerous institutions with nationally recognized programs, including Cal Tech, Carnegie Mellon, Washington University, the University of Iowa, UC Davis, Dartmouth College, Trinity College, the University of Michigan, SUNY Buffalo, SUNY Albany, the University of Wisconsin, Ohio State University, McGill University, and Texas. These trailblazing students included Peter Ordeshook, Kenneth Shepsle, Barbara Sinclair, Richard McKelvey, John Aldrich, David Rhode, Morris Fiorina, and others. This first generation of Rochester PhD students, coming from a then unknown program, would be crucial in transforming the study of politics in the decades ahead.

Other political science departments were quick to notice the marshaling of a leading program. Recruitment raids to acquire Riker himself were advanced by the University of Illinois, Rice University, Northwestern University, UC Berkeley, Emory University, and even the University of Michigan, which wanted Riker as its "dean" of operations to build a new political science program in 1965. The recruitment raids also extended beyond Riker to his carefully assembled faculty. A key to the Rochester school's success was its virtually impenetrable esprit de corps. Despite these constant attempts, in its first decade the department lost only Jerry Kramer (to Yale) and Arthur Goldberg (internally, to the Dean's office). During the entire process of institution building, Riker remained uncannily self-reflexive. In a letter to the graduate dean, he observed, "One main reason for this departmental success is, in my opinion, the fact that the department has had a coherent graduate program, centering on the notion of rational choice in political decision-making" ("Department of Political Science 10-Year Report, Sept. 1973," WHR papers).

By 1973, Riker had built up the infrastructure necessary to train students who would set forth from Rochester to contribute to the positive political theory research program and to spread the vision of a positive science of politics to political scientists in other programs. However, Riker's efforts on behalf of positive political theory extended beyond the confines of his home department at the University of Rochester. He maintained an active publication record, contributing so many articles to the flagship journal of political science, *The American Political Science Review*, that its editor Austin Ranney wrote to him, "There is some danger of turning this journal into the 'William H. Riker Review'" (March 22, 1967, WHR papers). Another step in establishing his method as a part of the discipline-wide currency was his co-authorship, with Ordeshook, of a textbook that elucidated the parameters of positive political theory. This text, entitled *An Introduction to Positive Political Theory* (1972), was aimed at advanced undergraduates and beginning graduate students, and it was an important step in defining positive political theory for a widespread audience. It introduced the assumption of rationality and the formal account of preference orderings, and it demonstrated the positive approach to political science by applying it to political problems, such as political participation, voting and majority rule, public goods, public policy, and electoral competition. The text also discussed formal theory and deductive results from formal theory, including *n*-person and two-person game theory, the power index, and the size principle. It is not clear that the textbook was introduced into the curriculum of many political science programs, but it was a necessary step in paving the way for a rational choice approach to politics to be widely recognized and well defined. It provided a resource for those outside Rochester who sought to participate in the research program launched by the Rochester school.

SECURING A LEGACY

If the 1962–1972 period was one of building up Riker's home institution, the next two decades were devoted to spreading the rational choice approach to departments across the nation and to steadily achieving institutional milestones indicating not only that the Rochester school had matured as a subfield of political science but that it had secured its legacy within the entire discipline of political science. Rochester's first generation of graduates built successful careers. They first introduced positive political theory to other departments and then made their skills indispensable to these departments. In addition to the array of appointments mentioned above, the Rochester school established strongholds and established new outposts through the appointment of its graduates to the relevant departments at Cal Tech, Carnegie Mellon, and Washington University. These programs, like Rochester's, became important centers of positive political theory. By 1985, Fiorina and Shepsle had attained appointments at Harvard, which Riker considered one of the greatest signs that positive political theory had arrived. His alma mater, which had long insisted on perpetuating what he took to be dated and nonscientific approaches to politics, had at last come around to acknowledge the leading role that his positive political science rightfully played. Meanwhile, back at Rochester, a second generation of students was prepared to reinforce those already practicing in the field, while another wave of students absorbed the steady pedagogy of Rochester's first progeny. The second generation of Rochester students, like their predecessors, have become leaders in many subfields of political science. Keith Poole, Keith Krehbiel, James Enelow, and others emerged as leading scholars of American politics in the positivist tradition. Michael Altfeld, James Morrow, David Lalman, and Woosang Kim made important early contributions to the development of a positive political theory of international relations. Subrata Mitra established a beachhead for rational choice models in the study of South Asian politics as Daryl Dobbs did in political theory. The consistent, thorough preparation of students who recognized themselves to be part of a distinct movement to alter political science, the camaraderie and tight-knit sense of community among those students, and their impressive scholarly productivity ensured that Riker's pioneering vision would become one of the field's standards. These scholars were steadfast in their commitment to positive political theory and unyielding in their efforts to research and advance the theoretical paradigm of rational choice. Their advances and branches of study are the subject of a following section.

Riker was nominated to the National Academy of Sciences (NAS) in 1974, and thus was among the first political scientists to be inducted into the elite society. He was later joined by other Rochesterians, including Fenno, Shepsle, McKelvey, and Fiorina, as well as such "fellow travelers" as John Ferejohn. Admittance into the NAS signaled the acceptance of political scientists into the community of natural scientists for having met the dictates of rigorous scientific inquiry. Furthermore, it emphasized that this acceptance was partly because of the facility with formal models so clearly displayed by Rochester school members. Thus, when political science made the grade of inclusion into the NAS, this was in no small part due to Riker's steadfast promotion of a quantitative and deductively rigorous approach to politics. Of the 14 political scientists who have been elected to the NAS over the past two and a half decades, one third were either faculty at or PhD graduates from the University of Rochester. This is all the more remarkable considering that the Rochester program was always very small, often enrolling fewer than 10 students per year. The induction of Rochester-trained political scientists into the NAS had the further effect of elevating the status of the political science departments and universities that could count them among their faculty for purposes of accreditation and national ranking.

Riker met with additional career successes that established his legacy and served as community recognition of his significant role in making over political science. His nomination to the American Academy of Arts and Sciences in 1975 was a significant accomplishment, even if overshadowed by the NAS triumph. In 1983, when Riker was chosen to serve as President of the American Political Science Association, all political scientists, whether sympathetic or not to the Rochester credo, had to acknowledge that positive political theory had changed the terrain of political science. In the next decade, all major departments would have faculty who worked within the rational choice/positive political theory research tradition.

ROCHESTER SCHOOL CONTRIBUTIONS

The Rochester school's contributions, ranging from Riker and his colleagues' work to that of his first- and second-generation students, fall into several categories: spatial models of preference aggregation, agenda control and heresthetics, game theory, democratic theory, and epistemological advances.

The insights and puzzles raised by spatial models of politics formed a core area of inquiry for the early contributors to the Rochester school. Black (1948) had shown that the Condorcet problem could be escaped by assuming single-peaked preferences. Kramer, Ordeshook, McKelvey, and Shepsle, as well as Hinich, Schwartz, Schofield, and Weingast, among others, began the systematic exploration of the spatial model. Excellent reviews of this work can be found in Ordeshook (1986), Hinich & Munger (1997), and Enelow & Hinich (1984). It quickly became apparent that Black's solution and his median-voter theorem could not be extended to multidimensional problems. In such problems, voters select from a possibility set of more than two linked outcomes. For example, voters must decide how to allocate resources over two or more program areas. If issues are linked, or are best represented in a space that is not unidimensional, then single-peakedness is insufficient to escape the problem of cyclical aggregated preferences. The observation is of profound importance because, if cyclical preferences are common (Niemi & Weisberg 1968), then positive political theorists face the challenge of explaining policy stability and constancy in politics. Thus, spatial model results provided an intellectual challenge to democratic theory. In addition, they prompted research with a game-theoretic orientation, with an emphasis on equilibria.

McKelvey and Schofield, working at first independently and then together, resolved a fundamental feature of the spatial puzzle and tied it to equilibrium concepts (McKelvey 1976, 1979; Schofield 1978; McKelvey & Schofield 1986). They proved that in a policy space of any dimensionality above one, if there is at least one more decision maker than there are dimensions, if majority rule applies, and if "voters" chose sincerely (that is, in accordance with their true preferences), then there is a rational basis for any possible combination of policy choices. If the aggregation of preferences to produce policy choices leads to stable outcomes in real politics, then it must be that one or more of the assumed conditions are violated in practice.

The resulting, aptly named chaos theorem suggests several explanations for stability and change in politics. It draws attention to agenda setting. By manipulating political agendas, politicians can shape and restrict the domain of political choices, limit the time within which logrolls could be pursued, and create opportunities for strategic voting to influence outcomes. The formation of political agendas became a central concern of the Rochester school and of Riker himself. His book *Agenda Formation* (1993) was published only days before he died. The collection of essays includes contributions from many members of the Rochester school, some within the spatial models framework (e.g. Poole & Rosenthal, Laver & Shepsle) and others within the framework of noncooperative game theory (e.g. Bueno de Mesquita & Lalman).

Agenda control was not the only means by which policy chaos could be averted. In conjunction with the literature on agenda formation, theorists examined how political institutions or political structure induce equilibria. Structure-induced equilibria (SIE) became a centerpiece of research by the first and second generations of Rochester students and faculty. Shepsle (1979) and later Shepsle & Weingast (1984, 1987) helped launch what today is called the new institutionalism in political science. Riker (1980) also was among the first to signal the importance of political institutions, such as congressional committees and voting rules, within a positive theory context. This research led to an intense intellectual debate. Shepsle & Weingast (1981, 1987, 1994) argued that preference outliers or extremists were institutionally advantaged and so came to dominate and steer congressional committees. A counterargument within the positivist model was launched by Gilligan & Krehbiel (1989) and Krehbiel (1991), who argued that the institutional power of committees comes from their expertise or specialized knowledge and that experts, rather than preference outliers, are granted the power through committees to shape congressional debate and outcomes.

Riker saw in the SIE debate a need for a theory of dimensionality. That is, he came to believe that whether issues were unidimensional (as in Gilligan-Krehbiel models) or multidimensional (as in Shepsle-Weingast models) was itself an endogenous, strategic decision. "Heresthetics," discussed below, was his label for this strategic effort to influence whether issues were linked or not. In *The Art of Political Manipulation* (1986) and in the posthumously published book, *The Strategy of Rhetoric* (1996), Riker brought together his concern for heresthetic maneuvering with his interest in political persuasion. Just as the Rochester school had been instrumental in returning political science to its early focus on institutions and constitutions, Riker helped return the discipline to an examination of the science behind persuasion and campaigning by reinvigorating the study of rhetoric as a strategic device. Most rational choice scholarship accepts the institutional structure in which preferences are aggregated to be given in the model, and Riker drew attention to the significance of structuring the environment in which preferences are coordinated into a collective outcome. Thus, Riker contrasted heresthetics with rhetoric. Whereas rhetoric involves persuasion, heresthetics involves strategic manipulation of the setting in which political outcomes are reached. Riker listed a number of examples of heresthetic actions, including strategic voting (expressing preference for a less favored outcome in order to avoid an even worse outcome); agenda manipulation; avoiding wasted votes on a guaranteed winner in order to achieve a secondary objective; creating a voting cycle to undermine a current winner; vote trading; altering the sequence of decisions; and interdicting new alternatives.

The spatial model of voting also led early Rochester pioneers, especially Fiorina, to reexamine voter decision making. By the beginning of the 1970s, the Michigan view of voting as attitudinal and psychological, driven by family-transmitted party identification, had gained intellectual ascendancy. By the next decade, as a result of the research especially by Fiorina (1976, 1981), Aldrich (1980), and Ferejohn (1986) and others, the notion that voters make policy decisions had proven the major rival to the Michigan party-identification perspective. Fiorina and others elaborated a theory of retrospective voting, in which voters evaluate the past performance of incumbents and base their votes on expectations about policy performance and shared preferences. Aldrich built on the growing body of theoretical literature on rational voting decisions to launch the first theoretical and empirical analysis of the presidential-primary process. Bueno de Mesquita (1984) and his colleagues (Bueno de Mesquita et al 1985, Bueno de Mesquita & Stokman 1994) built on the theoretical developments in the spatial model of voting to construct a practical, applied model that found broad use in the US government and in business to predict policy decisions in voting and nonvoting settings. Riker pointed to this work as further evidence that his vision of a predictive, positive political science was being realized. He observed of the median-voter theorem that

> a forecasting model based on the theorem has attracted repeat customers in the worlds of business and government (Bueno de Mesquita, Newman, and Rabushka 1985). While commercial success says nothing about scientific explanation, it does at least indicate that the model using the median-voter theorem is better for prediction than alternatives (which are mostly nontheoretical and intuitive). Unplanned reality testing of this sort gives me, at least, some confidence that rational choice theory is on the right track. [quoted in Alt & Shepsle (1990:180)]

As noted above, game theory was an important instrument in the Rochester school's tool box. By the early 1980s, advances in noncooperative game theory made it possible to analyze complex problems involving uncertainty about the payoffs of players or about the past history of play. Again, the Rochester school was at the forefront. With the additions of David Austen-Smith, Jeffrey Banks, and Randall Calvert to the faculty, Rochester began producing a new generation of students equipped to use noncooperative games to examine problems for which cooperative game theory proved inadequate. Austen-Smith & Banks (1988, 1990) investigated the complexity of voter choices in parliamentary systems, puzzling over the difficulty voters face in choosing their most preferred candidate or in choosing to enhance the prospects that their most preferred party will get to form a government. They also returned to the Condorcet jury theorem to evaluate its implications within an equilibrium framework (1996). Morrow (1989), Bueno de Mesquita & Lalman (1992), and Smith (1995), as well as fellow travelers Brams (1985, 1990), Powell (1990), Fearon (1994), Downs & Rocke (1990, 1995), and Zagare (1987), introduced noncooperative game theory to the study of international relations, casting doubt on many of the most widely accepted beliefs about international affairs in the process. Diermeier & Feddersen (1998) and Smith (1996), among others, are doing the same in comparative politics.

Riker's joint theoretical and empirical exploration of the nature of democracy, based on the social choice work of Arrow, indicates the power of positive political theory to influence our hopes and aspirations for democratic government. In his book *Liberalism Against Populism* (1982), Riker uses social choice theory to argue that the populism of Jean Jacques Rousseau is untenable, whereas the more limited liberalism of James Madison is realistic. Riker makes his case by recounting the lesson of Arrow's Impossibility Theorem, which proves that no means of democratically aggregating votes for more than two outcomes can be devised that has the desired properties of citizen sovereignty, Pareto optimality, non-dictatorship, independence of irrelevant alternatives, and universal domain. In effect, Arrow demonstrated the limits of democratic processes for reaching collective outcomes. Riker, who was often frustrated by political scientists' failure to recognize the implications of Arrow's work, used Arrow's result to question the efficacy of democratic government in producing outcomes that are somehow publicly beneficial. He put democratic theory to the test, asking what normative goal it postulated and what practical goals were attainable. He concluded that social choice theory undermined populism, but he supported the less ambitious Madisonian liberalism.

Comparative politics was slowest among substantive fields of study to utilize, if not embrace, the theoretical advances that positive political theory had brought to the study of American politics and international relations. In some ways, this is the most surprising and disappointing aspect of the efforts to spread the Rochester school's focus on rational action. It is surprising because Riker's focus on coalition formation had natural applications in comparative politics. Many picked up on the ideas in investigating coalitions (Groennings et al 1970, de Swaan 1973), but the area-studies focus of comparativists proved difficult to overcome. Coalition politics was not the only aspect of comparative politics that was examined using the new positive political theory. Rabushka & Shepsle (1972) showed how to utilize rational choice modeling to think about the sources of political instability in plural societies. Mitra (1978) developed theoretical insights and showed strong empirical support for them in his investigation of cabinet instability in India. Only relatively recently, however, has positivism begun to take hold in the study of comparative politics. Strom (1990), Laver & Shepsle (1994), and Laver & Schofield (1990) returned to the investigation of coalitions and cabinet formation. Fearon & Laitin (1996) have begun the systematic investigation of ethnic conflict, returning to the theme of research by Rabushka & Shepsle a quarter of a century earlier. And many others, both inside and outside the Rochester school, have undertaken rational choice studies of parliamentary voting, banking policy, political party politics, federalism, economic growth, and so on.

The Rochester school has done more than just contribute to a better understanding of specific questions about politics, although these contributions are not to be underestimated. The epistemology of positive political theory itself has drawn attention to basic problems in the previous conduct of political research. These advances include the following four general areas of insight: endogenous choices and their implications for path dependence; selection effects in theory and in data and how they can distort inferences from historical or statistical analysis; keeping arguments independent from the evidence used to evaluate their merits in order to distinguish between description, explanation, and prediction; and prediction as a means of evaluating the potential of scientific inquiry. These four items—endogeneity, selection effects, independence between argument and evidence, and prediction—represent areas where scientific inquiry into politics has proven to be helpful in clarifying problems that frequently arise in other modes of analysis. Table 1 summarizes these claims.

Each of the points summarized in the table represents an important difference between the epistemology characteristic of positive political theory and that of rival methods. The emphasis on endogenous choice draws attention to how strategic decisions influence the flow of events. We briefly offer two examples.

Students of American politics have observed that the presidential veto is rarely used. This traditionally was explained by claiming that the president was weak compared with the Congress. By focusing on endogenous choice,

Table 1   Some general insights into positive political theory

	Historical and Some Statistical Inductive Approaches	Positive Political Theory, Especially Noncooperative Game Theory
Flow of Events	Taken as given or as the product of "exogenous" developments	Endogeneity is analyzed. Events are linked to strategic decision making
Selection of Cases	Sampling on the dependent variable. Cases are chosen in which similar outcomes seem to be caused by similar factors. Cases with the same factors but without similar outcomes may be overlooked	Sampling on the independent variables. Cases are chosen to evaluate whether similar factors occur with similar outcomes when variation in factors and outcomes are both represented in the cases analyzed
Evidence	Often drawn from the same events that provided the basis for the hypotheses	Evidence should be independent of the information used to derive hypotheses
Objective of Study	To describe and explain specific events and actions in terms of contextual factors or in terms of patterns observed in the data	To make and test claims about causation as indicated by the proposed relations among variables so that those proposed relations can be evaluated repeatedly through empirical testing to assess predictability

rational choice models have drawn attention to a rival explanation that seems to fit the empirical record better. The president needs to invoke the veto only rarely because the threat that he will use it is sufficient to pursuade the Congress to pass legislation that the president will sign or that has enough support that a presidential veto can be overridden.

Students of international affairs observe that when a state with allies is attacked, the allies fail to come to the aid of their partner about 75% of the time. When decisions to attack are taken as exogenous, the implication is that alliances are unreliable. When decisions to attack are taken as endogenous, it becomes apparent that reliable alliance commitments are unlikely to be tested by adversaries. In fact, Smith (1995) has shown that the latter account fits the record of history, both with regard to attacks and successful deterrence, better than the alternative explanation.

An emphasis on selection effects is closely related to this focus on endogenous choice. The alliance example highlights selection effects based on observed and unobserved actions that make up an equilibrium strategy. Game-theoretic perspectives attend to counterfactual reasoning about what is expected to happen if actors follow different strategies. Actions are endogenous to the model precisely because actors select them with an eye to avoiding worse expected outcomes. This influences both the derivation of hypotheses and sampling decisions when hypotheses are tested. One important consequence is that rational choice models provide a natural and logical basis for thinking about counterfactual events and for structuring hypotheses that are contingent rather than monolithic explanations (Fearon et al 1996).

The Rochester school has emphasized deriving hypotheses from axioms. Doing so reduces the risk that hypotheses are restatements of already observed patterns in the data. Even when models are constructed specifically to account for known empirical regularities, they are likely to produce new propositions that have not previously been tested. These new propositions, of course, create demanding tests of the theory. Historical and statistical analyses tend not to hold the relations among variables constant from study to study and so are less likely to test inductively derived hypotheses against independent sources of evidence.

One of Riker's primary goals was the construction of a predictive science of politics. We referred above to a body of positive theory research that has an audited track record in making predictions about events that had not occurred when the research was published. Though in its infancy, this record seems to provide significant evidence that positivist methods are leading to a predictive science. A detailed accounting can be found elsewhere (Ray & Russett 1996, Feder 1995).

REVISITING THE "ECONOMICS IMPERIALISM THESIS"

Often, in presenting the accomplishments and history of rational choice theory in political science and the Rochester school, scholars put forth the "economics imperialism thesis" (see e.g. Miller 1997, Solow 1997). This thesis holds that the methods of economics, and the assumption that self-interested rational action characterizes human behavior, spread from economics and took over such disciplines as political science. Some evidence for this thesis exists in the early curriculum established by Riker at Rochester. The Chicago school of economics, and especially Stigler's (1966) price theory text, was a staple of graduate training at Rochester for many years. The problems with the economic imperialism thesis, however, are threefold. First, this thesis holds that rational choice theory was fully articulated within economics and then colonized, as it were, other fields, including political science. Second, this theory displaces the credit for innovation from political scientists to economists. Third, the economics imperialism scenario ignores that both economists and political scientists have had to reconsider their subject areas as market phenomena are increasingly seen to be interlaced with nonmarket "externalities," and "political economy" is taken to be a single unit of study which entails recognizing the unification of politics within economics.

The most glaring inaccuracy of the economics imperialism account is the idea that political scientists took the theory of rational action as articulated by economists and applied it to political events. This narrative ignores what Riker made obvious in *The Theory of Political Coalitions*—that traditionally the rationality of economic agents was thought of as mechanical rather than deliberate and conscious, was modeled using multivariate techniques of maximization, and copied the principle of least action from physics rather than the new mathematics of game theory. "Rational choice," denoting conscious decision making in a strategic environment with rational competitors, as originally articulated by von Neumann & Morgenstern (1944), became the status quo within political science before economists fully grasped its merits for their field. Certainly a number of the original contributions to the rational choice canon came out of the economics tradition, but they were marginal within their own discipline until the 1970s. It was not until the 1980s that game theory made its way into the heart of microeconomic theory, and the use of spatial models in economics is quite different from their use in studying politics.

Furthermore, as is evident from the fact that the Rochester school transformed political science and was comprised of political scientists and not economists, rational choice theory was articulated outside of economics. The Rochester political scientists were not pirates on economic waters, stealing concepts at their fancy. More accurately, Riker and his colleagues developed a rational choice approach to politics that was anchored in individual decisions and depended on a conception of rational agency entailing a strategic, thinking environment. This environment was foreign to most economists, to whom rational action resembled automatic, unthinking maximization (Knight 1963 [1956], Samuelson 1948). Riker could not have made headway without his predecessors von Neumann, Morgenstern, Black, Arrow, and Downs, and some of the important innovators in political economy within economics at Chicago, but a rational choice theory of politics existed only in an incomplete and inchoate form in the promise of these earlier theories. It took Riker's rigorous, analytic mind to develop a unified approach to politics that drew on the varied approaches of his predecessors. As he wrote in the preface to *Liberalism Against Populism*,

> One central question of political description—a question much disputed but little understood—is the problem of explaining why some issues are politically salient and others not. This problem has usually been investigated by reducing politics to something else—to economics, for example, as in Marxism, or to psychology, as in psychoanalytic visualizations—thereby producing an economic (or psychological) interpretation of politics. However,...I offer a political interpretation of politics, a theory about the rise and decline of the salience of issues that derives directly from social choice theory and is entirely political in form. (Riker 1982:ix)

Riker rescued and made mainstream a coherent method from a mixed bag of techniques that otherwise would probably not have been coalesced into positive political theory or a rational choice approach to politics.

DEBATES SURROUNDING RATIONAL CHOICE SCHOLARSHIP

Institutional victories and the high-profile status of Rochester-trained scholars, as well as consistent determination on the part of Rochester school members to displace other forms of political science, have positioned the Rochesterians and positive political theory at the center of much heated debate. As Riker was the first to opine, "the rational choice paradigm is the oldest, the most well established, and now,...the one that by its success is driving out all others" (unpublished manuscript "A Paradigm for Politics," 1983, WHR papers). Green & Shapiro (1994) both underscored the arrival of the rational choice method as an accepted and mainstream practice within political science and articulated reservations about its explanatory powers. Green & Shapiro raised concerns that the Rochesterians' commitment to universalizing formal models has taken on a life of its own, and they questioned to what extent their highly abstract formal theories are amenable to empirical testing. Green & Shapiro concluded that within the rational choice tradition, "very little has been learned...about politics" (1994:x). As cases in point, the authors discuss several anomalies the rational choice approach seems unable to explain. These include (*a*) the paradox of voting (the fact that voters apparently receive no tangible payoff from voting in a general election seems to undermine the idea that actors are motivated by rational expectations); (*b*) the tragedy of the commons and the free-rider problem that rational choice theory predicts from self-oriented behavior (Green & Shapiro argue that the narrowly construed concept of the rational actor does not leave room for communicative sociability, which actually drives interactive behavior and can forestall collective action calamities); (*c*) the predicted abundance of instability in democratic institutions (for which Green & Shapiro question the empirical support). Green & Shapiro also question the adequacy of the empirical evidence supporting the positivist political theorists' theory derived from spatial models supporting the median-voter theorem.

In defense of rational choice theory and the Rochester school, political theorist James Johnson has little patience with Green & Shapiro's "hostile" assessment of the rational choice research program (Johnson 1996). He is dissatisfied with their grasp of social science (1996:81) and defends the Rochesterians by arguing that layers of abstract theoretical research eventually result in breakthroughs with proved empirical relevance, many of which we have discussed here, and he notes that Green & Shapiro fail to discuss bodies of rational choice scholarship that make solid contributions to the knowledge of political events.

Debate over the efficacy of a rational choice theory of politics continued in a forum provided by the journal *Critical Review*, which devoted an entire issue to the swirling controversies (Friedman 1995). Here it is evident that the debate over the merits and efficacy of a rational choice theory of politics are contested on three levels. As described above, scholars disagree as to whether positive political theory's theoretical findings and empirical evidence provide meaningful insight into political phenomena. At a secondary level, scholars disagree over the definition and legitimate practice of social science, generally, and political science, particularly. At an even more inclusive level, the heated nature of the exchanges results from a fundamental disagreement as to whether the "rational actor" model of human behavior is sufficient. Whereas the debate of theoretical adequacy and empirical verification concentrates on specific models and theories, the latter discussion has interdisciplinary relevance as scholars in economics, sociology, philosophy, and jurisprudence take up the rational choice mantle. Whereas the Rochesterians often remain focused on the issues of theoretical validity, the debate over rational choice theory has become, in other corners, a debate over the fundamental character of human nature, human psychology, and human agency. The Rochester positive political theorists have focused on building predictive models that can be applied to such tasks as designing political institutions or structuring electoral processes. However, some of their colleagues in other fields have used the rational-actor account of human action to promulgate a vision of society governed by the proselytizing assumption that all social institutions and interactive collective events must be accounted for according to the assumption of self-interested reason: What can I get out of it? What are my payoffs? Thus, it is necessary to contrast the work of scholars who have constructed a set of normative prescriptions from the starting assumptions of rational choice (e.g. Buchanan 1975, Brennan & Buchanan 1985) with the work of the Rochesterian positivists, who strive to stay focused on using their theoretical constructs to draw predictive conclusions that are subject to empirical test.

CONCLUDING STATEMENT

Although a confluence of factors bolstered Riker's success in building a school of political science and transforming the discipline of political science, the story of the Rochester school demonstrates the impact that a single person can have on an entire field. Furthermore, although it is continually stated that rational choice theory worked its way from economists' workbooks to political scientists' heads, it must be remembered that rational choice theory, as a theory of deliberate, strategically calculating action originated by von Neumann

& Morgenstern's *Theory of Games and Economic Behavior*, was initially rejected by mainstream economists as external to their subject matter. While economists continued to work until the 1980s in the tradition of maximizing models couched in terms of differential calculus and a quasi-mechanical conception of reason, William H Riker both had the vision to construct a comprehensive science of politics grounded in the idea of strategic competition and grasped the potential of game theory to model these interactions. In the final analysis, the Rochester school's far-reaching institutional success, which resulted from both an ambitious research program and astute political maneuvering, is the most telling indication of the validity of its creed.

> Visit the *Annual Reviews home page* at
> http://www.AnnualReviews.org.

Literature Cited

Aldrich J. 1980. *Before the Convention: Strategies and Choices in Presidential Nomination Campaigns.* Chicago: Univ. Chicago Press

Alt J, Shepsle K, eds. 1990. *Perspectives on Positive Political Economy.* New York: Cambridge Univ. Press

Arrow KJ. 1950. A difficulty in the concept of social welfare. *J. Polit. Econ.* 58:328–46

Arrow KJ. 1963. *Social Choice and Individual Values.* London: Yale Univ. Press. 2nd ed.

Austen-Smith D, Banks J. 1988. Elections, coalitions, and legislative outcomes. *Am. Polit. Sci. Rev.* 82:405–22

Austen-Smith D, Banks J. 1990. Stable governments and the allocation of policy portfolios. *Am. Polit. Sci. Rev.* 84:891–906

Austen-Smith D, Banks J. 1996. Information aggregation, rationality, and the Condorcet jury theorem. *Am. Polit. Sci. Rev.* 90:34–45

Austen-Smith D, Banks J. 1998. Social choice theory, game theory, and positive political theory. *Annu. Rev. Polit. Sci.* 1:259–87

Black D. 1948. On the rationale of group decision making. *J. Polit. Econ.* 56:23–34

Brams SJ. 1985. *Superpower Games.* New Haven, CT: Yale Univ. Press

Brams SJ. 1990. *Negotiation Games: Applying Game Theory to Bargaining and Arbitration.* New York: Routledge

Brennan HG, Buchanan JM. 1985. *The Reasons of Rules.* Cambridge, UK: Cambridge Univ. Press

Buchanan JM. 1975. *The Limits of Liberty: Between Anarchy and Leviathan.* Chicago: Univ. Chicago Press

Buchanan JM, Tullock G. 1962. *The Calculus of Consent.* Ann Arbor: Univ. Mich. Press

Bueno de Mesquita B. 1984. Forecasting policy decisions: an expected utility approach to post-Khomeini Iran. *PS*(Spring):226–36

Bueno de Mesquita B, Lalman D. 1992. *War and Reason.* New Haven, CT: Yale Univ. Press

Bueno de Mesquita B, Newman D, Rabushka A. 1985. *Forecasting Political Events.* New Haven, CT: Yale Univ. Press

Bueno de Mesquita B, Stokman F. 1994. *European Community Decision Making.* New Haven, CT: Yale Univ. Press

Coase RH. 1998. Foreword. In *The Theory of Committees and Elections*, ed. I McLean, A McMillan, BL Monroe. Amsterdam: Kluwer. 2nd rev. ed.

Cook TI. 1950. The methods of political science, chiefly in the United States. *Contemporary Political Science: A Survey of Methods, Research and Teaching*, pp. 75–90. UNESCO

De Swaan A. 1973. *Coalition Theories and Cabinet Formations.* New York: Elsevier

Diermeier D, Feddersen T. 1998. Cohesion in legislatures and the vote of confidence procedure. *Am. Polit. Sci. Rev.* 92:611–21

Downs A. 1957. *An Economic Theory of Democracy.* New York: Harper

Downs GW, Rocke DM. 1990. *Tacit Bargaining, Arms Races, and Arms Control.* Ann Arbor: Univ. Mich. Press

Downs GW, Rocke DM. 1995. *Optimal Imperfection? Domestic Uncertainty and Institutions in International Relations.* Princeton, NJ: Princeton Univ. Press

Eisenmann C. 1950. On the matter and methods of the political sciences. *Contemporary Political Science: A Survey of Methods, Research and Teaching*, pp. 91–131. UNESCO

Fagen RR. 1963. Book review. *Am. Polit. Sci. Rev.* 57:446–47

Fearon JD. 1994. Domestic political audiences and the escalation of international disputes. *Am. Polit. Sci. Rev..* 88:577–92

Fearon JD, Laitin DD. 1996. Explaining interethnic cooperation. *Am. Polit. Sci. Rev.* 90:715–35

Feder S. 1995. Factions and policon: new ways to analyze politics. In *Inside CIA's Private World: Declassified Articles from the Agency's Internal Journal, 1955–1992*, ed. HB Westerfield, pp. 274–92. New Haven, CT: Yale Univ. Press

Ferejohn J. 1986. Incumbent performance and electoral control. *Public Choice* 50: 5–25

Fiorina MP. 1976. The voting decision: instrumental and expressive aspects. *J. Polit.* 38:390–415

Fiorina MP. 1981. *Retrospective Voting in American National Elections.* New Haven, CT: Yale Univ. Press

Friedman J, ed. 1995. Rational choice theory. *Critical Rev.* 9(1–2)

Gilligan T, Krehbiel K. 1989. Collective choice without procedural commitment. In *Models of Strategic Choice in Politics,* ed. P Ordeshook, pp. 295–314. Ann Arbor: Univ. Mich. Press

Green DP, Shapiro I. 1994. *Pathologies of Rational Choice Theory: A Critique of Applications in Political Science.* New Haven, CT: Yale Univ. Press

Groennings S, Kelly EW, Leiserson M, eds. 1970. *The Study of Coalition Behavior: Theoretical Perspectives and Cases from Four Continents.* New York: Holt, Rinehart & Winston

Hinich MJ, Munger MC. 1997. *Analytical Politics.* Cambridge, UK: Cambridge Univ. Press

Johnson J. 1996. How not to criticize rational choice theory: pathologies of "common sense." *Philos. Soc. Sci.* 26(1):77–91

Klausner SZ, Lidz VM, eds. 1986. *The Nationalization of the Social Sciences.* Philadephia: Univ. Penn. Press

Krehbiel K. 1991. *Information and Legislative Organization.* Ann Arbor: Univ. Mich. Press

Knight FH. 1963 (1956). *On the History of Method in Economics.* Chicago: Univ. Chicago Press

Laver M, Schofield N. 1990. *Multiparty Government: The Politics of Coalition in Europe.* New York: Oxford Univ. Press

Laver M, Shepsle K. 1994. *Cabinet Ministers and Parliamentary Government.* New York: Cambridge Univ. Press

Leonard RJ. 1992. Creating a context for game theory. In *Toward a History of Game Theory,* ed. ER Weintraub, pp. 29–76. Durham: Duke Univ. Press

McKelvey R. 1976. Intransitivities in multidimensional voting models and some implications for agenda control. *J. Econ. Theory* 12:472–82

McKelvey R. 1979. General conditions for global intransitivities in formal voting models. *Econometrica* 47:1085–1112

McKelvey R, Schofield N. 1986. Structural instability of the core. *J. Math. Econ.* 15: 179–98

Miller GJ. 1997. The impact of economics on contemporary political science. *J. Econ. Lit.* XXXV(Sept.):1173–1204

Mitra SK. 1978. *Governmental Instability in Indian States: A Study of West Bengal, Bihar, Uttar Pradesh and Punjab.* Delhi: Ajanta

Morrow JD. 1989. Capabilities, uncertainty, and resolve: a limited information model of crisis bargaining. *Am. J. Polit. Sci.* 33: 941–72

Niemi R, Weisberg H. 1968. A mathematical solution for the probability of the paradox of voting. *Behav. Sci.* 13:317–23

Olson M Jr. 1965. *The Logic of Collective Action.* Cambridge, MA: Harvard Univ. Press

Ordeshook PC. 1986. *Game Theory and Political Theory.* Cambridge, UK: Cambridge Univ. Press

Powell R. 1990. *Nuclear Deterrence Theory: The Search for Credibility.* New York: Cambridge Univ. Press

Rabushka A, Shepsle K. 1972. *Politics in Plural Societies.* Columbus, OH: Merrill

Ray JL, Russett BM. 1996. The future as arbiter of theoretical controversies: predictions, explanations and the end of the cold war. *Br. J. Polit. Sci.* 25:1578

Riker WH. 1953. *Democracy in the United States.* New York: Macmillan

Riker WH. 1957. Events and situations. *J. Philos.* 54:57–70

Riker WH. 1958. The paradox of voting and congressional rules for voting on amendments. *Am. Polit. Sci. Rev.* 52:349–66

Riker WH. 1959a. A test of the adequacy of the power index. *Behav. Sci.* 4:120–31

Riker WH. 1959b. Causes of events. *J. Philos.* 56:281–92

Riker WH. 1963. *The Theory of Political Coalitions*. New York: Yale Univ. Press

Riker WH. 1980. Implications from the disequilibrium of majority rule for the study of institutions. *Am. Polit. Sci. Rev.* 74: 1235–47

Riker WH. 1982. *Liberalism Against Populism: a Confrontation between the Theory of Democracy and the Theory of Social Choice*. San Francisco: Freeman

Riker WH. 1986. *The Art of Political Manipulation*. New Haven, CT: Yale Univ. Press

Riker WH. 1996. *The Strategy of Rhetoric: Campaigning for the American Constitution*. New Haven, CT: Yale Univ. Press

Riker WH, ed. 1993. *Agenda Formation*. Ann Arbor, MI: Univ. Mich. Press

Riker WH, Ordeshook PC. 1973. *An Introduction to Positive Political Theory*. Englewood Cliffs, NJ: Prentice Hall

Riker W, Schaps R. 1957. Disharmony in federal government. *Behav. Sci.* 2:276–90

Samuelson PA. 1948. *Foundations of Economic Analysis*. Cambridge, MA: Harvard Univ. Press

Schofield N. 1978. Instability of simple dynamic games. *Rev. Econ. Stud.* 45:575–94

Shapley LS, Shubik M. 1954. A method of evaluating the distribution of power in a committee system. *Am. Polit. Sci. Rev.* 54: 787–92

Shepsle K. 1979. Institutional arrangements and equilibrium in multidimensional voting models. *Am. J. Polit. Sci.* 23:27–60

Shepsle K, Weingast B. 1981. Structure induced equilibrium and legislative choice. *Public Choice* 37:503–19

Shepsle K, Weingast B. 1984. Uncovered sets and sophisticated voting outcomes with implications for agenda institutions. *Am. J. Polit. Sci.* 28:49–75

Shepsle K, Weingast B. 1987. The institutional foundations of committee power. *Am. Polit. Sci. Rev.* 81:85–104

Smith A. 1995. Alliance formation and war. *Int. Stud. Q.* 39:405–25

Smith A. 1996. Endogenous election timing in majoritarian parliamentary systems. *Econ. Polit.* 8:85–110

Solow RM. 1997. How did economics get that way and what way did it get? American academic culture in transformation: fifty years, four disciplines. *Daedalus* Winter: 39–58

Stigler G. 1966. *The Theory of Price*. New York: Macmillan

Strom K. 1990. *Minority Government and Majority Rule*. New York: Cambridge Univ. Press

Tetlock P, Belkin A, eds. 1996. *Counterfactual Thought Experiments in World Politics*. Princeton, NJ: Princeton Univ. Press

von Neumann J, Morgenstern O. 1944. *Theory of Games and Economic Behavior*. Princeton, NJ: Princeton Univ. Press

Zagare FC. 1987. *The Dynamics of Deterrence*. Chicago: Univ. Chicago Press

Annu. Rev. Polit. Sci. 1999. 2:297–321

BOUNDED RATIONALITY

Bryan D. Jones

Department of Political Science, University of Washington, Seattle, Washington
98195; e-mail: bdjones@u.washington.edu

KEY WORDS: decision making, behavioral organization theory, behavioral decision theory,
political psychology

ABSTRACT

Findings from behavioral organization theory, behavioral decision theory, survey research, and experimental economics leave no doubt about the failure of rational choice as a descriptive model of human behavior. But this does not mean that people and their politics are irrational. Bounded rationality asserts that decision makers are intendedly rational; that is, they are goal-oriented and adaptive, but because of human cognitive and emotional architecture, they sometimes fail, occasionally in important decisions. Limits on rational adaptation are of two types: procedural limits, which limit how we go about making decisions, and substantive limits, which affect particular choices directly. Rational analysis in institutional contexts can serve as a standard for adaptive, goal-oriented human behavior. In relatively fixed task environments, such as asset markets or elections, we should be able to divide behavior into adaptive, goal-oriented behavior (that is, rational action) and behavior that is a consequence of processing limits, and we should then be able to measure the deviation. The extent of deviation is an empirical issue. These classes are mutually exclusive and exhaustive, and they may be examined empirically in situations in which actors make repeated similar choices.

INTRODUCTION

Do people make rational decisions in politics and economics? Not if by "rational" we mean that they demonstrate conformity to the classic expected-utility model. There is no longer any doubt about the weight of the scientific evidence; the expected-utility model of economic and political decision making is not sustainable empirically. From the laboratory comes failure after failure of rational expected utility to account for human behavior. From systematic observation in organizational settings, scant evidence of behavior based on the expected-utility model emerges.

297

Does this mean that people (and therefore their politics) are irrational? Not at all. People making choices are intendedly rational. They want to make rational decisions, but they cannot always do so.

The implication for politics is that rational responses to the environment characterize decision making generally, but at points—often important points—rationality fails, and as a consequence there is a mismatch between the decision-making environment and the choices of the decision maker. We refer to this mismatch as "bounded rationality showing through" (Simon 1996b).

This conception has an important implication. In structured situations, at least, we may conceive of any decision as having two components: environmental demands (seen by the individual as incentives, positive or negative) and bounds on adaptability in the given decision-making situation. Ideally, an analysis based on rational choice should be able to specify what the environmental incentives are and to predict decisions based on those incentives. What cannot be explained is either random error (even the most rational of us may make an occasional mistake, but these are not systematic) or bounded rationality showing through. Standard statistical techniques give us the tools to distinguish systematic from random factors, so in principle it should be possible to distinguish the rational, adaptive portion of a decision from bounds on rationality.

One may think of any decision as arising from two sources. One is the external environment—how we respond to the incentives facing us. The other is the internal environment—those parts of our internal make-ups that cause us to deviate from the demands of the external environment (Simon 1996b).

We are not, however, thrown into a situation in which all residual systematic deviations from rational choices are treated prima facie as bounded rationality. A very limited set of facets of human cognitive architecture accounts for a very large proportion of the deviations from adaptation. These may be placed into two classes: procedural limits, which limit how we go about making decisions, and substantive limits, which affect particular choices directly. Of procedural limits, I cite two as being extraordinarily important in structured, institutional settings (such as voting in mass publics or in legislative bodies), attention and emotion. Of substantive limits, I cite but one—the tendency of humans to "overcooperate," that is, to cooperate more than strict adherence to rationality would dictate.

The primary argument in this essay is that most behavior in politics is adaptive and intendedly rational but that limits on adaptive behavior, imposed by human cognitive/emotional architecture, may be detected in even the most stable of environments. I advocate a research strategy that explicitly divides political action into the two categories of intended rationality and deviations from (or bounds on) intended rationality and explores empirically the implications for the outputs of institutions and the institutional processes responsible for those outcomes. [The analysis presented here is further developed in my *Traces of Eve: Adaptive Behavior and Its Limits in Political and Economic Institutions* (manuscript in preparation).]

BOUNDED RATIONALITY: BIRTH AND DEVELOPMENT

Bounded rationality is a school of thought about decision making that developed from dissatisfaction with the "comprehensively rational" economic and decision theory models of choice. Those models assume that preferences are defined over outcomes, that those outcomes are known and fixed, and that decision makers maximize their net benefits, or utilities, by choosing the alternative that yields the highest level of benefits (discounted by costs). The subjective expected-utility variant of rational choice integrates risk and uncertainty into the model by associating a probability distribution, estimated by the decision maker, with outcomes. The decision maker maximizes expected utility. Choices among competing goals are handled by indifference curves—generally postulated to be smooth (twice differentiable)—that specify substitutability among goals.

A major implication of the approach is that behavior is determined by the mix of incentives facing the decision maker. A second implication is that adjustment to these incentives is instantaneous; true maximizers have no learning curves.

Like comprehensive rationality, bounded rationality assumes that actors are goal-oriented, but bounded rationality takes into account the cognitive limitations of decision makers in attempting to achieve those goals. Its scientific approach is different; rather than making assumptions about decision making and modeling the implications mathematically for aggregate behavior (as in markets or legislatures), bounded rationality adopts an explicitly behavioral stance. The behavior of decision makers must be examined, whether in the laboratory or in the field.

The Birth of Bounded Rationality

Simon (1999; see also Simon 1996a) reminds political scientists that the notion of bounded rationality and many of its ramifications originated in political science. Over his long career, Simon made major contributions not only to political science (as the founder of the behavioral study of organizations) but also to economics (as a Nobelist), psychology (as a founding father of cognitive psychology), and computer science (as an initiator of the field of artificial intelligence).

In the 1940s and 1950s, Simon developed a model of choice intended as a challenge to the comprehensive rationality assumptions used in economics.

The model first appeared in print in *Administrative Behavior* (1947), which critiqued existing theories of public administration and proposed a new approach for the study of organizational decision making. Simon gave great credit for the initiation of his innovative work to the behavioral revolution in political science at the University of Chicago, where he studied for all of his academic degrees. Although most political scientists are aware of Simon's contributions, many fail to appreciate that bounded rationality was the first, and because of its ripple effects in so many disciplines, the most important idea (even academic school of thought) that political science has ever exported.[1]

A brief retelling of the tale is in order. As an undergraduate at the University of Chicago, Simon returned to his native Milwaukee in 1935 to observe budgeting in the city's recreation department. He wrote:

> I came as a gift-bearing Greek, fresh from an intermediate price theory course taught by the grandfather of Chicago-School neoclassical laissez-faire economics, Henry Simons.... My economics training showed me how to budget rationally. Simply compare the marginal utility of a proposed expenditure with its marginal cost, and approve it only if the utility exceeds the cost. However, what I saw in Milwaukee didn't seem to be an application of this rule. I saw a lot of bargaining, of reference back to last year's budget, and incremental changes in it. If the word "marginal" was ever spoken, I missed it. Moreover, which participants would support which items was quite predictable.... I could see a clear connection between people's positions on budget matters and the values and beliefs that prevailed in their sub-organizations.
>
> I brought back to my friends and teachers in economics two gifts, which I ultimately called "organizational identification" and "bounded rationality." (Simon 1999)

In his autobiography, Simon noted the importance of these two notions for his later contributions to organization theory, economics, psychology, and computer science. "I would not object to having my whole scientific output described as largely a gloss—a rather elaborate gloss, to be sure—[on these two ideas]" (Simon 1996a:88).

Bounded rationality and organizational identification (now considered a consequence of bounded rationality) won ready acceptance in political science, with its emerging empiricist orientation, but they were largely ignored in the more theoretical discipline of economics. Or, as Simon (1999) puts it,

---

[1]Two recent incidents convinced me of the need to remind political scientists that Simon's "tribal allegiance" (1999) is to our discipline. A well-regarded political scientist recently commented, "I didn't know that Simon was a political scientist." In a written review, a cognitive psychologist somewhat haughtily informed me that Simon's work on organizations, and in particular March & Simon's *Organizations* (1958), was intended to extend his work on problem solving to organizational behavior. Of course, the intellectual path was the other way around.

economists "mostly ignored [bounded rationality] and went on counting the angels on the heads of neoclassical pins."

Procedural Rationality

Simon spent a great deal of time and energy attacking the abstract and rarefied economic decision-making models. Much of his attack was negative—showing how the model did not comport with how people really made decisions. But Simon also developed what he termed a procedural model of rationality, based on the psychological process of reasoning—in particular his explanation of how people conduct incomplete searches and make tradeoffs between values.

> Since the organism, like those of the real world, has neither the senses nor the wits to discover an "optimal" path—even assuming the concept of optimal to be clearly defined—we are concerned only with finding a choice mechanism that will lead it to pursue a "satisficing" path that will permit satisfaction at some specified level of all of its needs. (Simon 1957:270–71)

Simon elaborated on his "satisficing" organism over the years, but its fundamental characteristics did not change. They include the following:

1. Limitation on the organism's ability to plan long behavior sequences, a limitation imposed by the bounded cognitive ability of the organism as well as the complexity of the environment in which it operates.

2. The tendency to set aspiration levels for each of the multiple goals that the organism faces.

3. The tendency to operate on goals sequentially rather than simultaneously because of the "bottleneck of short-term memory."

4. Satisficing rather than optimizing search behavior.

An alternative satisfices if it meets aspirations along all dimensions (attributes). If no such alternative is found, a search is undertaken for new alternatives.

Meanwhile, aspirations along one or more dimensions drift down gradually until a satisfactory new alternative is found or some existing alternative satisfices (Simon 1996b:30).

In detailing the general requirements of an organism operating under bounded (as contrasted with comprehensive) rationality, Simon (1983:20–22; see also Simon 1995) notes the following requisites: (*a*) "Some way of focusing attention," (*b*) "a mechanism for generating alternatives," (*c*) "a capacity for acquiring facts about the environment," and (*d*) "a modest capacity for drawing inferences from these facts."

I cannot do justice to the importance for other disciplines of Simon's "gloss" on bounded rationality. Just one note: The study of problem solving is grounded in the intended rationality of problem solvers, as is the study of judgment (Newell 1968, 1990). By imposing a task environment, experimenters can examine that part of the problem solver's behavior that may be explained objectively, via the nature of the task environment, and compare it with that part that can be explained only with reference to failures to overcome systematic internal limitations—bounded rationality showing through (Newell & Simon 1972, Simon 1996b).

The principle that rationality is intended but not always achieved, that what "shows through" from the inner environment of the problem solver can be systematically studied, is a principle that I consider extraordinarily useful in the study of human behavior in relatively set institutional task environments.

BOUNDED RATIONALITY IN POLITICAL SCIENCE

Bounded rationality has been a key component since the 1950s in public-administration and public-policy studies. In more recent times, partly in reaction to the attitudinal model of voting behavior, the approach has been used to understand political reasoning (Iyengar 1990, Sniderman et al 1991, Marcus & McKuen 1993). Nevertheless, bounded rationality, born in organization theory (Simon 1947), has had its greatest impact in political science in the study of governmental organizations.

The fundamental premise underlying organizational studies in political science is that the behavior of organizations mimics the bounded rationality of the actors that inhabit them (March 1994). This correspondence is not simply an analogy among phenomena at different levels; the relationship is causal. This premise characterized behavioral organization theory generally, along with the insistence that organizational science be grounded in the observation of behavior in (and analysis of data from) organizational settings. The most important components of the political theory of organizations were the concepts of limited attention spans, habituation and routine, and organizational identification. Behavioral organization theory, unlike the subjective expected-utility approach, viewed uncertainty not as simple probabilities attached to specified outcomes, but as infecting the very specification of outcomes themselves.

Over and over again, students of the behavior of public organizations reported findings that did not comport with the demands of "objective rationality" (Simon 1985:294). Search was incomplete, selective, and nonoptimal (Simon 1985, Jones & Bachelor 1994). Decision makers did not need simply to choose among alternatives; they had to generate the alternatives in the first place (Simon 1983, 1996b; Chisholm 1995). Problems were not givens; they had to be defined (Rochefort & Cobb 1994). Solutions did not automatically follow problems; sometimes actors had set solutions ready to apply to problems that could occur (Cohen et al 1972, Kingdon 1996, Jones & Bachelor 1994). Choice was based on incommensurate goals, which were ill-integrated (March 1978; Simon 1983, 1995; Jones 1994). Organizations seemed to have limited attention spans and, at least in major policy changes, serial processing capacity (Simon 1983, Jones 1994, Cobb & Elder 1972, Kingdon 1996).

The three most important strands of research stemming from behavioral organizational theory in political science focused on incremental budgeting, on the impacts of organizational routine on policy outputs, and on policy agendas.

Incremental Budgeting

Incremental decision making was developed not only as a descriptive model of decisions by bounded actors but as a normative mechanism for use in an uncertain world (Lindblom 1959). If people are handicapped by limited cognition, and if the world is fundamentally complex and ambiguous, then it made sense for a decision maker to (a) move away from problems, rather than toward solutions; (b) make only small moves away from the problem; and (c) be willing to reverse direction based on feedback from the environment. Wildavsky (1964; see also Fenno 1966, Meltsner 1971), in his classic observational studies of federal budgeting, noted that such incremental budgeting was governed by decision rules based on two norms: base and fair share. What was the agency's base, and what was a fair share given changes in the agency's environment since last year's budget meeting? Incrementalism was even criticized as too rational a characterization of budget processes, because of the adoption of roles by budget decision makers (Anton 1966, Crecine 1969). Incrementalism, in effect a small-step hill-climbing algorithm, implied adjustment to local optima rather than global ones.

Incrementalism in decision making implied incrementalism in organizational outcomes—so long as one also modeled exogenous "shocks" (Davis et al 1966, 1974). Students of the budgetary process concluded that incrementalism did not fit even endogenous decision processes (Wanat 1974, Gist 1982). Pure incrementalism did not seem to characterize governing organizations. In essence, there were too many large changes in budget processes. But it was realized that attentional processes are selective (as the incremental model recognized) and subject to occasional radical shifts. Incorporating this aspect of attentional processes better accounts for the distribution of budget outcomes (Padgett 1980, 1981; Jones et al 1996, 1997, 1998).

Organizational Habits and Routines

Cognitive limits of human decision makers imposed limits on the ability of the organization to adjust to its environment. Rather than maximizing, organizations tended to adopt task performance rules, which routinized even the most important decisions of the organization (March & Simon 1958). Firms routinized price and output decisions (Cyert & March 1963). Learning in organizations seemed to be a slow, evolutionary, conflictual process (Sabatier & Jenkins-Smith 1993, Lounamaa & March 1985, Ostrom 1990) rather than the instantaneous adjustment process that rational organization theory would imply. Participants identified with the rules of the organization, adhering to them even in the face of evidence of problems (Jones 1980, 1985). This could cause disjoint "lurches" as organizations were finally forced to adjust to changes in their environments (Dodd 1994).

Routines in service organizations invariably generated unintended consequences, many of which went unrecognized or unaddressed. For example, distributional consequences of supposedly neutral rules were often ignored (Levy 1974, Mladenka 1978).

In other cases, an organization might have contradictory demands on it. Such contradictory demands are handled in economics via indifference curves, which specify a decision maker's preferences under all combinations of the demands. Instead of a rational process for handling tradeoffs, public service organizations tended to develop task performance rules for each demand. The response of the organization depended on which set of rules was activated. A study of Chicago's Building Department revealed that two sets of task performance rules were in effect. One set directed resources in accordance with the severity of the problem. These rules embodied the classic administrative norm of neutral competence. A second set of rules, less explicit but just as important, directed resources based on responsiveness to political forces. The distribution of organizational outputs to neighborhoods depended on an attention rule, activated by middle management, that governed which set of rules was to be put in force. Neutral competence was the default; response to political forces required an override of standard operating procedures, but the attention rule override happened so often that it could easily be detected in organizational outputs (Jones 1985).

Policy Agendas

If individuals have limited attention spans, so must organizations. The notion of policy agendas recognizes the "bottleneck" that exists in the agenda that any policy-making body addresses (Cobb & Elder 1972). These attention processes are not simply related to task environments—problems can go for long periods of time without attracting the attention of policy makers (Rochefort & Cobb 1994). A whole style of politics emerges as actors must strive to cope with the limits in the attentiveness of policy makers—basically trying to attract allies to their favored problems and solutions. This style of politics depends on connections driven by time-dependent and often emotional attention processes rather than a deliberate search for solutions (Cohen et al 1972, March & Olsen 1989, Kingdon 1996, Baumgartner & Jones 1993).

Because attention processes are time dependent and policy contexts change temporally, connections between problems and solutions have time dependency built into them. As an important consequence, policy systems dominated by boundedly rational decision makers will at best reach local rather than global optima. Because of the time dependence of attentional processes, all policy processes will display considerable path dependence (March 1994).

OBJECTIONS TO THE EXPECTED-UTILITY MODEL: BEHAVIORAL DECISION THEORY

The expected-utility model incorporates risk and uncertainty into models of rational choice. Instead of maximizing utility, decision makers maximize expected utility in choice situations in which the consequences of choice are risky (may be characterized by known probabilities) or uncertain (are characterized by unspecified probabilities).

Numerous empirical studies of human decision making, from experiments in the laboratory to large-scale social surveys to observational studies in the field, have demonstrated that humans often do not conform to the strictures of choice theory (Slovak 1990). This study of how people actually behave in choice situations is known as behavioral decision theory. Even defenders of choice theory have retreated in the face of the onslaught of empirical findings. Expected-utility theory is no longer seriously entertained as an accurate descriptive theory (Halpern & Stern 1998b).

Again, this does not imply that people are irrational, nor that people interacting in large-scale institutions make large-scale mistakes. Intendedly rational actors in large-scale institutions may respond collectively to the tasks they face adaptively. Wittman (1995:16) notes that "even if some individuals make incorrect choices, the law of large numbers is likely to yield the correct majority choice."

Many of these objections are quite fundamental—so much so that it seems impossible to develop a serious empirical theory of choice without taking them into consideration. They address both (*a*) the limitations of humans to comprehend and act on inputs from the environment and (*b*) the fundamental complexity of the environment, which is vastly underestimated in standard rational choice theories.

The Nature of the Decision Maker

Empirical objections to rational choice are so voluminous that they are, in effect, a laundry list of problems. The first set has to do with the nature of the decision maker.

SEARCH BEHAVIOR   In general, people do not consider all aspects of a decision facing them. They must factor the decision to make it manageable, examining only relevant aspects. They do not undertake complete searches for information, and they ignore available information—especially if it is not relevant to the factors they have determined to characterize the structure of the problem.

SEARCH MUST INCLUDE BOTH ALTERNATIVES AND ATTRIBUTES   Different physiological and psychological mechanisms probably underlie the search for attributes (which is equated in ordinary language with understanding a problem) and the search for alternatives (which involves the choice under a given decisional structure, design, or understanding) (Jones 1996).

CALCULATIONS   People generally cannot perform the calculations necessary even for a reduced set of options in a decision-making situation. This is actually the least problematic limitation in decision making. They can, given time, write down and manipulate the numbers.

COGNITIVE ILLUSIONS AND FRAMING   When identical options are described in different terms, people often shift their choices. For example, if a choice is described in terms of gains, it is often treated differently than if it is described in terms of losses. This shift demonstrates the concept of framing, developed by psychologists Daniel Kahneman and Amos Tversky. They claim that this tendency violates a major, if often unstated, assumption of rational choice—namely the axiom of invariance, which states that the "preference order between prospects should not depend on the manner in which they are described" (Kahneman & Tversky 1983:343). They bolster their claim with numerous convincing experiments indicating that decision makers tend to choose different alternatives when they are described in positive terms (for example, in terms of the number of lives saved with a vaccine) than when they are described in negative terms (the number of people who will die). Kahneman & Tversky (1983:343) state, "In their stubborn appeal, framing effects resemble perceptual illusions more than computational errors."

SELF-CONTROL   People often seem to need to bind themselves in some way to establish self-control over their behavior in the future. A major mechanism for dealing with likely future lapses in self-control is to establish binding rules that prohibit the unwanted behavior. For example, Thaler (1991) has developed the notion of mental accounting to explain the tendency of people to separate categories of income and impose more constraints on some (investment income) than on others (a Christmas bonus). People also tend to treat gains differently from losses, applying different risk functions to them, essentially being more risk-adverse for gains than for losses (Kahneman & Tversky 1983, 1985).

INCOMMENSURATE ATTRIBUTES   In multi-attribute situations, people often have severe difficulties in making the tradeoffs that look so simple in consumer choice theories. They tend to use a variety of shortcuts that avoid making the direct tradeoff.

DESIGN   People have trouble figuring what factors are relevant to a given decision-making situation, and these framings are subject to radical shifts in a short period of time (Jones 1994).

UPDATING   People are "incomplete Bayesians." In uncertain situations, they do not update their choices in light of incoming information about the probability of outcomes in the manner predicted by calculations from probability theory (Bayes' rule is the relevant yardstick) (Edwards 1968; Kahneman & Tversky 1983, 1985; Piattelli-Palmarini 1994). Some literature in political science suggests that voters update partisan attachments in the aggregate in a Bayesian fashion (Gerber & Green 1998). Intendedly rational voters would update (if not strictly according to Bayes' rule). Whether the law of large numbers acts to push incomplete Bayesian voters toward a closer approximation to Bayes' rule in the aggregate remains an open question.

IDENTIFICATION WITH MEANS   In situations of repeated decision making, people often come to identify both cognitively and emotionally with the means, or subgoals, of a decision-making process. If they do, they are likely to become too conservative in shifting to a more effective means for solving a problem (March 1994). A scientist may, for example, become expert in a mode of analysis and apply it to all sorts of problems, even if the approach yields suboptimal results. The rational choice debate in political science has aptly illustrated the tendency to identify emotionally as well as cognitively with means (Green & Shapiro 1994).

A Note on Experimental Economics

In recent years, a vigorous experimental movement in economics has emerged. The methodology is direct: Derive a result from theoretical economics, set up a laboratory situation that is analogous to the real-world economic situation, and compare the behavior of subjects to the predicted behavior. These experiments have been criticized by practitioners of disciplines with much longer traditions of experimentation, such as psychology and biology; these criticisms are substantial. Perhaps most importantly, the economics experiments typically fail to study control groups (Green & Shapiro 1994:125–27). The justification is that the theoretical prediction serves as the comparison, or control.

In any case, two sets of findings have emerged. The first is that, in many situations that mimic real markets, in both animal and human experiments, market incentives have a major effect on behavior (Kagel et al 1995). On the other hand, the maximization models do not predict behavior very well—and they fail to predict behavior just where bounded rationality should show through in decision making. To cite but one very important result, the laboratory studies of Kagel & Levin (1986) show that auctions, and particularly auctions with numerous bidders, produce aggressive bidding that results in negative profits—the "winner's curse." Overbidding afflicts experienced as well as inexperienced bidders.

The Nature of the Environment

In addition to the objections based on the nature of the decision maker, there are objections to rational choice theory that involve the nature of the environment.

AMBIGUITY AND UNCERTAINTY   Proponents of limited rationality suggest that the environment is fundamentally more uncertain than is understood in prevailing choice models. Uncertainty, in rational choice models, means not knowing the probability of decisional consequences. In limited-rationality models, uncertainty also involves lack of knowledge of the attributes that characterize the problem (these are termed ill-structured problems). It can also involve ambiguity, which itself has two connotations. The first refers to situations in which the attributes are clear, but their relative importance is not (Jones 1996). The second, more fundamental ambiguity is one in which "alternative states are hazily defined or in which they have multiple meanings, simultaneously opposing interpretations" (March 1994:178).

Ambiguity and uncertainty in the environment feed back into characteristics of the decision maker. Preferences are desires about end states. In the rational choice model, people maximize the probabilities of achieving a desired state. But if end states are ambiguous, then our preferences must be ambiguous! If our preferences are ambiguous, then that mainstay of rational choice—fixed, transitive preferences—cannot hold (see March 1994:ch. 5, for an extended discussion).

REPEATED DECISIONS AND ENDS-MEANS CAUSAL CHAINS   People never make decisions in isolation. They interact with others, who themselves have decision strategies. They must modify their goals in light of the social milieu in which they find themselves. Indeed, some analysts have argued that preferences should be viewed as fluid, not fixed, because of the necessity to be flexible in the face of changing circumstances. It is common for decisions to exist in complex ends-means causal chains (Simon 1983). In many problems, as we take one step down the path toward solution, we preclude other options and we open new opportunities. That is, problem solving is an ongoing process involving interaction with the environment, which changes the set of constraints and opportunities we face.

THE COST OF INFORMATION

A major (he says *the* major) contribution of Downs' *An Economic Theory of Democracy* was to introduce the notion that search behavior is subject to a rational calculus (Downs 1957, 1993). The more valuable the likely outcome of a decision, the more extensive one's search should be. Where the decision maker possesses limited information about alternatives, it would be rational for that decision maker to use shortcuts, such as ideology or party identification, as cues to action in order to save expensive search time. The addition of a cost-of-search function to the model of rationality, along with the understanding of the role of risk and uncertainty, are the major additions to our understanding of rational choice (see Becker 1976). Downs' notion has been developed extensively in political science, especially in the study of voter turnout (Ferejohn & Kuklinski 1990). Lupia & McCubbins (1998) have explored the notion of source effects in cuing voting direction as a rational action, and they provide experimental evidence.

In my opinion, information cost functions cannot save comprehensive rationality. First, no studies have yet been directed at the search process in realistic political situations. And, make no mistake about it, this is an important process assumption. One will need to show that decision makers explicitly and consciously substitute such considerations as party and ideology for seeking information on public policy proposals. If the shortcut is buried in the backwaters of habit and routine, only bounded rationality can be used to understand the phenomenon.

Second, a model of rationality including search costs fails to incorporate the tendency of people to identify with means (organizational identification). If people act out of organizational loyalty rather than self-centered calculation, then the model fails. This is, in principle, testable, but again the proponents of information-cost functions have not done the empirical work.

It is possible to include organizational loyalty as part of the utility function—that is, as a separate goal. Then it will be necessary to map the trade-offs made by the decision maker between, for example, party loyalty and a policy goal—just the kind of trade-offs that laboratory studies show that people accomplish poorly.

Third, information costs cannot explain many of the observations of organizational behavior and laboratory results. These include at least the following: (*a*) the tendency of people to think of risk differently when they are losing than when they are winning, (*b*) the "winner's curse" in auctions, and (*c*) the tendency of people to fail to act according to Bayes' rule in updating information.

INFORMATION THEORY AND INFORMATION PROCESSING

Nowhere do comprehensive and bounded rationality differ more than in the treatment of information. The transmission of information has always been an important component of politics, but it has received renewed emphasis in recent years via signaling theory. Rational-actor theories of decision making require no theory of decision makers, because all behavior is explained in terms of incentives incoming from the environment (Simon 1979). Similarly, rational-actor theories of information need a theory of signals and a theory of senders but have no need of a theory of receivers. In modern signaling theory, information is costly and noisy; the receiver wants the information and the sender may or may not have incentive to supply correct information. If the sender does transmit the information, the signal will reduce the variance (noise) affecting the receiver's view of the world.

In information processing, the receiver must attend to and interpret incoming information. Often, the problem for the receiver is not a lack of information but rather an overload. The scarce resource is not information; it is attention (Simon 1996b). In essence, one needs a theory of the receiver to understand his or her response to a signal. If the receiver's frame of reference is multidimensional, then the concept of noise reduction is not enough to explain the receiver's response. The sender of the information may also try to influence the relative importance of the attributes that structure the multidimensional frame of reference held by the receiver (Jones 1996). Framing effects in political communication stem primarily from the limited attention spans (short-term memories) of decision makers and the necessity to retrieve coded patterns from long-term memory (Iyengar 1990).

WHAT SHOULD REPLACE RATIONAL CHOICE?

The response of social scientists to the onslaught of empirical findings showing the failure of the rational model may be divided into two camps. The first camp continues to do business as usual, ignoring the demonstrated weaknesses of the underlying assumptions—for example, denying that assumptions ought to be subject to empirical test. Then there has been a tendency to "discover" incentives in the environment that must have been there to account for any observed deviations. Green & Shapiro (1994) refer to this as post-hoc theorizing and offer numerous examples.

The second camp has begun a research program of incorporating elements of bounded rationality into models of political and economic decision making. Behavioral economist Colin Camerer (1998:56) recommends replacement assumptions that allow economic agents to be impulsive and myopic, to lack self-control, to keep track of earning and spending in separate "mental accounting" categories, to care about the outcomes of others (both enviously and altruistically), to construct preferences from experience and observation, to sometimes misjudge probabilities, to take pleasure and pain from the difference between their economic state and some set of reference points, and so forth.

This challenge has been taken seriously. In international relations, Kahneman & Tversky's prospect theory has been used to understand foreign policy decision making (Farnham 1994, Levy 1997, Quattrone & Tversky 1988). I have shown elsewhere that shifts of attention among the attributes that structure a situation can yield discontinuous behavior in political institutions—even when actors maximize utility (Jones 1994). In the study of voting behavior, Hinich & Munger (1994) predict that "rigorous formal models may someday account for emotion, history, and the idiosyncrasies of human cognition." Economists have directly modeled economic phenomena, using selected assumptions based on bounded rationality (Sargent 1993). Financial economists have incorporated decision-making models based on heuristic shortcuts, emotion, and contagion to understand large jumps in the behavior of asset markets (Lux 1995, 1998). This approach, though promising, is feasible in the long run only if rigorous empirical tests of the new models are undertaken.

There is a third possibility, as yet unexplored in political science. That is to use the rational model to estimate what fully rational actors would do given the external situation. This is a possibility only when one understands the structure of the situation and the frame that would be used by rational actors—as is the case when cognitive psychologists study problem solving in set task environments. This approach causes us to consider explicitly the conditions under which bounded rationality will show through in structured decision-making situations. It is not as useful in fluid, nonstructured environments.

THE PROBLEM OF PROBLEM SPACES

Results from problem-solving experiments in psychology laboratories and from studies in artificial intelligence suggest that decision makers process information by applying operators in a problem space constructed to search for solutions (Newell 1990). In these experiments, the task environment is tightly specified, so that the investigator knows exactly the preferences (goals) of the subject—to solve the problem. Process-tracing methods allow the study of the steps that subjects take to solve the problem (Newell & Simon 1972). Results suggest that, as the time allocated to solve the problem increases, the demands of the task environment overwhelm the limitations imposed by human cognitive architecture. However, some facets of the underlying architecture continue to show through even in tightly specified task environments.

What if task environments are uncertain, ambiguous, or contradictory? Then the direct representation of the task environment in the problem space of the decision maker is not so evident. Considerable work in political science has been directed at the study of how policy makers understand the problems they face (Rochefort & Cobb 1994). Perhaps the major problem with the use of rational choice in political science has been the confident postulation of a problem definition that may or may not fit the problem definition held by the decision maker. Even when the goals of decision makers are clear and unambiguous (such as the postulate that legislators wish to be reelected), subgoals may not be at all clear.

BOUNDED RATIONALITY SHOWING THROUGH

If, however, the task environment can be specified tightly enough to predict rational responses from decision makers, then it becomes possible to compare observed behavior with that expected from rational predictions (Jones 1999). We have already seen that this is the technique commonly used by experimental economists. (Unfortunately, the economists have no alternate hypothesis to accept when the null expectation is rejected.) But it is also possible to extend the approach to structured institutional decision making, in which the incentives generated by the institution are understood well enough to model quantitatively.

The "efficient market thesis" provides a powerful example. In what economists call an informationally efficient market, the price of a stock tomorrow cannot be predicted from the price of a stock today. The reason, as Samuelson (1965:41) put the enigma, is this: "In competitive markets, there is a buyer for every seller. If one could be sure that a price will rise, it would have already risen."

There will be plenty of price movement in the stock market. But because all participants are fully rational, they will use up all of the available systematic information. That means they will fully value the stock. The next move of the stock cannot be predicted—it could be up or down. But, because the factors that will affect the price of the stock (after it has been bid up or down by investors based on systematic information) are random, the distribution of the changes in a stock's prices—hourly, daily, or yearly—follow a random walk through time (Fama 1965).

The simplest form of the random-walk hypothesis may be written as follows:

$$P_t = \mu + P_{t-1} + \varepsilon_t, \qquad\qquad \varepsilon_t \sim \text{IID}\,(0, \sigma^2). \qquad\qquad 1.$$

Here the price at t is a function of $t-1$, a term μ (which assesses the long-run expected change, or drift, in the price series), and an error term that is assumed to be independently and identically distributed with finite variance. In this circumstance, markets would follow a random walk with drift, and prices would be Normally distributed because of the central limit theorem.

The implication of the efficient-market thesis is that a stock market (or other asset market, such as bonds) will follow a random walk.[2] In a random walk, we cannot predict the next step from previous steps. If we define the (daily) returns in a stock price as the price on day two minus the price on day one, and we make a frequency distribution of these daily returns over a long period of time, this frequency distribution will approximate a Normal. The many factors that could affect the price of a stock (or a whole market), when added up, mostly cluster around the average return, with very few changes a long way (either up or down) from the average return.

So we have a clear prediction for the behavior of market returns. Unfortunately, the evidence is not supportive. Asset market returns are invariably leptokurtic; they have slender peaks and fat tails in comparison to the Normal (see Figure 1). They are, in effect, subject to bubbles and crashes. Bubbles and crashes are not to be expected in the efficient-market thesis because sophisticated traders will be able to make money on the underlying dependence in the error-generating process (Fama 1965:38). This, in effect, would restore Normality to the price series.

Note that the observed leptokurtic distributions are not bizarre deviations from the Normal distribution, and that we have standard techniques for estimating the "excess kurtosis problem" (Lux 1998:149). Intendedly rational actors may deviate from fully rational actors, but the deviation will be attenuated in well-functioning institutions. The fat-tailed, slender-peaked distribution is what we would expect if we thought that market participants were intendedly rational. Markets would be affected by such factors as (a) non-Bayesian updating behavior in the face of incoming information (basically underreacting to some information and overreacting to other information, depending on the context), (b) contagion, and (c) emotion (Lux 1998). This disproportionate reaction to information would not be fully compensated by sophisticated traders, since they also would be subject to the same cognitive and emotional forces.

It may be objected that external shocks surprising to everyone are responsible for the observed fat tails. Experimental economists, however, have directly observed bubbles and crashes (the fat tails) in their toy economies (Smith et al 1988). The experimentalists have also directly observed leptokurtic distributions in simulated markets (Plott & Sunder 1982). It is unlikely that what occurs endogenously in the lab would be explained exogenously in real markets.

---

[2]The initial random-walk hypothesis has been supplemented by more sophisticated models of random processes. The theoretical justification and implications remain similar. See Campbell et al (1997) for a discussion.

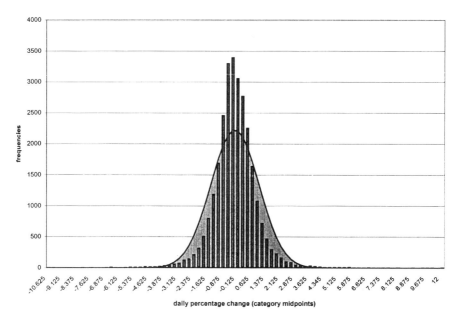

Figure 1 Frequency distribution of percentage changes in the Dow-Jones Industrial Average, 1896–1996, compared with a normal distribution with similar mean and variance.

We may use this approach in the study of politics. In the study of elections, there has been considerable debate about realignments. Electoral realignments imply leptokurtic distributions. If we were to plot election-to-election changes over a long period of time, we would expect to see most elections cluster around the center, with very little change in the pattern of standing allegiances to the parties for most elections. Once in a while, however, a major change would occur, falling in the fat tails. Very few cases would fall in the shoulders, or wings, of the distribution.

There is, however, a second hypothesis. In this approach, parties are the creations of ambitious, election-driven politicians (Aldrich 1995). Politicians play the part of entrepreneurs in market economies, immediately responding to the preferences of voters for "packages" of public policies. This suggests a relatively efficient response to information because of the activities of entrepreneurial politicians. Elections, under the hypothesis that elections are relatively informationally efficient, would have output distributions similar to the stock market.

Nardulli (1995) has produced a phenomenally complete analysis of presidential elections since 1824 at the county level. He finds scant evidence of national realignments but points to a series of "rolling realignments" that are regionally based.

Nardulli's data may be plotted in a frequency distribution, similar to the stock market data discussed above. Figure 2 plots 110,000 observations on election margin swings in US counties for presidential elections from 1824 through 1992. On the one hand, the distribution is leptokurtic—the fat tails and slender peaks are in evidence. On the other hand, the distribution is no more leptokurtic than the US stock market. It would seem that bounded rationality—not sweeping realignments or a fully rational interaction between voters and politicians—best characterizes the data.

Another way to look at distributional data is to subtract the observed relative frequency of categories from expected (based on the Normal). Figure 3 does this for Nardulli's election data. The graph makes clear how the election data deviates from what is expected based on the Normal. Specifically, the graph shows an excess of cases clustered around the central peak and in the tails of the distribution. There are too few cases in the shoulders of the distribution, in comparison to the Normal. This means that a great many elections are

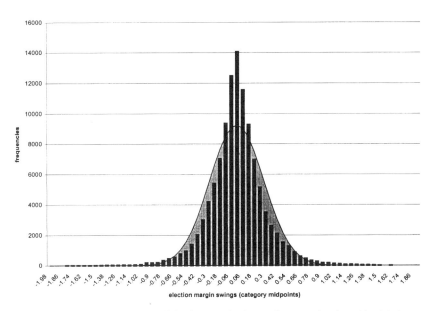

Figure 2 Frequency distribution of election margin changes in county-level presidential elections, 1824–1992, compared with a normal distribution with similar mean and variance. Election margin swing is the Democratic proportion of the two-party vote minus the Republican portion. Compiled from P Nardulli, personal communication.

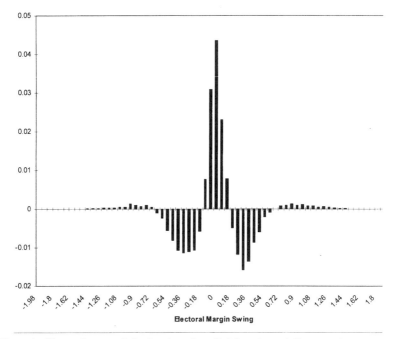

Figure 3   Observed-expected election data. Compiled from P Nardulli, personal communication.

incremental changes from the previous election, but a few exhibit considerable punctuations. There are too few modest changes in the distribution (again with the Normal as a standard).

Although I cannot make the full argument here, I note that this is the kind of distribution one would expect, given a set of intendedly rational actors subject to certain cognitive limits—particularly limits on attention—facing a world in which incoming information is approximately normally distributed.[3]

SUBSTANTIVE LIMITS ON RATIONALITY: OVERCOOPERATION

Riker's *The Theory of Political Coalitions* (1963) is an elegant analysis of political behavior in formal group decision-making situations, such as committees or legislative bodies. In many situations, committees must decide how to share a divisible good (one that can be broken up in any number of ways). The

[3]If decision makers are modeled based on a power function and if information is normally distributed, then the outcome distribution will be exponential. Substantial reasons exist for using a power function as a first approximation for bounded decision makers in institutional settings. Both elections and stock markets are exponential distributions (Jones 1999).

good could be streetlights that must be allocated to neighborhoods by a city council or highway projects to congressional districts or dollars to any number of worthy projects. Riker (1963) assumed that each member of the decision-making body had one vote and that a plurality was necessary for a proposal to win.

If decision makers are rational in such situations, they will form minimum winning coalitions, Riker reasoned. That is, rational legislators will find a way to divide the good up in such a way that the winning coalition will share all of the benefits while totally excluding the losers. In that way, each member of the winning coalition will maximize his or her part of the spoils. Any sharing with the minority will dilute the benefits gained by the majority.

Many political scientists spent a great amount of effort searching for the predicted minimum winning coalition, with mixed results at best. In the real world of democratic politics and government, there seemed to be too much co-operation. Moreover, participants often seemed to cooperate with the "wrong" others. In an early study of coalition formation in parliamentary democracies, Axelrod (1970; see also 1997) showed that parties tended to form coalitions based on ideological similarity rather than on the size of the governing coalition.

Why would rational actors seemingly overcooperate? Political scientists uncovered all sorts of reasons that minimum winning coalitions might not form on any given vote in a committee or legislature. The vote might not be on something divisible. It might be on something that was not excludable from the minority, as would be the case in voting for an increase in social security benefits in Congress. Social security recipients can live in any district. Political institutions are sometimes set up to require supermajorities, in effect forcing more cooperation than might be predicted from preferences alone.

Even on divisible goods, rational legislators might not form minimum coalitions because of what Axelrod (1984) called "the shadow of the future." In the language of game theory, a vote is not a one-shot game. Axelrod began studying cooperative (or coalitional) behavior in computer simulations of games in which rational players repeated play. Cooperative behavior indeed emerged in such situations, whereas it did not in a single play. If people know that they will be interacting with others over a long period of play, then they are more likely to use strategies that involve offers of cooperation in the rational hope that such offers will be reciprocated, making both parties better off. This sort of cooperation is rationally based—it is a reasoned response to the task environment.

Divide the Dollar

In a laboratory game that mimics political coalition formation, a subject is asked to divide a set amount among several players. The players can reject the offer, but they cannot modify it. This game, or a variant of it, has been played in laboratories many times. The inevitable result is that leaders give away too much of the spoils. They generally do not divide the results equally, but they do share too much. Remember that this is a one-shot game; there is no repeated play. The leader will not see these people again. (Repeated play and knowing the participants cause leaders to share even more.)

In contrast to the process limitations discussed earlier in this paper, how-ever, the limitations here are not that the leader was unable to do the necessary calculations or attend to the relevant factors. In the simplest form of this game, the ultimatum game, consisting of only two players (proposer and responder), the same results hold. The typical offer to the responder is 30–40% of the total. Even when the responder cannot reject the offer (the "dictator" game), the proposer offers more than predicted.(See Camerer & Thaler 1995 for a non-technical review of these findings.)

These games, which are not affected by the size of the reward but do seem to be affected somewhat by cultural differences, illustrate major deviations from strict self-centered rationality. Heuristic decision making took over, but this was not a heuristic that served as an informational shortcut. I term these and other similar heuristics substantive, because the heuristic directly affects the decisional outcome.

CONCLUSIONS: RATIONAL CHOICE AS TASK ENVIRONMENT

Political decision makers are invariably intendedly rational; they are goal-directed and intend to pursue those goals rationally. They do not always suc-ceed. I have detailed an approach to political choice that has three components: (a) the task environment, (b) the problem space constructed by the decision maker, and (c) the limits imposed by the cognitive/emotional architecture of human decision makers.

The behavior of a fully rational decision maker would be completely deter-mined by the task environment. If we know the environment and the goals of the decision maker, then we may deduce the decision maker's actions. If, however, the decision maker intends to be rational but may fail, then we will need to know something about the cognitive and emotional architecture of the decision maker.

This conception of decision making leads to two important hypotheses:

1. In relatively fixed task environments, such as asset markets and elections, observed behavior (B) of actors may be divided into two mutually exclusive and exhaustive categories: rational goal attainment (G) and limited ration-ality (L). This leads to the fundamental equation for fixed task environ-ments, $B = G + L$.

2. In uncertain, ambiguous, or contradictory task environments, behavior is a function of goals, processing limits, and the connection between the decision maker's problem space and the task environment (objectively characterized). In this far more complex situation, problem-space representations may interact nonlinearly with goals and processing limits.

The strategy I have suggested here is to divide these two separate situations for analytical purposes and treat them separately. In relatively fixed task environments, we should be able to divide behavior into adaptive, goal-oriented behavior and behavior that is a consequence of processing limits, and we should be able to measure the deviation. I have offered a first cut at such a strategy above for outcome distributions from structured institutional settings. Having so divided outcome behavior, we might want to reexamine the internal workings of such institutions—in effect, to trace the processes that lead to the outcomes of interest.

Visit the *Annual Reviews home page* at
http://www.AnnualReviews.org.

Literature Cited

Aldrich J. 1995. *Why Parties?* Chicago: Univ. Chicago Press

Anton T. 1966. *The Politics of State Expenditures in Illinois.* Urbana: Univ. Ill. Press

Axelrod R. 1970. *Conflict of Interest.* Chicago: Markham

Axelrod R. 1984. *The Evolution of Cooperation.* New York: Basic Books

Axelrod R. 1997. *The Complexity of Cooperation.* Princeton, NJ: Princeton Univ. Press

Baumgartner FR, Jones BD. 1993. *Agendas and Instability in American Politics.* Chicago: Univ. Chicago Press

Becker GS. 1976. *The Economic Approach to Human Behavior.* Chicago: Univ. Chicago Press

Camerer CF. 1998. Behavioral economics and nonrational organizational decision making. See Halpern & Stern 1998a, pp. 53–77

Camerer CF, Thaler RF. 1995. Ultimatums, dictators and manners. *J. Econ. Perspect.* 9:209–19

Campbell JY, Lo AW, MacKinlay AC. 1997. *The Econometrics of Financial Markets.* Princeton, NJ: Princeton Univ. Press

Chisholm D. 1995. Problem-solving and institutional design. *J. Public Admin. Res. Theory* 5:451–91

Cobb R, Elder C. 1972. *Participation in American Politics.* Baltimore, MD: John Hopkins Univ. Press

Cohen M, March JG, Olsen J. 1972. A garbage can model of organizational choice. *Admin. Sci. Q.* 17:1–25

Crecine JP. 1969. *Government Problem-Solving: a Computer Simulation of Government Budgeting.* Chicago: Rand McNally

Cyert RM, March JG. 1963. *A Behavioral Theory of the Firm.* Englewood Cliffs, NJ: Prentice Hall

Davis OA, Dempster MAH, Wildavsky A. 1966. A theory of the budget process. *Am. Polit. Sci. Rev.* 60:529–47

Davis OA, Dempster MAH, Wildavsky A. 1974. Towards a predictive theory of government expenditure: US domestic appropriations. *Br. J. Polit. Sci.* 4:419–52

Dodd LC. 1994. Political learning and political change: understanding development across time. In *The Dynamics of American Politics*, ed. LC Dodd, C Jilson, pp. 331–64. Boulder, CO: Westview

Downs A. 1957. *An Economic Theory of Democracy*. New York: Harper & Row

Downs A. 1993. The origins of an economic theory of democracy. In *Information, Participation, and Choice*, ed. B Groffman, pp. 197–99. Ann Arbor: Univ. Mich. Press

Edwards W. 1968. Conservatism in human information processing. See Kleinmuntz 1968, pp. 17–52

Fama E. 1965. The behavior of stock market prices. *J. Business* 12:34–105

Farnham B. 1994. *Avoiding Losses, Taking Risks*. Ann Arbor: Univ. Mich. Press

Fenno R. 1966. *The Power of the Purse: Appropriations Politics in Congress*. Boston: Little, Brown

Ferejohn J, Kuklinski J, eds. 1990. *Information and the Democratic Process*. Urbana: Univ. Ill. Press

Gerber A, Green DP. 1998. Rational learning and partisan attitudes. *Am. J. Polit. Sci.* 42:794–818

Gist JR. 1982. "Stability" and "competition" in budgetary theory. *Am. Polit. Sci. Rev.* 76:859–72

Green DP, Shapiro I. 1994. *Pathologies of Rational Choice Theory*. New Haven, CT: Yale Univ. Press

Halpern J, Stern R. 1998a. *Debating Rationality*. Ithaca, NY: Cornell Univ. Press

Halpern J, Stern R. 1998b. Beneath the social science debate: economic and social notions of rationality. See Halpern & Stern 1998, pp. 1–20

Hinich M, Munger M. 1994. *Ideology and the Theory of Political Choice*. Ann Arbor: Univ. Mich. Press

Iyengar S. 1990. Shortcuts to political knowledge: selective attention and the accessibility bias. In *Information and the Democratic Process*, ed. J Ferejohn, J Kuklinski, pp. 160–85. Urbana: Univ. Ill. Press

Jones BD. 1980. *Service Delivery in the City: Citizen Demand and Bureaucratic Rules*. New York: Longman

Jones BD. 1985. *Governing Buildings and Building Government. A New Perspective on the Old Party*. University: Univ. Ala. Press

Jones BD. 1994. *Reconceiving Decision-Making in Democratic Politics*. Chicago: Univ. Chicago Press

Jones BD. 1996. *Attributes, alternatives, and the flow of ideas: information processing in politics*. Presented at Annu. Meet. Am. Polit. Sci. Assoc., San Francisco

Jones BD. 1999. Bounded rationality, political institutions, and the analysis of outcomes.

In *Competition and Cooperation: Conversations with Nobelists about Economics and Political Science*, ed. J Alt, M Levi, E Ostrom. New York: Russell Sage Found. In press

Jones BD, Bachelor L. 1994. *The Sustaining Hand*. Lawrence: Univ. Press Kans. 2nd ed.

Jones BD, Baumgartner FR, True JL. 1996. *The shape of change: punctuations and stability in U.S. budgeting, 1947–94*. Presented at Annu. Meet. Midwest Polit. Sci. Assoc., Chicago

Jones BD, Baumgartner FR, True JL. 1998. Policy punctuations: US budget authority, 1947–1995. *J. Polit.* 60:1–33

Jones BD, True JL, Baumgartner FR. 1997. Does incrementalism stem from political consensus or from international gridlock? *Am. J. Polit. Sci.* 41:1319–39

Kagel J, Battalio R, Green L. 1995. *Economic Choice Theory*. New York: Cambridge Univ. Press

Kagel J, Levin D. 1986. The winner's curse and public information in common value auctions. *Am. Econ. Rev.* 76:894–920

Kahneman D, Tversky A. 1983. Choices, values, and frames. *Am. Psychol.* 39:341–50

Kahneman D, Tversky A. 1985. Prospect theory: an analysis of decision-making under risk. *Econometrica* 47:263–91

Kingdon J. 1996. *Agendas, Alternatives, and Public Policies*. Boston: Little, Brown. 2nd ed.

Kleinmuntz B, ed. 1968. *Formal Representation of Human Judgment*. New York: Wiley

Levy F. 1974. *Urban Outcomes: Schools, Streets, and Libraries*. Berkeley: Univ. Calif. Press

Levy JS. 1997. Prospect theory, rational choice, and international relations. *Int. Stud. Q.* 41:87–112

Lindblom CE. 1959. The science of muddling through. *Public Admin. Rev.* 19:79–88

Lounamaa PH, March JG. 1985. Adaptive co-ordination of a learning team. *Manage. Sci.* 33:107–23

Lupia A, McCubbins M. 1998. *The Democratic Dilemma*. Cambridge, UK: Cambridge Univ. Press

Lux T. 1995. Herd behaviour, bubbles and crashes. *Econ. J.* 105:881–96

Lux T. 1998. The socio-economic dynamics of speculative markets. *J. Econ. Behav. Org.* 33:145–65

March J. 1978. Bounded rationality, ambiguity, and the engineering of choice. *Bell J. Econ.* 9:578–608

March JG. 1994. *A Primer on Decision-Making*. New York: Free

March JG, Olsen JP. 1989. *Rediscovering Institutions.* New York: Free

March JG, Simon HA. 1958. *Organizations.* New York: Wiley

Marcus GE, McKuen M. 1993. Anxiety, enthusiasm, and the vote. *Am. Polit. Sci. Rev.* 87:688–701

Meltsner A. 1971. *The Politics of City Revenue.* Berkeley: Univ. Calif. Press

Mladenka K. 1978. Rules, service equity, and distributional decisions. *Soc. Sci. Q.* 59: 192–202

Nardulli P. 1995. The concept of a critical realignment, electoral behavior, and political change. *Am. Polit. Sci. Rev.* 89:10–22

Newell A. 1968. Judgment and its representation. See Kleinmuntz 1968, pp. 1–16

Newell A. 1990. *Unified Theories of Cognition.* Cambridge, MA: Harvard Univ. Press

Newell A, Simon HA. 1972. *Human Problem Solving.* Englewood Cliffs, NJ: Prentice Hall

Ostrom E. 1990. *Governing the Commons.* Cambridge, UK: Cambridge Univ. Press

Padgett JF. 1980. Bounded rationality in budgetary research. *Am. Polit. Sci. Rev.* 74: 354–72

Padgett JF. 1981. Hierarchy and ecological control in federal budgetary decision making. *Am. J. Sociol.* 87:75–128

Piattelli-Palmarini M. 1994. *Inevitable Illusions.* New York: Wiley

Plott CR, Sunder S. 1982. Efficiency of experimental security markets with insider trading. *J. Polit. Econ.* 90:663–98

Quattrone GA, Tversky A. 1988. Contrasting rational and psychological analyses of political choice. *Am. Polit. Sci. Rev.* 3: 719–36

Riker W. 1963. *The Theory of Political Coalitions.* New York: Yale Univ. Press

Rochefort D, Cobb R. 1994. *The Politics of Problem Definition.* Lawrence: Univ. Press of Kansas

Sabatier P, Jenkins-Smith H. 1993. *Policy Change and Learning.* Boulder, CO: Westview

Samuelson P. 1965. Proof that properly antici-

pated prices fluctuate randomly. *Ind. Manage. Rev.* 6:41–49

Sargent T. 1993. *Bounded Rationality in Macroeconomics.* Oxford, UK: Oxford Univ. Press

Simon HA. 1947. *Administrative Behavior.* New York: Macmillan

Simon HA. 1957. *Models of Man.* New York: Wiley

Simon HA. 1979. Rational decision-making in business organizations. *Am. Econ. Rev.* 69: 495–501

Simon HA. 1983. *Reason in Human Affairs.* Stanford, CA: Stanford Univ. Press

Simon HA. 1985. Human nature in politics: the dialogue of psychology with political science. *Am. Polit. Sci. Rev.* 79:293–304

Simon HA. 1995. Rationality in political behavior. *Polit. Psychol.* 16:45–61

Simon HA. 1996a. *Models of My Life, MIT Edition.* Cambridge, MA: MIT Press

Simon HA. 1996b. *The Sciences of the Artificial.* Cambridge, MA: MIT Press. 3rd ed.

Simon HA. 1999. The potlatch between political science and economics. In *Competition and Cooperation: Conversations with Nobelists about Economics and Political Science*, ed. J Alt, M Levi, E Ostrom. Cambridge, UK: Cambridge Univ. Press

Slovak P. 1990. Choice. In *Thinking: An Invitation to Cognitive Science*, ed. DN Osherson, EE Smith, 3:89–116. Cambridge, MA: MIT Press

Smith VL, Suchanek GL, Williams AW. 1988. Bubbles, crashes, and endogenous expectations in experimental spot asset markets. *Econometrica* 56:1119–51

Sniderman PM, Brody RA, Tetlock PE. 1991. *Reasoning and Choice: Explorations in Political Psychology.* Cambridge, UK: Cambridge Univ. Press

Thaler RH. 1991. *Quasi Rational Economics.* New York: Russell Sage Found.

Wanat J. 1974. Bases of budgetary incrementalism. *Am. Polit. Sci. Rev.* 68:1221–28

Wildavsky A. 1964. *The Politics of the Budgetary Process.* Boston: Little, Brown

Wittman D. 1995. *The Myth of Democratic Failure.* Chicago: Univ. Chicago Press

Annu. Rev. Polit. Sci. 1999. 2:323–43

THE DECAY AND BREAKDOWN OF COMMUNIST ONE-PARTY SYSTEMS

Stathis N. Kalyvas

Department of Politics, New York University, New York, New York 10003-6806;
e-mail: stathis.kalyvas@nyu.edu

KEY WORDS: political parties, political regimes, single-party rule, democratic transitions, communism

ABSTRACT

The failure to anticipate the collapse of communist one-party systems stands in striking contrast to the determinism of retrospective accounts. This essay reviews accounts of the decay and breakdown of one-party systems in order to uncover the causes behind political science's inability to both anticipate these developments and provide satisfactory explanations. These causes include the deterministic character of most accounts, the absence of a theory of single-party rule, the absence or misspecification of causal links between the major building blocks of the arguments put forth, and the analytic conflation of decay and breakdown. Understanding the decay and breakdown of one-party systems requires a methodologically conscious distinction between these two processes and a specification of their links (and the links between the variables affecting each process), grounded in a theory of single-party rule.

INTRODUCTION

The breakdown of communist one-party regimes took everyone by surprise, participants and observers alike (Kuran 1991:7, Bermeo 1992:1). Indeed, experts expected "just the opposite of what happened" (Lipset & Bence 1994:175). Their surprise was provoked not only by the breakdown itself but also by its characteristics: speed, smoothness, and nonviolence, all of which

323

stand in stark contrast to the seeming durability and immutability of single-party rule in earlier decades. Most ruling parties fell without resistance: They abdicated, "willingly gave up power," and "melted away" (Tismaneanu 1992: xi, Janos 1992:110). Thus, besides being a crucial political development, the breakdown of these one-party regimes is a "dismal failure of political science" (Przeworski 1991:1).

Even though a few observers had mentioned the possibility of the breakdown of one-party systems (e.g. Amalrik 1969, Brzezinski 1989), their "prediction" was spurious. Hence, theories of breakdown are retrospective. However, Elster et al (1998:2) remind us that even in retrospect we are far from a proven explanation of this amazing turn of history. This essay reviews retrospective accounts in order to pinpoint some of the causes behind political science's inability to both anticipate these events and provide satisfactory retrospective explanations. As it turns out, the shortcomings of retrospective accounts and the failure to anticipate the breakdown share common causes: the absence of a theory of one-party systems (or single-party rule), the absence or misspecification of links between the major building blocks of the arguments put forth, and the analytic conflation of decay and breakdown.

In the first section, I address the absence of a theory of one-party systems, survey past efforts to build such a theory, and account for their failure; in the second section, I review the main accounts of one-party system decay and breakdown. I argue that the central problem of these accounts lies in their determinism, which in turn is caused by the analytic conflation of decay and breakdown. I review the attempts to overcome this problem and point to the necessity of developing a theoretical understanding of single-party rule. The empirical focus of this essay is primarily on the communist one-party systems of Central and Eastern Europe because they were regarded as the most enduring and stable one-party systems. As a result, the great majority of social science efforts to understand and explain these processes have focused on these cases.

THE ABSENCE OF A THEORY OF SINGLE-PARTY RULE

In order to understand how the end came as such a surprise, it is necessary to understand how order was maintained for so long by ruling parties, whose fate is intertwined with that of one-party systems (Hosking et al 1992:205). However, single-party rule has been (and continues to be) studied in a nontheoretical and noncomparative way. The absence of a theory of single-party rule is striking—particularly when compared with the theoretical development of the research on political parties. This absence, I argue, can be traced to (*a*) political scientists' misdirected efforts during the 1960s and 1970s to integrate the study of political parties in both competitive and noncompetitive regimes into a single framework, (*b*) the emphasis on the production of typologies, and (*c*) the deleterious effects of functionalism, modernization theory, and "old institutionalism." The resulting failure left a theoretical void, which has yet to be filled.

Political science during the 1960s and 1970s tended to equate theory building with generating typologies. Most efforts (and related debates) focused on the construction and elaboration of such typologies, which served, in fact, as a substitute for what had to be explained. The most authoritative typology of party systems, which emerged after years of debate and remains in use, posits seven types of party systems: one-party (or single-party), hegemonic party, predominant party (or one-party dominant), two-party, limited pluralism, extreme pluralism, and atomized (Sartori 1976:125). Unfortunately, this typology confuses party systems and political regimes. Indeed, all types of party systems except the one-party (and perhaps the ambiguous hegemonic party) presuppose a competitive political regime. The "one-party system," on the other hand, is a misnomer for a noncompetitive political regime, i.e. one-party dictatorship. The problematic nature of this typology becomes obvious when one juxtaposes two almost adjacent types, the predominant party and the one-party systems. Their conceptual proximity should be expected to imply cognate properties; however, the opposite is the case. Governing parties in predominant party systems tend to be extremely competitive; they succeed in governing (on their own or as the primary and ongoing partners in coalitions) without interruption for substantial periods of time (often for three to five decades, dominating ten or more successive governments), despite open electoral competition, open information systems, respect for civil liberties, and the right of free political association (Pempel 1990:1–2). In contrast, governing parties in one-party systems do not compete; in the exceptional cases where they must, their performance is usually dismal, leading to the end of the one-party system. Predictably, this typology has been the source of considerable ambiguity and confusion, as Sartori himself recognized (1976:220). (To avoid more confusion, I use here the term "one-party system" in a generic way.) Yet the conceptual category of the one-party system survived and remains in use. Why did the effort to theorize single-party rule fail?

The phenomenon to be explained was new and important. Although authoritarian polities had existed throughout history, one-party systems were the principal form of authoritarian politics in the modern world—just as plural party systems were the principal manifestation of democracies and no-party regimes had been the main premodern form of authoritarianism (Huntington & Moore 1970a:509). Indeed, Duverger (1969:255) argued that the single party could be considered "the great political innovation of the twentieth century." Interest in one-party regimes was further fueled by their emergence and proliferation in the newly independent nations (particularly in Africa, where, at the beginning of 1964, two thirds of the continent's states could be described as one-party systems), their progressive political connotation (one-party systems were presented as essential for nation building and modernization), and the complex reality concealed behind the cloak of monolithic political unity (Finer 1967, Janos 1970, Wallerstein 1966:202–3).

The transformation by political scientists of one-party regimes into one-party systems and their inclusion in the party system typology was a deleterious effect of the dominant paradigms of the 1960s: modernization theory, functionalism, and old institutionalism. In the context of modernization theory, political parties were both a manifestation and a condition of the "thrust to modernity." They were expected to emerge wherever the activities of a political system reached a certain degree of complexity; just as bureaucracy emerged when public administration could no longer be adequately handled in the prince's household, the political party materialized when the tasks of recruiting political leadership and making public policy could no longer be handled by a small coterie of men unconcerned with public sentiments (LaPalombara & Weiner 1966a:3). This perspective was reinforced by functionalism (parties being expected to perform the same functions regardless of the regime in which they operated) and old institutionalism (which focused solely on the formal aspect of institutions). For instance, Duverger (1969:256) argued that "there is no fundamental difference in structure between single parties and the parties of democratic regimes." Although Epstein (1975: 232–33) was aware of the problematic nature of including "those entities, operating under the name of parties, that exist in noncompetitive electoral systems" within the party system typology, he nevertheless decided to include them because some of their activities "are plainly the counterpart of those performed elsewhere by competing parties, such as presenting candidates for elective public office and recruiting prospects for nonelective public office." For many years, a number of sovietologists argued that the Communist Party of the Soviet Union (CPSU) aggregated interests in much the same way that parties did in the West and had, therefore, evolved into a genuine party performing functions associated with parties in competitive regimes (Hill & Frank 1981). After all, elections in one-party regimes were seriously seen as "evidence of the regime's increasing ability to mobilize the population and to integrate them into the political system" (White 1979:87). One still encounters similar arguments. For example, Ware (1996:127) argues that "even though for most of their existence Baath parties [ruling parties in Iraq and Syria] have not had to devote resources to electoral mobilization, they resemble liberal democratic parties in that they involve the pooling of individual resources for exercising power over a state."

Thinking of one-party regimes as one-party systems was made easier by the booming research on parties and party systems. Although the foundations of party theory were laid by the pioneering works of Ostrogorski (1902) and Michels (1915), the theoretically informed study of political parties and party systems really took off in the 1960s and 1970s, following Duverger's (1969), Rokkan's (1970), and Sartori's (1976) pathbreaking contributions. Enthusiasm about the study of parties and its potential led to an overt effort to be as comprehensive as possible by extending the reach of the party system typology. As Sartori (1976:237–38) pointed out, "According to a broad estimate, a majority of the countries and nearly two-thirds of the world population are governed today by single parties. A framework that allows for two major types and five subtypes is hardly redundant vis-à-vis such an order of magnitude." Moreover, because the primary criterion of the party system typology was numerical, one-party regimes could neatly fit in, in a way that was as intuitively attractive as it was analytically flawed.

The inherent ambiguity of the one-party category prevented its theoretical development and failed to add any substantial analytical value. "To call a polity a one-party system does not really tell us very much apart from that" (Huntington 1970:6). Indeed, while the theoretically informed study of parties took off, the study of one-party systems stagnated, remaining descriptive, noncomparative, and atheoretical. Even the proponents of the party system typology seemed aware of its limitations. Sartori (1976:222) acknowledged that "when the study of parties came to the fore, it did not add much to what had already been discussed in terms of totalitarian or authoritarian dictatorships" (see Aron 1967 for a similar point). Years later, students of authoritarian regimes confirmed this failure by noting that the party systems typology had proved an "unsatisfactory" framework "because our approach to political parties has been overwhelmingly shaped by the liberal democratic experience within which the discipline of political science developed. As a result, the concepts used to understand parties are well adapted to those parties which operate in such systems, but have less immediate relevance to those bodies which call themselves parties and which operate in non-liberal-democratic systems" (Gill 1995:1). In addition, area specialists refused to accept a typology that crowded a vast array of one-party regimes across the world into a single category (Gill 1995:1, Bienen 1970:100). More detailed typologies, such as those distinguishing between "one-party totalitarian" and "one-party authoritarian" or "exclusionary" and "revolutionary" systems (Ware 1996:128–31, Clapham 1993:663, Sartori 1976:222, Huntington 1970, LaPalombara & Weiner 1966a: 37–41), remained without effect because they sacrificed generality without providing analytical gain. In short, the concept of the one-party system remained in use but was devoid of any theoretical content.

The only renewed attempt to develop a theory of one-party systems was Huntington's in 1970. It was grounded in modernization theory; the origins of single-party systems were to be found in highly polarized societies where modernization led to the breakdown of traditional society structures and the subsequent mobilization of new groups. In such contexts, Huntington (1970) argued, one-party systems represented the efforts of leaders of "more modern" social forces to suppress "more backward" social forces on the way to modernity. Huntington called for a focus on such key variables as the role of the ruling party in the political system, the strength of the party relative to other institutions, and the societal actors who interact with the single party. He linked the evolution of one-party systems to the shifting roles of competing actors vying with ruling parties for supremacy in the system. Huntington's approach suffered from a structuralist bias, inherited from modernization theory, which led him to posit incremental political reform "in the spirit of one-soul-at-a-time" as the only way out of single-party rule (1988:9). Still, it is unfortunate that Huntington's effort was not pursued further. The lack of a theory of single-party rule has unquestionably hurt political science's understanding of the decay and breakdown of one-party systems. However, the death of the most prominent one-party systems should not deter the development of such a theory. A theory of single-party rule should analytically and comparatively address such issues as the internal dynamics of one-party systems, their origins and growth, and their connection to the patterns and sequences of underlying societal cleavages and to the strategic choices of political actors. Such a theory could benefit from recent developments in party theory, particularly party formation (Kalyvas 1996, Aldrich 1995). The theoretical understanding of single-party rule holds more than mere historical interest, even in the hypothetical case of the total and definite disappearance of one-party systems. Such an understanding is also necessary for the study of post–single-party rule.

ACCOUNTS OF DECAY AND BREAKDOWN: BUILDING BLOCKS AND LINKS

Although the relaxation of geopolitical constraints by the Soviet Union (known as the Gorbachev effect) was an important factor in the breakdown of Eastern European one-party systems, there is widespread agreement that it did not cause it. Domestic factors prevailed over external ones; the impetus was internal (Hough 1997, Szelenyi & Szelenyi 1994, Tismaneanu 1992, Jowitt 1991, Przeworski 1991). A careful reading of the Hungarian and Polish "thaws" in 1989 suggests a process of interaction, whereby reforms were brought about by domestic developments and gained momentum because of the Gorbachev effect, which they in turn reinforced, thus contributing to the chain reaction in neighboring countries (Kaminski 1999). The same can be said about the pressures from the West, both direct ones (e.g. the cost of imperial overstretching and military build-up—including the effects of the "Star Wars" program of the Reagan administration) and indirect ones (e.g. the "demonstration effect" of western media-disseminated images and realities of prosperity, freedom, and democracy) (Arnason 1993).

Most retrospective accounts of the breakdown of communist one-party systems are built around the following core: One-party systems experienced a long economic decay due to massive economic inefficiency; this decay undermined their ideological legitimation. To respond, they undertook political and economic reforms. However, these reforms failed, and the regimes collapsed. The main building blocks of these accounts are economic decay, ideological delegitimation, and reforms.

Economic Decay

The fundamental role of economic decay is almost universally stressed. Socialist economics turned out to be a dismal failure. Growth rates began to decline in the late 1960s and early 1970s. By the 1980s, socialist economies were in serious trouble and growth rates had declined to near zero. The consequences were devastating. "The darkened streets of late communism, the empty shops and frustrated careers, the potholes and tawdry buildings, the general coarseness of social life, and the pervasive dishonesty of the ubiquitous bureaucracy degraded all that it came into contact with" (Sakwa 1993:28).

How did regimes with a transformational mission produce such stagnation (Roeder 1993)? Several analyses have focused on the key flaws of socialist economics (e.g. Brus 1975, Kornai 1980) or illustrated its basic problems (Maier 1997:73–97), but there is widespread disagreement about the exact causes of the dismal economic performance of the 1970s and 1980s (Szelenyi & Szelenyi 1994:214). Was economic failure induced mainly by international factors, including rapid technological change? Was it the exclusive outcome of the internal logic of command economies—the "unfeasibility of socialism" (Przeworski 1991)? Was it the result of a particular path of modernization, "thoroughly ambivalent, modern and traditional at the same time, giving rise to a distinctive alternative modernity" (Sakwa 1993:28–29), which transformed societies in a way that transcended their economic system (Hough 1997, Hosking 1991, Lewin 1988)? Was economic failure political in origin—did the reluctance of ruling parties to adopt measures that would undermine their control over society cause their inability to cope with the demands of the world market (Stokes 1993)? Was it part of a general systemic failure, interweaving the regime's functional failure to coordinate demand and supply, polity and economy, civilian and military sector (Arnason 1993)?

The debate is open; weakest is the modernization argument, which tends to confuse the process of industrialization with its effects (Fish 1995:19). Furthermore, the direction of causality remains unclear; economic failure affected politics and society, but it may also have resulted from political and societal factors, such as the regimes' lack of political legitimacy (Szelenyi & Szelenyi

1994:218). Finally, arguments that point exclusively to economic factors fail to specify the links between economic decline and the actual processes of decay and breakdown. In short, it would be overly reductionist to explain the dynamics of breakdown exclusively in economic terms (Szelenyi & Szelenyi 1994). Exactly how an economic system that proved hugely successful in industrializing and modernizing backward societies decayed after achieving its initial objective (rates of growth during the 1950s were excellent, as were many indicators of development, such as life expectancy rates) (Szelenyi & Szelenyi 1994, Therborn 1992) remains an open issue.

Ideological Delegitimation

A plausible link between economic failure and the decay of one-party systems is the erosion of political legitimacy (Mason 1992). In the absence of material benefits, the implicit social pact of socialist societies, whereby elites offered the prospect of material welfare in exchange for silence, could not be sustained (Przeworski 1991:2). In other words, political dynamics are generally seen as the mechanism that translated, so to speak, economic failure into decay and breakdown. It was the changing moral and political climate of Eastern Europe that eventually destroyed communism; the Marxist myth had exhausted its galvanizing power and was replaced by widespread cynicism (Tismaneanu 1992: 281, Chirot 1991:9). The decay of legitimacy and the erosion of commitment to the official ideology were tantamount to the destruction of the moral base of communism. This caused loss of elite confidence and the "rise and ripening" of a civil society, eventually leading to breakdown (Chirot 1991). One version of this argument goes as far as to deemphasize economic dynamics, viewing them as mere "accelerators" of fundamentally autonomous political processes (Tismaneanu 1992).

Authors pointing to the importance of ideological delegitimation (e.g. Fish 1995, Chirot 1991) criticize the sovietological literature for having focused too much on elites and too little on societal developments. However, their argument suffers from problems as well. Theoretically, we know that widespread disapproval of a government is not sufficient to mobilize large numbers of people for antigovernmental collective action (Kuran 1991:21). Empirically, we know that the mobilization of social forces played only a limited role in the breakdown of one-party systems, and only in the last stage of the crisis; in most cases, the emergence of civil society was part and parcel of the breakdown process, rather than its cause (Walder 1994:313). Public opinion data indicate that support for socialism in East Germany and Poland was not negligible and remained relatively stable until the mid-1980s (Kaminski 1999, Kuran 1991: 31). In most cases, the opposition consisted of "a set of weak, diverse, and fragmented organizations" (Bruszt & Stark 1992:30). Outside of Poland, there was an absence of revolutionary counterelites, ideologies, blueprints, and reasonably unified political agents rooted in socioeconomic cleavages and conflicts; the stultifying and demeaning communicative and associative conditions fostered by authoritarian rule produced widespread "semantic incompetence," "cognitive confusion," and "self-doubt" that hampered any formation of agency and made most people, most of the time, actually cooperate in their own repression (Elster et al 1998:13). Although today it may seem obvious that most people in Eastern Europe were profoundly hostile to communist rule, it is a fact that in Poland and Hungary (where political reforms were first launched), leaders of both the regime and the opposition grossly overestimated the popular appeal and electoral chances of communism (Kaminski 1999, Szakolczai & Horváth 1991:488). Likewise, when protests began in East Germany and Czechoslovakia, "neither dissidents nor regimes expected that they would produce fundamental political change within a few short weeks" (Karklins & Petersen 1993:588). All in all, there were few outward signs of active discontent until the very end, and many reasons to believe that 40 years of communist rule had socialized most people into a passive acceptance of the system (Arnason 1993:18). Moreover, popular action was least important to the process of breakdown where the discourse of civil society was most developed (Poland and Hungary), whereas revolutionary upheavals took place where civil society was weaker (East Germany, Czechoslovakia, Romania) (Arnason 1993:188, Ekiert 1991:307). In short, the people experienced the process of breakdown with the same degree of surprise and amazement as did outside observers (Elster et al 1998:25).

Reforms

The erosion of legitimacy appears, therefore, to be a correlate of decay rather than a causal link between economic failure and breakdown. This link can be sought more fruitfully in the failure of economic and political reforms. Economic failure and the erosion of legitimation did not necessarily doom the regimes; the problem was rather that these regimes could not adapt to changing conditions (Elster et al 1998:53). This point raises many questions. What was the initial scope of reforms? Why did initially limited reforms turn into revolutions? Could reforms have succeeded or were they doomed from the outset? If they were doomed, why? More generally, how did a remarkable long-term stability give way to almost instant breakdown?

In retrospect, most accounts insist on the inevitability of the failure of reforms: Communism was unreformable; it was doomed to collapse (e.g. Roeder 1993, Sakwa 1990). Various arguments have been put forward. "Closed systems" are fundamentally incapable of adaptation and self-transformation and can only produce a vicious circle of decline, inexorably leading to the exhaustion of resources and the reinforcement of blockages (Kaminski 1991); communist institutions are ultimately incapable of accommodating the explosion of participatory demands that follow the liberalization of political rights (Remington 1992:125); the institutional design of socialist regimes had replaced accountability to the people with a system of bureaucratic reciprocal accountability, which gave the Soviet political system vast resources to transform society but destroyed its ability to adapt to the changes it set in motion (Roeder 1993); instead of reinvigorating existing institutions through adaptation, reforms sapped their vitality, reduced their power, and corrupted their integrity, thus accelerating their decay (Pei 1994:205); one-party regimes became the victims of their alleged strength—the omniscience of the party and the omnipotence of the state deprived them of the capacity to learn how to adapt to social change (Elster et al 1998).

Yet, most experts assessing the situation during the implementation of the reforms thought that these reforms did not threaten the regimes. For instance, Colton (1984:219) stated that "the Soviet system, though it has no more prospect of eternal life than any other human construct, is at the present time stable in its fundamentals. The USSR is not Poland—its homegrown regime is far older, stronger, and ornerier, and the average citizen is more stoically acceptive of its continuance. There is no revolutionary crisis in the Soviet Union today." Huntington (1988:8) argued that although Mikhail Gorbachev might be a reformer, he clearly had no intention of abandoning the Communist Party's monopoly on power. Even when the breakdown in Eastern Europe was under way in November 1989, many observers were too caught up in the excitement and confusion of events to draw this conclusion with much confidence (Arnason 1993:18–19). Hence, one remains skeptical about arguments that posit the inevitability of breakdown; if the fate of reforms had indeed been sealed from their very inception, surely the experts would have noticed. As Kuran (1991: 12) points out, "if the revolution was inevitable, why was it not foreseen?" This problem brings to the fore the issue of retrospective determinism.

RETROSPECTIVE DETERMINISM

Most available retrospective examinations are deterministic. The breakdown was "inescapable" (Brown 1991:2), "inevitable" (Lohmann 1994:43), "decades in the making" (Hough 1997:495), "rooted in the vanguard regime created by the Bolsheviks after taking power in 1917" (Roeder 1993:246). Przeworski (1991:1) notes that "any retrospective examination of the fall of communism must not only account for the historical developments but also identify the theoretical assumptions that prevented us from anticipating these developments. For if we are wise now, why were we not equally sage before?"

It may well be true, as Kuran has argued (1991), that revolutions are inherently unpredictable because private preferences and individual thresholds of collective action are unknown and prone to tipping effects, thus bringing a society to the brink of a revolution without anyone knowing it. Even if this is the case, retrospective accounts are useful and necessary, but they need not be deterministic. There are good reasons to think that the breakdown was not inevitable. Kaminski (1999) demonstrates that the adoption of a different electoral law in the crucial 1989 elections in Poland would have translated the actual distribution of votes into an electoral outcome favorable to the regime. The particular social, economic, and political conditions, he argues, were not sufficient to predict the fate of communism, since a different electoral law was feasible for the Polish communists, and such a law could have affected deeply the course of events and possibly delayed or restrained the fall of communism in Poland and the rest of the Soviet Bloc altogether. As Arnason (1993:18–19) puts it, "Who knows how close the GDR [German Democratic Republic] or Czechoslovak regimes may have been to imposition of a 'Chinese solution'? When future historians examine the archives, they may find that there are possible worlds, close to ours, in which the GDR politburo orders the police to shoot on the demonstrators in Leipzig."

However, nondeterministic accounts remain the exception. Only a few authors have been willing to argue that the breakdown was only one among many possible outcomes (e.g. Kaminski 1999, Szelenyi & Szelenyi 1994, Arnason 1993, McAuley 1992). I argue that the proliferation of deterministic accounts is an indicator of the analytic conflation of decay (stagnation or crisis) and breakdown (or collapse). Although the self-destructive dynamics that so suddenly became visible had been undermining one-party systems for quite a long time before their demise, these dynamics did not cause their breakdown directly. Though decaying, the Soviet regime did not collapse until the abortive coup of August 1991. The one-party systems of China, Cuba, Vietnam, and North Korea are caught in a process of protracted decay which, so far, has not resulted in breakdown. The distinction between decay and breakdown entails a distinction between underlying causes and precipitating conditions. Przeworski (1991:1) uses a medical metaphor: "[M]ost terminal cancer patients die of pneumonia. And social science is not very good at sorting out underlying causes and precipitating conditions." Indeed, the inability to distinguish between decay and breakdown is widespread (e.g. Roeder 1993:20, Pipes 1990:16). In some cases, breakdown is altogether dismissed as merely the automatic and inevitable manifestation of decay (Gill 1995:178).

Decay

The decay of communist regimes was highly visible. Every specialist and many casual observers knew well what was wrong in Eastern Europe. More than 30 years ago, Brzezinski (1966) argued that the Soviet system faced a choice between degeneration and fundamental transformation. Yet, almost no one guessed that what had been a slowly developing situation for several decades might take such a sudden turn for the worse. None of them could answer the question, "Why 1989?" (Chirot 1991:12). Macrosocietal factors, now the cornerstone of retrospective accounts, were only recently treated as evidence of the remarkable collective stability of communist regimes throughout the world in the last half-century; indeed, arguments stressing systemic exhaustion can predict both self-perpetuation and self-destruction (Walder 1994:297, Arnason 1993:184). "While today we look back upon an inexorable cumulative crisis," Walder (1994:297) points out, "a few years ago one could just as easily be struck by how little all of these deeply-rooted problems seemed to shake these stable and stagnant regimes." The fact that observers could identify decay but not predict breakdown underlines the simple but widely overlooked fact that "the historical life-span of the Soviet model was not predetermined by its structural logic" (Arnason 1993:181). Distinguishing between decay and breakdown allows the formulation of key questions. When does decay give way to breakdown? Are particular modes of decay related to particular modes of breakdown? What modes of decay and breakdown are associated with democratic outcomes? I review some of these issues below.

Decay can linger on indefinitely. "The slowing economy was certainly creating problems," observes McAuley (1992:89) about Gorbachev's USSR, "but there is no reason to suppose that the administrative-command system under Communist Party rule could not have retained its essential features for ten, or perhaps twenty years." Garton Ash (1989:252–55), arguably one of the most astute observers of Eastern Europe, described a possible scenario involving a long and slow decay of the center and a gradual loss of control over the periphery, which he dubbed "Ottomanization of the Soviet Empire." In addition, decay is not an inexorable and cumulative process of change inevitably leading to democracy (Ekiert 1991:286); it can lead to a different kind of authoritarian system, such as a no-party system or some kind of corporatist order (Chirot 1980). Lewin (1988:133) expected that one-party systems would survive a protracted political crisis because "the party is the main stabilizer of the political system" and is "the only institution that can preside over the overhaul of the system without endangering the polity itself in the process." Huntington & Moore (1970a:517) argued that the most likely response to a crisis of legitimacy in a one-party system was institutionalization in an authoritarian rather than a democratic direction and the concomitant appeal to a corporatist rather than a competitive tradition. In China, the process of decay associated with the Cultural Revolution involved a reassertion rather than a relaxation of party authority (Townsend 1970:306). The decay of one-party systems in Africa in the 1960s suggested a return to more traditional, militaristic, or personalistic forms of authoritarianism (Huntington 1970:4).

Decay could also result in war. Bialer (1986) argued that the "Soviet paradox" was based on the connection between internal decline and external expansion. Luttwak (1983) thought that the growing awareness of decline was likely to prompt the Soviet leaders to make full use of their military advantages before it was too late. Finally, even if the eventual outcome is a democratic transition, it can be slow, gradual, and limited. In an article insightfully titled "Is Mexico the Future of East Europe?" Croan (1970) argued that post-totalitarianism would reject the totalitarian heritage only selectively and gradually.

Breakdown

Distinguishing between decay and breakdown carries important methodological consequences. First, it is a way to avoid the determinist trap; it makes it possible to theorize about contingency. Breakdown is a process full of highly contingent and subjective factors, wherein beliefs cause events and events change beliefs (Arnason 1993:19). Key developments, such as a decision to participate in a demonstration (or to shoot at demonstrators), are often shaped by perceptions. Perceptions matter because predictions about how others will act are at the core of decision making (Karklins & Petersen 1993). Second, this distinction makes it possible to treat the structural macro-factors accounting for decay as constraints that define a set of possibilities but do not determine the outcome. Because most theories of rebellion and revolution are of limited help in explaining what happened in Eastern Europe in 1989 (Karklins & Petersen 1993, Chirot 1991:17), the study of breakdown calls for a shift in focus—away from the association of macrostructural variables with outcomes and toward microanalytical approaches that seek to identify links, processes, and mechanisms.

Olson (1990) is among the first authors to have looked at the breakdown of one-party systems from a microanalytical perspective. He argues that the logic of collective action could keep unpopular dictators in power but could also be the source of tremendous instability because perceptions are the key mechanism at work. Where the repressive apparatus believe they will be rewarded if they carry out the leadership's orders and punished if they fail, an autocracy is secure. But perceptions can change in the blink of an eye if the regime is even once observed to be weak; then, future expectations will lead to coordination in an antiregime position. Kuran (1991) pushes this argument further by elaborating on the tipping logic of the breakdown process. He argues that individual choices to participate or not participate in antiregime collective action are contingent on the participation of a certain minimal proportion of fellow citizens, which constitutes the individual "revolutionary" threshold. Slight shifts in individual thresholds can produce revolutionary bandwagons, i.e. an explosive growth in public opposition leading to breakdown. In a similar vein, Lohmann

(1994) analyzes the demonstrations that took place in East Germany as "informational cascades" that made public some previously hidden information about the regime's popularity, thus undermining it. Likewise, Hirschman (1993) has applied to the East German case his theory of exit, voice, and loyalty, which identifies several ways that popular disaffection with a regime can induce political change. Karklins & Petersen (1993) extend Hirschman's insights by contextualizing them in a comparative framework and seeking to explain variation in patterns of breakdown. The focus is on the micro-foundations of the mass protests of 1989. The authors examine two distinct but interactive dynamics: the dynamics of increasingly large and frequent mass demonstrations and the simultaneous process of fragmentation, defection, and loss of confidence within the regime. The originality of this paper lies in the recognition of the heterogeneity of both the masses and the regime, which are treated as sets comprising different groups.

Microanalytical perspectives represent one of the most promising areas of research; they contain numerous insights waiting to be elaborated, tested, and extended. What is particularly needed is work on preference formation and on the elaboration of links between micro-dynamics and macro-constraints. Such links can be provided by a theory of single-party rule.

SINGLE-PARTY RULE AND DECAY

Party decay and regime decay are related processes. First, the inability of ruling parties to respond to challenges is seen as a major cause of regime decay and breakdown (Gill 1995:178). This process can be traced back to the 1960s, when the ruling parties of Central and Eastern Europe entered a period of protracted ideological decay. "Party bureaucrats were no longer able to spend their nights at meetings, to wear working-class uniforms, to march and shout slogans, to abstain from ostentatious consumption" (Przeworski 1991:2). A process of depoliticization took place when party leaders ceased to be political leaders and became bureaucrats (Lewin 1995:292). Second, where single-party rule overlaps with an economic environment in which the party exercises de facto property rights and controls or monopolizes decisions regarding production, investment, income, and careers (Walder 1994:298–99), we need a clear understanding of the links between economics and politics.

The connection between micro-processes and macro-structures requires a theoretical understanding of single-party rule. As I pointed out in the first section, such an understanding is missing. Single-party rule is treated in the literature in a casual and atheoretical way, almost always in a case-study context. Yet, implicit references to possible causal links are present in many accounts. Party decay and regime decay are connected through (*a*) the effects of political reforms, (*b*) the introduction of political competition, and (*c*) the interaction of political and economic reforms.

The Effects of Political Reforms

Single parties (the CPSU in particular) failed to adapt to the political and economic reforms they themselves initiated (Gill 1995, Jowitt 1991). Political reforms were apparently undertaken in order to spur economic change, but they inadvertently undermined the parties' leading role (Tompson 1993:105, McAuley 1992:95). The goal was to reform ruling parties by introducing some accountability and competition to elected bodies, reducing party functions in the society, allowing greater freedom of discussion (and the expression of contrary views) within the party, and opening up the sphere of politics to the public. Still, ruling parties were to remain firmly in control.

The case of the Soviet Union is illuminating. Reforms were introduced in the 19th Party Conference (held in 1988) and included such measures as the creation of the Congress of People's Deputies, which was to elect a smaller body from among its members to serve as a Supreme Soviet and act as a legislature. Two thirds of the seats in the Congress would be open to competition on the basis of universal suffrage. The reforms had three main effects. First, they enabled nonparty forces to intervene in party disputes and radicalize them. The publication of party disputes projected the image of a party continually at odds with itself; the televised critique of the government by the Congress of People's Deputies, in 1990, was a terrible blow to the regime. As a result, the intense struggle within the party elite opened new political spaces, creating an opportunity for the development of an opposition (Szelenyi & Szelenyi 1994: 227), while the sense of disillusionment and demoralization at lower party levels increased rapidly (Gill 1995:180). Second, the ruling parties' basic task—direct administrative supervision—was gradually removed, eroding the very grounds of their power. Ruling parties found themselves deprived of a role that fitted their organizational structures and culture (Gill 1995:184). The elimination of members' privileges (which were many, owing to the party's unprecedented degree of control over individual incomes and career opportunities) alienated party cadres and narrowed the gap between party and society (Szakolczai & Horváth 1991). Third, the introduction of competition into the political system irremediably hurt parties that had never faced competition in the past. This point brings up the effects of reforms on the central feature of one-party systems: the absence of political competition.

The Introduction of Political Competition

As a result of political reforms, single parties had to transform themselves into real parties that could appeal successfully for popular support. They failed;

their performance in the first semi-free elections (i.e. where a degree of competition was introduced, as in Poland and the Soviet Union) was dismal. In the Soviet Union, the March 1989 elections for two thirds of the seats of the Congress of People's deputies showed that unexpectedly many voters used their new rights to punish party candidates. Even where they ran unopposed, as in Leningrad, prominent party candidates lost. It had never occurred to them that they could lose; when the results came out there was stunned silence (McAuley 1992:98). These elections were a terrible blow to the parties' assumption of unqualified support.

Why did ruling parties fare so badly in these key elections? The obvious answer is that they lacked popular support. However, such an answer overlooks a number of other factors. Ruling communist parties had no understanding of electoral rules and committed gross miscalculations during electoral bargains (Kaminski 1999). The party apparatus did not know how to fight an election campaign (Colton 1990). The jobs of party officials were related to administration, not to political competition; for example, party activists complained that they could not answer impromptu questions during electoral campaigns because they had not had time to check back with party headquarters. Party discipline began to collapse; in the Soviet Union, most candidates who stood against the party were party members. The 1990 elections provided new opportunities to opponents, in a context where associative life began to boom (White 1991:406, Fish 1995). By the spring of 1991, the CPSU was dead as a political organization (McAuley 1992:110). In short, single-party rule had destroyed the ability of ruling parties to compete, even in a semi-free environment. As Kaminski (1999) points out, "The communists lost power when they began to experiment with the classical devices of democracy: polls, electoral laws, and electoral campaigns. By playing with these devices without necessary skills, they produced a series of mistakes. Lenin's prophecy that capitalists would sell communists a rope to hang themselves on reached an ironic finale."

The Interaction of Political and Economic Reforms

Finally, the interaction between economic and political reforms contributed in important ways to the decay of single-party rule. Market reforms eroded the bureaucratic coordination of ruling parties, launching a process that intertwined (internal) demoralization with (external) alternative options. This process led to the decay of communist parties (but not necessarily to the breakdown of the regimes) because, once reforms were undertaken, the penetration of market institutions increased the incentives for opportunism while political reforms weakened the monitoring and enforcement capacity of the party. The result was the massive exit of members and officials. Once reforms got under way, communist parties began losing members in a quasi-exponential way, until they eventually imploded (Gill 1995). This process began in ancillary organizations and later affected the core of the parties. The Soviet Communist Youth organization (Komsomol) lost some 12 million members in just five years (1985–1990); CPSU membership stagnated in 1989 and began declining in 1990; about a quarter of the party's members left it between January and July 1991. Even in countries where no regime breakdown occurred, party decay is pronounced. A study of 1358 Chinese Communist Party village branches in 1989 reported that only 32.4% of the party branches "could fully play their role," 59.5% were "mediocre," and 7.95% were "basically defunct"; in Vietnam, the Communist Party managed to attract 36,000 new members in 1991 compared with 100,000 in 1987 (Pei 1994, Gill 1995, Sakwa 1990). The key mechanism of decay was, therefore, the desertion of party officials because of a shift in the sources of their revenue and income (and consequently their interests and orientations), rather than the emergence of civil society and the resistance of ordinary citizens to the state (Nee & Lian 1994, Walder 1994).

The introduction of market elements caused a decline of state-controlled resources and a shift in the balance of power from state to society. Market reforms expanded the originally limited options of party bureaucrats. Departures from central planning (which included tolerance for the "second economy" or "informal sector") opened alternatives to rewards and careers formerly controlled by the party and weakened the incentives and capacity of local officials to monitor and sanction member and citizen behavior. As a separate and lucrative private sector emerged, officials found that it offered important new sources of revenue and personal income. They therefore turned away from former allegiances to bureaucratic superiors in favor of new business ventures with long-term colleagues from the ministries in their localities (Walder 1994). Most party grassroots organizations became redundant. Alternative options often amounted to corruption, since the boundaries between public and private sector remained blurred. McAuley (1992:111) provides many examples of local and regional party organizations simply turning into private businesses. In Perm, a city in the Urals, the party committee set up a firm that paid its shareholders dividends; the firm began to rent out party property, including the party hotel (still supplied by the state wholesale network), and based a lucrative taxi service for foreign businessmen on its car pool, using state fuel. Between 1982 and 1991, government prosecutors and disciplinary committees in the Chinese Communist Party investigated and prosecuted 1.78 million cases of corruption involving members of the party. Among 41,000 criminals implicated in major corruption cases in 1991, more than 50% had held positions in party organizations, government agencies, and state-owned enterprises. In short, by creating opportunities for quick self-enrichment that many government and party officials found irresistible, economic reforms facilitated the illicit conversion of political power into economic gains, causing a breakdown of the state's institutional discipline and fueling an exodus from the party (Cheng & Gong 1997, Pei 1995, Gill 1995). At the same time, an increasing number of party members, especially of the younger generation, became convinced that their party could never be reformed and would have to be destroyed or split from within (Hosking et al 1992:205). On the one hand, the key institutions of the communist party-state were especially vulnerable to accelerated decay because of their high level of interconnectedness and interdependence. The decaying of one institution infected another, degraded its integrity, and reduced its chances for self-renewal (Pei 1995). On the other hand, demoralization generated tipping effects; the waning of commitment was contagious, a consequence of both institutions and perceptions (Nee & Lian 1994, Walder 1994).

The distinction between decay and breakdown is crucial. Some ruling parties have been able to maintain their hold on power despite their decay, while others failed. This variation seems to be related to the modalities of reform, and in particular to the content, timing, and interaction of political and economic reforms. For instance, economic reforms in the absence of political reforms produced a situation wherein the illicit conversion of political power into economic gains led to the decay of the ruling party but did not diminish its ability to maintain control, since control was precisely the precondition for economic gains.

CONCLUSION

It is clear that explaining the decay and breakdown of one-party systems is a formidable task; the complexity of the issue is colossal and the size of the sample is small. This combination favors ad hoc explanations (Kaminski 1999).

However, it is realistic to expect progress in understanding aspects of this process. Advances in the field will have to be based on a careful distinction between decay and breakdown. They will combine microanalytical studies of breakdown (using approaches such as tipping models, models of informational cascades, etc) with a theoretically and empirically grounded understanding of single-party rule and decay (its social basis, institutional dynamics, content of reforms, structure of rewards and sanctions, etc).

They will specify explicitly the causal links between developments at the macro level (e.g. structural change, international factors) and processes at the micro level (e.g. individual decisions to defect from the party), as well as the links between processes and variables operating within each level of analysis (e.g. economic decay and ideological decay, political and economic reforms). They will be sensitive to context and grounded in comparative empirical research (formulating, deriving, and testing falsifiable hypotheses); finally, their substantive scope will extend beyond communist regimes to eventually include the universe of one-party regimes.

ACKNOWLEDGMENT

I wish to thank Marek Kaminski for valuable comments.

Visit the *Annual Reviews home page* at
http://www.AnnualReviews.org.

Literature Cited

Aldrich JH. 1995. *Why Parties? The Origin and Transformation of Political Parties in America.* Chicago/London: Univ. Chicago Press. 349 pp.

Amalrik A. 1969. *Will the Soviet Union Survive Until 1984?* New York: Harper & Row. 93 pp.

Arnason JP. 1993. *The Future That Failed: Origins and Destinies of the Soviet Model.* London: Routledge. 239 pp.

Aron R. 1967. Can the party alone run a one-party state? *Gov. Oppos.* 2 (2):165–71

Bermeo N. 1992. Introduction. In *Liberalization and Democratization: Change in the Soviet Union and Eastern Europe*, ed. N Bermeo, pp. 1–6. Baltimore/London: Johns Hopkins Univ. Press. 205 pp.

Bialer S. 1986. *The Soviet Paradox: External Expansion, Internal Decline.* New York: Knopf. 391 pp.

Bienen H. 1970. One-party systems in Africa. See Huntington & Moore 1970b, pp. 99–127

Brown JF. 1991. *Surge to Freedom: The End of Communist Rule in Eastern Europe.* Durham, NC: Duke Univ. Press. 338 pp.

Brus W. 1975. *Socialist Ownership and Political Systems.* Boston: Routledge/Kegan Paul. 222 pp.

Bruszt L, Stark D. 1991. Remaking the political field in Hungary: from the politics of confrontation to the politics of competition. *J. Int. Aff.* 45(1):201–45

Brzezinski Z. 1966. The Soviet political system: transformation or degeneration. *Probl. Communism* 15(1):1–15

Brzezinski Z. 1989. *The Grand Failure: The Birth and Decay of Communism in the Twentieth Century.* New York: Scribner. 278 pp.

Chen F, Gong T. 1997. Party versus market in post-Mao China: the erosion of the Leninist organization from below. *J. Communist Stud. Transit. Polit.* 13(3):148–66

Chirot D. 1980. The corporatist model and socialism. *Theory Soc.* 2:363–81

Chirot D. 1991. What happened in Eastern Europe in 1989? In *The Crisis of Leninism and the Decline of the Left: The Revolutions of 1989*, ed. D Chirot, pp. 3–32. Seattle: Univ. Washington Press. 245 pp.

Clapham C. 1993. One-party system. In *The Oxford Companion to Politics of the World*, ed. J Krieger, pp. 663–65. Oxford, UK: Oxford Univ. Press. 1056 pp.

Colton T. 1984. *The Dilemma of Reform in the Soviet Union.* New York: Counc. Foreign Relat. 115 pp.

Colton T. 1990. The politics of democratization: the Moscow election of 1990. *Sov. Econ.* 4(6):285–344

Croan M. 1970. Is Mexico the future of East Europe? Institutional adaptability and political change in comparative perspective. See Huntington & Moore 1970b, pp. 451–517

Duverger M. 1969. *Political Parties: Their Organization and Activity in the Modern State.* London: Methuen. 439 pp.

Ekiert G. 1991. Democratization processes in East Central Europe: a theoretical reconsideration. *Br. J. Polit. Sci.* 21(3):285–313

Elster J, Offe C, Preuss UK. 1998. *Institutional Design in Post-Communist Societies: Rebuilding the Ship at Sea*. Cambridge, UK: Cambridge Univ. Press. 350 pp.

Epstein LD. 1975. Political parties. In *Handbook of Political Science: Nongovernmental Politics*, ed. FI Greenstein, NW Polsby, 4:229–77. Reading, MA: Addison-Wesley. 285 pp.

Finer SE. 1967. The one-party regimes in Africa: reconsiderations. *Gov. Oppos.* 2(4): 491–509

Fish SM. 1995. *Democracy from Scratch: Opposition and Regime in the New Russian Revolution*. Princeton, NJ: Princeton Univ. Press. 300 pp.

Garton Ash T. 1989. *The Uses of Adversity: Essays on the Fate of Central Europe*. New York: Random House. 335 pp.

Gill G. 1995. *The Collapse of a Single-Party System: The Disintegration of the Communist Party of the Soviet Union*. New York: Cambridge Univ. Press. 258 pp.

Hill RJ, Frank P. 1981. *The Soviet Communist Party*. London: Allen & Unwin. 167 pp.

Hirschman AO. 1993. Exit, voice, and the fate of the German Democratic Republic: an essay in conceptual history. *World Polit.* 45(1):173–202

Hosking GA. 1991. *The Awakening of the Soviet Union*. Cambridge, MA: Harvard Univ. Press. 246 pp.

Hosking GA, Aves J, Duncan PJS. 1992. Triumph and foreboding. In *The Road to Post-Communism: Independent Political Movements in the Soviet Union, 1985–1991*, ed. GA Hosking, J Aves, PJS Duncan, pp. 202–12. London/New York: Pinter. 236 pp.

Hough JF. 1997. *Democratization and Revolution in the USSR, 1985–1991*. Washington, DC: Brookings Inst. 542 pp.

Huntington SP. 1970. Social and institutional dynamics of one-party systems. See Huntington & Moore 1970b, pp. 3–47

Huntington SP. 1988. One soul at a time: political science and political reform. *Am. Polit. Sci. Rev.* 82(1):3–10

Huntington SP, Moore CH. 1970a. Conclusion: authoritarianism, democracy, and one-party politics. See Huntington & Moore 1970b, pp. 509–17

Huntington SP, Moore CH. 1970b. *Authoritarian Politics in Modern Society: The Dynamics of Established One-Party Systems*. New York/London: Basic Books. 533 pp.

Janos A. 1970. The one-party state and social mobilization: East Europe between the wars. See Huntington & Moore 1970b, pp. 204–36

Janos A. 1992. Social science, communism, and the dynamics of change. In *Liberalization and Democratization: Change in the Soviet Union and Eastern Europe*, ed. N Bermeo, pp. 81–112. Baltimore/London: Johns Hopkins Univ. Press. 205 pp.

Jowitt K. 1991. The Leninist extinction. In *The Crisis of Leninism and the Decline of the Left: The Revolutions of 1989*, ed. D Chirot, pp. 74–99. Seattle: Univ. Washington Press. 245 pp.

Kalyvas SN. 1996. *The Rise of Christian Democracy in Europe*. Ithaca/London: Cornell Univ. Press. 300 pp.

Kaminski B. 1991. *The Collapse of State Socialism: The Case of Poland*. Princeton, NJ: Princeton Univ. Press. 264 pp.

Kaminski MM. 1999. How communism could have been saved: formal analysis of electoral bargaining in Poland in 1989. *Public Choice* 98(1–2):83–109

Karklins R, Petersen R. 1993. Decision calculus of protesters and regimes: Eastern Europe 1989. *J. Polit.* 55(3):588–614

Kennan G.[X.] 1947. The sources of Soviet conduct. *Foreign Aff.* 25(4):566–82

Kornai J. 1980. *Economics of Shortage*. Amsterdam: North Holland. 2 Vols.

Kuran T. 1991. Now out of never: the element of surprise in the East European revolution of 1989. *World Polit.* 44(1):7–48

LaPalombara J, Weiner M. 1966a. The origins and development of political parties. See LaPalombara & Weiner 1966b, pp. 3–42

LaPalombara J, Weiner M. 1966b. *Political Parties and Political Development*. Princeton, NJ: Princeton Univ. Press. 487 pp.

Lewin M. 1988. *The Gorbachev Phenomenon: A Historical Interpretation*. Berkeley: Univ. Calif. Press. 176 pp.

Lewin M. 1995. *Russia/USSR/Russia: The Drive and Drift of a Superstate*. New York: New Press. 368 pp.

Lipset SM, Bence G. 1994. Anticipations of the failure of communism. *Theory Soc.* 23(1):169–210

Lohmann S. 1994. The dynamics of informational cascades: the Monday demonstrations in Leipzig, East Germany, 1989–1991. *World Polit.* 47(1):42–101

Luttwak E. 1983. *The Grand Strategy of the Soviet Union*. New York: St. Martin's. 242 pp.

Maier CS. 1997. *Dissolution: The Crisis of Communism and the End of East Germany*. Princeton, NJ: Princeton Univ. Press. 440 pp.

Mason DS. 1992. *Revolution in East-Central Europe: The Rise and Fall of Communism and the Cold War*. Boulder, CO: Westview. 242 pp.

McAuley M. 1992. *Soviet Politics, 1917–1991.* Oxford, UK: Oxford Univ. Press. 132 pp.

Michels R. 1915. *Political Parties: A Sociological Study of the Oligarchical Tendencies of Modern Democracy.* New York: Hearst's Int. Libr. 416 pp.

Nee V, Lian P. 1994. Sleeping with the enemy: a dynamic model of declining political commitment in state socialism. *Theory Soc.* 23(2):253–96

Olson M. 1990. The logic of collective action in Soviet-type societies. *J. Sov. Nationalities* 1:8–27

Ostrogorski MI. 1902. *Democracy and the Organization of Political Parties.* New York: Macmillan. 2 Vols.

Pei M. 1994. *From Reform to Revolution: The Demise of Communism in China and the Soviet Union.* Cambridge, MA: Harvard Univ. Press. 253 pp.

Pempel TJ. 1990. Introduction. In *Uncommon Democracies: The One-Party Dominant Regimes*, ed. TJ Pempel, pp. 1–32. Ithaca/London: Cornell Univ. Press. 371 pp.

Pipes R. 1990. Gorbachev's Russia: breakdown or crackdown? *Commentary* 89(3): 13–25

Przeworski A. 1991. *Democracy and the Market: Political and Economic Reforms in Eastern Europe and Latin America.* Cambridge, UK: Cambridge Univ. Press. 210 pp.

Remington TF. 1992. Reform, revolution, and regime transition in the Soviet Union. In *Dismantling Communism: Common Causes and Regional Variations*, ed. G Rozman, pp. 121–51. Washington, DC: Woodrow Wilson Cent. 405 pp.

Roeder PG. 1993. *Red Sunset: The Failure of Soviet Politics.* Princeton, NJ: Princeton Univ. Press. 317 pp.

Rokkan S. 1970. *Citizens, Elections, Parties: Approaches to the Comparative Study of the Processes of Development.* New York: McKay. 470 pp.

Sakwa R. 1990. *Gorbachev and His Reforms, 1985–1990.* New York: Philip Allan. 459 pp.

Sakwa R. 1993. *Russian Politics and Society.* London/New York: Routledge. 506 pp. 2nd ed.

Sartori G. 1976. *Parties and Party Systems: A Framework for Analysis.* Cambridge, UK: Cambridge Univ. Press. 370 pp.

Stokes G. 1993. *The Walls Came Tumbling Down: The Breakdown of Communism in Eastern Europe.* New York: Oxford Univ. Press. 319 pp.

Szakolczai A, Horváth A. 1991. Political instructors and the decline of communism in Hungary: apparatus, nomenclatura and the issue of legacy. *Br. J. Polit. Sci.* 21(4): 469–88

Szelenyi I, Szelenyi B. 1994. Why socialism failed: towards a theory of system breakdown. *Theory Soc.* 23(1):211–31

Therborn G. 1992. The life and times of socialism. *New Left Rev.* 194:17–32

Tismaneanu V. 1992. *Reinventing Politics: Eastern Europe from Stalin to Havel.* New York: Free. 312 pp.

Tompson WJ. 1993. Kruschev and Gorbachev as reformers: a comparison. *Br. J. Polit. Sci.* 23(1):77–105

Townsend JR. 1970. Intraparty conflict in China: disintegration in an established one-party system. See Huntington & Moore 1970b, pp. 284–310

Walder AG. 1994. The decline of communist power: elements of a theory of institutional change. *Theory Soc.* 23(1):297–323

Wallerstein I. 1966. The decline of the party in single-party African states. See LaPalombara & Weiner 1966b, pp. 201–14

Ware A. 1996. *Political Parties and Party Systems.* Oxford, UK: Oxford Univ. Press. 435 pp.

White S. 1979. *Political Culture and Soviet Politics.* London: Macmillan. 234 pp.

White S. 1991. Rethinking the CPSU. *Sov. Stud.* 43(3):405–28

Annu. Rev. Polit. Sci. 1999. 2:345–62

ISAIAH BERLIN: Political Theory and Liberal Culture

Alan Ryan

New College, Oxford University, Oxford OX1 3BN, United Kingdom;
e-mail: Alan.Ryan@new.ox.ac.uk

KEY WORDS: Machiavelli, Herzen, pluralism, conversation

ABSTRACT

The essay provides a short outline of Berlin's career and an assessment of his contribution to pluralist and liberal thought. He was a British academic with a Russian cast of mind, and an inhabitant of the ivory tower who was very much at home in the diplomatic and political world. Similarly, he was neither a historian of ideas nor a political philosopher in the narrow sense usually understood in the modern academy. Rather, he engaged in a trans-historical conversation about the human condition with such figures as Machiavelli, Herzen, Vico, and Herder. The Russian liberal understanding of the historical and cultural setting was, in his view, much superior to that of familiar figures such as John Stuart Mill, just as the nonliberal Machiavelli cast a particularly vivid light on the problems of a pluralist world view.

INTRODUCTION

The vividness of the life and personality of the author whose more narrowly intellectual contributions are under discussion would not usually present a problem for the commentator (Ignatieff 1998). The case of Isaiah Berlin is rather different. Bertrand Russell led a vivid life and had a striking personality, but the academic treatment of his work prescinds from these, concentrating on the austerities of his contributions to formal logic and on his less formal analyses of problems in metaphysics and epistemology. The relationship between Berlin's personal history and his intellectual contributions is more intimate than that, however. Because Berlin practiced the history of ideas in a highly personal and imaginative fashion, the student of his analyses is also a student of

345

his sensibility. This is not an unusual state of affairs in more literary subjects, where we take it for granted that an understanding of the work involves an understanding of the interaction of the author's sensibility and experience, and criticism of the work properly roams back and forth between the author's experience and its subsequent transformation into art. Philosophers who do not write their autobiographies are commonly immune from such scrutiny. The exceptions prove the rule: Mill's *Autobiography* and Russell's; St. Augustine's *Confessions* and Rousseau's. These works invite a more personal and more intimate scrutiny from the reader—though Mill himself strenuously denies this (1981 [1873]:4). They do not merely assert and defend a doctrine but display a sensibility and a temperament; the cogency of their arguments demands discussion and so does the quality of their sensibility.

Here, then, I tread cautiously. I allow myself some biographical background and then drop Berlin's philosophical work out of sight as irrelevant to our present purposes. I then move to Berlin as a historian of ideas, a student of distinctively Russian social and political themes, and a defender of a distinctively pluralist, anti-utopian liberalism. The division is artificial in the extreme, and the issues raised in each area of discussion are inextricably intertwined. The not particularly liberal Machiavelli is invoked in aid of a liberal moral pluralism, as is the much more liberal Russian Alexander Herzen. Much of the apparently more formal argument of even such essays as Berlin's inaugural lecture, *Two Concepts of Liberty* (1958a), is carried by the invocation of historical figures with whom Berlin carried on those astonishing transhistorical conversations that his friends, students, and lecture audiences all over the world were allowed to overhear.

A LITTLE HISTORY

The *Guide Michelin* starts its readers on their journeys with a short introductory account of the history of the region, its people, its culture, and its way of life. Isaiah Berlin was born in Riga, Latvia, in 1909. Owing to an accident at birth, he had a permanently damaged left arm; whether he might otherwise have had athletic tastes and abilities may be doubted, but in any event, his favored place was the sofa rather than the mountain track. His family were upper-middle-class Jews; his father was a descendant of the founder of the Lubavicher sect, but the immediate family were thoroughly Europeanized, and their tastes were musical and literary. A comfortable life was disturbed by the First World War, which provoked anti-Germanism and anti-Semitism; the family moved to Petrograd in 1916 and there encountered both the Russian Revolutions of 1917. Although they suffered no violence, and not much deprivation, the family saw what might happen after the Civil War of 1920–1921, and made their way to England. Mendel Berlin, Isaiah's father, was a timber merchant with commercial ties to Britain, and he thought well of British schools.

Arriving with little English in a wholly strange environment, the twelve-year-old Berlin thrived. A suburban preparatory school, in the English sense of the term, was followed by public school, also in the English sense; from St. Paul's, where he followed the traditional classical syllabus, Berlin went to Corpus Christi College, Oxford. He made many friends, and his flair for conversation was a great resource in so doing. Late-1920s Oxford was both snobbish and mildly anti-Semitic, but it sheltered a society that was less attached to its social prejudices than to cleverness and charm. Both of these the young Berlin had in abundance.

To those who know them and their reputation, any account of All Souls' College, and any account of the pleasures of a Prize Fellowship 77 years ago, is otiose. For those who do not, it perhaps suffices to say that Berlin's situation combined the intellectual pleasures of a professorship at the Institute for Advanced Study with the social pleasures of a lifetime membership of the Century Club enhanced by an introduction to all the other members. Berlin was the first Jew to be elected to All Souls' and was duly congratulated by the Chief Rabbi and invited to dinner by Lord Rothschild (Ignatieff 1998:62). Intellectually, the 1930s were the time of logical positivism's bracing blasts of scientism and skepticism; the Oxford environment was not particularly hospitable to importations from Vienna, but among Berlin's friends were AJ Ayer, who had come back from Vienna full of Carnap and Schlick, and Gilbert Ryle, who had a clearer grasp of where the Wittgenstein of the *Tractatus* had been and where the later Wittgenstein was now going. Berlin's closest intellectual companions were John Austin and Stuart Hampshire, neither of them imbued with the belief in science that drove the logical positivists, but each in his own way entirely disaffected from old-fashioned, intuitionistic Oxford philosophy, though each in his own way a great admirer of Aristotle (Berlin 1973, reprinted in 1998:130ff).

Berlin wrote several deft, acute, and accurate essays on the logical positivists' favorite pieces of analysis—of sentences about the past and sentences describing physical objects in the world around us—but although these showed great philosophical talent, they did not offer any insights into what else he might do (Berlin 1978a). Berlin's own account of his development suggested that his philosophical career was essentially a prewar matter. This is not entirely accurate. It is true that his essay "Verification" dates from 1939, but *Concepts and Categories* (1978a) includes the chastely titled "Empirical Propositions and Hypothetical Statements" from 1950, in which he showed that categorical statements about the past and the external world cannot be reduced to hypothetical statements about what we would experience under various conditions, as well as the seminal essay "Equality" from 1956. The one piece of work from the 1930s that does offer such an insight is *Karl Marx* (Berlin 1996 [1939]). This was commissioned for the Home University Library in 1935 but delivered only in 1939. Berlin read very widely for it and was one of the first non-Marxists to take seriously Marx's youthful enthusiasm for the philosophy of Hegel and Hegel's critics, such as Strauss and Feuerbach. Marx's economics did not interest him in the least, however, and the book as a whole is a series of reflections on the temperament that leads its possessors to embrace utopian, determinist schemes of social improvement. (I return to Berlin's treatment of Marx below.)

Berlin's career was less interrupted than kick-started by the outbreak of the Second World War. It took him to New York for the Ministry of Information, whence he was poached by the Foreign Office for the Washington Embassy. From there, he sent back streams of dispatches to his masters in London (Nicholas 1981). It was partly this close contact with the makers of American foreign policy that reshaped his life, but more importantly, it was his postwar encounters with Russian poets, novelists, dramatists, and other intellectuals in the winter of 1945–1946.

Just what happened is hard to recapture, but it evidently persuaded him of two things. The first was that he was, after all, a Russian intellectual, for all his years in Oxford, and the other was that Stalin's attempts at the destruction of Russian cultural and intellectual life were appalling, not only because of the cruelty and thuggishness involved in all Stalin's actions, but also because there had been a vitality, vividness, and originality in Russian literature and political thinking from the 1840s onward that was unmatched in the West (Berlin 1998:198–254). At a personal level, it was his encounters with Anna Akhmatova and Boris Pasternak that persuaded him of this; at a more—but not very—austerely intellectual level, it was his reading of Alexander Herzen and Ivan Turgenev.

HIGH TIDE

From 1950 onward, Berlin was important in British academic life and more broadly in British culture as a lecturer for the BBC and as a general commentator on political and intellectual life in the context of the Cold War. Berlin wrote nothing about the Holocaust and little about German anti-Semitism as such. He was a Zionist and a good friend of Chaim Weizmann, who was the first President of Israel and the subject of one of Berlin's most heartfelt *éloges* (Berlin 1958b). His cousin Yitzhak Sadeh (born Isaac Landoberg) was a noted general in the Israeli War of Independence, and Berlin recalled him with immense affection. He described Sadeh as "a huge child," who did more for Israel than his exploits on the battlefield alone might suggest. In Berlin's words, he "introduced an element of total freedom, unquenchable gaiety, ease, charm, and a natural elegance, half bohemian, half aristocratic, too much of which would ruin any possibility of order, but an element of which no society should lack if it is to be free or worthy of survival" (Berlin 1998:89–90). Berlin wrote interestingly about Moses Hess's slow and reluctant movement from assimilationism to a liberal Zionism not wholly unlike his own (Berlin 1959b, reprinted in 1978b). And he wrote the most unlikely short double biography of all time when he discussed Karl Marx and Benjamin Disraeli as exemplars of mid-Victorian London Jewishness (Berlin 1970, reprinted in 1978b). Still, it was Stalinist totalitarianism, not Nazism, that concerned him. His interest lay in the way in which the rationalist and reformist impulses of the Enlightenment, sometimes in perverse combination with the anti-Enlightenment forces of Romanticism, had produced millenarian and totalitarian movements that had set back the cause of liberal, pluralist, humanitarian progress by a century and more. It was in arguing on behalf of a pluralist, indeterminist, open-ended liberalism that he invoked the memory of those figures in the history of ideas that he particularly made his own.

Let us begin by asking a slightly odd question: Why did Berlin invoke these figures at all? To put it another way, if Berlin wished to argue that values are many not one, that the future is open not closed, and that the quest for Utopia is more likely to arrive at hell than heaven, why did he need help from the dead? These are philosophical questions, or perhaps in the case of the last thought a matter of political prudence, that he could have argued on his own behalf, and without appealing to anyone else for support. [Of course, to say this is to gesture to the essays in which he did argue the case with less historical reference. Viewed as an essay in "pure" political philosophy, *Two Concepts of Liberty* (1958a) would seem heavily encrusted with historical allusion, but it is manifestly not an essay in the history of ideas. "From Hope and Fear Set Free" (1964) is similarly light on historical reference, and such essays as "Historical Inevitability" (1954) argue against determinist theories of history with relatively little further reference.] The answer to the odd question must go back to Berlin's treatment of Giambattista Vico (Berlin 1976).

Berlin was seized by Vico's concept of *fantasia*. To argue about Berlin's understanding of Vico's concept is fruitless here, though others have done so profitably in different contexts (Pompa 1975). The point here is Berlin's use of the idea as he understood it. Essentially, Berlin took over Vico's thought that human society was historical, that an understanding of the human mind was to be sought by an active effort of positive, imaginative recreation, and that understanding the moral and political concepts by which we make sense of our existence, both individual and collective, is a historical activity.

This last point, incidentally, suggests that Berlin's own account of having abandoned philosophy in favor of the history of ideas is misleading; as Bernard Williams observed (personal communication), the truth is rather that he abandoned the idea that philosophical analysis is always concerned with the timelessly valid explication of concepts. The logical positivist ideal of philosophical analysis was that it would eventuate in a definition that would hold true forever. But in Berlin's version of *fantasia*, the concepts of political philosophy are the reflection of transitional, if not necessarily transitory, attempts by human cultures to grasp their moral and political experience and to mold it as they desire. The other aspect of *fantasia* that provides the clue, not so much to the content as to the dazzling rhetorical form, of Berlin's work in the history of ideas is its emphasis on reenacting past thought as it was thought by past thinkers. I have elsewhere perhaps overused the image of Berlin taking his hearers to a party in the Elysian Fields; but the thought that conveying a full understanding of another writer is like bringing the reader into the physical presence of that writer is, with due allowances made, hard to escape.

Here is Berlin's account of the kind of knowledge that, he believed, Vico had identified.

> This is the sort of knowing that participants in an activity claim to possess as against mere observers: the knowledge of the actors as against that of the audience, of the 'inside' story as opposed to that obtained from some 'outside' vantage point; knowledge by 'direct acquaintance' with my 'inner' states or by sympathetic insight into those of others, which may be obtained by a high degree of imaginative power; the knowledge that is involved when a work of the imagination or of social diagnosis or a work of criticism or scholarship or history is described not as correct or incorrect, skilful or inept, a success or a failure, but as profound or shallow, realistic or unrealistic, perceptive or stupid, alive or dead. (Berlin 1969, reprinted in 1978b:117)

That description opens up the reason why Berlin so often invoked long-dead allies in making the case for pluralism, liberalism, and open-endedness. In effect, thinking our own way through the dichotomies of pluralism/monism, freedom/authoritarianism, and indeterminism/determinism is one side of a conversation with writers who happen to be dead. It is one facet of imagining our society set against others, so as to illuminate the virtues and vices of each. To know why we believe in—if we do believe in—negative liberty, for instance, is to know what we would want to say to Pericles about his beloved Athens, and what we would want to say to Benjamin Constant (1988 [1819]) about the contrast he drew between the liberty of the ancients and the liberty of the moderns. Seen in that light, Berlin's handling of the figures about whom he wrote becomes easy to understand.

Consider one of the most famous essays, "The Originality of Machiavelli" (Berlin 1972, reprinted in 1978b:25–79). The "originality" of Machiavelli is itself an interestingly ambiguous topic. Taken in a simple, literal sense, originality is producing ideas—about life, morality, politics, or whatever else—that were unprecedented, unheard of, not previously ventilated by other thinkers.

By that definition, Machiavelli might plausibly be said to have been unoriginal. He himself claimed that although his method was novel, what he was doing was reminding the rulers of the "Christian states," whose "proud indolence" he deplored, of truths about successful political practice that had been known to the ancients and forgotten by themselves.

> When we consider the general respect for antiquity, and how often—to say nothing of other examples—a great price is paid for some fragments of an antique statue, which we are anxious to possess to ornament our houses with, or to set before artists who strive to imitate them in their own works; and when we see on the other hand, the wonderful examples which the history of ancient kingdoms and republics presents to us, the prodigies of virtue and of wisdom displayed by the kings, captains, citizens and legislators who have sacrificed themselves for their country—when we see these I say more admired than imitated, or so much neglected that not the least trace of this ancient virtue remains, we cannot but be at the same time as much surprised as afflicted. (Machiavelli 1992 [1513]:90)

Another understanding of the concept of originality, however, gets us to a different result. We think of individuals as "originals" if we react to them with surprise, astonishment, and even something akin to shock; it is not that every single component of their thought and behavior is, taken separately, unprecedented, but that the ensemble strikes us with a certain awkwardness and unassimilability. Machiavelli has, of course, always been treated as a shocking figure. *The Prince* was the first book to be placed on the Index of works that Roman Catholics were forbidden to read; and it was so thoroughly banned that even priests who wished to preach against it were required to obtain special leave from their bishops to read the work they were about to assail.

It was this unassimilable quality that attracted Berlin's attention. "There is something surprising about the sheer number of interpretations of Machiavelli's political opinions. There exist even now over a score of leading theories of how to interpret *The Prince* and *The Discourses*—apart from a cloud of subsidiary views and glosses" (Berlin 1978b:25). Berlin's interpretation did not exactly deny the plausibility of, say, seeing Machiavelli as somehow the begetter of Italian nationalism, as Italian commentators of the nineteenth century, such as Pasquale Villari, had done; rather, as his remarks about Vico's interpretive methods suggest, Berlin implied that that was not a particularly illuminating insight into the extraordinariness of Machiavelli. As to what would provide a deeper insight, Berlin was not concerned to add a twenty-fifth or twenty-ninth interpretation to all the rest. His interpretation was intended to answer a present-centered and essentially philosophical question, and thus to deepen the present-day reader's encounter with Machiavelli. Of course, a man who observed that he preferred the city to the salvation of his own soul was a devout patriot. Machiavelli certainly had a strong sense of Italian identity; that is, he had a strong sense that the Italians were not like the French and Spanish who so often trampled through his country. To think of him as a nationalist was, however, unlikely to prove deeply illuminating; much of the intellectual interest of nineteenth-century nationalism lies in the fact that it was very unlike the patriotism and localism of previous ages.

So, when Berlin offered his picture of Machiavelli as a moral pluralist, this was to tell us something about how we can read him, rather than to tell us much about how his contemporaries might have read him. They, to be sure, found him difficult in somewhat the same way we do. Nonetheless, his superiors in the Florentine diplomatic service did not find him unreadable, merely somewhat too enthusiastic for overly subtle plans and schemes. By the same token, his friends were surprised that he spent so long in his study of an evening, dressed in the robes of a councillor, locked as it seemed to them in conversation with long-dead sages, generals, politicians, and other heroes. They could not, however, think of him as committed to an alarming form of moral pluralism. That was a way of conceptualizing the world that they did not possess. Berlin's writing, then, offers us a Machiavelli who is original in standing out against what Berlin thought of as the great hope of all European philosophy, the hope of demonstrating that beneath (or above or beyond) the chaotic flux of experience there lay a realm of order and harmony where conflict was once and for all dissolved. That was the realm in which reason and desire, impulse and conscience, and all the goods that a person might pursue would be shown to co-exist, and indeed to imply one another. Berlin thought, though he never did much to prove, that the Platonic ambition to uncover a timeless truth in which all values would be reconciled was the dominant urge in European thought. Machiavelli was interesting, not because he set out to show that Plato was wrong and that no such reconciliation was to be had, but because he simply took it for granted. The fact that he made a devastating philosophical point without taking the trouble to do so overtly was what made him philosophically unplaceable.

What Berlin wished to extract from Machiavelli was, however, a simple and slightly brutal point. This was that there is no overarching harmony in this world, that different moral universes and different cultural attachments are compelling, even equally compelling, but irreconcilable. Machiavelli did not argue that the values of tough, patriotic little city-states were superior to those of Christian self-abnegation; nor did he argue only that the self-abnegating were likely to make poorer soldiers and less aggressive statesmen than their classical predecessors. He certainly argued the latter, and we may guess that he believed the former. What was more off-putting was his insistence that his readers had to choose. If they wished to avoid the heat of the kitchen, they should retire to the monastery. Once they had decided to enter the kitchen, they should learn to endure the heat. Two exemplary little tales, one in *The Prince*

(1992 [1531]) and one in *The Discourses* (1975 [1531]) make this clear. In the first, Machiavelli commended Cesare Borgia for the cleverness with which he had first used a particularly nasty aide, Remirro de Orco, to subdue the Romagna, and then had ordered him murdered in order to appease the population and convey the impression that the cruelties of Remirro de Orco had nothing to do with Cesare Borgia. From the second, Machiavelli drew the moral that men do not know how to be truly good or truly wicked. Giovanpaolo Baglioni had the chance to kill Pope Julius II, and in the process make himself master of the whole of central Italy. He drew back—not, as Machiavelli was at pains to insist, because he was an admirable character. He was certainly a parricide, incestuous, and in general an object of loathing to almost all who knew him. What he lacked was the nerve to do something that everyone would have found astonishing as well as appalling.

This is part and parcel of the extraordinary casualness with which Machiavelli referred to *crudelita* and *terribilita* as part of the "virtue" *(virtu)* of heroes such as Hannibal. It is not that Machiavelli thought of cruelty and the ability to terrify one's subordinates as intrinsically good or attractive. He took for granted the everyday estimate of human action, and was in that sense not a moral innovator or a moral subversive. Leo Strauss' (1978) indictment of Machiavelli as a teacher of evil is less of an indictment than one might suppose; on the one hand, he taught men that they must do evil to achieve good ends in the political arena, but on the other, he did not suggest that that somehow makes the evil less evil. Under indictment, the political innovator who does evil for the safety of the state will argue not that he has done no evil, but that he did evil so that good might come. He will not expect his soul to be saved, only his city.

The peculiarity of Berlin's capture of Machiavelli for the pluralist cause is threefold. The first peculiarity is perhaps something of a quibble. Berlin was a pluralist; Machiavelli was more nearly a dichotomist. That is, he was not so much concerned to agree that there were many ways of life, each of which seemed good to its own practitioners, as to show that the moral values officially promoted in his own time and place were inimical to the welfare of the society that promoted them. What he pointed to was not pluralism but a head-on conflict between secular, political values and other-worldly values. The upshot was not that saints and generals inhabited different worlds but that a society of saints would be preyed upon by anyone who cared to do so. The reason why one might dismiss this point as quibbling is that Berlin does not deny it. To deepen the point: There cannot be a meeting of minds between the two sides of the conflict. It is no good telling the self-abnegating saint that he will fall prey to the brigand and the pirate; he knows it already. Nor is it any good telling Hannibal that he has behaved with brutality; he knows it already. The very currency in which they are willing to deal ensures that they will reject each other's calculations.

The second peculiarity about Berlin's appropriation of Machiavelli is that, whatever Machiavelli was, he was not a liberal. I shall recur below to two familiar anxieties about Berlin's pluralism, namely its connection to liberalism and its difference from relativism, so I shall say almost nothing on this point here. Still, it is worth recalling that Machiavelli's conception of freedom was not the liberal conception of freedom. In the terms that Constant (1988 [1819]) made famous, Machiavelli was concerned with "the liberty of the ancients" rather than "the liberty of the moderns." Hobbes almost made the point a century and a half before Constant, when he distinguished between the freedom of the city and the freedom of the person (Hobbes 1968 [1651]). That is, Hobbes thought Machiavelli and the enthusiasts for republican liberty were concerned with the city's independence from outside interference; the individual might, as Hobbes insisted, be less interfered with in a loosely governed despotism such as the Ottoman Empire than in Lucca (Hobbes 1968 [1651]). This is not quite right. Machiavelli was in fact concerned with the liberty of the individual as well as the independence of the polity. Above all, however, he emphasized the citizen's immunity from the predatory activities of the upper classes, and not Hobbesian or liberal *laissez-faire*. What counted as liberty was not license to do whatever we want, so much as it was freedom from the arbitrary, selfish, corrupt, and greedy whims of those whose power outran their self-control. The Romans, in this view, possessed individual liberty; rich men did not dare to affront the honor of the wives of their social inferiors, and nobody's property or person could be considered fair game. This was tough, tightly constrained republican freedom.

The third irony of Berlin's use of Machiavelli is that Machiavelli was willing, in a way that no twentieth-century writer could sensibly be, to envisage warfare as a permanent way of life. That states were at best in a state of suspended hostility to one another did not cause him any particular anxiety. The prince addressed in *The Prince* is encouraged to avoid the self-civilizing process that contemporary manuals on princely conduct urged; he was advised to confine himself to hunting, since that was an enjoyable way to learn the lay of the land in a way that he would need in time of war. The twentieth century has certainly been a time of war, but it has also, for that very reason, been a time when the desire for peace has been stronger than at any other time in human history. Liberalism is on the whole a pacific, if not exactly a pacifist, doctrine, and one would wonder at the invocation of Machiavelli in the pluralist cause, if that invocation were to carry any acceptance of Machiavelli's bellicose enthusiasms. Of course, the truth is that it does not.

Why then is it worth dwelling, in this mildly obsessive fashion, on this one instance of Berlin's invocation of an entire gallery of historical ancestors and instances? The reason is simple enough. It is not surprising to find Berlin invoking John Stuart Mill's *On Liberty* in his essay on Mill and the ends of life

(Berlin 1959a). Mill was insistent that the ends of life were many and varied and perhaps even "contradictory." It is not surprising to find Berlin appealing to Montesquieu; Montesquieu's pluralism is most famously sociological and political, but it would be strange to deny that he had an eye both for the importance of social pluralism as the reinforcement of the separation of powers and the moderate liberty of a state such as eighteenth-century Britain, and for the sheer variety of moral attachments and preconceptions that different societies and peoples exhibited. It is far from surprising to find Berlin invoking Alexander Herzen as the touchstone of liberal sensibility. By the same token, whatever one's anxieties about the sharpness of the line between relativism and pluralism, and whatever one's confidence about Herder's place on one side or other of that line, there is nothing surprising in Berlin's attention to his work. He was perhaps the earliest articulate critic of the Enlightenment's belief in the unity of human nature, and the unity of the goal toward which anything we might call progress must be tending. But what is astonishing is Berlin's ability to find in Machiavelli—an archaic thinker, a deliberate throwback to a vanished world, and a decided skeptic about anything we might dignify with the title of human rights—an ally in the metaphysical battle between the monists and the pluralists.

RUSSIAN THINKERS

It is time to say a very little about Berlin's Russian allegiances. If simple incapacity did not deter me from attempting to say much on this theme, the tremendous eloquence of Berlin's account of Herzen, Belinsky, Turgenev, and his own contemporaries such as Pasternak would render any commentary unnecessary. A feature of Berlin's treatment of all historical figures was that he wrote as if they were present in the room and in full flood. This has one slightly discouraging effect, which is that Berlin's work is not treated as seriously by historians of ideas as it might be. Because he did not draw much of a distinction between those elements of his account that were supposed to be taken absolutely straightforwardly as contributions to the strictly historical account of the subject and those that were supposed to open a way into another mind for beginners (or the merely puzzled), the more dogged sort of reader can become impatient. The one field where this is not true is in his treatment of nineteenth-century Russian writers. Although here too Berlin relied on what one might call the direct as opposed to the contextual approach, the fact that the writers who most interested him were part of the twentieth-century political struggle between communists and liberals within and without the Soviet Union meant that any account of them and their ideas involved taking sides in what might vulgarly be called the great debate over whose fault the Russian Revolution really was. Oddly enough, Berlin was on the opposite side to one of his oldest and best friends, Leonard Schapiro, on the question. Schapiro held that it was a chronic failing of the Russian intelligentsia of the nineteenth century to seek total solutions that laid the foundation for the contempt for individual rights that was such a marked characteristic of the Bolsheviks and then the Communist Party of the Soviet Union, whereas Berlin thought that what one might call the 1848 intelligentsia displayed an ambivalence about means and ends, about the compatibility of individual emancipation and social order, that were strikingly modern in themselves and in some form central to the liberal imagination (Kelly 1998). As Kelly has argued, Western commentators throughout the years of the Cold War tended to use "intellectual" as a term of condemnation; since the Soviet Union was not entirely inept in recruiting the intellectuals of both actual and recently emancipated colonies for nationalist, anti-American and anti-British political movements, it is not hard to see why they did so. Moreover, Stalinist propaganda was quick to attempt retrospectively to recruit radical nineteenth-century intellectuals as forerunners of modern communism. In a manner of speaking, Berlin's aim was to rescue writers such as Herzen from this embrace by people whom he would have loathed; writers on the other side were less inclined to dispute with Stalin the title to their memory but were more inclined to explain why they had rendered themselves vulnerable for such a takeover (Malia 1961).

The most famous of all Berlin's essays on Russian thinkers is the least relevant to this argument. *The Hedgehog and the Fox* (Berlin 1978c [1953]) explored the head-on conflict between Tolstoy's passionate conviction that he was called to give the world a unified moral vision and put all his rhetorical and literary talents behind it and his complete inability to see the world in such a unitary fashion. The title, as the whole world knows by now, comes from a fragment from a Greek poet, Archilocus, to the effect that the fox knows many things, but the hedgehog knows one big thing (Berlin 1978c [1953]:22). Tolstoy, in this view, was a fox who drove himself mad by trying to be a hedgehog. His genius was to be a fox, and it is that ability to see the world in a fragmentary but aesthetically coherent fashion (to the extent that art confers unity) that makes a novel such as *War and Peace* a masterpiece. Conversely, readers of *Anna Karenina* are not infrequently moved to complain that the novel is artistically damaged by Tolstoy's determination that the adulterous Anna shall come to a bad end. However that might be, my point is that in this one essay, Berlin's anti-monism is not a political doctrine, nor much freighted with metaphysics, but rather an insight into Tolstoy's increasingly fragile grasp on reality in his old age. It is of course a moral, metaphysical, and political doctrine elsewhere and often.

The more central essays, from the standpoint of politics, are Berlin's discussions of Herzen and Turgenev. Here I must admit to an uncertainty. Ignatieff (1998) maintains that it was Turgenev to whom Berlin felt closest. This strikes me as less than entirely persuasive because Berlin's accounts of Herzen (Berlin 1955, 1956b, 1968) seem to me more deeply felt, less apologetic, and far more convincing than the picture of Turgenev that he presents in *Fathers and Children* (Berlin 1972b). However, this raises only the question, convincing about what? If Berlin's liberalism is at least as much a matter of sensibility and attachment as it is a devotion to theories of freedom, human rights, political democracy, and the usual subject matter of political philosophy, what sensibility does that liberalism invoke, and to whom might it be most passionately and unswervingly attached? In *Fathers and Children*, Berlin devoted much of his energy, as had Turgenev, to the task of explaining to the young and enraged that the elderly liberal is not merely cowardly, not merely unable to give up his comforts. The liberal is torn between two distinct impulses; the first is to side with the violent indignation of the young and to assist in their destruction of the existing order; the existing order is, after all, always sufficiently replete with injustice, cruelty, oppression, and the rest to justify any amount of destruction; but the second impulse is the opposite. The existing order contains as much of civilization as we possess, and its cruelties can be palliated or even eliminated in due course, as can many of its injustices. The liberal cannot help noticing that people filled with indignation about the existing brutalities and injustices might be likely to commit a number of brutalities and injustices themselves, perhaps out of a failure to hit only and exactly the right targets for attack, perhaps out of a regrettable tendency to get carried away by zeal, and perhaps worst of all out of acquiring a taste for violently dispatching their enemies.

Ignatieff (1998) suggests that the identification with Turgenev that is visible in Berlin's Romanes Lecture of 1971 represents a liberalism under attack. That is true enough, but it marked something of a retreat from the more exuberant liberalism that Berlin had earlier derived from Herzen. Whether Herzen was in any straightforward sense a liberal is a large question that we may decently duck on this occasion. We can agree that he was a populist, a socialist, and sometimes a revolutionary, and still say that he possessed what Berlin considered the archetype of the liberal sensibility. For Herzen's creed was the importance of rescuing individuals from every form of oppression, including the oppression of duty, sociability, and solidarity. Even to call it a creed is something of a mistake, since creeds were another of the oppressions that Herzen was eager to battle. When he described himself as waging "a little guerilla war" against all restraints on individuality, he meant it. Herzen knew that this was a reckless way to think, and that one might easily be led into contradiction and confusion; but when praised by Dostoevsky for writing dialogues in which Herzen himself was always being driven into corners by his interlocutors, he replied, "but that is the point." More than a few of the building blocks of Berlin's liberalism were explicitly part of Herzen's anti-credal creed: the antipathy to distant goals that might be made the excuse for vast sacrifices of present happiness; a skepticism about abstractions, even including freedom, justice, democracy, and the nation; an insistence on the importance of small, concrete happinesses; a preference for the empirical and felt over the theoretical and rational.

LIBERALISM AND PLURALISM

Finally, what of the theoretical structure behind Berlin's liberalism? Is it proper that he should be remembered as the theorist of negative liberty and the writer who showed that pluralism and liberalism were natural allies? No short answer can be persuasive, and what follows is inevitably dogmatic. Berlin wrote a good deal in defense of a certain sort of liberalism, though not all of it was in an academic vein. Thus, *On the Pursuit of the Ideal* (Berlin 1988) was a mildly polemical attack on utopian thinking, delivered to a large audience who had come to see Berlin receive the Agnelli Prize for contributions to European ethics. Essays such as *John Stuart Mill and the Ends of Life* (Berlin 1959a) were partly about their ostensible subject matter—in this case John Stuart Mill and the inconsistency between Mill's official utilitarianism and his actual passion for individual freedom—and partly about the nature of freedom and a liberal society. The individual thinker illuminated the larger topic, and the larger topic framed the individual thinker. The discussions of Vico and Herder, like the lectures on Romanticism, were part of a larger strategy of casting doubt on some of the cherished beliefs of the Enlightenment, though always in such a way as to preserve many others.

What this means is that Berlin's liberalism is not like that of, say, Rawls (1971, 1983). Whereas Rawls deduced or at least derived the two principles of justice that for him define the basic framework of a liberal social, political, and economic order, Berlin supported a kind of liberalism with essentially cultural and historical arguments. Although he was, of course, concerned with human rights, he never thought it plausible to define liberalism in terms of its attachment to rights, save insofar as an attachment to rights is both instrumentally a way of enhancing freedom and expressively a way of insisting on the importance of freedom as a central human good. Berlin, like Herzen before him, was content to agree that the liberal's passion for individual freedom is historically, geographically, and culturally local, without thinking that this in any way impugns liberal ideals. That the individual with whom liberalism is concerned is a historical novelty does not diminish the appeal of freedom, any more than the fact that we were born rather recently and will not live forever excuses an unconcern with living happily and decently while we are alive. To say, as commentators sometimes do (Gray 1995), that Berlin's liberalism is not "Enlightenment liberalism" is both true and misleading (Kocis 1989, Galipeau 1994).

To the extent that the Enlightenment is identified with the view that morality is timeless, rationally derived, known a priori to be valid (or true), universal, and therefore no more culturally variable than mathematical truth, Berlin was a critic of the Enlightenment. He did not deny that human nature is in many ways uniform; Shylock's famous question, "If you prick us, do we not bleed?" is as powerful a question as Shylock supposed. Still, Berlin agreed with the Romantic critics of the Enlightenment that talk of "Man" in the abstract was unhelpful, and that what we encounter is human beings in an almost infinite variety. The insistence on this point was what Berlin found congenial in Marx's work; what he rejected was the semireligious faith in the existence of an ultimate solution to all of humanity's ills. Again, then, if utopianism is a feature of Enlightenment thought, Berlin's anti-utopianism is anti-Enlightenment.

What is not anti-Enlightenment is Berlin's hostility to irrationalism. Berlin's anti-rationalism was not irrationalism; he had, one might think, a great dislike of the cruelty that so often goes along with irrationalism. He could not but think that de Maistre was a precursor of Fascism, and that was almost the end of the matter. He was not much concerned to dissect de Maistre so as to distinguish the rationalizable, Burkean elements in his thought from the violently theocratic and irrationalist ones; it was as though the latter aspect of de Maistre struck him so forcefully that argument began and ended there (Berlin 1990). If what we are offered is anti-rationalist but not anti-rational, contextualist but not narrowly local, what sort of liberalism is it, and how is this cultural and historical account of it sustained by such relatively abstract essays as *Two Concepts of Liberty*?

The answer is not easy to sustain, but in outline it is simple enough. Berlin's inaugural lecture was not, appearances to the contrary, concerned to distinguish between two concepts of liberty, let alone to defend one against the other. The lecture was more nearly a broadside against everything Berlin deplored and a gesture in favor of all the things he wished to defend. There is not, and cannot be, one concept of liberty that holds together the Stoic conception of the freedom available to the slave whose self-control makes him freer than his master, the Hegelian/Marxian thought that freedom is the consciousness of necessity, the supposed collectivist conception stemming from Rousseau's thought that a person is free when obeying the *moi commun*, and the several other "positive" conceptions that Berlin presented to his hearers. Conversely, the several glosses on negative liberty that he offered did not identify one negative conception, let alone one that could neatly be set against one positive conception. Therefore, the conclusion to draw is not that *Two Concepts* was confused but that it was doing so many different things at once that even its author was not wholly in command of the plot. That may sound either frivolous or faintly insulting, but it is not meant to be so; if Herzen was prepared to argue against himself in the hope of illuminating a truth that could not be gained by simpler means, there is no reason why Berlin should not have been doing the same thing.

This, however, brings us to one of the standard cruxes. If Berlin was arguing for a kind of liberalism suited to a pluralist culture such as our own, why did he not confront more directly the difficulty that all commentators have pointed to, namely that pluralism is not particularly the natural ally of liberalism? That there are conservative varieties of pluralism is not news. The Ottoman Empire's millet system suffered non-Moslem communities to survive and, up to a point, to flourish. David Hume's defense of a conservatively understood balance of powers within the British constitution was not in Berlin's sense liberal, since it privileged order over liberty. It certainly advocated as much liberty as order would allow, and defended a secular, tolerant, accommodating society as good for both commerce and individual happiness. It was not, however, a pluralism that simultaneously claimed that values were multiple and that freedom was somehow special. Berlin seems to have contradicted himself in a way that Hume did not. In fact, appearances are again deceptive. Berlin's thought was culturally local. Once we have a society in which individuals are capable of feeling stifled by having to accommodate themselves to the prevailing norms simply to keep the peace, pluralism implies liberalism. This is what one might call the liberalism of non-suffocation; it is the liberalism implied in Herzen's revolt not only against the tsarist police but also against all the overbearing calls to acknowledge our duty in which nineteenth-century political writing was so rich. It is not so much philosophically grounded as culturally and psychologically grounded. The distinction between positive and negative liberty then turns into several distinctions, all of them doing a good deal of work. The refusal of the "retreat to the inner citadel" that characterizes Berlin's rejection of Stoicism is an affirmation of the modern confidence in our ability to act on and in the world. The rejection of the Rousseauian wish for a liberty that we can only share with fellow citizens is an affirmation of Constant's liberty of the moderns. The insistence that liberty is not justice, not equality, not democracy is Berlin's way of reminding us that we may have all of these and still be oppressed in the ways Mill and Herzen identified. The repudiation of an account of being one's own master that equates it with the control of our lower selves by higher and enlightened selves is Berlin's way of defending the empirical, here-and-now individual and his or her aspirations against anyone else's attempt to second-guess them. In some situations, pluralism would not support liberalism because these aspirations would be unattainable or would not be conceptually coherent. Where they are coherent, attainable, and deeply rooted in our sense of ourself, the connection holds.

This will not reassure critics who have thought that Berlin was doing an orthodox kind of political philosophy. The objection that liberty is always one thing, subject only to different understandings of what obstacles we wish to be free *from* and of what we wish to be free to *do*, is familiar (MacCallum 1967, Gray 1980), but it is beside the point. For one thing, it is not an entirely successful analysis of liberty—not all obstacles from which we may wish to be free are obstacles to freedom; for another, it only deflects the argument onto the question whether a purported obstacle really is an obstacle. The Stoic insists that no conventionally characterized obstacle is one; the Stoic's critic insists that most really are. More importantly, Berlin's case rested on the assumption that conventional philosophical analysis could not make a sufficient moral or political difference. It could perhaps help us see what might make such a difference, but it did not change anything itself. Whether Berlin was offering an unconventional philosophical analysis or engaging in a polemical exercise of another kind entirely may not matter very much; locating the difference between academic philosophical analysis and Berlin's work matters rather more. In so doing, the secondary literature is of limited use; the one indispensable aid is Hardy's meticulous bibliographical work (1997).

Visit the *Annual Reviews home page* at
http://www.AnnualReviews.org.

Literature Cited

Berlin I. 1939. Verification. *Proc. Aristot. Soc.* 39:225–48

Berlin I. 1950. Empirical propositions and hypothetical statements. *Mind* 59:289–312

Berlin I. 1954. *Historical Inevitability.* Auguste Comte Memorial Trust Lecture No. 1. Oxford, UK: Oxford Univ. Press

Berlin I. 1955. Herzen and Bakunin on individual liberty. In *Continuity and Change in Russian and Soviet Thought*, ed. EJ Simmons, pp. 437–99. Cambridge, MA: Harvard Univ. Press

Berlin I. 1956a. Equality. *Proc. Aristot. Soc.* 56:301–26

Berlin I. 1956b. Introduction. In *"From the Other Shore" and "The Russian People and Socialism,"* A Herzen, pp. vii–xxiii. London: Weidenfeld & Nicolson

Berlin I. 1958a. *Two Concepts of Liberty.* Oxford, UK: Clarendon

Berlin I. 1958b. *Chaim Weizmann.* London: Weidenfeld & Nicolson

Berlin I. 1959a. *John Stuart Mill and the Ends of Life.* London: Counc. Christ. and Jews

Berlin I. 1959b. *The Life and Opinions of Moses Hess.* Lucien Woff Memorial Lecture. Cambridge, UK: Heffer

Berlin I. 1964. From hope and fear set free. In *Proc. Aristotelian Soc. 1963–4*, pp. 1–30 Oxford, UK: Blackwell

Berlin I. 1968. Introduction. In *My Past and Thoughts*, A Herzen, pp. xiii–xxxvii. London: Chatto & Windus

Berlin I. 1969. A note on Vico's concept of knowledge. In *Giambattista Vico: An International Symposium*, ed. G Tagliacozzo, HV White, pp. 371–77. Baltimore, MD: Johns Hopkins Press, reprinted in Berlin 1978b

Berlin I. 1970. Benjamin Disraeli, Karl Marx, and the search for identity. *Trans. Jew. Hist. Soc. Engl.* 22:29–49

Berlin I. 1972a. The originality of Machiavelli. In *Studies on Machiavelli*, ed. MP Gilmore, pp. 149–206. Florence: Sansoni, reprinted in Berlin 1978b

Berlin I. 1972b. *Fathers and Children: Turgenev and the Liberal Predicament.* Oxford, UK: Clarendon

Berlin I. 1973. J. L. Austin and the early beginnings of Oxford philosophy. In *Essays on*

J.L. Austin, I Berlin et al, pp. 1–16. Oxford, UK: Clarendon

Berlin I. 1976. *Vico and Herder.* London: Hogarth

Berlin I. 1978a. *Concepts and Categories.* London: Chatto & Windus

Berlin I. 1978b. *Against the Current.* London: Chatto & Windus

Berlin I. 1978c (1953). *The Hedgehog and the Fox.* London: Weidenfeld & Nicolson

Berlin I. 1988. *On the Pursuit of the Ideal.* Turin, Italy: Giovanni Agnelli Found

Berlin I. 1990. Joseph de Maistre and the origins of Fascism. In *The Crooked Timber of Humanity*, pp. 91–174. London: John Murray

Berlin I. 1996 (1939). *Karl Marx.* London: Harper Collins. 4th ed.

Berlin I. 1998 (1980). *Personal Impressions.* London: Pimlico Books

Constant B. 1988 (1819). The liberty of the ancients compared with that of the moderns. In *Political Writings*, ed. B Fontana, pp. 307–28. Cambridge, UK: Cambridge Univ. Press

Galipeau C. 1994. *Isaiah Berlin's Liberalism.* Oxford: Clarendon

Gray JN. 1980. Negative and positive liberty. *Polit. Stud.* 28:507–26

Gray JN. 1995. *Isaiah Berlin.* London: Fontana

Hardy H. 1997. A bibliography of Isaiah Berlin. In *Against the Current,* I Berlin, pp. 356–89. London: Pimlico. 2nd ed.

Hobbes T. 1968 (1651). *Leviathan.* Harmondsworth: Penguin. 729 pp.

Ignatieff M. 1998. *Isaiah Berlin.* London: Chatto & Windus

Kelly A. 1998. *Toward Another Shore.* New Haven, CT: Yale Univ. Press

Kocis R. 1989. *A Critical Appraisal of Sir Isaiah Berlin's Political Philosophy.* Lewiston, ME: Edwin Mellen

MacCallum GC Jr. 1967. Negative and positive freedom. *Philos. Rev.* 76:312–34

Machiavelli N. 1975 (1531). *Discourses on Livy.* London: Walker, Routledge

Machiavelli N. 1992 (1531). *The Prince,* ed. RM Adams. New York: Norton

Malia M. 1961. *Alexander Herzen and the Birth of Russian Socialism.* New Haven, CT: Yale Univ. Press

Mill JS. 1981 (1873). *Autobiography.* Vol. 1 of *The Collected Works of John Stuart Mill.* Toronto: Univ. Toronto Press

Nicholas HG. 1981. *Washington Despatches, 1941–1945,* London: Weidenfeld & Nicolson

Pompa L. 1975. *A Study of the New Science.* Cambridge, UK: Cambridge Univ. Press

Rawls J. 1971. *A Theory of Justice.* Cambridge, MA: Harvard Univ. Press

Rawls J. 1983. *Political Liberalism.* New York: Columbia Univ. Press

Strauss L. 1978. *Thoughts on Machiavelli.* Chicago: Univ. Chicago Press. 348 pp.

Annu. Rev. Polit. Sci. 1999. 2:363–67
Copyright © 1999 by Noel Annan

ISAIAH BERLIN (1909–1997)

Noel Annan

45 Ranelagh Grove, London SW1W8PB, England

NOTE

This talk was originally presented at a memorial service honoring Isaiah Berlin at the Hampstead Synagogue, England, on January 14, 1998.

When I heard that Isaiah Berlin had died, I sat down and read the letters we had written each other since 1950, and he lived again. He wrote as he talked, and he was the most dazzling talker of his generation. Strangers might hardly understand a word because his tongue had to sprint to keep up with the pace of his thoughts. Ideas, similes, metaphors cascaded over each other. His talk was sustained by a fabulous memory for names, events, and the motives of the participants in his stories. It was like watching a pageant. As Dr. Johnson said of Richard Savage, "at no time in his life was it any part of his character to be the first of the company that desired to separate." At New College and All Souls he talked until his exhausted guest tottered to bed, only to find Berlin sitting on the end of it, unwilling to bring the evening to an end. On the historic occasion when he called on Anna Akhmatova they talked straight through the night.

No one else was remotely like him. Of course he had charm, but he had more than that. He was a magus, a magician when he spoke, and it was for his character and personality as much as for his published works that so many honors fell upon him. The *Evening Standard* spoke truth when it said, "the respectful sadness that met his death and the enormous regard in which he was held shows that intellectuals can still be prized as civilising influences in Britain." He was loved by people with whom he had nothing in common—millionaires, obscure writers, world-famous musicians, public figures, and young unknown scholars to whom he listened. Whatever the circle, he civilized it; and the world is a little less civilized now that he has left it.

Generosity came naturally to him. He was never sneaky or malevolent as a critic. Indeed he tried too hard, perhaps, to avoid giving offense. "I enjoy being able to praise," he said. He never intrigued to meet the geniuses of his time—Freud, Einstein, Virginia Woolf, Russell, Pasternak, Stravinsky—and he had no shame in admitting that he was greatly excited when he did meet them. His oldest friends, Stuart Hampshire or Stephen Spender, were especially dear to him. Yet he had an eye for human failings and noted feet of clay, even of people he esteemed. He did not censure, but he did not condone ungentle behavior or sexual exhibitionism. "I feel acutely uncomfortable," he wrote me, "in the presence of Beaverbrook, Cherwell, Radcliffe or Driberg." People who rejected equality as a goal were deeply unsympathetic to him. Equality had to give way often to liberty, but so did liberty sometimes to equality. For instance, he thought that the price England paid for the public schools was too high.

Nicolas Nabokov accused him of liking bores too much. But then Isaiah was meticulous in obeying the obligations of a scholar. No one was ever turned away who came to him genuinely wishing to discuss a problem. To watch him at Mishkenot Shc'ananim in Jerusalem, spending hours with those who queued to seek his advice, was to realize that he honored anyone in search of truth. Those who have never believed, he wrote of the days when the young Oxford philosophers met with Austin and Ayer, that they were discovering for the first time some new truth that might have profound influence upon philosophy, "those who have never been under the spell of this kind of illusion, even for a short while, have not known true intellectual happiness."

Very few people are able to write unforgettably about liberty. Rousseau did; John Stuart Mill did; and in our own times, Schumpeter and EM Forster did. But, as Forster once said of himself in a parody of Landor: "I warmed both hands before the fire of life,/And put it out." Isaiah made it blaze. He took the unfashionable view that liberty meant not being impeded by others. He distrusted Rousseau's and Hegel's theory of positive freedom as a perversion of common sense. To deny free will—to believe in the inevitability of a historical process—to portray man as imprisoned by the impersonal forces of history—that ran against our deepest experience. He believed the creation of the state of Israel proved that history is not predetermined. Israel owed its existence to Weizmann, yet all Weizmann's schemes were swept away by fortuitous events. And what could be less inevitable than the survival of Britain in 1940? To Berlin, the very methods that Marxists, economists, and sociologists used prevented them from discovering what is at the heart of men and women. He distrusted technocrats in government and sapient reports with their self-confident proposals for restructuring institutions. That was why he did not pontificate on daily issues. Monetarism, social security schemes, were not for him. He disappointed President Kennedy by not advancing views on the necessary number of ICBMs.

But there was one public issue on which he left no one in doubt. Above all, Isaiah was a Jew, and he never forgave those who forgot to conceal their anti-Semitism, the nastier ways of snubs, pin-pricks, acts of exclusion which we Gentiles inflict upon Jews, and in so doing defile ourselves. He was a Zionist precisely because he felt that however well Jews were treated and accepted by the country they lived in, they felt uneasy and insecure. That was why they needed a country of their own where Jews could live like other nations. As he lay dying, he declared that the partition of the Holy Land was the only solution to give Palestinians rights to their land and give Israel Jerusalem as its capital city with the Muslim holy places under a Muslim authority, and an Arab quarter under UN protection. He never felt the smallest difficulty in being loyal to Judah and loyal to Britain. When he worked during the war in Washington, he told American Zionists that he was the servant of the British government—but its servant, not its conscript. At any time, he could resign if he decided British policy was unforgivable. He was proud to belong to Britain, to that country which Weizmann had praised for its moderation, dislike of extremes, a humane democracy.

There was another claimant for his loyalty—Oxford. He thought he owed it a debt. He paid that debt when, against the advice of his most intimate friends, he agreed to become head of a new Oxford college. Who can doubt that it was Isaiah's personality that convinced Mac Bundy of the Ford Foundation and Isaac and Leonard Wolfson, renowned for their princely generosity, to build and endow a new college with Isaiah as President? President, not Master. The Master of Wolfson sounded to Isaiah too much like a Scottish laird, and he did not fancy himself in a kilt. Many of the chores he left to the faithful Michael Brock; but it was Isaiah who negotiated the deal with the University and strangled some dingy proposals for shackling the new place. And it was Isaiah who traveled 4000 miles to interview architects, select materials, and convince the 60 Fellows with barely a dissenting voice.

He was a man of invincible modesty. But for Henry Hardy, we would never have had his collected works. He genuinely believed that he was overrated and deserved few of the honors he was given. "I have a pathological dislike of personal publicity," he wrote me. "It is like a terror of bats or spiders. I am not a public figure like AJP Taylor, Graham Greene, Arthur Schlesinger, or Kenneth Clark. Nor an ideologue like Tawney, Cole, Oakeshott. Perhaps not as bad as Crossman and a good many others thought me to be, a well-disposed amiable rattle." For years he had no entry in *Who's Who*, until he found that the entry form he had left lying around had been filled in by Maurice Bowra, with scandalous fictitious achievements. Then he gave in.

To have lived without music would have been to him a nightmare. Unthinkable to live without Bach, unendurable without Beethoven and Schubert. He loved Verdi for the uninhibited tunes and for Verdi's hatred of aristocratic brutality and tyranny. No one, he thought, had ever played the Beethoven posthumous quartets like the Busch ensemble. He admitted that Toscanini was not the man for the thick brew of Wagner; but when one saw Toscanini as well as heard him, the authority was such that, so he wrote me, "this and this only was the truth—the intensity, the seriousness and the sublime *terribilità* totally subdued you." Walter, Klemperer, and Mahler and the luxuriant valleys of Furtwängler, yes—but Toscanini was Everest—compared with him, he said, the rest were not fit to tie his shoelaces, mere Apennines covered with villas. Yet in his later years he found a friend, an intellectual as well as a profound musician, in Alfred Brendel; and he and his old friend Isaac Stern have honored him today.

He was at his happiest in a small group of intimate friends in Oxford colleges or sitting in a corner of the Russian Tea Room on 57th Street a few blocks down from the offices of the *New York Review of Books* with Robert Silvers, Stuart Hampshire, and the Lowells. In Oxford as a bachelor—in the days before the war he was always called Shaya—renowned as the most amusing young don in Oxford—in those days his door was always open. Colleagues, pupils, friends from London dropped in to gossip. He loved gossip. An election to a chair in Oxford or Cambridge would inspire him to give a dramatic performance of the proceedings. The treachery of Bloggs, the craven behavior of Stiggins, the twitterings of the outside electors, and when it came to the vote, the *volte-face*, the defection of those you had imagined were your closest allies. Brought up to imagine that such proceedings were sacred and secret, priggish Cambridge visitors such as myself reeled.

What made those excursions into fantasy all the more enchanting was Isaiah's irrepressible sense of humor. It was not English humor. It came from the Russian part of his make-up; from Gogol, from Chekhov. He loved jokes. He loved games. Who was a hedgehog, who was a fox? What is the difference between a cad and a bounder? When others were maddened by the perverse, egoistic, self-satisfied speeches in a college meeting, Isaiah reveled in them—to him they revealed the perennial eccentricity of human beings. Let none of us, however, be deceived. The lot of human beings, he saw, was tragic. And why? They are made of crooked timber.

As the years pass, bachelor life in college becomes exhausting, and in 1956 occurred the greatest stroke of good fortune that ever befell him. He married Aline. She transformed his life without changing it—if the contradiction be permitted. She gave him what he had always needed: love. As solicitous as she was beautiful, she caressed his existence in Albany, in Portofino, and in Headington. Like him, she disliked ostentation. Aline had been a great competitor when she was golf champion of France, but she never competed with Isaiah. She was there as the setting in which he shone—perpetually anxious that all should go well for him, not for her. She brought him a family, her children Michel Strauss, Peter and Philippe Halban, and her young Gunzbourg cousins, for whom he was a new uncle. To the delight of Isaiah's friends, they created a new persona, calling him "Ton-ton Isaïe."

And now he is gone. If I have not spoken sufficiently of his defense of liberty or pluralism, or of his detestation of cruelty and ruthlessness, it is because I speak of him as a friend. Political thinkers and intellectuals, so I believe, have not yet understood how disquieting is his contention that good ends conflict. Isaiah Berlin was original, and he is as hard to come to terms with as Machiavelli or Hume. All I can say is that he seems to me to have offered the truest and most moving interpretation of life that my own generation made.

And I must add this. I owe everything to my teachers. They taught me to learn and, if I got above myself, how much more I had to learn. I was never, of course, one of Isaiah's students, but I never failed to learn from him. He taught me to think more clearly, to feel more deeply, to hope, and to put my trust in life.

Visit the *Annual Reviews home page* at
http://www.AnnualReviews.org.

Annu. Rev. Polit. Sci. 1999. 2:369–404
Copyright © 1999 by Annual Reviews. All rights reserved

HISTORICAL INSTITUTIONALISM IN COMPARATIVE POLITICS

Kathleen Thelen

Department of Political Science, Northwestern University, Evanston, Illinois 60208;
e-mail: thelen@nwu.edu

KEY WORDS: path dependency, rational choice, institutional change, critical junctures,
            policy feedbacks

ABSTRACT

This article provides an overview of recent developments in historical institutionalism. First, it reviews some distinctions that are commonly drawn between the "historical" and the "rational choice" variants of institutionalism and shows that there are more points of tangency than typically assumed. However, differences remain in how scholars in the two traditions approach empirical problems. The contrast of rational choice's emphasis on institutions as coordination mechanisms that generate or sustain equilibria versus historical institutionalism's emphasis on how institutions emerge from and are embedded in concrete temporal processes serves as the foundation for the second half of the essay, which assesses our progress in understanding institutional formation and change. Drawing on insights from recent historical institutional work on "critical junctures" and on "policy feedbacks," the article proposes a way of thinking about institutional evolution and path dependency that provides an alternative to equilibrium and other approaches that separate the analysis of institutional stability from that of institutional change.

INTRODUCTION

Institutional analysis has a distinguished pedigree in comparative politics, and the "new" institutionalist literature of the past two decades has both sustained this venerable tradition and deepened our understanding of the role of institutions in political life. At the same time, recent work has given rise to new debates. It is now conventional to distinguish three different varieties of institutionalism: rational choice institutionalism, historical institutionalism, and socio-

1094-2939/99/0616-0369$08.00

logical institutionalism.[1] Each of these three schools in fact represents a sprawling literature characterized by tremendous internal diversity, and it is often also difficult to draw hard and fast lines between them. The differences that have been identified amount to tendencies that apply unevenly across particular authors within each school of thought (Hall & Taylor 1996). The walls dividing the three perspectives have also been eroded by "border crossers" who have resisted the tendencies toward cordoning these schools off from each other and who borrow liberally (and often fruitfully) where they can, in order to answer specific empirical questions. A few examples will suffice to illustrate this point.

First, a group of prominent theorists working out of a rational choice perspective have become proponents of a more eclectic approach that combines elements of deductive theory—the hallmark of rational choice—with an explicit attempt to contextualize the analysis in ways that historical institutionalists have long advocated (Bates et al 1998b). This strategy, which they call analytic narratives, represents an attempt to construct explanations of empirical events through analyses that "respect the specifics of time and place but within a framework that both disciplines the detail and appropriates it for purposes that transcend the particular story" (Levi 1999). The analyses offered thus incorporate elements of deduction and induction in ways that overcome traditional distinctions between historical institutionalism's characteristic focus on specific contextual conditions and rational choice's characteristic search for generalizable features of political behavior rooted in the incentive structures that individuals face.

A second illustration of border crossing is the equally important impact of rational choice on the work of many historical institutionalists. One development has been an enhanced appreciation of the need for explanations that rest on firm micro foundations. Although much macro-historical work was already implicitly sensitive to these issues, articulating the micro-foundational logic of the arguments offered was not always a top priority, and recent work reflects a heightened appreciation for such issues. Many historical institutionalists have also taken on board the notion that institutions that solve collective action problems are particularly important in understanding political outcomes (Rothstein 1996:159). This has long been a central concern of rational choice theory, and it has set an important agenda for historical institutionalists as well. Thus, an increasing number of historical studies focus precisely on explaining the emergence and persistence of institutions that do (or do not) facilitate coordination among employers and other groups (see e.g. Hall 1994, Thelen & Kume 1999).

---

[1]The best treatment of the defining features, as well as the characteristic strengths and weaknesses, of each is in Hall & Taylor (1996). Other useful reviews include Lichbach & Zuckerman (1997), Immergut (1998), Rothstein (1996), Ikenberry (1994), Kato (1996b), and Remmer (1997).

Third, there has been some important borrowing and cross-fertilization between historical institutionalism and sociological institutionalism. The works that lie at this intersection often embrace a more expansive view of institutions, not just as strategic context but as a set of shared understandings that affect the way problems are perceived and solutions are sought.[2] Katzenstein's analysis of the evolution of Japanese security policy, for example, shows how collectively held norms define appropriate conduct, shape actor identities, and influence actor interests (1996:23), and in doing so, "inform how political actors define what they want to accomplish" (1996:ix). Katzenstein roots his cultural approach in a political analysis of how some norms (and not others) came to be institutionalized, and so his perspective resonates especially with those versions of institutional sociology that specifically incorporate considerations of power and/or legitimacy in explaining how institutions emerge and are reproduced (e.g. Fligstein 1991, DiMaggio 1988, Stinchcombe 1997). In sum, there have been some rather fruitful developments at the intersection of these various schools of institutionalism, and in my view historical institutionalism has been enriched by encounters with alternative perspectives.

This article provides an overview of recent developments within the historical institutional tradition. Given the vast scholarship in this area, this tour is necessarily selective. I attempt to capture the current state of the literature in two passes. First, I review some distinctions that are commonly drawn between the "historical" and the "rational" choice variants of institutionalism. This exercise reveals that there are more points of tangency than commonly assumed. However, differences remain, and here I focus on the difference between rational choice's emphasis on the coordinating functions of institutions (generating or maintaining equilibria) versus historical institutionalism's emphasis on how institutions emerge from and are embedded in concrete temporal processes. This discussion serves as the foundation for the second half of the essay, in which I revisit one of the key frontiers in historical institutionalism (identified in Thelen & Steinmo 1992) and assess the progress that has been made in our understanding of institutional formation and change. Taking up an important challenge by Orren & Skowronek (1994), and drawing on insights from recent historical institutional work on critical junctures and on policy feedbacks, I propose a way of thinking about institutional evolution and path dependency that provides an alternative to equilibrium and other approaches that separate the analysis of institutional stability from that of institutional change.

---

[2]Some of this literature also relates to ongoing work by rational choice theorists that emphasizes the role of culture in defining "focal points" that influence which of a number of possible equilibria is actually achieved (Ferejohn 1991, Greif 1994, Bates et al 1998a).

RED HERRINGS AND REAL ISSUES

Theoretical Versus Empirical Work

One of the lines that is frequently drawn between historical institutionalism and rational choice institutionalism is between "theoretical" and "empirical" work. In a well-known critique, Green & Shapiro (1994) charge that rational choice has produced elegant theories but has generated little to explain real observed events. From the other side, rational choice theorists have often argued that historical institutionalists are engaged in something less than theory building; they are stringing details together, "merely telling stories." Even where the distinction is not drawn so starkly, the assertion is that the difference is fundamental. Thus, for example, Levi argues (in opposition presumably to historical institutionalism) that rational choice is "almost always willing to sacrifice nuance for generalizability [and] detail for logic" (1997a:21).

This dichotomy is often exaggerated, and in my view it is misplaced, for the best work in both perspectives is concerned with generating hypotheses that are then brought to bear on empirical phenomena. For example, Luebbert's (1991) analysis of the origins of fascism, social democracy, and liberal democracy is based on a comparative analysis of class relations in the interwar period in Europe. Combining comparative method with close historical process tracing in individual cases, Luebbert singles out as the crucial explanatory variable the issue of how the landed peasantry was mobilized politically. Where working-class–based parties allied themselves with the landed peasantry, this produced the mass base necessary for the establishment of social democratic regimes. By contrast, where social democrats failed to forge this alliance, the landed peasantry turned against the working class and provided the mass base on which fascism grew. One can disagree with his findings, but Luebbert's work is an exemplary model of the testing, through the comparative method, of a strong and clear hypothesis that is obviously capable of being falsified.

Another example is Collier & Collier's (1991) impressive study of regime transformation in Latin America. Based on structured comparisons and historical process tracing for individual cases, they found that differences in patterns of labor incorporation were key to the type of regime that emerged. Like Luebbert's work, this study was not meant to capture every detail; on the contrary, Collier & Collier's account is precisely designed to probe the plausibility of alternative hypotheses. Much is thus lost in terms of a comprehensive history of each country, but the payoff is a set of general propositions about the way in which labor incorporation affected subsequent regime outcomes across a number of countries.

Many other works could be invoked that use the comparative historical method to sort out the causal mechanisms behind observed empirical patterns (see the discussion, below, of the critical junctures literature). All of them "go beyond conventional history's preoccupation with historical particularity and aim for theoretical generalization" (Rueschemeyer et al 1992:4). In this, they share much with rational choice analyses as characterized by Levi, sacrificing much detail in order to identify general causal patterns that hold across a number of countries.

Conversely, rational choice work in comparative politics arguably has become more empirical over time. For example, the authors of the "analytic narratives" project mentioned above specifically emphasize that the papers they present are "problem driven, not theory driven; they are motivated by a desire to account for particular events or outcomes. They are devoted to the exploration of cases, not to the elaboration of theory..." (Bates et al 1998b:11). Some of the analyses are comparative, others focus on single cases; however, like good single case studies by historical institutionalists, the latter use close analysis of critical cases to illuminate important general issues.

Although the difference between the historical and rational choice variants of institutionalism cannot be summed up accurately in a strict dichotomy of "empirically" versus "theoretically" oriented work, there do appear to be some differences between the two traditions' approaches to theory building. First, most historical institutionalists are working at the level of mid-range theory of the sort that Bendix and others have advocated. Often, though not always (e.g. Rueschemeyer et al 1992, Karl 1997), this involves focusing on a limited range of cases that are unified in space and/or time, for example, explaining transitions to democracy in Eastern Europe (Stark & Bruszt 1998) or the effects of new international pressures on the political economies of the advanced industrial democracies (Hall 1994). Rational choice theorists, by contrast, sometimes aspire to produce more general (even universal) theoretical claims[3] or use historical examples not so much for their intrinsic importance (e.g. as "critical cases") but to demonstrate how widely applicable are the theoretical claims (e.g. Knight 1992, Levi 1988, Tsebelis 1990). Still, the object of both is to test theoretical propositions against observed phenomena, in order not only to explain the cases at hand but also to refine the theory.

A second difference with respect to theory building lies in the ways that historical institutionalists and rational choice institutionalists approach hypothesis formation. Very frequently, historical institutionalists begin with empirical puzzles that emerge from observed events or comparisons: Why did the policies of the advanced industrial countries differ so much in response to the oil shock of 1973 (Katzenstein 1978)? Why have some industrial relations sys-

---

[3]This is not always the case, and in fact the tendency may be weaker among comparativists. For example, those who study the political economy of the advanced industrial countries (e.g. Scharpf and Soskice) tend to formulate their hypotheses and conclusions at the same, mid-range, level as most historical institutionalists.

tems proved more stable than others in the face of globalization pressures (Thelen 1993, 1994)? Why do some countries tax and spend more than others (Steinmo 1993)? The analyst then uses the comparisons to test hypotheses that can account for the observed differences. Rational choice theorists often proceed somewhat differently, deriving their puzzles from situations in which observed behavior appears to deviate from what the general theory predicts: Why, given free rider problems, do workers join unions (Wallerstein 1989)? Why would unions lead workers into hopeless battles (Golden 1997)? Why would citizens ever volunteer for war (Levi 1997b)? This difference in the analytic point of departure accounts for the extensive use of counterfactuals in rational choice research (e.g. Bates et al 1998a), which function much as cross-national comparisons often do in historical institutional research. The question is, what is "off the equilibrium path" (Levi 1997a:31)? The theory gives us prior expectations that we can then hold against the observed outcomes (see also Scharpf 1997:29).

The point is that it is not the case that one perspective's analysis is guided by clear hypotheses and the other's is not. The issue is where these hypotheses come from. Moreover, the difference in sources of hypotheses is not a hard and fast rule. As Scharpf points out, rational choice theories seek "to explicate what the authors of 'good' case studies always have in the back of their minds: a 'framework' that organizes our prior (scientific and prescientific) knowledge about what to expect in the province of the world that is of interest to us, that emphasizes the questions that are worthwhile asking, the factors that are likely to have high explanatory potential, and the type of data that would generally be useful in supporting or invalidating specific explanations" (1997:29–30).

Moreover, there is much overlap between the two perspectives when it comes to testing hypotheses against empirical cases, for this invariably involves contextualizing the theory (assumptions and propositions) and demonstrating that the hypothesized processes are actually at work (Pierson 1996: 158). As Scharpf puts it, "We need to have hypotheses that specify a causal model showing why and how a given constellation of factors could bring about the effect in question," but equally, "we need to have empirical evidence that the effect predicted by the hypothesis is in fact being produced" (1997:28). There is, in other words, no dichotomy between theoretical and empirical work because good analyses have to be both. The generation of the hypotheses is not the analysis, although it is the vital starting point for engaging the empirical material. The utility of a theory, after all, cannot be assessed apart from the empirical material it is meant to explain.

Preferences: Problematical or Not

In 1992, Steinmo and I argued that "one, perhaps *the* core, difference between rational choice institutionalism and historical institutionalism lies in the question of preference formation, whether treated as exogenous (rational choice) or endogenous (historical institutionalism)" (Thelen & Steinmo 1992:9, emphasis in original). I now think this may be a less stark difference than before. Setting aside some important ambiguities on this issue in both the rational choice and the historical institutionalist literature,[4] one of the core claims of historical institutionalism from the beginning was that institutions do more than channel policy and structure political conflict; rather, "the definition of interests and objectives is created in institutional contexts and is not separable from them" (Zysman 1994:244). In almost any version this is quite different from strong versions of rational choice theory, which begin with a (universal, not context-specific) rationality assumption.

Or is it? As Levi has suggested, in rational choice "the trick is in defining the preferences in general, ex ante to a particular application" (1997a:24). She notes that this is frequently difficult; for example, in the case of citizens, "given the range of interests [they] might have; there is nothing comparable to the economics dictum of getting the most for the least for one's money in the marketplace" (1997a:24).[5] In a candid discussion of the problem of imputing preferences, she notes the danger that assuming utility maximization "can...produce tautology: Whatever people do becomes a 'revealed preference'" (1997a:24).[6]

Even the assumptions traditionally considered "safe" may be trickier than we thought, the most common perhaps being that politicians are seeking re-election. This cannot be valid for Mexico, where the rules of the game (read: the specific institutional configuration) rule out, by law, reelection of legisla-

---

[4]Within the rational choice literature on norms, for example, there is some ambiguity as to whether norms affect *belief* formation or *preference* formation. "Beliefs" simply refer to how you think others will behave, whereas "norms" are collectively shared convictions (see Ferejohn 1991; Bates et al 1998a; Levi 1997b, 1998). (I am indebted to Guillermo Trejo for pointing this out to me.) Among historical institutionalists, Immergut (1997) argues that the claim that institutions shape preferences has often conflated several analytically separate issues, and she prefers "to distinguish more sharply between preferences, interests and choices" and to focus on interests as "publicly expressed, organized demands" rather than preferences in the sense of the views of individuals. She argues that "most institutionalists focus on how institutions may foster the emergence of particular definitions of mutual interest, or advantage particular political choices, without necessarily re-socializing citizens in a fundamental way" (1997:339–40).

[5]In economics, theories of the firm have been more successful than theories of consumption for this very reason. The assumption that firms seek to maximize profits is much more tangible, concrete, and therefore useful, than the assumption that consumers seek to maximize "utility" (whatever that might be). The quality of the theory appears to be a direct function of the degree of specificity of the core assumptions (G Trejo, personal communication). See also the discussion in Satz & Ferejohn 1994, esp. p. 72.

[6]See also Kuran (1991), who distinguishes between the private and public preferences of individuals and shows that people may in fact falsify their preferences for pragmatic reasons, making it impossible to know whether their behavior reflects their true preferences or is simply strategic. See also Rothstein (1996:148).

tors. (The same is true for presidents across a much larger number of countries.) In such cases, an analysis that starts with the reelection-seeking assumption will be widely off the mark. How do rational choice analysts deal with this situation? By and large they try to figure out, within a given context, what would make sense for a politician to seek, which is to say that they contextualize the preferences based on the particular institutional incentives that these politicians face in different settings.[7] This is not so different from how historical institutionalists often proceed. The point is that the move from general propositions about what political actors are seeking to maximize inevitably brings the theorist face to face with the question of what it means to, say, maximize power *within a given context*. Until this step is complete, the analysis cannot begin. This seems to be what Bates et al (1998a) mean when they note that the "'cultural' knowledge required to complete a rational choice explanation reveals the complementarity of the ['rational' and 'interpretive'] approaches. Game theorists often fail to acknowledge that their approach requires a complete political anthropology.... Game-theoretic accounts require detailed and fine-grained knowledge of the precise features of the political and social environment within which individuals make choices and devise political strategies" (1998a:628).

In addition, norms and culture, which for a long time were of concern mainly to historical institutionalists and institutional sociologists, appear to be assuming an increasingly important role in rational choice analysis.[8] Ferejohn's recent work, for example, argues that "culturally shared understandings and meanings" are crucial to selecting among the many possible strategic equilibria (1991:285). He argues that

> in social action, human agents make strategic or allocative choices while simultaneously enacting (ontologically) prior understandings about the nature of the strategic situation in which they find themselves, the characteristics or identities of the players (including themselves), and the common understandings or expectations as to how the game will be played. Thus, when it comes to explaining action, rational accounts, no less than interpretive ones, must appeal to principles external to the individual agents. (Ferejohn 1991: 285)

---

[7]A revision of the reelection assumption might say that politicians are seeking to maximize their careers or trying to increase their power, but again, what that means depends on the context—among other things, where power is located (institutionally) in different systems. For example, given the historical weakness of Congress in Latin America, "maximizing power" for a legislator there may mean angling for an appointive job in the bureaucracy. This is why rational choice theory works best in highly structured settings in which the players and the rules are stable and well known (Satz & Ferejohn 1994:72,81; Bates 1997:704; Bates et al 1998:222), in other words, where the structure itself does some of the analytical work.

[8]Actually, this interest goes back to Schelling (1960), and Elster (1989) too has long been concerned with norms and culture. More recently they have been joined by a host of others, including Ferejohn (1991), Bates et al (1998a), Levi (1998, 1999), North (1990), and Greif (1994). See also APSA-CP (1997), especially the contributions by Bates, Johnson, Laitin, Rogowski.

Many rational choice theorists follow North in his argument that norms constitute informal institutions—another set of rules that create incentives or constraints on behavior. However, theorists differ in explaining how norms and culture fit into the analysis of political outcomes. Some authors see cultural symbols and norms as resources invoked in strategic interactions (e.g. Johnson 1997); others view them as signaling devices in games of incomplete information (e.g. Bates et al 1998a); still others as focal points that affect which of a number of possible equilibria prevails (Rogowski 1997, Greif 1994). Here it is sufficient to note that in order to operate in any of these ways, norms must exert some independent power over individual behavior, and in this sense most of these works appear to go well beyond traditional "instrumental rationality" assumptions. In light of such developments, the issue of preferences (exogenous/endogenous) no longer seems to provide a clear line of demarcation between the different approaches.

Micro-Foundational Versus Macro-Historical Research

The issue of micro foundations is a third one that is typically cited as distinguishing historical institutional research from rational choice. The idea is that aggregate outcomes need to be understood in terms of the actions and behavior of individuals behaving strategically. This is frequently contrasted to broad macro-historical research that either sees interests as structurally generated in one way or another or stays at the level of aggregations (such as class) without regard for the way in which the strategic actions of individuals figure into the aggregation process.

But this too is a false dichotomy. The issue of the embeddedness of interests has been discussed above; however, there is the additional question of how to think about aggregate behavior. "Micro-foundational" obviously does not preclude dealing with collectivities, since most rational choice work deals with collective actors.[9] The analysis remains, nonetheless, "actor-centered" in the sense that the players are defined as "any individual or composite actor that is assumed to be capable of making purposeful choices among alternative courses of action" (Scharpf 1997:7). This may be unproblematical, as for example in Scharpf's case, since unions (or at least the union leadership) and not individual workers are the relevant players who actually engage in the strategic bargaining that generates the policy outcomes of interest. In other cases, however, it is worthwhile questioning whether the collectivities to which stra-

[9]Scharpf's (1997) work on economic policy outcomes, for example, examines the interaction of unions, employers, and the government. Golden (1997) explains apparently suicidal struggles on the part of unions by analyzing the behavior of union leaders, employers, and the rank and file. Weingast (1998) examines the incentives faced by Southern states in their interaction with the North. In all these cases, the relevant players are aggregations of individuals, that is to say, collectivities.

tegic action is attributed in fact constitute players in the sense that Scharpf identifies.

Take the example of Rogowski's (1987) analysis of coalitional alignments and realignments in the late nineteenth century. Rogowski's analysis hinges on the interaction of land (agricultural interests), labor, and capital, aggregations that are viewed as acting purposefully and strategically in the face of changing conditions in international trade. To be persuasive, we need to do more than impute (actor-centered) motives and strategies to these aggregations; we have to demonstrate that these actors were in fact players in Scharpf's sense, i.e. that these aggregations were cohesive and strategic. But we know from historical work—and indeed from the logic of Rogowski's own analysis—that these aggregations were not coherent players, each being riven by internal tensions that derive from precisely the changes in international trade that are the focus of Rogowski's analysis. Rogowski's argument itself suggests that business interests would have been divided, depending on whether firms were oriented toward the domestic market or the international market. And we know from historical work that this was in fact the case. Similarly, among labor, workers' interests frequently followed the divisions within business, opening the door for "cross-class alliances" that were crucial to the outcomes in which Rogowski is interested (Gourevitch 1986, Swenson 1989). Swenson's (1989) deeply inductive, historical approach is clearly more micro-foundational than Rogowski's rational choice approach in the sense that Swenson gets much closer to the actual players whose strategic interactions produced the outcomes at issue.

There is no dichotomy because taking micro foundations seriously means that we cannot be content to impute coherence to actors identified by the analyst; we must do the empirical work to make sure that the actors to whom we attribute certain strategic behaviors are in fact "players" in the first place.[10] In other words, the fact that a particular analysis employs a rational choice perspective does not necessarily mean that it stands on strong micro foundations. Conversely, historical institutional research is *not* necessarily not micro-foundational—quite the contrary, as we have seen.

Functional Versus Historical View of Institutions

It is frequently noted that, unlike most historical institutionalism, a good deal of rational choice theory embraces a functional view of institutions (e.g. Hall & Taylor 1996:943–44, Pierson 1996). This distinction probably originated in the two schools' differing approaches to the issue of institutions. Zysman notes

[10]A major theme in historical institutionalism is the way actors and their interests are constituted historically; see Thelen & Steinmo 1992, as well as the discussion, below, of the critical junctures and policy feedback literatures.

succinctly that "rational choice institutionalists start with individuals and ask where institutions came from, whereas historical institutionalists start with institutions and ask how they affect individuals' behaviors" (1992, comments at Conference of Europeanists, Chicago). Indeed, much of the early and pathbreaking work in rational choice did pose the question in the way Zysman suggests, and the question of why institutions emerge and are sustained has been answered in terms of the functions that they perform. One example is the literature on the US Congress and the way its rules eliminate "cycling"; another is the rational choice literature on institutions in international relations, which are viewed as mechanisms by which states can reduce transaction costs and achieve joint gains in an anarchic world (e.g. Shepsle & Weingast 1981, Shepsle 1986, Moravcsik 1993).

However, there has been much work within rational choice that, like historical institutionalism, embraces a non-functionalist, more historical view of institutions (Pierson 1996:131). North's later work (e.g. 1990), for example, is concerned with tracing, historically, the emergence of different kinds of institutional arrangements that either promote or distort development. Knight too has criticized a good deal of rational choice literature for embracing either an evolutionary or a spontaneous-creation view of institutions (1992:ch. 1). Against more functionalist accounts, Knight sets his own model of institutional formation and change, which places issues of distributional conflict at the center of the analysis.[11]

These works share much with the more historical view of institutions embraced by historical institutionalists. Zysman writes of political-economic institutions, "The institutional approach begins with the observation that markets, embedded in political and social institutions, are the creation of governments and politics" (1994:244). This is close to Knight's view, and for that matter March & Olsen's (1989); none of these works makes any assumptions about the social efficiency of institutional arrangements, and all of them allow for suboptimality and inefficiency. Differences remain, of course. Here I simply wish to point out that these differences do not boil down to the commonly cited divide between rational choice's "functionalist" and historical institutionalist's more "historical" approaches to institutions.

Synthesis or Creative Borrowing?

Should we conclude from the above that there has been a blending of these different approaches? In my view, no. What we see is a partial convergence of the

---

[11]Moreover, in some cases a functionalist view of institutions seems perfectly warranted because it is consistent with the historical record. Weingast's study of the "balance rule" in antebellum America, for example, provides evidence that this institution was precisely designed to perform the functions he identifies (1998:176–77).

issues at stake as, for example, historical institutionalists have come to a deeper appreciation of micro foundations and problems of collective action, and rational choice theorists have come to treat preferences, norms, and beliefs as a more central (also more complicated) issue than heretofore.[12] But, as pointed out above, differences remain—in how theorists working out of these different traditions approach these issues, in how they generate the hypotheses that guide their work, and in the level at which they attempt to build theory, for example.

Rather than a full-fledged synthesis, we might instead strive for creative combinations that recognize and attempt to harness the strengths of each approach. This seems to be the strategy advocated by prominent proponents within each school, Zysman from a historical institutionalist perspective and Scharpf from a rational choice perspective. Thus, for example, Zysman (1994: 277) argues that

> institutions and broad processes of social change certainly have micro-foundations. The "naked" institution emerging from a state of nature by rational choice and the "socially embedded" institution are one and the same, but they represent two different narratives whose perspectives highlight different processes within a common story. That is, the arguments built around institutions and historical dynamics should be consistent with notions of the "rational" dynamics of individual behavior. Inconsistencies are instructive to both those who would build micro-foundations and macro-theories.

He likens the difference between the two perspectives to that between "high-level computer languages (historical narrative) and the bit-level machine language of the computer (microeconomic narrative)" and maintains that "inherently they must work together, they must be consistent" (Zysman 1994:277) and that "issues must be segmented to make appropriate use of the perspectives, not to reject the insight of one or the other as part of an ideological quarrel" (1994:278; see also Ostrom 1995, esp. pp. 177–78).

Scharpf (1997) elaborates in some detail how this might be achieved. He advocates the use of rational choice and game theory as a way of generating hypotheses that can discipline empirical analysis, but he acknowledges that "even when we can rely on models with high predictive power, they are likely to be of limited scope and will only represent certain subsets of the complex, multiarena and multilevel interactions that are characteristic of real-world processes" (1997:31). This being the case, he argues that "it is usually necessary

[12]I am tempted to argue that the divide between rational choice and historical institutionalism is giving way to a divide between materialist-oriented analysis and norm-oriented analysis. The materialist-oriented side is exemplified in historical institutionalism by the work of Karl, Swenson, Immergut, and others, and in rational choice by the work of Knight, Tsebelis, and others. Analysis oriented toward ideational issues and norms in historical institutionalism includes recent work by Katzenstein and Hall; in rational choice, recent work by North and Levi.

to *combine* several such modules into a more complete explanation" (1997:31, emphasis in original). The composite explanation of particular processes

> is likely to be unique for each country but...the modules employed in constructing it may reappear more frequently in other cases as well and thus are more likely to achieve the status of empirically tested theoretical statements. Even then, however, the *linkages* between these modules remain problematical.... Thus we will often depend on narrative, rather than analytical, connections between partial theories that have analytical as well as empirical support—which also means that the composite explanation itself remains vulnerable to charges of being ad hoc. (Scharpf 1997:32)

Equilibrium Order Versus Historical Process

One area does seem to distinguish these two analytic approaches, at least in emphasis. This distinction can be characterized in terms of the relative centrality of "equilibrium order" versus "historical process" in the analysis of political phenomena.[13] One of the defining features of rational choice institutionalism is its assumption of equilibria and its view of institutions as coordinating mechanisms sustaining these equilibria (Levi 1997a:27, Scharpf 1997:10, Shepsle 1989:145). As Levi (1997a) has emphasized, this does not imply efficient equilibria; indeed, a major concern of rational choice has been to sort out the reasons why individual actors, behaving rationally, often produce suboptimal or inefficient collective outcomes. Nor does the equilibrium assumption imply that there exists a single, unique equilibrium outcome; another central problem in rational choice is to understand the process through which one equilibrium rather than another is reached. And finally, this assumption does not mean that rational choice theorists are uninterested in political change—merely that they tend to treat it as involving a transition between equilibrium orders. As Orren & Skowronek put it, "institutional politics appears as 'normal,' as politics as usual, explicitly or implicitly opposed to an extraordinary politics, in which equilibria are upset, norms break down, and new institutions are generated" (1994:316). Bates et al (1998a) appear to concur, also with the implicit critique: "The greatest achievement of rational choice theory has been to provide tools for studying political outcomes in stable institutional settings.... Political transitions seem to defy rational forms of analysis" (1998a:604–5). (Bates et al address this problem by incorporating elements of an "interpretivist" approach into the analysis).

---

[13]This section is strongly influenced by Orren & Skowronek (1994). I perhaps draw a less sharp distinction than they do between equilibrium analysis and process analysis, since the equilibria described by rational choice theories are not static but dynamic, and conversely, the "feedback" literature in historical institutionalism (see below) can be seen as a kind of equilibrium analysis as well.

Whereas rational choice theorists tend to view institutions in terms of their coordinating functions, historical institutionalists see institutions as the legacy of concrete historical processes. In embracing this view, historical institutionalism "brings questions of timing and temporality in politics [rather than equilibrium order] to the center of the analysis of how institutions matter" (Orren & Skowronek 1994:312). This does not mean that historical institutionalists are uninterested in regularities and continuities in politics;[14] it just means that the emphasis tends to be on political development as a (structured) process and on the way institutions emerge from particular historical conflicts and constellations (e.g. Steinmo 1993, 1994). As Pierson puts it, historical institutionalism "stresses that many of the contemporary implications of…temporal processes are embedded in institutions—whether these be formal rules, policy structures, or norms" (1996:126; see also Skocpol 1992:58–59).

Orren & Skowronek emphasize two features of political life that have been central to historical institutional analyses. The first is that "institutions, both individually and collectively, juxtapose different logics of political order, each with their own temporal underpinnings" (1994:320). That is, the various institutional arrangements that make up a polity emerge at different times and out of different historical configurations. For this reason, the various "pieces" do not necessarily fit together into a coherent, self-reinforcing, let alone functional, whole. For example, some analysts treat the German political economy as a well-integrated "system" in which various institutional subsystems—vocational education and training, collective bargaining institutions, financial institutions, bank-industry links—form a mutually reinforcing whole. Historical institutionalists, by contrast, are likely to be concerned with the origins rather than the functions of the various pieces, and indeed, historically oriented research has demonstrated that the evolution of the German model was highly dyssynchronous and full of unintended consequences (Streeck 1992; P Manow, unpublished manuscript; Thelen & Kume 1999). This has important implications for our view of the operation of this system. Streeck (1997), for example, has drawn attention to the ways in which industrial-relations institutions actively generate problems and pressures in other parts of the system, especially vocational education and social welfare institutions. As in the more functionalist view, the interdependencies among the various parts of the system are central to the analysis; however, in Streeck's work the frictions as well as the functional interdependencies come to the fore. The result is very much in the spirit of Orren & Skowronek's characterization: "The single presumption abandoned is that institutions are synchronized in their operations or synthetic

---

[14]As the large literature on comparative statics demonstrates, they are indeed interested (see Thelen & Steinmo 1992); see also the discussion of the "feedback effects" literature below.

in their effects; the more basic idea, that institutions structure change in time, is retained" (1994:321).

The second claim, related to the first, is that one important source of change comes from the interactions of different institutional orders within a society, as "change along one time line affects order along the others" (Orren & Skowronek 1994:321), that is, as interactions and encounters among processes in different institutional realms open up possibilities for political change.[15] Stark & Bruszt's (1998) work on the transition to democracy and market economy in Eastern Europe provides one example of what this looks like in practice. In language that resonates with Orren & Skowronek's, they argue that in Eastern Europe, "we see social change not as a transition from one order to another but as transformation—rearrangements, reconfigurations, and recombinations that yield new interweavings of the multiple social logics..." (1998:7). Like Orren & Skowronek, they stress the incongruities among the multiple processes as they unfold: "...within any given country, we find...many [transitions] occurring in different domains—political, economic, and social—and the temporality of these processes is often asynchronous and their articulation seldom harmonious" (Stark & Bruszt 1998:81). Change in one arena affects other ongoing processes, which is what drives institutional evolution.[16]

Pierson's (1996) analysis of the evolution of social policy in the European Union provides further examples. In one instance (the case of EU policy on gender equality), he shows how provisions adopted by the EU member states in one period—largely symbolic and without much effect—were later picked up by emergent women's groups, who were able to use these provisions to achieve gains at the EU level that had eluded them at the domestic level. Changes in the political and socioeconomic context brought new actors into the game (in Pierson's case, women's groups) who were able to use existing but previously latent institutions (in Pierson's case, Article 119 of the Treaty of Rome), whose new salience had important implications for political outcomes (Thelen & Steinmo 1992:16).

These examples point to the importance of examining politics as a dynamic process that frequently produces unintended consequences as different, ongo-

---

[15]Weir (1992) draws attention to this idea in her analysis of "collisions" between different policy streams; it is also related to Pierson's (1996) notion of "gaps" and "lags" in policy processes that produce openings for institutions to evolve in ways their designers did not anticipate (see below).

[16]The concept of institutional bricolage, which Stark and other students of Eastern Europe employ, describes "an innovative process whereby new institutions differ from but resemble old ones" (Campbell 1997:22). This echoes Orren & Skowronek's comment that "more often than not, we expect to find that continuities along one dimension of order and time will be folded into, and formative of, the extraordinary changes we are observing along another" (1994:322).

ing processes interact. Perspectives that conceive of change as the breakdown of one equilibrium and its replacement with another do not capture this well. Nor, however, do alternative conceptions, for example, some early versions of the new institutionalism in sociology, in which the definition of institutions as "shared cultural scripts" obscures political struggles among competing scripts and/or conceives of change as the displacement of one script by another.[17]

In sum, although historical institutionalists are just as interested as "other" institutionalists in the regularities of politics over time, they tend to emphasize historical process over equilibrium order. Whereas alternative conceptions view institutions in terms of their coordinating functions, historical institutionalists see them as the product of concrete temporal processes. Thus, rather than conceiving of institutions as "holding together" a particular pattern of politics, historical institutionalists are more likely to reverse the causal arrows and argue that institutions emerge from and are sustained by features of the broader political and social context. In this approach to institutions, path dependency involves elements of both continuity and (structured) change; institutions are conceived in relational terms (Immergut 1992, Katznelson 1997:104); and institutional arrangements cannot be understood in isolation from the political and social setting in which they are embedded.

PATH DEPENDENCY

Two ways of thinking about path dependency—one from the literature on economics and technology, the other from the work of "new" institutional sociologists—have gained prominence, and a brief discussion of each provides a baseline for a discussion of the historical institutional approach to path dependency. I argue that both contain insights into the mechanisms that sustain particular patterns of politics, but some of the most prominent formulations tend to obscure the distributional consequences of political institutions and blend out important sources of dynamism in political life.

Technological Models of Path Dependency from Economics

The most widely invoked model of path dependency is the one that comes out of the work of economists seeking to understand technological trajectories. Most closely associated with the "QWERTY keyboard," the argument developed by David (1985) and elaborated by Arthur (1989) holds that certain technologies, for idiosyncratic and unpredictable reasons, can achieve an initial

---

[17]See for example Meyer et al (1987) on "western ontology." More recent literature has confronted the issue of rival scripts (e.g. Friedland & Alford 1991, Dobbin 1994, Powell 1991, and Heimer 1999).

advantage over alternative technologies and prevail even if in the long run the alternatives would have been more efficient. (Krasner 1988, Kato 1996a, and Pierson 1997 all review these arguments in detail.) What political scientists have taken from this is the intuitively attractive idea that technology, like politics, involves some elements of chance (agency, choice), but once a path is taken, then it can become "locked in," as all the relevant actors adjust their strategies to accommodate the prevailing pattern.

Some features of politics are undoubtedly subject to the kinds of "positive feedback" effects to which the David/Arthur model of technological change draws attention, and the notion of increasing returns certainly has important applications to politics.[18] But as a general guide to understanding political development, the QWERTY model is both too contingent and too deterministic. It is too contingent in that the initial choice (call it a "critical juncture") is seen as rather open and capable of being "tipped" by small events or chance circumstances, whereas in politics this kind of blank slate is a rarity, to say the least.[19] The openness implied in this model is belied by the vast literature on critical junctures (discussed below) that traces divergent trajectories back to systematic differences either in antecedent conditions or in the timing, sequencing, and interaction of specific political-economic processes, suggesting that not all options are equally viable at any given point in time.

The QWERTY model is also too deterministic in that once the initial choice is made, then the argument becomes mechanical. There is one fork in the road, and after that, the path only narrows. In this model, actors adapt to prevailing institutions by investing in them in ways that reinforce the institutions (e.g. people learn to type in a particular way, firms make products that fit with the standard). In other words, in the world of firms and users of technology, adapting to the standard means adopting it; those who do not adapt lose, and—importantly—the losers disappear (for example, as firms go out of business).

Politics is characterized by disagreement over goals and disparities in power, and in fact institutions often reinforce power disparities (Hall 1986, Knight 1992, Riker 1980:444–45). However, the losers do not necessarily disappear, and their adaptation can mean something very different from embracing and reproducing the institution, as in the technology model. For those who are disadvantaged by prevailing institutions, adapting may mean biding their time until conditions shift, or it may mean working within the existing framework in pursuit of goals different from—even subversive to—those of the in-

[18]The best treatment of these issues is by Pierson (1997), and the policy feedback literature discussed below provides numerous examples of increasing returns arguments in politics.

[19]David (1985), especially, emphasizes "chance elements" (p. 332) and "essentially random" factors (p. 335) in determining among an apparently very wide range of possible outcomes; Arthur (1989) is overall more circumspect and nuanced.

stitution's designers.[20] Such considerations provide insights into the reasons why, in politics, increasing returns do not necessarily result in an irrevocably locked-in equilibrium; further choice points exist.

Path Dependency in Institutional Sociology

Another strong argument about path dependency emerges from the work of the new institutionalists in sociology. Whereas economic models start with individuals or firms in the market, sociological perspectives begin with society. Institutions, in this view, are collective outcomes, but not in the sense of being the product or even the sum of individual interests. Rather, institutions are socially constructed in the sense that they embody shared cultural understandings ("shared cognitions," "interpretive frames") of the way the world works (Meyer & Rowen 1991, Scott 1995:33, Zucker 1983:5). Specific organizations come and go, but emergent institutional forms will be "isomorphic" with (i.e. compatible with, resembling, and similar in logic to) existing ones because political actors extract causal designations from the world around them and these cause-and-effect understandings inform their approaches to new problems (DiMaggio & Powell 1991:11, Dobbin 1994). This means that even when policy makers set out to redesign institutions, they are constrained in what they can conceive of by these embedded, cultural constraints.

The strong emphasis on cognition in the new institutionalism in sociology gives us powerful insights into the persistence of particular patterns of politics over time, but as DiMaggio & Powell point out (1991, esp. pp. 1, 11–12), the early formulations (e.g. Meyer and colleagues) were less helpful in understanding change.[21] Some versions of new institutionalism in sociology make it hard to see any forks in the road at all; for example, Zucker (1991:85) argues that

> each actor fundamentally perceives and describes social reality by enacting it, and in this way transmitting it to the other actors in the social system....The young are enculturated by the previous generation, while they in turn enculturate the next generation. The grandparents do not have to be present to ensure adequate transmission of this general cultural meaning. Each generation simply believes it is describing objective reality.

---

[20]An example of the latter is the job classification system in American industrial relations. This system was originally imposed on unions by employers as a way of controlling labor. Unable to change the system, emergent unions adapted their strategies to it but sought to attach rules to these job classifications, and in doing so, they eventually turned it into a system of union control. In this case, "adapting" to the institution had the effect of transforming it altogether, so much so that now it is employers who attack the system, unions who defend it.

[21]*The New Institutionalism in Organizational Analysis* (Powell & DiMaggio 1991) is partly a response to these weaknesses. See also Powell & Jones (1999), which explicitly addresses institutional change.

The notion of institutions as shared scripts sometimes obscures conflicts among groups (because the scripts are by definition shared), and the notion of isomorphism emphasizes continuity across time and space (because new problems are solved using the same cultural template). Yet we know that dominant cultural norms emerge out of concrete political conflicts, in which different groups fight over which norms will prevail (Katzenstein 1996); we know that dominant policy paradigms can and do shift at times (Hall 1993); we know that organizational fields are often imposed by powerful actors (Fligstein 1991, DiMaggio 1991), and that legitimacy, not automaticity, explains why people follow scripts in the first place (Stinchcombe 1997). This is why recent formulations argue that the cognitive dimensions (though important) should not eclipse the strategic and political elements of action, and frequently find that in questions of institutionalization and institutional change, the political part of the story (and not the cognitive) is more important (DiMaggio & Powell 1991:27,31; see also Katzenstein 1996). At a minimum, then, much work remains to be done to sort out the relationship between the political (decision/power) and the cognitive (script) aspects of institutional stability and change.

Both the economic-technological and the sociological-institutional perspectives provide strong tools for understanding continuity, but by stipulating and privileging particular mechanisms of reproduction (coordination effects for the former, isomorphism for the latter) they have a hard time incorporating notions of conflict and power, and they are not particularly helpful in talking about change. Dynamism in both models has to come from some exogenous shock, or, as Orren & Skowronek (1994) argue for equilibrium models generally, these perspectives strongly imply that political change is not amenable to the same type of analysis we use to understand the operation of the institutions themselves.

PATH DEPENDENCY IN HISTORICAL INSTITUTIONALISM

Ikenberry captures the essence of a historical institutional approach to path dependency in his characterization of political development as involving "critical junctures and developmental pathways" (1994:16ff). As the phrase implies, this approach includes two related but analytically distinct claims. The first involves arguments about crucial founding moments of institutional formation that send countries along broadly different developmental paths; the second suggests that institutions continue to evolve in response to changing environmental conditions and ongoing political maneuvering but in ways that are constrained by past trajectories. These two lines of argument tend to be reflected in a bifurcation of the literature in this area. A number of important analyses of critical junctures explore the origins of diversity across nations (e.g. Skocpol 1979, Luebbert 1991, Ertman 1997); other studies focus on the logic and self-reinforcing properties of particular national trajectories over time, drawing out comparisons to other countries where relevant (e.g. Weir 1992, Skocpol 1992).[22]

Although obviously related, these two literatures have characteristic strengths and weaknesses, and each would be enriched by a more sustained engagement of the other. The great strength of the critical junctures literature lies in the way in which scholars have incorporated issues of sequencing and timing into the analysis, looking specifically at the different patterns of interaction between ongoing political processes and at the effect of these interactions on institutional and other outcomes. Where this literature has generally been weaker is in specifying the mechanisms that translate critical junctures into lasting political legacies. Here the policy feedback literature, which has provided many insights into the mechanisms that account for continuity over time, is useful. However, in this second literature, strong tools for understanding continuity are not matched by equally sophisticated tools for understanding political and institutional change. In the next three sections of this essay, I argue that greater insight into the different types of reproduction mechanisms behind different institutional arrangements holds the key to understanding what particular kinds of external events and processes are likely to produce political openings that drive (path-dependent) institutional evolution and change.

Historical Institutional Analyses of Critical Junctures

As Katznelson (1997) suggests, the macro-historical analysis of critical junctures that set countries along different developmental paths has long been the bread and butter of historical institutionalism. Rejecting a functionalist view of institutions, historical institutionalists see institutions as enduring legacies of political struggles. The classics in this genre (ably reviewed by others, e.g. Ikenberry 1994) include Moore (1966), Gerschenkron (1962), Lipset & Rokkan (1967), and Shefter (1977). All of these works emphasize sequencing and timing and, related to these issues, different patterns of interaction between ongoing political and economic processes in the formation and evolution of institutional arrangements. These studies are "configurative," as Katznelson (1997) puts it, in the sense that they do not view political processes in isolation but rather focus specifically on how the temporal ordering of, and interactions among, processes influence outcomes—in these cases, institutional outcomes.[23]

---

[22]There are, however, studies that treat both the cross-national differences and the over-time continuities within countries. Steinmo (1993) and Collier & Collier (1991) are good examples.

[23]However, I disagree with Katznelson's distinction between "configurative" and "variable centered" analyses. I understand one of the great strengths of these works to be the framing of key variables in a way that captures the interactive nature of these processes.

This venerable tradition is alive and well in historical institutional research, as a review of a few select works demonstrates.[24] Collier & Collier's landmark study, *Shaping the Political Arena*, links differences in patterns of labor incorporation to variation in party and regime outcomes across a wide range of Latin American countries. As in the earlier works cited above, Collier & Collier emphasize the central importance of sequencing and timing; their study "confront[s] the interaction between a longitudinal and a cross-sectional perspective: between the unfolding over time within each country of phases of political change, and a sequence of international developments that influenced all the countries roughly in the same chronological time, but often at a different point in relation to these internal political phases" (Collier & Collier 1991:19–20). In fact, one of the book's central themes is the way in which "common" international events or trends translate into different challenges in different countries as a result of their intersections and interactions with ongoing domestic processes (see also Locke & Thelen 1995, Collier 1993).

Another example of critical junctures work in historical institutional research is Ertman's *Birth of the Leviathan*, which traces the origins of state institutions across a broad range of European countries from the twelfth to the eighteenth century. Employing a logic that parallels Gerschenkron's, Ertman argues that "differences in the timing of the onset of sustained geopolitical competition go a long way toward explaining the character of state infrastructures found across the continent at the end of the 18th century" (1997:26). Like Collier & Collier, Ertman attends to variation in the ways in which common international forces intersect with ongoing domestic political developments. Where state-builders faced geopolitical competition early, they were forced into greater concessions to the financiers, merchants, and administrators who financed and staffed the bureaucracy, resulting in patrimonial systems. Where rulers confronted geopolitical pressures later, "they found themselves in a quite different world," where developments in education and finance made these side payments unnecessary, resulting in greater bureaucratic autonomy (Ertman 1997:28).

P Manow's analysis of union formation in Germany and Japan (unpublished manuscript) is also centrally concerned with how the intersection and interactions among different processes affect institutional outcomes. Against conventional analyses that attribute the different institutional forms adopted by the two labor movements to the triumph of social democratic ideology (Germany) or to employer strategies (Japan), Manow reveals that, in both

[24]In addition to works discussed briefly below, see Luebbert (1991), Spruyt (1994), Downing (1992), Gould (1999), Stark & Bruszt (1998), Dunlavy (1994), Esping-Anderson (1990), Rueschemeyer et al (1992), S Vitols (unpublished manuscript), Thelen & Kume (1999), and Karl (1997); this work is also featured in APSA-CP (1998).

cases, the evolution of state social policy intersected with union formation and affected it by systematically favoring certain organizational forms over others. A complementary analysis by Thelen & Kume (1999) reveals that the organizational forms ultimately embraced by the two labor movements were also powerfully supported by differences in the systems of vocational education and training as these emerged in the early industrial period. In both analyses, attention to the timing and sequencing of union development, in relation to and in interaction with other ongoing political processes (the institutionalization of social policy and of vocational training), helps to explain the organizational forms that the labor movement ultimately adopted.

What all of these comparative historical studies share is a perspective that examines political and economic development in historical context and in terms of processes unfolding over time and in relation to each other, within a broader context in which developments in one realm impinge on and shape developments in others. Each of these works demonstrates that "[c]ausal analysis is inherently sequence analysis" (Rueschemeyer et al 1992:4). All of them engage in close examination of temporal sequences and processes as they unfold, and perhaps even more importantly, as different processes at the domestic level or at the international and domestic levels unfold in relation to one another. They all focus on variables that capture important aspects of the interactive features of ongoing political processes, and in ways that explain important differences in regime and institutional outcomes across a range of cases.

However, many of these works tend not to emphasize or even sufficiently problematize how the outcomes of critical junctures are translated into lasting legacies. In other words, they neglect the mechanisms for the "reproduction" (Collier & Collier 1991) of the legacy over time within a particular country. (Collier & Collier 1991 and Skocpol 1992 are exceptions; see below.) A good deal of this literature, old and new, invokes a similar language, arguing that the events described are important because they had the effect of "filling the political space" in ways that were difficult to reverse or alter.[25] Pierson articulates what appears to be the logic behind such arguments when he suggests that feedback effects are likely to be "most consequential in issue-areas (or in countries...) where interest group activity is not yet well established.... Factors that give one set of organizations an initial advantage—even a small one—are likely to become self-reinforcing" (1993:602–3). However, it is not clear that this reasoning stands up to historical scrutiny. The history of organized labor—to consider one important interest group—is actually littered with organizational forms that, despite some early-comer advantages, did not manage to

---

[25]The metaphor of political space comes up, explicitly or implicitly, time and again in "legacies" arguments. See Lipset & Rokkan (1967:51ff), Valenzuela (1979:ch. 6), Luebbert (1991, e.g. pp. 9–11), Skocpol (1992, esp. pp. 52 and 530), Thelen & Kume (1999), and Herrigel (1993).

survive, let alone dominate the available political space (e.g. materials-based unions in Sweden and skill-based organizations in Germany). Instead, they withered for lack of mechanisms to reproduce themselves.[26]

Political space arguments (and related arguments about the "freezing" or "crystallization" of particular institutional configurations) obscure more than they reveal unless they are explicitly linked to complementary arguments that identify the mechanisms of reproduction at work. Without these, they are at best incomplete, for they cannot explain why these patterns persisted and how they continue to dominate the political space. Indeed, the language of freezing and crystallization can be deeply misleading because it suggests that things stand still, when in fact we know intuitively that organizations such as political parties or unions with roots in the nineteenth century must adapt to myriad changes in the environment in order to survive into the twentieth century. The reproduction of a legacy, in short, is a dynamic process, and this is not well captured in some of the dominant formulations.

With this perhaps in mind, several authors invoke Stinchcombe's (1968) arguments about "sunk costs" and "vested interests" that make embarking on alternative paths costly and uncertain. But such references, though a promising starting point for the analysis, cannot themselves replace the analysis; these concepts need to be applied, not just invoked. Among other things, we need to know exactly who is invested in particular institutional arrangements, exactly how that investment is sustained over time, and perhaps how those who are not invested in the institutions are kept out. Attending to these issues is likely to generate insights into differences in the mechanisms of reproduction that sustain different kinds of institutional arrangements, or even the same kinds of institutions in different contexts.

Within the critical junctures literature, Collier & Collier stand out in explicitly drawing attention to the issue of the reproduction of critical junctures legacies, as well as the related matter of a legacy's duration (1991, esp. pp. 31–34). For example, the authors describe a pattern of labor incorporation for Mexico that is based on the ability of the labor-mobilizing party, Partido Revolucionario Institucional (PRI), to use the resources of the state to maintain the link to labor at all levels. The legacy of this type of labor incorporation, in other words, is reproduced through patronage, and indeed a form of patronage that reaches deep into society, so that ordinary workers (who may owe their jobs to the governing PRI party) are also materially invested in this system. This pattern of reproduction is quite different from, say, Brazil, where (as Collier & Collier show) labor incorporation involved harassment, repression, and coercion and left a legacy of labor alienation that was sustained by ongoing labor exclusion.

[26]To argue that the groups institutionalized first were the ones that "stuck" is to beg the question of why some were institutionalized and others not.

The general point I wish to make is that the different forms of labor incorporation identified by Collier & Collier are sustained by different mechanisms of reproduction—at the extreme, broad-based patronage in Mexico versus repression and control in Brazil. These considerations are crucial to understanding differences in the duration of the various legacies [some critical junctures produce very stable regimes, whereas others seem to contain the seeds of their own destruction (Collier & Collier 1991:34)], but also—maybe more importantly—they are crucial to understanding what kinds of events or processes have the capacity to undermine the legacy in different countries. In the Mexican case, for example, the reproduction of the legacy was (predictably) especially vulnerable to developments that make it hard for the PRI to continue to deliver patronage benefits. And so we find that ongoing economic crisis in recent years has shaken the hegemonic position of the PRI by interfering with the party's use of state resources to shore up political support (Collier & Collier 1991:759).

Summing up, the critical junctures literature has taught us a great deal about the politics of institutional formation and the importance of the timing, sequencing, and interaction of ongoing political processes in accounting for cross-national variation. Where many of these analyses have been somewhat less explicit, however, is in explaining what sustains the institutional arrangements that emerge from these critical junctures. The issue of continuity over time and feedback mechanisms that sustain institutions dynamically are at the center of a related body of work, to which I now turn.

Feedback Effects

The literature on policy feedback in historical institutionalism has been elegantly and thoroughly summarized (see especially Pierson 1993 and Ikenberry 1994). This literature follows on Krasner's observation that "path dependent patterns are characterized by self-reinforcing positive feedback" (1988:83).[27] The literature in this area points to two broad types of feedback mechanisms (Ikenberry 1994:20), though, as the examples below indicate, many analyses combine elements of both. One set of mechanisms, which Ikenberry refers to as functional, is perhaps better described as incentive structure or coordination effects (see also North 1990). What this means is that once a set of institutions is in place, actors adapt their strategies in ways that reflect but also reinforce the "logic" of the system. Zysman captures the essence of these arguments when

---

[27]As Krasner (1988:84) and Pierson (1997) point out, many of these arguments could be put in the language of "increasing returns," here understood simply as a situation in which once a particular path is chosen, actors adapt to the existing institutions in ways that push them further along that trajectory (and in so doing, also render the path not chosen increasingly remote) (see also Levi 1997:28ff).

he states that "the institutional structure induces particular kinds of...behavior by constraining and by laying out a logic to the market and policy-making process" (1994:243). A few examples from recent work can illustrate this idea.

Streeck's (1992) work on the political economy of Germany has shown that the existence of particular institutional arrangements (e.g. a national system for vocational education and training and centralized collective bargaining) affects firm strategies in ways that not only reflect but also actively reinforce these institutions. These arrangements, as he puts it, "force and facilitate" the pursuit of strategies based on high-skill, high–value-added production. As business adapts its strategies to institutional incentives and constraints, its adaptation encourages further movement along this trajectory, as firms come to depend on the existence of these institutions for their continued success in international markets. PA Hall & D Soskice (unpublished manuscript) take this argument a step further by suggesting that the presence of certain institutions (e.g. strong works councils) can raise the returns to the presence of other, complementary institutions (e.g. strong bank-industry links). The authors use this argument to explain why certain kinds of labor market arrangements tend to be associated in many advanced industrial economies with certain kinds of financial arrangements (especially "patient capital"). Esping-Anderson's (1990) "conservative-corporatist" welfare state provides another example of this feedback mechanism. Since the conservative-corporatist welfare state is premised on the notion of a single breadwinner, family structures adapt to the incentives and disincentives it embodies, which is one reason why female labor market participation in such economies is low by international standards.

Schneider's (1997–1998) analysis of the developmental state in Latin America provides another example. Schneider shows that the structures and policies of developmental states often have the effect of fragmenting business interests. Where states distribute economic benefits on a discretionary basis, firms orient their strategies toward direct, individual appeals to the government. State activity of this sort generates very weak incentives for firms to engage in collective action, resulting in anemic business associations. Levy (1999) comes to similar conclusions for France, showing how the traditionally dominant role of the state in the French political economy actively discouraged the emergence of strong intermediate (political-economic) associations. In what he calls "Tocqueville's revenge," recent attempts by the state to withdraw from its traditionally pivotal role in economic life have failed for lack of viable associations that can step into the regulatory void created by the state's retreat. In other words, historically, the more the French state compensated for France's weak associations, the less able it was to do anything else.

Vogel's (1996) analysis of the politics of deregulation in the political economies of the advanced industrial countries also tracks the path-dependent evolution of institutions. His study looks at "how political-economic institutions shape policy choices and also…how these choices in turn reshape the institutions" (Vogel 1996:9), and he identifies feedback mechanisms at both the ideational and the structural levels. Against contemporary theories predicting cross-national convergence in the face of globalization, Vogel finds that the regulatory reforms that individual governments have actually undertaken reflect and reinforce distinctive national trajectories based on different underlying ideas about the appropriate role of the state in the market and on structural features of the political-economic context. The picture that emerges from his analysis is one of evolution and change, but countries move along (nationally specific) well-worn paths, because the search for solutions to new international pressures is structured by prevailing domestic institutions.

The second feedback mechanism identified by Ikenberry (1994) has to do with the distributional effects of institutions. The idea is that institutions are not neutral coordinating mechanisms but in fact reflect, and also reproduce and magnify, particular patterns of power distribution in politics (see especially Pierson 1997). This body of work emphasizes that political arrangements and policy feedbacks actively facilitate the organization and empowerment of certain groups while actively disarticulating and marginalizing others. The distributional biases in particular institutions or policies "feed back" so that "over time, some avenues of policy become increasingly blocked, if not entirely cut off" as "decisions at one point in time can restrict future possibilities by sending policy off onto particular tracks" (Weir 1992:18,19).

Some of the best work in this area has been done by Skocpol and her collaborators. *Protecting Soldiers and Mothers* (Skocpol 1992) is an important contribution that reiterates but also elaborates some central themes of Skocpol's earlier work. Skocpol explicitly problematizes the issue of interest formation, arguing that institutional arrangements "affect the capabilities of various groups to achieve self-consciousness, organize, and make alliances" (1992:47). (This is a major theme in Rueschemeyer et al 1992 and Weir 1992 as well.) For example, drawing on work by Shefter, Skocpol shows how the fragmentation of the state, as well as the organization of party competition along patronage lines, actively mediated against the development of a unified working class that could then spearhead the movement for comprehensive social policies in the United States. At the same time, the policies the government did devise powerfully shaped future possibilities for more comprehensive schemes. Specifically, the policy of granting social benefits to Civil War veterans contributed to the emergence of a self-conscious interest group (veterans and their widows) and endowed it with material and ideational resources that threw up barriers to other groups who might appeal to the state for protection on other grounds.

To take another example, Esping-Anderson (1990) draws attention to the "decommodifying" effects of universal welfare states, demonstrating that these arrangements actively shore up the power of the political and economic organizations of the working class. The resulting pattern of politics contrasts sharply with patterns in the United States, where, as Skocpol and Katznelson emphasize, political institutions and government policy have if anything operated to disarticulate working class organizations and to disempower working class interests. Rather than taking the interests of political actors as given, all these authors step back to ask how groups originally got constituted in the particular ways they did, then to consider how this affects the groups' understanding and pursuit of their interests. As Hall (1993:51) puts it, "The social construction of identities in other words is necessarily prior to more obvious conceptions of interest: a 'we' needs to be established before its interests can be articulated." Weir has brought these insights to bear on the issue of coalition formation. "By channeling the way groups interact in politics and policy making,...institutions greatly affect the possibilities for diverse groups to recognize common interests and construct political alliances" (Weir 1992:24). The result is that, in some institutional settings, groups with the same "objective material interests" cannot find common cause.

My final example of the feedback literature emphasizing distributional effects is Karl's (1997) study of "petro-states," which paints an especially vivid portrait of path dependency that emphasizes the power-distributional biases of institutions. In countries as diverse in regime type, social structure, and culture as Venezuela, Iran, Nigeria, Algeria, and Indonesia, Karl finds that the adaptation of political-economic institutions to the oil economy produces pathologies that actively reinforce the dependence of these economies on oil, despite explicit efforts by many governments to use oil revenues to fuel more balanced economic development. Her view of path dependency stresses political-distributional feedback effects, arguing that the incentives embedded in political-economic institutions are "above all else...the reflection and product of power relations" (1997:xvi). In her cases, both societal and state institutions are irresistibly drawn to organize themselves around the oil economy (e.g. the domestic bourgeoisie shifts its activities to those linked to oil—where the money is—and the state becomes the center of rent-seeking behavior, so that state jurisdiction expands massively with the expansion of oil-related activities even as state autonomy and authority atrophy). For one case, Venezuela, Karl examines specific choice points in detail and shows how the various decisions "demonstrate that there was never an equal probability that other choices would be made in their place; that each decision was related and grew from the previous one; and that, except during uncertain moments of regime change, the range of choice narrowed from one decision to another as Venezuela moved further into its oil-led trajectory" (1997:226). In the end, the perverse and paradoxical effect is that oil revenues, rather than leading the way to development, perpetuate a dependence on oil and a failure to develop.

These works have taught us a great deal about the dynamic processes that help explain how stable patterns of politics persist and indeed reproduce themselves over time (Ikenberry's "developmental pathways"). However, by emphasizing the mechanisms through which previous patterns are reproduced, many of these works downplay the factors that might tell us how they can be changed. The language of "lock-in" frequently obscures the fact that, because institutions are embedded in a context that is constantly changing, stability—far from being automatic—may have to be sustained politically. [Weingast's (1998) analysis of antebellum America is a good case in point, for his characterization suggests that the balance rule was not at all automatic but had to be actively nurtured in light of changing external conditions.] Where the context is changing, those who are invested in particular institutions reevaluate their investment in light of these changes. Moreover, changes in one institutional arena can reverberate, provoking changes in other, complementary institutions (Skocpol 1992:59; PA Hall & D Soskice, unpublished manuscript). These considerations lead us to a discussion of institutional evolution and political change.

Institutional Evolution and Political Change

If positive feedback and increasing returns were the whole story, then prediction would be easy, since we could simply read the outcomes off the institutional configuration. But institutions evolve and change over time, and this is where Orren & Skowronek's (1994) arguments about temporality and the unfolding of different processes over time become important. Above I argued that two alternative views of path dependency are overly deterministic; this weakness is at least partly attributable to the fact that both of them stipulate, at a very high level of abstraction, particular reproduction mechanisms that obscure conflict and make it difficult to talk about change. Orren & Skowronek, by contrast, present a more dynamic alternative, which—very importantly—focuses on the incongruities and intersections between different processes and institutional logics as they unfold over time. Illustrations of this approach in practice can be found in recent work by Weir and Pierson, among others. Weir's (1992) study of US welfare policy demonstrates that the unexpected "collision" of two (previously) unconnected policy streams in the 1960s—the "War on Poverty" and the civil rights movement—had a profound impact on the evolution of employment policy in the United States, turning it in a direction that policy makers did not originally intend. Similarly, in his study of the evolution of the European Union, Pierson (1996) shows how "gaps" (between different levels of action—domestic and European-level) and "lags" (produced by disjunctures between short- and long-term events and considerations) created openings that allowed non-state actors (in his cases, women's groups and EU bureaucrats) to influence institutional development in ways that the EU member states did not anticipate and could not control.

In some ways, however, Orren & Skowronek's characterization is *too* fluid. The intersection and interaction of different processes unfolding in time is certainly an important feature of political life; the "collisions," "gaps," and "lags" to which Weir and Pierson have directed our attention are also clearly pervasive in politics. But what we need to know is which particular interactions and collisions are likely to be politically consequential—which of these, in other words, have the potential to disrupt the feedback mechanisms that reproduce stable patterns over time, producing political openings for institutional evolution and change. I suggest that the kinds of openings that particular institutional configurations offer depends on the particular mechanisms of reproduction that sustain them.

Institutions rest on a set of ideational and material foundations that, if shaken, open possibilities for change. But different institutions rest on different foundations, and so the processes that are likely to disrupt them will also be different, though predictable. Take the case of the welfare state. Esping-Anderson's (1990) three models—social-democratic, conservative-corporatist, and liberal welfare systems—not only rest on different levels of support (from broad and diffuse to narrow and weak) but also rely on different mechanisms of reproduction, and therefore they are differently affected by specific other "external" trends. For instance, changes in gender relations and family structures are likely to reinforce elements of the universalistic and liberal welfare states (which both, though in different ways, support a high level of labor-force participation by women), but these changes create new frictions and contradictions for conservative welfare states, which are premised on the single-breadwinner model of the family. In other words, we might well expect a (politically consequential) collision between changing gender roles and welfare state development, but only in the conservative welfare states.[28]

Universal welfare states, on the other hand, may be especially susceptible to other kinds of pressures. Rothstein's (1998) analysis of the universal welfare state, for example, suggests that middle-class support is crucial (because this is the pivotal electoral group) but that—unlike the working class—the middle classes are neither clear material beneficiaries nor clear losers in the universal welfare state. Whereas working-class support for the system includes a very strong material component, Rothstein argues that the support of the middle class is premised more on their belief that the system is fair, in the sense that they are not shouldering an undue burden, and that all citizens are contributing their fair shares (this is what Rothstein, following Levi 1998, calls contingent

---

[28]See also Pierson's (1994) comparative analysis of welfare state retrenchment in Britain and the United States. But in contrast to Pierson, I wish to emphasize that it is not just a question of whether policies are more locked in or less, but rather of the different ways in which the policies are reproduced, which makes them vulnerable to different kinds of pressures.

consent). This type of analysis raises the issues flagged above, concerning who has vested interests in particular institutions and what sustains these investments over time. Rothstein's study reveals that the foundations of working-class support for the welfare state are fundamentally different from those of the middle class; both are invested, but in different ways. The coalition behind the universal welfare state, far from being self-reinforcing (as in increasing returns arguments), may in fact have to be politically re-invented from time to time, as the environment changes and as these various groups reevaluate their investment in light of these changes. As Rothstein (1998) points out, one development that could complicate the reproduction of the system is the emergence of individualized private-sector social services, which open up opportunities for those with sufficient resources to opt out of the standardized univeralistic programs. The growth of such alternatives could then upset the contingent consent of the middle classes, who would resent paying privately for their own more individualized services while also shouldering the burden of the standardized system on which they no longer draw. In short, a rise in individualism associated with demands for more choice and less standardization is potentially subversive to the universal welfare state, given its particular material and moral foundations.

Understanding the different mechanisms of reproduction that sustain different institutions is also the key to understanding why common international trends frequently have such different domestic consequences, disrupting previously stable patterns in some countries while washing over others seemingly without effect (see Locke & Thelen 1995). As many authors have noted, the political-economic institutions of the advanced industrial democracies have proven surprisingly resilient in the face of globalization pressures, and this certainly speaks for the strong feedback mechanisms at work. However, some countries have in fact seen important changes. Prominent examples are wage bargaining institutions in Denmark and Sweden, both of which have experienced substantial reconfiguration in the last 15 years. How do we make sense of the special vulnerability of the Swedish and Danish systems of wage bargaining to these putatively common international trends? The crucial starting point for any such analysis is to examine what ideological and material foundations sustained these institutions prior to the onset of these new pressures (Swenson 1989). Both the Danish and the Swedish models of the 1960s and 1970s were characterized by a high degree of egalitarianism, which rested on (and also re-produced) a particular coalition of interests and a set of ideational claims supporting egalitarianism. These arrangements were highly resilient in the face of several important changes—both domestic and international— through the 1970s, but they began to unravel in the face of market changes in the 1980s that systematically enhanced the bargaining power of skilled over unskilled workers (Pontusson & Swenson 1996). Specifically, the trend toward "diversified quality production" was deeply subversive to systems like the Danish and the Swedish ones because it encouraged the development of shop-floor structures that were completely at odds with the overarching national wage bargaining institutions. By contrast, the trend toward diversified quality production did not subvert, and in some ways reinforced, key institutions in the German political economy because these were premised on a very different foundation and different mechanisms of reproduction, which accommodated (indeed nurtured) certain kinds of inequalities between skilled and unskilled workers.

A final example is the stability of party systems. Lipset & Rokkan (1967) may be right in arguing that party systems become "frozen" at particular junctures, but we know from Shefter's work (1977) that the mechanisms that sustain and stabilize different party systems vary. Shefter's distinction between patronage-based and programmatic parties clearly makes a difference to the kinds of events that are likely to disrupt stable patterns of politics. For instance, throughout the postwar period, both Italy and Sweden had very stable party systems that revolved around the dominance of a single hegemonic party, the (patronage-oriented) Christian Democrats in Italy and the (more programmatic) Social Democrats in Sweden. The Swedish party system could absorb a defeat of the Social Democrats at the polls (as in 1976, for example) without a full-scale breakdown. In Italy, however, the defeat of the Christian Democrats (not coincidentally, precipitated by corruption scandals) prevented the party from continuing to use state resources to shore up its political support, and so the crisis of the Italian Christian Democrats created a massive opening that quickly brought about a major reconfiguration of the political landscape.

In all of these cases, understanding moments in which fundamental political change is possible requires an analysis of the particular mechanisms through which the previous patterns were sustained and reproduced. In contrast to equilibrium and other models that separate the question of stability from the question of change and propose that they require different analytic tools, the examples above suggest that an understanding of political change is inseparable from—and indeed rests on—an analysis of the foundations of political stability (Skowronek 1995:96, Orren & Skowronek 1994:329–30).

CONCLUSION

Gourevitch (1986) is responsible for the memorable aphorism that, among comparativists, happiness is a crisis that hits a lot of countries—for in moments of crisis, the elements that previously held a system together come into full relief. This is essentially what I have argued here. It is possible to do better than to separate questions of institutional reproduction from those of institutional change, resigning ourselves to the idea that each requires an entirely different toolkit. Instead, drawing together insights from the critical junctures literature and the literature on path dependency and policy feedbacks, I have argued that the key to understanding institutional evolution and change lies in specifying more precisely the reproduction and feedback mechanisms on which particular institutions rest. I take from Orren & Skowronek the important insight that much of what moves politics is the intersection and interaction of different ongoing processes, although I qualify this by arguing that only some of the resulting collisions are likely to be politically consequential, specifically those that interfere with the reproduction mechanisms at work in particular cases.

Attention to these matters will provide insights into some of the provocative issues raised but not necessarily fully answered by recent historical institutional work. These include the important issue of differences in the duration of critical junctures legacies, as well as the related question of why some institutional legacies seem to contain the seeds of their own destruction. Understanding these issues will require work that is "genuinely historical" (Skocpol 1992:59) in the sense that it tracks the unfolding of processes, individually and in relation to one another, over time. The link between the critical junctures literature (on institutional formation) and the feedback literature (on institutional reproduction) is thus clear: Knowing how institutions were constructed provides insights into how they might come apart.

Functionalist perspectives will not take us far, since they skirt the issue of the origins of institutions and the all-important matter of the material and ideological coalitions on which institutions are founded. This does not mean that borrowing from other perspectives is impossible; on the contrary, it may be quite fruitful. One can imagine conceiving and analyzing consequential policy collisions as "nested games," for example, employing some of the tools of rational choice to sort out the logic of the situation and the responses of the actors. This could certainly form one of the "modules," as Scharpf (1997) puts it, in a more comprehensive analysis. It will not, however, substitute for the process-oriented analysis that is characteristic of historical institutionalism, which is often the only way to understand how some games came to be nested within others in the first place.

Many of the insights from the recent feedback literature will certainly play a role as well; this work has provided invaluable tools for exploring the key issues of who, exactly, is invested in particular institutions, and what sustains these institutions dynamically over time. Institutional research's traditional focus on continuity and stability is thus maintained, but in some cases this should be combined with greater attention to what specific mechanisms sustain that stability, for it is there that we will find clues as to the particular external processes that can produce political opening and change. Attention to the different mechanisms of reproduction will also lend insight into the distinctive ways that different countries are affected by putatively common international forces and trends. In short, a more precise specification of the reproduction mechanisms behind particular institutions is the key to understanding important elements of both stability and change in political life.

ACKNOWLEDGMENTS

For their comments on this paper, I thank David Collier, Frank Dobbin, Peter Hall, Peter Katzenstein, Margaret Levi, Paul Pierson, Nelson Polsby, Walter Powell, Bo Rothstein, Fritz Scharpf, Ben Schneider, Stephen Skowronek, Sven Steinmo, Guillermo Trejo, and the participants in the faculty seminar "The New Institutionalism in Comparative Politics" at the Centro de Investigación y Docencia Económicas in Mexico City.

> **Visit the *Annual Reviews home page* at
> http://www.AnnualReviews.org.**

Literature Cited

APSA-CP. 1997. *Newsletter of the APSA Organized Section in Comparative Politics. Culture and Rational Choice.* 8:2 (Summer)

APSA-CP. 1998. *Newsletter of the APSA Organized Section in Comparative Politics. Comparative-Historical Analysis: Where Do We Stand?* 9:1 (Summer)

Arthur WB. 1989. Competing technologies, increasing returns, and lock-in by historical events. *Econ. J.* 99:116–31

Bates RH. 1997. Comparative politics and rational choice: a review essay. *Am. Polit. Sci. Rev.* 91(3):699–704

Bates RH, de Figueiredo RP Jr, Weingast BR. 1998a. The politics of interpretation: rationality, culture, and transition. *Polit. Soc.* 26(4):603–38

Bates RH, Greif A, Levi M, Rosenthal JL, Weingast B. 1998b. *Analytic Narratives.* Princeton, NJ: Princeton Univ. Press.

Campbell JL. 1997. Mechanisms of evolutionary change in economic governance: interaction, interpretation and bricolage. In *Evolutionary Economics and Path Dependence*, ed. L Magnusson, J Ottosson, pp. 10–32. Cheltenham, UK: Elgar

Collier RB. 1993. Combining alternative perspectives: internal trajectories versus external influences as explanations of Latin American politics in the 1940s. *Comp. Polit.* 26(1):1–30

Collier RB, Collier D. 1991. *Shaping the Political Arena.* Princeton, NJ: Princeton Univ. Press

David PA. 1985. Clio and the economics of QWERTY. *Am. Econ. Rev.* 75(2):332–37

DiMaggio P. 1988. Interest and agency in institutional theory. In *Institutional Patterns and Organizations: Culture and Environment,* ed. LG Zucker, pp. 3–21. Cambridge, MA: Ballinger

DiMaggio P. 1991. Constructing an organizational field as professional project: US art museums, 1920–1940. See Powell & DiMaggio 1991, pp. 267–92

DiMaggio P, Powell W. 1991. Introduction. See Powell & DiMaggio 1991, pp. 1–40

Dobbin F. 1994. *Forging Industrial Policy: The United States, Britain and France in the Railway Age.* New York: Cambridge Univ. Press

Dodd LC, Jillson C, eds. 1994. *The Dynamics of American Politics.* Boulder, CO: Westview

Downing BM. 1992. *The Military Revolution and Political Change: Origins of Democracy and Autocracy in Early Modern Europe.* Princeton, NJ: Princeton Univ. Press

Dunlavy C. 1994. *Politics and Industrialization: Early Railroads in the U.S. and Prussia.* Princeton, NJ: Princeton Univ. Press

Elster J. 1989. *The Cement of Society: A Study of Social Order.* New York: Cambridge Univ. Press. 311 pp.

Ertman T. 1997. *Birth of the Leviathan.* New York: Cambridge Univ. Press. 363 pp

Esping-Anderson G. 1990. *Three Worlds of Welfare Capitalism.* Princeton, NJ: Princeton Univ. Press

Ferejohn J. 1991. Rationality and interpretation: parliamentary elections in early Stuart England. In *The Economic Approach to Politics,* ed. K Monroe, pp. 279–305. New York: Harper-Collins

Fligstein N. 1991. The structural transformation of American industry. See Powell & DiMaggio 1991, pp. 311–36

Friedland R, Alford RR. 1991. Bringing society back in: symbols, practices, and institutional contradictions. See Powell & DiMaggio 1991, pp. 232–63

Gerschenkron A. 1962. *Economic Backwardness in Historical Perspective.* Cambridge, MA: Harvard Univ. Press

Golden M. 1997. *Heroic Defeats: The Politics of Job Loss.* New York: Cambridge Univ. Press

Gould A. 1999. *Origins of Liberal Dominance.* Ann Arbor: Univ. Mich. Press. In press

Gourevitch P. 1986. *Politics in Hard Times.* Ithaca, NY: Cornell Univ. Press

Green D, Shapiro I. 1994. *The Pathologies of Rational Choice.* New Haven, CT: Yale Univ. Press

Greif A. 1994. Cultural beliefs and the organization of society. *J. Polit. Econ.* 102: 912–50

Hall PA. 1986. *Governing the Economy: The Politics of State Intervention in Britain and France.* New York: Oxford Univ. Press

Hall PA. 1993. Policy paradigms, social learning and the state. *Comp. Polit.* 23:275–96

Hall PA. 1994. Central bank independence and coordinated wage bargaining. *Ger. Polit. Soc.* 31:1–23

Hall PA, Taylor RCR. 1996. Political science and the three new institutionalisms. *Polit. Stud.* 44:936–57

Heimer C. 1999. Competing institutions: law, medicine, and family in neonatal intensive care. *Law Soc. Rev.* 33:1

Herrigel G. 1993. Identity and institutions: the social construction of trade unions in nineteenth-century Germany and the United States. *Stud. Am. Polit. Dev.* 7: 371–94

Ikenberry GJ. 1994. History's heavy hand: institutions and the politics of the state. Presented at conf. on The New Institutionalism, Univ. Maryland, Oct. 14–15, 1994

Immergut EM. 1992. The rules of the game. See Steinmo et al 1992, pp. 57–89

Immergut EM. 1997. The normative roots of the new institutionalism: historical institutionalism and comparative policy studies. In *Theorieentwicklung in der Politikwissenschaft: Eine Zwischenbilanz,* ed. A Benz, W Seibel, pp. 325–55. Baden-Baden, Ger.: Nomos Verlagsgesellschaft

Immergut EM. 1998. The theoretical core of the new institutionalism. *Polit. Soc.* 26(1): 5–34

Johnson J. 1997. Symbol *and* strategy in comparative political analysis. See APSA-CP 1997, pp. 6–9

Karl TL. 1997. *The Paradox of Plenty: Oil Booms and Petro-States.* Berkeley: Univ. Calif. Press

Kato J. 1996a. Path dependency as a logic of comparative studies: theorization and application. Presented at APSA meet., San Francisco, Aug. 29–Sept. 1, 1996

Kato J. 1996b. Review article: institutions and rationality in politics: three varieties of neo-institutionalists. *Br. J. Polit. Sci.* 26: 553–82

Katzenstein PJ, ed. 1978. *Beyond Power and Plenty.* Madison: Univ. Wisc. Press

Katzenstein PJ. 1996. *Cultural Norms and National Security: Police and Military in Postwar Japan.* Ithaca, NY: Cornell. 307 pp.

Katznelson I. 1997. Structure and configuration in comparative politics. See Lichbach & Zuckerman 1997, pp. 81–112

Knight J. 1992. *Institutions and Social Conflict.* New York: Cambridge Univ. Press

Krasner SD. 1988. Sovereignty: an institutional perspective. *Comp. Polit. Stud.* 21(1):66–94

Kuran T. 1991. Now out of never: the element of surprise in the East European revolution of 1989. *World Polit.* 44(1):7–48

Levi M. 1988. *Of Rule and Revenue.* Berkeley: Univ. California Press

Levi M. 1997a. A model, a method and a map: rational choice in comparative and historical analysis. See Lichbach & Zuckerman 1997, pp. 19–41

Levi M. 1997b. *Consent, Dissent and Patriotism.* New York: Cambridge Univ. Press

Levi M. 1999. Producing an analytic narrative. In *Critical Comparisons in Politics and Culture,* ed. J Bowen, R Petersen. New York: Cambridge Univ. Press. In press

Levi M. 1998. Conscription: the price of citizenship. See Bates et al 1998b, pp. 109–47

Levy J. 1999. *Tocqueville's Revenge: State, Society and Economy in Contemporary France.* Cambridge, MA: Harvard Univ. Press. In press

Lichbach MI, Zuckerman AS, eds. 1997. *Comparative Politics: Rationality, Culture and Structure.* New York: Cambridge Univ. Press. 321 pp.

Lipset SM, Rokkan S. 1967. Cleavage structures, party systems, and voter alignments: an introduction. In *Party Systems and Voter Alignments,* ed. SM Lipset, S Rokkan, pp. 1–64. New York: Free

Locke R, Thelen K. 1995. Apples and oranges revisited: contextualized comparisons and the study of comparative labor politics. *Polit. Soc.* 23(3):337–67

Luebbert G. 1991. *Liberalism, Fascism, or Social Democracy: Social Classes and the Political Origins of Regimes in Interwar Europe.* New York: Oxford Univ. Press

March JG, Olsen JP. 1989. *Rediscovering Institutions.* New York: Free

Meyer JW, Rowan B. 1991. Institutionalized organizations: formal structure as myth and ceremony. See Powell & DiMaggio 1991, 41–62

Meyer J, Boli J, Thomas G. 1987. Ontology and rationality in the western cultural account. In *Institutional Structure: Constituting State, Society, and the Individual,* ed. G Thomas, J Meyer, R Francisco, J Boli, pp. 9–32. Newbury Park, CA: Sage

Moore B. 1966. *Social Origins of Dictatorship and Democracy.* Boston: Beacon Books

Moravcsik A. 1993. Preferences and power in the European community. *J. Common Market Stud.* 31:473–524

North DC. 1990. *Institutions, Institutional Change and Economic Performance.* New York: Cambridge Univ. Press

Orren K, Skowronek S. 1994. Beyond the iconography of order: notes for a "new" institutionalism. See Dodd & Jillson 1994, pp. 311–32

Ostrom E. 1995. New horizons in institutional analysis. *Am. Polit. Sci. Rev.* 89(1):174–78

Pierson P. 1993. When effect becomes cause: policy feedback and political change. *World Polit.* 45(4):595–628

Pierson P. 1994. *Dismantling the Welfare State? Reagan, Thatcher, and the Politics of Retrenchment.* Cambridge, UK: Cambridge Univ. Press

Pierson P. 1996. The path to European integration: a historical institutionalist approach. *Comp. Polit. Stud.* 29(2):123–63

Pierson P. 1997. Path dependency, increasing returns, and the study of politics. Cent. Eur. Stud. Work. Pap. No. 7.7 (September). Cambridge, MA: Cent. Eur. Stud., Harvard Univ.

Pontusson J, Swenson P. 1996. Labor markets, production strategies, and wage bargaining institutions. *Comp. Polit. Stud.* 29(2): 223–50

Powell WW. 1991. Expanding the scope of institutional analysis. See Powell & DiMaggio 1991, pp. 183–203

Powell WW, DiMaggio P, eds. 1991. *The New Institutionalism in Organizational Analysis.* Chicago: Univ. Chicago Press

Powell WW, Jones D, eds. 1999. *Bending the Bars of the Iron Cage: Institutional Dynamics and Processes.* Chicago: Univ. Chicago Press. In press

Remmer KL. 1997. Theoretical decay and theoretical development: the resurgence of institutional analysis. *World Polit.* 50(1): 34–61

Riker WH. 1980. Implications from the disequilibrium of majority rule for the study of institutions. *Am. Polit. Sci. Rev.* 74(2): 432–46

Rogowski R. 1987. Political cleavages and changing exposure to trade. *Am. Polit. Sci. Rev..* 81(4):1121–37

Rogowski R. 1997. Rational choice as a Weberian view of culture. See APSA-CP 1997, pp. 14–15

Rothstein B. 1996. Political institutions: an overview. In *A New Handbook of Political Science,* ed. RE Goodin, H-D Klingemann, pp. 133–66. Oxford, UK: Oxford Univ. Press

Rothstein B. 1998. *Just Institutions Matter: The Moral and Political Logic of the Universal Welfare State.* New York: Cambridge Univ. Press. 254 pp.

Rueschemeyer D, Stephens EH, Stephens JD. 1992. *Capitalist Development and Democracy.* Chicago: Univ. Chicago Press. 387 pp.

Satz D, Ferejohn J. 1994. Rational choice and social theory. *J. Phil.* 91:71–87

Scharpf FW. 1997. *Games Real Actors Play.* Boulder, CO: Westview. 318 pp.

Schelling TC. 1960. *The Strategy of Conflict.* Cambridge, MA: Harvard Univ. Press

Schneider BR. 1997–1998. Organized business politics in democratic Brazil. *J. Interam. Stud. World Aff.* 39(4):95–127

Scott WR. 1995. *Institutions and Organizations.* Thousand Oaks, CA: Sage

Shefter M. 1977. Party and patronage: Germany, England, and Italy. *Polit. Soc.* 7(4): 403–51

Shepsle KA. 1986. Institutional equilibrium and equilibrium institutions. In *Political Science: The Science of Politics,* ed. H Weisberg, pp. 51–81. New York: Agathon

Shepsle KA. 1989. Studying institutions: some lessons from the rational choice approach. *J. Theor. Polit.* 1(2)131–47

Shepsle K, Weingast B. 1981. Structure-induced equilibrium and legislative choice. *Public Choice* 37:503–19

Skocpol T. 1979. *States and Social Revolutions.* Cambridge, UK: Cambridge Univ. Press

Skocpol T. 1992. *Protecting Soldiers and Mothers: The Political Origins of Social Policy in the United States.* Cambridge, MA: Belknap. 714 pp.

Skowronek S. 1995. Order and change. *Polity* 28(1):91–96

Spruyt H. 1994. *The Sovereign State and Its Competitors.* Princeton, NJ: Princeton Univ. Press

Stark D, Bruszt L. 1998. *Postsocialist Pathways: Transforming Politics and Property in East Central Europe.* New York: Cambridge Univ. Press. 284 pp.

Steinmo S. 1993. *Taxation and Democracy: Swedish, British and American Approaches to Financing the Modern State.* New Haven, CT: Yale Univ. Press

Steinmo S. 1994. American exceptionalism reconsidered: culture or institutions? See Dodd & Jillson 1994, pp. 106–31

Steinmo S, Thelen K, Longstreth F, eds. 1992. *Structuring Politics: Historical Institutionalism in Comparative Analysis.* New York: Cambridge Univ. Press. 257 pp.

Stinchcombe AL. 1968. *Constructing Social Theories.* New York: Harcourt, Brace and World

Stinchcombe AL. 1997. On the virtues of the old institutionalism. *Annu. Rev. Soc.* 23:1–18

Streeck W. 1992. *Social Institutions and Economic Performance.* Newbury Park, CA: Sage

Streeck W. 1997. German capitalism: does it exist? Can it survive? In *Political Economy of Modern Capitalism: Mapping Convergence and Diversity,* ed. C Crouch, W Streeck, pp. 33–54. Thousand Oaks, CA: Sage

Swenson P. 1989. *Fair Shares.* Ithaca, NY: Cornell Univ. Press

Thelen K. 1993. European labor in transition:

Sweden and Germany compared. *World Polit.* 46(1):23–49

Thelen K. 1994. Beyond corporatism: toward a new framework for the study of labor in advanced capitalism. *Comp. Polit.* 27:107–24

Thelen K, Kume I. 1999. The rise of nonmarket training regimes: Germany and Japan compared. *J. Jpn. Stud.* 25(1):33–64

Thelen K, Steinmo S. 1992. Historical institutionalism in comparative politics. See Steinmo et al 1992, pp. 1–32

Tsebelis G. 1990. *Nested Games: Rational Choice in Comparative Politics.* Berkeley: Univ. Calif. Press

Valenzuela JS. 1979. *Labor movement formation and politics: the Chilean and French cases in comparative perspective, 1850–1950.* PhD thesis. Columbia Univ.

Vogel SK. 1996. *Freer Markets, More Rules: Regulatory Reform in Advanced Industrial Countries.* Ithaca, NY: Cornell Univ. Press

Wallerstein M. 1989. Union organization in advanced industrial democracies. *Am. Polit. Sci. Rev.* 83(2):481–501

Weingast B. 1998. American democratic stability and the Civil War: institutions, commitment, and political behavior. See Bates et al 1998b, pp. 148–93

Weir M. 1992. *Politics and Jobs: The Boundaries of Employment Policy in the United States.* Princeton, NJ: Princeton Univ. Press. 238 pp.

Zucker LG. 1983. Organizations as institutions. In *Research in the Sociology of Organizations,* ed. SB Bacharach, pp. 1–42. Greenwich, CT: JAI

Zucker LG. 1991. The role of institutionalization in cultural persistence. See Powell & DiMaggio 1991, pp. 83–107

Zysman J. 1994. How institutions create historically rooted trajectories of growth. *Ind. Corp. Change* 3(1)243–83

Annu. Rev. Polit. Sci. 1999. 2:405–28

EFFECTS OF INSTITUTIONAL ARRANGEMENTS ON POLITICAL STABILITY IN SOUTH ASIA

Subrata Kumar Mitra

Department of Political Science, South Asia Institute, The University of Heidelberg, Im Neuenheimer Feld 330, 69120 Heidelberg, Germany; e-mail: js3@ix.urz.uni-heidelberg.de

KEY WORDS: postcolonial state, neo-institutionalism, governance, legitimacy, India

ABSTRACT

Despite high mass poverty, illiteracy, and religious and linguistic heterogeneity, the states of South Asia enjoy a moderately high level of orderly and democratic government. This contrast to other comparable parts of the world is explained to some extent by the cultural, institutional, and social legacies of British colonial rule and the orderly transfer of power in these successor states. However, 50 years after decolonization, one needs to look beyond colonial rule for explanations. The essay develops a general model based on a rational choice perspective to explain political stability through institutional arrangements. In its application of this model to South Asia, the chapter suggests that political stability is conditional (*a*) on the capacity of the postcolonial state to innovate new institutions and (*b*) on the ability of its new political elites to integrate modern and premodern political structures and values within the institutional set-up and to consult the masses periodically through a democratic political process. This model is illustrated with reference to state-society, state-economy, and interstate relations within South Asia.

INTRODUCTION

The rival nuclear tests of India and Pakistan in May 1998 and the specter of Hindu and Muslim fundamentalism on the ascendance (Huntington 1996) have added a new urgency to the question, how stable is South Asia? In spite of

405

1094-2939/99/0616-0405$08.00

India and Pakistan's long-standing conflict over Kashmir and several high-profile assassinations in India (Mahatma Gandhi in 1948, Indira Gandhi in 1984, and Rajiv Gandhi in 1991) and Sri Lanka (SWRD Bandaranaike in 1959 and Ranasinghe Premadasa in 1993), as well as similar threats to stability in Pakistan and Bangladesh, the states of South Asia present a picture of relative resilience compared with the Middle East, large parts of Africa, central Asia, and Latin America, or Eastern Europe. [Political order, understood as a situation in which ordinary people perceive life and property to be secure, is measureable in terms of survey of individual attitudes or by aggregate indicators such as violent death or riots per million inhabitants. Resilience refers to "strong and unique equilibrium" (Riker & Ordeshook 1973:150–51), denoting the capacity of structures, rules, and processes to bounce back after a temporary deviation from the norm.] There is of course great variation in the level of political stability within the region. As a whole, India stands out as an exemplar of political stability.[1] Recent Indian data compared with the trends predicted in the 1980s (Akbar 1988, Kohli 1990) do not support conjecture about growing disorder [e.g. "...the current political situation features an outpouring of diverse new social demands, ad hoc and vacillating responses by the state, and a growing sense that order and authority—and perhaps even democracy—may be disintegrating in India" (Kohli 1990:6)] (see Figure 1a,b). Nor is non-Indian South Asia lagging far behind. New scholarly studies show a lower level of challenges to governance in Pakistan (Hussain & Hussain 1994), Sri Lanka (de Silva 1994), and Bangladesh (Sobhan 1993) than one might expect on the basis of media reports.[2] Furthermore, although India is once again the leader of the pack (Butler et al 1995), elected, democratic governments now rule all the other states of the region as well.

Nevertheless, in spite of these positive indications, political stability in South Asia carries a residual sense of uncertainty. Even in India, justifiably called the world's largest democracy in view of the size of the electorate and the frequency, regularity, and significance of competitive elections (Table 1), political institutions carry an undertone of fragility. Put to the acid test of religious fanaticism, seen at its extreme in the destruction of the Babri Mosque by a mob of Hindu fanatics in the North Indian city of Ayodhya in 1992, the authority of the world's largest democracy has sometimes failed to assert itself. The democratic regime itself was held in abeyance for 18 months during the National Emergency of 1975–1977. The Indian National Congress, an effective institution based on consensus and accommodation since its inception in 1885,

[1]*Crime in India* (Government of India 1991) reports an average of about four times as many murders in the United States as in India. See Mitra (1996:722).

[2]The following comment speaks for many: "A series of upheavals in South Asia has set off a chain reaction that is pushing this historically unstable country [Pakistan]—now capable of building nuclear weapons—to the edge of political and economic chaos..." (Filkins 1998).

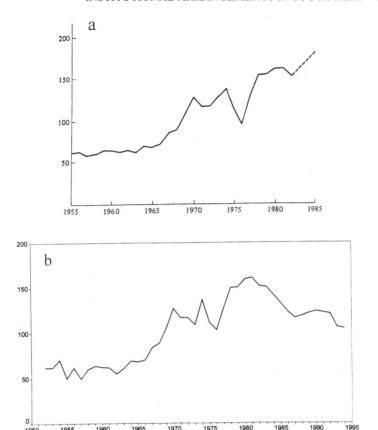

Figure 1 (*a*) Number of riots in India per million population, 1955–1985 (Government of India, various years). From Kohli 1990:7, Figure 1.1. (*b*) Number of riots in India per million population, 1952–1994 (Government of India, various years).

has left center stage, bowing down to a coalition of over a dozen different political parties, with the constant threat of defection by disgruntled partners. At the center of this ruling coalition is the Bharatiya Janata Party, whose advocacy of *hindutva*—the incorporation of Hinduism as the core value of the state—is vigorously opposed by other religious groups and political parties committed to the separation of religion and the state. A plethora of ethnonationalist movements in various parts of the region, such as Punjab, Kashmir, Assam, Sindh, and Northeastern Sri Lanka, further complicate the situation of concern (Brown & Ganguly 1997).

Seen from outside the region, the general character of South Asian politics thus comes across as somewhat schizophrenic: enormous strength and resil-

Table 1 Indian parliamentary elections, 1952–1998[a]

Year	Seats	Candidates	Polling stations	Electorate (in millions)	Vote polled (in millions)	Turnout (%)
1952	489	1,874	132,560	173.2	79.1	45.7
1957	494	1,519	220,478	193.7	92.4	47.7
1962	494	1,985	283,355	217.7	120.6	55.4
1967	520	2,369	267,555	250.6	153.6	61.3
1971	518	2,784	342,944	274.1	151.6	55.3
1977	542	2,439	373,908	321.2	194.3	60.5
1980	529	4,629	434,742	363.9	202.7	56.9
1984	542	5,493	479,214	400.1	256.5	64.1
1989	529	6,160	579,810	498.9	309.1	62.0
1991	534	8,780	588,714	511.5	285.9	55.9
1996	543	13,952	767,462	592.6	343.3	57.9
1998	539	4,708	765,437	602.3	373.3	62.0

[a]Source: Data Unit, Centre for the Study of Developing Societies, Delhi

ience laced with vulnerability. While the strength and resilience contradicts the predictions of comparative democratic theory (Lipset 1959) and South Asia–specific scholarship (Harrison 1960), the vulnerability calls into question some rather optimistic explanations of South Asia's exceptionalism (Dahl 1989:253, Lijphart 1996, Varshney 1998). This double puzzle is the main theme of this article, which presents a theoretical explanation of South Asia's relative stability in terms of the goals, perceptions, and strategies of the region's political actors and the institutional contexts in which they are placed.

MODERN INSTITUTIONS AND POLITICAL STABILITY IN SOUTH ASIA

The relationship of institutional arrangements and political stability is part of a larger debate within South Asian studies. Institutions, understood as "rules of the game in a society…the humanly devised constraints that shape human interaction" (North 1990:3), are grounded in basic assumptions regarding relative autonomy and choice on the part of political actors. These canons of human behavior are not seen as typical of South Asia by some theorists, who conceptualize South Asia in terms of a religious essence. For this line of thinking, which goes back to Marx and Weber, political stability is possible only through oriental despotism (Wittfogel 1957) or through social hierarchy based on the caste system (Dumont 1966). However, in contrast to this mode of thinking, which can conceptualize politics in South Asia only as an epiphenomenon, some political scientists (Kothari 1970, Gould 1990) and statesmen from the onset of independence have placed their faith in institutions as the cutting edge of social change and political order. When Nehru inaugurated the Republic of India with his famous speech on *Freedom at Midnight*, he rested the task of laying the foundations of a modern state squarely on the institutional structure of the new Republic (Rushdie & West 1997). These institutions—mainly the police, the armed forces, and the administration, but also those more directly connected with politics of the day, such as the parliament, the bureaucracy, the courts, and the federal structure of the state—were creations of the British Raj (Weiner 1989:78). Those unfamiliar with South Asia would marvel at the faith that the leader of a successful anticolonial movement placed in colonial institutions. Actually, the belief of Nehru and other leaders of the Republic in the ability of modern, secular institutions to ensure progress can be traced back to the Utilitarians, whose thinking contributed a great deal to the design of colonial regulations and institutions (Stokes 1959). In India and Ceylon (later Sri Lanka), and to a lesser degree in Pakistan, the Freedom Movement was characterized by the dual phenomenon of competition and collaboration with the colonial government. Not surprisingly, therefore, the successors' regimes were deeply impregnated with the values of British-style parliamentary democracy put into effective use through the "agency of India's freedom movement" (Varshney 1998:38).

The continuation of the "steel frame of the Empire," particularly the Indian Civil Service (Potter 1986) and the Indian Police (Bayley 1983), gave the successor state a great measure of continuity (Brown 1985:308). But the capacity of the institutions to carry this burden was questioned right at the outset by Harrison's much-cited *India: The Most Dangerous Decades* (1960). Harrison's apprehensions arose out of the entry of caste, region, and religion into mainstream politics as a result of independence and the sudden expansion of participation. Those primordial identities, which had lain in a state of suspended animation just beneath the surface of colonial institutions, bounced into life under the impact of accelerated popular participation and the simultaneous loosening of central control. Another angle from which skepticism arose about the ability of the institutions to maintain both stability and legitimacy was that of Moore (1966) and Myrdal (1968). Drawing on the combination of rising expectations induced by independence, limited resources for redistribution available to the new regimes, and the likely difficulty of serious structural change by institutions under democratic control, these theorists saw the emergence of a "soft state" (Myrdal 1968) more likely to lead to "peaceful paralysis" (Moore 1966) than to stable, legitimate, democratic governments.

This early skepticism regarding the capacity of modern institutions to sustain democracy, development, and governance continues to cast its long shadow on theories of political stability in South Asia. It underpins much of recent literature (Manor 1983, Saberwal 1986, Morris-Jones 1987, Kothari 1988, Kohli 1990). With the possible exceptions of Rudolph & Rudolph

(1987) and Lijphart (1996), scholars of government and politics in India are unanimous in their diagnosis of the malaise. Voicing this common concern, Morris-Jones (1987:262) questions the complacent view of the incremental evolution of the modern state and traditional society in India and reports that, in some parts of the country, "the process of peaceful interpenetration is certainly present but its character has become hugely conflictual...a condition of intermittent civil war has become virtually normal, with caste-based 'armies' serving the interests of landlord groups by carrying out terrorist killings." The dire predictions of some scholars are further reinforced by nongovernmental organizations [see e.g. Amnesty International's *India: Torture, Rape & Deaths in Custody* (1992)] and the popular press.[3]

Those who emphasize violent conflict as the more important aspect of contemporary South Asia point toward other such pathologies that blight the political landscape. Pakistan, carved out of British India as a homeland for Muslims following the advocacy of the two-nation theory by Jinnah and the Muslim League, could not accommodate the demand of the Bengali population of East Pakistan for regional autonomy and identity. However, the bloody division of the country, which produced the sovereign, democratic, secular, socialist state of Bangladesh, in retrospect strengthened the resilience of Pakistan—and, after some initial problems with state formation, Bangladesh appears to have found a steady path of development as well. Sri Lanka, which achieved universal adult franchise and the status of a welfare state long before India, went through a major transformation of the Republic as a result of the "Sinhala only" policy, which transformed the Tamil population into second-class citizens. Although a determined government under the recently elected President Kumaratunga is trying to cope with this challenge through a combination of repression and accommodation, the anger and frustration that spawned the Tamil separatist movement continues to produce violent unrest in Sri Lanka's domestic politics as well as in its relations with India (de Silva 1994).

Political upheavals in South Asia are explained mostly with reference to structural (Huntington 1968; Frankel & Rao 1989/1990), sociopsychological (Gurr 1970), or ethnic (Brass 1991) accounts. In identifying institutions of the modern state as the critical variable underpinning their models, these theorists merely assert that institutions are important for political stability without trying to derive them from within the world view of actors whose movements those institutions were meant to constrain. Saberwal (1986:197–98) describes India's crisis of legitimacy

---

[3]For a report on the increase in "violence, defiant indiscipline and lawlessness" by "not just the armed militants of the Jammu and Kashmir Liberation Front or the Khalistan Commando Force, but ordinary people, lawyers, policemen, shopkeepers, civil servants, students, trade unionists," see *India Today* (1990).

as a consequence of our collective difficulty in working with institutions of Western derivation which have been implanted in India during and after the colonial period: legislatures, courts, universities, banks and so forth. Our difficulty arises perhaps in a lack of fit between the principles which have gone into the designing of these institutions over many long centuries in Europe, and those informal institutions to which we in India have traditionally been heir: family, caste, village, pilgrimage center, little kingdom, and so forth.

A RATIONAL CHOICE CRITIQUE OF CONVENTIONAL EXPLANATIONS

In hindsight, there was startlingly little public debate about the lack of fit between acquired institutions and the political culture at the onset of independence. No consistent attempt was made to derive or adapt the principles of government to local and regional cultural and political traditions. Inden (1990: 197–98) criticizes this essentialized view of the modern state in South Asia as a "nation-state that remains ontologically and politically inaccessible to its own citizens." From the point of view of scholars and statesmen—for whom a strong, modern state in India, reinforced by such institutions as the separation of religion from the state, is a fixed point of analysis—all outbreaks of public disorder and violent secessionist movements appear "misguided" and possibly "acts of the foreign hand" (Saberwal 1986:ix).[4] However, from the perspective of the political actors, who see themselves as a wronged people, anti-state violence is a necessary step in the direction of a preferred future (Juergensmeyer 1994). A theory that takes the actor seriously must incorporate the actor's perception of reality as an endogenous variable in its operational model.

Against the background of this unsatisfactory state of explanation, it is necessary to start with an assumption that requires of politics no more than the fact that political actors seek to maximize their interests. This main assumption needs to be reinforced by further assumptions that ordinary people are able to perceive their interests, to order them in terms of preferences, to pursue them by drawing on their political resources [both conventional resources and those that they can mobilize through protest action (Mitra 1992)], and to combine alternative courses of action, both risky and certain, in an optimal fashion (Riker & Ordeshook 1973, Mitra 1978, Little 1991).

For the purpose of constructing a formal model of political stability, I assume that rational individuals will be orderly if and only if they perceive rule obedience to be worth their while, i.e. if the expected utility of undertaking the transaction in accordance with the rule is higher than that of breaking the rule. Rules are thus a critical explanatory variable for the likelihood of political sta-

---

[4]The allegation of a conspiracy to destabilize India with the collusion of foreign powers dominated the political rhetoric of Indira Gandhi in the 1970s (Wariavwala 1992).

bility [see Hechter 1990, Bueno de Mesquita & Cohen 1995; Saberwal & Sievers (1998) provide insights into the origin and functioning of rules in the South Asian context], which is high when the rules of transaction are obeyed by those subject to them. In order to link the preferences of political actors in the real world and the options that they may select to pursue for strategic reasons, I next turn to ideal type situations in which two players (who in real life might represent competing political forces) are engaged in guessing each other's options and choosing their alternatives in a manner that maximizes their expected utility (Mitra 1997:26).

The payoff matrix presented in Figure 2 depicts the alternatives available to two actors who can each choose either to carry out the transaction at hand according to the rule or to maximize his expected gain by breaking the rule. For the sake of simplicity, I assume symmetry, so when both actors obey the rule, each is likely to get K. (For simplicity I assume K as a payoff for each player, but it need not be, since no interpersonal comparison of utility is involved.) For a variety of reasons, however, actor 1 (or/and 2) might consider breaking the rule. The actor in charge of some public function might charge a fee [*pyravi* in South Indian usage (Reddy & Hargopal 1985)] for carrying out his duties (i.e. rent seeking); he might plunder public funds (corruption) or act unfairly in favor of his kin (nepotism). Rule violations at higher reaches of the system cascade downward with a cumulative multiplier effect, leading to the collapse of law and order.

In each of the situations depicted in Figure 2, two players are considering whether to carry out the transaction according to the rule or in a manner not allowed by the rule. The cells denote payoffs to the players. By convention, the payoff to actor 1 is denoted first. The figures to the right of the matrix (outside the box) indicate the minimum payoff that actor 1 can expect; the figures at the bottom indicate minimum gains expected by actor 2. The rewards of rule

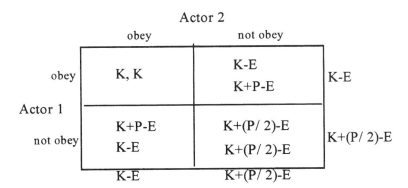

Figure 2   Payoff matrix for a two-person non-zero-sum "rules" game.

breaking for each actor are P, so alternative "not obey" can fetch $K + P$. However, the other actor might get wind of the rule-breaking activity. Discovery of rule breaking creates some apprehension in the mind of the rule-abiding player because there is a possibility of collective punishment for disorderly conduct. The closing of a public-sector undertaking that continues to lose money, for example, will invite sanction from above. The closing of the enterprise will put all the employees out of a job. So the knowledge that one's colleague is not playing the game according to the rule is likely to have an expected cost E to the rule-bound player. Therefore, when the rule breaker expects $K + P$ (or, to be more rigorous, $K + P - E$), the rule-abiding player expects $K - E$.

When both players decide to break the rule, the additional reward P, being finite in nature, has to be shared. We can anticipate that the players will think in terms of a fraction of P (for the sake of symmetry, $P/2$) as the additional gain, less E, the cost of rule breaking. The minimum gains the players can expect are $K - E$ for rule obedience and $K + P/2 - E$ for rule breaking. It is easy to see that maximin players (i.e. players who choose their options in a manner that maximizes their minimum gain) will prefer rule breaking to rule obedience, so rule breaking is the likely outcome of this two-person noncooperative "rules" game. Seen as a general model, this Prisoner's Dilemma outcome can lead to a situation of lawlessness and political instability.

Rule breaking by substantial parts of the population results in anarchy, which, once started, holds the potential for spreading (as Table 2 demonstrates). However, anarchy resulting from mass rule breaking is not inevitable. Just as unregulated competition for power creates a Hobbesian state of nature where life can be solitary, poor, nasty, brutish, and short, given the effective constraint of institutions, civilized social intercourse and orderly rule are possible. As we learn from the concept of "new institutionalism" (March & Olson 1989), political institutions, as interfaces of society and state, are crucial in this context.[5] This concept alerts us to the importance of the maneuvering room that institutions can provide the new elites. As Remmer's critical reevaluation of the impact of Huntington's (1965) article on political development reminds us, "Standing at the intersection of political inputs and outputs, political institutions represent the 'black box' of politics through which societal interests are translated into policies and policy outcomes" (Remmer 1997:50).

The modernizing approach that underpins some of the early general works on South Asia saw the state as the unproblematic purveyor of modernity and progress. Theoreticians of this genre conceptualized the state as a neutral

[5]March & Olson (1984) stressed the importance of norms and values in defining how political institutions should and would function (Peters 1996). Seen in this light, institutions define a "logic of appropriateness" that guides the actions of their members. In this view, the most important element defining an institution is "the collection of values by which decisions and behaviors of members are shaped, not any formal structures, rules, or procedures" (Peters 1996:208).

Table 2   Trust and confidence in political institutions and actors (%)

Institutions/Actors	Great deal	Somewhat	Not at all
Election commission	45.9	31.3	23.0
Judiciary	41.6	34.2	24.2
Local government	39.0	37.8	23.2
State government	37.2	43.6	19.2
Central government	35.2	42.5	22.3
Elected represantatives	19.9	40.4	39.7
Political parties	17.4	43.6	39.0
Government officials	17.2	40.4	42.3
Police	13.0	29.9	57.1

enforcer of unity and guarantor of progress, above everyday politics. When empirical studies showed the state to be far from this ideal and a key player in politics, the modernizing approach had to resort to such concepts as fundamentalism (Huntington 1996) and deinstitutionalization (Kohli 1990:24), which were more in the nature of Kuhnian anomalies than falsifiable conjectures. Being actor-oriented, a neo-institutionalist model is able to look at politics within, below, above, and outside the state. It builds on the basic assumptions that political actors need to amass power and that institutions function as constraints on this competition for power. Conditions can be created under which rational actors prefer to be rule-oriented through effective political and administrative action. Such conditions may include self-policing (a likely outcome in the context of a recursive game in which actors can communicate) and reciprocity through a combination of rewards and sanctions (Axelrod 1984). Such conditions can be produced by creating smaller, culturally cohesive political units through decentralization. Rational actors in such units perceive the long-term cost of rule breaking (E) to be significantly greater than the immediate gain (P), so that the members of the community have incentive to become the agents of rule enforcement. The creation of a firm, fair, effective police force, which guarantees the punishment component of rule breaking (E) to be greater than its benefits (P), can keep rational actors on the right side of the law. Effective social and economic reform, which improve the normal payoff (K) to a point where the expected benefits of rule breaking are lower than its costs, can transform poachers into gamekeepers. Finally, if the rule is offensive to an actor's identity and dignity, so that E is seen not as a cost but as a benefit greater than K [illustrated by collective resistance movements ranging from terrorism to Gandhian *satyagraha* (Parekh 1989:107–71)], the situation can be made orderly by substituting the rule with one that reflects the core beliefs and values of the actors (Das Gupta 1970, Shastri 1997).

There are, however, two boundary conditions, exogenous to the game situations depicted here. First, the rule violators, rather than being interested in policy outcomes, might simply wish to be rid of the specific governing elites concerned. If one were an East Bengali politician in 1971, with one's country ravaged and community devastated, the top priority might be to get the existing government, seen as aggressors, off one's soil. Under these circumstances, no orderly political transaction is possible, particularly if there is no overlap between rulers and their challengers. However, if there is an intersection between the two, then, depending on the relative weight of the intersection, it is possible to anticipate an orderly transfer of power (rather than a disorderly coup d'etat, rebellion, or riot). Following this conjecture, policies based on regular elections, electoral reform, and the creation of new political arenas that facilitate the recruitment of new elites would enhance the legitimacy of political institutions.

Another exogenous factor that affects legitimacy and political order is geopolitical in nature. If a neighboring state exports disaffection downstream through agents provocateurs or armed secessionists and encourages law breaking by providing protection, then there is not much the government can do in terms of domestic public policy. Political stability of the states of the region is thus part of the larger issue of global and regional security.

A NEO-INSTITUTIONAL MODEL OF POLITICAL STABILITY IN SOUTH ASIA

A neo-institutional model of political stability should incorporate at least four parameters: a bureaucratic state machinery that combines policy responsiveness and law-and-order management (Bayley 1983); local protest movements contributing to agenda setting (Omvedt 1993); political elites using two-track strategies that combine protest and participation (Mitra 1991); and constitutional change as a political resource (Austin 1966, Sen Gupta 1991, Iftekharuzzaman 1998, Shastri 1997). This model, which approaches the problem of challenges to political stability, distinguishes itself from the structural-functional approaches because of its methodological individualism, its incorporation of rules as an endogenous variable, and its specification of cultural and historical contexts as exogenous constraints rather than as fuzzy tradition surrounding modern institutions.

Once we conceptualize the political process—law and order, policy making, and constitution—as an explanatory variable, any empirical analysis in the Indian context reveals several interesting factors, including civil disobedience, riots, caste and tribal conflict, insurgency, and terrorism. What unites these disparate acts is the fact that the government is invariably a key target. Underneath the challenge to the government of the day, there usually lurks a political agenda that wholly or partly questions the legitimacy of the established authority and institutions of the state. For that very reason, the articulation of such demands takes place outside conventional political institutions. Thus, in a broader sense, the agents responsible for a "governability crisis" are political actors—a status that the representatives of the state resolutely resist granting them until they cannot do otherwise.

As we learn from both successful and failed cases of conflict management in South Asia, in the event of the outbreak of political instability, one of three situations is likely to occur: persistent crisis, which slowly brings most social institutions to a standstill, leading to a radical change in the constitutional rules governing conflict (e.g. takeover by a military dictator); quick escalation of the crisis into violent conflict, leading to civil war or military insurgency; or political accommodation of the agenda of the challengers through state action—administrative, legal, or constitutional. Liberal democratic theory holds that the breakdown of law and order is unlikely if political parties and pressure groups, which act as intervening structures between government and society, can articulate and aggregate political demands. The state and the constitution in which it is embedded provide an overarching framework that acts as the boundary condition to the competition, collaboration, and occasional conflict of the actors concerned. An intelligent and effective government, i.e. one that listens to the society and one whose bureaucracy manages to implement what is legally ordained, can be presented in terms of the model depicted in Figure 3.

Almond & Powell (1996:88) explain why the political process described in Figure 3 becomes problematic in postcolonial societies where rapid economic and social change combined with inadequate institutionalization and parties with a narrow social base can lead to violent protest, crisis, and declining legitimacy. This theoretical linkage, postulated by Huntington (1968) and Gurr (1970), can be specified in the form of the Gurr-Huntington "polarization" model (Figure 4). The factors that Kohli (1990) points out in his account of political change in India leading to the governability crisis, namely "the deinstitutionalizing role" of national and regional leaders, "weak political institutions," the "undisciplined political competition," politicization of "all types of social divisions, including caste, class and ethnic cleavages," and "numerous strategies, including…violence [which] have been used to gain access to the state's resources" (1990:385), substantiate the conjectures of this model.

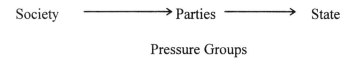

Figure 3   The liberal model of state-society linkage.

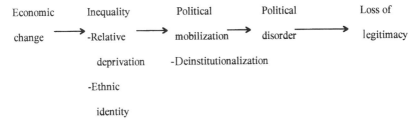

Figure 4   The Huntington-Gurr polarization model.

Kohli's comparison of the levels of governability crisis in different States of India is a major advance on previous studies because it helps isolate the causal factors that underpin governmental stability. Thus, whereas Bihar is found virtually in a state of war of each against all, and Gujarat is caught in intense political conflict on communal lines, West Bengal provides a contrasting case because of generally successful conflict management by a marxist party turned into a reform-minded ruling coalition with cohesive leadership and a disciplined rank and file, which has managed to plant itself firmly between the people and the government. The West Bengal situation thus resembles that of the model presented in Figure 2. The transformation of a radical marxist opposition party into a ruling party within the confines of a parliamentary democracy with a written constitution is the main explanation for West Bengal's achieving this high level of conflict management. Factors such as effective initiation and implementation of reform and law-and-order management, which enhance the explanatory power of the model, can be specified in terms of the model presented in Figure 5.

Crucial to the neo-institutionalist model are (*a*) the maneuvering room that the constitution permits the political elite in the first place (a democratic regime offers greater scope for negotiation and bargaining than does military rule) and (*b*) the political accountability of the elites, which obliges them to engage in purposeful social intervention. These two factors solve the central puzzle of Huntington (1968:55), namely how institutional change can add to stability rather than undermining it (Remmer 1997:36). Further dynamism is added to the model by leaving the criteria of legitimate political action to political actors at the local and regional levels. The response of the government, in terms of law-and-order management, redistributive policies, and constitutional change, acts as a feedback loop that affects the perception of the people at the local and regional levels. The perception of a fair, responsive, and firm state lowers the level of relative deprivation. Compared with the model presented in Figure 4, the model in Figure 5 introduces a few additional parameters, such as policy responsiveness. In a case of successful transaction, competing elites choose their options in a manner that maximizes benefits and

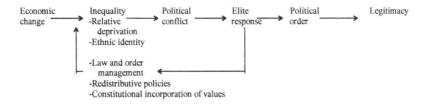

Figure 5   A dynamic neo-institutional model of political stability.

minimizes costs of transaction, and they negotiate on the basis of a complex repertoire that combines instruments of rational protest with elements of participation, such as contacts with higher level decision makers, lobbying, voting, and sending petitions.[6] India's significant achievement in the area of positive discrimination, which has successfully severed the cultural and economic links between caste and occupation, and legislation that has transformed social privilege into a politically contested concept bear ample testimony to the change that has come about democratically. When redistributive policies and constitutional change are the results, they lead to the reduction of perceived inequality and provide necessary political accommodation to such "transcendental" issues as group identity. Once the transcendental issues are incorporated into the constitution through appropriate changes in the rules of the game and creation of new arenas, politics within the reconstituted units reverts back to the transactional themes of material benefits.

A PARTIAL TEST OF THE MODEL

This section examines the implications of the two models described in Figures 4 and 5 with regard to some salient aspects of South Asia relevant to political stability, namely, state and nation building, social transformation, economic change, and the security dilemma. In each case, although the Indian state and government are often faced with serious problems and appear to be on the brink, they confound predictions of disaster by somehow bouncing back (Manor 1994; Mitra 1978, 1997). The high governmental stability of the 1950s was followed in the 1960s by the rapid rise and fall of governments and the first indications of the use of unruly crowds by opposition parties to press their demands for political change. Indira Gandhi's populist rhetoric, authoritarian

[6]The point is made by Bueno de Mesquita & Root (2000), who present a model of endogenous institution formation and link it to government performance and the ability of political leaders to survive. The chapter by Root refers to the incentive for corruption among bureaucrats in India. For testable hypotheses based on the neo-institutional model of political stability, see Mitra (1997: 37–38).

politics, and use of mass mobilization as an alternative to parliamentary approval of her policies characterized the Emergency of 1975–1977. The restoration of parliamentary democracy in 1977 also returned political disorder to pre-Emergency levels (Figure1a,b). The period that followed saw a rapid rise in the challenges to stability, such as large crowds on the rampage and violent separatist movements. However, the liberalization of the economy (Lewis 1995) loosened the low-level equilibrium trap of the mixed economy that managed to cumulate the suboptimal aspects of the command economy and private enterprise, described graphically by Bardhan (1984). Orderly rule was restored during the government of Narasimha Rao, the last in recent memory to have served its full term. These changes can claim to have restored India to a level where it has ceased to be the subject of dire predictions.

The resilience of the postcolonial state in India (Mitra 1990:79–82) and the skill with which the state has managed to accommodate leaders of anti-state movements through a combination of sanctions, rewards, and reform (Mitra & Lewis 1996) have played a crucial role in the restoration of the orderly political process. India, once a segmentary state based on zones of influence (Stein 1980), has acquired the quintessential characteristics of a modern state. It has secure boundaries, in the northwest and northeast in particular; its multilinguistic and multireligious population identifies with the Indian state; it has achieved sovereign control over domestic politics through an astute combination of concentration of power in the hands of the government and cultivation of an international profile through nonalignment; and now it has achieved globalization. In the course of this transition, the state in India has successfully combined the twin roles of providing a relatively neutral point of reference for competing social forces and providing a sense of direction for social and economic change. Rudolph & Rudolph's characterization of the state in India shows how it has successfully incorporated some apparently contradictory values in order to create a space where different social groups can periodically negotiate the priorities for the politics of the day (1987:400–1).

> Like Hindu conceptions of the divine, the state in India is polymorphous, a creature of manifold forms and orientations. One is the third actor whose scale and power contribute to the marginality of class politics. Another is a liberal or citizens' state, a judicial body whose legislative reach is limited by a written constitution, judicial review, and fundamental rights. Still another is a capitalist state that guards the boundaries of the mixed economy by protecting the rights and promoting the interest of property in agriculture, commerce, and industry. Finally a socialist state is concerned to use public power to eradicate poverty and privilege and tame private power. Which combination prevails in a particular historical setting is a matter for inquiry.

The double transformation of state and society has been possible through a written and judicially enforceable constitution that clearly lays down the fundamental rights of the regions through a federal division of powers and that protects liberty through a separation of powers between the three wings of government (Austin 1966) but has nevertheless enough flexibility to incorporate changing social values and norms and to bring about social and economic reform through constitutional amendment (Sen Gupta 1991). Constitutional change in the 1950s brought India's political regions in line with her cultural divisions, in effect promoting mother tongue to the official language for the bulk of the population while safeguarding the interests of the minorities through a complex three-language formula (Brass 1974). Failure to undertake similar reforms eventually split Pakistan, leading to the birth of Bangladesh as a separate country (Rashiduzzaman 1989), and is the root cause of the Tamil problem in Sri Lanka today. Recent amendments have brought about such radical changes in India's federal structure by adding a third level, which has already devolved autonomous political and financial powers to the *gram panchayats*—elected councils in India's half million villages (Government of India 1978)—with a constitutional guarantee of one third of the seats to women and new units of the federation to accommodate distinct subnational groups.

This rigid-flexible stance of the constitution also facilitates both the enactment and repeal of major legislation, to keep institutions in tune with changing political environments, both national and international. A good example is the liberalization of the economy, which has radically transformed India's state-dominated, command economy into one poised at the threshold of a full integration into the international market economy. Finally, beyond the constitution and legislation is the informal process of politics and administration. The mediating role of a plethora of commissions, informal quota systems, and symbolic recognition, meticulously documented by Lijphart (1996), shows the combination of the features of federalism and consociationalism that effectuates majoritarian democracy in India while protecting the rights of minorities. A second arena where administrative initiatives have produced some regional coordination is the South Asian Association for Regional Cooperation (SAARC), supplemented with a number of formal and informal institutional initiatives referred to as regional confidence-building measures (Ganguly & Greenwood 1996; see Ahmed 1998 for a series of concrete measures for regional cooperation).

Earlier scholarship (Kothari 1970) had presented the Indian National Congress, bearing the legacy of the Freedom Movement, as the main founder of India's institutions. The puzzle of political stability despite the decline of the Congress Party is partly explained by the existence of a relatively fair and effective electoral process, which has become an agent of the creation of a stable and legitimate political order. When consensus building is posed as a prime concern, the existence and availability of the electoral option act as an incentive for political parties to concede, coalesce, compromise, and come to a consensus. In spite of their tendency to produce unstable political groupings, single-member constituencies and the first-past-the-post system have made it virtually impossible for any political party to concentrate its efforts on only a single social group. Thus, the national and regional parties have an incentive to look for allies beyond the arena in which they are placed. This is the dynamics behind the political integration of India and the larger involvement of the citizenry in its politics. The electoral principle, effective at the macro, meso, and micro levels of the system, is the cutting edge of social change in India. As recent experience shows, although competitive elections in India hold the potential for mobilization on communal lines, the need for compromise sets the limits beyond which parties consider it politically imprudent to go, particularly when their issue positions appear to threaten the survival and dignity of other communities. The ruling Hindu nationalist coalition's jettisoning of three of its salient programs (the removal of the separate status of Kashmir, the enactment of a uniform personal law to replace current legislation that permits a separate status to Muslims, and the dropping of a commitment to build a temple to Rama in Ayodhya on the spot where the Babri Mosque once stood) is an indication of this informal but effective safety mechanism built into the Indian political system (see the *National Agenda for Governance: BJP & Alliance Partners* 1998).

The direct entry of traditional social and religious symbols into the political arena is seen by some scholars (Vanaik 1997) as an assault on the secular structure and modern institutions of the state. On the other hand, the fact that culture and ritual, in their multiple local and regional ways, have steadily voted their way into the public space, and that radical right-wing religious movements have been transformed into parties of governance functioning within the constraints of the constitution, is an indication of the vibrancy of the political process that has steadily expanded the scope and depth of modern institutions. This polarization and debate on the issue of "secularism" requires students of Indian politics to look at social rituals in the electoral context not merely as an exotic and amusing backdrop to the serious business of party ideology and campaign but as a possible attempt to relate abstract and alien ideas to local and regional contexts, or even to find indigenous moorings for exotic institutions. Rudolph & Rudolph (1967), in their early disagreement with the uncritical acceptance of modernization, argued that the incorporation of social ritual into modern political institutions could be the basis of a negotiated solution to the problems of modernization of traditional societies.[7] The political experi-

---

[7]The continuation of the administration of rights of various groups of interests that form part of the Jagannath Temple and religious communities within the secular State of Orissa, with the Gajapati King of Puri playing a significant role both in administration and ritual, provides an interesting regional model of the accommodation of the secular state and the sacred beliefs of important groups of people (Mitra 1994).

ence of the past five decades provides evidence for the prescient character of their early prognosis.

WHY DO INSTITUTIONS WORK IN SOUTH ASIA SOMETIMES?

This section analyzes the mixed record of South Asia's attempts to achieve political stability through institutional change with reference to the important theoretical insights provided by North (1990). North describes the process of institutional change as a

> complicated process because the changes at the margin can be a consequence of changes in rules, in informal constraints, and in kinds and effectiveness of enforcement. Moreover, institutions typically change incrementally rather than in discontinuous fashion. How and why they change incrementally and why even discontinuous changes (such as revolution and conquest) are never completely discontinuous are a result of the embeddedness of informal constraints in societies. Although formal rules may change overnight as the result of political or judicial decisions, informal constraints embodied in customs, traditions and codes of conduct are much more impervious to deliberate policies. These cultural constraints not only connect the past with the present and future, but provides us with a key to explaining past historical change. (North 1990:6)

North identifies two major factors that are responsible for incremental institutional change, namely, "the lock-in that comes from the symbiotic relationship between institutions and the organizations that have evolved as a consequence of the incentive structure provided by those institutions, and the feedback process by which human beings perceive and react to changes in the opportunity set" (North 1990:7). North's locked-in symbiosis suggests a close relationship between sacred beliefs of important groups in society and their main interests. As long as this convergence holds fast, these groups do not question the legitimacy of the rules of the game. Legitimacy of the political system requires that their effect be continuously reflected in appropriate changes in the constitution. But this feedback may not take place for a variety of reasons. The key decision-making elites may simply fail to perceive the rationale behind demands from below or may not consider them politically advantageous enough. Thus, the original impetus for Pakistan was created through a fortuitous convergence of Islam and a good career move for Muslim elites of British India, but when the equally important Bengali nationalism manifested itself, as did the resentment of the Bengali elite against the quasi-monopoly of the West Pakistani elite over the economy and administration, these changes were not effectively communicated into Pakistan's high politics. Within India, the emergence of Tamil and Telugu nationalism have found an institutional home

within the Indian Republic, but the same cannot be said about Sikh nationalism, which is still testing the limits of India's secular state. Nor can this be said
of Kashmiri nationalism. The institutionalized hiatus between the political and
economic market of Kashmir and the rest of India gave Kashmir a special
status within the Indian Union in the form of Article 370 of the Indian constitution. This special status and the fraudulent nature of elections in Kashmir in the
past stopped an emergent post-independence generation of Kashmiri elites
from getting into power (as in other regions of India). As such, the political
process of Kashmir has not succeeded in finding its home within the constitution of the Indian Republic despite the repeated claims of India's leadership
that Kashmir is an integral part of Indian territory.

From the above discussion, it is apparent that actors' perception of institutions is a key factor in political stability. The results of a recent survey (Mitra
& Singh 1999) provide the empirical evidence that, interpreted in the manner
of North (1990), explains why institutions in India appear simultaneously
strong and weak. The data are drawn from a sample of 10,000 men and women,
representing the Indian electorate, interviewed in May–June 1996 in the wake
of the parliamentary elections. Responses to the question "how much trust/
confidence do you have in different institutions of India?" are highly positive
for institutions but more negative for those who are in charge of those institutions (Table 2).

The comparatively high trust in India's independent and highly effective
Election Commission and in the Supreme Court, which has recently played a
key role in fighting corruption and injustice, shows evidence of what North
describes as lock-in of the institution of the rule of law and main organs of the
state. The regular renewal of this trust through political participation at the
three levels of the federation reaching down to the village, which gets moderate support from the respondents, is also significant. However, the precipitous
decline of trust in the actual repositories of power, namely the elected representatives, political parties, government officials, and police reveal the Achil-
les' heel of the Indian political system.

A situation in which individual voters are assertive about their identity and
interests but have little confidence in the elected representatives and civil servants responsible for implementing policy does not augur well for political
stability. A stable democracy requires reasonably high trust in institutions as
well as a high sense of personal efficacy on the part of citizens. In a context of
high legitimacy and low efficacy one can expect an authoritarian regime with
limited participation. When personal efficacy overtakes system legitimacy, the
field is open for intervention from outside the political system by such potential challengers as protest movements, the church, students, the army, and any
organized group with the means to convince the masses that it can deliver better results. The negative evaluation of government officials and the police, on

the one hand, and the plethora of corruption and other scandals involving political leaders, on the other, explain the uncertain feeling many Indians have
about their own political system. In order to test the strength of association of
efficacy and legitimacy, these two variables were cross-tabulated. The results
are presented in Table 3.

We learn from the cross-tabulation of efficacy and legitimacy that the overall relationship between the two is positive, although the strength of association is rather low. This helps explain both the general political stability of India
and its occasional collapse. The center of the political spectrum is occupied by
a large group of people, constituting 41.5% of the electorate, who are moderately efficacious and hold the system to be moderately legitimate. The main
source of challenge to the stability of the system is at the bottom left corner of
the matrix—namely, the 4.1% of the population who are highly efficacious but
for whom system legitimacy is at its lowest; the 15.2% who are moderately efficacious but hold system legitimacy to be low; and the 14.4% who are highly
efficacious but hold system legitimacy to be only moderate. But balancing this
substantial group of about 34.0% are the 14.2% of Indian electorate, resembling Almond's parochials, who occupy the top right corner of the matrix,
where legitimacy overtakes efficacy. Although greater research is needed to
identify the various social groups in terms of their location in the matrix, this
interesting evidence provides new insights into India's political stability as
well as to the sources of its vulnerability.

Table 3   Cross-tabulation of efficacy and legitimacy[a]

Efficacy	Legitimacy			
	Low	Medium	High	Total
Low	36.8	56.0	7.2	100
	21.9	12.9	9.5	14.7
	5.4	8.3	1.1	
Medium	24.7	67.4	7.9	100
	61.5	64.6	43.5	61.5
	15.2	41.5	4.8	
High	17.2	60.8	22.0	100
	16.5	22.5	47.0	23.7
	4.1	14.4	5.2	
Total	100	100	100	100
	24.7	64.2	11.1	

[a]The first entry in each cell refers to the row percentage, the second to the
column percentage, and the third to the percentage of cases in each cell.
Kendall's tau = 0.17.

CONCLUSION

Those familiar with Kuhn's account of scientific paradigms understand why scientists sometimes choose to ignore or demonize what they do not fully understand. The political scientist's dismissal of what he considers merely ritual, primordial, idiosyncratic, or fundamentalist may be indicative of the limitations of the instruments that he applies to the analysis of political behavior in unfamiliar settings. Familiar tools of comparative politics, applied to political behavior in a postcolonial context, might fall short of appreciating the inner logic and motivation that connect individual action (or lack of it) with institutions and larger social processes. This essay argues that a rational choice approach can cut through the obscurity of many modern and traditional institutions to connect political actors, bridge the conceptual gap between social and political spaces, and, in the hands of imaginative policy makers, become a useful building block of an indigenous modernity.

The fond notion of an enlightened and authoritarian elite ruling over a diverse society as a precondition of political stability is a chimera that characterized social theory of nonwestern societies in the colonial era. Much criticized by Said (1978), Inden (1990), and many others as "orientalist," these theories have nevertheless spawned their postwar versions in the form of models of political order and political development. New writings on South Asian politics (Haynes & Prakash 1991, Chatterjee 1997, Malik & Kapur 1998), which are considerably more actor-oriented and take politics from below seriously, are engaged in making the complexities of South Asian politics accessible so that those whose lives are being thus described might recognize themselves. Scholarly research on South Asia has now redirected its focus toward the identification of precolonial political institutions (Dirks 1993:3–5). Both postcolonial institutions and postcolonial discourse (Naipaul 1990) are engaged in devising policies and processes to help create a legitimate political order.

In sum, political stability in South Asia remains critically conditional on (*a*) the ability of the modern institutions to accommodate traditional values, (*b*) the effective implementation of social and economic reform of the kind that can meet popular entitlements (Kohli 1987, Drèze & Sen 1995), and (*c*) the difficult balancing of force and cooption for the management of law and order. Of equal importance is the commitment of the state to individual rights as the cornerstone of democracy rather than as the derivation of legitimacy from some predefined ideological, cultural, or religious essence.[8] The existing literature gives empirical shape to the question of why political order in South Asia

[8]Variously described as Islamic, Guided People's, or Basic "Democracies," these systems describe the slippery slope to authoritarian rule, leading to their violent rejection. The failure to make the distinction between individual rights and collective values is responsible for some scholarly equivocation between the political systems of India and Pakistan (Jalal 1995).

evinces the dual tendency to go off track occasionally and then to bounce back again. Drawing on the broader comparative, rational choice, and new institutionalism literature, this essay has attempted to give a theoretical solution to this interesting puzzle. The challenge for comparative politics is to understand how a moderate degree of political stability has been possible in South Asia in the first place and which political processes and institutional arrangements might take it further.

ACKNOWLEDGEMENTS

I wish to thank the German Research Council (DFG) for their support for field work and research assistance, both of which have been made available under a project entitled "Governance in India: A Cross-Region Analysis of Six Indian States" (no. M1535|1-2).

> **Visit the *Annual Reviews home page* at**
> **http://www.AnnualReviews.org.**

Literature Cited

Ahmed M. 1998. Confidence-building measures between Pakistan and India: an argument for change. *Contemp. South Asia* 7(2):137–45

Akbar MJ. 1988. *Riot after Riot: Reports on Caste and Communal Violence in India.* Delhi: Penguin. 168 pp.

Almond G, Powell GB. 1996. *Comparative Politics Today.* New York: Harper Collins. 846 pp.

Amnesty International. 1992. *India: Torture, Rape & Death in Custody.* London: Amnesty Int. 195 pp.

Austin G. 1966. *The Indian Constitution.* Oxford, UK: Oxford Univ. Press. 390 pp.

Axelrod RA. 1984. *The Evolution of Cooperation.* New York: Basic Books. 241 pp.

BJP. 1998. *National Agenda for Governance: BJP & Alliance Partners.* New Delhi: BJP. 8 pp.

Bardhan P. 1984. *The Political Economy of Development in India.* New York: Basil Blackwell. 118 pp.

Bayley DH. 1983. The police and political order in India. *Asian Surv.* 23(4):486–96

Brass PR. 1974. *Language, Religion and Politics in North India.* Cambridge, UK: Cambridge Univ. Press. 467 pp.

Brass PR. 1991. *Ethnicity and Nationalism:* *Theory and Comparison.* New Delhi: Sage. 358 pp.

Brown J. 1985. *Modern India: The Origin of an Asian Democracy.* Delhi: Oxford Univ. Press. 429 pp.

Brown M, Ganguly S, eds. 1997. *Government Policies and Ethnic Relations in Asia and the Pacific.* Cambridge, MA: MIT Press. 607 pp.

Bueno de Mesquita B, Cohen L. 1995. Self-interest, equity and crime control: a game-theoretic analysis. *Criminology* 33:483–518

Bueno de Mesquita B, Root H. 2000. *Governing for Prosperity.* New Haven, CT: Yale Univ. Press

Butler D, Lahiri A, Prannoy R. 1995. *India Decides. Elections 1952–1995.* Delhi: Books & Things. 405 pp.

Chatterjee P, ed. 1997. *State and Politics in India.* Delhi: Oxford Univ. Press. 576 pp.

Dahl R. 1989. *Democracy and Its Critics.* New Haven, CT: Yale Univ. Press

Das Gupta J. 1970. *Language Conflict and National Development: Group Politics and National Language Policy in India.* Bombay: Oxford Univ. Press. 293 pp.

de Silva KM. 1994. *Sri Lanka: Problem of Governance.* Delhi: Konark. 289 pp.

Dirks N. 1993. *The Hollow Crown: Ethnohistory of an Indian Kingdom.* Ann Arbor: Univ. Mich. Press. 433 pp.

Drèze J, Sen AK. 1995. *Economic Development and Social Opportunities.* Oxford, UK: Oxford Univ. Press. 292 pp.

Dumont L. 1966. *Homo Hierarchicus: The Caste System and its Implications.* Chicago: Univ. Chicago Press. 490 pp.

Filkins D. 1998. Pakistan ripe for radicals: unrest in wake of US sanctions and attacks enhances appeal of Islamic fundamentalism. *NY Herald Tribune*, Aug. 26, p. 1

Frankel F, Rao MSA, eds. 1989/1990. *Dominance and State Power in Modern India: Decline of a Social Order.* Delhi: Oxford Univ. Press. Vol. 1, 443 pp.; Vol. 2, 555 pp.

Ganguly S, Greenwood T, eds. 1996. *Mending Fences: Confidence and Security-Building Measures in South Asia.* Boulder, CO: Westview. 241 pp.

Gould H. 1990. *The Hindu Caste System: The Sacralization of a Social Order.* Delhi: Chanakya. 193 pp.

Government of India, Ministry of Home Affairs. 1951–1993. *Crime in India.* New Delhi: Gov. Press

Government of India. 1978. *Report of the Committee on Panchayati Raj Institutions.* New Delhi: Minist. Agric. Irrig., Dep. Rural Dev. 301 pp.

Gurr TR. 1970. *Why Men Rebel.* Princeton, NJ: Princeton Univ. Press. 421 pp.

Harrison S. 1960. *India: The Most Dangerous Decades.* Delhi: Oxford Univ. Press. 350 pp.

Haynes D, Prakash G, eds. 1991. *Contesting Power: Resistance and Everyday Social Relations in South Asia.* Berkeley: Univ. Calif. Press. 310 pp.

Hechter M, Opp KD, Wippler R, eds. 1990. *Social Institutions: Their Emergence, Maintenance and Effect.* Berlin: de Gruyter. 342 pp.

Huntington SP. 1965. Political development and political decay. *World Polit.* 17: 386–430

Huntington SP. 1968. *Political Order in Changing Societies.* New Haven, CT: Yale Univ. Press. 488 pp.

Huntington SP. 1996. *The Clash of Civilisations and the Remaking of World Order.* New York: Simon & Schuster. 367 pp.

Hussain M, Hussain A. 1994. *Pakistan: Problem of Governance.* Delhi: Konark. 166 pp.

Iftekharuzzaman, ed. 1998. *Ethnicity and Constitutional Reform in South Asia.* Delhi: Manohar. 190 pp.

Inden R. 1990. *Imagining India.* Oxford: Blackwell. 298 pp.

India Today. 1990. Cult of anarchy. 31:7

Jalal A. 1995. *Democracy and Authoritarianism in South Asia: A Comparative and Historical Perspective.* Cambridge, UK: Cambridge Univ. Press. 295 pp.

Juergensmeyer M. 1994. *Religious Nationalism Confronts the Secular State.* Delhi: Oxford Univ. Press. 292 pp.

Kohli A. 1987. *The State and Poverty in India: The Politics of Reform.* Cambridge, UK: Cambridge Univ. Press. 260 pp.

Kohli A. 1990. *Democracy and Discontent: India's Growing Crisis of Governability.* Cambridge, UK: Cambridge Univ. Press. 420 pp.

Kothari R. 1970. *Politics in India.* Boston: Little Brown. 461 pp.

Kothari R. 1988. Decline of the moderate state. In *State Against Democracy*, ed. R Kothari, pp. 14–36. Delhi: Ajanta

Lewis JP. 1995. *India's Political Economy. Governance and Reform.* Oxford, UK: Oxford Univ. Press. 401 pp.

Lijphart A. 1996. The puzzle of Indian democracy: a consociational interpretation. *Am. Polit. Sci. Rev.* 90(2):258–68

Lipset SM. 1959. Some social requisites of democracy: economic development and political legitimacy. *Am. Polit. Sci. Rev.* 53: 69–105

Little D. 1991. Rational choice models and Asian studies. *J. Asian Stud.* 50(1)35–52

Malik Y, Kapur A, eds. 1998. *India: Fifty Years of Democracy and Development.* New Delhi: APH. 489 pp.

Manor J. 1983. Anomie in Indian politics: origins and potential impact. *Econ. Polit. Wkly.* 18(1/2):725–34

Manor J. 1994. *Nehru to Nineties: The Changing Office of Prime Ministers in India.* London: Hurst. 261 pp.

March JG, Olsen JP. 1989. *Rediscovering Institutions: The Organizational Basis of Politics.* New York: Free. 227 pp.

Mitra SK. 1978. *Governmental Instability in Indian States: West Bengal, Bihar, Uttar Pradesh and Punjab.* Delhi: Ajanta. 150 pp.

Mitra SK, ed. 1990. *Post-colonial State in Asia: The Dialectics of Politics and Culture.* Hemel Hempstead, UK: Harvester. 257 pp.

Mitra SK. 1991. Room to maneuver in the middle: local elites, political action and the state in India. *World Polit.* 43(3):390–413

Mitra SK. 1992. *Power, Protest, Participation: Local Elites and the Politics of Development in India.* London: Routledge. 315 pp.

Mitra SK. 1997. Religion, region and identity: secular beliefs and sacred power [Orissa]

in a regional state tradition of India. In *Aspects of India: Essays on Indian Politics and Culture*, ed. N O'Sullivan, pp. 87–127. Delhi: Ajanta

Mitra SK. 1996. India. See Almond & Powell 1996, pp. 669–729

Mitra SK, Alison Lewis R, eds. 1996. *Subnational Movements in South Asia*. Boulder, CO: Westview. 256 pp.

Mitra SK. 1997. Legitimacy, governance and political institutions in India. In *Legitimacy and Conflict in South Asia*, ed. SK Mitra, D Rothermund, pp. 17–49. Delhi: Manohar. 279 pp.

Mitra S, Singh VB. 1999. *Democracy and Social Change in India: A Cross-sectional Analysis of the National Electorate*. Delhi: Sage.

Moore B. 1966. *Social Origins of Dictatorship and Democracy: Lord and Peasant in the Making of the Modern World.* Boston: Beacon. 559 pp.

Morris-Jones WH. 1987. *The Government and Politics of India.* Wistow, UK: Eothen. 296 pp.

Myrdal G. 1968. *Asian Drama: An Inquiry into the Poverty of Nations.* 3 vols. New York: Pantheon. 2284 pp.

Naipaul VS. 1990. *India: A Million Mutinies Now.* London: Heinemann. 520 pp.

North D. 1990. *Institutions, Institutional Change and Economic Performance.* Cambridge, UK: Cambridge Univ. Press. 152 pp.

Omvedt G. 1993. *Reinventing Revolution: New Social Movements and the Socialist Tradition in India.* London: Sharpe. 353 pp.

Parekh B. 1989. *Colonialism, Tradition and Reform: An Analysis of Gandhi's Political Discourse.* New Delhi: Sage. 288 pp.

Peters BG. 1996. Political institutions, old and new. In *A Handbook of Political Science*, ed. RE Goodin, pp. 205–23. New York: Oxford Univ. Press

Potter DC. 1986. *India's Political Administrators, 1978–1983.* Oxford, UK: Oxford Univ. Press. 289 pp.

Rashiduzzaman M. 1989. East-west conflicts in Pakistan: Bengali regionalism, 1947–1970. In *The States of South Asia: Problems of Integration*, ed. AJ Wilson, D Dalton, pp. 111–30. London: Christopher Hurst. 345 pp.

Reddy R, Hargopal K. 1985. The pyraveekar:

the fixer in rural India. *Asian Surv.* 25(11): 1148–62

Remmer KL. 1997. Theoretical decay and theoretical development. *World Polit.* 50: 34–61

Riker W, Ordeshook P. 1973. *An Introduction to Positive Political Theory.* Englewood Cliffs, NJ: Prentice Hall. 387 pp.

Rudolph LI, Rudolph SH. 1967. *The Modernity of Tradition: Political Development in India.* Chicago: Univ. Chicago Press. 306 pp.

Rudolph LI, Rudolph SH. 1987. *In Pursuit of Lakshmi: The Political Economy of the Indian State.* Chicago: Univ. Chicago Press. 529 pp.

Rushdie S, West E, eds. 1997. *The Vintage Book of Indian Writing, 1947–1997.* London: Vintage. 578 pp.

Saberwal S. 1986. *The Roots of Crisis.* New Delhi: Oxford Univ. Press. 90 pp.

Saberwal S, Sievers H, eds. 1998. *Rules, Laws and Constitutions.* Delhi: Sage. 289 pp.

Said E. 1978. *Orientalism.* London: Vintage. 368 pp.

Sen Gupta PK. 1991. *India: Constitutional Dynamics in a Changing Polity.* Delhi: Chugh. 403 pp.

Shastri A. 1997. Constitution-making as a political resource: crisis of legitimacy in Sri Lanka. See Mitra & Rothermund 1997, pp. 173–206

Sobhan R. 1993. *Bangladesh: Problem of Governance.* New Delhi: Konark. 289 pp.

Stokes E. 1959. *The English Utilitarians and India.* Oxford, UK: Clarendon. 350 pp.

Stein B. 1980. *Peasant State and Society in Medieval South India.* Delhi: Oxford Univ. Press. 533 pp.

Vanaik A. 1997. *Communalism Contested: Religion, Modernity and Secularization.* New Delhi: Vistaar. 374 pp.

Varshney A. 1998. India defies the odds. *J. Democr.* 9(3):36–50

Wariavwala B. 1992. Security issues in domestic politics. In *A Changing Landscape: Electoral Politics in India*, ed. SK Mitra, J Chiriyankandath, pp. 125–36. New Delhi: Segment. 285 pp.

Weiner M. 1989. *The Indian Paradox: Essays in Indian Politics.* New Delhi: Sage. 336 pp.

Wittfogel KA. 1957. *Oriental Despotism: A Comparative Study of Total Power.* New Haven, CT/London: Yale Univ. Press. 556 pp.

Annu. Rev. Polit. Sci. 1999. 2:429–44

INSTITUTIONALISM AND THE EUROPEAN UNION: Beyond International Relations and Comparative Politics

J. Jupille and J. A. Caporaso

Department of Political Science, University of Washington, Seattle, Washington
98195; e-mail: caporaso@u.washington.edu

KEY WORDS: institutions, preferences, explanation, integration

ABSTRACT

The growing use of institutional analysis in the study of the European Union
(EU) has improved EU scholarship and rendered it more integral to the discipline of political science. Institutionalist analyses differ regarding the theoretical role of institutions and actor preferences. We classify institutionalist
approaches to the EU by their theoretical treatment (exogenous or endogenous) of institutions and preferences. Analyses at the research frontier transcend these categories and offer the promise of an improved understanding
of EU politics and a greater contribution by EU studies to the broader discipline of political science.

INTRODUCTION

Although born of international diplomacy and law, the European Union (EU)
implicates and exhibits authority over its constituent members in ways reminiscent of a domestic polity. The study of the EU thus stands ambiguously
astride the fields of international relations (IR) and comparative politics.
Whereas some have inferred from the EU's uniqueness the need for a specialized theory of European integration, others have analyzed the EU with
standard theories from established fields in political science and economics.

1094-2939/99/0616-0429$08.00

However, no single-stranded approach satisfactorily explains the creation, change, and operation of EU institutions.

EU scholarship both reflects and reinforces broader trends in political science. Currently, students of EU politics and policy making are taking up insights from the new institutionalism in political science, economics, sociology, and law. In this chapter, we survey and assess institutional approaches to the EU. We proceed in three steps. First, we survey recent debates over the relative applicability of IR and comparative politics for understanding the EU. Second, we conceptually map prevailing institutional approaches to EU politics and policy making. Third, we proceed to the research frontier, suggesting that the best current work transcends both the traditional categories of institutionalism and the divide between IR and comparative politics. We conclude that the institutional turn has improved EU scholarship and made it more integral to the discipline of political science.

BETWEEN INTERNATIONAL RELATIONS AND COMPARATIVE POLITICS

Wallace's (1983) celebrated characterization of the EU as "less than a federation, more than a regime" speaks to the problematic ontology of the EU. American students of the EU have predominantly used the toolkit of IR. They have focused on the ways in which sovereign states have come together and, through "conventional statecraft" (Moravcsik 1991), created a set of rules permitting them collectively to achieve outcomes unavailable to them individually. The EU, from this perspective, is a functional transaction cost regime, an international organization not qualitatively different from others insofar as states create, control, and can exit it.

Europeans, by contrast, have tended to use analytical tools drawn from policy analysis or public administration, more reminiscent of comparative politics. Hix (1994) has argued in favor of a comparative-politics approach to the EU. Hix distinguishes between "integration," understood as the process of system transformation from a decentralized balance-of-power system to an authoritative polity, and "politics," understood as policy making and interaction within a given and authoritative institutional structure. According to Hix, integration theory "describes a 'process', whereas a theory of 'politics' assumes a certain degree of 'stasis'" (1994:11–12). He argues that the study of EU politics should take precedence over the study of integration and that comparative politics performs better in this area than do approaches based in IR.

Hix claims that comparative politics and IR have different empirical foundations. He bases this assertion on a particular vision of the trajectories of the two fields. In particular, he suggests that "the academic discourse of IR scholars and comparativists has grown apart as the fields have matured" (1994:23).

We dispute this assessment for the following reasons. First, both fields have a sustained tradition of cross-level (international-domestic) analysis and inference. The recent explosion of two-level games analysis (Evans et al 1993) goes beyond the older traditions of second image IR theorizing (Katzenstein 1978) and second-image-reversed comparative work (Gourevitch 1978, Rogowski 1989) in its synthesis of IR and comparative concerns.

A second and related objection is that important empirical trends in the international political economy have led the comparative and IR research agendas to converge. Whether the interest lies in cross-national organizational isomorphism in the face of otherwise pervasive differences (Finnemore 1996) or the common pressure on all countries resulting from international economic globalization (Keohane & Milner 1996), broadly similar substantive concerns motivate the fields. EU studies may best exemplify this convergence, a point to which we return below.

Third, comparative and IR scholars are increasingly using institutional analysis, making common cause with the notion that institutions matter. From this perspective, it matters less whether politics occurs within or among nations. What matters more is that politics occurs within a framework of mutually understood principles, norms, rules, or procedures—that is, within an institutional context. Institutionalism, for its proponents, promises a logic that can unify the analysis of politics and policy making at and across levels of analysis, contributing to the increasing transcendence of the traditional comparative-IR divide. Institutionalism also characterizes much (and the best) of recent work on the EU.

INSTITUTIONALISM AND THE EUROPEAN UNION

The new institutionalism is a disparate set of ideas with diverse disciplinary origins, analytic assumptions, and explanatory claims (Hall & Taylor 1994; Koelble 1995; Kato 1996; Goodin 1996; Shepsle 1986, 1989). Institutions are generally seen as "the rules of the game" or the "humanly devised constraints that shape human interaction" (North 1990:3). Actors' preferences and institutions are the raw materials of institutionalist explanation (Van Hees 1997). Among the many possible organizing principles, we organize the literature according to the respective theoretical roles of (and relationships between) institutions and actor preferences.

Two Dimensions of Institutional Analysis

The first dimension of institutional analysis concerns the theoretical role of institutions. Are they exogenous (i.e. given outside of theory) or endogenous (explained in theoretical terms)? Where institutions are exogenous, analysts invoke them in explaining noninstitutional political dynamics and outcomes.

Such institutional explanations examine the ways in which institutions structure incentives, instantiate norms, define roles, prescribe or proscribe behavior, or procedurally channel politics so as to alter political outcomes relative to what would have occurred in the absence of (or under alternative) institutions. If institutions are the dependent variable, they are endogenous, and we are in the realm of explaining institutions. Here, analysts ask about institutional origins, why certain ones take hold but others do not, the dynamics of institutional choice, and so forth.

There are good reasons not to overdraw this distinction. Approaches concerned with explaining the origins of institutions almost always rely on the assumption of prior or deeper institutional arrangements as part of their explanatory apparatus (Field 1981, 1984). Indeed, it is hard to imagine what an institution-free world would look like (would it have language, common understandings, respect for elementary property rights?). Institutional explanations of policy and other outcomes may themselves require the acceptance of prior institutional conditions. Keeping this caveat in mind, we nonetheless find it useful to identify the principal explanatory role of institutions, as indicated by their presence or absence on the left-hand (dependent-variable) side of explanatory equations, as one way of differentiating institutionalist analyses.

The second dimension along which institutional approaches cleave concerns the theoretical place of actor preferences. By preferences, we mean fundamental goals (over outcomes) rather than strategies. From one perspective, actors' preferences over alternative outcomes are exogenously given and remain stable (or at least uninfluenced by institutions). Institutions alter the relative costs and benefits of various strategies but do not affect actors' underlying motivations. Where rationality is bounded, institutions may make available new information about strategies and/or outcomes. Even here, however, fundamental preferences remain unaltered. From a second perspective, preferences over outcomes are partially or wholly endogenous to institutions. Institutions may work their effects directly (e.g. by specifying the outcomes to be desired) or indirectly (e.g. through effects on actors' identities). Whatever the causal pathway, actors' goals do not (or, at the limit, cannot) exist independently of institutions.

Combining these two dimensions yields a fourfold classification of the institutional literature, within which we place approaches to the EU (Figure 1). Approaches in the northwest cell, including federalism, spatial analysis, and network approaches, take both institutions and preferences as exogenous and use them in different mixes to explain changes in policy and behavior. In the northeast cell, rational institutional choice approaches seek to explain institutions (endogenous) on the basis of exogenous preferences and other variables such as power resources. In the southwest cell, populated by sociological new institutionalists, exogenous institutions shape actors' preferences, although

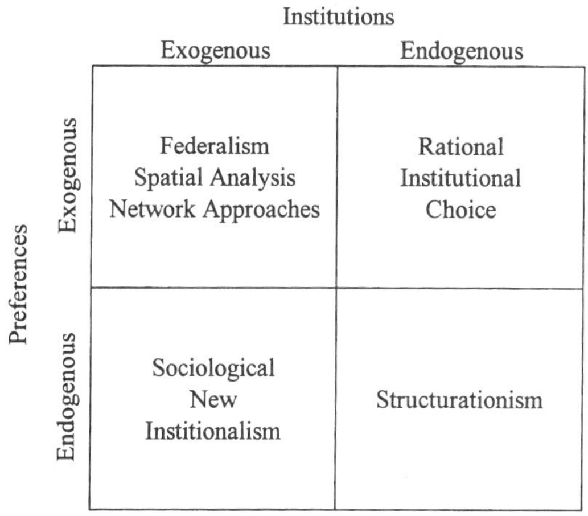

Institutions

	Exogenous	Endogenous
Exogenous	Federalism Spatial Analysis Network Approaches	Rational Institutional Choice
Endogenous	Sociological New Institionalism	Structurationism

Preferences

Figure 1   Two dimensions of institutional analysis.

preferences might also depend on other (noninstitutional) explanatory elements. Because preferences depend on institutions, the latter also take priority in explaining actors' power and bargaining or policy outcomes. Structurationist approaches à la Wendt (1987), in which both explanatory elements are endogenous, lie in the southeast cell. Here, preferences and institutions are said to coconstitute each other through complex iterative processes involving, among other elements, socialization and learning. This approach poses tremendous explanatory challenges, among which is the difficulty of identifying the causal (and thus sequential) relationships between preferences and rules.

Institutionalism and the European Union: Prevailing Approaches

We organize institutional approaches to the EU within our fourfold classification. Because we cannot provide a detailed accounting here, we satisfy ourselves with a rapid survey to give the flavor of institutional approaches to the EU.

Institutional analyses in which both institutions and preferences are exogenous have recently proliferated. An older tradition of federalist analysis has been updated and is gaining currency. Scharpf's (1988) analysis of the "joint-decision trap" seeks to explain the prevalence of suboptimal policy outcomes in systems characterized simultaneously by multiple levels of political authority, unanimity decision rules, and a status quo default option. Sbragia (1991) calls for comparative federalist analysis of the EU. Her portrayal of federalism as the interplay of territorial and nonterritorial interests (Sbragia 1993) rejects the naive assumption, found in some earlier federalist analyses of the EU, that the EU is progressing toward sovereign (Westphalian) statehood. That the EU is not nominally a federal system has not blinded these and other analysts to the growing relevance of federalist concepts to the evolving EU.

Spatial theories analyze the effects of different EU legislative procedures on power and policy outcomes. Whereas intergovernmentalists imply that EU legislative procedures reflect and serve the interests of the states that create them, Tsebelis (1994) argues that the cooperation procedure created by the Single European Act (SEA) enhanced the political power of the European Parliament (EP) at member states' expense, possibly in ways not foreseen by the states themselves (Tsebelis & Kreppel 1998). Specifically, the procedure affords the EP "conditional agenda setting power," meaning that, with the help of the European Commission, the EP can offer amendments to legislative proposals that member states can more easily adopt than amend. Where supranational actors can conditionally set the policy agenda, outcomes will depart from the lowest common denominator of the member states and will better serve supranational interests.

The spatial-analytic research agenda has been an active one. The cooperation procedure has been subjected to additional analysis (Tsebelis 1995, Crombez 1996, Steunenberg 1994; Moser 1996, 1997a; Hubschmid & Moser 1997; Tsebelis 1996), and the basic approach has been applied to intergovernmental, interinstitutional, and international bargaining (Schneider 1995, Cooter & Drexl 1994, Meunier 1998, Jupille 1999), among other areas. Analyzing the Maastricht Treaty's new codecision procedure, Garrett and Tsebelis have concluded that the EP is worse off under codecision than it was under the cooperation procedure because codecision replaces its highly effective conditional agenda-setting power with a less effective unconditional ex post veto (Garrett 1995a, Tsebelis 1997, Tsebelis & Garrett 1997a, Garrett & Tsebelis 1998). Others have challenged this claim on conceptual, methodological, and empirical grounds (Steunenberg 1994, Earnshaw & Judge 1995, Jacobs 1997, Crombez 1997, Scully 1997a,b). Finally, spatial analysts (Garrett et al 1995; Garrett & Tsebelis 1996; Tsebelis & Garrett 1996, 1997b) have directly challenged the validity of voting power analysis (e.g. Hosli 1993), accusing it of neglecting both the spatial arrangement of preferences and the role of supranational actors. Voting power analysts have responded with general improvements to their approach (Widgrén 1995, Hosli 1996).

Network approaches, finally, seek to explain EU policy outcomes based on three characteristics of sectoral policy networks: membership stability, insularity, and the relative strength of resource dependencies between actors (Peterson 1995a). As these characteristics increase, the network approaches the polar type of a policy community, and outcomes tend to be highly stable over time. At the other extreme, mere "issue networks" produce fluid and changeable policies. The precise relationship between policy networks approaches and institutionalism is contested (Jordan 1990, Blom Hansen 1997). However, broad institutional factors, such as issue-by-issue variations in EU competence, clearly condition network characteristics and effects (Peterson 1995a:82, 1995b; Kassim 1994). In addition, implicit in descriptions of strong networks (policy communities) are norms and standard operating procedures that assimilate easily to institutionalist ideas. Given the growing use of network analysis (especially among Europeans), its debatable relationship to other institutional approaches, and the relative success of similarly situated approaches, this approach warrants continued attention.

The northeast cell, in which analysts explain EU institutions and view preferences as exogenous to them, finds its clearest expression in the rationalist literature on EU institutional choice. Moravcsik's "liberal intergovernmentalism" (1993), for example, seeks to explain the outcomes of the EU's grand institutional bargains, such as the Treaty of Rome, the SEA, and the Maastricht Treaty. Moravcsik (1998) explains these institutional choices as a three-step process. First, domestic societal actors form preferences for cooperation or policy coordination at the EU level, partly as a result of their position in the international political economy. States aggregate societal interests and thereby demand some level of European cooperation. Second, armed with these preferences, state executives bargain in the EU arena, attempting to supply their constituents with the desired outcomes. Third, states choose institutional arrangements that maximize the credibility of their commitment to cooperate. Outcomes, according to Moravcsik, result from the interaction of preferences and bargaining power. Although others have embellished this basic approach with formal treatments of strategic interaction (Garrett 1992, Garrett & Weingast 1993), explicit consideration of transactions problems (Weber 1997), and sectoral variation by Lowian policy type (Pollack 1995), the explanatory goals (explaining institutions) and premises (goals exogenous to EU institutions) are largely similar.

Sandholtz (1993) seeks to explain the choice of Economic and Monetary Union by the member states at the 1990–1991 Intergovernmental Conference that culminated in the February 1992 signing of the Maastricht Treaty. Sandholtz argues, counter to intergovernmentalism, that "the national interests of EC [European Community] states do not have independent existence; they are not formed in a vacuum and then brought to Brussels. Those interests are defined and redefined in an international and institutional context that includes the EC. States define their interests in a different way as members of the EC than they would without it" (Sandholtz 1993:3). Sandholtz attempts to endogenize both preferences and institutions. EU institutions provide information and options that boundedly rational states would otherwise lack, on the basis of which they choose new institutions. The endogeneity only of strategic, rather than fundamental, preferences keeps Sandholtz in the northeast rather than the southeast quadrant of our matrix, wherein both goals and institutions are fully endogenous.

Approaches that explicitly adopt the label "new institutionalism" and claim to endogenize preferences, taking EU institutions and interactions as explanatory variables, populate the southwest quadrant of our matrix. Although he characterizes the EU as an emerging state, Bulmer (1993, 1998) is more interested in explaining the effects of EU institutions than their origins. Bulmer explicitly adopts the mantle of historical institutionalism, arguing that institutions shape not only strategies, but also actors' underlying goals. Although Bulmer (1993) admirably maps the EU "governance regime," his empirical examination of EU merger control rules (Bulmer 1994) fails to establish the dependence of member state preferences on these rules.

Kerremans similarly argues that the EU decisively and consistently reshapes state preferences. EU institutions not only provide information and alternatives under conditions of uncertainty, they also effectively socialize participants into EU-defined norms of behavior. In particular, Kerremans (1996: 232) asserts that national representatives in EU Councils (including ministers, lower-level political officials, and administrators) are socialized such that "national affiliations are often thwarted by the affiliations with the councils" in which an individual participates. He is careful not to overstate the case; we are not witnessing wholesale redefinition of national interests in European terms. Instead, à la March & Olsen (1989), national representatives take on new roles as European agents in the domestic arena as well as being domestic agents in the European arena, and they act in ways appropriate to those roles. More research, carefully designed, is called for to assess the perfectly plausible expectation that, in the EU, "membership matters" by, among other things, shaping state preferences (Sandholtz 1996).

Work in the southeast cell is only beginning to emerge. Wind (1996), relying largely on Wendt, advances structurationism as a fruitful approach to the study of the EU, although the nuts and bolts of such an approach remain unclear. Christiansen (1998) seeks to examine the interrelationships between three "layers of change" (at the policy-making, constitutional, and macrosocietal levels), each of which operates in a different historical time frame. His version of historical institutionalism, combined with structurationism and constructivism, would endogenize "the current configuration of actors, interests and powers" (1998:113) to the structures within which they act. Through the medium of actors, interests, and powers, structures thus condition the policy-making process, which conditions constitutional reforms, which contribute in turn to long-term structural (deep institutional) change. The approach, though currently lacking specification, would effectively endogenize both preferences and institutions in a comprehensive explanation of EU (and, indeed, European) politics.

To summarize, institutionalism has permeated the study of the EU, replacing older, and less fruitful, ad hoc approaches. We have suggested that institutional analyses distinguish themselves according to the theoretical place of their two primary explanatory elements, institutions and actor preferences. We have surveyed institutional approaches to the EU that take different stances on this issue. The latest and best work, we suggest below, attempts to erase these distinctions in the quest for a more comprehensive understanding of EU politics.

INSTITUTIONALISM AND THE RESEARCH FRONTIER

The adequacy or quality of a research strategy must be judged with reference to the questions asked or problems raised. There is nothing inherently wrong in seeking only to explain institutions or preferences or to keep one or both of them exogenous in explaining other phenomena. However, such choices produce problems of integration and cumulation of knowledge for the literature as a whole. Older debates between intergovernmentalists and neofunctionalists now risk being rehashed as debates between those who seek to explain "grand bargains" (institutions) and those who construct institutional explanations of "day-to-day politics" (see Wincott 1995a, Moravcsik 1995). All too often, these differences have been cast as the differences between IR and comparative-politics approaches to the EU. However, as Puchala (1972) argued about an earlier generation of integration theory, allegedly competing approaches actually examine different aspects of the EU and are, to that extent, incommensurable. The latest wave of EU studies progresses beyond Puchala's problem of blind men and elephants. Indeed, approaches that transcend and synthesize the different institutional approaches identified above constitute the frontier of research regarding EU politics and policy making.

Institutions and Explanation

Several analysts have transcended the putative divide between explaining institutions and institutional explanation. Pierson (1996) departs from the intergovernmentalist premises of member state control and efficient institutions at the time of institutional design. He proceeds to challenge intergovernmentalist conclusions in two steps. First, he argues that, over time, gaps can emerge between the intentions of institutional designers and institutional (and political) outcomes. Such gaps result from the autonomous actions of supranational organizations (see e.g. Cram 1993, Wincott 1995b), decision makers' restricted time horizons (Alter 1998), the large potential for unanticipated consequences, and the changing preferences of national executives. Second, member states cannot easily regain control because supranational organizations may resist such efforts, institutional obstacles to reform may be substantial, or sunk costs may be high and path dependence strong (see also Marks et al 1996). Pierson shows how principals choose institutions to serve their needs at one time point only to see those institutions acquire their own interests and autonomy and move in directions that depart from the choosers' original goals. All of this can be shown within a principal-agent framework. It does not require a shift to another language, such as systems theory or macropolitical economy.

Pollack's (1996, 1997) institutionalist cut on EU governance bears a strong family resemblance to Pierson's. Pollack, too, departs from intergovernmentalist premises. He argues that institutions can "lock in," or take on a life of their own. This occurs by two means. First, certain decision rules, such as unanimity, make it difficult to change the status quo [Scharpf's (1988) "joint decision trap"]. Second, societal actors adjust to, invest in, and may resist changes to institutions, which Pollack terms micro-level adaptation. Once locked in, institutions can cease to reflect optimally the wishes of their creators. Pollack (1996:442–43) goes further in drawing attention to cross-sectoral variation in the degree of lock-in. In particular, the joint decision trap, requiring a status quo reversion (default) outcome and unanimity decision making, does not apply always and everywhere (see also Peters 1997). Similarly, societal actors may be variably invested in the continuation of EU policies. Pollack (1996, 1997) also pays greater attention than does Pierson to the dynamics of delegation between member states and supranational institutions, considering both the monitoring and sanctioning problems inherent in their principal-agent relationship and the extent and limits of supranational agenda setting.

The explicitly institutional analyses of Pierson and Pollack are effective, among other reasons, because they begin to trace reciprocal and dynamic causal relations between institutional choices and institutional effects. Both are better at institutional explanation, especially of policy outcomes, than at explaining institutions (Pollack 1996:454). However, they are not content to explain only institutional choices (as is intergovernmentalism) or institutional effects. By contemplating the ways in which member states can and might react to institutionally driven gaps or lock-ins, they provide suggestive ideas about the feedback, over time, between day-to-day politics and institutional choices. The resulting accounts, though less parsimonious than Moravcsik's intergovernmentalism, offer the promise of a fuller theory of European integration and politics.

Europeanization and Domestication

Other approaches cross the institutional divide we have identified as well as the putative divide between domestic and supranational levels of analysis (Caporaso 1997). Research on the Europeanization of domestic polities, for example, attempts to explain variations in domestic institutions (e.g. strength of parliaments, executive-judicial-legislative relations, state-society relations) by appealing to institutional and economic changes at the European level. Clearly, in this formulation, institutions do work on both sides of the explanatory equation. Cowles et al (MG Cowles, T Risse, JA Caporaso, unpublished manuscript) define Europeanization as "the emergence and development at the European level of a distinct political system, a set of political institutions that formalizes and routinizes interactions among the actors, and the growth of policy networks specializing in the creation of authoritative European rules." Denying the premise of long-run exogenous preferences and stable domestic institutions, analysts of Europeanization seek to assess changes in domestic structures resulting from the growth of European institutions and politics. Their framework suggests a three-step process. First, European policy and institutional changes generate adaptational pressure on the member states. Second, pressure varies from state to state as a function of the "goodness of fit" (consistency) between what happens in Europe and what exists on the ground in the member states. Third, these institutional pressures, amplified or attenuated by preexisting domestic institutions, generate domestic structural change. Because changed domestic structures may entail different state preferences, they may feed back onto Europeanization. By this logic, domestic institutions serve as the dependent variable at one time point and become the independent variable at the next.

Domestication, by contrast, implies the "taming" of international politics (a mode of interaction based on power and interest within an anarchy) and the transformation of anarchic relations into something more rule-like. Suganami's (1989) domestic analogy suggests a continuum ranging from the most asocial, anarchic international system to centralized world government under a common legal and value system. Whereas the Europeanization approach takes different levels of analysis as given and seeks to derive valid generalizations about cross-level effects, the domestication approach conceptually assimilates the institutional model of international politics into the model of domestic politics. Both kinds of polities are ideal types in any event. Domestic society has elements of anarchy (contract enforcement and cheating are problematic); the international system has substantial elements of governance and rule. The domestication approach merely completes the task of demonstrating that anarchy and hierarchy are ideal types. The challenge of explaining change involves explaining how specific historical cases can move from one to another.

The legal integration literature, explaining the establishment and growth of the rule of law at the European level, has gone farthest in addressing the issue of domestication. Two schools have dominated the scholarly agenda. On the one hand, Garrett and his coauthors (Garrett 1992, 1995b; Garrett & Weingast 1993; Garrett et al 1998) argue that the growth of EU law is explicable in terms of the interests of and strategic interaction between the European Court of

Justice and the member states. "Domestication" is probably a misnomer here, because what is at issue is the creation of a dispute-resolution mechanism permitting member states to monitor and sanction defection and thus to cooperate rationally in the realization of otherwise unattainable collective gains.

On the other hand, neofunctionalists and legal integration scholars have suggested that domestication represents a much more complex fusion of European and domestic legal orders. According to this formulation (Burley & Mattli 1993; Mattli & Slaughter 1995, 1998), the European Court of Justice is not an agent instructed by member state principals. Instead, through a complex process of legal integration termed "constitutionalization," a consolidation of domestic and international orders is taking place (Stone 1994). Constitutionalization refers to a process by which a treaty, essentially a compact among states horizontally differentiated from one another, becomes relevant for the individuals within those states. Over time, the Rome Treaty (the founding document of today's EU) has evolved from a set of legal arrangements binding only on states themselves into a vertically integrated regime conferring judicially enforceable rights and obligations on all legal persons and entities (firms, corporations, and public bodies) within EU territory. The process of constitutionalization describes something quite radical, namely the transformation of a traditional international organization governed by international treaty law into a multitiered system of governance resembling a domestic polity (Stone Sweet & Caporaso 1998:102).

In short, the process of domestication goes beyond two-level games and partial equilibrium analyses, in which institutions are exogenous or endogenous. Instead of institutions at one level affecting institutions at another level, the two are fused into a single, though differentiated, legal order.

CONCLUSION

The literature on EU politics and policy making is increasingly turning away from specialized theories of integration or parochial applications of IR or comparative tools in favor of more generic (and broadly intelligible) forms of institutionalism. The best of the new EU literature transcends prevailing categories of institutional analysis and promises a fuller account of EU politics, one that considers both integration (system transformation) and politics within an existing institutional structure.

Much remains to be done to complete the changes wrought by the introduction and sophisticated application of institutionalism to the EU. In particular, although the EU's highly institutionalized system would seem to be fertile social soil within which actors' preferences might be transformed, a truly constructivist alternative to the dominant rationalism has not emerged. What has emerged has tended to be exploratory (Wind 1996, Christiansen 1998) or to make relatively weak claims about the endogeneity of strategies rather than goals. Rigorous and carefully designed empirical tests of stronger constructivist claims are called for. More generally, EU studies should confront and contribute to the resolution of conceptual ambiguities and epistemological tensions in the broader edifice of institutionalism (Aspinwall & Schneider 1997).

The institutional turn in EU studies may be judged positively for four related reasons. First, it increasingly borrows from successful literatures, including principal-agent analysis, spatial theories of legislative politics, transaction cost economics, and the new economics of organization.

A second and related reason is that these newly applied lenses tend toward a rigor that broad waves of earlier EU literature lacked. This point applies to both realist and neofunctional theories of integration.

Third, this conceptual borrowing has not necessitated conceptual stretching (Sartori 1970). Indeed, the ability to generalize across contexts while incorporating local specificity is a signal advantage of institutional analysis.

Fourth, the institutional turn has rendered EU studies more integral to the broader concerns of the discipline and has permitted EU studies to contribute in kind. The theory of conditional agenda setting is a novel contribution to the positive theory of legislative institutions. The engagement of spatial and voting-power approaches has led to improvements in the latter, especially through the incorporation of preferences (Widgrén 1995, Hosli 1996). These improvements promise to transcend their narrow application to the EU. Finally, just as the EU itself represents the greatest transcendence of the Westphalian nation-state in the face of economic, social, and environmental forces, the EU literature has gone farthest in erasing the boundaries between the fields of IR and comparative politics. This erosion of disciplinary boundaries might be the most lasting contribution of EU studies to political science.

> Visit the *Annual Reviews home page* at
> http://www.AnnualReviews.org.

Literature Cited

Alter KJ. 1998. Who are the "masters of the treaty"? European governments and the European Court of Justice. *Int. Organ.* 52(1):121–48

Aspinwall MD, Schneider G. 1997. *Same menu, separate tables: the institutionalist turn in political science and the study of European integration.* Presented at Res. Sess. Eur. Consort. Polit. Res., Bergen

Blom Hansen J. 1997. A "new institutional" perspective on policy networks. *Public Admin.* 75:669–93

Bulmer S. 1993. The governance of the EU: a new institutionalist approach. *J. Public Policy* 13(4):351–80

Bulmer S. 1994. Institutions and policy change in the European Communities: the case of merger control. *Public Admin.* 72:423–44

Bulmer S. 1998. New institutionalism and the

governance of the single European market. *J. Eur. Public Policy* 5(3):365–86

Burley A-M, Mattli W. 1993. Europe before the Court: a political theory of legal integration. *Int. Organ.* 47(1):41–76

Caporaso JC. 1997. Across the great divide: integrating comparative and international politics. *Int. Stud. Q.* 41(4):563–92

Christiansen T. 1998. "Bringing process back in": the *longue durée* of European integration. *J. Eur. Integration* 21(1):99–121

Cooter R, Drexl J. 1994. The logic of power in the emerging European constitution: game theory and the division of powers. *Int. Rev. Law Econ.* 14:307–26

Cram L. 1993. Calling the tune without paying the piper? Social policy regulation: the role of the Commission in European Community social policy. *Policy Polit.* 21(2): 135–46

Crombez C. 1996. Legislative procedures in the European Community. *Br. J. Polit. Sci.* 26(2):199–228

Crombez C. 1997. The co-decision procedure in the EU. *Legis. Stud. Q.* 22(1):97–119

Earnshaw D, Judge D. 1995. Early days: the European Parliament, co-decision and the EU legislative process post-Maastricht. *J. Eur. Public Policy* 2(4):624–49

Evans PB, Jacobson HK, Putnam RD, eds. 1993. *Double-Edged Diplomacy: International Bargaining and Domestic Politics*. Berkeley: Univ. Calif. Press. 490 pp.

Field AJ. 1981. The problem with neoclassical institutional economics. *Explor. Econ. Hist.* 18:174–98

Field AJ. 1984. Microeconomics, norms, and rationality. *Econ. Dev. Cult. Change* 32: 683–711

Finnemore M. 1996. Norms, culture, and world politics: insights from sociology's institutionalism. *Int. Organ.* 50(2):325–48

Garrett G. 1992. International cooperation and institutional choice: the European Community's internal market. *Int. Organ.* 46(2):533–60

Garrett G. 1995a. From the Luxembourg compromise to codecision: decision making in the EU. *Elect. Stud.* 14(3):289–308

Garrett G. 1995b. The politics of legal integration in the EU. *Int. Organ.* 49(1):171–82

Garrett G, Kelemen RD, Schulz H. 1998. The European Court of Justice, national governments, and legal integration in the EU. *Int. Organ.* 52(1):149–76

Garrett G, Tsebelis G. 1996. An institutional critique of intergovernmentalism. *Int. Organ.* 50(2):237–68

Garrett G, Tsebelis G. 1998. More on the co-decision endgame. *J. Legis. Stud.* 3(4):139–43

Garrett G, Weingast BR. 1993. Ideas, interests, and institutions: constructing the European Community's internal market. In *Ideas and Foreign Policy*, ed. J Goldstein, RO Keohane, pp. 173–206. Ithaca, NY: Cornell Univ. Press. 308 pp.

Garrett G, McLean I, Machover M. 1995. Power, power indices, and blocking power: a comment on Johnston. *Br. J. Polit. Sci.* 25(4):563–68

Goodin RE. 1996. Institutions and their design. In *The Theory of Institutional Design*, ed. RE Goodin, pp. 1–53. New York: Cambridge Univ. Press. 288 pp.

Gourevitch P. 1978. The second image reversed: the international sources of domestic politics. *Int. Organ.* 32(4):881–911

Hall PA, Taylor RCR. 1994. Political science and the three new institutionalisms. *Polit. Stud.* 44:936–57

Hix S. 1994. The study of the European Community: the challenge to comparative politics. *West Eur. Polit.* 17(1):1–30

Hosli MO. 1993. Admission of European Free Trade Association states to the European Community. *Int. Organ.* 47(4):629–43

Hosli MO. 1996. Coalitions and power: effects of qualified majority voting in the Council of the EU. *J. Common Mark. Stud.* 34: 255–73

Hubschmid C, Moser P. 1997. The cooperation procedure in the EU: why was the European Parliament influential in the decision on car emission standards? *J. Common Mark. Stud.* 35(2):225–42

Jacobs F. 1997. *Legislative co-decision: a real step forward?* Presented at Bienn. Meet. Eur. Comm. Stud. Assoc., 5th, Seattle, WA

Jordan G. 1990. Policy community realism versus "new" institutionalist ambiguity. *Polit. Stud.* 38:470–84

Jupille J. 1999. The EU and international outcomes. *Int. Organ.* 53(2):In press

Kassim H. 1994. Policy networks, networks and EU policy making: a sceptical view. *West Eur. Polit.* 17(4):15–27

Kato J. 1996. Institutions and rationality in politics: three varieties of neo-institutionalists. *Br. J. Polit. Sci.* 26(4):553–82

Katzenstein PJ, ed. 1978. *Between Power and Plenty: Foreign Economic Policies of Advanced Industrial States*. Madison: Univ. Wisc. Press. 344 pp.

Katzenstein PJ. 1996. Introduction: alternative perspectives on national security. In *The Culture of National Security*, ed. PJ Katzenstein, pp. 1–32. New York: Columbia Univ. Press

Keohane RO, Milner HV, eds. 1996. *Internationalization and Domestic Politics*. New York: Cambridge Univ. Press. 308 pp.

Kerremans B. 1996. Non-institutionalism, neo-institutionalism, and the logic of common decision-making in the EU. *Governance* 9(2):217–40

Koelble TA. 1995. The new institutionalism in political science and sociology. *Comp. Polit.* 27(2):231–43

March JG, Olsen JP. 1989. *Rediscovering Institutions*. New York: Free. 227 pp.

Marks G, Hooghe L, Blank K. 1996. European integration from the 1980s: state-centric v. multi-level governance. *J. Common Mark. Stud.* 34(3):341–77

Mattli W, Slaughter A-M. 1995. Law and politics in the EU: a reply to Garrett. *Int. Organ.* 49(1):183–90

Mattli W, Slaughter A-M. 1998. Revisiting the European Court of Justice. *Int. Organ.* 52(1):177–210

Meunier S. 1998. *Europe divided but united: institutional integration and EC-US trade negotiations since 1962.* PhD thesis. Mass. Inst. Technol., Cambridge, MA

Moravcsik A. 1991. Negotiating the Single European Act: national interests and conventional statecraft in the European Community. *Int. Organ.* 45(1):19–56

Moravcsik A. 1993. Preferences and power in the European Community: a liberal intergovernmentalist approach. *J. Common Mark. Stud.* 31(4):473–524

Moravcsik A. 1995. Liberal intergovernmentalism and integration: a rejoinder. *J. Common Mark. Stud.* 33(4):611–28

Moravcsik A. 1998. *The Choice for Europe: Social Purpose and State Power From Messina to Maastricht.* Ithaca, NY: Cornell Univ. Press. 514 pp.

Moser P. 1996. The European Parliament as a conditional agenda setter: what are the conditions? *Am. Polit. Sci. Rev.* 90(4):834–38

Moser P. 1997a. A theory of the conditional influence of the European Parliament in the cooperation procedure. *Public Choice* 91:333–50

Moser P. 1997b. The benefits of the conciliation procedure for the European Parliament. *Aussenwirtschaft* 52(1/2):57–62

North DO. 1990. *Institutions, Institutional Change, and Economic Performance.* New York: Cambridge Univ. Press. 152 pp.

Peters BG. 1997. Escaping the joint-decision trap: repetition and sectoral politics in the EU. *West Eur. Polit.* 20(2):22–36

Peterson J. 1995a. Decision-making in the EU: towards a framework for analysis. *J. Eur. Public Policy* 2(1):69–93

Peterson J. 1995b. Policy networks and EU policy making. *West Eur. Polit.* 18(2):389–407

Pierson P. 1996. The path to European integration: a historical institutionalist analysis. *Comp. Polit. Stud.* 29(2):123–63

Pollack MA. 1995. Creeping competence: the expanding agenda of the European Community. *J. Public Policy* 14(2):95–145

Pollack MA. 1996. The new institutionalism and EC governance: the promise and limits of institutional analysis. *Governance* 9(4):429–58

Pollack MA. 1997. Delegation, agency, and agenda setting in the European Community. *Int. Organ.* 51(1):99–134

Puchala DJ. 1972. Of blind men, elephants and international integration. *J. Common Mark. Stud.* 10(2):267–84

Rogowski R. 1989. *Commerce and Coalitions: How Trade Affects Domestic Political Alignments.* Princeton, NJ: Princeton Univ. Press. 208 pp.

Sandholtz W. 1993. Choosing union: monetary politics and Maastricht. *Int. Organ.* 47(1):1–39

Sandholtz W. 1996. Membership matters: limits of the functional approach to European institutions. *J. Common Mark. Stud.* 34(3):403–29

Sartori G. 1970. Concept misformation in comparative politics. *Am. Polit. Sci. Rev.* 64(4):1033–53

Sbragia AM. 1991. Thinking about the European future: the uses of comparison. In *Euro-Politics: Institutions and Policymaking in the "New" European Community*, ed. AM Sbragia, pp. 257–92. Washington, DC: Brookings. 303 pp.

Sbragia AM. 1993. The European Community: a balancing act. *Publius* 23(3):23–38

Scharpf FW. 1988. The joint-decision trap: lessons from German federalism and European integration. *Public Admin.* 66:239–78

Schneider G. 1995. The limits of self-reform: institution-building in the EU. *Eur. J. Int. Rel.* 1(1):59–86

Scully RM. 1997a. The European Parliament and the co-decision procedure: a reassessment. *J. Legis. Stud.* 3(3):58–73

Scully RM. 1997b. The European Parliament and co-decision: a rejoinder to Tsebelis and Garrett. *J. Legis. Stud.* 3(3):93–103

Shepsle KA. 1986. Institutional equilibrium and equilibrium institutions. In *Political Science: The Science of Politics*, ed. HF Weisberg, pp. 51–81. New York: Agathon. 307 pp.

Shepsle KA. 1989. Studying institutions: some lessons from the rational choice approach. *J. Theor. Polit.* 1(2):131–47

Steunenberg B. 1994. Decision making under different institutional arrangements. *J. Inst. Theor. Econ.* 150(4):642–69

Stone A. 1994. What is a supranational constitution? An essay in IR theory. *Rev. Polit.*
56(3):441–74

Stone Sweet A, Caporaso J. 1998. From free
trade to supranational polity: the European
Court and integration. In *European Inte-
gration and Supranational Governing,* ed.
W Sandholtz, A Stone Sweet, pp. 92–133.
New York: Oxford Univ. Press

Suganami H. 1989. *The Domestic Analogy and
World Order Proposals.* Cambridge, UK:
Cambridge Univ. Press. 251 pp.

Tsebelis G. 1994. The power of the European
Parliament as a conditional agenda setter.
Am. Polit. Sci. Rev. 88(1):128–42

Tsebelis G. 1995. Conditional agenda-setting
and decision-making inside the European
Parliament. *J. Legis. Stud.* 1(1):65–93

Tsebelis G. 1996. More on the European Parliament as a conditional agenda setter. *Am.
Polit. Sci. Rev.* 90(4):839–44

Tsebelis G. 1997. Maastricht and the democratic deficit. *Aussenwirtschaft* 52:36–56
(spec. issue)

Tsebelis G, Garrett G. 1996. Agenda setting
power, power indices, and decision making in the EU. *Int. Rev. Legis. Econ.* 16:
345–61

Tsebelis G, Garrett G. 1997a. Agenda setting,
vetoes and the EU's co-decision procedure. *J. Legis. Stud.* 3(3):74–92

Tsebelis G, Garrett G. 1997b. Why power indices cannot explain decisionmaking in the
EU. In *Constitutional Law and Economics
of the EU,* ed. D Schmidtchen, R Cooter,
pp. 11–31. Cheltenham, UK: Elgar. 314
pp.

Tsebelis G, Kreppel A. 1998. The history of
conditional agenda-setting in European institutions. *Eur. J. Polit. Res.* 33(1):41–71

Van Hees M. 1997. Explaining institutions: a
defense of reductionism. *Eur. J. Polit. Res.*
32(1):51–69

Wallace W. 1983. Less than a federation, more
than a regime: the Community as a political system. In *Policy-Making in the European Community,* ed. H Wallace, W Wallace, C Webb, pp. 403–36. New York:
Wiley & Sons. 451 pp.

Weber K. 1997. Institutional choice in international politics: a glimpse at EU members'
industrial policies. Presented at Annu.
Conv. Int. Stud. Assoc., 38th, Toronto

Wendt A. 1987. The agent-structure problem
in international relations theory. *Int. Organ.* 41(3):335–70

Widgrén M. 1995. Probabilistic voting power
in the EU Council: the cases of trade policy
and social regulation. *Scand. J. Econ.*
97(2):345–56

Wildavsky A. 1987. Choosing preferences by
constructing institutions: a cultural theory
of preference formation. *Am. Polit. Sci.
Rev.* 81(1):3–21

Wincott D. 1995a. Institutional interaction and
European integration: towards an everyday critique of liberal intergovernmentalism. *J. Common Mark. Stud.* 33(4):
597–609

Wincott D. 1995b. The role of law or the rule
of the Court of Justice? An "institutional"
account of judicial politics in the European
Community. *J. Eur. Public Policy* 2(4):
583–602

Wind M. 1996. *Europe Towards a Post-
Hobbesian Order? A Constructivist The-
ory of European Integration. EUI Working
Papers No. 96/31.* Florence: EUI

Annu. Rev. Polit. Sci. 1999. 2:445–63

AMERICAN EXCEPTIONALISM

Byron E. Shafer

Nuffield College, Oxford University, Oxford OX1 1NF, United Kingdom;
e-mail: byron.shafer@nuffield.oxford.ac.uk

KEY WORDS: exceptionalism, American exceptionalism, de Tocqueville, American politics, comparative politics

---

ABSTRACT

American exceptionalism is the oldest and most contentious of the alleged national exceptionalisms—arguments that a given nation must be understood in essentially idiosyncratic fashion. John Winthrop, Alexis de Tocqueville, and Karl Marx helped develop and sustain an American variant for the first 350 years of a separate American political life. Modern political scientists have addressed the notion in a more systematic and methodologically self-conscious manner during the past half century. Nevertheless, much of the argument revolves around conceptual issues, operational difficulties, and empirical traps, so that these must provide the contours of the subject here. Two major recent books with sharply divergent conclusions, both marshaling extensive empirical evidence, serve not only as a means of updating the classical argument and of presenting its modern opposition. Both also suggest—indeed, contribute—further reasons for the continuing lure of a difficult and divisive notion.

If men define situations as real, they are real in their consequences.
WI Thomas, *The Child in America*, p. 572

INTRODUCTION

Exceptionalism is the notion that a phenomenon must be analyzed in terms, essentially, of itself. That is, it must be understood with regard to its own creation and its own evolution, rather than as an adjusted version of otherwise familiar variables and trends. Comparison remains integral to the notion, in the sense that the exceptional can only be located comparatively. Thereafter, however,

1094-2939/99/0616-0445$08.00

analysis must proceed in terms of idiosyncratic difference. American exceptionalism is thus the notion that the United States was born in, and continues
to embody, qualitative differences from other nations. Understanding other
nations will not help in understanding it; understanding it will only mislead in
understanding them.

CONCEPTUAL ISSUES

Within the realm of practical politics, exceptionalism is real or not, true or
false, depending on its motive impact. If political actors believe in it or, indeed,
if they are agnostic but can nevertheless use the symbolism of difference—to
move public opinion, to influence public policy, or to shape the policy process—then exceptionalism is a genuine and confirmedly empirical phenomenon. The accuracy or inaccuracy, the truth or falsity, of the propositions allegedly constituting this exceptionalism are not important. It is the use of the
theme, and its successful motive impact, that matters. Much of the remainder
of the exceptionalist debate is, alas, definitional. Proponents make assertions
that cannot be falsified. Opponents focus on indicators that cannot produce
qualitative difference. But the realm of practical politics is one with specifiable
empirical referents, where exceptionalism could be falsified or confirmed.

An example from this realm may be helpful at the start. At the end of the
Second World War, the institutional framework for pursuit of a looming Cold
War had to be created (or not). In the United States, conservative opponents of
its creation adopted, in part, an exceptionalist argument. What made this great
power different from every other, in their view, was that it had no standing
military, no military-industrial complex to go with it, and no "entangling" alliances to commit this (nonexistent) military establishment. It relied instead on
the inherent attractiveness of an exceptional society to produce international
"victories," by example and in the long run. Accordingly, it was important to
the success of this (exceptional) foreign policy not to forge the Cold War order,
but it was even more important to the domestic character of American society
not to do so (Muston 1997).

This was actually a general argument of some 300 years' standing, memo-
rably articulated by John Winthrop, colonial governor of Massachusetts:

> For we must consider that we shall be a city upon a hill. The eyes of all people
> are upon us, so that if we shall deal falsely with our God in this work we have
> undertaken, and so cause Him to withdraw His present help from us, we shall
> be made a story and a byword through the world. (Winthrop 1630)

The factual premises of this specific application against the Cold War were, in
the middle years of the twentieth century, largely true: no standing military establishment, an armaments industry normally focused on the private market,

with few international treaties of any kind. Nevertheless, the argument failed to carry the day. One result was that a standing military was established, with all those other accoutrements. Another result was that this argument for American exceptionalism effectively disappeared. But note the chain of causality: an appeal to exceptionalism was mobilized; it lost; and thereafter, its empirical premises were destroyed.

Within the realm of political science, exceptionalism has had an even more contentious career. On the one hand, pursuit of national distinctions sufficient to qualify for this designation was a reasonable activity for a newly self-conscious social science. Studies of "national character," in particular, proceeded on this basis in the immediate postwar years, and American society was at the center of this work (Riesman 1950, Potter 1954, Whyte 1956). Yet the social science disciplines brought with them a methodological presumption implicitly hostile to exceptionalism, namely that nations could not only be compared but ranked—scaled, even—on a variety of dimensions which would collectively constitute, say, a national economy, a national society, or a national political system. Such an approach did not countenance discrete exceptions. Or at least, it raised the threshold sharply.

The acknowledged progenitor of the social science of American exceptionalism was Alexis de Tocqueville. Writing in the 1830s, he could not bring the tools of modern political science to bear. Yet de Tocqueville certainly did focus on the collective character of American society and its polity. And he certainly found them to be distinctive:

> I have said enough to put the character of Anglo-American civilization in its true light. It is the result (and this should be constantly kept in mind) of two distinct elements, which in other places have been in frequent disagreement, but which the Americans have succeeded in incorporating to some extent one with the other and containing admirably. I allude to the spirit of religion and the spirit of liberty....
>
> Men sacrifice for a religious opinion their friends, their family, and their country; one can consider them devoted to the pursuit of intellectual goals which they came to purchase at so high a price. One sees them, however, seeking with almost equal eagerness material wealth and moral satisfaction; heaven in the world beyond, and well-being and liberty in this one.
> (de Tocqueville 1945 [1835]:45)

De Tocqueville wrote in a time when it was much easier to make such a judgment. Essentially, in the family of seriously "modernized" nations, there were the major states of Western Europe and there was the United States. Yet a sense for this same distinctiveness lasted within the new social science community at least into the early postwar years. In 1950, Sir Harold Butler, Warden of Nuffield College, Oxford, one of the premier institutions for the social sciences in Europe, could still note, "None of us realized what a different type of western civilization had grown up in the United States in the nineteenth century, how under American conditions a different social philosophy and a different political system had evolved" (Butler 1950:162–63).

By then, the notion of an explicitly American exceptionalism had been reinforced from a different quarter, in a line of argument that began in the early twentieth century and lasted well into the Cold War years. Like many of the exceptionalist arguments focused explicitly on the United States, this too was nurtured in ideology and then transplanted into social science. It was, of course, the Marxist view that the nations of the world would naturally follow a certain common path, toward dictatorship of the proletariat and establishment of international communism, and that the major developed nations were in fact well along in this trajectory, though it was harder to perceive this in the case of the United States. Indeed, while the concept ran back to the original settlers, the term "American exceptionalism" is determinedly marxist vocabulary, designed to deal with precisely this problem.[1]

On the other hand, exceptionalism is not in principle an exclusively American phenomenon. Bell (1991:47) has suggested that most great powers, in the period of their rise, develop a comparable notion of themselves, nationally, as exceptionalist. Britain in the late nineteenth century was surely imbued with this notion. Japan in the late twentieth has produced its counterpart. Yet there is no reason to stop with great powers rising. France, for example, has a long tradition of self-proclaimed exceptionalism. Moreover, that tradition—and hence French exceptionalism—continues to be real, in the sense that an argument that the government must do thus-and-such because it is essential to preserving the distinctiveness of French culture can still hope to prevail (Lovecy 1992).

What gives American exceptionalism its added bite, making it the nub of the exceptionalist argument in our time, is an array of other factors. Some of these are historical, as above, explaining why the debate with regard to the United States long preceded and far outlasted the particular terminology. Some of them are ruthlessly contemporary. As this is written, there appears to be only one superpower remaining on planet Earth. Simple passage of time may be unkind to this exception as a social fact, but as long as it is true, American exceptionalism, if it existed in additional realms, would simply matter more. Lastly, there is the massive and manifest irony intrinsic, at the time of this writing, only to the American case. This is the question of whether the global reach of American cultural and social trends, from suburbanization to financial derivatives to fast food, means that American exceptionalism is nec-

---

[1]As it developed, Josef Stalin, for one, was not an exceptionalist, and expelled Jay Lovestone, founding figure in the American Communist Party and godfather to this vocabulary, from party membership.

essarily waning, because Marx did get this one right—and the rest of the developed world is becoming more like the United States every day.

OPERATIONAL DIFFICULTIES

Those are the major issues of definition. Some fundamental problems of operationalization follow hard upon them, with the first being undeniably the toughest. This is the issue of generalizability versus uniqueness, and it plunges the empirical analyst—whether supportive, agnostic, or skeptical—into questions of the level of analysis right from the start. Seen closely enough, all social phenomena are distinctive, and every nation is unique. Seen from a sufficient distance, all social phenomena blur, and most nations resemble each other. Yet pitching the analysis in some sensible middle ground is easier said than done. Too close to individual cases, the analyst will still find numerous unique combinations of traits. Too far from individual cases, the possibility of judging any exceptionalist argument disappears.

Once more, a concrete example may be helpful. Seen from inside one nation while teaching the politics of another, differences abound and distinctions matter. Thus the opening lecture in a series labeled "Introduction to American Politics," when delivered in Britain, needs to set out the largest relevant background differences, the ones that explain why American politics is not just British politics with the dials adjusted. Note that this approach to the topic serves a useful heuristic function, and often bears the label "American exceptionalism." Yet it cannot in principle discover, much less confirm, any such implicit particularity. For there is no exceptionalism in the comparison of any two nations. The moment a third is added, however, the problem of which distinctions to count, and then of how to aggregate them, becomes insistent.

The number of individual items upon which nations might differ is effectively infinite. Worse yet, the differences on any one item, observed closely enough, are as extensive as the number of nations considered. If exceptionalism is not thereby to be crushed out of existence (or defined into existence everywhere), some way to group major realms of analysis is the only way around this dilemma. If that can be accomplished, then some way to isolate distinctive dynamics within those realms becomes the main empirical challenge. And comparison of those central dynamics does have the potential to mark one nation as exceptional, or to confirm that there is no empirical exceptionalism left.

The great exhortation toward operating in this way was articulated by Robert Merton.

> ...Middle-range theory...is intermediate to general theories of social systems which are too remote from particular classes of social behavior, organization, and change to account for what is observed and to those detailed orderly

descriptions of particulars that are not generalized at all. Middle-range theory involves abstractions, of course, but they are close enough to observed
data to be incorporated in propositions that permit empirical testing.... (Merton 1968:39)

Sociological theory, if it is to advance significantly, must proceed on
these interconnected planes: (1) by developing special theories from which
to derive hypotheses that can be empirically investigated and (2) by evolving, not suddenly revealing, a progressively more general conceptual scheme
that is adequate to consolidate groups of special theories. (Merton 1968:51)

Shafer (1991:viii) has attempted to adapt this formulation to American exceptionalism,

to highlight distinctively American *clusters* of characteristics, even distinctively American ways of organizing the major *realms* of social life. Such an
approach aspires to be more than a focus on individual peculiarities; it accepts the need to be less than a summary of world-wide patterns and their
violation.

Said differently, this approach to American exceptionalism looks for
peculiarly American approaches to major social sectors...and to their interaction in the larger society around them. Such an approach has the advantage of
bringing a grander focus than 'details producing uniqueness'. It has the advantage at the same time of not requiring some grand and general model by
which the rest of the world will progress. In essence, it searches for 'the
American model,' different from other nations in some larger regards, without implying that those other nations follow some single alternative.

A historical example from the specific sequence of American political development shows how theories (or at least perspectives) of the middle range
can help in dealing with the problem of what to count, the problem of universality and uniqueness. Historically, many authors have made much of the fact
that the United States granted universal white male suffrage before the rise of
organized labor (Zieger 1986), a fact which is alleged to have had major implications for working-class consciousness and labor-union behavior. But in
terms of political institutions on an even grander scale, the United States was
also argued to be, in its time, the only nation to be a democracy before acquiring a bureaucracy, having the institutions of a polity before the institutions of a
state (Skowronek 1982). The questions for anyone examining a putative exceptionalism in the realm of political development are thus very straightforward: Is this an accurate reading of political history? Do continuing consequences follow from it? And do these remain distinctive by comparison with
other nations? Note that as the developed world expands to include Japan and
Korea, and even India and China in time, the central developmental sequence
imputed here need not become any less exceptional.

Careful work along such lines is still easier to describe than to do—especially since the essence of the underlying problem, defining some middle

ground between universal-but-vague and precise-but-unique, leads quickly to the further problem of how to aggregate the resultant empirical findings. Again, however, an approach guided by middle-level theory is the only way forward, and a common line of exceptionalist argument from the contemporary world, one involving the basic nature of social organization, can provide an example (Lipset 1991, Bell 1991, Greeley 1991). What makes the United States distinctive here is that it is the society rather than the polity which really matters there—a society characterized by voluntarism rather than statism, one where liberty trumps security.

In this line of argument, the United States becomes the "civil society" par excellence, and other distinguishing characteristics follow from that status. For example, there is a distinctive model of policy making, emphasizing the manipulation of incentives rather than the implementation of outcomes (Rose 1991, Howard 1997). But is this an actual model of American public policy? Does it really differ from that of, say, Germany and Japan? And is it rooted in that complex of values and institutions which combine to constitute the civil society? Accurate answers have gained practical relevance in our time, as the newly independent nations of Eastern Europe, in particular, think consciously about the reestablishment of civil society, its prospects, and its implications.

The first two operational questions, then, are what to count and how to aggregate it. The third of these grand questions concerns change in these measures across time, that is, the comparative evolution of whatever is counted and aggregated. As long as research is constructed so that there can be exceptionalist polities, there is no reason to believe that they are reliably eternal and every reason to suppose that normally they are not. What exists at one time may disappear at another, perhaps only to reappear at a third. Yet unless a proper invocation of middle-level theory guides the resulting inquiry, an evolutionary judgment is effectively hopeless. The basic standard is easy enough to offer: In order for a society to generate and then sustain an exceptionalist politics, it must both maintain the essence and change the specifics of that politics. But this will quickly degenerate either into guaranteed exceptionalism or its "proven" disappearance merely by assertion—the inevitable change is either evidence of continuity or of its opposite—unless the level of conceptualization has been carefully specified in advance.

For example, a great power without a standing military was once truly exceptional. By that standard, this nation, the United States, no longer is.[2] In a trenchant exposition on the American economy, Temin (1991:71) makes the same kind of argument in another major realm, steering neatly through this evolutionary dilemma.

[2]However, contemporary fears about a "new American isolationism" suggest that not everyone views this door as permanently closed.

The American economy has seemed unique to generations of foreign observers. Its growth was a wonder of the Western world for more than a century. The organization of economic life provided a model for others to emulate. For a while after the Second World War, the United States even appeared capable of transforming the world economy into a larger version of itself. These images all seem to be fading like an old photograph...

I shall argue that the American economic experience until very recently was unique. Its uniqueness derived from two characteristics of the economy. First was the pervasive effect of 'free land'....

The second influence emanated from the federal system of American government created in the late eighteenth century that limited the political power of large land-holders...

EMPIRICAL TRAPS

What to count, how to aggregate it, and how to track its changes over time are large and difficult but not self-evidently impossible questions. Proper specification followed by empirical investigation is absolutely essential with all three, in order to move any exceptionalist debate forward. Yet there are three further pitfalls in existing efforts to do so, recurrent pitfalls so damaging to the resultant product that they need to be recognized early. The first of these involves the problem known more generally as the choice of a proper unit of analysis. The second involves the problem known more generally as the choice of measures with an appropriate range of variance. And the third is just a further twist on the generic problem, in a peculiar variant involving inconsistent—even circular—specification of the argument. Failure to recognize one or another of these problems appears to be the main flaw undercutting serious empirical work which does otherwise attempt to address these prior theoretical questions and which aspires to speak to the issue of exceptionalism.

The unit-of-analysis problem is probably the most common—is almost, indeed, endemic to this field. Here, the analyst specifies substantive realms carefully, guaranteeing that they are large and consequential, and then uses one or more other nations to highlight differences from (or similarities with) the United States. Sweden seems a favorite, but there are other far-flung contenders, including Belgium and South Africa. Proponents of American exceptionalism use such cases to show just how different the United States is. Opponents use them to demonstrate the existence of a continuum, with the United States merely at some different point. The risk in these comparisons, however, lies less in matters of theoretical specification and numerical aggregation, and more in the fact that the particular choice is often inappropriate by definition, thereby defining its answer rather than discovering it.

For example, one of the great fueling questions about American exceptionalism in the early twentieth century—one which had ideological origins, produced social-scientific explanations, and ramifies down through our time—

concerned the absence of a European class structure and associated industrial tradition. Sombart (1976 [1906]) addressed it most provocatively, in *Why Is There No Socialism in the United States?*, but successors have also asked, "Why no Labor Party?", "Why no Family Allowance?", and so on. Yet an inappropriate unit of comparison will undercut any answer, from the start. It must be granted that these are comparative questions, which should be addressed comparatively. Yet the choice of comparison still matters enormously.

Thus, if Australia is the comparative base for considering the United States—both "settler societies," after all, in the Anglo-American mode—the problem can be simply stated. Nation to nation, different things did happen historically. Yet Australia is more akin to some subregion of the United States, so that if the comparison were focused there instead, then very similar things often actually happened. In this line of reasoning, if the sparsely settled but highly unionized states of America are instead compared with Australia, then "why no Labor Party?" is patently the wrong question. In those states, there was a labor party; it just managed to seize the Democratic party label. As a result, either there was no labor-party exceptionalism, because essentially the same things did happen, or the exceptionalism lies in the way the United States (not Australia) was constituted and organized.

The problem of adequate variation—of insuring an adequate range of statistical variance—is in some ways the opposite of the unit-of-analysis problem. In the latter, examples chosen for their variance are not sensibly comparable. With inadequate variation, the measures chosen cannot vary greatly in principle. It is then no discovery when they do not vary greatly in practice; these data are irrelevant to an exceptionalist argument. The most frequent examples are items which are integral parts of economic development. Admittedly, appropriate comparisons of nations must often be among the developed nations. Yet many ostensible "measures" are actually part and parcel of being a developed nation—are essentially defined into the analysis for their similarity at the start—so that their variation, and the place of any outlier, is inherently limited. Economic stabilization programs, for example, may be roughly similar among these developed nations, with the United States merely at one end of the continuum. Yet it is very unlikely that a nation can be developed without some substantial capacity for economic stabilization, along with some generalized desire to use that capacity.

There is no point—no point for an exceptionalist argument, though many points for other purposes—in comparing the developed nations for their average life expectancies, housing units with indoor plumbing, or public policies on waste management, unless this comparison is to imply no exceptionalism by definition. This is not, however, as dire an empirical problem as it sounds. Or at least, it contains two main implications for how to proceed. One way is to focus on realms which are not such obvious concomitants of economic development. If it is difficult to imagine a developed nation without a major role for the automobile, and thus without substantial expenditures on public highways, it is easier to imagine one with radically different notions about crime and punishment, and thus criminal justice. The opposite approach is to take advantage of apparent concomitants to economic development by looking at those which are actually violated by some major developed nation.

Perhaps the outstanding example of the latter strategy involves the role of religion in national life, where the argument has long been that economic development will go hand in hand with secularization (Wilson 1982). Once again, this is a generalization that has not been violated by the movement of Japan and the East Asian tiger economies into the ranks of developed nations. Yet it has a major exception: the United States. Indeed, here, further specification of the differences is additionally useful. Among all the nations of the world, the United States is hardly distinctive for the role that religion and religiosity play in national political life. Yet among the developed nations, the most developed is apparently deviant. Moreover, this apparent finding links to other large arguments about American exceptionalism, arguments about whether the most developed nation on most measures shows major similarities with the less developed, and not with its developed counterparts; whether it needs to be treated instead as a "developing nation."

The last of the recurrent pitfalls, those interpretive traps awaiting even the methodologically wary, traces to a peculiar but nonetheless frequent confusion in the specification of the underlying argument. As with the problems in unit of analysis and range of variance, this one need not produce any interpretive difficulty in principle. Yet it often does so in practice, thanks to a peculiarly circular confrontation with the evidence. There are many ways to describe this pitfall in the abstract. But it normally surfaces with evolutionary interpretations, especially with regard to nations that innovate. Three simple, hypothetical questions for empirical research about change over time can illustrate this dilemma very concretely:

1. Are the macroeconomies of the developed nations becoming more like those of the United States, or France?

2. Are the popular cultures of the developed nations becoming more like those of the United States, or Germany?

3. Are the electoral politics of the developed nations becoming more like those of the United States, or Japan?

Most commonly, if the answers prove to be (in this example) France, Germany, and Japan, respectively, then the conclusion is that there are many national differences, but no exceptional nations. Yet it is surprising how often the opposite answer (the United States, three times) produces the same conclusion: dismissal of claims for national (in this case American) exceptionalism as well. There are grounds for reaching either of these conclusions, depending on prior conceptualization and prior operationalization. There are no grounds for reaching both simultaneously, much less for moving from one to the other after doing the empirical work. This time, however, the canonical texts would certainly counsel one of these perspectives rather than the other. Or at least, John Winthrop, Alexis de Tocqueville, and Karl Marx would all have viewed the second answer—the United States, the United States, and the United States—as evidence of American exceptionalism, not of its absence.

CONTINUING RESEARCH

In the face of all those difficulties—hard choices in definition, followed by multiple difficulties in operationalization—it may seem that investigations into even the grandfather of exceptionalisms might gradually have withered. They have not. There are inevitably cycles, fads, and fashions in tackling such topics and the associated research is entitled to ebb and flow. Yet we appear to be in the midst of a modest flow. It might also seem that there would be a further disciplinary bias to this. Historians, with their disciplinary concern for the specifics of the case, institutionally responsible for "context" as a variable, and charged with the lasting impact of earlier developments, might be expected to be more tolerant. Political scientists, with their disciplinary concern for operational measurement, responsible for structural influences in society, and aspiring, above all, to generalization as the goal, might be expected to move away. Yet in his overview of the many recent approaches to the topic, Kammen (1993:1–2) confirms that this has not become the case.

> Several new and important publications have appeared recently concerning a subject that has engaged many of us for decades—one that we discuss with colleagues and advanced students on a regular basis. I am inclined to suspect that we continue to do so largely because the issue remains so intriguing. One striking feature of the latest contributions is that they differ so radically among themselves. The most visibly polarized are Ian Tyrrell's "American Exceptionalism in an Age of International History" (which repudiates American exceptionalism) and a collection of essays edited by Byron Shafer entitled *Is American Different? A New Look at American Exceptionalism* (which reaffirms the notion).
> ...An admittedly impressionistic pattern began to occur to me that is curious, indeed, because it seems the reverse of what one might expect. For about a quarter of a century following World War II, while tough-minded social scientists became increasingly wary of national character studies in general and American exceptionalism in particular, professional historians of diverse ideological persuasions...continued to make inquiries and ventured generalizations about such slippery subjects. Subsequently, however, and for more than a decade now, historians...have expressed profound scepticism

and have made American exceptionalism extremely unfashionable in their guild, whereas prominent social scientists...have comfortably resuscitated and reaffirmed the whole gnarly matter and have done so largely on the basis of empirical study.

Kammen gathers many recent works addressing exceptionalism, American-style. His honor roll of disputants is formidable: Daniel Boorstin, David Potter, Frank Tannenbaum, Carl Degler, John Higham, Laurence Veysey, C Vann Woodward, Eric Foner, Sean Wilentz, Akira Iriye, Daniel Bell, Seymour Martin Lipset, Alex Inkeles, Sanford Jacoby, Samuel Huntington, Mona Harrington, John Roche, Peter Temin, Aaron Wildavsky, and Richard Rose (Kammen 1993). And that is before consideration of recent work which has implications for the concept but is not organized around it. Nevertheless, what Kammen also does for our purposes, having offered at least an opening catalog of recent findings, is to suggest a further focus on a few recent works in political science organized explicitly around American exceptionalism, to demonstrate both the problems and the prospects inherent in the concept.

Two recent books attempt a comprehensive synthesis of empirical work on the subject. Both are explicitly comparative. And they come to sweeping—opposite—conclusions. One is Lipset's *American Exceptionalism: A Double-Edged Sword* (1997). Because this brings his thinking up to date since the original and path-breaking *The First New Nation: The United States in Historical and Comparative Perspective* (1963), a short overview can provide a concise statement of the classical argument by those who have attempted to make the case. The second book is Wilson's *Only in America? The Politics of the United States in Comparative Perspective* (1998); while it focuses more exclusively on politics, it still ranges widely within and around that domain. As a result, a short overview states the contrary case for the skeptics. A comparison then demonstrates the importance of an answer to the three main operational questions (above) in distinguishing between these two points of view.

Lipset (1997) brings together recent essays related to the main theme, along with others which acquire new meaning when organized through this relationship. It is easy—and accurate—to say that this is the grand integrative approach to an alleged exceptionalism, beginning with the central theme and its explanation, then applying that theme to a series of major realms: ideology, politics, social deviance, economics, religion, welfare policy, socialism and unionism, domestic subgroups, international competitors. Lipset takes great pains to separate himself from the judgmental school of exceptionalist writings—neither Winthrop nor Stalin, he—but otherwise his is very much the comprehensive approach.

Yet there is a strong central argument to the book. For this is exceptionalism as a product of, and hence as embodied in, culture and institutions. In Lipset's line of argument, cultural values influence institutional arrangements, and their interaction then reinforces cultural patterns while institutionalizing them in new arrangements for a new (and changing) era. This is an argument in which original, foundational developments are important, and remain important precisely because the mechanisms by which they are adapted over time can be specified. Disruptive events and crises are free to change this evolution, so that exceptionalism can decline (or, presumably, advance). The Revolutionary War, for example, guaranteed that Canada would not be an integral part—a northern copy—of American exceptionalism. The Civil War, had the outcome gone the other way, would surely have altered this cultural and institutional pattern for a major part of what had been the United States.

On the other hand, such breaks were, if anything, confirmatory rather than disruptive in the case of the United States—the curious question is whether the New Deal and World War II were the real disruptions, now being "put right"—so that the American exception can, in Lipset's interpretation, be straightforwardly specified. An American creed provides the central cultural pattern, involving liberty, equality, individualism, populism, and laissez-faire. As this was confirmed, it resulted in an aggregate "Americanism," also centrally defining. Other nations, with the possible exception of the former Soviet Union, defined themselves by a common history as birthright communities. The United States defined itself, at bottom, as an ideology. (For a different route to the same conclusion, see Hartz 1956.)

The institutionalization of this Americanism was aided by the developmental fact that this was not a postfeudal society; it was aided by the social fact that it was a Protestant sectarian nation. Both facts meant that the Revolution itself could be about the incipient protection of those five linked values. Both facts sustained those values—that creed—forcefully in the aftermath of independence. They made a lasting Constitution, enshrining individual rights, more appropriate; they contributed to a hugely litigious society in the process. They also contributed large and ongoing tensions, for example the tendency to imbue most arguments over public (and foreign) policy with a heavy moralism, going hand in hand with a generalized disdain for formal authority, leading to such diverse outcomes as a continuing veneration of the Constitution and a continuing denigration of public figures. Where other nations learned to turn to government, to the state, this evolving America learned to turn to voluntarism, to civil society.

What resulted in politics was the most classically liberal polity in the world, from the founding to the present. This society, with that polity, had clear and natural emphases in public policy. It put a heavy investment in mass education, a way both to inculcate Americanism and to allow individuals to seek their own (individual) fortunes. By contrast (though also by logical extension), it put little investment into orthodox welfare programs, arriving late in this realm, eschewing many presumed essentials, and preferring opportunities for achievement rather than the redistribution of established wealth. Put back together, these developments leave Lipset in no doubt about a summary judgment.

> America continues to be qualitatively different. To reiterate, exceptionalism is a two-edged phenomenon; it does not mean better. This country is an outlier. It is the most religious, optimistic, patriotic, rights-oriented, and individualistic. With respect to crime, it still has the highest rates; with respect to incarceration, it has the most people locked up in jail; with respect to litigiousness, it has the most lawyers per capita of any country in the world, with high tort and malpractice rates. It also has close to the lowest percentage of the eligible electorate voting, but the highest rate of participation in voluntary organizations. The country remains the wealthiest in real income terms, the most productive as reflected in worker output, the highest in proportions of people who graduate from or enroll in higher education (post-grade 12) and in postgraduate work (post-grade 16). It is the leader in upward mobility into professional and other high-status and elite occupations, close to the top in terms of commitment to work rather than leisure, but the least egalitarian among developed nations with respect to income distribution, at the bottom as a provider of welfare benefits, the lowest in savings, and the least taxed....
> (Lipset 1997:26)

INTERPRETIVE DIFFERENCES

Wilson (1998) has revisited the more explicitly political implications of this argument, though he goes on to define the political very broadly. Wilson focuses on five main realms where any political exceptionalism ought to manifest itself: cultural influences, substantive agenda, governmental size, social pluralism, and institutional structure. Within these, he draws upon four main forms of exceptionalist argument: sociological explanations, cultural explanations, institutional explanations, and "path dependency," which might also be called historical explanations. A richly textured analysis results. The method is self-consciously comparative. The attitude is self-evidently skeptical. The result is unambiguous.

> How different, then, is American politics? The overall argument of this book is that while American politics is different, it is not unique. The issues, trends, and problems evident in American politics are by and large familiar to citizens of other modern democracies. Indeed, American politics has more in common with the politics of several other advanced industrialized democracies today than with American politics in the past....
>
> If this conclusion is acceptable, it should prompt a host of further questions. The role of the United States in comparative politics and policy analysis has long been that of the Great Exception. Generalizations about comparative political systems have generally been followed by the statement "but not in America". My argument has been that such statements would be expressed more accurately in the form "with minor differences in America".... (Wilson 1998:126–27)

Wilson begins by questioning not so much the notion as the implications of the United States as a liberal polity. He notes that many other traditions have gone into the American experience, and if liberalism is still the dominant one, it also masks a great deal of variety. In any case, much of Western Europe now looks more like America, ideologically, than it did in the days when the main contrast was American liberalism versus a European combination of organic conservatism and social democracy. A trawl through the mass attitudinal data then presents a contemporary nation that is, indeed, an outlier in saluting abstract democratic norms, not an outlier in saluting their concrete application.

More difficult to address with quantitative evidence is the content of American politics—the issue substance of the national agenda—but proxy measures can still ask whether this has changed within the United States, as well as whether the result is more or less like the rest of the developed world. Some change (redistributional issues down, sociocultural issues up) and some stability (for fiscal issues and foreign affairs) appears to be the case, with foreign affairs showing perhaps the greatest difference from other developed nations in its degree of emphasis. When the focus is instead the actual output of government, on the other hand, the data can speak more decisively. What they say is that the conventional measures, of governmental employment, governmental control of the economy, and size of social-welfare programs in particular, all show the United States as an outlier. Yet if these measures are supplemented by tax allowances and regulatory regimes, this outlier status is sharply reduced.

More problematic for interpretation, but leaning back toward an incipient exceptionalism, is the realm of social pluralism and national identity, where a continuing drift toward ethnic and racial pluralism mixes with strong pressures toward social conformity, both formal (through the schools) and informal (through the marketplace). Moreover, here, the stakes for a proper interpretation rise, since many of the older states of Western Europe are themselves experiencing an upsurge of ethnic diversity, with very different traditional means of addressing it. Likewise, in the realm of governmental arrangements, "no stable First World democracy is based on the institutions of the United States" (Wilson 1998:103). Yet the behavioral characteristics alleged to go along with this distinctiveness, such as fragmentation of governmental power and insecurity for political elites, do increasingly describe the process of government and politics elsewhere—again, not so very different at the end of the day.

Read closely and together, there is much overlap between the "two-edged" picture from Lipset and the "conditional" portrait from Wilson. If they nevertheless come to opposite conclusions, much of the difference inheres—as it must?—in different ways of approaching the three great challenges in operationalizing the concept of (American) exceptionalism. The "facts of the case," piece by piece, are not normally at issue. The grounds for contrasting conclusions are instead based upon (*a*) which pieces are central to the argument, (*b*) how to aggregate these central pieces, and (*c*) what to make of their evolution across time.

The first question, what to count on the way to an exceptionalist judgment, appears everywhere. Both Lipset and Wilson, for example, are well aware that approval of abstract democratic norms outstrips approval of their concrete application, so that the United States is by definition an outlier on the former but not on the latter. For Lipset, however, this is precisely the distinction between "values," central to a cultural definition of exceptionalism and available as a basis for political appeals across time, and "attitudes," which are associated with specific references and events of the day; whereas, for Wilson, this is the necessary evidence that the reality of behavior is not so very different in the United States. In the same way, for Wilson, the combination of hostility to unions with approval of working people, on top of hostility to corporations with approval of business, shows that the dominance of the liberal tradition does not go nearly as far as advertised; whereas, for Lipset, these are the classic attributes of populism—they form a coherent perspective—and a suspicion of "big government" combined with approval of social insurance programs belongs rightfully with them.

The second question, how to aggregate differences and similarities so as to reach a sound exceptionalist judgment, is, if anything, even more integral to this difference. There are huge difficulties in comparing public policy outcomes across nations when an implied exceptionalism is the focus, in guaranteeing comparability without simultaneously guaranteeing similarity. But when this is attempted, as it must always be in this debate, Wilson notes that aggregating governmental size, tax allowances, and regulatory reach makes the United States only a nation leaning in the "small government" direction. Conversely, Lipset, in searching for distinctive practical dynamics in different social realms, would presumably not lump these measures together. And if the analyst does not lump them, what appears instead is a nation distinguished by the fact that it is much less likely to use orthodox governmental programs to fulfill its public policy wishes, and much more likely to use tax allowances or governmental regulations to do so! Yet when the focus is social welfare programs, as it so often has been in this debate, the Esping-Anderson scale (Esping-Anderson 1990:52) still puts what is the largest political economy in the world almost two standard deviations short of the mean among developed nations.

Finally, the third question, what has been happening to these distinctions across time and how to make sense of it, gets equally (and diagnostically) different answers from these two books. Wilson sees a United States which is less like itself in the past than it is like other developed nations today. Lipset sees an America where the differences from those nations in other times have been translated into new social conditions, generating parallel differences for the world of today. All of the ancillary issues for an evolutionary interpretation also appear. On the one hand, if social pluralism increasingly characterizes the developed nations but they do not adopt American responses to it, does that diminish American exceptionalism or not? On the other hand, if ideological strands within other developed nations begin to resemble those in the United States, does that diminish American exceptionalism or (again) not?

THE FATE OF "BIG IDEAS"

What sustains a debate of this character? One simple, accurate, but insufficient answer lies in the very differences which comprehensive works such as Lipset's and Wilson's highlight, and in the potential that those differences contain for further conflict, not to mention further research. These need not, in principle, sustain a debate: Many arguments fall to the cumulating weight of scholarly evidence, and/or to a scholarly consensus. Yet this may be one where moving the lines of operationalization—up in abstraction or down in concreteness, out on social realms or in on political particulars—will always have a great deal to do with the results.

That shifting possibility is not nearly all that sustains the exceptionalist debate, in any case. A further part of its lasting character is effectively ideological. From one side, domestic nationalists find an opportunity to enjoy the features which make their society exceptionally itself, while foreign admirers look for ways to import what they see as distinctive virtues. From the other side, home-grown critics deny these alleged singularities, while foreign detractors worry simultaneously about their spread—though both are usually united by a belief that some other factor is explaining whatever they decry. There may even be an implicit methodological division in the social sciences to go with this ideological division in more general intellectual circles. On theoretical grounds, scholars do implicitly differ in their presumptions as to whether there is a societal exceptionalism or an international pattern "out there" to be discovered. More practically, scholars also differ as to whether getting the specifics right or producing generalization is the more important task.

In the end, however, what also sustains the debate about exceptionalism, perhaps especially of the American kind, is something else. In a world in which social scientists themselves can lament, albeit informally and off the record, that they know "more and more about less and less," exceptionalism remains one of those grand teasing concepts that purports to organize a broad array of knowledge and then come to a single strong conclusion. American exceptionalism can be sustained in this way only as long as American institutional influence and military power, or American cultural artifacts and social

462   SHAFER

practices, retain disproportionate sway. Yet as long as they do—and as long as de Tocqueville can continue to provide organizing hypotheses for their study—there is no reason to expect an end to the pursuit of American exceptionalism.

ACKNOWLEDGMENTS

Seymour Martin Lipset, Nelson Polsby, and Graham Wilson all encouraged a return to the topic of American exceptionalism. David Bell, Gordon Marshall, and Robert Mason helped track down particular parts of the story. A round-table on the topic at the 1998 annual meetings of the American Political Science Association then sharpened the argument. And Elaine Herman, as ever, converted the total package into a manuscript.

> **Visit the *Annual Reviews home page* at**
> **http://www.AnnualReviews.org.**

Literature Cited

Bell D. 1991. The "Hegelian secret": civil society and American exceptionalism. See Shafer 1991, pp. 46–70

Butler H. 1950. *Confident Morning*. London: Faber & Faber

de Tocqueville A. 1945 (1835). *Democracy in America*, 2 Vols. Transl. H Reeve. New York: Vintage Books (from French); originally *De la Democratie en Amérique*, 2 Vols. Paris: Charles Gosselin

Esping-Anderson G. 1990. *The Three Worlds of Welfare Capitalism*. Princeton, NJ: Princeton Univ. Press

Greeley AM. 1991. American exceptionalism: the religious phenomenon. See Shafer 1991, pp. 94–115

Hartz L. 1955. *The Liberal Tradition in America*. New York: Harcourt Brace Jovanovich

Howard C. 1997. *The Hidden Welfare State: Tax Expenditures and Social Policy in the United States*. Princeton, NJ: Princeton Univ. Press,

Kammen M. 1993. The problem of American exceptionalism: a reconsideration. *Am. Q.* 45:1–43

Lipset SM. 1963. *The First New Nation: The United States in Historical and Comparative Perspective*. New York: Basic Books

Lipset SM. 1997. *American Exceptionalism: A Double-Edged Sword*. New York: Norton

Lovecy J. 1992. Comparative politics and the Fifth Republic: la fin de l'exception française? *Eur. J. Polit. Res.* 21:385–408

Merton RK. 1968. On sociological theories of the middle range. In *Social Theory and Social Structure*, ed. RK Merton, pp. 39–72. New York: Free

Muston JD. 1997. *The end of exceptionalism in the foreign affairs debate? The resistance to internationalism in the US Senate, 1944–52*. DPhil thesis. Oxford Univ.

Potter DM. 1954. *People of Plenty: Economic Abundance and the American Character*. Chicago: Univ. Chicago Press

Riesman D, with N Glazer, R Denny. 1950. *The Lonely Crowd: A Study of the Changing American Character*. New Haven, CT: Yale Univ. Press

Rose R. 1991. Is American public policy exceptional? See Shafer 1991, pp. 187–221

Shafer B. 1991. *Is America Different?* Oxford, UK: Clarendon

Skowronek S. 1982. *Building a New American State*. Cambridge, UK: Cambridge Univ. Press

Sombart W. 1976 (1906). *Why Is There No Socialism in the United States?* Transl. C Husbands. London: Macmillan (from German); originally *Warum gibt es in den Vereinigten Staaten keinen Sozsialismus?* Türbingen: Mohr

Temin P. 1991. Free land and federalism: American economic exceptionalism. See Shafer 1991, pp. 71–93

Whyte WH Jr. 1956. *The Organization Man.* New York: Simon & Schuster

Wilson BR. 1982. *Religion in Sociological Perspective.* Oxford, UK: Oxford Univ. Press

Wilson GK. 1998. *Only in America? The Politics of the United States in Comparative Perspective.* Chatham, NJ: Chatham House

Winthrop J. 1630. A model of Christian charity, sermon delivered on board the *Arabella*

Zieger R. 1986. *American Workers, American Unions.* Baltimore, MD: Johns Hopkins Univ. Press

Annu. Rev. Polit. Sci. 1999. 2:465–91

AMERICAN DEMOCRACY FROM A EUROPEAN PERSPECTIVE

Sergio Fabbrini

Department of Sociology and Social Research, Trento University, 38100 Trento, Italy;
e-mail: fabbrini@soc.unitn.it

KEY WORDS: American exceptionalism, political development, institutional change,
comparative constitutionalism

ABSTRACT

This article analyzes American democracy from a European perspective. It
argues that American democracy (like European democracies) is based on
antinomies, two societal and two institutional, deeply rooted in American
constitutional development. Thus, each time American democracy has been
used as a model and exported, the attempt has ended in failure. An antinomic
model can be studied but not imitated. The article concludes that what is interesting for non-Americans is the way American democracy has historically
dealt with these antinomies, more than the American model per se. The
American method has to do with a peculiar constitutional structure that, having had the chance to institutionalize liberal principles, has tended to promote a positive-sum solution to those antinomies, in accord with individualistic values. Here resides the great divide between American and European
constitutional structures; for opposite reasons, the European constitutional
structure tends to promote a zero-sum solution to similar antinomies, in
agreement with collectivistic values. In both structures, something important
may be lost—private freedom in the latter and public good in the former.
Could a reciprocal constitutional learning process allow both sides to learn
the missing side of the story?

THE ARGUMENT

This paper analyzes American democracy[1] through a European lens. That is, I
discuss American democracy through a comparison with the only comparable

---

[1] I use the expressions "democracy in America" or "American democracy" in homage to the
Tocquevillian tradition, although it would be more accurate, as well as more respectful to the
multinational nature of the American continent, to speak of "democracy in the United States" or
"United States democracy."

1094-2939/99/0616-0465$08.00

experience (for historical and structural reasons), that of European democracy. In both cases, the term democracy is intended in a Tocquevillian sense—as the constitutional ordering of societal and institutional relations. I argue that, in constitutional terms, America and Europe are clearly distinguishable. This distinction is the effect of two separate political traditions embodied in different constitutional settings. The institutionalization of these settings facilitated different politicocultural approaches in America and Europe to the problems connected to democratization. These two approaches (liberal in America and democratic in Europe) still divide the two shores of the Atlantic. In this comparison, I try to arrange and connect the vast literature on the two democracies. The time has come to bridge the studies of both. For too long, unfortunately, those who pursued one study have ignored those who pursued the other.

A DEFINITION

Before discussing American democracy it is advisable to define the term. Because the United States is the longest-lived constitutional democracy in the world, it is inevitably conditioned by its long history and by its specific institutional structure. In the United States, history and institutional development are closely intertwined and have reciprocal influence [the issues involved in that development are well reconstructed by Ware (1997a)]. This helps to explain why all attempts to export American democracy have failed (or largely so). Constitutions can be imitated, but history cannot be repeated. Moreover, American democracy is the outcome of such specific geographical and environmental conditions that it is difficult to imagine another national context displaying similar characteristics (Mezey 1989). In sum, "American politics is in part the product of quite a lot of good luck, such as the fact that the nation possesses abundant natural resources and territory, enjoyed peace during its period of modernization, never had to overcome the class divisions of a feudal heritage, and had an expanding economy that could absorb and welcome successive waves of immigrants" (Polsby 1986:11).

This said, it is wise not to confuse recognition of (American) specificity with celebration of (American) exceptionalism. American democracy is unique, but so are all the national democracies.

> All nations are to some extent unique in one way or another. The idea of "exceptionalism", as it has been used to describe American history and institutions, assumes not only that the United States has been unlike other nations, but that it is exceptional in the sense of being *exemplary*. (Bell 1989:41)

The claim that American democracy is exemplary is not easily justifiable on empirical or normative grounds (see the debate in Wilson 1998, Lipset

1996, Kammen 1993, and Shafer 1991). In consequence, it is advisable to free ourselves of the exceptionalist dogma and fix the basic criteria with which to not only define American democracy but also compare it with European democracies (in particular). If all contemporary democracies are based on opposing views and contrasting interests, American democracy appears to be the antinomic democracy par excellence.

In fact, America has been an experiment in creating unity out of plurality. "E pluribus unum" was not only a motto but a necessity, given that America started from a lack of centralizing authority and an abundance of dispersed powers. I assume American democracy to be distinguished by four constitutive antinomies. Two are societal in nature; I define them as (*a*) the maximum of market vs the minimum of state and (*b*) a society of groups vs a nation of individuals. The other two antinomies are institutional, and I define them as (*a*) separated government vs popular participation and (*b*) composite republic vs democratic empire. These antinomies underlie American political development, here interpreted as the development of American constitutional structure, and they are my criteria for comparison.

An antinomic democracy is anything but static. In fact, American democracy has been an ongoing democracy, punctuated by historic changes in the national interpretation of its principles—the constitutional principles that reflected America's antinomies and tried to order their development. Of course, post facto, those principles seemed to have continuity. Ante facto, on the contrary, they are perceived as introducing discontinuity. The America of the Philadelphia constitutional convention of 1787 and of the first 10 Amendments of 1789 reinterpreted the principles that had arisen from the anti-English Revolution of 1776, thereafter consolidating itself in the first half of the nineteenth century. The America of the Civil War of 1861–1865 and of Amendments XIII, XIV, and XV reinterpreted the principles of the previous constitutional revolutions, thereafter consolidating itself at the turn of this century. The America of the New Deal years, 1933–1940, and of the Supreme Court decisions that followed, reinterpreted the principles in question, thereafter consolidating itself during the remainder of this century. In other words, although those reinterpretations were the outcome of conflict between different political traditions (Smith 1993), it is plausible to detect a "red line" connecting one to the other.

> American history has been punctuated by successful exercises in *revolutionary reform*—in which protagonists struggled over basic questions of principle that had ramifying implications for the conduct of large areas of American life. (Ackerman 1991:19)

Thus, American democracy is the outcome of a creative exercise in constitutional politics, an exercise that periodically unites the masses and élites in a dialogue at once conflictual and cooperative. More than anywhere else, democracy and constitution are synonymous in America. Assuming the American constitution to be the body of accumulated interpretations of the principles celebrated in the Declaration of Independence and in the Preamble of the Philadelphia document—reinterpretations imposed by the operation of one or the other of America's antinomies—then inquiry into those antinomies involves investigation of the regulatory as well as reflective capacity of the Constitution. I pursue this inquiry below by considering the comparable experience of European democracy, with the clarification that, by European democracy, I mean the democracy not only of the countries of continental Western Europe but also of Britain.

Of course, I know that the historical developments of the continent differ from those of Britain, not least because continental democratic experiences, unlike Britain's, are distinguished by a common statist matrix.[2] Nevertheless, this difference should not be exaggerated, if it is true that "[i]n Britain the concept of the Crown replaces the continental European concept of the state" (Rose 1996:74). Moreover, my concern here is the constitutional structure of democracy (and not the degree of its "stateness"), meaning the peculiar institutionalization of the constitutional principles realized in European countries. From this point of view, America differs unequivocally from all the (Western) European countries. All Western European countries have developed a monist constitution based on British design, i.e. a constitution that does not distinguish between decisions of the people and decisions of their representatives. America, on the contrary, has a dualist constitution, in which the types of decisions are not only distinguished but hierarchically ordered (in the sense that the decisions of the representatives must be taken in the institutional context defined by the decisions of the people). In America, constitutional politics is a business involving "We the People"; in Europe,"We the Representatives" (Ackerman 1991:6–10). This distinction has been clear since the beginning. James Madison wrote, "Even in Great Britain, where the principles of political and civil liberty have been most discussed,... it is maintained that the authority of the Parliament is transcendent and uncontrollable, as well with regard to the Constitution as the ordinary objects of legislative provisions" (*The Federalist Papers* No. 53, quoted in Beard 1964:234). Holmes (1995:144) thus comments, "Although the British government is moderate, therefore, it is not 'constitutionalist' in the American sense. In a passage well-known to all the American founders and framers, Blackstone himself had driven this point home:

---

[2]"The English case...represented a happy deviation from the 'normal' pattern on the continent: a center forming early, but never becoming a locus of absolute power, a pluralist order evolving slowly, legitimacy remaining strong, and 'responsible government' and the 'rule of law' being a more natural shorthand description for political beliefs than any reference to an abstract state" (Daalder 1995:117).

'Acts of parliament derogatory from the power of subsequent parliaments bind not'."

I start by discussing the above antinomies as they interacted with the Constitution until the Civil War of 1861–1865.

The Societal Antinomies

The first pair of antinomies concern the societal nature of American democracy. The one that sets the market against the state has been a subject of vast research. Despite the neofeudal model installed in the south by fugitive English aristocrats (fleeing the parliamentary revolution of 1688, known as the Glorious Revolution), the United States has been influenced much more sharply by the culture of the antiaristocratic English fugitives who had landed about 70 years previously on the East Coast. It was this antiaristocratic culture that impressed itself on the entire subsequent socioeconomic evolution of the colonies (first) and of the confederation and federation (later) (Lipset 1986). As we know, this culture was accordingly defined as "naturally" Lockean (Hartz 1955), in the sense that it was able to assert a sort of contractualist view of American democracy [although that view was challenged, especially with the ending of the nineteenth century (see Smith 1993)]. It was able to do so because neither group of fugitives was confronted by the political and social circumstances that have significantly and negatively conditioned the development of European democracy.

In fact, "[i]n sharp contrast to many European nations, the United States did not have a premodern polity characterized by monarchical absolutism, a locally entrenched standing army and bureaucracy, or recurrent mobilization for land warfare against equal competitors" (Skocpol 1992:235), nor did the United States have to set up a social system to distribute scarce resources to an exponentially growing population. In the absence of effective institutional and social constraints inherited from a feudal past, the American colonies and then states could promote their own commercial activities, gradually giving rise to what has been defined (post hoc) as a market system. It is not necessary to be in thrall to the exceptionalist myth to recognize that, in America, the market arose before the state—to recognize, in other words, that although economic freedom (of enterprise) may have been restricted by communitarian religious constraints, it preceded the birth and therefore guaranteed the growth of political freedom (of speech and action). This is why "America began and continues as the most anti-statist, legalistic, and rights-oriented nation" (Lipset 1996:20).

The market was the first institution able to impose order on social relations or, at any rate, to rationalize their development. There were no other institutions (such as the state) at the time, and when other institutions did arise, they labored to acquire the authoritative capacity that the market already had. Of course, the concrete construction of the market and therefore its development in the first half of the nineteenth century (in the North especially) required constant intervention by the states, the driving force behind the construction of the necessary legal and material infrastructures of the young American democracy (Toinet 1989). Nevertheless, the market was able to preserve its independence from these infrastructures (because it was powerfully protected by a constitution that hampered the formation of a centralized state authority), and this is why the market assumed a societal connotation—that is, it gained recognition as the paramount source of individual freedom. In sum, in the nineteenth century, "[t]he state did little and intruded less. By Max Weber's familiar definition of the state as the agency that monopolizes violent means of coercion, America was a virtual anarchy" (Wiebe 1995:15). In European democracy, by contrast, the market was imposed (with the help of the state and not despite it) on the basis of a preeminently economic rationale. In short, in Europe, the market has labored to find justification as an institution of efficiency; in America, it has not been obliged to justify itself because it was perceived from the beginning as a "natural" institution of freedom (Lipset 1979).

I now turn to the second societal antinomy, the contrast between groups and individuals. When Jefferson managed to convince the political élite of his country to sweep the dust of religious conflict under the carpet (Matthews 1984), by means of that astute declaration of freedom of conscience that celebrated the rigid separation of state and church, at that moment (whether or not he was aware of it), he laid the foundation for a modern pluralist society. For it is from the (recognized) pluralism of religious sects that the (encouraged) pluralism of social interests derives. America had to invent pluralism because only recognition of the plurality of religious preferences in the country could save it from confessional disintegration. However, once religious pluralism had been ratified, recognition of the pluralism of social, economic, and cultural interests inevitably followed (Dahl 1967).

This religious origin of pluralism is a curious phenomenon indeed when set in the context of European democracies. And yet, no European democracy originated as a country of emigrants prompted to leave their homelands by faith as well as socioeconomic necessity (Lipset 1979). The pluralism of the groups that emerged from this historical circumstance (which was given theoretical formalization in Madison's *Federalist Papers* no. 10)[3] would have had an unusually (for the period) dynamic character. These groups displayed transitory forms of identification, not the permanent ones that came about in Europe (following its modernization) with the formation of broad economic

[3]Madison wrote, "The latent causes of faction are...sown in the nature of man; and we see them every where brought into different degrees of activity, according to the different circumstances of civil society. A zeal for different opinions concerning religion, government, and many other points.... But the most common and durable source of factions has been the various and unequal distribution of property" (quoted in Beard 1964:70).

categories or inclusive social classes. The failure of the Articles of Confederation (1776–1787), with their attempt to institutionalize distinct (quasicorporative) territorial belongings, testifies to America's initial impermeability to the temptations of permanent subentities (Wood 1969).

At the same time, without a past, America was more aware than Europe of the need to invent a present. Without a state, America was more aware than Europe of the need to invent a nation. It is difficult to determine the degree of cultural awareness possessed by the American founding fathers (and I do not refer only to those who gathered in Philadelphia in the summer of 1787). Nevertheless, one is obliged to stress the novelty of their undertaking—to create a nation based on a constitution and not already justified by the state (Bellamy 1996), a nation that recognized itself as such on the basis of a pact among individuals rather than an accord or a compromise among institutional powers (as occurred in Europe in the nineteenth century, with the compromise between monarchical and parliamentary powers).

> [T]he parts that make up the United States...are individual men and women. The United States is an association of citizens. Its "anonymity" consists in the fact that these citizens don't transfer their collective name to the association. It never happened that a group of people called Americans came together to form a political society called America. The people are Americans only by virtue of having come together.... If the manyness of America is cultural, its oneness is political. (Walzer 1996:27, 29)

Thus, in America, from the very beginning of the new republican experience, there arose a dual society that in Europe was the outcome of a laborious process. On the one hand, there was the society of individuals, without which it would have been impossible to conceive the idea of the constitutional pact (an idea summed up by the "We the People" with which the Preamble of the Constitution begins); on the other hand, there was the society of groups, which was given the task of guaranteeing the social equilibrium on which the individual-oriented constitutional pact rested.

In short, America was the first country (and remains today, I believe, the only one) that not only began as a nation without a state but managed to keep the two separate when the state finally took shape, interposing the Constitution between them. Thus, in America, the nation has a constitutional basis, that is, a basis that is neither statist nor identitarian. Under the aegis of the Constitution the country's national diversities have been able to live together, as have its numerous religious sects and its contrasting socioeconomic interests. Anchored in the Constitution, the nationalities present in America have had to democratize their respective identitarian claims, lest they exclude themselves from the republican pact. In this sense, the American and European experiences differ radically. For America, the nation has never been, to use the celebrated formulation of Ernest Renan (1882:27), a "daily plebiscite" (as it was in Europe); it has been a constitutional accord to be daily verified—an accord among different national individuals and not an agreement among different nationalities. In short, "the United States is not a literal 'nation of nationalities' or a 'social union of social unions'" (Walzer 1996:27), but simply a nation of individuals with different nationalities.

The Institutional Antinomies

The second pair of antinomies concerns the institutional nature of American democracy. I start with the antinomy that sets separation of governmental power against its electoral legitimacy. Contrary to widespread belief, a system of separated government was created in America, not a presidential system (Neustadt 1990). What was celebrated at Philadelphia was the principle of the institutional separation of powers, not that of their centralization in the president; America forged a system "the chief distinctive feature of which is not a strong president but a strong Congress" (Polsby 1997:176). From this point of view, the Constitution of the United States is still the only authentically liberal constitution among the consolidated democracies. Of course, given that the Philadelphia constitutional convention was made necessary by the failure of the previous constitution (the Articles of Confederation, which regulated the country between 1781 and 1787), the practical liberalism of the new constitution had to distance itself to some extent from the theoretical liberalism of its inspirers (Locke and Montesquieu in particular). This practical liberalism might be more appropriately called Madisonian, for it was Madison who sought to conjugate the fear of power with the necessity of its use (Dahl 1956).

America inaugurated a system of government that, because it was influenced by Tudor England, proved very different from the system that was about to be institutionalized in Europe (and in post-Tudor England). Whereas Europe was laboriously seeking to bring the king into parliament, America decided to exclude its king (the president) from parliament. Whereas Europe strove to unify power, America strove to divide it. "Thus America perpetuated a fusion of functions and a division of power, while Europe developed a differentiation of functions and a centralization of power" (Huntington 1968:110). However, from the outset, this operational separation of powers [operational, that is, because of the principle of checks and balances introduced by Madison and intended to make the separation of powers workable (Ostrom 1987)] had to come to terms with a historical experience that fitted poorly with the reasons adduced to justify it. In short, constitutional liberalism very soon found itself forced to adapt to electoral democracy.

Indeed, the ink on the Constitution was hardly dry when Congress set about dividing itself into two caucuses (or what today we would term parliamentary parties), which endorsed distinct programs and which, more importantly, were politically hostile to each other. The Constitution therefore hardly had time to settle down when the wind of the electorate blew in through its windows. Hence, although liberal America had established itself on the principle of the fear of power—also, and perhaps principally, of power sustained by the majority—the new nation could not gainsay its principles by evading the necessity for a democratic (or, better, popular) legitimation of that power. Thus, America was the first country to introduce universal suffrage and therefore the first to create a modern party system as the indispensable means to substantiate the recognized right to vote. Of course, suffrage was "universal" only for white, male citizens (Shklar 1991), not for blacks and other minorities (Foner 1990) or for women (Baker 1984). In any case, in America, "[n]ineteenth century democratic politics revolved around elections...[and] each election reenacted the levelling of authority and renewed each voter's share of sovereign power" (Wiebe 1995:66), whereas "[t]he typical pre-1914 European government was a *constitutional oligarchy.* Government acted according to the rule of law, but the power to make and administer the law was in the hands of relatively few" (Rose 1996:25, italics in the original). In America coexisted, on the one hand, the insistent endeavor to preserve the constitutional limits on power, and, on the other hand, the equally insistent pressure to legitimize power electorally [as Morone (1990) brilliantly explains].

I now turn to the antinomy that opposes the composite republic against the democratic empire. American democracy was the first federal democracy in the world. In America, federalism was born from a rooted antimajoritarian and anticentralist prejudice. The enduring ambiguity that characterized the (confederalist) theory of the preeminence of the right of states over the right of the state can be explained only in light of the deep-seated (federalist) theory of the diffusion of state power. After all, as Sbragia (1992:260) reminds us, "until after the Civil War popular usage referred to the United States in the plural. 'The United States are' rather than 'the United States is' was the common formulation." In sum, the Civil War was waged to resolve this ambiguity—but not definitively. Although the shift from the plural to the singular highlighted the national character progressively acquired by American democracy, its institutionally and territorially compound nature nevertheless barred the way to any attempt at centralization.

A democracy is defined as compound when it is based on "[a] federal system of government...characterized by equilibrating structures that enable people to search out resolution in commonly defined realms of choice bounded by the limits of multiple veto points" (Ostrom 1987:23). By contrast, in nineteenth-century Europe, there were no effective veto points on the road toward a centralized state (Rokkan 1970). In fact, from 1815 to 1918, all European politics was concerned not only with the creation of new states coterminous with a particular nationality (Rose 1996:84) but also with the creation of a strong, central, all-powerful government. This centralization was imposed, sometimes by necessity (i.e. by the national élites' need to protect the territorial sovereignty of the state from the appetites of powerful neighbors), and sometimes by conviction (i.e. by the national élites' will to imitate what was then considered to be the successful model, the French one).

From its beginnings, however, the American compound republic had to reckon with the logic of a state of large territorial size (or rather, a state not prevented from becoming large). Indeed, it was long thought, following Madison,[4] that large size was the antidote to despotism (the illness typical of small states), and that federalism was the antidote to the expansionist instinct or spirit of power (the illness suffered by large states, and, a fortiori, those of continental extension). Thus it was that America expanded territorially for more than a century and yet remained composite. In this case, too, the Constitution established an equilibrium, both fragile and stable, between the centralizing tendencies of a country with evident expansionist potential and the anticentralizing tendencies of a democracy born from evident federalist need. This equilibrium was reflected in the growing role granted to the Supreme Court and, in any case, its preservation promoted a diffuse judicialization of intergovernmental relations (see Hodder-Williams 1992, Watts 1987, Caraley 1986).

Of course, the balance between the America of "ward democracy" (as Jefferson called it[5]) and the America of "imperial democracy"[6] could only be a delicate one, such was the cultural difference between them. Nevertheless, the balance proved surprisingly stable until the Civil War, thanks to the constitutionally protected balanced arrangement of the social and cultural forces associated with each of the two Americas. When the logic of the great continental state came to predominate, any minor mishap sufficed to galvanize the forces

[4]"Extend the sphere, and you take a greater variety of parties and interests; you make it less probable that a majority of the whole will have a common motive to invade the rights of other citizens; or if such a common motive exists, it will be more difficult for all who feel it to discover their own strength, and to act in unison with each other" (Madison, *Federalist Papers* No. 10, in Beard 1964:74).

[5]In a letter to Joseph C Cabell, written February 2, 1816, Jefferson wrote, "The elementary republics of the wards, the county republics, the State republics, and the republic of the Union, would form a gradation of authority, standing each on the basis of a law, holding every one its delegated share of powers, and constituting truly a system of fundamental balances and checks for the government. Where every man is a sharer in the direction of his ward-republic…and feels that he is a participator in the government of affairs…he will let the heart be torn out of his body sooner than his power be wrested from him by a Caesar or a Bonaparte" (see Koch & Peden 1944:661)

[6]Strangely enough, the same Jefferson, champion of ward democracy in theory, was (as president in the period 1801–1808) the promoter of the imperial democracy in practice, starting with the presidential Louisiana Purchase by treaty in 1803. "If the federal government, as Jefferson had always claimed, possessed no power not expressly granted, the President had no right to increase the national domain by treaty, much less to promise incorporation in the Union to people outside its original limits" (Morison 1972:92). Nevertheless, President Jefferson acted as a pure Hamiltonian, doing what the Constitution does not prohibit rather than doing only what it explicitly says to do. See the documented article by Tucker & Hendrickson (1990).

of local America or the interests of isolationist America. In the same way, when the logic of the ward democracy seemingly triumphed, its institutions and economy soon spawned the interests and cultures of anti-isolationist America, which was concerned with making the world safe, if not for democracy, then certainly for the market. This is why American federalism looks like a pendulum, moving from decentralization to centralization and back again according to historical needs and prevailing coalitions of interests (as Beer 1993 explained; see also Ostrom 1991, Grodzins 1962).

ANTINOMIES AND CHANGE

If those antinomies just described were the foundations of American democracy as established up to and through the Civil War, then it is worth investigating how they reacted to the subsequent changes in that democracy.

I begin with the opposition of state and market. With the formation of the great corporations in the second half of the nineteenth century, the market lost its role as the natural arena of societal interchange. Jefferson's yeomen was replaced by the great capitalists—great because they proved themselves able to gain monopoly over crucial production sectors. The challenge raised by the monopolistic reorganization of the market could not be countered by the minimal state. And yet it was a challenge that had to be neutralized if the market were to be preserved as the source of social mobility via economic competition. This dilemma prompted, in the New Deal years of the 1930s, a radical reinterpretation of constitutional principles in order to enable the creation of a federal state endowed both with increasingly broad regulatory powers and with an increasingly tight administrative organization—a federal state, nevertheless, that had been acquiring some of those regulatory powers since the 1880s, and some of those administrative capacities since the turn of the century (Skowroneck 1982).

Of course, the market has never entirely accepted such intervention by the state, which it deems a threat to its self-regulatory capacity. "To a greater degree than business people in many other capitalist nations, U.S. capitalists...distrust their state" (Skocpol 1992:242), even though the American federal state has always portrayed its intervention as necessary to revitalize and not to supplant the market's productive capacity (Stettner 1993). Of course, this regulatory intervention of the state has encountered growing difficulties as the current century of globalism comes to an end. Today, in fact, the relationships between state and market can no longer be defined solely in domestic terms, since they are powerfully influenced by the process of economic globalization.

I now turn to the second antinomy, that between groups and individuals. Partly as a result of federal centralization, but mainly as the outcome of the functional complexity of industrial society, the pluralism of groups also came to assume an oligopolistic configuration in the New Deal years. Public policies have been increasingly conditioned by great organized interests, in accord with the pattern that has been called "liberalism of interest groups" (Lowi 1979). In short, the individualistic basis of liberalism has been progressively eroded, with repercussions on the cultural identity of the country. Individual interests have been able to achieve recognition for themselves only by becoming organized groups, for only by organizing could they consistently influence the formation and outcomes of national public policies. Nonetheless, this organization has never acquired the neocorporatist features of some postwar European countries, centered on socially encompassing and peak-organized interest associations (Berger 1981).

Once the identity of the functional group lost its temporary and instrumental character (in pursuit of a specific public policy objective) and acquired a permanent one, the conditions were created for transformation of the very identity of the cultural group, in the sense that the melting pot, where the ingredients are blended, was gradually superseded by the salad bowl, where they retain their original features; the single-colored nation was gradually replaced by the rainbow-hued nation (Lind 1995). From this arose the risk of an ineluctable erosion of the constitutional bases of American identity (Schlesinger 1993, Fuchs 1990). Indeed, at the end of the twentieth century, the America of the hyphen (which joined and subordinated original national identity to subsequently acquired American identity) is now proving for the first time less attractive than the America without a hyphen, the America of distinct and separate identities. "It is very much like the dissidence of Protestant dissent in the early years of the Reformation, with many sects dividing and subdividing and many prophets and would-be prophets all talking at once" (Walzer 1997:96). Of course, it is obviously difficult to reconcile a cultural America of permanently separated group identities with the creed of the constitutional America of the preeminence of individuals. And, above all, once permanently organized groups succeed in controlling the policy-making process, then public policies tend to preserve the good of their interests and values even when the effects of that preservation are detrimental to the public good.[7]

The third antinomy, concerning the relationship between government and parties, has also undergone significant changes. Under the pressure exerted by changes in the environment, as well as by the processes of democratization set in motion by dissatisfied publics, separated government was translated into

---

[7]"Conservatism is literally sown in the nature of an organization itself. In this sense, we can say that formed groups are inherently conservative regardless of the nature of the goals of the organization or the predispositions of its members. [In summary]...our system is uniquely designed for maintenance" (Lowi 1971:52–54).

presidential government. More precisely, separated government with congressional primacy (as it had been throughout the nineteenth century) became, gradually with the new century and definitively after the crash of 1929, separated government with presidential primacy (Fabbrini 1999). However, although congressional government had looked with favor on the growth of modern party organizations, presidential government did not. Indeed, "the Democratic party became during the late 1930s the party to end all parties. Under Roosevelt's leadership, it was dedicated to a program that eventually lessened the importance of the two-party system and established a modern executive as the principal focus of representative government in the United States" (Milkis 1993:5).

But when there is no institutional incentive for the fusion of powers, it is unlikely that institutionally cohesive parties will form, because parties tend to adapt to the features of the institutional system and not vice versa (Avril 1986). In fact, the ascent of the presidency, without the simultaneous descent of the Congress (whose prerogatives continued to be guaranteed by the constitutional separation of powers), gave rise to a different hierarchization of decision making between the two governmental institutions, not to a rearrangement of the government around the president. In sum, there are political and institutional reasons for the progressive weakening of American parties in the presidential era; it could not have been otherwise in a system of government that has grown increasingly separated. In the congressional period, the separation was less marked simply because the presidency was not yet sufficiently institutionalized to compete effectively with the much more institutionalized Congress. In the presidential period (initiated by Roosevelt in the 1930s), separation grew more accentuated because both institutions of government were able to use their institutional resources fully (Mezey 1989).

Of course, weak parties are bound to become weaker, in the sense that they are unable to raise effective resistance against pressures for their further weakening. An example is the reform of the system of presidential candidate selection introduced by the Democrats in 1972 and then also adopted by the Republicans (Polsby 1983). This weakening of the parties further reduced the weight of partisan loyalties in the electorate (Polsby & Wildavski 1996, Wattenberg 1994). Thus, first gradually and then rapidly, there ensued the phenomenon of "ticket splitting" (Fiorina 1992), which led, after 1968, to the quasi-institutionalization of a full-blown regime of "divided government" (Ginsberg & Shefter 1990). Controlled by opposed party majorities, the two separated institutions transformed an ordinary partisan conflict into an extraordinary institutional conflict (see McKay 1994 for a review of the interpretations of divided government). The outcome was a drift toward a largely adversarial decision-making process between the two governmental branches [although the conflict was focused on policies of national and distributive significance because of the different electoral bases of the House, the Senate, and the president (Peterson & Greene 1993)], which rousing rhetoric by the president (Kernell 1992) and silent offers of coalitional cooperation by Congress attempted to resolve. This context, although it eventually led to a policy decision,[8] nevertheless complicates the identification of those who are responsible for it, because it further obscures that already opaque distinction between government and opposition allowed by the system of separation of powers. "Gridlock," Lowi (1994:414) remarks, "can better be characterized as the unresponsiveness of the government to changes in the economy and society" (see, for similar criticism of the American governmental system, Sundquist 1992 and Robinson 1989). Although many scholars are much less sanguine on the perils of gridlock, because they consider "split-party government as legitimate in a system of separated and disconnected elections" (Jones 1995:viii), it is nevertheless plausible to assert that "there is some truth in the conundrum that America is difficult to govern because governing is difficult in America" (Ware 1997b:xxviii).

I turn finally to the changes that have occurred in the fourth antinomy, regarding relationships between states and the state. First rapid industrial growth and then America's international ascendancy subjected the institutional structure of the compound republic to powerful pressures. If the New Deal had begun the nationalization process of American politics (Lunch 1987), the Cold War accelerated its internationalization. Power was increasingly transferred from the states to the state, but this transfer found no justification in a coherent culture of the state. Indeed, in the past 50 years, "[t]here was virtually no serious political science inquiry into whether the changes in constitutional doctrine, governmental structure, and policy commitments constituted a regime change" (Lowi 1992:5). Thus, the America of the imperial state was forced to coexist with the antistate America of the states—the America of overarching power with the America of the small county.

In short, nationalization and internationalization imposed themselves without being able to pervade the logic that drove the institutional system. "All politics is local," was the oft-repeated dictum of Tip O'Neill, the popular Democratic Speaker of the House in the early 1980s. This was an exaggeration, of course, but one nevertheless justified in this century by the enduring influence of Congress (that is, of local and state interests) on national policies (Bensel 1984). The enduring influence of localism gave rise to the see-saw motion of the relationship between states and the state. The ascent of the state has never been definitive; indeed, today we witness its descent (partly due to

---

[8]In fact, that conflict did not prevent the approval of several important bills when solid consensus formed among legislators and the president concerning the solution of an (electorally) important issue (Mayhew 1991).

contingent factors), to the advantage of the states.[9] Although a pendulum seems to drive the relations between the two institutional powers, the nature of those relations appears to be continually challenged.

In some ways, the changes in post–World War II European democracies were analogous to America's, although their antinomies were activated by pressures from precisely the opposite direction. In Europe, it is the market that has challenged the regulatory primacy of the state, especially in the wake of the growing economic and monetary integration of the continent (Majone 1994). In Europe, a culture of individual rights has called into question a policy-making process designed to serve groups or collective interests (for a comparison, see Safran 1997, Crawford 1993, Brubaker 1992). In Europe, strong governmental leaderships have emerged to contend with the control of the government by the parties (Mair 1994, Fabbrini 1994). In Europe, the explosion of regional political identities (stimulated and protected by the process of sovra-national integration) has pressed for the creation of national and subnational compound polities (Richardson 1996, Jones & Keating 1995). In fact, for a decade now, a discussion of the "Americanization of European politics" has proceeded—an argument (Manin 1993) that is, in many European public opinions, as implausible as the argument of the "Europeanization of American politics" was. The analogy between the two democracies resides in the nature of the antinomies, not in the strategies for dealing with them. In fact, the historical-institutional differences between America and Europe, as they are reflected and ordered in the constitutions, tend to promote dissimilar solutions to similar problems.

A MODEL OR A METHOD?

If my argument is plausible, and if an "American model" exists (Beyme 1987), that model is nevertheless founded on unequivocal antinomies (of course, formally, an antinomic model is a contradiction in terms, given that models necessarily consist of internally coherent and closed-ended patterns; empirically, however, it is a common reality). If one bears in mind this historically grounded antinomic nature of the American model, it becomes easier to understand why, in most cases, the model has dramatically failed when it has been exported. Accordingly, rather than imitating or, worse, importing the American model,[10] it is much more interesting for Europeans and for non-Americans

[9]Intractable macroeconomic, macrosocial, and macropolitical problems have obliged the federal state to resort to the well-known strategy of blame avoidance, transferring the task of solving these problems (and the potential blame for failure) to the states. On the ambiguity and complexity of the new federalist trends, see Walker (1995, 1996).

[10]On the issue of importing constitutions, there is a vast literature, which spans from Friedrich (1967) to Greeberg et al (1993) and does not stop there.

in general to investigate how the American antinomies have been dealt with. In short, we should concern ourselves less with an American model than with an American method to resolve these antinomies, given that they are not unique to American democracy, as we have seen. Of course, by a method I mean the specific tools of political culture with which to create the categories of thought (translatable, therefore, into political and institutional choices) necessary to conciliate the antinomies in question, or at least to try.

What has been the American method to handle the societal antinomies? I begin with the antinomy between states and market. Although America has never lacked proponents of a zero-sum solution, America's history displays a predominantly competitive approach to this antinomy. America has never undertaken the "statization" of the market, although frequent attempts have been made to "marketize" the state. The American approach, inaugurated in the 1880s and then confirmed by developments in the 1930s to 1960s, has been to transform the state into the regulator of the market, not into its replacement as in Europe (Majone 1991)—a regulation justified by empirical reasons, since, if left to itself, the market tends to generate oligopolies that suffocate competition. Hence, the market must be regulated to save it from itself, that is, to make it a competitive institution (Brinkley 1995).

The antinomy between groups and individuals has not lacked proponents of a zero-sum solution either. One solution would involve the complete "corporativization" of national policies, another the reassertion of their uniquely individualistic character. Yet, American history shows the emergence of a very different approach, seeking to counterbalance the power of groups with individual leaderships (of the president and sometimes of leading institutional members of Congress). Presidential leadership, in particular, has provided (disorganized) outsiders with their principal resource against (organized) insiders (Shklar 1991). Thanks to the progressive democratization of his electoral investiture, the president has become the guarantor of the nation. In sum, "[a] people's champion, preferably one in the White House, was as significant to advancing the cause of ordinary people as absolute monarchs had once been to opposing it" (Kazin 1995:24). Of course, the importance of individual leadership is a structural feature of American democracy, if it is true that "[i]n America the individual rather than the state is the foundation of political authority. [And in fact]...the study of American government emphasizes the political behavior of individuals, whether voters, members of Congress, or the president" (Rose 1996:74).

What has been the American method to deal with the institutional antinomies? Once again the proponents of a zero-sum solution abound. However, regarding the antinomy between government and parties, advocates of a government without parties have been much more numerous than those defending the importance of a government of parties. Yet, in the presidential era, the inevitable approach has been to deal with the antinomy not only by individualizing the responsibility of those in power (president and members of Congress), but also by subordinating party cohesion to institutional independence. This, of course, has reinvigorated the competition between the two governmental institutions, Congress and the presidency, more than between the two rival parties—let us say, freeing Madison from Jefferson.[11] In short, members of Congress have tended to decide (and thus to vote) with the interests of their electoral districts in mind more than those of their party caucus or their president. It is after all in the district, not in the party, that a politician needs to gain reelection. "In most democratic countries, the fate of most politicians depends, not primarily on their own endeavors, but on the fate—locally, regionally or nationally—of their party. If their party does well in an election, so do they.... [In the United States, on the contrary, the] candidate's party is a background factor. It is the candidate himself who is in the foreground" (King 1997:37, 39).

If it is plausible to say that in America today, "office seeking is candidate centered," that is, "candidates are autonomous and individually responsible for their own fates" (Aldrich 1995:161; see also Katz & Kolodny 1994, Wattenberg 1991), then, consequently, it is also plausible to claim that, in America, (party) responsibility has been increasingly interpreted as primarily (individual) accountability. Thus, identification of accountability is entrusted to the process of reciprocal checks and balances between institutions, more than to the process of mutual control between the party in government and the party in opposition (Fabbrini 1995). Hence, in the antinomy between states and the state, there have been few proponents of a return to the preeminence of states [although Ostrom (1997) makes a powerful argument in favor of it], compared with those who envisage the centralization of the federalist state. Here too, however, the prevalent solution has been a much more pragmatic one, the formation of a federal set-up with competition between states and the state (Dye 1990). In both of the institutional antinomies, the constitution plays a strategic role in setting the boundaries within which the competition (between the Congress and the presidency and between the federal center and the states) has to take place.

Seen from this perspective, the American method seems quite distinct from the one adopted by European democracy to deal with European antinomies.

---

[11]Hudson (1996:38) states, "The separation-of-powers structure erected formidable barriers in the way of forming a coherent governing majority in the United States.... The key to uniting the branches was the political party, and the first practitioner of the method was the third U.S. president, Thomas Jefferson." But he then adds, "Although the Jeffersonian model is the historical strategy for successful democratic politics in the United States, it does not overcome completely the antimajoritarian bias of the separation of powers" (1996:39). In fact, today, the parties in the government are less and less able to bridge the distance between the branches.

Regarding the societal antinomies, Europe has been traditionally suspicious of the culture of competition and has ambiguously eschewed the culture of leadership. Europe has feared competition because of its capacity to upset established social equilibria. Europe has downplayed the individual and emphasized the collective (i.e. party) role because, in its predominant political, religious, and communitarian movements (i.e. the Christian Democratic and Social Democratic parties), society has been perceived as a sum of groups of belongings more than as a sum of independent individuals. In fact, traditionally, European party leaders have tried to confirm existing social identities more than to mobilize dispersed electors.

America's economic dynamism and social integration derive from its twofold adherence to the principles of competition and leadership. The social legitimation that these two principles continue to enjoy may explain America's marked social mobility (Huntington 1981) but also its economic unfairness. This is a paradox from a European perspective, if it is true that "[t]he United States in the 1990s is socially, though not economically, a more egalitarian place than it was fifty or sixty years ago" (Walzer 1997:96). The fact that the United States is socially—but not economically—egalitarian is no paradox from an American perspective because "[t]he American commitment to equality of opportunity implies that achievement should reflect ability [and] justifies higher differentials in reward" (Lipset 1996:72). In any case, considering the capacity of the American system to integrate millions of immigrants into both economic and public policy systems, it is plausible to assert that competition and leadership have checked each other. In sum, although "the American emphasis on competitive individualism seems to have paid off" in America (Lipset 1996:58), Europeans think it will not in Europe.

Europe is quite distinct from America regarding the resolution of institutional antinomies as well. Europe's rigidly partitist tradition, with its emphasis on collective partisanship, continues to set it apart from the trend of political personalization, at the cost of downplaying individual political accountability. Europe's rigidly statist heritage, with its emphasis on hierarchical relations and paternalistic attitudes, appears to be inhospitable to the culture of institutional competition. Indeed, the institutional logic of contemporary European democracies requires (*a*) that responsibility must pass through the distinction between political options rather than individuals acting through opposing institutional branches, although that distinction has been recently altered by the emergence of political leaderships obliged to overcome party boundaries in order to deal with a growing, individualistic-oriented society; and (*b*) that competition among central and peripheral institutions be attuned to the necessity of their cooperation, although this cooperation has been recently jeopardized by the explosion of territorial interests addressing their conflictual claims to the center.

After all, first, European democracies (all with fusion of powers)[12] continue to be organized along party lines, which leaves limited chances for a democracy of leaders or candidates. Second, European democracies (all of state derivation) continue to be directed by the center through its extensive administrative apparatuses, which leaves limited chances for a democracy of the localities. This also occurs in noncentralized European countries. [An interesting discussion on the need to distinguish between noncentralization and decentralization is provided by Elazar (1976).] In fact, in Germany, where the state was demolished by a dramatic military defeat, the federal system had nevertheless to be based on cooperation between *Länder* and *Bund*. The same applies to Belgium, where a federalist reform of the state was introduced in 1993; to Austria, where the power of the *Bund* (or federal center) compared with that of the *Länder* (or regions) is unequivocally overwhelming; and to Spain, where recognition of regional autonomies by the new democratic constitution of 1978 was coupled with recognition, not abolition, of the center's prerogatives (Burgess 1993). After all, European federalisms arose from a process of disintegration of once unitary states, in which the center tried to retain as much as possible of its previous powers, whereas American federalism arose from a process of integration of once independent colonies, which tried to retain as many as possible of their previous powers (Sbragia 1992).

America and Europe have two different methods to deal with analogous antinomies. It is time to advance in the qualitative evaluation of their results, although this is a burden too heavy for my shoulders. Here, I limit myself to stressing that, in both cases, learning from the other method requires an investigation of the operative principles that distinct constitutional structures have historically shaped, protected, and fostered.

POSITIVE VERSUS ZERO-SUM SOLUTIONS

America has shown that there is an operational link between freedom and change. If America is the homeland of modern constitutionalism, it is so because it has been able to preserve its spirit as well as its form. America has been able to preserve the spirit of its constitution because it has been willing to change it. Not coincidentally, constitutional politics—that is, the politics of

---

[12]Even the genuinely semipresidential systems (like that of France of the Fifth Republic and, to a lesser extent, Finland) belong to the family of fused power systems, in that the executive cannot govern unless it has the confidence (albeit implicit) of the legislature (Fabbrini 1995). Of course, those systems that envisage the popular election of the president of the republic with powers solely of guarantee, not of government (e.g. those of Austria, Ireland, Iceland, and Portugal), cannot be regarded as semipresidential.

constitutional change—was born in America; the Constitution was amended (with the famous Bill of Rights) just two years after its approval. And when the amending process proved difficult to pursue, then (as has happened since the New Deal) the amendment took the form of a Supreme Court decision. This is why America had one constitution (or rather two, the first being the Articles of Confederation) but several constitutional regimes. Precisely because it is the homeland of constitutional change [whether through amendments (see Bernstein & Angel 1993) or judicial rulings (see Ackerman 1998a)], America cannot be conceived as a model to imitate.

Europe, by contrast, has often found itself in the position of replacing one constitution with another, either to protect the incumbent regime or to move from an old to a new regime. Since 1789, France has had 16 constitutions, but only five republics. Probably, this has also been because the American constitution is a frame of government, which "delineates the basic structure, institutions and procedures of the polity...[and] declares certain rights to be basic and provides means for their protection in civil society...[whereas] European constitutional codes tend to be far more rigid and require precise and deliberate formal textual change to be tuned or adopted" (Elazar 1985:233, 234). This rigidity surely results from the fact that "[m]ost European countries are governed under the Roman or the civil law, in which legal principles are regarded as comprehensive and fixed" (Rose 1996:80), which is not the case in common-law countries such as America (and Britain).

Yet, the difference between America and Europe seems to call for a deeper divergence in political culture. Although both have recognized the contrasts, inevitable and irresolvable, that underlie modern democracy, they have used historically opposite methods to deal with their antinomies. Since 1787 (with the crucial exception of the Civil War), American political culture has sought what I call a positive-sum solution to the antinomies that sprang from the republican experience [although it was not always able to live up to its own promises, as Hochschild (1995) and Sullivan et al (1982) remind us]. This approach, however, had its countereffect, if Sunstein (1993:198) is right in stressing that America has forgotten "the existence of a common good distinct from the aggregation of private interests," just as Madison feared. This search for a positive-sum solution contrasts with European political culture which, since the revolutionaries' decision to cut off Louis XVI's head in 1792, has preferred a zero-sum solution to the contradictions that obstruct the growth of democracy (of course, in the name of a transcendent public good). This suspicion of zero-sum solutions and this quest for positive-sum empirical solutions is perhaps characteristic of American political culture. In contrast, the ideological search for zero-sum solutions and the suspicion of bargained positive-sum solutions is characteristic of European political culture (see Franklin & Baun 1995 for a good introduction to some of these issues). In short, the distance between America and Europe is the stretch of ocean that divides perfecti-bility from perfection.[13] In sum, it was in America, not in Europe, that the constitution tried to create a regime "adequate to the precious human capacity for self-correction" (Holmes 1995:177).

But where does political culture come from? It comes from history and institutions, as they are reciprocally connected through the constitutional structure of the country (see Steinmo 1995 and, for a different view, Ellis 1993). Historically, for America, power was a problem, whereas for Europe it was a solution. The constitutional structures of the two democracies reflected, and then developed, these different preoccupations.

> The idea of checks and balances influenced the authors of the U.S. constitu-tion, which guards against the abuse—or even the use—of power. However, in Europe the idea did not take so strong a hold. Unchecked authority has been justified by arguments drawn from such very different principles as ab-solute monarchy, parliamentary democracy, or social democracy. (Rose 1996:78)

The Founders' view of power gave rise to the dualist constitution of Amer-ica, which, distinguishing between the decisions of the people and those of their representatives, enlarges the number of actors involved in constitutional change (making possible the search for positive-sum solutions through nego-tiations). The greater number of actors slows the onset of constitutional change but does not delay its impact.Thus, constitutional principles are freed from identification with the constitutional views of the incumbent power holders.

From a different view of power derive the monist constitutions of European countries, which, collapsing the decisions of the people and those of their representatives, reduce the number of actors involved in constitutional change, thus accelerating constitutional change. But a monist constitution imprisons constitutional principles within the view of the incumbent power holders. This monism is proper of the constitutions of all European countries, majoritarian and consensual, insular and continental, starting with Britain. In fact, "[s]o far as the monist is concerned, the British design captures the essence of democ-racy" (Ackerman 1991:8), a design America did not adopt (or failed to adopt). In sum, whereas "the British Constitution is essentially a *political* constitution, one whose operation depends upon the strength of political factors and whose interpretation depends upon the will of its political leaders" (Bogdanor 1988: 71), Americans, on the contrary,

---

[13]On November 10, 1787, George Washington wrote to Bushered Washington (see Levinson 1995:3), "The warmest friends and the best supporters the constitution has do not contend that it is free from imperfections." Since the founding of the new republic, the Founding Fathers' problem was to respond to imperfection, rather than to look for perfection (Levinson 1995). Lipset (1998) rightly insists on the important "ideological" role played by Washington.

[r]ather than granting a power monopoly to a single, popularly elected House of Representatives,...tolerate a great deal of insubordination from branches whose electoral connection is suspect or nonexistent. While the Senate gets its share of lumps, the principal object is the Supreme Court. Whoever gave Nine Old Lawyers authority to overrule the judgements of democratically elected politicians?" (Bogdanor 1988)

To be sure, it was none of the European democracies (see Jacob et al 1996).

Precisely because it was born in sequence with a liberalism that had the time to introduce its institutional and conceptual innovations, the American culture of democracy (prompted by liberalism) was forced to grow within a sufficiently established liberal institutional and intellectual context. This context made it difficult to conceive of perfect governments, much less of "angelic" governors. [After all, "If men were angels, no government would be necessary," as Madison wrote in the *Federalist Papers* no. 51 (Beard 1964:225). For a critique of Madison's (presumed) "heartlessness," see Matthews (1995).] The separation between people and power (that is, between principles and power-holders) and the diffusion of power have driven the search for pragmatic compromises among a plurality of actors and institutions. Nobody can claim to have the (constitutional) truth. The "city on the hill," if it exists, is not "down here" but "up there." And, in any case, appeals to that city serve as a populist antidote to the possible elitist degeneration of the liberal-pluralist feature of the constitution.[14] "Through populism, Americans have been able to protest social and economic inequalities without calling the entire system into question" (Kazin 1995:2).

By contrast, the European culture of democracy, precisely because it arose simultaneously with a liberalism that feared democracy since it wanted to overcome its procedural perspective, inevitably asserted (in opposition to liberalism) that perfect governments and angelic governors are possible. The city on the hill is down here, although only very few may see it. In fact, the parliamentary and centralized institutions thus created, once legitimized as the embodiment of the people's sovereignty, authorized the power holders to claim the constitutional truth. Deprived of an effective liberal antidote, European democratic movements have traditionally looked suspiciously on everything that might hamper the historical march toward the "hill," starting from individuals, that is, from individual rights and choices. The result is a society more protected (for groups) than America's but also less open (for individuals).

[14]American populism has its roots in that "We the People" with which the 1787 Constitution begins. Since the onset of republicanism, populism was legitimized as a current of thought that served to redress the defects of liberalism. In contrast to European populism (think of the European experience between the two world wars), it has never carried an antipolitical or indeed antidemocratic message, limiting itself to assert an excluded people's will against the included elites (see Ackerman 1998b).

CONCLUSION

If it is true that continuity is given to a social community not by contingent solutions proposed for its conflicts but by the principles that sustain the search for those solutions, one may suggest that America's constitution, by institutionalizing liberal principles, has enabled it to conduct a pragmatic search for democratic solutions. The experimentalism of this search has been contrasted in Europe, owing to the weak institutionalization of the liberal premises of Europe's democratic constitutions. Given that values live through institutions, perhaps the different degrees of institutionalization of liberal principles in Europe and democratic principles in America may explain why America and Europe still represent two different interpretations of a constitutional liberal democracy.

Thus, for Europe, studying the American method requires self-interrogation on the liberal rationale underlying its democratic institutions; that is, European democracy needs to take a step backward, to clarify its own liberal premises [as Dahrendorf (1990) and Habermas (1990) began to do in the wake of the fall of the Berlin wall], in order to strengthen the liberal institutions and practices of its constitutions (see Touraine 1997 and Preuss 1995). For America, reflecting on its own method from a European perspective requires self-interrogation regarding the democratic expectations added to America's liberal institutions (as suggested by Dahl 1998 and Brinkley 1998, but also Shklar 1998 and Sunstein 1997, from different theoretical perspectives). That is, America needs to take a step forward in order to neutralize the negative economic consequences produced by those liberal premises, if left alone.

Probably, in both cases, the respective constitutional structures need to be reassessed, if the purpose is to reach a more satisfactory equilibrium between liberalism and democracy. It remains to be seen whether it will be more difficult for America to meet the democratic criteria of the public good or for Europe to meet the liberal criteria of private freedom—given their distinctive constitutional structures.

Visit the *Annual Reviews home page* at
http://www.AnnualReviews.org.

Literature Cited

Ackerman B. 1991. *We the People. Foundations.* Cambridge, MA: Harvard Univ. Press. 369 pp.

Ackerman B. 1998a. *We the People. Transformations.* Cambridge, MA: Harvard Univ. Press. 515 pp.

Ackerman B. 1998b. The broken engine of progressive politics. In *Am. Prospect* 38: 34–43

Aldrich JH. 1995. *Why Parties? The Origin and Transformation of Political Parties in America.* Chicago: Univ. Chicago Press. 349 pp.

Avril P. 1986. *Essais sur les Parties.* Paris:

Libr. gén. droit Jurisprud. 216 pp.

Baker P. 1984. The domestication of politics: women and the American political society, 1780–1920. *Am. Hist. Rev.* 90(3):620–47

Beard C, ed. 1964. *The Enduring Federalist.* New York: Ungar. 396 pp. 2nd ed.

Beer SH. 1993. *To Make a Nation: the Rediscovery of American Federalism.* Cambridge, MA: Harvard Univ. Press. 474 pp.

Bell D. 1989. "American exceptionalism" revisited: the role of civil society. *Public Interest* 95:38–56

Bellamy R, ed. 1996. *Constitutionalism, Democracy and Sovereignty: American and European Perspectives.* Aldershot, UK: Avebury. 162 pp.

Bensel RF. 1984. *Sectionalism and American Political Development, 1880–1980.* Madison: Univ. Wis. Press. 494 pp.

Berger S, ed. 1981. *Organizing Interests in Western Europe: Pluralism, Corporatism and the Transformation of Politics.* Cambridge, MA: Cambridge Univ. Press. 426 pp

Bernstein RB, Angel J. 1993. *Amending America. If We Love the Constitution So Much, Why Do We Keep Trying to Change It?* Lawrence: Univ. Press Kans. 392 pp.

Beyme K. 1987. *America as a Model. The Impact of American Democracy in the World.* Aldershot, UK: Gower. 137 pp.

Bogdanor V, ed. 1988. Britain: the political constitution. In *Constitutions in Democratic Politics,* pp. 53–72. Aldershot, UK: Gower. 395 pp.

Brinkley A. 1995. *The End of Reform. New Deal Liberalism in Recession and War.* New York: Vintage. 371 pp.

Brinkley A. 1998. *Liberalism and Its Discontent.* Cambridge, MA: Harvard Univ. Press. 372 pp.

Brubaker WR. 1992. *Citizenship and Nationhood in France and Germany.* Cambridge, MA: Harvard Univ. Press. 270 pp.

Burgess M, ed. 1993. *Federalism and Federation in Western Europe.* London: Croom Helm. 227 pp.

Caraley D. 1986. Changing conceptions of federalism. *Polit. Sci. Q.* 101(2):289–306

Crawford YM, ed. 1993. *The Rising Tide of Cultural Pluralism: the Nation State at Bay?* Madison: Univ. Wis. Press. 305 pp.

Daalder H. 1995. Paths toward state formation in Europe: democratization, bureaucratization, and politicization. In *Politics, Society, and Democracy, Comparative Studies,* ed. HE Chehabi, A Stepan, pp. 113–30. Boulder, CO: Westview

Dahl RD. 1956. *A Preface to Democratic Theory.* Chicago: Univ. Chicago Press. 154 pp.

Dahl RD. 1967. *Democracy in the United States: Promise and Performance.* Chicago: Rand McNally. 514 pp.

Dahl RD. 1998. *On Democracy.* New Haven, CT: Yale Univ. Press. 217 pp.

Dahrendorf R. 1990. *Reflections on the Revolution in Europe.* London: Chatto & Windus. 163 pp.

Dye TR. 1990. *American Federalism. Competition Among Governments.* Lexington, MA: Lexington Books. 219 pp.

Elazar DJ. 1985. Constitution-making: the pre-eminently political act. In *Redesigning the State. The Politics of Constitutional Change,* ed. KG Banting, R Simeon, pp. 232–48. Toronto: Univ. Toronto Press

Elazar DJ. 1976. Federalism versus decentralization: the drift from authenticity. *Publius* 6(4):9–19

Ellis R. 1993. *American Political Cultures.* New York: Oxford Univ. Press. 251 pp.

Fabbrini S. 1994. Personalization as Americanization? The rise and fall of leader-dominated governmental strategies in Western Europe in the eighties. *Am. Stud. Int.* 32(2):51–65

Fabbrini S. 1995. Between parliamentarianism and presidentialism. A comparative perspective on governmental systems. *J. Behav. Soc. Sci.* 2:109–29

Fabbrini S. 1999. The American system of separated government: an historical-institutional interpretation. *Int. Polit. Sci. Rev.* 20(1):95–116

Fiorina M. 1992. *Divided Government.* London: Macmillan. 138 pp.

Foner E. 1990. Blacks and the US Constitution 1789–1989. *N. Left Rev.* 183:63–74

Franklin DP, Baun MJ, eds. 1995. *Political Culture and Constitutionalism. A Comparative Approach.* Armonk, NY: Sharpe. 246 pp.

Friedrich CJ. 1967. *The Impact of American Constitutionalism Abroad.* Boston: Boston Univ. Press. 359 pp.

Fuchs L. 1990. *American Kaleidoscope: Race, Ethnicity, and the Civic Culture.* Hannover, NH: Wesleyan. 618 pp.

Ginsberg B, Shefter EM. 1990. *Politics by Other Means. The Declining Significance of Elections in America.* New York: Basic Books. 226 pp.

Greeberg D, Katz SN, Oliviero MB, Wheatley SC, eds. 1993. *Constitutionalism and Democracy. Transitions in Contemporary World.* New York: Oxford Univ. Press. 391 pp.

Grodzins M. 1962. Centralization and decentralization in the American federal system. In *A Nation of States,* ed. R Goldwin, pp. 1–23. Chicago: Rand McNally.

Habermas J. 1990. *Die Nachholende Revolution.* Frankfurt: Suhrkamp. 223 pp.

Hartz LB. 1955. *The Liberal Tradition in America.* New York: Harcourt Brace Jovanovich. 329 pp.

Hochschild J. 1995. *Facing up to the American Dream: Race, Class and the Soul of the Nation.* Princeton, NJ: Princeton Univ. Press. 412 pp.

Hodder-Williams R. 1992. Six notions of "political" and the United States Supreme Court. *Br. J. Polit. Sci.* 22(1):1–20

Holmes S. 1995. *Passions and Constraints. On the Theory of Liberal Democracy.* Chicago: Univ. Chicago Press. 337 pp.

Hudson WE. 1996. *American Democracy in Peril. Seven Challenges to America's Future.* Chatham, NJ: Chatham House. 322 pp. 2nd ed.

Huntington SP. 1968. *Political Order in Changing Societies.* New Haven: Yale Univ. Press. 488 pp.

Huntington SP. 1981. *American Politics: the Promise of Disharmony.* Cambridge, MA: Harvard Univ. Press. 303 pp.

Jacob H, Blankenburg E, Kritzer H, Provine DM, Sanders J. 1996. *Courts, Law and Politics in Comparative Perspective.* New Haven, CT: Yale Univ. Press. 408 pp.

Jones CO. 1995. *Separate but Equal Branches. Congress and the Presidency.* Chatham, NJ: Chatham House. 262 pp.

Jones B, Keating K, eds. 1995. *The European Union and the Regions.* Oxford, UK: Clarendon. 306 pp.

Kammen M. 1993. The problem of American exceptionalism. *Am. Q.* 45(1):1–43

Katz RS, Kolodny R. 1994. Party organization as an empty vessel: parties in American politics. See Katz & Mair 1994, pp. 23–50

Katz RS, Mair P, eds. 1994. *How Parties Organize.* London: Sage. 375 pp.

Kazin M. 1995. *The Populist Persuasion. An American History.* New York: Basic Books. 381 pp.

Kernell S. 1992. *Going Public. New Strategies of Presidential Leadership.* Washington, DC: Congr. Q. 251 pp. 2nd ed.

King A. 1997. *Running Scared. Why America's Politicians Campaign Too Much and Govern Too Little.* New York: Free. 244 pp.

Koch A, Peden W, eds. 1944. *The Life and Selected Writings of Thomas Jefferson.* New York: Random House. 756 pp.

Levinson S, ed. 1995. *Responding to Imperfection. The Theory and Practice of Constitutional Amendment.* Princeton, NJ: Princeton Univ. Press. 330 pp.

Lind M. 1995. *The Next American Nation. The New Nationalism and the Fourth American Revolution.* New York: Free. 436 pp.

Lipset SM. 1979. *The First New Nation. The United States in Historical and Comparative Perspective.* New York: Norton. 366 pp. 2nd ed.

Lipset SM. 1986. Historical traditions and national characteristics. A comparative analysis of Canada and the United States. *Can. J. Sociol.* 11(2):113–55

Lipset SM. 1996. *American Exceptionalism. A Double-Edged Sword.* New York: Norton. 352 pp.

Lipset SM. 1998. George Washington and the founding of democracy. *J. Democr.* 9(4): 24–38

Lowi T. 1978. Europeanization of America? From United States to United State. In *Nationalizing Government: Public Policies in America,* ed. T Lowi, A Stone, pp. 15–29. Beverly Hills, CA: Sage

Lowi T. 1979. *The End of Liberalism. Ideology, Politics and the Crisis of Public Authority.* New York: Norton. 331 pp. 2nd ed.

Lowi T. 1992. The State in political science: how we become what we study. *Am. Polit. Sci. Rev.* 86(1):1–6

Lowi T. 1994. Presidential democracy in America: toward the homogenized regime. *Polit. Sci. Q.* 109(3):401–15

Lowi TJ. 1971. *The Politics of Disorder.* New York: Norton. 193 pp.

Lunch WM. 1987. *The Nationalization of American Politics.* Berkeley: Univ. Calif. Press. 408 pp.

Mair P. 1994. Party organizations: from civil society to the state. See Katz & Mair 1994, pp. 1–22

Majone GD. 1991. Cross-national sources of regulatory policy-making in Europe and the United States. *J. Public Policy* 11(1): 79–106

Majone GD. 1994. The rise of regulatory state in Europe. *W. Eur. Polit.* 17(3):78–102

Manin B. 1997. *The Principles of Representative Government.* Cambridge, UK: Cambridge Univ. Press. 243 pp.

Matthews RK. 1984. *The Radical Politics of Thomas Jefferson. A Revisionist View.* Lawrence: Univ. Press Kans. 171 pp.

Matthews RK. 1995. *If Men Were Angels. The Heartless Empire of Reason.* Lawrence: Univ. Press Kans. 297 pp.

Mayhew DR. 1991. *Divided We Govern. Party Control, Lawmaking, and Investigations.* New Haven, CT: Yale Univ. Press. 228 pp.

McKay D. 1994. Review article: divided and governed? Recent research on divided government in the United States. *Br. J.Polit. Sci.* 24(3):517–34

Mezey ML. 1989. *Congress, the President and Public Policy.* Boulder, CO: Westview. 255 pp.

Milkis SM. 1993. *President and the Parties. The Transformation of the American Party System Since the New Deal.* Oxford, UK: Oxford Univ. Press. 404 pp.

Morone J. 1990 *The Democratic Wish. Popular Participation and the Limits of American Government.* New York: Basic Books. 402 pp. 2nd ed.

Morison SE. 1972. *The Oxford History of the American People. Vol. 2: 1789 Through Reconstruction.* New York: Oxford Univ. Press. 540 pp. 2nd ed.

Neustadt RE. 1990. *Presidential Power and the Modern Presidents. The Politics of Leadership from Roosevelt to Reagan.* New York: Free. 371 pp. 3rd ed.

Ostrom V. 1987. *The Political Theory of a Compound Republic. Designing the American Experiment.* Lincoln: Univ. Nebr. Press. 240 pp. 2nd ed.

Ostrom V. 1991. *The Meaning of American Federalism.* San Francisco: ICS. 299 pp.

Ostrom V. 1997. *The Meaning of Democracy and the Vulnerability of Democracies. A Response to Tocqueville's Challenge.* Ann Arbor: Univ. Mich. Press. 329 pp.

Peterson PE, Greene JP. 1993. Why executive-legislative conflict in the United States is dwindling. *Br. J. Polit. Sci.* 24(1): 33–55

Polsby NW. 1983. *Consequences of Party Reform.* Oxford, UK: Oxford Univ. Press. 267 pp.

Polsby NW. 1986. *Congress and the Presidency.* Englewood Cliffs, NJ: Prentice Hall. 287 pp. 4th ed.

Polsby NW, Wildavsky A. 1996. *Presidential Elections. Strategies of American Electoral Politics.* Chatham, NJ: Chatham House. 358 pp.

Polsby NW. 1997. Constitutional angst: does American democracy work? In *New Federalist Papers. Essays in Defense of the Constitution,* ed. A Brinkley, NW Polsby, KM Sullivan, pp. 159–79. New York: Norton

Preuss U. 1995. *Constitutional Revolution. The Link Between Constitutionalism and Progress.* Atlantic Highlands, NJ: Humanities. 135 pp.

Renan E. 1882. *Qu'est-ce qu'un Nation.* Paris: Calman Lévy. 30 pp.

Richardson J, ed. 1996. *European Union. Power and Policy-making.* London: Routledge & Keagan Paul. 300 pp.

Robinson DL. 1989. *Government for the Third American Century.* Boulder, CO: Westview. 204 pp.

Rokkan S. 1970. *Citizens, Elections, Parties.* Oslo, Norway: Universitetsforlaget. 470 pp.

Rose R. 1996. *What is Europe? A Dynamic Perspective.* New York: Harper Collins. 363 pp.

Safran W. 1997. Citizenship and nationality in democratic systems: approaches to defining and acquiring membership in the political community. *Int. Polit. Sci. Rev.* 18(3):313–35

Sbragia AM. 1992. Thinking about the European future: the uses of comparison. In *Euro-politics. Institutions and Policy-making in the New European Community,* ed. AM Sbragia, pp. 257–91. Washington DC: Brookings Inst.

Schlesinger AM. 1993. *The Disuniting of America. Reflections on a Multicultural Society.* New York: Norton. 160 pp.

Shafer BE, ed. 1991. *Is America Different? A New Look at American Exceptionalism.* Oxford, UK: Clarendon. 266 pp.

Shklar J. 1991. *American Citizenship. The Quest for Inclusion.* Cambridge, MA: Harvard Univ. Press. 120 pp.

Shklar J. 1998. *Redeeming American Political Thought,* ed. S Hoffmann, DF Thompson. Chicago: Univ. Chicago Press. 209 pp.

Skocpol T. 1992. State formation and social policy in the United States. In *Reexamining Democracy,* ed. G Marks, L Diamond, pp. 227–49. Newbury Park, CA: Sage

Skowroneck S. 1982. *Building a New American State. The Expansion of National Administration Capacities.* New York: Cambridge Univ. Press. 389 pp.

Smith R. 1993. Beyond Tocqueville, Myrdal and Hartz. *Am. Polit. Sci. Rev.* 87(3): 549–66

Steinmo S. 1995. Why is government so small in America? *Governance* 8(3):303–34

Stettner EA. 1993. *Shaping Modern Liberalism. Herbert Croly and Progressive Thought.* Lawrence: Univ. Press Kans. 225 pp.

Sullivan JL, Pierson JE, Marcus GE. 1982. *Political Tolerance and American Democracy.* Chicago: Univ. Chicago Press. 278 pp.

Sundquist JL. 1992. *Constitutional Reform and Effective Government.* Washington, DC: Brookings Inst. 344 pp. 2nd ed.

Sunstein CR. 1993. The enduring legacy of republicanism. In *A New Constitution. Designing Political Institutions for a Good Society,* ed. SL Elkin, KE Soltan, pp. 174–206. Chicago: Univ. Chicago Press

Sunstein CR. 1997. *Free Markets and Social Justice.* New York: Oxford Univ. Press. 407 pp.

Toinet MF, ed. 1989. *L'Etat en Amérique.* Paris: Fond. Natl. des Sci. Polit. 337 pp.

Touraine A. 1997. *What Is Democracy?* Boulder, CO: Westview. 224 pp.

Tucker RW, Hendrickson DC. 1990. Thomas Jefferson and American foreign policy. *Foreign Aff.* 66(2):135–66

Walker D. 1995. *The Rebirth of Federalism.* Chatham, NJ: Chatham House. 370 pp.

Walker D. 1996. The advent of an ambiguous federalism and the emergence of new federalism III. *Public Admin. Rev.* 56(3): 271–80

Walzer M. 1996. *What It Means to Be an American. Essays on the American Experience.* New York: Marsilio. 124 pp.

Walzer M. 1997. *On Toleration.* New Haven, CT: Yale Univ. Press. 126 pp.

Ware A, ed. 1997a. *The United States,* Vols. I–III. Aldershot: Dartmouth. Vol. I, 514 pp.; Vol II, 510 pp.; Vol. III, 501 pp.

Ware A. 1997b. Introduction. See Ware 1997a, Vol. I, pp. xi–xxviii

Wattenberg B. 1991. *The Rise of Candidate-Centered Politics: Presidential Elections of the 1980s.* Cambridge, MA: Harvard Univ. Press. 186 pp.

Wattenberg B. 1994. *The Decline of American Political Parties.* Cambridge, MA: Harvard Univ. Press. 227 pp. 2nd ed.

Watts RL. 1987. The American constitution in comparative perspective: a comparison of federalism in the United States and Canada. *J. Am. Hist.* 101(3):769–91

Wiebe RH. 1995. *Self Rule. A Cultural History of American Democracy.* Chicago: Univ. Chicago Press. 321 pp.

Wilson GK. 1998. *Only in America? The Politics of the United States in Comparative Perspective.* Chatham, NJ: Chatham House. 166 pp.

Wood G. 1969. *The Creation of American Republic, 1776–1787.* Chapel Hill, NC: Univ. NC Press. 653 pp.

Annu. Rev. Polit. Sci. 1999. 2:493–535

COPING WITH TRAGEDIES OF THE COMMONS

Elinor Ostrom

Workshop in Political Theory and Policy Analysis; Center for the Study of Institutions, Population, and Environmental Change, Indiana University, Bloomington, Indiana 47408-3895; e-mail: ostrom@indiana.edu

KEY WORDS: adaptive systems, polycentricity, rational choice, irrigation, forestry, fisheries

ABSTRACT

Contemporary policy analysis of the governance of common-pool resources is based on three core assumptions: (*a*) resource users are norm-free maximizers of immediate gains, who will not cooperate to overcome the commons dilemmas they face; (*b*) designing rules to change incentives of participants is a relatively simple analytical task; and (*c*) organization itself requires central direction. The chapter shows that these assumptions are a poor foundation for policy analysis. Findings from carefully controlled laboratory experiments that challenge the first assumption are summarized. A different assumption that humans are fallible, boundedly rational, and norm-using is adopted. The complexity of using rules as tools to change the structure of commons dilemmas is then discussed, drawing on extensive research on rules in field settings. Viewing all policies as experiments with a probability of failure, recent research on a different form of general organization—that of complex adaptive systems—is applied to the process of changing rules. The last sections examine the capabilities and limits of a series of completely independent resource governance systems and the importance of encouraging the evolution of polycentric governance systems.

THE POLICY PUZZLE

Since the influential article by Hardin (1968), "the tragedy of the commons" has been used as a metaphor for the problems of overuse and degradation of natural resources including the destruction of fisheries, the overharvesting of timber, and the degradation of water resources. Many policy analysts, scholars, and public officials agree with Hardin's conclusion that the participants in

493

1094-2939/99/0616-0493$08.00

a commons dilemma are trapped in an inexorable process from which they cannot extract themselves. External authorities are presumably needed to impose rules and regulations on local users, since they will not do this themselves. Viewing resource users as trapped in a tragedy of their own making is consistent with contemporary textbooks on resource economics and the predictions derived from noncooperative game theory for finitely repeated dilemmas (E Ostrom et al 1994).

Further, the way that "scientific management of natural resources" is taught to future regulators of natural resources keeps fisheries, forests, and water resources as relatively homogeneous units that are closely interrelated across a vast domain. Irrigation systems are interlinked along watersheds of major river systems. Fish and wildlife species tend to migrate over a large range. This approach, as it has been applied to fisheries management, is described by Acheson et al (1998:391–92).

> For those trained in scientific management, it is also an anathema to manage a species over only part of its range. From the view of fisheries scientists and administrators, it is not rational to protect a species in one zone only to have it migrate into another area where it can be taken by other people due to a difference in regulations. As a result, the units to be managed range along hundreds of miles of coast and can only be managed by central governments with jurisdiction over the entire area. Lobsters, for example, extend from Newfoundland to the Carolinas; swordfish migrate from the Caribbean to Newfoundland and Iceland. From the point of view of the National Marine Fisheries Service, it makes sense to have a set of uniform regulations for the entire US coast rather than one for each state. (See Sherman & Laughlin 1992)

Contemporary policy analysts also share a belief in the feasibility of designing optimal rules to govern and manage common-pool resources for a large domain utilizing top-down direction. Because common-pool resources are viewed as relatively homogeneous and interlinked, and because simple models exist of how they work, officials acting in the public interest are considered capable of devising uniform and effective rules for an entire region. What is needed is to gather reliable, statistical information on key variables, determine what the optimal harvesting pattern should be, divide the harvesting level into quotas, and assign quotas to users. Prescriptions calling for central governments to impose uniform regulations over most natural resources are thus consistent with important bodies of theoretical work, as well as the most advanced scientific approaches to resource policy.

These prescriptions are not, however, supported by empirical research. Field studies in all parts of the world have found that local groups of resource users, sometimes by themselves and sometimes with the assistance of external authorities, have created a wide diversity of institutional arrangements for coping with common-pool resources (McCay & Acheson 1987, Fortmann & Bruce 1988, Berkes 1989, V Ostrom et al 1993, Netting 1993, Bromley et al 1992, Tang 1992, Blomquist 1992). Examples also exist of commons dilemmas that have continued unabated. One conclusion that can firmly be made in light of extensive empirical evidence is, however, that overuse and destruction of common-pool resources is not a determinant and inescapable outcome when multiple users face a commons dilemma. Scholars have begun to identify the conditions of a resource, and of the users of a resource, that are most conducive to local users self-organizing to find solutions to commons dilemmas (see E Ostrom 1992, 1998b; Baland & Platteau 1996). Further, the broad design principles that characterize robust self-organized resource governance systems have been identified (E Ostrom 1990) and found basically sound by other scholars (Morrow & Hull 1996).

Another important set of findings is that national governmental agencies are frequently unsuccessful in their efforts to design effective and uniform sets of rules to regulate important common-pool resources across a broad domain. Many developing countries nationalized all land and water resources during the 1950s and 1960s. The institutional arrangements that local users had devised to limit entry and use lost their legal standing, but the national governments lacked funds and personnel to monitor these resources effectively. Thus, common-pool resources were converted to a de jure government-property regime but reverted to a de facto open-access regime (Arnold 1998, Arnold & Stewart 1991). The incentives of a typical commons dilemma were accentuated because local users were implicitly told that they would not receive the benefits of adopting a long-term view in their use of the resource. When resources that were previously controlled by local participants have been nationalized, state control has usually proved to be less effective and efficient than control by those directly affected, if not disastrous in its consequences (Curtis 1991, Panayotou & Ashton 1992, Ascher 1995). The harmful effects of nationalizing forests that had earlier been governed by local user-groups have been well documented for Thailand (Feeny 1988), Africa (Shepherd 1992, Thomson 1977, Thomson et al 1992), Nepal (Arnold & Campbell 1986), and India (Gadgil & Iyer 1989; Jodha 1990, 1996). Similar results have occurred in regard to inshore fisheries taken over by state or national agencies from local control by the inshore fishermen themselves (Cordell & McKean 1992, Cruz 1986, Dasgupta 1982, Higgs 1996, Pinkerton 1989).

Tang (1992) and Lam (1998) have also both found that large-scale government irrigation systems do not tend to perform at the same level as smaller-scale, farmer-managed systems (see also Mehra 1981, Levine 1980, Bromley 1982, Hilton 1992). In a study of over 100 irrigation systems in Nepal, Lam (1998) finds that the cropping intensity and agricultural yield of crudely constructed irrigation systems using mud, rock, timbers, and sticks is significantly higher than the performance of systems built with modern concrete and iron headworks operated by national agencies.

A considerable disjunction exists between currently accepted policy recommendations, based on well-received theories of human behavior in commons dilemmas, and evidence from the field (Berkes et al 1989). These findings challenge three of the most important theoretical foundations of contemporary policy analysis. One foundation is the model of the human actor that is used. Resource users are explicitly thought of as norm-free maximizers of immediate gains, who will not cooperate to overcome the perverse incentives of dilemma situations in order to increase their own and others' long-term benefits unless coerced by external authorities. Government officials are implicitly depicted, on the other hand, as seeking the more general public interest and being able to analyze long-term patterns in order to design optimal policies.

A second foundational belief is that designing rules to change the incentives of participants is a relatively simple analytical task best done by objective analysts not intimately related to any specific resource. Analysts view most resources in a particular sector as relatively similar and sufficiently interrelated that they need to be governed by the same set of rules. Third is the view that organization itself requires central direction. Consequently, the multitude of self-organized resource governance systems are viewed as mere collections of individual agents out to maximize their own short-term returns. The groups who have actually organized themselves are invisible to those who cannot imagine organization without rules and regulations issued by a central authority (see, for example, Lansing 1991, Lansing & Kremer 1994).

I propose to show that these three assumptions are a poor foundation for public policy recommendations. To do this, I first need to define what is meant by a common-pool resource, which is done in the next section. I then use the Institutional Analysis and Development (IAD) framework to show how the seven components of an action situation can be used to construct an appropriation dilemma—the central common-pool resource problem identified in most policy texts. To address the adequacy of the model of the human actor used, I summarize the findings from a series of carefully controlled laboratory experiments of appropriation dilemmas. Given that predictions based on the model of a norm-free, myopic, and maximizing individual are not supported, I then present a closely related but alternative conception of human behavior—applicable to resource users and government officials alike. Humans are viewed as fallible, boundedly rational, and norm-using. In complex settings, no one is able to do a complete analysis before actions are taken, but individuals learn from mistakes and are able to craft tools—including rules—to improve the structure of the repetitive situations they face.

I go on to explore the complexity of using rules as tools to change the structure of commons dilemmas. First I describe the seven clusters of rules that affect the components of any action situation, and then describe the specific rules that are used in field settings by resource users and government agencies. An examination of the types of rules used in the field yields several important findings. First, the number of rules actually used in field settings is far greater than generally recognized. Second, the type of rules is different. Some rules recommended in the policy literature are not found among the rules used by self-organized systems.

Given the complexity of the process of designing rules to regulate the use of common-pool resources, I argue that all policy proposals must be considered as experiments. No one can possibly know whether a proposed change in rules is among the more optimal rule changes or even whether a rule change will lead to an improvement. All policy experiments have a positive probability of failing. I draw on recent research by Holland (1995) and colleagues at the Sante Fe Institute to discuss the attributes and mechanisms of a different form of general organization—a complex adaptive system—that is not the result of central direction. Complex adaptive systems cannot be understood if one tries to fit these systems into the image of an organization with a central director.

I show how the parallel efforts by a large number of local resource users to search out and design local rule configurations may find better rule combinations over the long term, whereas top-down design processes are more limited in their capacities to search and to find appropriate rules. All forms of decision making have limits. I discuss the limits of a series of completely independent resource governance systems and the importance of building polycentric governance systems with considerable overlap to combine the strengths of parallel search and design processes with the strengths of larger systems in conflict resolution, acquisition of scientific knowledge, monitoring the performance of local systems, and the regulation of common-pool resources that are more global in their scope. The resulting polycentric governance systems are not directed by a single center. They, too, are complex adaptive systems, requiring policy analysts to change their fundamental views of organization in order to cope more effectively with tragedies of the commons and many of the other problems facing modern societies.

THE COMPONENTS OF A COMMONS PROBLEM

The Definition of a Common-Pool Resource

A common-pool resource, such as a lake or ocean, an irrigation system, a fishing ground, a forest, or the atmosphere, is a natural or man-made resource from which it is difficult to exclude or limit users once the resource is provided, and one person's consumption of resource units makes those units unavailable to others (E Ostrom et al 1994). Thus, the trees or fish harvested by one user are not available for others. The difficulty of excluding beneficiaries is a characteristic that is shared with public goods, and the subtractability of the resource units is shared with private goods. The focus in this chapter is primarily on renewable natural resources as exemplars of common-pool resources, but the theoretical arguments are relevant to man-made common-pool resources.

When the resource units produced by a common-pool resource have a high value and institutional constraints do not restrict the way resource units are appropriated, individuals face strong incentives to appropriate more and more resource units, leading to congestion, overuse, and even the destruction of the resource itself. Because of the difficulty of excluding beneficiaries, the free-rider problem is a potential threat to efforts to reduce appropriation and improve the long-term outcomes achieved from the use of the common-pool resources. When free riding is a major problem, those who would willingly reduce their own appropriations if others did are unwilling to make a sacrifice for the benefit of a large number of free riders.

Consequently, one important problem facing the joint users of a common-pool resource is known as the appropriation problem, given the potential incentives in all jointly used common-pool resources for individuals to appropriate more resource units when acting independently than they would if they could find some way of coordinating their appropriation activities. Joint users of a common-pool resource often face many other problems, including assignment problems, technological externality problems, provision problems, and maintenance problems (E Ostrom et al 1994, E Ostrom & Walker 1997). And the specific character of each of these problems differs substantially from one resource to the next. In this chapter, I focus more on appropriation problems, since they are what most policy analysts associate with "the tragedy of the commons."

A Baseline Appropriation Situation

No single model adequately captures the essential structure of all common-pool resources. There are instead universal components of all situations in which individuals interact on a structured and repetitive basis. These components take multiple values and combine to produce an incredible variety of action situations. The structure of any action situation can be analyzed by identifying seven components and how they generate a set of incentives for those involved. The components include (*a*) participants, (*b*) positions, (*c*) actions, (*d*) outcomes, (*e*) transformation functions linking actions and outcomes, (*f*) information, and (*g*) payoffs (including both positive returns and negative sanctions where relevant). Basically, one is interested in learning about the number and characteristics of participants in positions where they must choose among diverse actions in light of the information they possess about how actions are linked to potential outcomes and about the costs and benefits assigned to actions and outcomes (see E Ostrom et al 1994:ch. 2). Although it is possible to identify the component parts, the resulting action situation is a complex system whose structure is derived from the combination of parts. Appropriation situations have many structures, depending on the combination of particular attributes of each of these seven components.

In order to understand the process of coping with appropriation problems, we need to start with a static, baseline situation that is as simple as we can specify without losing crucial aspects of the problems that real appropriators face in the field. Further, we need to start with an "institution-free" baseline situation so that we can understand the outcomes predicted and achieved in such a baseline situation and the processes involved in changing the structure by changing rules that affect it. I outline the baseline appropriation situation that is based on accepted theory and has been used in a large number of laboratory experiments (see E Ostrom et al 1992, 1994). This institution-free, static, baseline situation has the following characteristics:

1. It involves a set of n symmetric appropriators who are interested in withdrawing resource units from a common-pool resource over a finite time horizon.

2. No differentiation exists in the positions these appropriators hold relevant to the common-pool resource. In other words, there is only one position of appropriator.

3. Appropriators must decide how to allocate their time and effort in each time period. One can think of these appropriators as being "endowed" with a set of assets, e, that they allocate each time period to two activities. Each day, for example, appropriators must decide whether to spend time trying to harvest resource units from the common-pool resource or to use time in their next best opportunity, such as working in a local factory. To simplify the problem, we posit that all appropriators have the same endowment, face the same labor market, and can earn a fixed wage for any time they allocate to working for a factory.

4. The actions affect the amount of resource units that are appropriated from the common-pool resource or wages earned in the labor market.

5. Transformation functions map the actions of all appropriators, given the biophysical structure of the resource itself, onto outcomes. Although these functions are frequently stochastic in field settings and are affected by many variables in addition to the actions of individuals, here I consider only determinant functions of appropriation actions in the baseline setting. The wage function simply multiplies the amount of time allocated to it by what-

ever is the standard wage. The appropriation function is a concave function, F, that depends on the number of assets, x_i, allocated to appropriation from the common-pool resource. Initially, the sum of individuals' actions, Σx_i, generates better outcomes than a safe investment in wage labor. If the appropriators decide to allocate a sufficiently large number of their available assets, the outcome they receive is less than their best alternative. In other words, allocating too many assets to the common-pool resource is counterproductive. Such a function is specified in many resource-economics textbooks based on the pathbreaking articles by Gordon (1954) and Scott (1955).

6. As an initial information condition, we assume that appropriators know the shape of the transformation function and know that they are symmetric in assets and opportunities. Information about outcomes is generated after each decision round is completed.

7. Payoff rules specify the value of the wage rate and the value of the resource units obtained from the common-pool resource. Specifically, the payoff to an appropriator is given by

we if $x_i = 0$, or

$w(e - x_i) + (x_i\ /\ \Sigma x_i)\ F\ (\Sigma x_i)$ if $x_i > 0$.

If appropriators put all of the assets into wage labor, they receive a certain return equal to the amount of their endowment times the wage rate. If appropriators put some of their endowed assets into wage labor and some into the common-pool resource, they get part of their return from wages and the rest from their proportional investment in the common-pool resources times the total output of the common-pool resource as determined by function F.

Assumptions about Actors

To explain and predict the outcome of any situation, one needs to specify four key characteristics of the actors who are participating in the situation: (a) the type of preferences held, (b) how information is processed, (c) the formula or heuristic used for making decisions, and (d) the resources brought to the situation. The theory of complete rationality uses the assumptions that (a) individuals have a complete and transitive ordering of preferences over all outcomes that is monotonically related only to their own objective payoffs, (b) all relevant information generated by the situation is used in making decisions, (c) actors maximize their own expected payoffs, and (d) all needed resources to act in this situation are possessed.

The theory of norm-free, complete rationality has proved to be extremely useful in a diversity of circumstances where the institutional arrangements reduce the number of options and complexity of the situation and reward those who maximize expected returns to self while punishing those who do not. When such situations are completely specified, clear predictions of equilibrium outcomes are derived. Behavior in experimental laboratories and in the field closely approximates the predicted equilibrium in simple action situations where selection pressures retain those who maximize their own expected returns and thin out those who do not.

The theory of norm-free, complete rationality is also useful in a variety of other situations to enable the analyst to undertake a full analysis and predict equilibrium outcomes. If behavior deviates from the predicted outcomes, one has a clear benchmark for knowing how far behavior deviates from that predicted by this theory. Below, therefore, I initially use the theory of norm-free, complete rationality and the theory of finitely repeated games to predict what the outcome would be if a set of experimental subjects were to face a fully specified baseline appropriation situation as outlined above. I then modify this set of assumptions in light of the evidence obtained in the experimental laboratory (and supplemented by field studies).

Predicted Outcomes for a Common-Pool Resource in the Laboratory

Laboratory experiments provide an opportunity to observe how humans behave in situations that are simple compared with field settings but nonetheless characterize essential common elements of relevant field situations. In the laboratory experiments conducted at Indiana University, we thought it crucial to examine behavior in an appropriation situation with a nonlinear transformation function and a sufficient number of players so that knowledge of outcomes did not automatically provide information about each player's actions. In this chapter, I can only briefly discuss the results of these experiments. All procedures and specifications are thoroughly documented in E Ostrom et al (1994) and in journal articles cited therein. In the baseline experiments, we utilized the following equation for the transformation function, F:

$$23 \left(\Sigma x_i \right) - 25 \left(\Sigma x_i \right)^2$$

Eight experienced subjects participated in all experiments discussed in this chapter. Each subject was assigned either 10 tokens, in the low-endowment condition, or 25 tokens, in the high-endowment condition, in each round of play. Their outside opportunity was valued at $0.05 per token. They earned $0.01 on each outcome unit they received from investing tokens in the common-pool resource. Subjects were informed that they would participate in an experiment that would last no more than two hours. The number of rounds in each experiment varied between 20 and 30. Instead of asking subjects to pretend they were fishing or harvesting timber, we described the situation as involving a choice between investing in either of two markets having the structure specified above. In addition to being told the payoff function specifically, subjects were provided with look-up tables that eased their task of estimating outcomes.

With these specifications, the predicted symmetric equilibrium strategy for a finitely repeated game in which subjects do not discount the future is for each subject to invest 8 tokens in the common-pool resource, for a total of 64 tokens. The prediction is the same for both endowment levels. At this level of investment, each subject would earn $0.66 per round in the 10-token experiments and $0.70 per round in the 25-token experiments (players were paid half of their computer returns in the 25-token experiments to keep the payoffs roughly similar). The players could, however, earn considerably more if the total number of tokens invested in the common-pool resource was 36, rather than 64. This optimal level of investment would earn each subject $0.91 per round in the 10-token experiment and $0.83 per round in the 25-token experiment. The baseline experiment is an example of a commons dilemma in which the predicted outcome involves substantial overuse of a common-pool resource. A much better outcome could be reached if subjects were to lower their joint use.

BEHAVIOR IN A SPARSE EXPERIMENTAL N-PERSON, REPEATED APPROPRIATION DILEMMA

As predicted, subjects interacting in baseline experiments substantially over-invested (documented in E Ostrom et al 1994). Subjects in the 10-token experiments achieved, on average, 37% of the maximum available to them and subjects in the 25-token experiments received –3% (E Ostrom et al 1994:116). At the individual level, however, subjects rarely invested 8 tokens, which is the predicted level of investment at equilibrium. Instead, all experiments provided evidence of an unpredicted and strong pulsing pattern in which individuals appear to use a simple heuristic. They increase their investments in the common-pool resource until there is a strong reduction in yield, at which time they tend to reduce their investments. As the yield again goes up, they repeat the cycle. At an aggregate level, behavior approximates the predicted Nash equilibrium in the 10-token experiment but is much lower than predicted in the 25-token experiment. No game-theoretic explanation exists for the pulsing pattern or the substantial difference between the 10-token and the 25-token experiments.

These laboratory experiments have been replicated by other researchers (Rocco & Warglein 1995) with similar results. An extremely interesting study was recently completed (Deadman 1997) in which artificial agents were programmed to use a variety of heuristics similar to those used by the human subjects in these experiments and to interact in a simulated environment that exactly replicated the baseline experiments. Deadman found that the specific results obtained in any series of runs depended on the particular heuristic (or mix of heuristics) programmed. Artificial agents did consistently produce the same kind of pulsing returns, and the consistent difference between 10-token and 25-token environments was also observed. Deadman (1997:175–76) described his results as follows:

> As in CPR [common-pool resource] experiments, the group performance for the simulation follows an oscillating pattern in which high performance leads to over investment in the CPR and the resultant drop in performance causes a reduction in group-wide investment in the CPR.... Still more interesting is the observation that the simulations perform similarly to subjects in laboratory experiments in terms of average performance over time. At the ten token endowment, the simulations perform near the Nash equilibria over time. At the 25 token endowment, the simulations perform near zero percent of optimum over time.

Consequently, both human subjects and artificial agents programmed to use heuristics performed similarly in the baseline environment.

STRUCTURAL CHANGE IN THE LABORATORY

In addition to the baseline experiments, we have explored how rule changes affect outcomes. Rule changes were operationalized in the set of instructions given to subjects and in the procedures adopted within the experiment. The first structural change was an information rule change. Instead of forbidding all communication among subjects, as in the baseline experiments, subjects were now authorized to communicate with one another in a group setting before returning to their terminals to make their own private decisions. This introduction of an opportunity for "cheap talk," where agreements are not enforced by an external authority, is viewed as irrelevant within the context of a noncooperative game with a Pareto deficient equilibrium.[1] The same outcome is predicted as in the baseline experiment. In a second series of experiments, we changed the authority and payoff rules to allow subjects to sanction one another at a cost to themselves. Because using this option produces a benefit for all at a cost to the individual, the game-theoretic prediction for a finitely repeated game is that no one will choose the costly sanctioning option. In a third series, we changed the authority rule to allow subjects to covenant with one another to determine their investment levels and to adopt a sanctioning system if they wished. Again, the predicted outcome is the same. In all three of these structurally changed appropriation experiments, however, subjects demon-

---

[1]In coordination games, on the other hand, cheap talk helps players agree on which equilibrium to select among several. In coordination games, individuals have an incentive to keep a promise of a future action that leads both players to a better equilibrium. In a social-dilemma game, each player has an incentive to use cheap talk to deceive the other player into switching strategies so that the first player can reap a much higher payoff. It is for this reason that cheap talk is considered irrelevant in dilemma games but useful in coordination games (see Farrell & Rabin 1966).

strated their willingness and ability to search out and adopt better outcomes than those predicted.

Face-to-Face Communication

In the repeated communication experiments, subjects made 10 rounds of decisions in the context of the baseline appropriation game. At this point, subjects listened to an announcement that told them they would have an open group discussion before each of the continuing rounds of the experiment. The subjects left their terminals and sat in a group facing one another. After each discussion, they returned to their terminals and entered anonymous decisions. Subjects used face-to-face communication to discuss what strategy would gain them the best outcomes and to agree on what everyone should invest in the subsequent rounds. After each decision round, as in the baseline experiments, they learned what their aggregate investments had been, but they did not learn the decisions of individual players. Thus, they learned whether total investments were greater than their agreement. Although in many rounds, subjects did exactly as they had promised one another, some defections did occur. If promises were not kept, subjects used this information to castigate the unknown promise breaker.

This opportunity for repeated face-to-face communication was extremely successful in increasing joint returns in the 10-token experiments, where subjects obtained close to 100% of the maximum available returns. There were only 19 instances out of 368 total opportunities in which a subject invested more in the common-pool resource than agreed upon—a 5% defection rate (E Ostrom et al 1994:154). In the 25-token experiments, subjects also improved their overall performance, but the temptation to defect was greater. Subjects in the 25-token baseline experiments had received total returns that were slightly below zero, while in the communication experiments, they obtained on average 62% of the maximum available returns (with considerable variance across experiments). The defection rate was 13% percent. Our conclusion in completing an analysis of these experiments was as follows:

> Communication discussions went well beyond discovering what investments would generate maximum yields. A striking aspect of the discussion rounds was how rapidly subjects, who had not had an opportunity to establish a well-defined community with strong internal norms, were able to devise their own agreements and verbal punishments for those who broke those agreements.... In many cases, statements like "some scumbucket is investing more than we agreed upon" were a sufficient reproach to change defectors' behavior. (E Ostrom et al 1994:160)

That subjects had internalized norms regarding the importance of keeping promises is evidenced by several of their behaviors. First, simply promising to cut back on their investments in the common-pool resource led most subjects to change their investment pattern. Second, subjects were indignant about evidence of investment levels higher than that promised and expressed their anger openly. Third, those who broke their promise tended to revert to the promised level after hearing the verbal tongue-lashing of their colleagues. These findings are consistent with a large number of studies by other researchers (Sally 1995).

Sanctioning Experiments

Participants in field settings are usually able to communicate with one another on a face-to-face basis, at least from time to time, either in formally constituted meetings or at social gatherings. In most field settings, however, participants have also devised a variety of formal or informal ways of sanctioning one another if rules are broken. Engaging in costly monitoring and sanctioning behavior is, however, not consistent with the theory of norm-free, complete rationality (Elster 1989:40–41). Thus, it is important to ascertain whether subjects in a controlled setting would actually pay in order to assess a financial punishment on the behavior of other participants. The short answer to this question is yes.

All sanctioning experiments used the 25-token design because defections were much higher in this design. Subjects played 10 rounds of the baseline game, modified so that the individual as well as total contributions were reported. Subjects were then told that in the subsequent rounds they would have an opportunity to pay a fee in order to impose a fine on the payoffs received by another player. The fees ranged in diverse experiments from $0.05 to $0.20 and the fines from $0.10 to $0.80. In brief, the finding from this series of experiments is that much more sanctioning occurs than the predicted zero level. Subjects reacted both to the cost of sanctioning and to the fee-to-fine relationships. They sanctioned more when the cost of sanctioning was less and when the ratio of the fine to the fee was higher. Sanctioning was primarily directed at those who invested more in the common-pool resource, but some sanctioning appeared to be directed by those who had been fined in a form of "blind revenge" against those whose investments were lower than others and were thus suspected of having sanctioned them. In this set of experiments, subjects were able to increase their returns modestly to 39% of maximum, but when the costs of fees and fines were subtracted from the total, these gains were wiped out. When subjects were given a single opportunity to communicate prior to the implementation of sanctioning capabilities, they were able to gain an average of 85% of the maximum payoffs (69% when the costs of the fees and fines were subtracted).

Covenanting Experiments

In self-organized field settings, participants rarely impose sanctions on one another that have been devised exogenously, as the experimenters did in the above sanctioning experiments. Sanctions are much more likely to emerge from an endogenous process of crafting their own rules, including the punishments that should be imposed if these rules are broken. Spending time and effort designing rules creates a public good for all involved and is thus a second-level dilemma no more likely to be solved than the original dilemma. This is the foundation for the repeated recommendation that rules must be imposed by external authorities who are also responsible for monitoring and enforcing these rules.

Subjects experienced with baseline and sanctioning experiments were recalled and given an opportunity to have a "constitutional convention" in the laboratory to decide whether or not they would like to have access to a sanctioning mechanism like the one described above, how much the fines and fees should be, and what joint investment strategy they would like to adopt. All of these groups were endowed with 25 tokens in each round. Four out of six experimental groups adopted a covenant in which they specified the number of tokens they would invest and the level of fines to be imposed. The fines determined by the participants ranged from \$0.10 to \$1.00. The groups that crafted their own agreements were able to achieve an average of 93% of the maximum available returns in the periods after their agreement, and the defection rate for these experiments was only 4%. The two groups that did not agree to their own covenant did not fare as well. They averaged 56% of the maximum and faced a defection rate of 42%. In other words, those subjects who used an opportunity to covenant with one another to agree on a joint strategy and choose their own level of fines received very close to optimal results, based entirely on their own promises and their own willingness to monitor and sanction one another when necessary (see Frohlich et al 1987 for similar findings).

WHAT THEORY OF HUMAN BEHAVIOR IS CONSISTENT WITH EVIDENCE FROM LABORATORY EXPERIMENTS?

The appropriation experiments briefly summarized above provide the following picture of behavior in N-person commons-dilemma situations:[2]

1. When individuals are held apart and unable to communicate face to face (or via the type of signalling that is feasible in two-person situations), they overuse a common-pool resource.

2. Individuals use heuristics in dealing with complex problems.

3. Heuristics vary in their capabilities to cope with a changing configuration of actions by other participants.

---

[2]This picture is also consistent with the experimental results obtained by Abbink et al 1996, Andreoni 1989, Frey & Bohnet 1996, Frohlich & Oppenheimer 1970, Güth et al 1982, Hackett et al 1994, Hoffman et al 1996, Isaac & Walker 1988, and Orbell & Dawes 1991.

4. Individuals initially use an opportunity for face-to-face discussions to share their understanding of how their actions affect the joint outcomes and arrive at a common understanding of the best joint strategy available to them.

5. Individuals are willing to promise others, whom they assess as being trustworthy, that they will adopt a joint plan of action. Most individuals keep their promises (in situations where substantial advantage can accrue for breaking the promise).

6. If agreements are broken, individuals become indignant and use verbal chastisements when available. They are also willing to use costly sanctions, and even tend to overuse them, but they do not use grim trigger strategies.

7. When given an opportunity to craft their own rules and sanction nonconformance to these rules, many groups are willing to do so. Through their own efforts, these groups achieve close to optimal results. Those who forego such an opportunity are not able to sustain a high level of performance.

In other words, individuals initially rely on a battery of heuristics in response to complexity. Without communication and agreements on joint strategies, these heuristics lead to overuse. On the other hand, individuals are willing to discuss ways to increase their own and others' payoffs over a sequence of rounds. Many are willing to make contingent promises when others are assessed as trustworthy. A substantial number of individuals, but not all, are trustworthy and reciprocate the trust that has been mutually extended. When behavior not consistent with reciprocity is discovered, individuals are willing to use retribution in a variety of forms but not the form used to predict the possibility of optimal outcomes when these situations are modeled as indefinitely repeated games.

The assumption that individuals are able to engage in problem solving to increase long-term payoffs, to make promises, to build reputations for trustworthiness, to reciprocate trustworthiness with trust, and to punish those who are not trustworthy, leads to a different type of policy analysis than the assumption that individuals seek their own short-term, narrow interests even when presented with situations where everyone's joint returns could be substantially increased. Using the latter theory leads to the policy advice that rules to reduce overuse must be devised by external authorities and enforceably imposed on local users. This has been the foundation for most policy prescriptions regarding the regulation of common-pool resources during the second half of the twentieth century.

A better foundation for public policy is to assume that humans may not be able to analyze all situations fully but that they will make an effort to solve complex problems through the design of regularized procedures and will be able to draw on inherited capabilities to learn norms of behavior, particularly reciprocity (E Ostrom 1998a, Bendor 1987). Such a behavioral theory of boundedly rational and norm-using behavior views all policies as experiments and asks what processes of search and problem solving are more likely to arrive at better experiments. The key problems to be solved are how to ensure that those using a common-pool resource share a similar and relatively accurate view of the problems they need to solve, how to devise rules to which most can contingently agree (Levi 1988), and how to monitor activities sufficiently so that those who break agreements (through error or succumbing to the continued temptations that exist in all such situations) are sanctioned, ensuring that trust and reciprocity are supported rather than undermined (Bendor & Mookherjee 1990).

The dilemma never fully disappears, even in the best operating systems. Once an agreement has been reached, however, appropriators are no longer making their decisions in a totally independent manner that is almost guaranteed to lead to overuse. But the temptation to cheat always exists. No amount of monitoring and sanctioning reduces the temptation to zero. Instead of thinking of overcoming or conquering tragedies of the commons, effective governance systems cope better than others with the ongoing need to encourage high levels of trust while also monitoring actions and sanctioning rule infractions.

Presenting this difference in a theoretical perspective based on carefully designed laboratory experiments is the first task that I set out to accomplish. Boundedly rational, local users are potentially capable of changing their own rules, enforcing the rules they agree upon, and learning from experience to design better rules. The next task is to show why multiple, boundedly rational, local users are better at designing rules than a single team of boundedly rational officials in a central agency. To do this, I draw on research about the type of rules used in the field.

EXPERIMENTING WITH RULES IN THE FIELD

With this change in perspective, we can think of appropriators trying to understand the biophysical structure of a common-pool resource and how to affect each other's incentives so as to increase the probability of sustainable and more efficient use over the long term. Instead of being given a set of instructions with the transformation function fully specified, they have to explore and discover the biophysical structure of a particular resource that will differ on key parameters from similar resources in the same region. Further, appropriators have to cope with considerable uncertainty related to the weather, complicated growth patterns of biological systems that may at times be chaotic in nature, and external price fluctuations affecting the costs of inputs and value of outcomes (see Wilson et al 1991, 1994). In addition to the physical changes that they can make in the resource, they can use tools to change the structure of the action situations they face. These tools consist of seven clusters of rules that directly affect the components of their own action situations:

1. Boundary rules affect the characteristics of the participants.

2. Position rules differentially affect the capabilities and responsibilities of those in positions.

3. Authority rules affect the actions that participants in positions may, must, or must not do.

4. Scope rules affect the outcomes that are allowed, mandated, or forbidden.

5. Aggregation rules affect how individual actions are transformed into final outcomes.

6. Information rules affect the kind of information present or absent in a situation.

7. Payoff rules affect assigned costs and benefits to actions and outcomes.

Given the nonlinearity and complexity of action situations, it is rarely easy to predict what effect a change in a particular rule will produce. For example, a change in a boundary rule to restrict the entry of appropriators reduces the number of individuals who are tempted to break authority rules, but it also reduces the number of individuals who monitor what is happening or contribute funds toward hiring a guard. Thus, the opportunities for rule breaking may increase. Further, the cost of a rule infraction will be spread over a smaller group of appropriators, and thus the harm to any individual may be greater. Assessing the overall effects of a change in boundary rules is a nontrivial analytical task (for examples, see Weissing & Ostrom 1991a,b). Instead of conducting such a complete analysis, appropriators are more apt to use their intuitive understanding of the resource and each other to experiment with different rule changes until they find a combination that seems to work in their setting.

To understand better the types of tools that are available to appropriators, let us examine in some detail the kind of boundary, authority, payoff, and position rules used in field settings. These four clusters of rules are the major tools used to affect appropriation situations in many common-pool resources, whereas information, scope, and aggregation rules are utilized to complement changes induced by these four rules.

For the past 14 years, colleagues at or associated with the Workshop in Political Theory and Policy Analysis at Indiana University have studied a very large number of irrigation systems, forests, inshore fisheries, and groundwater basins, as well as other common-pool resources (see Schlager 1990; Tang 1992; Schlager et al 1994; Lam 1998; E Ostrom 1990, 1996; Gibson et al 1999). We have collected an immense archive of original case studies con-

Table 1 Variables used in boundary rules to define who is authorized to appropriate from a resource

Residency or membership	Personal characteristics	Relationship with resource
National	Ascribed	Continued use of resource
Regional	Age	
Local community	Caste	Long-term rights based on:
Organization (e.g. co-op)	Clan	Ownership of a proportion of
	Class	annual flow of resource units
	Ethnicity	Ownership of land
	Gender	Ownership of non-land asset
	Race	(e.g. berth)
	Acquired	Ownership of shares in a private
	Education level	organization
	Skill test	Ownership of a share of the resource
		system
		Temporary use-rights acquired
		through:
		Auction
		Per-use fee
		Licenses
		Lottery
		Registration
		Seasonal fees
		Use of specified technology

ducted by many different scholars on all sectors in all parts of the world (Martin 1989/1992, Hess 1996, see http://www.indiana.edu/~workshop). Using the IAD framework, we developed structured coding forms to help us identify the specific kinds of action situations faced in the field as well as the types of rules that users have evolved over time to try to govern and manage their resources effectively. In order to develop standardized coding forms, we read hundreds of cases describing how local common-pool resources were or were not regulated by a government agency, by the users themselves, or by a nongovernmental organization (NGO).

Affecting the Characteristics of Users through Boundary Rules

Boundary rules affect the types of participants with whom others interact. An important way of enhancing the likelihood of using reciprocity norms in a commons is to increase the proportion of participants who are well known in a community, have a long-term stake in that community, and find it costly to have their reputation for trustworthiness harmed in that community. Reducing the number of users but opening the resource to strangers willing to pay a license fee, as is frequently recommended in the policy literature, introduces participants who lack a long-term interest in the sustainability of a particular resource, reduces the level of trust and willingness to use reciprocity, and thus increases enforcement costs substantially.

As shown in Table 1, we identified 27 boundary rules described by case-study authors as having been used in at least one common-pool resource somewhere in the world (E Ostrom et al 1989). Although some systems use only a single boundary rule, many use two or three of these rules in combination. Boundary rules can be broadly classified in three general groups defining how individuals gain authority to enter and appropriate resource units from a common-pool resource. The first type of boundary rule relates to an individual's citizenship, residency, or membership in a particular organization. Many forestry and fishing user groups require members to have been born in a particular location. A second broad group of rules relates to individual ascribed or acquired personal characteristics. User groups may stipulate that appropriation depends on ethnicity, clan, or caste. A third group of boundary rules relates to the relationship of an individual with the resource itself. Using a particular technology or acquiring appropriation rights through an auction or a lottery are examples of this type of rule. About half of the rules relate to the characteristics of the users themselves. The other half involve diverse relationships with the resource.

In a systematic coding of case studies about inshore fisheries in many parts of the world, Schlager (1990, 1994) coded 33 user groups out of the 44 groups identified as having at least one rule regarding the use of the resource. All 33 groups used some combination of 14 different boundary rules (Schlager 1994:258). None of these groups relied on a single boundary rule. Thirty out of 33 groups (91%) limited fishing to those individuals who lived in a nearby community, and 13 groups also required membership in a local organization. This indicates that most inshore fisheries organized by the users themselves restrict fishing to those individuals who are well known to each other, have a relatively long-term time horizon, and are connected to one another in multiple ways (see Taylor 1982, Singleton & Taylor 1992).

After residency, the next most frequent type of rules, used in two thirds of the organized subgroups, involved the type of technology that a potential fisher must use. These rules are often criticized by policy analysts, since gear restrictions tend to reduce the "efficiency" of fishing. Gear restrictions have many consequences, however. Used in combination with authority rules that assign fishers using one type of gear to one area of the fishing groups and fishers using another type of gear to a second area, gear restrictions solve conflicts among incompatible technologies. Many gear restrictions also reduce the load on the fishery itself and thus help to sustain longer-term use of the resource.

Other rules were also used by the groups in Schlager's study. A scattering of groups used ascribed characteristics—age (two groups), ethnicity (three groups), or race (five groups). Three types of temporary-use rights included government licenses (three groups), lottery (five groups), and registration (four groups). Seven groups required participants to have purchased an asset, such as a fishing berth, and three groups required ownership of nearby land. Schlager did not find that any particular boundary rule was correlated with higher performance levels, but she did find that the 33 groups who had at least one boundary rule tended to be able to solve common-pool problems more effectively than the 11 groups who had not crafted boundary rules.

In a closely related study of 43 small- to medium-sized irrigation systems managed by farmers or by government agencies, Tang (1992) found that the variety of rules used in irrigation was smaller than among inshore fisheries. The single most frequently used boundary rule, used in 32 of the 43 systems (74%), was that an irrigator must own land in the service area of an irrigation system (Tang 1992:84–85). All of the government-owned and -operated irrigation systems relied exclusively on this rule. Many of the user-organized systems relied on other rules or land ownership combined with other rules. Among the other rules used were ownership of a proportion of the flow of the resource, membership in a local organization, and payment of a per-use fee. Tang (1992:87) found a strong negative relationship between performance and reliance on land as the sole boundary requirement. Over 90% of the systems using other boundary rules, or a combination of rules including land ownership, were rated positively in the level of maintenance achieved and in the level of rule conformance, while less than 40% of those systems relying solely on land ownership were rated at a higher performance level ($P = 0.001$).

This paradoxical result can be understood by a deeper analysis of the incentives facing engineers who design irrigation systems. Many government systems are designed on paper to serve an area larger than they are actually able to

Table 2   Types of authority rules

Allocation formula for appropriation rights	Basis for allocation formula
Percentage of total available units per period	Amount of land held
Quantity of resource units per period	Amount of historical use
Location	Location of appropriator
Time slot	Quantity of shares of resource owned
Rotational order	Proportion of resource flow owned
Appropriate only during open seasons	Purchase of periodic rights at auction
Appropriate only resource units meeting criteria	Rights acquired through periodic lottery
Appropriate whenever and wherever	Technology used
	License issued by a governmental authority
	Equal division to all appropriators
	Needs of appropriators (e.g. type of crop)
	Ascribed characteristic of appropriator
	Membership in organization
	Assessment of resource condition

serve when in operation, due to a variety of factors, including the need to show as many posited beneficiaries as possible to justify the cost of construction and to gain user support (see Palanisami 1982, Repetto 1986). The government must then use ownership in the authorized service area as the criterion for having a right to water. After construction, authorized irrigators find water to be very scarce because of the unrealistic plans. They are unwilling to abide by authority rules or contribute to the maintenance of the system because of the unpredictability of water availability.

Many of the rich diversity of boundary rules used by appropriators in the field attempt to ensure that the appropriators will relate to others who live nearby and have a long-term interest in sustaining the productivity of the resource. One way of coping with the commons is thus to change the composition of those who use a common-pool resource so as to increase the proportion of participants who have a long-term interest in sustaining the resource, who are likely to use reciprocity, and who can be trusted. Central governments tend to use a smaller set of rules, and some of these may open up a resource to strangers without a longer-term commitment to the resource or may generate conflict and an unwillingness to abide by any rules.

Affecting the Set of Allowable Actions through Authority Rules

Authority rules are also a major type of rule used to regulate common-pool resources. In the coding manual, we identified a diversity of authority rules used in field settings. Some rules involve a simple formula. Many forest resources, for example, are closed to all forms of harvesting during one portion of the year and open for extraction by all who meet the boundary rules during an open season. Most authority rules, however, have two components. In Table 2, the eight allocation formulas used in the field are shown in the left column. A fisher might be assigned to a fixed location (a fishing spot) or to a fixed rotational schedule; a member of the founding clan may be authorized to cut timber anywhere in a forest; an irrigator might be assigned to a fixed percentage of the total water available during a season or to a fixed time slot. In addition to the formula used in an authority rule, most rules required a basis for the assignment. For example, a fisher might be assigned to a fixed location based on a number drawn in a lottery, the purchase of that spot in an auction, or his or her historical use. An irrigator might be assigned to a fixed rotation based on the amount of land owned, the amount of water used historically, or the specific location of the irrigator.

If all of the bases were likely to be combined with all of the formulas, there would be 112 different authority rules (8 allocation formulas × 14 bases). A further complication is that the rules for one product may differ from those for another product in the same resource. In regard to forest resources, for example, children may be authorized to pick fruit from any tree located in a forest if it is for their own consumption; women may be authorized to collect so many headloads of dead wood for domestic firewood and certain plants for making crafts; *shaman* may be the only ones authorized to collect medicinal plants from a particular location in a forest (Fortmann & Bruce 1988). Appropriation rights to fish are frequently related to a specific species. Thus, the exact number of rules that are actually used in the field is difficult to compute because not all bases are used with all formulas, but many rules focus on specific products. A still further complication is that the rules may regularly change over the course of a year depending on resource conditions.

Schlager (1994:259–60) found that all 33 organized subgroups used one of the five basic formulas in their authority rules. Every user group included in her study assigned fishers to fixed locations using a diversity of bases including technology, lottery, and historical use. Thus, spatial demarcations are a critical variable for inshore fisheries. Nine user groups required fishers to limit their harvest to fish that met a specific size requirement, while seven groups allocated fishers to fishing spots using a rotation system and seven other groups only allowed fishing locations to be used during a specific season. Four groups allocated fishing spots for a particular time period (a fishing day or a fishing season).

An important finding—given the puzzles addressed in this chapter—is that the authority rule most frequently recommended by policy analysts (see Anderson 1986, 1992; Copes 1986) is not used in any of the coastal fisheries included in Schlager's study. No attempt was made "by the fishers involved to directly regulate the quantity of fish harvested based on an estimate of the yield. This is particularly surprising given that the most frequently recommended policy prescription made by fishery economists is the use of individual transferable quotas based on estimates on the economically optimal quantity of fish to be harvested over the long run" (Schlager 1994:397). In an independent study of 30 traditional fishery societies, Wilson and colleagues also noted the surprising absence of quota rules (Acheson et al 1998:397; see Wilson et al 1994):

> All of the rules and practices we found in these 30 societies regulate "how" fishing is done. That is, they limit the times fish may be caught, the locations where fishing is allowed, the technology permitted, and the stage of the life cycle during which fish may be taken. None of these societies limits the "amount" of various species that can be caught. Quotas—the single most important concept and tools of scientific management—is conspicuous by its absence.

Local inshore fishers, when allowed to manage a riparian area, thus use rules that differ substantially from those recommended by advocates of scientific management. Fishers have to know a great deal about the ecology of their inshore region, including spawning areas, nursery areas, the migration routes of different species, and seasonal patterns, just to succeed as fishers. Over time, they learn how "to maintain these critical life-cycle processes with rules controlling technology, fishing locations, and fishing times. Such rules in their view are based on biological reality" (Acheson et al 1998:405).

In the irrigation systems studied by Tang (1992:90–91), three types of authority rules are used most frequently: (*a*) a fixed time slot for each irrigator (19 out of the 37 cases for which data is available, and in 10 out of 12 government-owned systems), (*b*) a fixed order for a rotation system among irrigators (13 cases), and (*c*) a fixed percentage of the total water available during a period of time (5 cases). Three poorly performing systems with high levels of conflict use no authority rule at all. A variety of bases were used in these rules, such as "amount of land held, amount of water needed to cultivate existing crops, number of shares held, location of field, or official discretion" (Tang 1994:233). Farmers also do not use rules that assign a specific quantity of water to irrigators except in the rare circumstances where they control substantial amounts of water in storage (see Maass & Anderson 1986). Fixed-time-slot rules allow farmers considerable certainty as to when they will receive water without an equivalent certainty about the quantity of water that will be available in the canal. When the order is based on a share system, simply owning land next to an irrigation system is not enough. A farmer must purchase one or more shares to irrigate for a particular time period. Fixed-time allocation systems, which are frequently criticized as inefficient, do economize greatly on the amount of knowledge farmers have to have about the entire system and on monitoring costs. Spooner (1974) and Netting (1974) described long-lived irrigation systems in Iran and in Switzerland where there was perfect agreement on the order and time allotted to all farmers located on a segment of the system, but no one knew the entire sequence for the system as a whole.

Tang also found that many irrigation systems use different sets of rules depending on the availability of water. During the most abundant season, for example, irrigators may be authorized to take water whenever they need it. During a season when water availability is moderate, farmers may use a rotation system in which every farmer is authorized to take water for a fixed amount of time during the week based on the amount of land to be irrigated. During scarcity, the irrigation system may employ a special water distributor who is authorized to allocate water to those farmers who are growing crops authorized by the irrigation system and are most in need.

The diversity of rules devised by users greatly exceeds the limited authority rules that are recommended in textbook treatments of this problem. Appropriators thus cope with the commons by using a wide variety of rules that affect the actions available to participants and thus affect their basic set of strategies. Given this wide diversity of rules, it is particularly noteworthy that rules assigning appropriators a right to a specific quantity of a resource are used so infrequently in inshore fisheries and irrigation systems. [They are used more frequently when allocating forest products, where both the quantity available and the quantity harvested are much easier to measure (Agrawal 1994).] To assign an appropriator a specific quantity of a resource unit requires that those making the assignment know the total available units. In water resources where there is storage of water from one season to another and reliable information about the quantity of water is available, such rules are more frequently utilized (Blomquist 1992, Schlager et al 1994).

Affecting Outcomes through Payoff and Position Rules

One way to reduce or redirect the appropriations made from a common-pool resource is to change payoff rules so as to add a penalty to actions that are prohibited. Many user groups also adopt norms that rule breakers should be socially ostracized or shunned, and individual appropriators tend to monitor each other's behavior rather intensively. Three broad types of payoff rules are used extensively in the field: (*a*) the imposition of a fine, (*b*) the loss of appropriation rights, and (*c*) incarceration. The severity of each of these types of sanctions can range from very low to very high and tends to start out on the low end of the scale. Inshore fisheries studied by Schlager relied heavily on shunning and other social norms and less on formal sanctions. Thirty-six of the 43 irrigation systems studied by Tang used one of these three rules and also relied on vigorous monitoring of each other's behavior and shunning of rule breakers. The seven systems that did not self-consciously punish rule infractions were all rated as having poor performance. Fines were most typically used (in 21 cases) and incarceration the least (in only 2 cases). Fines tend to be graduated depending on the seriousness of the infractions and the number of prior infractions. The fines for a first or second offense tended to be very low.

Passing rules that impose costs is relatively simple. The difficult task is monitoring behavior to ascertain if rules are being broken. Self-organized fisheries tend to rely on self-monitoring more than the creation of a formal position of guard. Most inshore fishers now use short-wave radios as a routine part of their day-to-day operations, allowing a form of instant monitoring to occur. An official of a West Coast Indian tribe reports, for example, that "it is not uncommon to hear messages such as 'Did you see so-and-so flying all that net?' over the short-wave frequency—a clear reference to a violation of specified gear limits" (cited in Singleton 1998:134). Given that most fishers will be listening to their short-wave radios, "such publicity is tantamount to creating a flashing neon sign over the boat of the offender. Such treatment might be proceeded [sic] or followed by a direct approach to the rule violator, advising him to resolve the problem. In some tribes, a group of fishermen might delegate themselves to speak to the person" (cited in Singleton 1998:134).

Among self-organizing forest governance systems, creating and supporting a position as guard is frequently essential because resource units are highly valuable and a few hours of stealth can generate substantial illicit income. Monitoring rule conformance among forest users by officially designated and paid guards may make the difference between a resource in good condition and one that has become degraded. In a study of 279 forest *panchayats* in the Kumaon region of India, Agrawal & Yadama (1997) found that the number of months a guard was on duty was the most important variable affecting forest conditions. The other variables that affected forest conditions included the number of meetings held by the forest council (a time when infractions were discussed) and the number of residents in the village.

> It is evident from the analysis that the capacity of a forest council to monitor and impose sanctions on rule-breakers is paramount to maintaining the forest in good condition. Nor should the presence of a guard be taken simply as a formal mechanism that ensures greater protection. It is also an indication of the informal commitment of the *panchayat* and the village community to protect their forests. Hiring a guard costs money. The funds have to be generated within the village and earmarked for protection of the resource. If there was scant interest in protecting the forest, villagers would have little interest in setting aside the money necessary to hire a guard. (Agrawal & Yadama 1997:455)

Whether an irrigation system creates a formal position as guard depends both on the type of governance of the system and on its size. Of the 15 government-owned irrigation systems included by Tang (1992), 12, or 80%, have established a position of guard. Stealing water was a problem on most government-owned systems, but it was endemic on the three systems without guards. Of the 28 farmer-organized systems, 17 (61%) utilized the position of water distributor or guard. Of the 11 farmer-organized systems that did not employ a guard, farmers on 5 systems (45%) were vigilant enough in monitoring each other's activities that rule conformance is high. That means, of course, that self-monitoring was not sufficient on the other 6 systems to support routine conformance with their own rules. A study of 51 communal irrigation systems in the Philippines illustrated the effect of size (de los Reyes 1980). Of the 30 systems that were less than 50 hectares, only 6 (20%) had established a position of guard; of the 11 systems that served between 50 and 100 hectares, 5 (45%) had established guards; and of the 10 systems over 100 hectares, 7 (70%) had created guards. De los Reyes also found, in a survey of over 600 farmers served by these communal irrigation systems, that most farmers also patrolled their own canals even when they were patrolled by guards accountable to the farmers for distributing water. Further, the proportion of farmers who reported patrolling the canals serving their farms increased to 80% on the largest self-organized systems compared with 60% on the smallest systems.

Creating the position of guard also requires a change in payoff rules so that the guard can be remunerated. Several formulas are used. On government-owned irrigation systems, guards are normally paid a monthly wage that is not dependent on the performance of a system or on farmers' satisfaction. Wade (1994) describes self-organized systems in South India where the water distributor–guard is paid in kind as the harvest is reaped by going to each farmer to collect his share based on the amount of land owned by the farmer. Sengupta (1991:104) describes another system in which, immediately after appointment, the guards "are taken to the temple for oath taking to remain impartial. With this vow, they break a coconut. They are paid in cash at the rate of Rs 10 per acres...per month by the cultivators. The *neerpaichys* themselves collect the money." With such subtle ways of changing the way the payment is made to this position, farmers are able to monitor the monitor more effectively.

Boundary and authority rules also affect how easy or difficult it is to monitor activities and impose sanctions on rule infractions. Closing a forest or an inshore fishery for a substantial amount of time, for example, has multiple impacts. It protects particular plants or fish during critical growing periods and allows the entire system time to regenerate without disturbance. Further, during the closed season, rule infractions are obvious to anyone, since any appropriator in the resource is almost certainly breaking the rules. Similarly, requiring appropriators to use a particular technology may reduce the pressure on the resource, help to solve conflicts among users of incompatible technologies, and make it very easy to ascertain if rules are being followed. Many irrigation systems set up rotation systems so that only two persons need to monitor actions at any one time and thus keep monitoring costs lower than they would otherwise be. Changing payoff rules is the most direct way of coping with commons dilemmas. In many instances, dilemma games can be transformed into assurance games—a much easier situation to solve.

Affecting Outcomes through Changes in Information, Scope, and Aggregation Rules

These rules tend to be used in ways that complement changes in boundary, authority, payoff, and position rules. Individual systems vary radically in regard to the mandatory information that they require. Many smaller and informal systems rely entirely on a voluntary exchange of information and on mutual monitoring. Where resource units are very valuable and the size of the group is larger, more and more requirements are added regarding the information that must be kept by appropriators or their officials. Scope rules are used to limit harvesting activities in some regions that are being treated as refugia. If no appropriation from these locations is allowed, the regenerative capacity of a system can be enhanced. Aggregation rules are used extensively in collective-choice processes and less extensively in operational settings, but one aggregation rule that is found in diverse systems is a requirement that harvesting activities be done in teams. This increases the opportunity for mutual monitoring and reduces the need to hire special guards.

It is important to note that we have not yet found any particular rules to have a statistically positive relationship to performance. The absence of any boundary or authority rule, however, is consistently associated with poor performance. Relying on a single type of rule for an entire set of common-pool resources is also negatively related to performance. Although specific rules are not systematically related to performance, self-governed systems appear to have two advantages in adopting rules to fit a local resource—more knowledge of the resource and efficient monitoring options.

POLICIES AS EXPERIMENTS

The Daunting Search for Better Rules

It should now be obvious that the search for rules that improve the outcomes obtained in commons dilemmas is an incredibly complex task involving a potentially infinite combination of specific rules that could be adopted. To ascertain whether one has found an optimal set of rules to improve the outcomes achieved in a single situation, one would need to analyze how diverse rules affect each of the seven components of such a situation, and, as a result, the likely effect of a reformed structure on incentives, strategies, and outcomes. Because there are multiple rules that affect each of the seven components, conducting such an analysis would be an incredibly time- and resource-consuming process. For example, if only five changes in rules per component were considered, there would be 5^7, or 75,525, different situations to analyze. This is a gross simplification, however, since some of the important rules used in field settings include more than five rules—at least 25 in the case of boundary rules, and over 100 variants in the case of authority rules. Further, how these changes affect the outcomes achieved in a particular location depends on the biophysical characteristics of that location and the type of community relationships that already exist. No set of policy analysts (or even all of the game theorists in the world today) could ever have sufficient time or resources to analyze over 75,000 combinations of rule changes and resulting situations, let alone all of the variance in these situations due to biophysical differences.

Experimenting with Rule Changes

Instead of assuming that designing rules that approach optimality, or even improve performance, is a relatively simple analytical task that can be undertaken by distant, objective analysts, we need to understand the policy design process as involving an effort to tinker with a large number of component parts (see Jacob 1977). Those who tinker with any tools—including rules—are trying to find combinations that work together more effectively than other combinations. Policy changes are experiments based on more or less informed expectations about potential outcomes and the distribution of these outcomes for participants across time and space (Campbell 1969, 1975). Whenever individuals agree to add a rule, change a rule, or adopt someone else's proposed rule set, they are conducting a policy experiment. Further, the complexity of the ever-changing biophysical world combined with the complexity of rule systems means that any proposed change of rules faces a nontrivial probability of error.

With each policy change, when there is only a single governing authority, policy makers tend to experiment simultaneously with all of the common-pool resources within their jurisdiction. A central government can undertake pilot programs to experiment with various options, but the intent is usually to find the set of rules that work best for an entire jurisdiction. The process of experimentation is usually slow. Information about results may be contradictory and difficult to interpret. Thus, an experiment that is based on erroneous data about one key structural variable or one false assumption about how actors will react can lead to a very large disaster (see Wilson et al 1999). In any design process that involves substantial probability of error, having redundant teams of designers has been shown to be advantageous (see Landau 1969; 1973, Bendor 1985).

SELF-ORGANIZED RESOURCE GOVERNANCE SYSTEMS AS COMPLEX ADAPTIVE SYSTEMS

As discussed in the introduction, many scholars consider the very concept of organization to be closely tied to the presence of a central director who has designed a system to operate in a particular way. Consequently, the mechanisms used by organized systems that are not centrally directed are not well understood in many cases. Many self-organized resource governance systems are invisible to the officials of their own country or those from donor agencies. A classic example of this occurred in the Chitwan valley of Nepal several years ago, when an Asian Development Bank team of irrigation engineers recommended a large loan to build a dam across the Rapti River to enable the farmers there to irrigate their crops. What the engineering design team did not see were the 85 farmer-managed irrigation systems that already existed in the valley and had achieved relatively high performance. Most farmers in the Chitwan valley already obtained three irrigated crops a year as a result of their participation in the activities of these irrigation systems (see Benjamin et al 1994).

In contrast to forms of organization that result from central direction, most self-organized groups—including the types of locally organized fisheries, forests, grazing areas, and irrigation systems discussed in this chapter—are better viewed as complex adaptive systems. Complex adaptive systems are composed of a large number of active elements whose rich patterns of interactions produce emergent properties that are not easy to predict by analyzing the separate parts of a system. Holland (1995:10) views complex adaptive systems as "systems composed of interacting agents described in terms of rules. These agents adapt by changing their rules as experience accumulates." Complex adaptive systems "exhibit coherence under change, via conditional action and anticipation, and they do so without central direction" (Holland 1995:38–39). Holland points out that complex adaptive systems differ from physical systems that are not adaptive and that have been the foci of most scientific effort. It is the physical sciences that have been the model for many aspects of contemporary social science. Thus, the concepts needed to understand the adaptivity of systems are not yet well developed by social scientists.

Properties and Mechanisms of Complex Adaptive Systems

No general theory of complex adaptive systems yet exists to provide a coherent explanation for processes shared by all such systems. Biologists have studied many different adaptive systems but within separate fields of biology. Thus, even biologists have not recognized some of the similarities of structures and processes that characterize the central nervous system, the immune system, and the evolution of species. Recent work at the Sante Fe Institute has begun to identify central attributes, mechanisms, and processes used by all complex adaptive systems, including biological systems as well as markets and other social systems that are not centrally directed (Anderson et al 1988).

It appears that complex adaptive systems share four basic properties: nonlinearity, flows, diversity, and aggregation. The first three properties clearly characterize the types of self-organized resource governance systems discussed in this chapter involving nonlinear flows of diverse products from common-pool resources. The term aggregation refers to the "emergence of complex larger-scale behavior from the aggregate interactions of less complex agents" (Holland 1995:11). For example, many irrigation systems are divided into several tiers and multiple units at each tier. All of the farmers on a field channel are responsible for distributing the water to this small channel as well as keeping it in good repair. All farmers whose field channels are served by a branch canal may send a representative to a branch canal organization that focuses on the distribution of water among all branches and on the maintenance of the distribution canals. The branch canal organization may send a representative to a central committee that is responsible for the headworks that divert the water from a river into the system in the first place. The rules used on one branch canal or one field channel may be quite different from the rules used on others. There is no single center of authority for these systems that makes all relevant decisions on how to get water from the river to a farmer's field, but in many farmer-organized systems, the water is distributed in an organized fashion and all of the waterworks are maintained as a result of the aggregation of decisions and actions at multiple levels (see Yoder 1994; E Ostrom 1992; Coward 1979, 1985; Wade 1988).

In addition to these four attributes, complex adaptive systems also use three mechanisms that are key to the adaptive process itself. These include the use of tags, internal models, and building blocks.

THE USE OF TAGS   Tagging is a universal mechanism for boundary formation and aggregation of units in complex adaptive systems. "Tags are a pervasive feature of [complex adaptive systems] because they facilitate selective interactions. They allow agents to select among agents or objects that would otherwise be indistinguishable" (Holland 1995:14). All rules involve tags of some sort. The boundary rules shown in Table 1 involve the specification of the tags that are used to determine who is authorized to be a co-appropriator from a common-pool resource. Residency, prior membership, and personal characteristics are attributes that already exist and are easy to use as boundary tags. Boundary rules that focus on an individual's relationship with a resource are acquired specifically related to that resource. Local governance systems rely heavily on tags that identify individuals who are already known to each other, who have a long-term stake in the sustainability of a resource, who have an incentive to build a reputation for being trustworthy, and who are thus likely to extend reciprocity rather than recalcitrance in dealing with joint problems.

Tags are also used extensively to mark locations in a resource, to warn rule breakers, and even to mark individual organisms that need to be treated in a special way. An example of the latter occurs along the Maine coast, where it is forbidden to harvest berried lobsters (those with eggs). Such lobsters are V-notched and returned to the sea (Acheson 1988, 1989). Any fisherman who captures a V-notched lobster is also supposed to return it to the sea. If someone has put a lobster trap in the wrong place, Maine lobstermen tie a rope on the trap in a noticeable location to warn the fisher that his infraction has been noticed. If a fisher ignores this initial warning, the lobster traps themselves are likely to be destroyed the next time they are noticed in the wrong location.

INTERNAL MODELS   The appropriators from a common-pool resource build internal models of the resource, the relationships among the components of the resource, and frequently where their own actions are positively or negatively related to one another and the resource. Among the shared lore for most fishing villages is a clear understanding of where fish breed, where young fish tend to cluster, the length of time it takes for fish to be mature and reproduce, the migration patterns of fish, the food chain in a location, etc. Many inshore fishers develop their own maps of all of the fishing spots in their grounds (see, for example, Berkes 1986). In an effort to reduce the interference of one boat with another boat's fishing, these are frequently defined so that if all fishing spots are filled, all boats are still able to have a good chance to catch fish. These maps are then used in a variety of allocation rules that specify how any particular boat is assigned to a particular fishing spot. Users of forests also map their forests and may create refugia—sometimes as sacred forests—for sections that are particularly rich in biodiversity. By not harvesting from these refugia, users maintain a source of regeneration for other nearby locations that are disturbed through harvesting. Similarly, farmers who manage their own irrigation systems have clear mental (and frequently, paper) maps of these physical systems. These system models are called upon when maintenance responsibilities are allocated, so that their more vulnerable locations are assigned more time and resources than locations that are stable without much maintenance.

BUILDING BLOCKS   Building blocks are ways of breaking down complex processes into small chunks that can be used in multiple ways and can be combined and recombined repeatedly and at diverse levels. Once an authority rule that allocates resource units on some basis is determined, for example, using the same basis again to allocate responsibility for maintenance work is considered to be a fair allocation of benefits and costs in many cultures and is relatively easy to remember. On the large Chhattis Mauja farmer-organized system in Nepal, for example, water was originally allocated by the land area served. In the 1950s, the formula used for maintenance work was that each branch canal was responsible for sending one person to work on the main canal for each 17 hectares of area it irrigated. "The term used for a person-day of labor for canal maintenance was *kulara*. Since the share of water a branch canal is entitled to receive is the same as the resource mobilization requirement, water allocation is now also referred to as 'so many *kulara* of water'" (Yoder 1991:7). As the system has grown, the total number of *kulara* has now been set at 177 shared among 44 branch canals. Voting rights are now also set in terms of *kulara*. "Therefore, a branch canal with five *kulara* was entitled to 5/177 of the water in the main canal, responsible to supply 5/177 of the resources mobilized for the irrigation, and had five of the total 177 votes in all important decisions" (Yoder 1991:7).

Changing Rules as an Adaptive Process

Given the logic of combinatorics, it is impossible—as shown above—to conduct a complete analysis of the expected performance of all of the potential rule changes that could be made by the individuals served by a self-organized resource governance system trying to improve its performance. A similar impossibility also exists for many biological systems. Let us explore these similarities.

Self-organizing resource governance systems have two structures that are somewhat parallel in their function to the concepts of a genotype and a phenotype in biology. Phenotypic structures characterize an expressed organism—how bones, organs, and muscles develop, relate, and function in an organism in a particular environment. The components of an action situation characterize an expressed situation—how the number of participants, the information available, and their opportunities and costs create incentives, and how incentives lead to types of outcomes in a particular environment. The genotypic structure characterizes the set of instructions encoded in DNA to produce an organism with a particular phenotypic structure. A rule configuration is a set of instructions on how to produce the structure of relationships among individuals in an action situation that is also affected by the biophysical world and the kind of community or culture in which an action situation is located.

The evolution of social systems does not follow the same mechanisms as the evolution of species (Boyd & Richerson 1985, Campbell 1975, Nelson & Winter 1982). In any evolutionary process, there must be the generation of new alternatives, selection among new and old combinations of structural attributes, and retention of those combinations of attributes that are successful in a particular environment. In evolving biological systems, genotypic structures are changed through mechanisms such as crossover and mutation, and the distribution of particular types of instructions depends on the survival rate of the phenotypes they produce in given environments. Instead of blind variation, human agents do use reason and persuasion in their efforts to devise better rules, but the process of choice always involves experimentation. Self-organized resource governance systems use many types of decision rules to make collective choices. These range from deferring to the judgment of one person or elders, to using majority voting, to relying on unanimity. The subject of what collective-choice rules are better for coping with tragedies of the commons is too large to discuss here.

Most systems are likely to start with one or two simple rules. An obvious first candidate is to use tags to close the boundary to outsiders in order to enhance the likelihood of contingent cooperation and conformance to agreements. By changing only a few rules at the beginning, everyone can come to understand those rules while evaluating how they work. A second candidate is to use the shared model of the environment built up through years of interaction in an environment to refine where appropriation should be undertaken and when. Space and time are candidates for allocating access to resources in a manner that is relatively low-cost to sustain. If the community is small enough and shares common norms at a high enough level, it may be unnecessary to create formal sanctions, guards, records, and other rules.

Changes in specific rules may come about through accident (forgetting or innovating on the spot) or through specific collective-choice processes, in which considerable time and effort are devoted to considering why performance needs to be enhanced and which rules might be changed. Since many appropriators have experience with more than one product, rules tried in regard to one product may be tried in regard to others if they are successful. Migration of individuals into a community brings individuals with repertoires of different rules used in other locations. Commerce with other groups lets appropriators see and learn about other groups who may be doing better (or worse) than they are in regulating a sustainable and efficient resource system. Thus, a self-organized resource governance system with a higher level of in-migration or greater communication with other localities is more likely to adapt and change rules over time than is a system where new ideas concerning how to use rules as tools are rarely brought in. Trial-and-error processes may give relatively rapid feedback about rules that obviously do not work in a particular environment, but this is not always the case when the effect of human action on the environment has a long time delay. If all self-organized resource governance systems are totally independent and there is no communication among them, then each has to learn through its own trial-and-error process. Many will find that rules that they have tried do not work. Some will fail entirely.

The rate of change differs among self-organized resource governance systems. As with all learning theories, the rate of change is an important variable affecting performance over time. If change occurs too rapidly, little is learned from each experiment before another experiment is launched. Respect for tradition and even religious mystification has been used to increase the retention of rules considered effective by at least some participants. If the heavy hand of tradition is too heavy, however, and innovation is stymied, a system that was well adapted to a past environment may find itself faltering as external changes occur without adaptation.

THE ADVANTAGES AND LIMITS OF PARALLEL SETS OF LOCAL USERS IN POLICY EXPERIMENTS

The last major task of this chapter is to discuss why a series of relatively autonomous, self-organized resource governance systems may do a better job of regulating small common-pool resources than a single central authority. In such systems, individuals who have the greatest interest in overcoming tragedies of the commons learn the results of their experimentation with rules and can adapt to this direct feedback. In this section, I discuss the advantages and limits of a fully decentralized system, where all responsibility for making decisions related to smaller-scale common-pool resources is localized. In the final section, I discuss why a polycentric governance system involving higher levels of government as well as local systems is able to cope even more effectively with tragedies of the commons.

Among the advantages of authorizing the users of smaller-scale common-pool resources to adopt policies regulating the use of these resources are the following:

1. Local knowledge. Appropriators who have lived and appropriated from a resource system over a long period of time have developed relatively accurate mental models of how the biophysical system itself operates, since the very success of their appropriation efforts depends on such knowledge. They also know others living in the area well and know what norms of behavior are considered appropriate by this community.

2. Inclusion of trustworthy participants. Appropriators can devise rules that increase the probability that others are trustworthy and will use reciprocity. This lowers the cost of relying entirely on formal sanctions and paying for extensive guarding.

3. Reliance on disaggregated knowledge. Feedback about how the resource system responds to changes in actions of appropriators is generated in a disaggregated way. Fishers are quite aware, for example, when the size and species distribution of their catch changes over time. Irrigators learn whether a particular allocation system is efficient by comparing the net yield they obtain under one set of rules versus others.

4. Better adapted rules. Given the above, appropriators are more likely to craft rules that are better adapted to each of the local common-pool resources than any general system of rules.

5. Lower enforcement costs. Because local appropriators have to bear the cost of monitoring, they are apt to craft rules that make infractions highly obvious so that monitoring costs are lower. Further, by creating rules that are seen as legitimate, appropriators encourage higher conformance.

6. Redundancy. Multiple units are experimenting with rules simultaneously, thereby reducing the probability of failure for an entire region.

There are, of course, limits to all ways of organizing the governance of common-pool resources. Among the limits of a highly decentralized system are the following:

1. Some appropriators will not organize. Although the evidence from the field is that many local appropriators do invest considerable time and energy into their own regulatory efforts, other groups of appropriators do not. There appear to be many reasons why some groups do not organize, including the presence of low-cost alternative sources of income and thus a reduced de-

pendency on the resource, conflict among appropriators along multiple dimensions, lack of leadership, and fear of having their efforts overturned by outside authorities.

2. Some self-organized efforts will fail. Given the complexity of the task involved in designing rules, some groups will select combinations of rules that generate failure. They may be unable to adapt rapidly enough to avoid the collapse of a resource system.

3. Local tyrannies may prevail. Not all self-organized resource governance systems will be organized democratically or rely on the input of most appropriators. Some will be dominated by a local leader or a power elite who only make changes that will be an advantage to them. This problem is accentuated in locations where the cost of exit is particularly high and reduced where appropriators can leave.

4. Stagnation may occur. Where local ecological systems are characterized by considerable variance, experimentation can produce severe and unexpected results, leading appropriators to cling to systems that have worked relatively well in the past and stop innovating long before they have developed rules likely to lead to better outcomes.

5. Inappropriate discrimination may result from the use of identity tags. The use of tags is frequently an essential method for increasing the level of trust and rule conformance. Tags based on ascribed characteristics can, however, be the basis of excluding some individuals from access to sources of productive endeavor regardless of their trustworthiness.

6. Access to scientific information may be limited. Although time and place information may be extensively developed and used, local groups may not have access to scientific knowledge concerning the type of resource system involved.

7. Conflict may arise among appropriators. Without access to an external set of conflict-resolution mechanisms, conflict within and across common-pool resource systems can escalate and provoke physical violence. Two or more groups may claim the same territory and may continue to make raids on one another over a long period of time.

8. Appropriators may be unable to cope with larger-scale common-pool resources. Without access to some larger-scale jurisdiction, local appropriators may have substantial difficulties regulating only a part of a larger-scale common-pool resource. They may not be able to exclude others who refuse to abide by the rules that a local group would prefer to use. Given this, local appropriators have no incentives to restrict their own use.

THE CAPABILITIES OF POLYCENTRIC SYSTEMS IN COPING WITH TRAGEDIES OF THE COMMONS

Many of the capabilities of a parallel adaptive system are retained in a polycentric governance system while obtaining some of the protections of a larger system. By polycentric, I mean a system where citizens are able to organize not just one but multiple governing authorities at differing scales (see V Ostrom et al 1961; V Ostrom 1987, 1991, 1997). Each unit may exercise considerable independence to make and enforce rules within a circumscribed scope of authority for a specified geographical area. In a polycentric system, some units are general-purpose governments, whereas others may be highly specialized (McGinnis 1999a,b,c). Self-organized resource governance systems, in such a system, may be special districts, private associations, or parts of a local government. These are nested in several levels of general-purpose governments that also provide civil equity as well as criminal courts.

In a polycentric system, the users of each common-pool resource would have authority to make at least some of the rules related to the use of that particular resource. Thus, they would achieve many of the advantages of utilizing local knowledge as well as the redundancy and rapidity of a trial-and-error learning process. On the other hand, problems associated with local tyrannies and inappropriate discrimination can be addressed in larger, general-purpose governmental units that are responsible for protecting the rights of all citizens and for the oversight of appropriate exercises of authority within smaller units of government. It is also possible to make a more effective blend of scientific information with local knowledge where major universities and research stations are located in larger units but have a responsibility to relate recent scientific findings to multiple smaller units within their region. Because polycentric systems have overlapping units, information about what has worked well in one setting can be transmitted to others, who may try it out in their settings. Associations of local resource governance units can be encouraged to speed up the exchange of information about relevant local conditions and about policy experiments that have proved particularly successful. And when small systems fail, there are larger systems to call upon—and vice versa.

Polycentric systems are themselves complex adaptive systems without one dominating central authority. Thus, there is no guarantee that such systems will find combinations of rules at diverse levels that are optimal for any particular environment. In fact, one should expect that all governance systems will be operating at less than optimal levels, given the immense difficulty of fine-tuning any very complex, multitiered system.

In the United States, many examples of dynamic, polycentric resource governance systems exist where there is strong evidence of high performance. One example is the Maine lobster fishery, which is noteworthy because of the long-term, complementary roles adopted by both local and state governance systems. Maine is organized into riparian territories along most of the coast. Boundary rules and many of the day-to-day fishing regulations are organized by harbor gangs (Acheson 1988).

> In order to go fishing at all, one must become a member of a "harbor gang," the group of fishermen who go lobstering from a single harbor. Once one has gained admittance into such a group, one can only set traps in the traditional territory of that particular harbor gang. Members of harbor gangs are expected to obey the rules of their gang concerning fishing practices, which vary somewhat from one part of the coast to another. In all areas a person who gains a reputation for molesting others' gear or for violating conservation laws will be severely sanctioned. Incursions into the territory of one gang by fishers from another are ordinarily punished by surreptitious destruction of lobster gear. There is strong statistical evidence that the territorial system, which operates to limit the number of fishers exploiting lobsters in each territory, helps to conserve the lobster resource. (Acheson et al 1998:400)

In addition, the state of Maine has long-established formal laws that protect the breeding stock and increase the likelihood of high regeneration rates. "At present, the most important conservation laws are minimum and maximum size measures, a prohibition against catching lobsters with eggs, and a law to prohibit the taking of lobsters which once had eggs and were marked—i.e. the 'V-notch' law" (Acheson et al 1998:400). Neither the state nor any of the harbor gangs have tried to limit the quantity of lobster captured. The state does not make any effort to limit the number of fishers because this is already done at a local level. However, the state has been willing to intercede when issues exceed the scope of control of local gangs. In the late 1920s, for example, when lobster stocks were at very low levels and many local areas appear to have had substantial compliance problems, the state took a number of steps—including threats to close the fishery—that supported informal local enforcement efforts. By the late 1930s, compliance problems were largely resolved and stocks had rebounded.

Recently, in response to changes that were breaking down the harbor gang system, the state has formalized the system by dividing Maine into zones with democratically elected councils. Each council has been given authority over rules that have principally local impacts—trap limits, days and times fished, etc. Interestingly, the formalization of local zones was followed, almost immediately, by the creation of an informal council of councils to address problems at a greater-than-local scale. It is expected that the council of councils will be formalized soon (Wilson 1997).

Today, the state needs only about six patrol officers on the water to police the activities of 6800 lobstermen, all the other fisheries, and coastal environmental laws. During the 1990s, the fishery has been growing substantially with increased yields (Acheson 1993). At the same time, there is strong evidence that the number of reproductive-age female lobsters in the Maine waters is large and that the recruitment levels will remain high.

The system of co-management of the Pacific salmon fisheries in the state of Washington is another noteworthy example of a recently evolved polycentric system that appears to be working much better than an earlier system that was dominated primarily by state and federal agencies (see Singleton 1998). The change in the system came as a result of a major court decision in the mid-1970s, which stated that the Indian tribes who had signed treaties more than a century earlier had protected rights to 50% of the fish that passed through the normal fishing areas of the tribes. This has required the state to develop a "co-management" system that involves both the state of Washington and the 21 Indian tribes in diverse policy roles related to salmon. This is a large, transboundary resource utilized by major commercial firms as well as by the Indian tribes. The active involvement of the state means that it is "safe" for local groups to agree to follow strong conservation practices because they know that other local groups are involved in the same practices. At the same time, the earlier, centrally regulated system had focused on aggregations of species and spent little time on the fresh-water habitats that are essential to maintain the viability of salmon fisheries over the long term. Individual tribal authorities have concentrated their attention on the specific stocks and their management. Co-management of migrating fishery stocks has also been evaluated as successful in British Columbia and other locations (Pinkerton 1989, Poffenberger & McGean 1996). Alcorn & Toledo (1998) stress the complementary institutional systems at the national level in Mexico, supportive of *ejidos* and *communidades* at a local level, as generating a more sustainable governance system than exists in other, similar ecological conditions.

Coping with potential tragedies of the commons is never easy and never finished. Now that we know that those who depend on these resources are not forever trapped in situations that will only get worse over time, we need to recognize that governance is frequently an adaptive process involving multiple actors at diverse levels. Such systems look terribly messy and are hard to understand. The scholars' love of tidiness must be resisted. Instead, we need to develop better theories of complex adaptive systems, particularly those that have proved themselves able to utilize renewable natural resources sustainably over time.

ACKNOWLEDGMENTS

The author is grateful for continuing support from the National Science Foundation (Grants SBR-9319835 and SBR-9521918) and from the MacArthur Foundation. Versions of this chapter have been presented at seminars or lectures given at the University of Stockholm; University of Massachusetts, Amherst; University of Texas, Dallas; and University of Pittsburgh, and have benefitted from discussion with participants. Comments by Joanna Burger, Juan Camelo Cardenes, Sue Crawford, Michael McGinnis, Bruce Buena de Mesquita, James Wilson, Margaret Levi, Vincent Ostrom, and Duncan Watts and the thorough editing skills of Patty Dalecki are much appreciated.

Visit the *Annual Reviews home page* at
http://www.AnnualReviews.org.

Literature Cited

Abbink K, Bolton GE, Sadrieh A, Tang FF. 1996. *Adaptive learning versus punishment in ultimatum bargaining. Discussion paper #B-381.* Bonn: Rheinische Friedrich-Wilhelms-Univ. Bonn

Acheson JM. 1988. *The Lobster Gangs of Maine.* Hanover, NH: N. Engl. Univ. Press. 181 pp.

Acheson JM. 1989. Management of common-property resources. In *Economic Anthropology,* ed. S Plattner, pp. 351–78. Stanford, CA: Stanford Univ. Press

Acheson JM. 1993. Capturing the commons: legal and illegal strategies. In *The Political Economy of Customs and Culture: Informal Solutions to the Commons Problem,* ed. TL Anderson, RT Simmons, pp. 69–83. Lanham, MD: Rowman & Littlefield

Acheson JM, Wilson JA, Steneck RS. 1998. Managing chaotic fisheries. See Berkes & Folke 1998, pp. 390–413

Agrawal A. 1994. Rules, rule making, and rule breaking: examining the fit between rule systems and resource use. See E Ostrom et al 1994, pp. 267–82

Agrawal A, Yadama GN. 1997. How do local institutions mediate market and population pressures on resources? Forest *panchayats* in Kumaon, India. *Dev. Change* 28(3): 435–65

Alcorn JB, Toledo V. 1998. Resilient resource management in Mexico's forest ecosystems: the contribution of property rights. See Berkes & Folke 1998, pp. 216–49

Anderson LG. 1986. *The Economics of Fisheries Management.* Baltimore, MD: Johns Hopkins Univ. Press. 296 pp. Rev. ed.

Anderson LG. 1992. Consideration of the potential use of individual transferable quotas in U.S. fisheries. *Natl. ITQ Study Rep.* 1:1–71

Anderson PW, Arrow KJ, Pines D, eds. 1988. *The Economy as an Evolving Complex System.* Redwood City, CA: Addison-Wesley. 317 pp.

Andreoni J. 1989. Giving with impure altruism: applications to charity and ricardian equivalence. *J. Polit. Econ.* 97(6):1447–58

Arnold JEM. 1998. *Managing Forests as Common Property.* Rome: Food & Agric. Organ. UN, FAO Forestry Pap. No. 136

Arnold JEM, Campbell JG. 1986. Collective management of hill forests in Nepal: the community forestry development project. In *Proc. Conf. Common Property Resource Management,* Natl. Res. Counc., pp. 425–54. Washington, DC: Natl. Acad. Sci.

Arnold JEM, Stewart WC. 1991. *Common Property Resource Management in India.* Oxford, UK: Oxford Forestry Inst., *Trop. Fore. Pap. No. 24*

Ascher W. 1995. *Communities and Sustainable Forestry in Developing Countries.* San Francisco: ICS. 177 pp.

Baland J-M, Platteau J-P. 1996. *Halting Degradation of Natural Resources: Is There a Role for Rural Communities?* Oxford, UK: Clarendon. 423 pp.

Bendor JB. 1985. *Parallel Systems. Redundancy in Government.* Berkeley: Univ. Calif. Press. 322 pp.

Bendor JB. 1987. In good times and bad: reciprocity in an uncertain world. *Am. J. Polit. Sci.* 31(3): 531–58

Bendor JB, Mookherjee D. 1990. Norms, third-party sanctions, and cooperation. *J. Law Econ. Organ.* 6:33–63

Benjamin P, Lam WF, Ostrom E, Shivakoti G. 1994. *Institutions, Incentives, and Irrigation in Nepal.* DFM proj. rep. Burlington, VT: Assoc. Rural Dev.

Berkes F. 1986. Local-level management and the commons problem: a comparative study of Turkish coastal fisheries. *Marine Policy* 10:215–29

Berkes F, ed. 1989. *Common Property Resources. Ecology and Community-Based Sustainable Development.* London: Belhaven. 302 pp.

Berkes F, Feeny D, McCay BJ, Acheson JM. 1989. The benefits of the commons. *Nature* 340(6229):91–93

Berkes F, Folke C, eds. 1998. *Linking Social and Ecological Systems. Management Practices and Social Mechanisms for Building Resilience.* Cambridge, MA: Cambridge Univ. Press

Blomquist W. 1992. *Dividing the Waters: Governing Groundwater in Southern California.* San Francisco: ICS. 415 pp.

Boyd R, Richerson PJ. 1985. *Culture and the Evolutionary Process.* Chicago: Univ. Chicago Press. 331 pp.

Bromley DW. 1982. *Improving Irrigated Agriculture. Institutional Reform and the Small Farmer.* Washington, DC: World Bank Staff Work. Pap. No. 531

Bromley DW, Feeny D, McKean MA, Peters P, Gilles J, et al, eds. 1992. *Making the Commons Work: Theory, Practice, and Policy.* San Francisco: ICS. 339 pp.

Campbell DT. 1969. Reforms as experiments. *Am. Psychol.* 24(4):409–29

Campbell DT. 1975. On the conflicts between biological and social evolution and between psychology and moral tradition. *Am. Psychol.* 30(11):1103–26

Copes P. 1986. A critical review of the individual quota as a device in fisheries management. *Land Econ.* 62(3):278–91

Cordell JC, McKean, MA. 1992. Sea tenure in Bahia, Brazil. See Bromley et al 1992, pp. 183–205

Coward EW Jr. 1979. Principles of social organization in an indigenous irrigation system. *Hum. Organ.* 38:28–36

Coward EW Jr. 1985. Technical and social change in currently irrigated regions: rules, roles, and rehabilitation. In *Putting People First: Sociological Variables in Rural Development,* ed. MM Cernea, pp. 27–51. New York: Oxford Univ. Press

Cruz WD. 1986. Overfishing and conflict in a traditional fishery: San Miguel Bay, Philippines. In *Proc. Conf. Common Property Resource Management,* Natl. Res. Counc., pp. 115–35. Washington, DC: Natl. Acad. Sci.

Curtis D. 1991. *Beyond Government: Organisations for Common Benefit.* London: Macmillan. 216 pp.

Dasgupta P. 1982. *The Control of Resources.* Cambridge, MA: Harvard Univ. Press. 223 pp.

Deadman P. 1997. *Modeling individual behavior in common pool resource management experiments with autonomous agents.* PhD thesis. Univ. Ariz., Tucson

de los Reyes RP. 1980. *Managing Communal Gravity Systems: Farmers' Approaches and Implications for Program Planning.* Quezon City, Philipp.: Ateneo de Manila Univ., Inst. Philipp. Cult. 125 pp.

Downing TE, Gibson M, eds. 1974. *Irrigation's Impact on Society.* Tucson: Univ. Ariz. Press

Elster J. 1989. *The Cement of Society. A Study of Social Order.* Cambridge, UK: Cambridge Univ. Press. 311 pp.

Farrell J, Rabin M. 1996. Cheap talk. *J. Econ. Persp.* 10(3):103 18

Feeny DH. 1988. Agricultural expansion and forest depletion in Thailand, 1900–1975. In *World Deforestation in the Twentieth Century,* ed. JF Richards, RP Tucker, pp. 112–43. Durham, NC: Duke Univ. Press

Fortmann L, Bruce JW. 1988. *Whose Trees? Proprietary Dimensions of Forestry.* Boulder, CO: Westview. 341 pp.

Frey BS, Bohnet I. 1996. Cooperation, communication and communitarianism: an experimental approach. *J. Polit. Philos.* 4(4):322–36

Frohlich N, Oppenheimer JA. 1970. I get by with a little help from my friends. *World Polit.* 23(1):104–20

Frohlich N, Oppenheimer JA, Eavey CL. 1987. Choices of principles of distributive justice in experimental groups. *Am. J. Polit.* 31(3):606–36

Gadgil M, Iyer P. 1989. On the diversification of common-property resource use by Indian society. See Berkes 1989, pp. 240–72

Gibson C, McKean MA, Ostrom E, eds. 1999. *People and Forests: Communities, Institutions, and the Governance of Forests.* Cambridge, MA: MIT Press. In press

Gordon HS. 1954. The economic theory of a common property resource: the fishery. *J. Polit. Econ.* 62:124–42

Güth W, Schmittberger R, Schwarze B. 1982. An experimental analysis of ultimatum bargaining. *J. Econ. Behav. Organ.* 3(4):367–88

Hackett S, Schlager E, Walker J. 1994. The role of communication in resolving commons dilemmas: experimental evidence with heterogeneous appropriators. *J. Env. Econ. Manage.* 27(2):99–126

Hardin G. 1968. The tragedy of the commons. *Science* 162:1243–48

Hess C. 1996. *Common-Pool Resources and Collective Action: A Bibliography,* Vol. 3. Bloomington: Indiana Univ., Workshop Polit. Theory Policy Anal.

Higgs R. 1996. Legally induced technical regress in the Washington salmon fishery. In *Empirical Studies in Institutional Change,* ed. LJ Alston, T Eggertsson, DC North, pp. 247–79. New York: Cambridge Univ. Press

Hilton R. 1992. Institutional incentives for resource mobilization: an analysis of irrigation schemes in Nepal. *J. Theor. Polit.* 4(3):283–308

Hoffman E, McCabe K, Smith V. 1996. *Behavioral foundations of reciprocity: experimental economics and evolutionary psychology. Work. Pap.* Tucson: Univ. Ariz., Dept. Econ.

Holland JH. 1995. *Hidden Order. How Adaptation Builds Complexity.* Reading, MA: Addison-Wesley. 185 pp.

Isaac RM, Walker J. 1988. Communication and free-riding behavior: the voluntary contribution mechanism. *Econ. Inquiry* 26(4):585–608

Jacob F. 1977. Evolution and tinkering. *Science* 196(4295) (June 10):1161–66

Jodha NS. 1990. Depletion of common property resources in India: micro-level evidence. In *Rural Development and Population: Institutions and Policy,* ed. G McNicoll, M Cain, pp. 261–83. Oxford, UK: Oxford Univ. Press

Jodha NS. 1996. Property rights and development. In *Rights to Nature,* ed. SS Hanna, C Folke, K-G Mäler, pp. 205–22. Washington, DC: Island

Lam WF. 1998. *Governing Irrigation Systems in Nepal: Institutions, Infrastructure, and Collective Action.* Oakland, CA: ICS. 275 pp.

Landau M. 1969. Redundancy, rationality, and the problem of duplication and overlap. *Public Admin. Rev.* 29(4):346–58

Landau M. 1973. Federalism, redundancy, and system reliability. *Publius* 3(2):173–96

Lansing JS. 1991. *Priests and Programmers. Technologies of Power in the Engineered Landscape of Bali.* Princeton, NJ: Princeton Univ. Press. 183 pp.

Lansing JS, Kremer JN. 1994. Emergent properties of Balinese water temple networks: co-adaption on a rugged fitness landscape. In *Artificial Life III. Studies in the Sciences of Complexity,* ed. CG Langton, XVII: 201–23. Reading, MA: Addison-Wesley

Levi M. 1988. *Of Rule and Revenue.* Berkeley: Univ. Calif. Press. 253 pp.

Levine G. 1980. The relationship of design, operation, and management. In *Irrigation and Agricultural Development in Asia,* ed. EW Coward Jr., pp. 51–64. Ithaca, NY: Cornell Univ. Press

Maass A, Anderson RL. 1986. *...And the Desert Shall Rejoice: Conflict, Growth, and Justice in Arid Environments.* Malabar, FL: Krieger. 447 pp.

Martin F. 1989/1992. *Common-Pool Resources and Collective Action: A Bibliography,* Vols. 1, 2. Bloomington: Indiana Univ., Workshop Polit. Theory Policy Anal.

McCay BJ, Acheson JM. 1987. *The Question of the Commons: The Culture and Ecology of Communal Resources.* Tucson: Univ. Ariz. Press. 439 pp.

McGinnis M, ed. 1999a. *Polycentric Governance and Development: Readings from the Workshop in Political Theory and Policy Analysis.* Ann Arbor: Univ. Mich. Press. In press

McGinnis M, ed. 1999b. *Polycentricity and Local Public Economies: Readings from the Workshop in Political Theory and Policy Analysis.* Ann Arbor: Univ. Mich. Press. In press

McGinnis M, ed. 1999c. *Polycentric Games and Institutions: Readings from the Workshop in Political Theory and Policy Analysis.* Ann Arbor: Univ. Mich. Press. In press

Mehra S. 1981. *Instability in Indian Agriculture in the Context of the New Technology.* Washington, DC: Int. Food Policy Res. Inst., *Res. Rep. No. 25*

Morrow CE, Hull RW. 1996. Donor-initiated common-pool resource institutions: the case of the Yanesha forestry cooperative. *World Dev.* 24(10):1641–57

Nelson RR, Winter SG. 1982. *An Evolutionary Theory of Economic Change.* Cambridge, MA: Harvard Univ. Press. 437 pp.

Netting RM. 1974. The system nobody knows: village irrigation in the Swiss Alps. See Downing & Gibson 1974, pp. 67–75

Netting RM. 1993. *Smallholders, Householders: Farm Families and the Ecology of Intensive, Sustainable Agriculture.* Stanford, CA: Stanford Univ. Press. 389 pp.

Orbell JM, Dawes RM. 1991. A "cognitive miser" theory of cooperators' advantage. *Am. Polit. Sci. Rev.* 85(2):515–28

Ostrom E. 1990. *Governing the Commons: The Evolution of Institutions for Collective Action.* New York: Cambridge Univ. Press. 280 pp.

Ostrom E. 1992. *Crafting Institutions for Self-Governing Irrigation Systems.* San Francisco: ICS. 111 pp.

Ostrom E. 1996. Incentives, rules of the game,

and development. In *Proc. Annu. World Bank Conf. Development Economics 1995,* pp. 207–34. Washington, DC: World Bank

Ostrom E. 1998a. A behavioral approach to the rational choice theory of collective action. *Am. Polit. Sci. Rev.* 92(1):1–22

Ostrom E. 1998b. Self-governance of common-pool resources. In *The New Palgrave Dictionary of Economics and the Law,* ed. P Newman, 3:424–33. London: Macmillan

Ostrom E, Agrawal A, Blomquist W, Schlager E, Tang SY, et al. 1989. *CPR Coding Manual.* Bloomington: Indiana Univ., Workshop Polit. Theory Policy Anal.

Ostrom E, Gardner R, Walker JM. 1994. *Rules, Games, and Common-Pool Resources.* Ann Arbor: Univ. Mich. Press. 369 pp.

Ostrom E, Walker JM. 1997. Neither markets nor states: linking transformation processes in collective action arenas. In *Perspectives on Public Choice: A Handbook,* ed. DC Mueller, pp. 35–72. Cambridge, UK: Cambridge Univ. Press

Ostrom E, Walker JM, Gardner R. 1992. Covenants with and without a sword: self-governance is possible. *Am. Polit. Sci. Rev.* 86(2):404–17

Ostrom V. 1987. *The Political Theory of a Compound Republic: Designing the American Experiment.* San Francisco: ICS. 240 pp. 2nd rev. ed.

Ostrom V. 1991. *The Meaning of American Federalism: Constituting a Self-Governing Society.* San Francisco: ICS. 301 pp.

Ostrom V. 1997. *The Meaning of Democracy and the Vulnerability of Democracies: A Response to Tocqueville's Challenge.* Ann Arbor: Univ. Mich. Press. 329 pp.

Ostrom V, Feeny D, Picht H, eds. 1993. *Rethinking Institutional Analysis and Development: Issues, Alternatives, and Choices.* San Francisco: ICS. 486 pp. 2nd ed.

Ostrom V, Tiebout CM, Warren R. 1961. The organization of government in metropolitan areas: a theoretical inquiry. *Am. Polit. Sci. Rev.* 55:831–42

Palanisami K. 1982. *Managing tank irrigation systems: basic issues and implications for improvement.* Presented at workshop on Tank Irrigation: Problems and Prospects, Bogor, Indonesia, CIFOR

Panayotou T, Ashton, PS. 1992. *Not by Timber Alone: Economics and Ecology for Sustaining Tropical Forests.* Washington, DC: Island. 282 pp.

Pinkerton E, ed. 1989. *Co-operative Management of Local Fisheries: New Directions for Improved Management and Community Development.* Vancouver: Univ. BC Press. 299 pp.

Poffenberger M, McGean B. 1996. *Village Voices, Forest Choices: Joint Forest Management in India.* New Delhi: Oxford Univ. Press. 356 pp.

Repetto R. 1986. *Skimming the water: rent-seeking and the performance of public irrigation systems. Res. Rep. No. 4.* Washington, DC: World Resources Inst.

Rocco E, Warglein M. 1995. *Computer mediated communication and the emergence of 'electronic opportunism'. Work. Pap. RCC#13659.* Univ. degli Studi di Venezia

Sally D. 1995. Conservation and cooperation in social dilemmas: a meta-analysis of experiments from 1958–1992. *Rationality Soc.* 7(January):58–92

Schlager E. 1990. *Model specification and policy analysis: the governance of coastal fisheries.* PhD thesis. Indiana Univ., Bloomington

Schlager E. 1994. Fishers' institutional responses to common-pool resource dilemmas. See E Ostrom et al 1994, pp. 247–65

Schlager E, Blomquist W, Tang SY. 1994. Mobile flows, storage, and self-organized institutions for governing common-pool resources. *Land Econ.* 70(3):294–317

Scott AD. 1955. The fishery: the objectives of sole ownership. *J. Polit. Econ.* 63: 116–24

Sengupta N. 1991. *Managing Common Property: Irrigation in India and the Philippines.* New Delhi: Sage. 283 pp.

Shepherd G. 1992. *Managing Africa's Tropical Dry Forests: A Review of Indigenous Methods.* London: Overseas Dev. Inst. 117 pp.

Sherman K, Laughlin T, eds. 1992. *NOAA Technical Memorandum NMFS-f/NEC 91. The Large Marine Ecosystem (LME) Concept and Its Application to Regional Marine Resource Management.* Woods Hole, MA: Northeast Fish. Sci. Cent.

Singleton S. 1998. *Constructing Cooperation. The Evolution of Institutions of Co-management in Pacific Northwest Salmon Fisheries.* Ann Arbor: Univ. Mich. Press. 170 pp.

Singleton S, Taylor M. 1992. Common property economics: a general theory and land use applications. *J. Theor. Polit.* 4:309–24

Spooner B. 1974. Irrigation and society: the Iranian plateau. See Downing & Gibson 1974, pp. 43–57

Tang SY. 1992. *Institutions and Collective Action: Self-Governance in Irrigation.* San Francisco: ICS. 151 pp.

Tang SY. 1994. Institutions and performance in irrigation systems. See E Ostrom et al 1994, pp. 225–45

Taylor M. 1982. *Community, Anarchy, and*

Liberty. New York: Cambridge Univ. Press. 184 pp.

Thomson JT. 1977. Ecological deterioration: local-level rule making and enforcement problems in Niger. In *Desertification: Environmental Degradation in and around Arid Lands*, ed. MH Glantz, pp. 57–79. Boulder, CO: Westview

Thomson JT, Feeny D, Oakerson, RJ. 1992. Institutional dynamics: the evolution and dissolution of common-property resource management. See Bromley et al 1992, pp. 129–60

Wade R. 1988. The management of irrigation systems: how to evoke trust and avoid prisoners' dilemmas. *World Dev.* 26(4): 489–500

Wade R. 1994. *Village Republics: Economic Conditions for Collective Action in South India.* San Francisco: ICS. 238 pp.

Weissing FJ, Ostrom E. 1991a. Crime and punishment: further reflections on the counterintuitive results of mixed equilibria games. *J. Theor. Polit.* 3(3):343–50

Weissing FJ, Ostrom E. 1991b. Irrigation institutions and the games irrigators play: rule enforcement without guards. In *Game Equilibrium Models II: Methods, Morals,* *and Markets,* ed. R Selten, pp. 188–262. Berlin: Springer-Verlag

Wilson JA. 1997. Maine fisheries management initiative. In *The Social Impacts of Individual Transferable Quotas*, ed. G Palsson, pp. 335–53. Copenhagen: Tema-Nord

Wilson JA, Acheson JM, Kleban M, Metcalfe M. 1994. Chaos, complexity, and community management of fisheries. *Marine Policy* 18:291–305

Wilson JA, French J, Kleban P, McKay SR, Townsend, R. 1991. Chaotic dynamics in a multiple species fishery: a model of community predation. *Ecol. Model.* 58:303–22

Wilson JA, Low B, Costanza R, Ostrom E. 1999. Scale misperceptions and the spatial dynamics of a social-ecological system. *Ecol. Econ.* In press

Yoder RD. 1991. Peer training as a way to motivate institutional change in farmer-managed irrigation systems. In *Proc. Workshop on Democracy and Governance, Decentralization: Finance & Management Proj. Rep.*, pp. 53–67. Burlington, VT: Assoc. Rural Dev.

Yoder RD. 1994. *Locally Managed Irrigation Systems*. Colombo, Sri Lanka: International Irrigation Management Inst. 97 pp.

Annu. Rev. Polit. Sci. 1999. 2:537–65

DEMOCRACY AND DICHOTOMIES: A Pragmatic Approach to Choices about Concepts

David Collier and Robert Adcock

Department of Political Science, University of California, Berkeley, California 94720-1950; e-mail: dcollier@socrates.berkeley.edu

KEY WORDS: methodology, concept formation, validity, levels of measurement, regimes

ABSTRACT

Prominent scholars engaged in comparative research on democratic regimes are in sharp disagreement over the choice between a dichotomous or graded approach to the distinction between democracy and nondemocracy. This choice is substantively important because it affects the findings of empirical research. It is methodologically important because it raises basic issues, faced by both qualitative and quantitative analysts, concerning appropriate standards for justifying choices about concepts. In our view, generic claims that the concept of democracy should inherently be treated as dichotomous or graded are incomplete. The burden of demonstration should instead rest on more specific arguments linked to the goals of research. We thus take the pragmatic position that how scholars understand and operationalize a concept can and should depend in part on what they are going to do with it. We consider justifications focused on the conceptualization of democratization as an event, the conceptual requirements for analyzing subtypes of democracy, the empirical distribution of cases, normative evaluation, the idea of regimes as bounded wholes, and the goal of achieving sharper analytic differentiation.

INTRODUCTION

Should scholars engaged in comparative research on democracy treat the distinction between democracy and nondemocracy as a dichotomy, or in terms of gradations? This recurring and much debated question has important implica-

1094-2939/99/0616-0537$08.00

tions for how research is organized, for how data are collected and analyzed, and for inferences about the causes and consequences of democracy. It also serves as a reminder that discussions of research design in political science must pay central attention to conceptual issues.

Among the authors who have advocated an approach based on grading and ranking, Bollen & Jackman argue that "democracy is always a matter of degree" and that treating it as dichotomous is a "flawed" practice (1989:618, 612). A graded perspective is likewise adopted by Dahl, using the term polyarchy (1971:2, 8, 231–35; 1989:241, 316–17), and later by Coppedge & Reinicke (1990). By contrast, Sartori finds that treating the distinction between democracy and nondemocracy in graded terms is an analytically "stultifying" exercise in "degreeism," which misses the basic fact that political systems are "bounded wholes" (1987:184; also 1991:248). Other scholars who have adopted a dichotomous approach include Linz (1975:184–85), Huntington (1991:11–12), and Geddes (1999). Przeworski and collaborators have specifically rejected Bollen & Jackman's argument as "confused" because it does not recognize that regimes "cannot be half-democratic: there is a natural zero point" (Alvarez et al 1996:21). Their position is especially striking because their larger project (Przeworski et al 1996, Przeworski & Limongi 1997) is based on quantitative data and sophisticated forms of statistical analysis. Yet when it comes to measuring democracy versus nondemocracy, they select a dichotomy.

We see an interesting puzzle here. The choice of a dichotomy in effect places this distinction at what is traditionally viewed as the lowest level of measurement (Stevens 1946, Roberts 1976:492–93). This choice thereby appears to underutilize more fine-grained information that may routinely be available about differences among regimes. Yet both Sartori and Przeworski and collaborators are convinced that this lowest level of measurement is more valid in conceptual terms. This puzzle points to a question: What, indeed, are the grounds for viewing this as a valid dichotomy, and not a "false dichotomy"?

This is an important question. First, quite apart from the scholars who are explicitly debating this choice, large numbers of qualitative researchers (on the one side) and quantitative researchers (on the other side) in effect take a position on this issue without ever directly addressing it. Second, this choice is important because it affects substantive findings of research on democracy. Although alternative dichotomous and graded measures are strongly correlated with one another (Alvarez et al 1996:21), Elkins (1999) has shown that, in assessing the impact of regime type on the initiation of war, a graded measure reveals interesting incremental effects that would not be detected with a dichotomy. He likewise shows that, in studies of the effect of regime type on political stability, the use of a single cut-point can mask a relationship that emerges only if one looks at a different cut-point. Similarly, Coppedge (1997: 181, 189–97) finds that in cross-national tests evaluating explanations for levels of polyarchy, different results emerge depending on which cut-point is employed in creating a dichotomous measure of polyarchy. Restricting the analysis to any single dichotomous cut-point can thus obscure potential findings.

Given that the findings of research can be influenced by these choices, it is important to examine the conceptual reasoning that justifies alternative approaches. However, somewhat surprisingly, recent methodological writing in political science provides insufficient guidance for dealing with such questions, and various contributors to recent debates on research design have called for greater attention to conceptual issues (Laitin 1995:455–56, Collier 1995: 463, Brady 1995:16–18, Munck 1999).

This paper examines the conceptual justifications that lead scholars to choose a dichotomous or graded approach. Part 1 focuses on general methodological arguments about concept formation, dichotomies, and gradations. Part 2 reviews examples of the generic justifications employed by prominent authors in the literature on democracy. Part 3 considers more specific justifications, which we believe provide a better rationale for the choice between dichotomies and gradations.

In favoring these more specific justifications, we adopt a pragmatic position.[1] While recognizing that usage is shaped and constrained by the broader scholarly understanding of a concept's meaning, we hold that specific methodological choices are often best understood and justified in light of the theoretical framework, analytic goals, and context of research involved in any particular study. As theory, goals, and context evolve, choices about concepts likewise may evolve.

To explicate our pragmatic approach, it is useful to identify two interrelated priorities that underlie this perspective. First, it rejects the idea that there is a single correct, or "best," meaning for all concepts and views the search for a single best meaning as frequently being an unproductive enterprise. Second, this approach focuses on understanding how alternative meanings are connected with the specific goals and context of research. Thus, how scholars understand and operationalize a concept can and should depend in part on what they are going to do with it.

Our approach thus shares important concerns with the tradition of concept analysis that, in conjunction with a broad focus on the structure of meaning,

---

[1] In developing our position, we have drawn on discussions of concepts and measurement in Popper (1976:17–31), Kaplan (1964:34–81), Adams & Adams (1987), Jones (1974), Shapiro (1989), and Collier (1998). In relation to recent debates on the philosophy of science, we see our position on concepts as compatible with the general position of "pragmatic realism" advocated by Shapiro (1990:231–38).

explores variations in concept usage among different authors and different schools of thought. This tradition is identified both with the field of political theory (Gallie 1956, Pitkin 1967, Freeden 1996), and also with studies that draw directly or indirectly on Sartori's (1984b:40–42) methodology for the reconstruction of concepts. Examples of this latter approach include studies of consensus (Graham 1984), elite (Zannoni 1978), ideology (Gerring 1997), political culture (Patrick 1984), revolution (Kotowski 1984), and social movement (Diani 1992). This tradition generally avoids preemptively ruling out particular meanings or usages, and instead focuses on understanding each usage in its own terms.

Our pragmatic approach also shares important concerns with the focus on "construct validity," which is one central consideration in efforts by quantitative researchers in political science to evaluate choices about concepts and operationalization (Zeller & Carmines 1980:79–81). A central goal in assessments of construct validity is to evaluate whether a given operationalization of a concept, when used in testing a well-established hypothesis, yields results that are plausible and interesting in light of theoretical expectations regarding that hypothesis. With regard to the concept of democracy, Elkins (1999) is an excellent example of this approach.

We share with the construct validity approach a concern with the details of how particular concepts are actually used in exploring specific research questions. However, in contrast to this approach, we address this concern in relation to a broader range of issues about how concepts are applied and understood in empirical research. For example, we consider the implications of treating democratization as a well-bounded "event" and the conceptual requirements for analyzing subtypes of democracy, as well as issues of the empirical distribution of cases and normative assessment that arise in specific contexts of research.

These questions of justifying choices about concepts are complex, and we wish to underscore two issues not addressed here. First, we take as given the procedural definition of democracy that has predominated in the recent comparative literature on democratization. The interesting question of dichotomies in relation to other definitions of democracy is not addressed. Second, if a scholar adopts gradations, a further choice concerns the choice of procedures for aggregating observations in scales.[2] This choice is crucial but is likewise beyond our focus.

---

[2]For example, among advocates of a graded approach, Bollen (1993) and Bollen & Paxton (2000) begin with eight ordered scales (each involving between two and seven categories) and employ structural equation models with latent variables to produce an aggregated scale that ranges from 0 to 100. Coppedge & Reinicke (1990) begin with five graded measures (each involving either three or four categories) and employ Guttman scale analysis to produce an aggregated scale that ranges from 0 to 10.

1. CONCEPT FORMATION AND THE BURDEN OF DEMONSTRATION

This section explores two claims about dichotomies: (*a*) they are fundamental because concept formation is inherently based on classificatory reasoning; and (*b*) they can be justified through arguments about object concepts and bounded wholes. We conclude this section by considering where the burden of demonstration should lie in justifying a dichotomous or graded approach. For more than three decades, Sartori has been the scholar most centrally concerned with these issues.[3] Focusing on his views offers a productive way of exploring this debate, particularly because his position continues to be important in research on concept formation and on democracy (e.g. O'Kane 1993:170, 191; Vanhanen 1997:40), and because, in a number of respects, it is parallel to the approach of Przeworski and collaborators discussed below.

Is Concept Formation Inherently Based on Classificatory Reasoning?

Central to Sartori's view of concepts, as formulated in his classic article on "concept misformation" (1970), is the argument that concept formation is inherently based on classification and that dichotomies are therefore fundamental to reasoning about concepts. We focus on two parts of Sartori's argument. First, he suggests that the process of human reasoning that underlies concept formation involves thinking in terms of classification and cut-points. Thus, "human understanding—the way in which our mind works—requires cut-off points which basically correspond (in spite of all subsequent refinements) to the slices into which a natural or qualitative language happens to be divided" (Sartori 1970:1038). Second, Sartori applies essentially the same argument to norms of scholarly inquiry. He states that "whatever their limits, classifications remain the requisite, if preliminary, condition for any scientific discourse" (1970:1040).

With regard to the first point, since the time of Sartori's formulation of his position in 1970, a large body of research in linguistics, cognitive psychology, and cognitive science has yielded strong empirical evidence supporting a more multifaceted view of human cognition. Although classification is fundamental

---

[3]Sartori's arguments are by no means the only relevant point of reference. For example, Kalleberg (1966) also defends the primacy of classificatory reasoning. However, DeFelice (1980:120–23) and Jackman (1985:167–69) have effectively shown that Kalleberg's argument is undermined by a logical error, and hence it appears unnecessary to address it here. As DeFelice (1980:122–23) points out, this flawed argument is echoed in Sartori's 1970 article. Yet Kalleberg's argument is but one of several arguments that Sartori makes in favor of classification; our focus is on those not directly addressed by DeFelice and also on a major argument that Sartori advanced in 1987, after DeFelice's and Jackman's articles were published.

to human cognition, reasoning about gradations is likewise fundamental. Linguists employ terms such as cline, scale, and pragmatic scale to characterize graded understandings, and even prior to the full development of the contemporary field of cognitive linguistics, Lakoff's (1973) work on "hedges" pointed to the complexity of gradations away from central instances of a concept that are established by the application of modifiers to nouns. Rosch (1978) provided an empirical demonstration of the centrality of prototypes (i.e. cases that are understood as exemplifying a concept) in conceptual reasoning, and of graded reasoning in relation to prototypes (see also Lakoff 1987). It is further argued that, far from providing an unreliable and uncertain foundation for human cognition, a system of thought centrally organized around ideas of gradation is more stable, flexible, and reliable in the face of changing empirical reality (Taylor 1995:53–54). Overall, we are convinced that viewing human understanding as fundamentally anchored in classification presents an incomplete picture that fails to capture the remarkable capacity of the mind to conceptualize different modes of gradation and different forms of the partial occurrence of any given phenomenon.

Sartori's second point concerns norms of social science inquiry. Here we are likewise convinced that the reasoning about similarities and differences that underlies concept formation encompasses not only ideas about sharp contrasts and cut-points but also ideas about different forms of gradation and ordering. Both are fundamental to the conceptual work entailed in formal measurement theory. The axioms and conceptual reasoning that are a logical underpinning for measurement encompass simultaneously ideas about equal versus nonequal, which provide the foundation for categorization, and ideas about greater than versus less than, which provide the foundation for graded reasoning (Roberts 1976:476–78; Michell 1990:166–70). Both are also fundamental to less formal procedures for reasoning about conceptualization and operationalization. The choice of an approach based on either classification or gradation in fact involves a complex process of simplifying the available information about the cases under consideration. Although the "output" of this choice is presented in terms of cut-points or gradations, the "input" routinely includes observations and intuitions both about sharply defined contrasts and about gradations.

This conclusion has an important implication for Sartori's well-known argument that "concept formation stands prior to quantification" and that "the progress of quantification should lag—in whatever discipline—behind its qualitative and conceptual progress" (1970:1038). To the extent that Sartori is asserting that the process of assigning numbers to cases should be preceded by careful conceptual reasoning, he is correct. But it is important not to link this essential assertion to his other claim that classificatory reasoning based on cut-points is necessarily the first step in concept formation. We emphasize instead, following our argument above, that such conceptual reasoning is specifically not limited to classificatory thinking.

Object Concepts and Bounded Wholes

Sartori (1987:182–85, 1993:118–20) has subsequently developed a more flexible argument about dichotomies that focuses on "object concepts" and "bounded wholes." He begins by distinguishing between "contraries" and "contradictories," a distinction he uses in conjunction with an approach that explores the meaning of concepts by examining their opposites. Sartori states that in the case of conceptual oppositions that are contraries, intermediate positions exist. Examples are big vs small, hot vs cold, and rich vs poor. By contrast, in the case of oppositions that are contradictories, there is no intermediate possibility. The opposing concepts "are not only mutually exclusive but *also* exhaustively exclusive" (1987:182). Sartori's formulation thus echoes the traditional idea in philosophical logic of the "excluded middle" (Honderich 1995:256–57). He offers alive vs dead, married vs single, and biped vs quadruped as examples of contradictories, and he argues that democracy vs nondemocracy should be treated as a contradictory (1987:182–84). Sartori's distinction represents a flexible approach in that it validates the use of graded comparisons in treating some conceptual oppositions, while underscoring the importance in other instances of the dichotomous treatment entailed in contradictories.

In discussing contraries and contradictories, Sartori (1987:182–85) utilizes a related distinction between "object concepts" and "property concepts." This distinction, in effect, provides a rationale for treating certain concepts as contradictories and hence approaching them dichotomously. When a concept is construed as an object concept, then it designates what Sartori refers to as a type or an entity, and applying such a concept to empirical cases involves "identifying an entity" (1987:183). The type in question may be a complex phenomenon, such as a given form of political system. Sartori argues that such systems are constituted by multiple attributes, all of which must presumably be present for a case to be classified as an instance of the concept. Thus, it can be thought of as a bounded whole. When an object concept is applied to a particular case, one must establish, in dichotomous terms, whether or not the case corresponds to the concept. Sartori contrasts the idea of object concepts with a property concept approach, in which the concept is viewed as a characteristic that cases display to varying degrees and that hence calls for a graded treatment (1987:183–84; see also 1975:28–29).

We wish to underscore two contributions of this approach. First, Sartori explicitly presents it as a flexible perspective that allows for alternative ways of approaching the logical treatment of concepts. Concept formation thus involves "deciding which logical treatment is appropriate for what purpose" (1987:185). Relatedly, he discusses how particular concepts are construed as being suitable for one or the other of these logical treatments (1987:183; see also 1975:29). Choice is involved, and the choice could presumably be influenced by the goals of the investigator. We believe that this pragmatic emphasis on the goals of research takes the discussion in a good direction. Second, Sartori's argument about object concepts is promising because it focuses attention on the idea of an interaction among the component attributes of democracy. In Part 3, we address this interaction via the distinctively conceptual idea that each component attribute can potentially take on a different meaning, depending on the presence of other attributes.

At the same time, it is essential to sound a note of caution. We have a vivid label for the mistake of overstating the degree to which the attributes one seeks to conceptualize cohere as if they were like an object—this error is "reification." We present two observations concerning the potential problem of reifying bounded wholes, one about what is involved in "naming" phenomena, the other about changing empirical knowledge and evolving scholarly usage.

The observation about naming concerns a tacit belief, or what cognitive scientists call a folk theory, that people routinely hold about concepts. It is widely believed that, in relation to many phenomena in the real world, it is possible to identify an inherently correct name or system of names. People believe it is possible to identify "*the* name of a thing, the one that tells what it 'really is'" (Brown 1958:17; see also Lakoff 1987:9, 118–21). This tacit belief about naming has both an up side and a down side. On the up side, if a specific name is understood as designating what the phenomenon under discussion "really is," the use of this name can facilitate communication and make it easier to remember the argument being presented. Indeed, if the analyst has in fact meaningfully summarized a complex body of information as consisting of two distinct types, this impressive analytic accomplishment deserves to be clearly communicated. On the down side, if a particular name resonates primarily due to this tacit belief, rather than because it provides an analytically appropriate slicing of reality, then this name can become a slogan that is employed in a sloppy and uncritical manner, with serious risk of reification. One possible consequence could be that the idea of bounded wholes is uncritically embraced for the wrong reasons.

Our other basic observation about bounded wholes and reification is that in the face of changing social reality, shifting definitions of the subject matter, and evolving theoretical understanding and empirical knowledge, conceptualizations that initially serve to justify a dichotomy based on a particular cut-point can subsequently break down. This breakdown can be illustrated with some of Sartori's examples of contradictories. Social change in recent decades has, in many different ways, surely made married vs single a more complex distinction than it once was. The scholar studying evolving social relationships and related political and legal debates in contemporary society needs to consider a variety of alternative cut-points in defining married vs single as a dichotomy. Similarly, evolution in medical technology has led to complex legal, ethical, and policy debates about the definition of alive vs dead, as well as to the introduction of intermediate concepts such as "brain dead." More broadly, in many domains of knowledge, what initially appeared to be clear distinctions sometimes break down and are reconceptualized. For example, zoology has seen a long history of distinctions that initially appeared clear-cut but that subsequently were superseded (e.g. Gould 1983). Overall, it can be argued that in a variety of disciplines, (*a*) dichotomies are of central importance, (*b*) the cutpoints that establish dichotomies may evolve over time, and (*c*) scholars face an ongoing choice between retaining the use of dichotomies, based on these potentially evolving cut-points, or shifting to a graded approach that employs multiple cut-points.

Shifting the Burden of Demonstration

In light of these issues of changing social reality and evolving theoretical understanding, we suggest a pragmatic approach that places Sartori's distinction between object and property concepts on firmer ground. We carry even further Sartori's idea, noted above, of "deciding which logical treatment is appropriate for what purpose." It may often be the case that Sartori's distinctions provide a useful way to characterize a specific approach to the formulation and definition of a concept. Thus, a scholar may well develop a particular understanding and application that precludes intermediate alternatives, making it appropriate to view the concept as if it designated an object consisting of a set of interrelated parts, all of which are treated as definitionally necessary. On the other hand, the broad claim that a concept itself necessarily has object-like characteristics involving interrelated parts may be far more problematic.

Indeed, conceptual disputes are often only deepened when different groups of scholars involved in the dispute each treat their own particular approach as if it were a valid overall characterization of the concept. In her influential study of representation, Pitkin demonstrates how recognizing the multiple competing views of a concept, each of which mistakes its own "partial view" for the "complete structure," can help us to understand and overcome conceptual confusion (1967:10–11). A variety of other accounts of the complexity of concepts likewise supports this conclusion, including Gallie's (1956) discussion of the multifaceted structure of many important concepts, Lakoff's (1987) theory of the cognitive models that provide complex sources of conceptual meaning, and Freeden's (1996:60–67) view of conceptual "morphology" in which the potential meaning of a concept encompasses a spectrum of "quasi-contingent" features. Hence, scholars should be cautious in claiming to have come up with a definitive interpretation of a concept's meaning. It is more productive to establish an interpretation that is justified at least in part by its suitability to their immediate research goals and to the specific research tradition within which they are working.

This flexible, pragmatic approach shifts the burden of demonstration in justifying choices about concepts. Rather than treating the distinction between object concepts and property concepts as a permanent status, we understand this distinction as depending on the specific meanings and definitions that particular authors give to a concept, and on the goals and context of research.

2. EXAMPLES OF GENERIC JUSTIFICATIONS

We now consider justifications for gradations or dichotomies that have been advanced by prominent authors in the comparative literature on democracy and democratization. These authors focus most of their arguments on generic claims that the concept of democracy inherently requires one approach or the other. These examples suggest to us that this dispute is hard to resolve at the level of these generic claims, which is a further motivation for shifting the focus of justification to more specific arguments.

Justifying Gradations

Bollen and collaborators have strongly aligned themselves with the argument that the distinction between democracy and nondemocracy should be viewed in graded terms. Over a series of publications, Bollen (1980, 1993; Bollen & Grandjean 1981; Bollen & Jackman 1989; Bollen & Paxton 2000) has developed graded measures that treat political democracy as a property that regimes display in varying degrees. He incorporates gradations into his definition, defining democracy as "the extent to which the political power of the elite is minimized and that of the non-elite is maximized" (1980:372; see also 1993: 1208).

Bollen defends his choice of a graded approach with the generic conceptual assertion that it is dictated by the concept of democracy. Bollen & Jackman describe the use of a dichotomy as "hard to justify" because the resulting measures fail to reflect the "inherently continuous nature of the concept of political democracy" (1989:617, 612). Likewise, Bollen asserts that "the concept of political democracy is continuous" and hence we "unnecessarily compromise the concept by considering it a dichotomous phenomenon" (1990:13).

Bollen builds on this conceptual claim to make a further argument in favor of gradations based on a concern about measurement error (1990:14). He argues that, although both approaches introduce substantial measurement error because they fail to capture fully the continuous nature of political democracy, there are reasons to favor a graded approach. Bollen believes that "we can do better than dichotomous or three-point scales" and that a dichotomy is "crude" relative to the ordinal scales we can produce (1990:18). He favors scales with more than two or three categories because the "error introduced by analyzing ordinal indicators as if they were continuous generally is less, the greater the number of categories" (1990:18). His argument about error obviously depends on his conceptual argument, given that his assessment of the error entailed in ordinal versus dichotomous approaches focuses on how well they can capture a phenomenon he presumes to be continuous. Bollen specifically rules out statistical procedures that assume the underlying concept entails distinct categories. He considers them "not appropriate since the concept is continuous" (1990:18).

Dahl, in his influential writings on democracy, likewise incorporates gradations into his conceptualization and definition. He argues that "countries vary enormously in the extent to which their governments meet the criteria of the democratic process" (1989:233). In *Polyarchy*, he adopts a view of democracy that defines it in relation to an ideal type and thereby lays the foundation for his graded approach. Hence, as "one end of a scale, or a limiting state of affairs, it can (like a perfect vacuum) serve as a basis for estimating the degree to which various systems approach this theoretical limit" (1971:2).

Having used the term democracy to refer to this ideal, Dahl introduces the term polyarchy for discussing actual regimes. Following Dahl, Coppedge & Reinicke (1990) have employed Guttman scale analysis to operationalize a graded treatment of polyarchy, and Dahl's preference for gradations is also reflected in his use of their scale (1989:241).

Dahl is quite clear about the inadequacy of a classificatory approach. His conceptualization of polyarchy focuses on "opposition, rivalry, or competition between a government and its opponents" (1971:1), and he takes it as a conceptual given that there is "an underlying, hypothetical continuum that extends from the greatest to the least opportunity for oppositions" (1971:231). From this perspective, a classificatory treatment is an undesirable simplification. Thus, after identifying the two main dimensions with which he is concerned, Dahl states that "since a regime may be located, theoretically, anywhere in the space bounded by the two dimensions, it is at once obvious that our terminology for regimes is almost hopelessly inadequate, for it is a terminology invariably based upon classifying rather than ranking" (1971:6).

Obviously, Dahl and Bollen have both made outstanding contributions to the study of democracy. They offer carefully formulated definitions that incorporate a graded approach, and their use of the concept appropriately follows their own definitions. Yet establishing a definition based on gradations does not preclude the possibility that other scholars will employ conceptualizations and definitions based on a dichotomy, and it does not provide a basis for adjudicating the dispute over democracy and dichotomies.

Justifying a Dichotomy

Sartori argues that the distinction between democracy and nondemocracy should be treated as dichotomous (1962:150–52; 1987:156, 182–85, 205–7; 1991:248–49; 1993:118–20). Hence, the essential initial task is to establish exhaustive and mutually exclusive categories of democracy and nondemocracy (1987:182–85). In Sartori's view, approaches that treat the difference between democracy and nondemocracy as a matter of degree are fundamentally flawed. "What is completely missed by this degreeism, or continuism, is that political systems are *systems*, that is, bounded wholes characterized by constitutive mechanisms and principles that are either present (albeit imperfectly) or absent (albeit imperfectly)" (1987:184).

Sartori's claim about bounded wholes might appear to state an empirical hypothesis according to how imperfectly these mechanisms and principles are present or absent. However, our reading of Sartori's position is that he invokes empirical cases to illustrate a generic conceptual assertion that is treated as a necessarily valid claim about the concept of democracy, rather than to offer a validation of a potentially falsifiable claim. Sartori illustrates the need for dichotomies by pointing to sharp empirical differences—for example, between the United States and the Soviet Union, and between regimes that are so harsh as to produce large numbers of political refugees and those that receive these refugees (1987:184, 185). In these examples, he does not focus on the problem of comparing intermediate cases, among which the idea of gradations of democracy might potentially be especially relevant. Thus, he does not appear to look for evidence that would call his bounded-whole thesis into question.

Despite his arguments against a gradation-based approach, Sartori does not preclude the use of gradations altogether but argues that such a treatment should be applied only to countries deemed democratic in terms of an initial dichotomy. Thus, "what makes democracy *possible* should not be mixed up with what makes democracy *more democratic*" (Sartori 1987:156). Sartori argues that both issues can be addressed in a single, integrated framework as long as the analyst follows a specific two-step procedure. First, regimes must be classified as democracies or nondemocracies. Then, only as a second step, a further set of criteria can be applied to those regimes deemed democratic by the initial dichotomy. Only with regard to these cases should we inquire as to how democratic they are (1987:182–83). Sartori asserts that "unless the two problems are treated in this order, the oxen may well wreck the cart rather than pull it" (1987:156).

Sartori does not propose his two-step procedure for all concepts but specifically for those conceptualized as bounded wholes. His assertion of the need for the two-step procedure hence presupposes his previous claim that democracy must be treated as a bounded whole. To be plausible, this two-step procedure would require a fuller elaboration of the bounded-whole idea and a defense of its appropriateness for a particular definition of democracy. In Part 3, we suggest what such an elaboration and defense might look like.

Przeworski, Alvarez, Cheibub, and Limongi's argument for their dichotomy is based both on a generic claim about how democracy should be conceptualized and on a more specific claim about measurement and the empirical distribution of cases (see Part 3). Regarding the first claim, their definition of democracy requires the selection of the chief executive and the legislature through contested elections, the presence of more than one party, and the actual rotation of the incumbents out of office after a reasonable interval (Alvarez et al 1996:19). They argue that the graded approach is flawed because it fails to recognize that any regimes in which executive and legislative offices are not contested should not be considered democratic to any degree (Przeworski et al 1996:52, Alvarez et al 1996:21). To argue that there are borderline cases that call for a graded approach is, in their view, "ludicrous," because in a carefully applied classification of regimes, the ambiguous status of a case can only reflect "bad rules" or "insufficient information" (Alvarez et al 1996: 21–22). If a treatment of regimes fails to distinguish clearly democracies from nondemocracies, this does not undermine the attempt to apply a dichotomy; rather, it means that the scoring procedures need to be modified to remove the ambiguity.

Although Przeworski and collaborators thus make a broad claim about democracy, they go further than does Sartori in basing their justification on a specific understanding of the interaction among the attributes of democracy. Yet this justification still does not provide as complete an argument as we would like. For example, in our view it remains unclear why a regime that has competitive elections for the presidency, rotation in the presidential office, and more than one party—but lacks competitive elections for legislative office—is not at least partially democratic. This approach could also be helped by a specific justification of why each of the component attributes should be understood dichotomously, and not in terms of gradations.

Przeworski and collaborators do not rule out all graded comparisons among democracies but instead advocate the same two-step procedure as Sartori, with the first, dichotomous step essentially based on the idea of bounded wholes. They argue that

> while some regimes are more democratic than others, unless offices are contested, they should not be considered democratic. The analogy with the proverbial pregnancy is thus that while democracy can be more or less ad-

vanced, one cannot be half-democratic: there is a natural zero-point. (Alvarez et al 1996:21)

Przeworski and collaborators offer a criticism of Bollen & Jackman that explicitly challenges a basic assumption of gradation-based approaches.

> Note that Bollen and Jackman (1989) are confused: it is one thing to argue that some democracies are more democratic than others and another to argue that democracy is a continuous feature over all regimes, that is, that one can distinguish the degree of "democracy" for any pair of regimes. (Alvarez et al 1996:21; see also Przeworksi et al 1996:52)

For the purpose of comparing regimes that fall short of their standard, Przeworski and colleagues thus preclude the option of reasoning about them as partial democracies. Instead, they propose a separate conceptualization involving three dimensions of "dictatorship": whether it is mobilizing or exclusionary, how many formal centers of power it has (executive, legislative, and parties), and whether it rules within a framework of law or in some more arbitrary manner (Alvarez et al 1996:16–19).

In principle, we are sympathetic to this two-step procedure. Nevertheless, it would be valuable to formulate a more sharply focused argument about why certain core attributes entailed in a particular definition must occur together if a regime is to be considered minimally democratic according to this definition. As with the arguments for gradations noted above, such an argument may support the choice made in a particular research project, yet it should not be interpreted as a generic prescription that applies across all conceptualizations of democracy.

3. TOWARD MORE SPECIFIC JUSTIFICATIONS

We now turn to examples of justifications for dichotomies that are more specifically linked to the theoretical and analytic goals of the research and to the particular context being studied. We do not seek to cover all possible justifications but rather to illustrate some issues that arise in offering more specific justifications. An important counterpoint runs through the discussion. Although each of these justifications is initially meant to defend dichotomies, we find, in relation to each justification, a counterjustification that favors the use of gradations.

A major goal of the literature considered here is to understand the causes and consequences of democracy. However, the goals most relevant to our discussion are more specific. We first consider the implications of two analytic concerns that have been central in much of the comparative literature on democracy, namely a focus on events and a focus on subtypes of democracy. We then examine justifications—based on the empirical distribution of cases and normative concerns—that we believe provide part of the underlying rationale for a dichotomous approach. Finally, we explore how the idea of bounded wholes could be more fully developed as a justification for a dichotomy, and we consider some implications of a concern with achieving sharper analytic differentiation.

Studying Events and Subtypes

EVENTS   An important part of recent research on democratization is routinely called the "transitions literature" because of its concern with the event called a transition. The study of events has recently become an important focus in comparative social science (Abbott 1992, Griffin 1993, Sewell 1996), and, as Riker (1957) demonstrated in his classic article on defining events, the analytically rigorous study of events requires establishing their boundaries in dichotomous terms. Correspondingly, O'Donnell & Schmitter (1986:6) define a transition as "the interval between one political regime and another" (see also Huntington 1991:11). This definition in turn calls for a dichotomous approach that establishes the cut-point or threshold in relation to which the event of a transition to democracy is identified.

In studies based on complex comparisons across countries and over time, important problems can arise in establishing a threshold that meaningfully delimits the onset of democracy. Bollen & Jackman raise two concerns about such dichotomous treatments. First, they point to the difficulty of establishing conceptual equivalence among cases of democratization that occur in different historical contexts. This concern with equivalence centers on the fact that "the nature of political democracy (especially inclusiveness) has changed considerably over the past decades" (1989:619; see also Markoff 1996:4,116–17). Second, for many cases, they question the feasibility of locating a point in time at which democracy, conceived dichotomously, began. They argue that "it is meaningless to claim that democracy was inaugurated in a given country on a single date," and that "dating the inauguration of democracy conceived in binary terms is an inherently ambiguous task.... In fact, it is an impossible task" (1989:618, 619).

One plausible response to Bollen & Jackman's first concern is to adopt a context-specific approach to conceptual equivalence. A central problem in establishing equivalence lies in the fact just noted, that the plausible agenda of "full" democratization has changed dramatically over time. What could be viewed as full democratization by the standards of an earlier period might be seen as incomplete democratization by later standards. For example, in the late 20th century, universal suffrage and the protection of civil rights for the entire national population are routinely seen as essential features of democracy, whereas in the 19th century they were not (Huntington 1991:7, 16). In light of this problem of equivalence, one solution is to compare regimes according to whether they have achieved full democratization in relation to the norms of the relevant time period (RB Collier 1999:ch. 1, Russett 1993:15). This context-specific conceptualization allows for a dichotomous classification of cases distinguishing those that are fully democratized from those that are not.[4]

The goal of conducting strong tests of hypotheses can provide a rationale for adopting this conceptualization, and hence for sticking with a dichotomy. Thus, the analyst may accept the standard of equivalence of full democratization according to the norms of the historical period, in part because it leads to the inclusion of what may be considered "inconvenient facts" (Weber 1958: 147) from the standpoint of a major hypothesis being entertained in the study. For example, Russett (1993:15) wishes to include 19th-century cases in his tests of the democratic peace hypothesis because that inclusion pushes him to deal with a greater number of conflicts that could be interpreted as wars between democracies. Similarly, RB Collier (1999:ch. 1) is skeptical about some arguments concerning the pivotal role of the working class in democratization, and to make her case, she wishes to include late nineteenth- and early twentieth-century cases that were the basis for classic arguments about the working class role.

A plausible response to Bollen & Jackman's second concern, regarding the problem of establishing a single starting date for democracy, is to temper the idea of a strict dichotomy. Recognizing that important distinctions are lost by employing a single threshold (Paxton 1995:4, 18–19), the analyst may focus on two or more successive thresholds, which potentially are crossed at widely separated dates. By conceptualizing democratization as a sequence of steps, rather than as a single event, this approach in effect introduces gradations. Examples are found in Rueschemeyer et al (1992:160–62, 205, 304–8) and RB Collier (1999:ch. 1). This approach allows both the author and the reader to evaluate the implications of alternative thresholds for the findings of the analysis. Along these lines, Geddes' comparative study of democratic transitions that have occurred since 1946 is another example of an analysis that reports the consequences of alternative thresholds (1999: Table 1). We strongly endorse this practice.

Notwithstanding the importance of this concern about meaningful starting dates, we would reject a blanket pronouncement in favor of the universal use of gradations in research on democratization. Although Bollen & Jackman are correct to suggest that a focus on democratization as a single event is flawed for many cases, this does not imply that it is inapplicable in all cases. Those cases where democratization is an abrupt, rather than protracted, process might

[4]An important example of a context-specific approach that was constructed to deal with differences across regions, rather than across historical periods, is found in Lipset 1959:73–74.

be adequately analyzed using a dichotomy that treats democratization as a single, well-bounded event.

SUBTYPES OF DEMOCRACY   In some studies, the larger set of arguments advanced by the authors is concerned with assessing the causes or consequences of what may be called "classical" subtypes of democracy (Collier & Levitsky 1997:435). These subtypes are understood as corresponding to countries that are definitely democratic and that have some further differentiating attribute. The focus on these subtypes presupposes a concern with delimiting the set of democracies, within which the subtypes are differentiated.

A prominent example of this focus on subtypes is found in studies of the consequences for regime stability of parliamentary democracy, as opposed to presidential democracy (Stepan & Skach 1993, Linz & Valenzuela 1994, Sartori 1994). The inclusion of cases in this comparison strongly implies a dichotomous standard for establishing which countries are democratic and therefore can be considered instances, more specifically, of the parliamentary and presidential subtypes of democracy.

Another example is found in comparisons of what O'Donnell (1994) has called "delegative democracies," i.e. regimes with strong presidencies in which the "horizontal accountability" of the executive to the legislature is attenuated. O'Donnell is convinced that among democracies, this delegative pattern has the consequence of eroding political institutionalization. He specifically defines delegative democracies as regimes that are above a basic threshold of democracy (1994:56). Hence, inclusion in the set of delegative democracy assumes inclusion in a larger, dichotomously defined set of democratic countries. Still another example is found in the democratic peace literature, which explores the effect of national regime types on the likelihood that countries will go to war with one another. Elman (1997) argues that political scientists need to specify the democratic peace hypothesis more carefully by looking at the consequences of particular types of democracy for international conflict behavior, and she likewise focuses on the parliamentary and presidential subtypes. Her analysis, like O'Donnell's, is specifically concerned with understanding a set of countries that are democratic.[5]

Research questions conceptualized in terms of democratic subtypes may appear to require a dichotomous approach, yet, as with events, an alternative is available. These studies could ask, for example, whether the consequences of a presidential versus parliamentary organization of legislative-executive rela-

[5]Geddes' (1999) analysis of transitions from authoritarianism to democracy parallels these studies of democratic subtypes. She combines a dichotomous treatment of democracy vs nondemocracy with a focus on the consequences for regime stability of different (classical) subtypes of authoritarianism.

tions vary according to the degree of democracy, with different patterns emerging in borderline cases as opposed to cases that fully meet some accepted standard for democracy. This is a distinct, but certainly related, question. Delegative democracy could be analyzed in the same way. This graded approach is in fact followed in Shugart's new study, which seeks to explain the emergence of parliamentarism versus presidentialism. At one point in the analysis he looks at the strength of one explanatory factor among both (*a*) countries that are either semidemocracies or democracies and (*b*) countries that are specifically democracies (Shugart 1999:Table 5). Shugart thus moves away from the underlying notion of democracy as a well-bounded type by conceptualizing it in graded terms.

In their writing on delegative democracy, democratic peace, and parliamentarism versus presidentialism, O'Donnell (1994:56), Elman (1997), and Stepan & Skach (1993:3) are quite specific in stating that they are concerned with regimes that are democracies. This focus clearly depends on a prior dichotomous understanding of democracy as a type. The question then becomes, how does one justify the choice between this dichotomous understanding and a graded alternative?

Underlying Justifications

We are convinced that these choices about the study of events and subtypes often rest on underlying assumptions regarding the empirical distribution of cases and normative judgments. By recognizing these assumptions and defending them, scholars could provide better justifications for these choices.

EMPIRICAL DISTRIBUTION OF CASES   One of the important ways in which the context of research affects choices about concepts involves the empirical distribution of the cases being studied. In a given context, scholars may observe a gap between democracy and nondemocracy, either across national units or over time within a given country, with observed cases generally either possessing or lacking most of the defining attributes of democracy. Given this gap, a dichotomy may provide an adequate summary of the empirical contrasts among cases. The use of a dichotomy in this context is not a conceptual assertion that rejects a graded approach as inherently flawed. On the contrary, the empirical hypothesis that regimes do cluster in this manner must be evaluated within a graded approach that can assess whether a gap exists. Thus, by looking for gradations, scholars may justify the conclusion that, for a given context, a dichotomy is good enough.

The idea of an empirical gap between democratic and nondemocratic regimes was of great importance to the recent literature on democratization, which was routinely concerned with relatively dramatic shifts in which many attributes of regimes changed in a relatively short span of time. Correspondingly, this literature made extensive use of a dichotomous conception of democracy/nondemocracy and of the idea of a regime transition as a well-bounded event.

Arguments about the empirical distribution of cases have also been used to justify a dichotomous approach, based on a concern with measurement error. Przeworski and collaborators argue that a "more refined classification will have a smaller error" if the distribution of cases is unimodal and approximately symmetric, whereas "there is less measurement error when a dichotomous scale is used" if cases are uniformly distributed (Alvarez et al 1996:31). Furthermore, if the distribution is "u-shaped," as they suggest the distribution of democracy versus nondemocracy tends to be, then the advantage of a dichotomy in terms of reducing error is even greater than it is for a uniform distribution (Alvarez et al 1996:31). Although Elkins (1999) has raised questions about the way these authors treat error, this unquestionably is an argument in which the criterion of justification focuses on the empirical distribution of cases.

If the choice of a dichotomy can be justified on the basis of the empirical distribution of cases, then a change in this distribution can lead to a different choice. Huntington's *Third Wave* treated democracy as dichotomous, though he noted a few intermediate cases (1991:12). Yet in a more recent article, he observes that "as formal democratic institutions are adopted by more and more diverse societies, democracy itself is becoming more differentiated." He therefore sees the need to focus on a "democratic-nondemocratic continuum," on which one finds "a growing number of countries somewhere in the middle" (Huntington 1996:10). Diamond makes the same argument with reference to Latin America, where he finds that the shift toward democracy has made it "more fruitful to view democracy as a spectrum, with a range of variation in degree and form." Owing to this changing empirical reality, treating democracy as something "merely present or absent" has become "a sterile perspective" (Diamond 1996:53). More recently, on the basis of a world-wide comparison of regimes, Diamond (1999:Table 2.4) shows that the proportion of intermediate cases has doubled between 1990 and 1997.

Although information about the empirical distribution of cases should play an important role in choices about dichotomies versus gradations, it should not be taken as the sole determinant of all such choices. It needs to be balanced against the potential value of sharp analytic distinctions, such as those offered by the classical subtypes discussed above, and against normative concerns that we discuss in the next section. In sum, we argue that although a graded approach is needed to adequately capture a highly uniform distribution, for more discontinuous distributions the choice between dichotomies and gradations remains open, and the various other considerations discussed throughout this paper may play a decisive role.

Finally, in certain limited situations, a dichotomy may be justifiable regardless of the empirical distribution of cases. For example, in exploring certain research questions, the analyst's treatment of democracy vis-à-vis nondemocracy may need to reflect the viewpoint of the individuals who are being studied. With such an actor-defined, emic approach to differentiating among regimes, a dichotomy would be justifiable independently of the empirical distribution of cases, provided that the actors whose behavior is being examined do in fact think of the world in terms of a democracy/nondemocracy dichotomy.[6] Starr's recent discussion of the democratic peace hypothesis provides an example of such an argument. He interprets the causal mechanism at work in the hypothesis as including the idea that "each side must understand that the other *is* a democracy." Hence, Starr argues that analysts can best evaluate this hypothesis if they establish a "threshold point" above which the relevant political actors in other nations view a given country as democratic (1997: 129–30). In specific instances, such an approach may not always win universal agreement, yet in principle it is an appropriate justification.

NORMATIVE EVALUATION   Normative concerns play an important role in comparative research on democracy (Dahl 1971:ch. 2; Sartori 1987:7–8), and these concerns can provide another source of justification for a dichotomous or graded approach. Indeed, it appears likely that normative concerns lurk behind many arguments in favor of dichotomies, even though they are not made explicit. Although the idea of a fact-value distinction remains a familiar point of reference for many social scientists, we must recognize that the general choice of research topics, and more specific choices concerning what outcomes are explained and how they are conceptualized, routinely have a normative component. A study tends to be viewed as more important if it seeks to explain a humanly important outcome, and viewing an outcome as humanly important involves normative appraisal.

An example of a study that is careful and self-conscious in explicating the normative criteria that can underlie the choice of a dichotomy is the summary volume by O'Donnell & Schmitter (1986) in the *Transitions from Authoritarian Rule* series. Their point of departure was explicitly normative (1986:5, 11, 13) and was formulated in light of the political and social parameters, as of the 1980s, faced by the Latin American and Southern European countries with which they were concerned. Given these parameters, the authors were convinced that a plausible target for advocates of regime transitions was a "procedural minimum" version of democracy that encompassed free and fair elections, universal suffrage, and broad protection of political and civil liberties. They labeled this constellation of features "political democracy" (1986:8,

---

[6]On the emic-etic distinction, see Headland et al 1990.

13),[7] and they employed a dichotomous distinction to establish it as a democratic target. In establishing this target, they were deliberately positioning themselves in relation to scholars and political actors who aimed at a lower or higher standard.

Although normative concerns may lead scholars to adopt a dichotomous treatment and may serve to justify the choice of a particular cut-point, similar concerns can also motivate a graded approach. In *Democracy and Its Critics,* Dahl expresses concern that in the evaluation of regimes, a dichotomous approach may "impose upon the moral and empirical complexities of the world a false Manichean orderliness" (1989:316). A dichotomy is "empirically misleading" because it overlooks the fact that "countries below a reasonable threshold for full polyarchy are of extraordinary variety." As a consequence, such an approach is "morally inadequate and likely to lead to inept policies" (1989:316). Dahl's concern for flexibility and subtlety in normative appraisal is further reflected in his suggestion that such appraisal needs "to make judgments about the *dynamics of change*, and particularly the *direction* and *rate* of change," because "even highly repressive regimes are not morally and empirically equivalent if their dynamics of change are radically different" (1989: 316).

These two perspectives on normative evaluation reflect the different purpose of the authors. O'Donnell & Schmitter were writing in the midst of a dramatic, world-wide episode of democratization. They sought to identify what they saw as appropriate targets (neither too low nor too high) at which political actors should aim in pursuing democratization within this context. By contrast, Dahl is making a more general statement about normative evaluation that is not embedded in a specific historical episode, and hence his more flexible approach is also appropriate.

Further Issues of Justification

DEVELOPING THE IDEA OF BOUNDED WHOLES   Given the emphasis on bounded wholes in the conceptual discussions reviewed in Parts 1 and 2, it is somewhat surprising that we have not found what we consider fully elaborated versions of this potential justification for a dichotomous, type-based conceptualization of democracy. We seek here to develop the notion of bounded wholes by focusing on conceptual interaction among the defining attributes of democracy.[8] Specifically, we explore the argument that if each component attribute within the definition is to be meaningfully understood as reflecting an aspect of democracy, then the other attributes must also be present. It seems likely

[7]O'Donnell & Schmitter (1986:8) also include horizontal accountability in their initial definition, but it does not appear to play a role in their subsequent analysis.

[8]An alternative theoretical approach to developing the notion of bounded wholes might build on the idea of equilibrium.

that if such an argument is to be effective, it would not be a generic argument about democracy but rather would be tied to a specific definition based on a particular set of component attributes, and potentially also a specific context of analysis.

Although we have not encountered examples of full conceptual justifications along these lines, we have found partial examples in which authors do consider this kind of interaction among certain attributes of democracy. Specifically, they assert that the meaning of some defining attributes of democracy is changed if an additional attribute is not present. Thus, a "negative score" on one key attribute in effect cancels the meaning of a "democratic score" on others. Whereas the bounded whole criterion entails the expectation that all of the attributes are interrelated in this manner, this more limited thesis holds that the score on one of the attributes affects the meaning of the others. Thus, the arguments presented in this section are not in themselves full justifications for a dichotomy, but they are an example of the kind of conceptual reasoning that, if applied to all defining attributes, could provide such a justification.[9]

One example is found in discussions of "electoralism" (Karl 1986). This term is applied to regimes that hold elections in which substantial competition occurs, with uncertain electoral outcomes, yet where widespread violations of civil liberties continue to be a fundamental feature of political life. Various analysts argue that the electoral arena should not be seen as genuinely competitive and uncertain if civil liberties are not respected. Thus, one finds an interaction among these attributes of democracy, in that the absence of civil liberties specifically cancels the interpretation of the other attributes as being democratic.

Another example is found in discussions of the problem that some "democratically" elected governments lack effective power to govern.[10] In several Latin American countries, one legacy of authoritarian rule has been the persistence of "reserved domains" of military power over which elected governments have little or no authority (Valenzuela 1992:70). Hence, despite free or relatively free elections, civilian governments in these countries are seen by

---

[9]If X_1, X_2, X_3, and X_4 are dichotomous components of democracy that assume a value of 0 or 1, the idea of a bounded whole might be represented by $X_1*X_2*X_3*X_4$. This bounded-whole formulation assumes the value 1 if all the component scores are 1, and zero if any of them are zero. In contrast, the idea of partial interaction being discussed here, in which a score of zero on one key attribute (X_4) cancels the meaning of a democratic score on the others, can be represented by $(X_1+X_2+X_3)*X_4$. This partial-interaction formulation would not lead to the simple zero/one dichotomy of the bounded-whole formulation because if X_4 has a value of 1, the overall expression can assume a value of either 0, 1, 2, or 3. However, the conceptual reasoning in the partial-interaction formulation regarding the relationship between X_4 and the other attributes does provide an example of the kind of arguments that would be necessary for each attribute if the idea of a bounded whole is to be fully justified.

[10]The following discussion draws on Collier & Levitsky (1997:442–45).

some analysts as lacking effective power to rule. In light of these authoritarian legacies, and often in response to claims that these countries are "democratic" because they have held free elections, some scholars sought to modify the definition of democracy by specifying as an explicit criterion that the elected government must have a reasonable degree of effective power. With this revised approach, some scholars have excluded countries such as El Salvador and Chile, during certain periods, from the set of cases classified as democracies, even though they held relatively free elections (Karl 1990:2; Valenzuela 1992:70; Loveman 1994:108–13). This revised definition has received substantial acceptance (Huntington 1991:10, Markoff 1996:102–4), although there has not been full agreement on the treatment of specific cases (Rabkin 1992:165).

In the context of our discussion of the conceptual reasoning that could provide a full justification of a dichotomous approach, the point here is as follows: In cases where the elected government lacks effective power to rule, it is not valid to treat the other defining attributes of democracy (e.g. competitive elections) as meaningfully measuring the presence of democracy. The absence of effective power to rule does not merely make countries somewhat less democratic; it undermines the meaningfulness of the other defining attributes of democracy.

If the search for interactions among attributes is to be convincing, it is important that, in principle, the investigator be able to find negative cases, i.e. instances in which such a conceptual interaction might be found but is not. An example appears in the debate over the observation that in many new democracies, elected presidents at times make extensive use of decree power, circumvent democratic institutions such as the legislature and political parties, and govern in a plebiscitarian manner that is seen as having strong authoritarian undercurrents. Such tendencies are addressed by definitions of democracy that include checks on executive power and hence exclude cases of weakly constrained presidentialism (Schmitter & Karl 1991:76, 87; Ball 1994:45–46).

However, this innovation has not been widely adopted. In this example, a crucial point is that these presidents are elected leaders. Hence, it might be appropriate to treat these regimes as meeting a minimal standard for democracy and to avoid any further adjustment in the definition—as long as they maintain presidential elections, a more-or-less viable legislature, and a general respect for civil liberties, and as long as opposition parties are not banned or dissolved. Scholars have considered the option of viewing the weakness of checks on executive power as invalidating the democratic characterization of these regimes, but instead they have concluded that it represented additional useful information about regimes that should be considered democratic (O'Donnell 1994:56).

This discussion of checks on executive power is a useful negative example, in which scholars conclude that the absence of one attribute does not invalidate or diminish the meaning of other attributes in relation to the concept of democracy. Scholars concerned with refuting a bounded-whole approach could usefully devote more attention to making such arguments about the absence of this specific kind of interaction among attributes. Rather than endorsing or rejecting the bounded-whole approach in general terms, we urge scholars to carefully address themselves to the attributes of a particular definition of democracy, and to ask whether all the attributes display the kind of conceptual interaction which we have explored.

SHARPER DIFFERENTIATION   Achieving sharper, more fine-grained differentiation is an important goal in the comparative analysis of democracy, and a standard view of the advantages of a graded, as opposed to dichotomous, approach is that it more effectively promotes this goal. The practice of giving explicit names to categories that group together similar cases is also a means of pinpointing and differentiating crucial attributes of regimes. In this section, we explore two strategies that pursue the goal of sharper differentiation by combining gradations with named categories.

First, with an ordinal scale based on a limited number of categories, names can be given to the categories. An example is Dahl's adaptation of the Coppedge-Reinicke scale of polyarchy. Dahl applies to the marginally democratic categories in this scale such names as "dominant party regimes" and "multiparty nondemocratic regimes" (Dahl 1989:241). Diamond (1996:57) offers a similar ordinal scale, based on Freedom House data, in which the categories have names such as "partially illiberal democracy" and "semicompetitive authoritarian." To the extent that these names meaningfully identify important empirical differences among the categories, this form of the scale may convey more information than does the scale without the names. For example, Dahl's label "multiparty nondemocratic regime" conveys more information about the cases in this category than would a simple numerical score on his scale. He thus adds, in relation to the ordinal idea of "more or less," sharper differentiation concerning "more of what."

A second combined strategy that achieves sharper differentiation begins on the side of categories but incorporates the idea of gradations. As Collier & Levitsky (1997:437–42) have shown, in the names of "diminished subtypes" such as semidemocracy, the adjective serves to cancel part of the meaning of democracy, creating a type that is less than fully democratic by whatever definition the author is using but that still retains some attributes of democracy. The subtype thus expresses the idea of a gradation away from democracy.

The use of diminished subtypes presents an interesting alternative to employing an ordinal scale. Consider, for example, three diminished subtypes formed in relation to standard procedural definitions of democracy, which routinely include universal suffrage, fully contested elections, and civil liberties.

In relation to that definition, one finds diminished subtypes that characterize cases as missing one of these attributes. Thus, "male democracy" is used for cases that lack women's suffrage; "controlled democracy" is used for cases with some important limitation on contestation, such as the banning of one political party; and "illiberal democracy" is used for cases where civil liberties are attenuated (Collier & Levitsky 1997:440). With each of these subtypes, one attribute is missing, but other attributes in this procedural definition remain present.

Consider how this same information would be conveyed using an additive scale of zero to three, based on the sum of a dichotomous (zero-one) version of these three component attributes. With the alternative configurations of attributes that correspond to these three diminished subtypes, the score in all three instances would be a two, conveying no information about which attribute is lacking. By contrast, if diminished subtypes are carefully employed, that information is clearly conveyed in the names of the subtypes. In this case, the concern with sharper differentiation parallels a concern, expressed by Gleditsch & Ward (1997:381) in their recent assessment of the Polity III data, that the use of aggregated scales can divert attention from important insights that emerge at a more disaggregated level. In sum, in relation to the idea of "more or less," diminished subtypes convey sharper, more disaggregated differentiation regarding "less of what."

However, along with this advantage, scholars should note a down side: this approach can encourage an undesirable proliferation of subtypes. If this occurs, the potential gains in sharper differentiation could be cancelled by the conceptual confusion that may result.

CONCLUSION

The debate on democracy and dichotomies raises basic issues, faced by both qualitative and quantitative researchers, concerning appropriate standards for justifying choices about the formation and application of concepts. We have argued that justifications for the use of a dichotomous or graded approach are most productive when they focus on specific arguments about the goals and context of research. Throughout the discussion, a counterpoint emerged in which arguments that initially appeared to favor a dichotomy could, with modification, be compatible with, or even require, the use of gradations. This counterpoint reinforces our conviction that justifications should be as specific as possible, and that scholars should recognize that conceptual choices may prove more ambiguous than they initially appear.

We have shown that decisions about gradations versus dichotomies are often built into the framing of research questions. Research that focuses on democratization as a well-bounded event and on classical subtypes of democracy favors dichotomies. However, alternative ways of viewing events and sub-types are also available that allow for the introduction of graded notions. In relation to these conceptual choices, we hold that, although gradations are necessary in certain contexts, in other contexts the empirical distribution of cases or normative concerns may justify a dichotomy. Justifications based on the conceptualization of regimes as bounded wholes are also promising but have not been adequately developed. Finally, our discussion of the goal of sharper differentiation points to the value of combining gradations with named categories.

Our pragmatic approach, which recognizes that concepts, definitions, and operationalization may evolve with changes in the goals and context of research, should not be seen as neglecting an essential concern with standardization and rigor. We certainly do not favor an "epistemological anarchism" in which "anything goes" (Feyerabend 1973). Rather, the specific goals of standardization and rigor are most productively pursued in conjunction with a realistic focus on how other goals influence the use and application of concepts. For certain concepts, it is not plausible, and may even be counterproductive, to assume that the accumulation of knowledge requires that all scholars adopt a standardized meaning. Instead, for such concepts, it is more realistic to aim for an accumulation of knowledge grounded in mutual comprehension among scholars who self-consciously recognize their conceptual decisions as real choices. Thus, they are choices from a range of alternatives, which, although they are justified in light of certain context-specific criteria, still allow the scholar to recognize the validity of other decisions in other contexts.

ACKNOWLEDGMENTS

Among the many colleagues who have provided helpful comments on this paper, we especially thank Jake Bowers, James Mahoney, and Gerardo Munck, as well as Nathaniel Beck, Kenneth Bollen, Henry Brady, Jack Citrin, Zachary Elkins, Andrew Gould, Donald Green, Ernst Haas, Robert Kaufman, Gary King, Peter Kingstone, Steven Levitsky, Matthew McCubbins, Martin Rein, Sally Roever, Giovanni Sartori, and Richard Snyder. The usual caveats apply. Robert Adcock's work on this project was supported by a National Science Foundation Graduate Fellowship.

> **Visit the *Annual Reviews home page* at**
> **http://www.AnnualReviews.org.**

Literature Cited

Abbott A. 1992. From causes to events: notes on narrative positivism. *Sociol. Methods Res.* 20:428–55

Adams EW, Adams WY. 1987. Purpose and scientific concept formation. *Br. J. Philos. Sci.* 38:419–40

Alvarez M, Cheibub JA, Limongi F, Przeworski P. 1996. Classifying political regimes. *Stud. Comp. Int. Dev.* 31:3–36

Ball AR. 1994. *Modern Politics and Government.* Chatham, NJ: Chatham House. 5th ed.

Bollen KA. 1980. Issues in the comparative measurement of political democracy. *Am. Sociol. Rev.* 45(June):370–90

Bollen KA. 1990. Political democracy: conceptual and measurement traps. *Stud. Comp. Int. Dev.* 25:7–24

Bollen KA. 1993. Liberal democracy: validity and method factors in cross-national measures. *Am. J. Polit. Sci.* 37:1207–30

Bollen KA, Grandjean B. 1981. The dimensions of democracy: further issues in the measurement and effects of political democracy. *Am. Sociol. Rev.* 46:651–59

Bollen KA, Jackman RW. 1989. Democracy, stability, and dichotomies. *Am. Sociol. Rev.* 54:612–21

Bollen KA, Paxton P. 2000. Subjective measures of liberal democracy. *Comp. Polit. Stud.* In press

Brady HE. 1995. Doing good and doing better. Part 2 of a symposium on *Designing Social Inquiry. Polit. Methodol.* 6:11–19

Brown R. 1958. How shall a thing be called? *Psychol. Rev.* 65:14–21

Collier D. 1995. Translating quantitative methods for qualitative researchers: the case of selection bias. *Am. Polit. Sci. Rev.* 89:461–66

Collier D. 1998. Putting concepts to work: toward a framework for analyzing conceptual innovation in comparative research. Presented at Annu. Meet. Am. Polit. Sci. Assoc., Sept. 3–6, Boston, MA

Collier D, Levitsky S. 1997. Democracy with adjectives: conceptual innovation in comparative research. *World Polit.* 49:430–51

Collier RB. 1999. *Paths Toward Democracy: Working Class and Elites in Western Europe and South America.* Cambridge, UK:Cambridge Univ. Press. In press

Coppedge M. 1997. Modernization and thresholds of democracy: evidence for a common path and process. In *Inequality, Democracy, and Economic Development,* ed. M Midlarsky, pp. 177–201. New York: Cambridge Univ. Press

Coppedge M, Reinicke WH. 1990. Measuring polyarchy. *Stud. Comp. Int. Dev.* 25:51–72

Dahl RA. 1971. *Polyarchy: Participation and Opposition.* New Haven, CT: Yale Univ. Press

Dahl RA. 1989. *Democracy and Its Critics.* New Haven, CT: Yale Univ. Press

DeFelice EG. 1980. Comparison misconceived: common nonsense in comparative politics. *Comp. Polit.* 13:119–26

Diamond L. 1996. Democracy in Latin America: degrees, illusions, and directions for consolidation. In *Beyond Sovereignty: Collectively Defending Democracy in the Americas,* ed. T Farer, pp. 52–104. Baltimore, MD: Johns Hopkins Univ. Press

Diamond L. 1999. *Developing Democracy: Toward Consolidation.* Baltimore, MD: Johns Hopkins Univ. Press. In press

Diani M. 1992. The concept of social movement. *Sociol. Rev.* 40: 1–25

Elkins Z. 1999. Gradations of democracy: empirical tests of alternative conceptualizations. Presented at Seminar on Democratization, Inst. Int. Stud., Stanford Univ., Jan. 21, Stanford, CA

Elman MF. 1997. Unpacking democracy: presidentialism, parliamentarism, and the democratic peace theory. Presented at Annu. Meet. Am. Polit. Sci. Assoc., Aug. 28–31, Washington, DC

Feyerabend P. 1973. *Against Method: Outline of an Anarchistic Theory of Knowledge.* London: Verso

Freeden M. 1996. *Ideologies and Political Theory: A Conceptual Approach.* Oxford, UK: Oxford Univ. Press

Gallie WB. 1956. Essentially contested concepts. *Proc. Aristotelian Soc.* 51:167–98

Geddes B. 1999. What do we know about democratization after twenty years? *Annu. Rev. Polit. Sci.* 2:115–44

Gerring J. 1997. Ideology: a definitional analysis. *Polit. Res. Q.* 50:957–94

Gleditsch KS, Ward MD. 1997. Double take: a reexamination of democracy and autocracy in modern politics. *J. Confl. Resol.* 41:361–83

Gould SJ. 1983. What, if anything, is a zebra? In Gould, *Hen's Teeth and Horses' Toes.* New York: Norton

Graham GJ. 1984. Consensus. See Sartori 1984a, pp. 89–124

Griffin LJ. 1993. Narrative, event-structure analysis, and causal interpretation in historical sociology. *Am. J. Sociol.* 98: 1094–1133

Headland TN, Pike KL, Harris M. 1990. *Emics and Etics: The Insider-Outsider Debate.* Newbury Park, CA: Sage

Honderich T. 1995. *The Oxford Companion to Philosophy.* Oxford, UK: Oxford Univ. Press

Huntington SP. 1991. *The Third Wave: Democratization in the Late Twentieth Century.* Norman: Univ. Oklahoma Press

Huntington SP. 1996. Democracy for the long haul. *J. Democr.* 7:3–13

Jackman RW. 1985. Cross-national statistical research and the study of comparative politics. *Am. J. Polit. Sci.* 29:161–82

Jones CO. 1974. Doing before knowing: concept development in political research. *Am. J. Polit. Sci.* 18:215–28

Kalleberg AL. 1966. The logic of comparison: a methodological note on the comparative study of political systems. *World Polit.* 19: 69–82

Kaplan A. 1964. *The Conduct of Inquiry.* San Francisco: Chandler

Karl TL. 1986. Imposing consent? electoralism vs. democratization in El Salvador. In *Elections and Democratization in Latin America, 1980–1985,* ed. PW Drake, E Silva, pp. 9–36. La Jolla, CA: Cent. Iberian and Latin Am. Stud., Univ. Calif., San Diego

Karl TL. 1990. Dilemmas of democratization in Latin America. *Comp. Polit.* 23:1–21

Kotowski CM. 1984. Revolution. See Sartori 1984a, pp. 403–51

Laitin D. 1995. Disciplining political science. *Am. Polit. Sci. Rev.* 89:454–60

Lakoff G. 1973. Hedges: a study of meaning criteria and the logic of fuzzy concepts. *J. Philos. Logic* 2:458–508

Lakoff G. 1987. *Women, Fire, and Dangerous Things: What Categories Reveal About the Mind.* Chicago: Univ. Chicago Press

Linz JJ. 1975. Totalitarian and authoritarian regimes. In *Handbook of Political Science,* ed. FI Greenstein, NW Polsby, 3:175–353. Reading, MA: Addison-Wesley

Linz JJ, Valenzuela A, eds. 1994. *The Failure of Presidential Democracy.* Baltimore, MD: Johns Hopkins Univ. Press

Lipset SM. 1959. Some social requisites of democracy: economic development and political legitimacy. *Am. Polit. Sci. Rev.* 53: 69–105

Loveman B. 1994. "Protected democracies" and military guardianship: political transitions in Latin America, 1979–1993. *J. Interam. Stud. World Aff.* 36:105–89

Markoff J. 1996. *Waves of Democracy: Social Movements and Political Change.* Thousand Oaks, CA: Pine Forge

Michell J. 1990. *An Introduction to the Logic of Psychological Measurement.* Hillsdale, NJ: Erlbaum

Munck G. 1999. Canons of research design in qualitative analysis. *Stud. Comp. Int. Dev.* 34:In press

O'Donnell G. 1994. Delegative democracy. *J. Democr.* 5:55–69

O'Donnell G, Schmitter PC. 1986. *Transitions from Authoritarian Rule: Tentative Conclusions about Uncertain Transitions.* Baltimore, MD: Johns Hopkins Univ. Press

O'Kane RHT. 1993. The ladder of abstraction: the purpose of comparison and the practice of comparing African coups d'état. *J. Theor. Polit.* 5:169–93

Patrick GM. 1984. Political culture. In *Social Science Concepts: A Systematic Analysis,* ed. G Sartori, pp. 265–314. Beverly Hills, CA: Sage

Paxton P. 1995. *Women in the measurement of democracy: problems of operationalization.* Presented at Annu. Meet. Am. Sociol. Assoc., Aug. 21, Washington, DC

Pitkin HF. 1967. *The Concept of Representation.* Berkeley, CA: Univ. Calif. Press

Popper K. 1976. *Unended Quest: An Intellectual Autobiography.* La Salle, IL: Open Court

Przeworski A, Alvarez M, Cheibub JA, Limongi F. 1996. What makes democracies endure? *J. Democr.* 7:39–55

Przeworski A, Limongi F. 1997. Modernization: theories and facts. *World Polit.* 49: 155–83

Rabkin R. 1992. The Aylwin government and "tutelary" democracy: a concept in search of a case? *J. Interam. Stud. World Aff.* 34:119–94

Riker WH. 1957. Events and situations. *J. Philos.* 54:57–70

Roberts FS. 1976. *Discrete Mathematical Models, with Applications to Social, Biological, and Environmental Problems.* Englewood Cliffs, NJ: Prentice-Hall

Rosch E. 1978. Principles of categorization. In *Cognition and Categorization,* ed. E Rosch, BB Lloyd, pp. 27–48. Hillsdale, NJ: Erlbaum

Rueschemeyer D, Stephens EH, Stephens JD. 1992. *Capitalist Development and Democracy.* Chicago: Univ. Chicago Press

Russett B. 1993. *Grasping the Democratic Peace: Principles for a Post–Cold War World.* Princeton, NJ: Princeton Univ. Press

Sartori G. 1962. *Democratic Theory.* Detroit, MI: Wayne State Univ. Press

Sartori G. 1970. Concept misformation in comparative politics. *Am. Polit. Sci. Rev.* 64:1033–53

Sartori G. 1975. The Tower of Babel. In *Tower*

of Babel: On the Definition and Analysis of Concepts in the Social Sciences, ed. G Sartori, FW Riggs, H Teune, pp. 7–38. Occas. Pap. No. 6, Int. Stud. Assoc., Univ. Pittsburgh

Sartori G, ed. 1984a. *Social Science Concepts: A Systematic Analysis.* Beverly Hills, CA: Sage

Sartori G. 1984b. Guidelines for concept analysis. See Sartori 1984a, pp. 15–85

Sartori G. 1987. *The Theory of Democracy Revisited.* Chatham, NJ: Chatham House

Sartori G. 1991. Comparing and miscomparing. *J. Theor. Polit.* 3:243–57

Sartori G. 1993. *Democrazia, cosa è.* Milan: RCS Rizzoli Libri, SPA

Sartori G. 1994. *Comparative Constitutional Engineering: An Inquiry into Structures, Incentives, and Outcomes.* New York: New York Univ. Press

Schmitter PC, Karl TL. 1991. What democracy is...and is not. *J. Democr.* 2:75–88

Sewell WH. 1996. Three temporalities: toward an eventful sociology. In *The Historical Turn in the Human Sciences*, ed. TJ McDonald. Ann Arbor: Univ. Mich. Press

Shapiro I. 1989. Gross concepts in political argument. *Polit. Theory* 17:51–76

Shapiro I. 1990. *Political Criticism.* Berkeley: Univ. Calif. Press

Shugart MS. 1999. Presidentialism, parliamentarism and the provision of collective goods in less-developed countries. *Const. Polit. Econ.* 10:53–88

Starr H. 1997. *Anarchy, Order and Integra-tion: How to Manage Interdependence.* Ann Arbor: Univ. Mich. Press

Stepan A, Skach C. 1993. Constitutional frameworks and democratic consolidation: parliamentarianism versus presidentialism. *World Polit.* 46:1–22

Stevens SS. 1946. On the theory of scales of measurement. *Science* 103(2684):677–80

Taylor J. 1995. *Linguistic Categorization: Prototypes in Linguistic Theory.* Oxford, UK: Oxford Univ. Press

Valenzuela JS. 1992. Democratic consolidation in post-transitional settings: notion, process, and facilitating conditions. In *Issues in Democratic Consolidation: The New South American Democracies in Comparative Perspective*, ed. S Mainwaring, G O'Donnell, JS Valenzuela, pp. 57–104. Notre Dame, IN: Univ. Notre Dame Press

Vanhanen T. 1997. *Prospects of Democracy: A Study of 172 Countries.* London: Routledge

Weber M. 1958. Science as a vocation. In *From Max Weber: Essays in Sociology*, ed. HH Gerth, CW Mills, pp. 129–56. New York: Oxford Univ. Press

Zannoni P. 1978. The concept of elite. *Eur. J. Polit. Res.* 6:1–30

Zeller RA, Carmines EG. 1980. *Measurement in the Social Sciences: The Link Between Theory and Data.* Cambridge, UK: Cambridge Univ. Press

SUBJECT INDEX

A

Ability to intervene
civil-military relations and, 226, 229
Activism
political parties and democracy, 256–57, 259, 261, 263
Actors
bounded rationality and, 313, 318
institutional arrangements in South Asia, 408, 410–12, 414, 419, 423, 425
institutionalism and the European Union, 429–41
tragedies of the commons and, 496, 500–1
Adaptive systems
complex
tragedies of the commons and, 493–530
rational
bounded rationality and, 297–319
Administrative chief
presidency and, 9
Africa
communist one-party systems and, 325, 334
democratization and, 116, 119–20, 122, 124–26, 129, 132–33, 138–39
electoral coordination and, 157
ending revolutions and building new governments, 51, 60, 64, 67
historical institutionalism and, 395
institutional arrangements in South Asia, 406
political economy of international trade, 107
Agenda setting
spatial modeling of Rochester school and, 269, 271, 284
Aggregate public opinion
perceptual bias and, 202–5
Aggregation rules
tragedies of the commons and, 509, 518–19

Algeria
electoral coordination and, 157
ending revolutions and building new governments, 60
historical institutionalism and, 395
Allegiances
party
bounded rationality and, 314
Alliances
deterrence and international conflict, 39
political economy of international trade, 105
Allowable actions
tragedies of the commons and, 513–16
Amateurization hypothesis
term limits and, 176
Ambiguity
bounded rationality and, 308, 312, 319
American democracy
from a European perspective
antinomies and change, 475–79
argument, 465–66
definition, 466–72
institutional antinomies, 472–75
model or method, 479–81, 483
overview, 487
positive vs zero-sum solutions, 483–86
societal antinomies, 469–72
American exceptionalism
"big ideas," 461–62
conceptual issues, 446–49
continuing research, 455–58
empirical traps, 452–55
interpretive differences, 458–61
introduction, 445–46
operational difficulties, 449–52

Analytical narratives
historical institutionalism and, 370
Analytic differentiation
democracy and dichotomies, 537
Anarchy
historical institutionalism and, 379
Angola
democratization and, 135
Antinomies
American democracy from European perspective, 465, 467, 469–79
Appropriations
baseline
tragedies of the commons and, 498–501
Arab-Israeli conflict
deterrence and international conflict, 27, 35–36, 42–43
Archival methods
presidency and, 1–21
Argentina
democratization and, 121, 123–24, 128, 138
Arizona
term limits and, 183
Arkansas
term limits and, 179, 181
Armed forces
civil-military relations and, 211–36
Arrow's Impossibility Theorem
Rochester school and, 275, 286
Artificial agents
tragedies of the commons and, 503
Asia
American exceptionalism and, 454
democratization and, 119, 126, 135, 139
deterrence and international conflict, 26, 42, 44
electoral coordination and, 148, 151–53, 156–58
ending revolutions and building new governments, 51

Vietnam
  communist one-party sys-
    tems and, 339
Vietnam War
  civil-military relations and,
    213, 234, 236
  presidency and, 18
"V-notch" law
  tragedies of the commons
    and, 522, 529
Voluntarism
  American exceptionalism
    and, 457
Voters
  bounded rationality and,
    314, 317
  democratization and, 135,
    137
  electoral coordination and,
    145, 154–55
  institutional arrangements
    in South Asia, 408,
    423–24
  institutionalism and the
    European Union, 441
  perceptual bias and,
    192–95
  political economy of inter-
    national trade, 98
  political parties and democ-
    racy, 248–63
  spatial modeling of
    Rochester school and,
    269, 283–86, 291
  term limits and, 166

W

War
  American exceptionalism
    and, 446–48, 457
  civil-military relations and,
    212–13, 220, 230–32,
    234–36
  communist one-party sys-
    tems and, 335
  deterrence and, 25–46
  institutional arrangements

  in South Asia, 416
  political economy of inter-
    national trade, 109–10
  presidency and, 10–11, 18
Ward democracy
  American democracy from
    European perspective,
    474
Warsaw Pact
  civil-military relations and,
    224
Washington consensus
  political economy of inter-
    national trade, 105
Washington State
  term limits and, 165
  tragedies of the commons
    and, 530
Weakness
  presidency and, 16
Weimar Republic
  ending revolutions and
    building new govern-
    ments, 59, 62–63, 65
Western Europe
  American democracy from
    European perspective, 468
  American exceptionalism
    and, 447, 459
  civil-military relations and,
    217
  deterrence and international
    conflict, 42
West Germany
  ending revolutions and
    building new govern-
    ments, 62, 68
Westphalian statehood
  institutionalism and the
    European Union, 433, 441
Winner's curse
  bounded rationality and,
    308–9

Women
  historical institutionalism
    and, 397
World Bank
  political economy of inter-

  national trade, 106–7, 111
World Trade Organization
  (WTO)
  political economy of inter-
    national trade, 93–94, 106
World War I
  civil-military relations and,
    235
  deterrence and international
    conflict, 27, 42
  ending revolutions and
    building new govern-
    ments, 63
World War II
  American democracy from
    European perspective, 479
  American exceptionalism
    and, 446, 452, 455, 457
  civil-military relations and,
    220
  deterrence and international
    conflict, 27
  ending revolutions and
    building new govern-
    ments, 55, 59, 62
  political economy of inter-
    national trade, 93, 105,
    111
  Rochester school and, 271
Wyoming
  term limits and, 183–84

Z

Zaire
  ending revolutions and
    building new govern-
    ments, 64
Zero-sum solutions
  American democracy from
    European perspective,
    465, 480, 483–86
Zimbabwe
  democratization and, 125
  ending revolutions and
    building new govern-
    ments, 64

NAME

ADDRESS

CITY   STATE/PROVINCE   COUNTRY   POSTAL CODE

TODAY'S DATE   DAYTIME PHONE

E-MAIL ADDRESS   FAX NUMBER

Phone
Orders **800-523-8635** (U.S. or Canada)
650-493-4400 ext. 1 (worldwide)
8 a.m. to 4 p.m. Pacific Time, Monday–Friday

Mention priority code **BB99** when placing phone orders

FAX
Orders **650-424-0910**
24 hours a day

STEP 4 : CHOOSE YOUR PAYMENT METHOD

☐ Check or Money Order Enclosed (US funds, made payable to "Annual Reviews")

☐ Bill Credit Card ☐ AmEx ☐ MasterCard ☐ VISA

Account No.

Signature

Exp. Date _____ / _____ Name _____
(print name exactly as it appears on credit card)

    # $

    #   ☐ Yes, save 10% ☐ No $

    #   ☐ Yes, save 10% ☐ No $

    #   ☐ Yes, save 10% ☐ No $

30% STUDENT/RECENT GRADUATE DISCOUNT (past 3 years) Not for standing orders. Include proof of status.

CALIFORNIA CUSTOMERS: Add applicable California sales tax for your location. $

CANADIAN CUSTOMERS: Add 7% GST (Registration # 121449029 RT).

STEP 3 : CALCULATE YOUR SHIPPING & HANDLING

HANDLING CHARGE (Add $3 per volume, up to $9 max. per location). **Applies to all orders.** $

SHIPPING OPTIONS:
(No UPS to P.O. boxes)

U.S. Mail 4th Class Book Rate (surface). Standard option. FREE.
UPS Ground Service ($3/ volume. 48 contiguous U.S. states.) $ **N/C**

Please note expedited shipping preference:

☐ UPS Next Day Air ☐ UPS Second Day Air ☐ US Airmail
☐ UPS Worldwide Express ☐ UPS Worldwide Expedited

Note option at left. We will calculate amount and add to your total

Abstracts and content lists available on the World Wide Web at
http://AnnualReviews.org. E-mail orders: service@annurev.org   **TOTAL $**

Orders may also be placed through booksellers or subscription agents or through our Authorized Stockists.
From Europe, the UK, the Middle East and Africa, contact: **Gazelle Book Service Ltd.** Lancaster, England,
Fax (0) 1524-63232. From India, Pakistan, Bangladesh or Sri Lanka, contact: SARAS Books, New Dehli,
India, Fax 91-11-941111.

Annual Reviews

ANNUAL REVIEW OF:

	INDIVIDUALS		INSTITUTIONS	
	U.S.	Other countries	U.S.	Other countries
ANTHROPOLOGY				
Vol. 28 (avail. Oct. 1999)	$55	$60	$110	$120
Vol. 27 (1998)	$55	$60	$110	$120
ASTRONOMY & ASTROPHYSICS				
Vol. 37 (avail. Sept. 1999)	$70	$75	$140	$150
Vol. 36 (1998)	$70	$75	$140	$150
BIOCHEMISTRY				
Vol. 68 (avail. July 1999)	$68	$74	$136	$148
Vol. 67 (1998)	$68	$74	$136	$148
BIOMEDICAL ENGINEERING New Series!				
Vol. 1 (avail. August 1999)	$62	$67	$124	$134
BIOPHYSICS & BIOMOLECULAR STRUCTURE				

ANNUAL REVIEW OF:

	INDIVIDUALS		INSTITUTIONS	
	U.S.	Other countries	U.S.	Other countries
FLUID MECHANICS				
Vol. 31 (avail. Jan. 1999)	$60	$65	$120	$130
Vol. 30 (1998)	$60	$65	$120	$130
GENETICS				
Vol. 33 (avail. Dec. 1999)	$60	$65	$120	$130
Vol. 32 (1998)	$60	$65	$120	$130
IMMUNOLOGY				
Vol. 17 (avail. April 1999)	$64	$69	$128	$138
Vol. 16 (1998)	$64	$69	$128	$138
MATERIALS SCIENCE				
Vol. 29 (avail. Aug. 1999)	$80	$85	$160	$170
Vol. 28 (1998)	$80	$85	$160	$170
MEDICINE				
Vol. 50 (avail. Feb. 1999)	$60	$65	$120	$130
Vol. 49 (1998)				

ANNUAL REVIEW OF:

	INDIVIDUALS		INSTITUTIONS	
	U.S.	Other countries	U.S.	Other countries
PHYTOPATHOLOGY				
Vol. 37 (avail. Sept. 1999)	$62	$67	$124	$134
Vol. 36 (1998)	$62	$67	$124	$134
PLANT PHYSIOLOGY & PLANT MOLECULAR BIOLOGY				
Vol. 50 (avail. June 1999)	$60	$65	$120	$130
Vol. 49 (1998)	$60	$65	$120	$130
POLITICAL SCIENCE New Series!				
Vol. 2 (avail. June 1999)	$60	$65	$120	$130
Vol. 1 (1998)	$60	$65	$120	$130
PSYCHOLOGY				
Vol. 50 (avail. Feb. 1999)	$55	$60	$110	$120
Vol. 49 (1998)	$55	$60	$110	$120
PUBLIC HEALTH				
Vol. 20 (avail...)				

Annual Reviews

A nonprofit scientific publisher • P.O. Box 10139
4139 El Camino Way •
Palo Alto, CA 94303-0139 USA

STEP 1: ENTER YOUR NAME & ADDRESS

BB99

STEP 2: ENTER YOUR ORDER

QTY	ANNUAL REVIEW OF:	VOL.	Place on Standing Order? SAVE 10% NOW WITH PAYMENT	PRICE	TOTAL
		#	☐ Yes, save 10% ☐ No	$	$
		#	☐ Yes, save 10% ☐ No	$	$

Annual Reviews
THE INTELLIGENT SYNTHESIS OF SCIENTIFIC LITERATURE

ANNUAL REVIEW OF:	INDIVIDUALS U.S.	Other countries	INSTITUTIONS U.S.	Other countries
ANTHROPOLOGY				
Vol. 28 (avail. Oct. 1999)	$55	$60	$110	$120
Vol. 27 (1998)	$55	$60	$110	$120
ASTRONOMY & ASTROPHYSICS				
Vol. 37 (avail. Sept. 1999)	$70	$75	$140	$150
Vol. 36 (1998)	$70	$75	$140	$150
BIOCHEMISTRY				
Vol. 68 (avail. July 1999)	$68	$74	$136	$148
Vol. 67 (1998)	$68	$74	$136	$148
BIOMEDICAL ENGINEERING New Series!				
Vol. 1 (avail. August 1999)	$62	$67	$124	$134
BIOPHYSICS & BIOMOLECULAR STRUCTURE				
Vol. 28 (avail. June 1999)	$70	$75	$140	$150
Vol. 27 (1998)	$70	75	$140	$150
CELL & DEVELOPMENTAL BIOLOGY				
Vol. 15 (avail. Nov. 1999)	$64	$69	$128	$138
Vol. 14 (1998)	$64	$69	$128	$138
COMPUTER SCIENCE (suspended)				
Call Customer Service or see our Web site for pricing.				
EARTH & PLANETARY SCIENCES				
Vol. 27 (avail. May 1999)	$70	$75	$140	$150
Vol. 26 (1998)	$70	$75	$140	$150
ECOLOGY & SYSTEMATICS				
Vol. 30 (avail. Nov. 1999)	$60	$65	$120	$130
Vol. 29 (1998)	$60	$65	$120	$130
ENERGY & THE ENVIRONMENT				
Vol. 24 (avail. Oct. 1999)	$76	$81	$152	$162
Vol. 23 (1998)	$76	$81	$152	$162
ENTOMOLOGY				
Vol. 44 (avail. Jan. 1999)	$60	$65	$120	$130
Vol. 43 (1998)	$60	$65	$120	$130

BACK VOLUMES ARE AVAILABLE Visit http://AnnualReviews.org for information

ANNUAL REVIEW OF:	INDIVIDUALS U.S.	Other countries	INSTITUTIONS U.S.	Other countries
FLUID MECHANICS				
Vol. 31 (avail. Jan. 1999)	$60	$65	$120	$130
Vol. 30 (1998)	$60	$65	$120	$130
GENETICS				
Vol. 33 (avail. Dec. 1999)	$60	$65	$120	$130
Vol. 32 (1998)	$60	$65	$120	$130
IMMUNOLOGY				
Vol. 17 (avail. April 1999)	$64	$69	$128	$138
Vol. 16 (1998)	$64	$69	$128	$138
MATERIALS SCIENCE				
Vol. 29 (avail. Aug. 1999)	$80	$85	$160	$170
Vol. 28 (1998)	$80	$85	$160	$170
MEDICINE				
Vol. 50 (avail. Feb. 1999)	$60	$65	$120	$130
Vol. 49 (1998)	$60	$65	$120	$130
MICROBIOLOGY				
Vol. 53 (avail. Oct. 1999)	$60	$65	$120	$130
Vol. 52 (1998)	$60	$65	$120	$130
NEUROSCIENCE				
Vol. 22 (avail. March 1999)	$60	$65	$120	$130
Vol. 21 (1998)	$60	$65	$120	$130
NUCLEAR & PARTICLE SCIENCE				
Vol. 49 (avail. Dec. 1999)	$70	$75	$140	$150
Vol. 48 (1998)	$70	$75	$140	$150
NUTRITION				
Vol. 19 (avail. July 1999)	$60	$65	$120	$130
Vol. 18 (1998)	$60	$65	$120	$130
PHARMACOLOGY & TOXICOLOGY				
Vol. 39 (avail. April 1999)	$60	$65	$120	$130
Vol. 38 (1998)	$60	$65	$120	$130
PHYSICAL CHEMISTRY				
Vol. 50 (avail. Oct. 1999)	$64	$69	$128	$138
Vol. 49 (1998)	$64	$69	$128	$138
PHYSIOLOGY				
Vol. 61 (avail. March 1999)	$62	$67	$124	$134
Vol. 60 (1998)	$62	$67	$124	$134

ANNUAL REVIEW OF:	INDIVIDUALS U.S.	Other countries	INSTITUTIONS U.S.	Other countries
PHYTOPATHOLOGY				
Vol. 37 (avail. Sept. 1999)	$62	$67	$124	$134
Vol. 36 (1998)	$62	$67	$124	$134
PLANT PHYSIOLOGY & PLANT MOLECULAR BIOLOGY				
Vol. 50 (avail. June 1999)	$60	$65	$120	$130
Vol. 49 (1998)	$60	$65	$120	$130
POLITICAL SCIENCE New Series!				
Vol. 2 (avail. June 1999)	$60	$65	$120	$130
Vol. 1 (1998)	$60	$65	$120	$130
PSYCHOLOGY				
Vol. 50 (avail. Feb. 1999)	$55	$60	$110	$120
Vol. 49 (1998)	$55	$60	$110	$120
PUBLIC HEALTH				
Vol. 20 (avail. May 1999)	$64	$69	$128	$138
Vol. 19 (1998)	$64	$69	$128	$138
SOCIOLOGY				
Vol. 25 (avail. Aug. 1999)	$60	$65	$120	$130
Vol. 24 (1998)	$60	$65	$120	$130

Also Available From Annual Reviews:

	INDIVIDUALS U.S.	Other countries	INSTITUTIONS U.S.	Other countries
The Excitement & Fascination Of Science				
Vol. 4 (1995)	$50	$55	$50	$55
Vol. 3 (1990) 2-part set, sold as set only	$90	$95	$90	$95
Vol. 2 (1978)	$25	$29	$25	$29
Vol. 1 (1965)	$25	$29	$25	$29
Intelligence and Affectivity by Jean Piaget (1981)	$8	$9	$8	$9
Paperback Collections				
The Cytoskeleton	$21	$21	$21	$21
Genetic Flow	$21	$21	$21	$21
AIDS	$15	$18	$15	$18
Origins of Planets and Life	$15	$20	$15	$20
Hydrologic Processes from Catchment to Continental Scales	$15	$20	$15	$20

Annual Reviews

A nonprofit scientific publisher
4139 El Camino Way • P.O. Box 10139
Palo Alto, CA 94303-0139 USA

BB99

STEP 1 : ENTER YOUR NAME & ADDRESS

NAME

ADDRESS

CITY   STATE/PROVINCE   COUNTRY   POSTAL CODE

TODAY'S DATE   DAYTIME PHONE

E-MAIL ADDRESS   FAX NUMBER

Phone **800-523-8635** (U.S. or Canada)
Orders **650-493-4400 ext. 1** (worldwide)

8 a.m. to 4 p.m. Pacific Time, Monday–Friday

| Mention priority code **BB99** when placing phone orders |

FAX **650-424-0910**
Orders 24 hours a day

STEP 4 : CHOOSE YOUR PAYMENT METHOD

☐ Check or Money Order Enclosed (US funds, made payable to "Annual Reviews")
☐ Bill Credit Card   ☐ AmEx   ☐ MasterCard   ☐ VISA

Account No.

Signature

Exp. Date ___/___   Name _____ (print name exactly as it appears on credit card)

STEP 2 : ENTER YOUR ORDER

Qty	Annual Review of:	Vol.	Place on Standing Order? SAVE 10% NOW WITH PAYMENT	Price	Total
		#	☐ Yes, save 10% ☐ No	$	$
		#	☐ Yes, save 10% ☐ No	$	$
		#	☐ Yes, save 10% ☐ No	$	$
		#	☐ Yes, save 10% ☐ No	$	$
		#	☐ Yes, save 10% ☐ No	$	$

30% STUDENT/RECENT GRADUATE DISCOUNT (past 3 years) Not for standing orders. Include proof of status.

CALIFORNIA CUSTOMERS: Add applicable California sales tax for your location. $

CANADIAN CUSTOMERS: Add 7% GST (Registration # 121149029 RT). $

STEP 3 : CALCULATE YOUR SHIPPING & HANDLING

HANDLING CHARGE (Add $3 per volume, up to $9 max. per location). **Applies to all orders.** $

SHIPPING OPTIONS:
(No UPS to P.O. boxes)

U.S. Mail 4th Class Book Rate (surface). Standard option. FREE. $ **N/C**
UPS Ground Service ($3/ volume. 48 contiguous U.S. states.)

Please note expedited shipping preference:
☐ UPS Next Day Air ☐ UPS Second Day Air ☐ US Airmail
☐ UPS Worldwide Express ☐ UPS Worldwide Expedited

| Note option at left. We will calculate amount and add to your total |

TOTAL $

Abstracts and content lists available on the World Wide Web at
http://AnnualReviews.org. **E-mail orders: service@annurev.org**

Orders may also be placed through booksellers or subscription agents or through our Authorized Stockists. From Europe, the UK, the Middle East and Africa, contact: **Gazelle Book Service Ltd.**, Lancaster, England, Fax (0) 1524-63232. From India, Pakistan, Bangladesh or Sri Lanka, contact: SARAS Books, New Delhi, India, Fax 91-11-941111.